ENGLISH LOCAL GOVERNMENT

THE PARISH AND THE COUNTY

ENGLISH LOCAL GOVERNMENT

A series of eleven volumes on the growth
and structure of English Local Government
by SIDNEY and BEATRICE WEBB

*Volumes 10 and 11 were originally published separately, but are now
included to make the scope of the work more comprehensive.

The Parish and the County

SIDNEY and BEATRICE WEBB

With a new Introduction by
B. KEITH-LUCAS

*Senior Lecturer in Local Government
in the University of Oxford*

FRANK CASS AND CO. LTD.
1963

First published by Longmans Green & Co. in 1906

This edition published by Frank Cass & Co., 10, Woburn Walk, London, W.C.1., by the kind permission of the Trustees of the Passfield Estate.

First published   1906
Reprinted   1963

Printed in Great Britain by
Thomas Nelson and Sons Ltd, Edinburgh

Beatrice and Sidney Webb were not by nature historians ; they were too much absorbed in the problems of the world in which they lived, and the social questions of the day, to be inclined to spend laborious years in the detailed investigation of seventeenth and eighteenth century records dealing with the minutiæ of parochial affairs. Yet for thirty years they spent much of their time on this research, and in writing the nine large volumes which constitute their *History of English Local Government from the Revolution to the Municipal Corporations Act*.

Beatrice Webb has described in *My Apprenticeship*[1] and in *Our Partnership*[2] the way in which she was led to undertake this great work. It was not a desire to elucidate the past for the sake of knowledge alone that inspired her. Essentially she was concerned to understand and to improve the world around her. She had come to believe that the regeneration of society was to be sought in an extension of the conceptions of the co-operative movement. She had studied the trade unions and the co-operative societies carefully, and came to see through them a pattern of a new form of state, and a new vision of social development.

Meanwhile Sidney Webb was himself actively involved in local government as a member of the London County Council, and he had for some years been writing on the subject of municipal socialism. She saw the need to replace the capitalist system by " associations of consumers "; he, always more practical, was thinking in terms of municipal provision of essential services. In the parish vestries, improvement commissions and municipal councils of England she recognized institutions which had for a long time been working on the principles which she advocated ; working as associations of consumers, not activated by the desire for profit but by the demand for services. So they both saw in the municipal institutions of the country an instrument through which the principles of Socialism could be developed. " It was important to discover by what means the various parishes and counties and municipalities were in fact governed ; how their several administrations had arisen in the past and how they were now developing ;

[1] pp. 377-395.
[2] pp. 147-180.

and by what extensions and improvements their social institutions could best be fitted for the additional tasks that they would find themselves undertaking ".[1]

Thus they decided to undertake a survey of local institutions in the nineteenth century, as a basis on which to build the structure of a new political and social organisation. But they soon found that they could not study the developments of that era without making a special study of the period before the reforms of 1832–35. So they decided to start with an account of the local government of England from 1688 to 1835. But the more they and their assistants collected facts on their card index, the more they realised that there was yet more to be done. So it was that by 1929, after thirty years' work, they had published the introductory survey in nine volumes, but had not started on the main account of local government in the nineteenth century ; Sidney was already seventy, and Beatrice seventy-one ; the major part of the project was never undertaken.

This somewhat indirect approach to the history of local government inevitably had its effect on the nature of the work. The authors were not attempting to write a history of local government so much as a history of the institutions of local government. They did not see the subject against the broader background of the social and political scene, in the way that Dr. Redlich, writing in the last years of the nineteenth century, had done.[2] They were not concerned with the place of local government in the theories of the State, as expounded by Rudolf von Gneist[3] and Joshua Toulmin Smith[4], nor with the legal niceties of Merewether and Stephens.[5] They were concerned primarily to find out how the institutions worked. But behind this lay their conception of them as associations of consumers. So there runs through these volumes the theme of municipal and parochial co-operation, and they interpreted historical events greatly in this light. Thus, while Redlich had seen the Municipal Corporations Act as a part of the long national

[1] *Our Partnership*, p. 150.

[2] *Englische Lokalverwaltung* by Josef Redlich, translated into English as *Local Government in England* by Josef Redlich and Francis W. Hirst.

[3] *Englische Verwaltungsrecht*.

[4] *Local Self-Government and Centralisation*.

[5] *The History of the Boroughs and Municipal Corporations* by H. A. Merewether and A. J. Stephens.

struggle for self-government, and an epilogue to the Reform Act, the Webbs saw it in a different light—" The Reformers of 1835, as we have seen, only dimly realised the nature of the fundamental defect in the conception of membership of the old Corporations. They recognised the invidious character of the shrinking into close Bodies, the trade restrictions and the exclusive privileges that flowed, as we have seen, from the very nature of the Association of Producers. They adopted, as the basis of their reform, the diametrically opposite conception of universality of membership, corresponding to that of the Association of Producers."[1]

The nature of these books was also influenced by the Webbs' method of work. Most of the investigation was done by research assistants, who recorded each separate fact on a separate sheet of quarto paper. In the course of time they accumulated many tens of thousands[2] of these sheets ; then they sat down together at the table, Sidney Webb writing, while Beatrice manipulated the enormous card index. The result was inevitably more an accumulation of facts than an interpretation of historical trends ; more an array of detail than a picture of local government as part of the development of the nation.

Sometimes, it must be admitted, this tendency went too far, and the text got almost lost in the mass of explanatory footnotes ; it is not uncommon to find pages in which there are five or six lines of footnotes for every line of text. The size of their footnotes is due in part to the caution which led them to include any reference available which had any bearing, however remote, to the subject of the text. For example, on page 249 of *The Parish and the County* there is a footnote about the corruption of the select vestries in London in the seventeenth century. It ends with the comment that " It may be added that the dummy bill which is introduced every session into the House of Lords, as an assertion of its right to debate before the King's Speech is read, is entitled 'A Bill to reform Select Vestries '. This is believed to date from a couple of centuries back. It is mentioned in the *Further Memoirs of the Whig Party* by

---

[1] *The Manor and the Borough*, p. 752. See also Ibid, p. 731 ; *Statutory Authorities*, pp. 437-445.
[2] *Our Partnership*, p. 156 n.

Lord Holland, 1905, p.250." This reference is in fact unlikely to
help the student interested in the select vestries of the seventeenth
century, as it refers to an episode in the House of Lords in 1817 ;
all that Lord Holland wrote was ; "Accordingly, on the resumption
of the House, before the Select Vestry Bill was moved, or the Lord
Chancellor had read the speech from the Woolsack, up rose my
Lord Sidmouth, and with more than his usual solemnity (sufficient
though it be to that or almost any other occasion) stated that the
Prince, on his return through the Park, had been grossly insulted
and assailed ".

Despite these failings, the Webb's History of Local Government
is, and will remain the definitive work on the subject. No previous
writer had attempted to cover the whole field ; Toulmin Smith
was a romantic of the Gothic Revival, concerned more with the
Witanagemote and the Anglo-Saxon Golden Age than with the
details of administrative history ; Merewether and Stephens were
lawyers, deeply involved in the intricacies of corporation law, and
concerned with the rights and priveleges created by mediæval
charters, rather than with the actual events of later centuries.
The Webbs on the other hand started with two great advantages ;
they had a team of meticulous research workers, and they were free
from the romantic and legal bias of their predecessors. They and
their assistants turned not to the mediæval charters and legal text
books, but to the minutes and files of the local authorities themselves to discover how the towns and villages were actually
governed. Here they found an enormous wealth of material, ill kept
and little regarded, scattered in local solicitors' offices, town halls
and parish chests.

Out of these researches there came, first, a new and much
greater understanding of the practical working of municipal corporations, Quarter Sessions and parish vestries. But in some ways
more important was the realisation that these bodies were only a
part of the system of local administration in the Eighteenth
Century. Previous historians had concentrated on these general
local authorities and had ignored the complicated tangle of special
authorities established by Private Acts—Improvement Commissioners, Incorporated Guardians of the Poor, Turnpike Trusts and

other statutory bodies. The Webbs were the first to realise that it was here, rather than in the municipal corporations and vestries, that lay the germs of the new ideas that were to transform English local government in the Nineteenth Century. In the thousands of previously unregarded Local Acts,[1] and in the forgotten minutes of Improvement and Paving Commissions they found the really fertile ground of new ideas and methods. It was perhaps in this realization that they made their greatest contribution to the history of English local government.

Despite the time and care that the Webbs themselves, Mr. and Mrs. Spencer, and their other assistants gave to their research, there remains much to be done on this subject. Between them they never managed to read through all the Local Acts of the period ; they certainly never had an opportunity to look more closely into the working of more than a few dozen of the boards and commissions of which they wrote. The Local Acts of the Nineteenth Century have not yet been explored even to this degree.

Beatrice and Sidney Webb were primarily concerned with the statutory authorities because these were the pioneers of modern administrative methods, the first to employ salaried professional officers, and to evolve the committee system as we know it today. But they were also pioneers in other ways ; it is in these Local Acts that one finds the seeds of the sanitary legislation of the Nineteenth Century, of the new Poor Law of 1834, of National Insurance and also of the secret ballot, town planning, protection of animals from human cruelty, smoke control, traffic regulation, and much else besides.[2] There remains here a vast field for historical research, which the Webbs discovered, but could not possibly explore in every detail.

[1] The Webbs (*Statutory Authorities*, p. 7.) state that " Even omitting the four thousand Enclosure Acts, and all the " Private " and " Personal " legislation, the statutes specifically establishing or continuing one or other of the eighteen hundred Local Authorities described in the present volume, or altering their powers or obligations, must number something like ten thousand ".

[2] See also *Municipal Origins* by F. H. Spencer ; A Local Act for Social Insurance in the Eighteenth Century, *Cambridge Law Journal* Vol. 11. No. 2, 1952 ; Some Influences affecting the Development of Sanitary Legislation in England, *Economic History Review* Vol. VI, No. 3 ; Influence of Local Experiments on Social Legislation, *Municipal Journal*, October 30, 1953, by B. Keith-Lucas ; *Local Government in St. Marylebone 1688–1835* by F. H. W. Sheppard.

In the volume on the *Parish and the County* the outstanding contribution made by the Webbs was their exposition of the role of Quarter Sessions, not as a judicial body, but as an administrative and legislative assembly, managing the affairs of the county, supervising the Poor Law, and also advising and being consulted by Parliament. Moreover, in their general power to interpret Acts of Parliament, and to enforce them in whatever manner seemed to them appropriate, the magistrates performed a legislative function, which might be compared with the part played by Statutory Instruments today, in amplifying and defining the general provisions of parliamentary statutes.

The tendency of the Webbs to think in terms of Associations of Consumers and Associations of Producers shows perhaps most clearly in the last part of the *Manor and the Borough*. Here, in assessing the Municipal Corporation of 1835 and the report of the Royal Commission, they paid little attention to the political forces of the time, but reiterated that the old corporations had failed because they were Associations of Producers, with all the defects and dangers that this involved. The Report had criticized the corporations severely and somewhat indiscriminately, holding, rather dogmatically, that the close corporations were bad, and elected bodies good. With this judgment the Webbs could not agree. They were in some ways authoritarian in their impatience for social reform, and distrustful of popular elections as a means of achieving it. In particular they deplored the failure of the reformers to recommend the establishment of central control, supervision, inspection, audit and control over the new corporations, and they saw the dangers inherent in an elected bench of magistrates.

While admitting that abuses existed in the old corporations, they accused the commissioners of exaggeration and of unjustified generalisations in their account of the corporations. In criticizing the Report they found themselves in alliance with one of the original Commissioners, Sir Francis Palgrave, who had refused to sign the Report, and issued a violent protest against it, which was published by the Government.[1] He was the odd man out among the

[1] *Protest of Sir Francis Palgrave, One of the Commissioners for inquiring into Municipal Corporations in England and Wales, in the matter of the Report presented to His Majesty by the said Commissioners. P.P. Eng. 1835. 135.*

Commissioners ; nearly all were young Whig barristers ; he was a distinguished historian, and probably included in the Commission because, although a Tory, he had already published a criticism of the existing system of municipal government.[1]

The Webbs appear to have accepted too readily his views on the Report, which coincided with their own ; they describe his *Protest* as " an able and instructive document by the most distinguished of the Commissioners ", while they call the Report itself " a violent political pamphlet being, to serve Party ends, issued as a judicial report."

With this judgment one may well disagree. Palgrave was justified in some of his complaints, but he was himself guilty of some misrepresentation. He objects to the wholesale condemnation of the corporations on what he regards as inadequate grounds, and gives a number of examples. Closer inspection of individual cases shows that he was at least as misleading as his colleagues. An instance of this is afforded by the case of Penryn. Palgrave wrote of this town :

" In a certain number of towns the dissatisfaction of the inhabitants is ascribed to particular causes, not unfrequently to the assertion of rights which, though legal, are unpleasing to the inhabitants, or of which the inhabitants contest the legality. The ' public mind ' is dissatisfied in Penryn because the Corporation holds a property of which it has been in uninterrupted possession since 1669 ". The implication is clearly that there are no real grounds for the allegation of public dissatisfaction with the corporation.

He has here glossed over the principal causes of the alleged discontent. The Report stated that " The system by which the corporation are elected, and the secrecy with which their proceedings are conducted, together with their refusal to account for the distribution of the Park Helland property, to which the inhabitants deem themselves entitled, all contribute to create dissatisfaction in the public mind ". This sentence he did in fact print in the lengthy appendix of extracts from the Report, in small type at the end of his *Protest*, but did not reproduce the information on which

[1] *Observations on the Establishment of New Corporations*, 1832.

it was based. The Report itself did in fact show that the method of election of the corporation was such as to give good grounds for dissatisfaction ; the Governing Body of 24 Chief Burgesses was entirely self-elected, and excluded all but professional men. Six of the seats were vacant, and of the remaining eighteen members, seven were non-resident. They held office for life.

Another instance of Palgrave's understatement is the town of Camelford, of which he states that the Report disclosed only " bad management of property " and " borough under patronage ". In fact the Report recorded that " For many years the Corporation can scarcely be said to have existed ; even its small revenue, which constituted all the little power it possessed, having been surrendered into the hands of the patron. Taking no part in the administration of civil or criminal justice, it was kept on foot for no other purpose than that of creating electors of the borough . . . A more complete system of corruption has not existed in any Cornish borough.

" For municipal purposes also, the corporation is ill adapted. It is self-elected ; it is irresponsible, and the inhabitants are entirely excluded from taking any part in the government of the town. The usual consequences have followed. The public money has been squandered ; no accounts whatever of its application have been kept ; the trusts for the school have been abused ; and the character of the corporation has been brought to disrepute.

" The revenue, although small, might with good management have been rendered very beneficial to the town. But not a single instance of its application to a work of public improvement was pointed out to me ".

Many more such instances could be quoted to show that *Palgrave's Protest* is not in fact so reliable a document as the Webbs took it to be.

They themselves were to some extent guilty of the same offence as Palgrave. They state, for example, that[1] "A repeated use of the words, ' frequently ', ' generally ' and ' in many instances ' coupled with reference to the notorious cases, enabled the Commissioners to imply that the whole two hundred Municipal Corporations were

[1] *The Manor and the Borough* p. 718.

guilty of ' the alienation in fee of the corporate property to individual corporators ', ' the execution of long leases for nominal consideration '; the voting of ' salaries to sinecure, unnecessary or overpaid officers '; the devotion of their income to ' entertainments of the Common Council and their friends '; and the misappropriation of trust funds ' to gain or reward votes both at the Municipal and Parliamentary elections '. On the Commissioners' own showing not one of these statements is true of more than half a dozen out of the couple of hundred corporations ; yet the impression is skilfully conveyed that these evils are characteristic of all of them."

In fact the Commissioners only alleged that lavish expenditure of this kind was found " in many of the important Corporations ", though the practice of having periodic dinners at the corporate expense was alleged to prevail " almost universally ". A detailed inspection of the reports of individual towns shows that such irresponsible expenditure was widespread, and the habit of dining at the public expense was specifically referred to in at least seventy corporations—not, as the Webbs allege, in less than half a dozen.

Reading through the detailed reports sent in by the individual Commissioners one cannot help being impressed by the very widespread mismanagement and abuse that existed ; the Report itself does exaggerate here and there, and generalises sometimes too widely, but the mass of evidence of how the corporations had been corrupted is overwhelming. It may be that the Chairman and Secretary, when they wrote the Report, were determined to damn the Corporations in general, but the evidence, as it came in, justified nearly everything they said.

The Webbs, it would seem, were unduly persuaded by Palgrave's Protest, and too much influenced by their own conception of the Associations of Producers and Associations of Consumers to see the picture clearly. Above all, they failed to see the corporations against the social and political background of the time, and to appreciate the extent to which the corruption of the municipal institutions sprang from their role as electoral colleges for Parliament.

This, it would seem, was the principal cause of the decay. The municipal corporations had two main functions ; the government of the town, and the returning of Members to Parliament. This second function had outgrown the first. Many of the corporations had been bought and bribed by the boroughmongers, and had become the notorious rotten and pocket boroughs of the Eighteenth Century. In some, local government functions had been almost forgotten, or neglected by corporations composed greatly of strangers whose functions began and ended with the election of Members of Parliament. In others, noble patrons controlled the corporation by bribes or by their power as landlords. The passing of the Reform Act had drastically altered the picture ; many of the small boroughs had lost what had now become their only purpose ; in others, the change in the franchise had altered the whole pattern of influence.

Though in this one matter we may criticize their views and interpretation, this does not imply any criticizm of the work as a whole. Essentially these volumes stand as an unequalled collection of the detailed facts which, taken together, constitute the mosaic of English administration in the Eighteenth Century. The value of this work lies not so much in the general picture as in the worth of each individual tessera out of which the mosaic is composed—the instances and examples drawn from the varied quarries of munici-pal records and archives.

Had they been able to extend their writing to the period after 1835 the result would without doubt have been of equal, or even greater, value. But this they never did. Some of the raw material exists in the library of the London School of Economics ; notes of what they found in the town halls and archives up and down the country, many of them in Beatrice's abominable writing, describing anything that might possibly one day prove to be relevant. But all that they published on this later period, apart from the history of the Poor Law, is contained in a series of lectures given by Sidney at the London School of Economics in 1899—before they had under-taken their main researches. These lectures were published in the *Municipal Journal and London* in 1899, and Dr. Redlich acknow-ledged that he had made substantial use of them in writing his *Local Government in England.* They were re-published by the *Municipal Journal* in 1951 as a pamphlet—*The Evolution of Local*

Government. At most however they are but a shadow of what the projected work would have been.

So, though the Webb's great plan was never completed, and though one may disagree with their judgment on the Royal Commission on Municipal Corporations, their work remains a great monument of research and learning. It presents an unrivalled picture of English local administration in the Eighteenth and early Nineteenth Centuries, not based on inspired intuition or penetrating social psychology, but built up, piece by piece, from the thousands of relevant facts which their researches disclosed. When the first volumes were published in 1908 they received an enthusiastic and detailed review from A. L. Smith in the English Historical Review[1]; he pointed out how much the Webbs' researches did to elucidate historical developments outside the field of local government, and how much new light they shed on the administration of English towns and counties. He hailed their work as a major contribution to the understanding of Eighteenth Century England. To-day these volumes still stand as the unchallenged authority in their field. As they have long been out of print, their republication is an act of public service.

NUFFIELD COLLEGE,
August, 1962.   B. KEITH-LUCAS.

---

[1] Vol. XXV pp. 353-364. See also review of *Statutory Authorities* by J. H. Clapham, Vol. XXXIX pp. 288-292.

PREFACE

THE thirteen chapters now published form the first instalment of a detailed description of the Local Government of England and Wales as it existed between 1689 and 1835. This description, which will extend to five or six volumes, falls into two main divisions, dealing respectively with Structure and Function. In the first three volumes we restrict ourselves to the constitutional form and the administrative procedure of the various kinds of local governing authorities; the changes in these organisations from decade to decade; and the principles on which their development proceeded. We start in the present instalment, which has a unity of its own, with the two forms of Local Government that were practically ubiquitous, the Parish and the County. The second volume will deal similarly with the various immunities, franchises and liberties, which, embodied in Manorial Jurisdictions and Municipal Corporations, stood out as exceptions. This will still leave undescribed the form of Local Government that was the most characteristic product of the eighteenth century, the Statutory Authority for Special Purposes—known in the slang of the hour as the Ad Hoc Body—and to these authorities, together with our general summary of and judgment upon English Local Government between the Revolution and the Municipal Corporations Act, we shall devote our third volume. We have also in preparation the remainder of the work, in which we shall describe the action of all these authorities in respect to the various functions entrusted to Local Government, such as the Relief of Destitution, the Prevention of Crime, the Suppression of Nuisances, the Maintenance of Highways, the Provision of Markets and the Regulation of Trade.

We may frankly confess that when, nearly eight years ago, we began our investigations into Local Government history, it was, in the main, the practical problems of the Local Government of the present day that aroused our interest. What we contemplated, indeed, was an analysis of the Local Government of this generation, with merely a preliminary chapter about the antiquities, anterior to 1835, which it had superseded. But in the course of our journeyings up and down the country, we found even the present Local Government so firmly rooted in the past, and the past so complicated and obscure, that it became indispensable to us to make a special study of the period immediately preceding the reforms of 1832-35. At first we intended to restrict ourselves to the first three decades of the nineteenth century. Further study convinced us that we could neither understand nor make intelligible by itself what was but the tag-end of a period opening with the Revolution.

The century and a half lying between the dismissal of the Stuarts and the Reform Parliament constitutes, for the historian of the internal administration of England and Wales, a distinct period of extraordinary significance. For the first, and perhaps for the last, time in English History, the National Government abstained from intervention in local affairs, practically leaving all the various kinds of local governing bodies to carry out their several administrations as they chose, without central supervision or central control. Even when Parliament was appealed to for legislation, it allowed the different localities to have practically whatever constitutions and whatever powers they asked for; contenting itself with ratifying, in the innumerable Local Acts of the eighteenth-century Statute-book, the particular projects and compromises of the local interests concerned. The experiments in Poor Law and Municipal Enterprise thus initiated are, we think, instructive to the reformers of to-day. But besides these experiments in function, the varied constitutions of the eighteenth-century Local Authorities, and their several developments and results, seem to us of interest to the political student. There is a great deal of the eighteenth century still surviving in the Local Government of the twentieth; and those who are familiar with its working—whether in England or in the United States—will, we believe, find warning, suggestion, and encouragement from an intimate acquaintance with the story of the past.

It is remarkable that practically the only treatise dealing with the subject as a whole, for the period that we are describing, is by a German author; and it is, we think, even less creditable to us that this monumental work of Rudolf von Gneist never found an English translator.[1] We attribute the neglect of the subject by our own historians to its magnitude and complexity, and to the bulk of the materials to be studied. For, as we ourselves found, the English Local Government of the eighteenth century is not a subject that can be adequately dealt with in compartments. The Parish cannot be understood without the County, nor the Municipal Corporation without the Manor, nor the Statutory Authorities for Special Purposes without all the rest. The historian who should confine his researches to the archives of any one kind of local governing body, cannot, any more than if he restricted himself to the experience of any one town, arrive at a correct appreciation even of the narrow field that he selects. To understand the part played by the parish officers, we have had to consult, not the parish archives alone, but also the voluminous orders of Quarter Sessions. To unravel the complications connected with the Jury of Sewers, it was necessary to discover the working of the Leet Jury of the Manorial Court, the Ward Inquest of the Municipal Corporation, and the Hundred Jury of the County. To gain an

---

[1] We give bibliographical footnotes in connection with each chapter.

explanation of certain features in the government of the City of London, we found ourselves exploring the church chests of villages in Northumberland.

It may be of interest in this connection to give here a short survey of the materials. The indispensable foundation for any study of local governing bodies is an investigation of their own official records. We have found the manuscript minutes of the Parish Vestries and the primitive accounts of the parish officers—sometimes dating back four and even five centuries—a storehouse of facts and figures, and deserving both of more careful preservation and of more extensive publication than they have yet been favoured with. The voluminous "Order Books" and Sessions Papers of the Courts of Quarter Sessions in the different counties constitute precious materials for the social historian, whilst the scantier records of Petty and Special Sessions, and the manuscript diaries of Justices of the Peace, yield even more intimate knowledge than the formal records of the larger bodies. The Rolls of those Manors which still continued to do Local Government work go far to elucidate the manuscript minutes of the innumerable "Courts" and assemblies of which the Municipal Corporations of the period were made up. We broke ground that was quite new to us when we explored the proceedings of the Courts of Sewers, the Street Commissioners, the Turnpike Trustees, and the Incorporated Guardians of the Poor. To go through these local archives, all of which were indispensable to our task, has involved many a sojourn in provincial centres from Newcastle to Plymouth, and journeys innumerable into the remotest corners of England and Wales.

After the manuscript records, the student of English Local Government finds most useful the contemporary local newspapers, which give flesh and blood to the skeleton provided by the official minutes. It is here that the student makes acquaintance with the personalities whose administration he is unravelling; here, too, he will find much that is not recorded, or not intelligibly recorded, in the minute books. These old local newspapers have been but imperfectly preserved, and it is to the excellent collection in the British Museum that we owe most of the information that they have afforded to us. We rejoice that the destruction of this collection, by the distribution of its contents among the various provincial towns—actually proposed by the Treasury a few years ago has been happily averted. The dispersal of these unique files all over England—the virtual destruction as an accessible source of perhaps the most valuable of all the materials for the social history of the eighteenth century—would, in our judgment, be an act of gross Vandalism.

Next in importance to the manuscript records and the newspapers, we rank the contemporary pamphlets, especially those which are controversial in character. These (together with novels, plays, and even sermons) let us—often by their incidental allusions—into many secrets which neither minutes nor newspapers divulge. We have done our best to explore the local histories, to which we have found Dr. Gross's bibliography a most convenient guide. But their yield to the student of the eighteenth century is, as a rule, disappointingly small; partly because their authors commonly lose all interest in their task after the cessation of what they consider the picturesque incidents of the Middle Ages, and partly because their lack of general knowledge of Local Government prevents their knowing what to select for record. Least important of all the books that we have consulted are the general histories of the period, which concern themselves with other topics.

An indispensable supplement to the records and contemporary descriptions of local governing bodies is furnished by the correspondence and the decisions on local matters of the various branches of the National Government, especially the Privy Council, the Secretary of State's Office, and the Treasury, to all of which the student will be able to obtain access in the Public Record Office. The more scanty records of the appointment and dismissal of Justices of the Peace may be explored in the Crown Office. The printed Journals of the House of Lords and House of Commons, together with the reports of their debates, and the voluminous blue-book literature, have been of great incidental use. We have not found time to do more than dive, for certain specific incidents, into the unprinted archives—petitions, abortive bills, etc.—of the House of Lords.

Finally, we come to the law, upon which alone Rudolph von Gneist based his account of English Local Government. Here we have found most useful, not the general statutes, though these are the only ones usually resorted to even by historians of repute, but the far more interesting Local Acts, which created new local governing bodies in nearly every town and county, and modified the constitution and enlarged the powers of most of those of ancient origin. The bewildering array of these thousands of separate statutes—unanalysed, undigested, even unindexed—nearly daunted us. But English Local Government was not to be understood without them; and their systematic analysis yielded, in fact, some indispensable results. The statutes, however, whether general or local, public or private, afford but little information as to what the Local Government really was. Even the formal constitutions that they enacted were, more frequently than not, very different from the real constitutions that actually existed; and the student has always to be on his guard against assuming that, because an Act of Parliament ordered something to be done, it therefore was done. Hence we have had to treat the statute law as merely one of the causes, or modifying influences, of the working constitutions. More instructive than the statutes, will sometimes be found the reports of cases, yielding a view both of Common Law and local custom, but unfortunately scattered among hundreds of volumes, stowed away in which we have occasionally found instructive visions of the Local Government as it was carried on. With these we may cite also the best legal text-books of each successive generation, and especially the footnotes in which their authors sometimes described their own experience as local administrators.

So extensive a field of research could not be covered by one person, or even by two persons. At the outset of our work eight years ago we had the good fortune to secure as a colleague Mr. F. H. Spencer, LL.B., and, three years later, Miss Amy Harrison, B.A., D.Sc. (Econ.) (now Mrs. Spencer), both of the London School of Economics and Political Science. To these two fellow-investigators we owe the greater part of the material upon which our work is based, and many suggestions and criticisms of which we have endeavoured to make use. More recently they have been joined in this work by Miss M. E. Bulkley, B.Sc. (Econ.), also of the London School of Economics and Political Science; and we have also had the advantage of help for particular subjects, or in particular districts, of Mr. L. L. Matthews (now Assistant Attorney-General in the Transvaal Colony), Miss Mildred Sturge (Newnham College, Cambridge), and Miss M. M. Crick (St. Hugh's Hall, Oxford). The notes taken by these helpers and by ourselves, from the various manuscript and printed sources described above, have all been written on separate sheets of paper of uniform size, each recording only a single fact, of one local governing authority, in one place and at one date. It is only by this elaborate system of note-taking, and the incessant mechanical shuffling and reshuffling which it permits, that we have been able to keep control of so great an accumulation of material, and to assemble on our table from time to time all the facts relating to a particular subject, or to a particular place, or to a particular date, without being distracted by irrelevant considerations. These sheets of paper—numbering perhaps something like fifty thousand, and consisting, as they usually do, of precise extracts from sources not easily accessible—form a collection which, we

believe, may be of as much use to other workers as is already
the much smaller collection on similar lines that we made on
Trade Unionism in 1891-97. Like that, it will presently be
deposited for the convenience of all students in the British
Library of Political Science, in connection with the London
School of Economics and Political Science, Clare Market,
Kingsway.

In spite of the help that we have received in this investigation, it would be absurd to suppose that we have either
exhausted all the possible sources or deduced from them all
the inferences that they might be made to yield. What we
have aimed at is rather the mapping out of the whole field of
English Local Government for this period, without assuming
to have dealt exhaustively with any part of it. We have
carried our own investigations into the development of each
kind of local governing authority up to the point where
further researches seemed to bring us nothing but repetition.
Thus, after we had gone through the Quarter Sessions records
of some five-and-twenty counties, we discovered nothing
further that seemed new to us; and we contented ourselves,
for the rest, with such printed material as we could come
across. Still more conscious are we that our dealing with
the material itself has necessarily been restricted by the
limitations of individual culture. For this reason, if for no
other, each generation must write its own history, exactly as
it has to formulate its own physics and its own chemistry. It
is, indeed, a testimony to the fertility of any historical
treatise, as it is to that of any physical or chemical work,
that it should quickly become superseded by subtler and
more exhaustive analysis of the phenomena with which it
deals.

The mistakes of fact which we cannot fail to have made, we
hope will be promptly pointed out by other students. To ensure
this correction, we have been even punctilious in giving exact
references. We are inclined to agree with a biographer of a

former generation that "not the most honest and veracious of
historians is to be depended upon for a matter of fact. It may
seem a harsh judgment, but I believe it to be a just one, that
when the best of men in the best of language makes an
averment for which he gives no authority, there is an equal
chance whether it be false or whether it be true ; and if he
founds it upon an unnamed document, there is always a high
probability that the document will bear another construction.
No man can write from his own knowledge of that which
passed before he was born : he must take his notions from
some evidence or from some authority ; and he who conceals
from those whom he teaches the grounds of his own belief may
be suspected of caring more for his own views than for the
truth of the matter." [1]   For a similar reason we have forgone
any attempt to produce a work of literature, by burdening our
volume with footnotes and our text with actual quotations.
We can only hope that the student, bent on further research
of his own, will welcome that which the general reader may
resent.

Thus have we, to quote the words of a famous sixteenth-
century forerunner in the study of English Local Government,
"by the favour of God brought this treatise to an end :
wherein if many things have escaped me unseen, I do not
greatly marvel, when I look back and behold the variety and
multitude of the matter that I have passed through ; and it
shall not be hard for him that meeteth with such estrays to
take and lodge them in their right titles here.   Again, if I
shall be thought to have heaped up too many conceits . . .
I make answer that I have omitted many and have made
the best choice that I could. . . . Finally, whatsoever other
thing is done amiss, I protest that it hath escaped out of
unskill, and not proceeded of wilfulness, and therefore I desire
that I may be allowed the benefit of that pardon which (as I

---

[1] *Memoirs of . . . Sir William Temple, Bart.,* by the Rt. Hon. T. P.
Courtenay, 1836, p. ix.

told you even now) is in like case grantable to a Justice of the Peace." [1]

The amount of friendly assistance that we have received in the course of our eight years' investigation has been so large, and the number of those to whom we are indebted is so great, that we have necessarily to forgo the pleasure of expressing our thanks to them individually by name. From all the hundreds of authorities to whom we have applied for permission to peruse the manuscript records in their possession —from the Incumbents and Churchwardens of many scores of rural parishes up to the busiest of Bishops and the most assiduous of Town-Clerks; from the most ancient Court of Sewers up to the newest County Council; from the Lords and Stewards of the most archaic rural Manors up to the Library Committee, the hard-worked Librarian and the learned Archivist of the Corporation of the City of London itself—we have invariably met with the politest of reception, without the reservation of any document or the exaction of any fee. To all those whom we have thus troubled with our insatiable curiosity about the past we can only tender our sincere thanks. The public libraries at Manchester and Glasgow, those of the Universities of Oxford and Cambridge, the great accumulation of City archives and pamphlets at the Guildhall, the newer library of the London County Council, the manuscripts at Lambeth Palace, the unique collection of official documents at the London School of Economics and Political Science, but above all the invaluable storehouses of the British Museum and the Public Record Office, have been of the greatest service to us; in all cases rendered by their custodians with that willing courtesy which marks the common citizenship of the Republic of Letters.

---

[1] *Eirenarcha, or of the Office of the Justices of the Peace*, by William Lambard, of Lincoln's Inn, gentleman (1581). We may here say, once for all, that we have modernised the spelling of quotations, and always given the year's date in the new style (thus, 172½ we print as 1722).

To various friendly critics, notably Mr. G. L. Gomme, Miss
Hadley, the Rev. William Hudson, Mr. J. A. Hyett, J.P., Mr.
and Mrs. Phillimore, Mr. Bernard Shaw, Lady Strachey,
Mr. George Unwin, and Mr. Graham Wallas, who have read
one or more of our chapters in manuscript, we owe various
helpful criticisms and suggestions ; but our thanks are specially
due, in this connection, to Mr. Hubert Hall, of the Public
Record Office and the London School of Economics and
Political Science, who has found time, amid a constant press of
occupations, to go through the greater part of our work, and
to enrich it by many a suggestive hint and comment.

SIDNEY AND BEATRICE WEBB.

41 GROSVENOR ROAD, WESTMINSTER,
    September 1906.

CONTENTS

BOOK I

THE PARISH

CHAPTER I

CHAPTER II

CHAPTER III

CHAPTER IV

CHAPTER V

CHAPTER VI

CHAPTER VII

BOOK II

THE COUNTY

CHAPTER I

CHAPTER II

CHAPTER III

CHAPTER VI

BOOK I

THE PARISH

INTRODUCTION

In the constitutional development of English Local Government from 1689 to 1835 our attention is claimed first by the parish. The Municipal Corporations, the Courts of Sewers, and the various kinds of statutory bodies, were all specialised structures, peculiar to comparatively small portions of the kingdom. The manorial courts survived, as local governing authorities, in but a minority of districts, and were everywhere rapidly falling to decay. Even the County Justices, who elsewhere exercised so dominating an influence, were jealously excluded from the towns which had secured the privilege of government by their own corporate magistracy. But throughout England and Wales the parochial organisation was practically ubiquitous.[1] The parish officers were to be found exercising their manifold functions among and beneath all other authorities in town and country alike; within the walls of powerful chartered municipalities; among the fens and marshes governed by ancient Courts of Sewers, and from end to end of the most highly organised counties. The financial importance of the parish was equally overwhelming. In mere public ownership of real and personal property, the

[1] The relative numbers are sufficiently striking. Exclusive of the manor and the parish, the aggregate total of local governing authorities in England and Wales—the County Justices in Quarter Sessions assembled, the Municipal Corporations, the Courts of Sewers, and the bewildering variety of statutory bodies created for turnpike, street, harbour, and Poor Law purposes—did not amount to a couple of thousands. Of active manorial courts in the eighteenth century there may have been several thousands. But right down to 1835 there continued to be no fewer than "15,635 parishes or places separately relieving their own paupers" (*First Annual Report of the Poor Law Commissioners*, 1835, p. 6); that is to say, parishes or townships levying their own rates, by their own officials, as distinct units of local administration.

thousands of parishes, with their churches and burial-grounds, their parish cottages and workhouses, their common lands and endowed charities, their market-crosses, pumps, pounds, whipping-posts, stocks, cages, watch-houses, weights and scales, clocks and fire-engines, excelled in the aggregate the whole reputed wealth and apparatus of the couple of hundred Municipal Corporations then in being. Measured by the amount of its taxation alone, the parish outweighed all other local governing authorities. By 1835 it was spending, not only more than all the other local bodies put together, but not far short of one-fifth of the budget of the national government itself. In the number and variety of regulative and administrative functions, the eighteenth century parish simply bewilders the modern student, accustomed to authorities having strictly limited spheres of action. The maintenance of the church and its services, the keeping of the peace, the repression of vagrancy, the relief of destitution, the mending of roads, the suppression of nuisances, the destruction of vermin, the furnishing of soldiers and sailors—even to some extent the enforcement of religious and moral discipline—were among the multitudinous duties imposed on the parish and its officers by the law of the land. By custom, the right and power of the parish to provide for its inhabitants whatever services or regulative ordinances were deemed locally expedient was so vaguely extensive as to be practically without ascertained limits. But this was not all. It was in no abstract sense that every citizen was said to "belong" to his parish. The responsible householder found himself bound to serve in succession in the onerous and wholly unpaid public offices of Churchwarden, Overseer, Surveyor of Highways, and Constable. The whole parish had to turn out, when summoned, to join in the "hue and cry" after suspected robbers. Once a year every one was called upon in church to send his team or go in person to labour for six days on the roads. The property-less man escaped the parish taxes and received, when destitute, the parish pay, but under the law of settlement found himself, at the discretion of the Overseers of the Poor, legally confined to his parish for the term of his natural life. The wealthy classes in town or country could buy exemption from, or commute for money, the innumerable personal obligations imposed by the parish, and thought of it therefore only as a taxing authority.   To the historian of England between the Revolution and the Municipal Corporations Act, if he is not to leave out of account the lives of five-sixths of the population, the constitutional development of the parish and the manifold activities of its officers will loom at least as large as dynastic intrigues, the alternations of Parliamentary factions, or the complications of foreign politics.

To define with any certainty or precision the legal constitution of the parish at the accession of William and Mary is, we think, impracticable.   Neither the King by charter, nor the High Court of Parliament by statute, had ever endowed it with a precise or even any written constitution. In respect to some of the most important of its features— such, for instance, as its area and boundaries, the number and method of appointment of its most characteristic officers, and their powers of taxation—it had no better warrant than ancient tradition, handed down from generation to generation, seldom embodied in any document, and admittedly differing from place to place according to local usages, of which no one outside the localities concerned had any exact knowledge. During three or four centuries at least, the national government or the Established Church had from time to time made use of such parish organisation as existed, for the fulfilment of new social obligations or the enforcement of measures of public policy.   But there had been no systematic treatment of the parish as a whole and no attempt at co-ordination in any general scheme of constitutional development.   Each imposition of a new duty, such as the provision of " harness " and arms for soldiers, the repression of vagrancy, the destruction of vermin, the mending of roads, the suppression of drunkenness, and, most important of all, the successive Acts for the relief of destitution, had prescribed for the parish (or tacitly assumed it to possess) a particular set of officers and a more or less definite procedure ; each, moreover, had placed the parish, so far as that particular function was concerned, under a separate code of law and in a different relationship to external authorities.   For, whatever may have been its origin, the parish was, in respect of all these new duties at any rate, in no sense an autonomous and independent entity, but merely the base of a more or less elaborate hierarchy of government. Thus, at the close of the seventeenth century, the student will discern few parishes exactly alike in their constitutions. The customary and statutory powers and obligations are found, as a matter of fact, divided in confused and inexplicable ways among all the different functionaries and dignitaries —among the Churchwardens, Surveyors of Highways, and Overseers of the Poor, on the one hand; and on the other, among the Lord of the Manor, his Steward and other officers, the Incumbent and the Archdeacon, and the Justices of the Peace in their individual capacities, or sitting in Petty or Quarter Sessions; whilst " the principal inhabitants " or the parishioners at large intervene or co-operate to a different degree, and in a different way, with each set of officers for each of the various functions. Yet to enable the student to follow our account of the constitutional developments in parish government from 1689 to 1835 we must attempt to give some conception of the legal relations between the different elements in the parish—we cannot say as they existed in the normal legal constitution, for there was no such constitution; but as they would, we think, have been interpreted by the law courts of the end of the seventeenth century if a series of cases from different parts of the country on all the different points had been brought before them.[1]

---

[1] There exists no trustworthy and satisfactory book on the parish as a unit of administration, though innumerable manuals have been published on the law relating to parish officers.

The chief works dealing with parish government are *The Parish,* by Joshua Toulmin Smith (1st edition, 1854 ; 2nd edition, 1857) ; and *Self-Government, Communalverfassung und Verwaltungsgeschichte in England,* by H. Rudolph von Gneist, first published in 1857 and finally revised in the 1871 edition. These works, both of great erudition, deal rather with parish organisation as it should have been according to the view taken by them of the law, than as it really existed. Toulmin Smith was able to examine only an inadequate selection of the records of the government that he describes, and Gneist examined none at all. The former was unwarranted in his ascription of a civil origin and practically unlimited powers to the Open Vestry, which he uncritically connected with the supposed free village community of Anglo-Saxon times, and nevertheless assumed to be identical with the Court Leet. His book is, in fact, untrustworthy in its quotations, and especially in its translations of terms, and is so passionately biassed as to be positively misleading to the student. Gneist, on the other hand, was historically accurate and exhaustive in detail, but derived his information almost exclusively from the statutes and Parliamentary papers. This led him, in contrast with Toulmin Smith, unduly to minimise the Vestry meeting, and to exaggerate the position of the Justices of the Peace. Both authors deal really only with the old rural England, and are inadequate as to the towns and new urban districts. Their common want of sympathy with representative institutions makes their work useless for the period after 1835. Gneist's book, however, remains of value from its exhaustive survey of official material, and it is remarkable that no English translation has ever appeared. There was a French edition in 1867-1870, by T. Hippert, entitled *La Constitution Communale de l'Angleterre.* A more balanced view is presented in *Die englische Lokal-Verwaltung,* by Dr. J. Redlich, 1901 ; translated as *Local Government in England,* by J. Redlich and F. W. Hirst, 1903, which, however, deals less adequately with the parish than with some more modern developments. For material as to the parish we have had recourse chiefly to the MS. parish archives, which exist in vast numbers in the shape of Vestry minutes and Churchwardens' accounts, and have hitherto been little noticed even by local historians. Comparatively few of these valuable documents have been printed, and then usually only in scanty fragments. The Shropshire County Council, setting an example which it is to be hoped will be followed, has made a systematic inspection of these village archives, and published a valuable inventory and description of them, in a volume of 378 pages (*Shropshire Parish Documents,* n.d.). Useful lists of published accounts of parish officers— of which perhaps the best are Dr. Edwin Freshfield's reproduction of the books of half a dozen minute parishes of the City of London, and Mr. Kitto's sumptuous volume on those of St. Martin's-in-the-Fields—will be found in the *English Historical Review,* vol. xv. April 1900, pp. 335-341 (by Miss Phillips), and *Notes and Queries,* 9th series, vols. iv. and v., 1899-1900 (by Miss Hutchins). Among published Vestry minutes we may instance those in *Memorials of Stepney,* by G. W. Hill and W. H. F. Frere, 1890 ; *History of Tooting Graveney,* by W. E. Morden, 1897 ; *Memoirs of the Life of Mr. Ambrose Barnes,* vol. l., Surtees Society, 1867 ; and *The Annals of St. Helen's, Bishopsgate,* by J. E. Cox, 1876. A valuable collection of the MS. Vestry minutes and other parish archives of many of the small parishes of the City of London, from the sixteenth to the nineteenth century, is to be found in the Guildhall Library (see Catalogue of Manuscripts).

CHAPTER I

THE LEGAL FRAMEWORK OF THE PARISH

AT the very threshold of our subject we are confronted with its indeterminate complexity. What, in 1689, constituted a parish as a unit of local government? What were its boundaries? Were these the same for all purposes? Was parish organisation actually ubiquitous throughout every part of England and Wales? Was there any, and, if so, what connection between the boundaries of parishes and those of townships, manors, boroughs, hundreds, and counties? Finally, was every English resident a parishioner? To all these questions the facts, so far as we know them, present a confused and uncertain answer.

(a) *The Area and Membership of the Parish*

The division of England into parishes was determined by no statute, and, so far as can be ascertained, by no royal decree or authoritative commission.[1] From the ecclesiastical standpoint, a parish was a "shrift-shire," the sphere of reciprocal duties between a duly commissioned priest and the inhabitants in his charge; the one party administering the sacraments and supplying religious services generally, whilst the other yielded tithes and oblations. "As these duties

---

[1] "The settling parochial rights or the bounds of parishes," says Archbishop Stillingfleet, "depends upon an ancient and immemorial custom. For they were not limited by any Act of Parliament, nor set forth by special commissioners, but as the circumstances of times and places and persons did happen to make them greater or lesser" (*Ecclesiastical Cases relative to Duties and Rights of Parochial Clergy*, etc., by Edward Stillingfleet, 1698, Part I. p. 348; also an able pamphlet on *The Rise of the Parochial System in England*, by Rev. Oswald Reichel, 1905; see also *Constitutional History of England*, by W. Stubbs, vol. i. p. 227 of 1880 edition; and *English Dioceses*, by Geoffrey Hill, 1900).

and profits are limited," said Archbishop Stillingfleet in 1698, "by undefined geographical bounds, it is necessary that these bounds should be carefully preserved, as they generally are, by annual perambulations." When, by some express act of the legislature or decision of the law courts, civil rights and duties were associated with the parish, the existing boundaries, whatever they were, seem to have been tacitly accepted. The Parliaments of the sixteenth century, for instance, habitually assumed the parish as the common unit of local administration. In so doing, however, they went beyond the facts. It was not merely that the Constable, whom, as we shall see, they associated with the Churchwardens in parochial functions, was an officer of the manor and not of the parish. Even for such a semi-ecclesiastical service as the relief of the poor, the actual units of administration, which had existed time out of mind, were in some parts of the country not parishes but separate vills, townships, or tithings within a parish. Moreover, there were many little corners, and some considerable stretches of country, which were included in no parish, either because they had been expressly exempted from parish jurisdiction, or because they had, from time immemorial, been simply ignored.[1] For practical purposes, however, we may take it

---

[1] In many cases the privilege of extra-parochiality had been granted by the King, or rarely by Parliament, or had grown up by prescription, in favour of lands occupied by monasteries, colleges, inns of court, cathedrals, bishops' palaces, forests, royal castles or residences, and even shire halls, together with the precincts of these places. Up and down the country a considerable number of small manors, parks, or ancient houses asserted a similar privilege on analogous grounds. (See the decided cases in such a book as Sir James Burrows' *Series of the Decisions of the Court of King's Bench on Settlement Cases*, 1768 ; *Cases of supposed Exemption from Poor Rate claimed on the Ground of Extra-parochiality*, by Edward Griffith, 1831 ; *Third Report of Dean Forest Commissioners*, 1835 ; *Report of the late important Trial . . . respecting the Parochial Rates . . . from . . . Richmond Terrace*, 1834.) "Catchland," says an eighteenth-century writer, we know not with what legal authority, "is land that is not known to what parish it belongs of certainty, so that the tithe for that year belongs to the first parson that tithes it, provided the liberties of his parish join the land. There is such in the east part of Norfolk" (*The Complete Steward*, by John Mordant, 1761, vol. i. p. 36). Canvey Island, at the mouth of the Thames, was, time out of mind, extra-parochial, and Mr. Round alludes to a fringe of land on the coast of Essex which was common ground between several villages (*Victoria County History of Essex*, vol. i. p. 369).

Some, at least, of these extra-parochial areas had originally been merely disregarded interstices between parishes ; see the interesting case of the "Ash Meadow" lying between certain parishes near Warkworth in Northamptonshire, which, in the seventeenth century at any rate, annually divided the commonage by lot among their parishioners, and appointed Fieldmen and "Crocusmen" by

that, in 1689, the ecclesiastical parish was, with few exceptions, the unit of local government all over England and Wales, the only deviation that we need note being that in many large parishes, chiefly in the North of England and Wales, the jurisdiction of particular Constables, Overseers of the Poor, and Surveyors of Highways was determined, unlike that of their Churchwardens, not by the boundaries of the parish, but by those of the separate manors or townships within the parish. Whatever may have been the original parcelling out of England into separate parishes, these, as they existed in 1689, presented every conceivable variety in size, shape, and population, from a mere handful of families in a rural hamlet, or the tiny but densely peopled fragment of area immediately surrounding each of the many churches of an ancient walled town, up to the one or two hundred square miles of sparsely inhabited moorland of a Northern county,[1] or the relatively early large aggregations of population of such London parishes as St. Giles's, Cripplegate, or St. Martin's-in-the-Fields, which, already by 1689, must each have numbered their twenty thousand souls. In Suffolk the average area of a parish was two square miles; in Northumberland it was six times as great. These heterogeneous units coincided in their boundaries, except by chance, with those of no other local governing authority. Even the county boundary, often the oldest and deepest cleavage in English historical geography, is not infrequently seen cutting parishes in halves, with the practical result that such parish officers as Overseers of the Poor and Surveyors of Highways might find themselves under the orders of different sets of Justices of the Peace in respect of the paupers or of the roads in different parts of their parishes.[2] With regard to the

an archaic joint meeting (*History of Northamptonshire*, by John Bridges, 1791, vol. i. p. 219; Brand's *Observations on Popular Antiquities*, vol. ii. p. 12 of 1841 edition; see also *The Growth of the Manor*, by P. Vinogradoff, 1905, p. 167).

[1] The parish of Whalley, in Lancashire, extended over 161 square miles (*History of the original Parish of Whalley*, by T. D. Whitaker, 1818, book iv. p. 243; *Growth of the Manor*, by P. Vinogradoff, 1905, pp. 166, 167). Such a parish as Halifax, in Yorkshire, was, in 1689, not only large but also very populous; presently claiming, in fact, to be the most populous in England (*Tour through the whole Island of Great Britain*, by D. Defoe, vol. iii. p. 82 of 1748 edition).

[2] Thus, to give two among many instances, the old parish of St.

relation of the parish to the manor it seems difficult to make any general statement.   In ancient times, we are told, " when the Lord of the Manor was at the charge to erect a new church," or found his manor subject to tithes, he would contrive to arrange that the area of the parish should coincide with " the unity of possession," even at the cost of constituting the new ecclesiastical division out of discontinuous pieces of land. Whether or not from this cause, we find many of the parishes of 1689 coinciding exactly with manors, others stretching over several manors, whilst others again seem to have had no connection at all with manorial divisions.   The municipal boroughs contained usually each a number of parishes, the boundaries of which often extended far beyond the walls, and occasionally even beyond the " liberties " of the municipality. On the other hand, some municipal corporations, such as Liverpool and Leeds, were exactly coterminous with a single parish.   Within the municipal borough there might be wards and precincts, each with its own set of officers, but the boundaries of these municipal subdivisions seldom coincided with those of the parishes.   The uncertainty of all these boundaries was as great as their complexity.   There were, in 1689, we may say, no accurate surveys and no detailed published maps.[1]   The various local governing authorities (except the county) would periodically arrange for formal perambulations of their areas, for the purpose of perpetuating testimony.   But this custom was already beginning to die out. " In some parishes," we read in 1787, " thirty or even fifty years elapse without the bounds and limits of the parish being ascertained, and it frequently happens, in case of law-suits, that the jury are obliged to depend on the memory of some old man." [2]   It was not even known how many parishes

Nicholas, Deptford, extended into both Surrey and Kent; it included the Manor of Hatcham and part of the Manor of East Greenwich, the latter itself extending into two counties ; and when, in 1730, the new parish of St. Paul, Deptford, was cut out of the mother parish, its boundaries were made to coincide with none of these.   The parish of Halesowen had fifteen vills or townships, twelve in Shropshire and three in Worcestershire (R. v. Justices of Salop, 1832, in *Reports of Cases*, by R. V. Barnewall and J. L. Adolphus, 1833, vol. iii. pp. 910-915).

[1] The Extents and Surveys among the Exchequer records had been made for special and political purposes, and, like monastic and other private surveys, chiefly related to the Manor or some particular estate.

[2] *Gentleman's Magazine*, January 1787, p. 5.

there were. As new churches were built, or old ones destroyed
by fire or non-repair, the ecclesiastical authorities had, from
time to time, subdivided parishes or amalgamated them ; and
it depended on particular legal decisions, arrived at in different
decades, whether the parish, as a unit of local government,
would or would not be affected by these ecclesiastical re-
arrangements.[1] The parishes were, in fact, constantly
changing in total number, and therefore in individual area,
without any note being taken. The most probable estimate
that can be framed puts the total number, at the time of the
Revolution, at about 9000.[2] The number of separately
organised townships—certainly several thousands—was quite
unascertained, and varied from decade to decade, according to
local usage and the spasmodic decisions of the law courts.[3]

[1] Thus, when in 1655 some persons were prosecuted in Newcastle-on-Tyne
for non-attendance at their parish church, they pleaded that "the whole town
of Newcastle and some other places adjoining are accounted all one parish, and
not certainly distinguished " ; and they proved that it was customary to repair
"as occasion serveth" to one or other of the various churches with which the
town was then provided, each of which had its own parish (*Memoirs of the
Life of Mr. Ambrose Barnes*, vol. l., Surtees Society, 1867, Appendix, p. 323).
Eventually it became settled that, even if the ecclesiastical authorities re-
arranged parishes for religious purposes, this did not affect the parish as a unit
of local government, which was not even a matter of ecclesiastical jurisdiction.
"The cognisance touching the bounds of parishes," says Ayliffe in 1726, "is
not allowed by our common lawyers to belong to the jurisdiction of the spiritual
court" (*Parergon Juris Canonici Anglicani*, by John Ayliffe, 1726, p. 408).
The Bishop could, of his own authority, consecrate a new church, and assign to
it a new parish : this might possibly carry with it legally the appointment of
Churchwardens and the making of a Church Rate (*Directions to Churchwardens
for the faithful Discharge of their Office*, by Humphrey Prideaux, 1701) ; though
the latter might be doubted.   But it certainly affected no other matters of parish
government.
[2] Coke had said, at the beginning of the seventeenth century, that there
were 8803 "towns" which were neither cities nor boroughs.   The total number
of "parishes and parochial chapelries" steadily increased, by subdivision
(though there were also a few amalgamations by ecclesiastical authority), until,
in 1821, John Rickman reported that it had reached 10,693 (*Preliminary
Observations*, to Census of 1821, p. xii.).   Including the uncertain number of
separately organised townships, there were, in 1835, as before mentioned,
"15,635 parishes or places separately relieving their own paupers" (*First
Annual Report of the Poor Law Commissioners*, 1835, p. 6).
[3] Whether or not particular places were entitled to be treated as separate
units for the relief of the poor, became the subject of considerable litigation.
Villages which were actually separated as reputed parishes prior to 1601, even if
originally mere vills, were held to be distinct units.   Whether a customary
separate existence, begun subsequent to 1601, would be upheld, was more
doubtful.   If the place consisted of more than two or three houses, if it had a
Constable of its own, and if it was reputed to be a hamlet, "constablewick," or
vill, its claim might be admitted.   On the other hand, the mere possession of

What we may call the membership of the parish was as indeterminate as its boundaries. Both law and custom assumed that "the inhabitants" of a parish were those who were reputed to "belong" to it. Whether by this was meant all who actually resided in the parish, or those who owned or rented lands or houses within the parish—including the "outsitters"—or merely the heads of households, or the adult men only, or those only who possessed what was called a legal settlement in the parish, was never generally determined by law, and differed according as particular rights or obligations were in question. The obligation of the parish to set the poor to work, maintain the aged and impotent, and apprentice the children, extended only to those who had a legal settlement therein; and this status depended, not on residence at all, but on a whole range of other considerations, such as parentage or marriage; the ascertained place of birth, of completed apprenticeship, or of continued service; the occupation of a tenement; the acting as a parish officer; or the payment of rates; the whole interpreted by a long and ever-growing series of statutes and legal decisions. On the other hand, the obligation of the individual to mend the roads depended merely on residence or occupation of a tenement within the parish, whilst that of serving the various parish offices depended, according as one or other of them was concerned, on varied and never generally determined combinations of residence and occupation.[1] The parish had the right to require the payment of rates from all occupiers of

a separate chapel, or long-continued separate rates, would not alone suffice, without the existence of a Constable or the reputation of being a vill. Moreover, a vill had to contain at least several houses, and not be proved to be a mere extra-parochial place. See the cases cited in *The Laws relating to the Poor*, by Francis Const, edition of 1805, which deserve more study from constitutional historians. It may possibly be that, as Mr. Round asserts, "parochial divisions are artificial and comparatively modern. The formula that the parish is the township in its ecclesiastical capacity is . . . not historically true" (*The Commune of London*, by J. H. Round, 1899, p. 10). In Northumberland, at least, it can be said that the ecclesiastical and civil boundaries are "rarely conterminous" (J. C. Hodgson, in *History of Northumberland*, 1892, vol. vi. p. 348).

[1] The few recorded cases (apart from the law of settlement), as to who was a parishioner, were cited in R. *v.* Adlard in 1824 (*Reports of Cases*, etc., by R. V. Barnewall and C. Cresswell, vol. iv. pp. 772-780). Non-resident occupiers were liable to pay rates, to receive an apprentice, and to serve as Overseer; but not to serve as Constable nor to attend the Court Leet.

lands or houses within its area, whether they were actually resident or not; but as payment of rates carried with it a legal settlement, the parish was chary of exercising this right as regards the occupiers of cottages, or newcomers who might become destitute. As for the right to be present at the Vestry meetings, and thus to take part in the government of the parish, it had apparently never been thought of sufficient importance to obtain either statutory or judicial decision, whether it was confined to the payers of one or other of the parish rates, or to residents in the parish, or to heads of households, or to male adults.[1] Thus we may conclude that there was at all times a considerable body of English subjects who, for one or other purpose, did not belong to any parish, whilst there must have been a less numerous migratory population which, for all purposes whatsoever, was completely outside parish membership.

(b) *The Officers of the Parish*

For the execution of the obligations and the fulfilment of the functions of parochial government, the parish had as its organs the four principal offices of Churchwarden, Constable, Surveyor of Highways, and Overseer of the Poor. Though these offices, as we shall see, differed widely in their origin, in their antiquity, and in their scope, they had many attributes in common. They all rested upon a different basis from the modern conception of a public official. They were unpaid. Service in them was compulsory, with certain legal exemptions,[2] upon all who belonged to the parish. The holder of

---

[1] A few cases decided particular points, but these decisions obtained neither publicity nor general authority. Thus, in Olive *v.* Ingram in 1739, it was held that, in the absence of proved local custom to the contrary, women ratepayers might vote at an election of Sexton, "this being an office that did not concern the public, or the care and inspection of the morals of the parishioners" (*Reports of Adjudged Cases*, etc., by Sir John Strange, vol. ii. p. 1114 of edition of 1795). As late as 1819 we find an indignant ratepayer asking the Home Secretary to pass a law excluding from the Vestry meetings women, minors, and persons not belonging to the parish (Home Office Domestic State Papers in Public Record Office, No. 324, 19th September 1819).

[2] The legal grounds for claiming exemption from parish offices were partly at common law and partly statutory; and it was never definitely settled whether all of them applied to all the offices. It seems that these exemptions included "all peers of the realm by reason of their dignity; all clergymen by reason of their order; and all Parliament men by reason of their privilege" (Gibson's

the office for the time being was personally responsible to the
law for the due execution of his duties, and personally clothed
with all the necessary authority for that purpose, irrespective
of the decisions or commands of the parish as a corporate
entity.   Though, as we shall explain, the method of selection
varied, both by statute and at common law, we find surviving
or growing up a widespread local custom that each of these
offices ought to be served in rotation by all parishioners
qualified according to certain traditional requirements.   " In
some places," said Chief-Justice Holt in 1698, " people are to
be Constables by house-row," or rotation among occupiers.[1]
" As it is an office of great burden," wrote Thomas Gilbert, in
1786-1787, of the office of Overseer, " it generally goes by
house-row in rotation through the parish." [2]   " In fact," summed
up Dr. Burn in 1764, " the office goes by rotation from one
householder to another "[3]—in "indiscriminate rotation," records
another observer, " among all those whose occupations
render them liable to the office." [4]   In rural parishes the
customary obligation to serve the parish offices was often
connected with the tenure of ancient farms or units of

Codex Juris Ecclesiastici Anglicani, p. 215 ; The Laws relating to the Poor, by
Francis Const, vol. i. p. 9 of 1807 edition) ; attorneys, practising barristers,
revenue officers, Justices of the Peace, aldermen of the City of London, members
of the Royal College of Physicians (by 32 Henry VIII. c. 40, 1540, as regards
City of London) ; dissenting ministers (by 1 William and Mary, c. 18, sec. 11,
1688) ; apothecaries (by 6 and 7 William III. c. 4, 1694) ; practising members
of the Royal College of Surgeons (by 18 George II. c. 15, sec. 10, 1745) ; and
latterly also non-commissioned officers and men of the militia (by 42 George III.
c. 90, sec. 174, 1802), yeomen of the guard, and officers of the army, navy, or
marines, on full or half-pay.   So little were these grounds of exemption settled
by law that in 1742 we find the Corporation of the City of London praying the
Privy Council to restrain the Attorney-General from his habit of protecting (by
noli prosequi) excise or customs officers, or Post-Office letter-carriers, who had
been indicted for refusing to serve as Constables, Churchwardens, or on the
Wardmote Inquest.   The Privy Council refused to restrain the Attorney-General
(MS. Minutes, Privy Council, 13th and 17th February and 24th August 1742,
George II. vol. viii. pp. 76, 88, 218).   The Home Secretary stated in 1835
that there was no legal objection to a revenue officer or a Justice of the Peace
serving as Overseer (Home Office Domestic Entry Book in Public Record Office,
vol. lxxii. 15th January 1835).

[1] R. v. Barnard ; see Cases and Resolutions of Cases adjudged in the Court of
King's Bench concerning Settlements and Removals, pp. 216-218 of edition of
1742.

[2] A Plan of Police, by Thomas Gilbert, 1786, p. 31 ; see also his Considerations on the Bills for the Better Relief and Employment of the Poor, 1787, p. 11.

[3] History of the Poor Laws, by Richard Burn, 1764, p. 211.

[4] General View of the Agriculture of Shropshire, by J. Plumley, 1803,
p. 133.

land-holding. Thus in the parish of Stoke-on-Trent, in Staffordshire, we are told that "an ancient custom prevailed by which three Churchwardens were annually appointed, one for Burslem, one for Sneyd, and one for Hulton; and the occupiers of certain ancient messuages and farms in those three townships . . . were bound to serve the office in rotation. This custom, with a list of the tenants then liable to serve, is recorded in the parish register under the date 1657, and attested by the Minister, as being the then ancient order in the parish; and we believe it continued to prevail, generally, until the year 1789 or thereabouts, when, on account of the decay of many of the ancient messuages and the alteration of property, it was broken through; and the appointment of the three Churchwardens has since been made without regard to the old routine; but so that one of them is yearly nominated for each hamlet, besides a fourth chosen of late years by the Rector."[1] Such a custom explains why we find a parish Vestry appointing a particular person to an office "for" a specified farm, or "for his mother's estate,[2] no service having been done for the said little parcel of land these forty years";[3] or why a woman would be appointed "because the turn had come to her house."[4] Traces of similar service by tenure are specially frequent in the case of the Constable. Thus, about the middle of the seventeenth century, the inhabitants of Cole Aston, in Derbyshire, petition the Justices in Quarter Sessions against the refusal of some of their neighbours to accept the office in their turn, alleging "that whereas there be twenty-four oxgangs of land within the village and hamlet of Cole Aston . . . and for nine of the said twenty-four oxgangs of land your petitioners or their tenants have served . . . and the owners . . . of fifteen oxgangs have not served."[5] A similar custom even

[1] *The Borough of Stoke-on-Trent*, by John Ward, 1843, p. 213.

[2] MS. Vestry Minutes, Burton Bradstock, Dorsetshire, 29th March 1703. At Stretford, a township of Manchester, we see the Chapelwardens in 1714, 1723, and other years, appointed "for" particular estates (*History of the Ancient Chapel of Stretford*, by H. T. Crofton, Chetham Society, vol. xlii. 1899, p. 108).

[3] *History of the Parish of Ribchester*, by Tom C. Smith and Rev. Jonathan Shortt, 1890, p. 160.

[4] Thus, the records of Ribchester (Lancashire) show that the Overseers, who evidently served habitually "for" particular hereditaments, were, between 1660 and 1800, at least six times women (viz. in 1674, 1675, 1779, 1782, 1786, and 1795), who appointed deputies (*ibid.* p. 175).

[5] *Three Centuries of Derbyshire Annals*, by J. C. Cox, 1890, vol. i. p. 108.

grew up with regard to the new statutory office of Overseer of the Poor. At Arundel, for instance, the Manorial Borough claimed to nominate one Overseer, who was always its retiring Mayor. "In the parish of Bodekern, in Anglesea," we are told in 1833, "the mode of determining who are to be Overseers is singular. A list was, in 1811, made out by a general Vestry, of all the farms and holdings in the parish, and they were so arranged that holdings in opposite parts of the parish should follow each other on the list. In the first year the occupiers of the two first on the list were the Overseers, and so on in rotation till 1836, when the list will expire."[1] Whether in all these cases the local custom would have been enforced by the law courts, if the case had been tried, cannot now be ascertained.[2] It is abundantly clear that such customs existed and were, in the parishes themselves, universally accepted as binding.

The common disinclination to serve differed in intensity according to the office. The position of Churchwarden was one of dignity and importance, without very onerous duties, and was therefore little objected to. Those of Surveyor of Highways and Overseer of the Poor involved unpleasant relations with one's neighbours, besides considerable work and responsibility; and they were accordingly avoided. But the post most objected to was that of Petty Constable, which was either abandoned to humble folk, attracted by its perquisites, or else invariably filled by a substitute.[3] It was, indeed, a

---

[1] MS. Minutes, Town Council, Arundel (Sussex), 4th April 1769; First Report of Poor Law Inquiry Commissioners, Appendix A, Walcott's Report, p. 184. At Dolgelly in 1753, the Justices recognised a similar custom, appointing alternately from town and country (MS. Sessions Rolls, Merionethshire, 1753). An "agreement" to similar effect, for both Overseer and Constable, by the parish of Penderin is "confirmed" by the Justices in 1702 (MS. Minutes, Quarter Sessions, Breconshire (1st July 1702). In Dorsetshire parishes, in the early part of the eighteenth century, service as Overseer evidently went by farms, the women occupiers serving in their turn (see, for instance, MS. Vestry Minutes, Burton Bradstock, Dorsetshire, 1700-1721).

[2] Though the Overseer held a statutory office, of recent institution, filled by appointment at the hands of the Justices of the Peace, the custom, at Taunton in 1635, that each householder should serve in turn, was deemed locally of such authority as to override the legal right of a practising attorney to claim exemption from service altogether. This the judges would not allow, but they did not demur to the possibility of any good legal custom existing with regard to service as Overseer (R. v. Prouse, Reports of Sir George Croke, 1657, p. 389).

[3] There was thus a recognised gradation among these local offices. "Here in the country with us," writes a seventeenth century Bishop, "if a man's

common feature of all these offices that the duties could be performed by deputy. Service, moreover, could be avoided by payment of a fine to the parish funds, according to the scale customary in the parish. In many of the crowded parishes of London, and to a lesser extent in some other cities, these fines became, as we subsequently describe, an important source of income. There was yet another way of escaping the onerous obligation of parish office. By an Act of Parliament of 1699,[1] the person prosecuting a felon to conviction, or the first assignee of such person, was given the privilege of exemption from all parish offices in the parish in which the felony was committed. Under this section, the "Tyburn Ticket," as it was universally called, was habitually sold, sometimes for a large sum, to some wealthy parishioner desiring exemption.

It was common to all these parish offices that, whilst the normal term of service was one year, the occupant of the position habitually had to remain in office until his successor was installed. When, for any reason, the new appointment had not been made, we frequently find the same person serving for a second or a third year; and coming to the Justices of the Peace in Quarter or Petty Sessions to ask to be relieved of the burden of office. It thus became an object with the holder of any of these offices to find a successor, and the custom grew up of allowing the existing officers, in the absence of any reason to the contrary, the privilege of nominating those who were to be appointed to succeed them.[2] Finally, we may add that as parochial office was a burden and not a privilege, there was no property or other qualification, and not even a religious test.

stock of a few beasts be his own, and that he lives out of debt, and pays his rent duly and quarterly, we hold him a very rich and a sufficient man ; one that is able to do the king and the country good service, we make him a Constable, a Sidesman, a Headborough, and at length a Churchwarden ; thus we raise him by degrees, we prolong his ambitious hopes, and at last we heap all our honours upon him. Here is the greatest governor amongst us " (*The Fall of Man*, by Rev. Godfrey Goodman, 1616, p. 139).

[1] 10 and 11 William III. c. 23, sec. 2 (called also 10 William III. c. 12 ; repealed by 7 and 8 George IV. c. 27, 1827).

[2] Some of the early law manuals even contained a form of precept to the Constables directing them to signify to the existing Overseers that they should nominate persons to succeed them in the office (see *Complete Guide for a Justice of Peace*, by J. Bond, 1696, p. 458 ; *Choice Precedents upon all Acts of Parliament relating to the Office and Duty of a Justice of the Peace*, by Richard Kilburn, 1703, p. 343).

The foremost of these parish officers, alike in representative character, extent of functions, and financial responsibility, were the Churchwardens (called also *procuratores, yconimi, guardiani ecclesiae, supervisores fabricae, custodes bonorum et ornamentorum ecclesiae,* and in English, "proctors," "kirkmasters," "keepers of the goods and chattels," "churchmasters," "churchreeves," "churchmen," or simply "wardens")[1]—two, three, four, or even more parishioners, annually chosen to fill this ancient office, the origin of which is unknown. These Churchwardens were directly responsible by custom and common law, to say nothing of the Canons of the Church, to "the Ordinary"— that is, the Bishop or his Archdeacon—as well as to the ecclesiastical courts, for the maintenance and repair of the whole, or at any rate the greater part, of the church fabric,[2] for the provision of the materials and utensils necessary for the church services, and, in conjunction with the Incumbent, for the allocation of seats in the church, the keeping up of "churchways," and the administration of the churchyard.

[1] These officers appear under one or other of these titles in monastic archives, in the first reported cases in the Year Books, and in the earliest known parish accounts (see, for instance, the admirable *Churchwardens' Accounts of Croscombe, etc. . . . ranging from A.D. 1349 to 1560,* edited by Bishop Hobhouse for the Somerset Record Society, vol. iv. 1890, and *Churchwardens' Accounts of St. Edmund and St. Thomas, Sarum, 1443-1702,* edited by H. J. F. Swayne for the Wilts Record Society, 1896); and as Churchreeves in Chaucer's "Friar's Tale" (1386). Sometimes they are distinguished by special titles as "Renter Warden," "College Warden," "Bell Warden," "Newcomen Warden," and "Warden of the Great Account," in St. Saviour's, Southwark ; or, frequently, as "Rector's Warden" and "People's Warden"; or elsewhere (as in the township of Manchester) the "head" or "chief" or "elder" or "senior" Churchwarden had different duties from those of the "acting" or "second" or "younger," and these again from the work of the third or "junior" Churchwarden. (See the *Report of the Associated Leypayers of the Township of Manchester,* 1794, p. x. ; or Dr. Edwin Freshfield's *Vestry Minute Book of St. Margaret, Lothbury,* 1887. At Birmingham one of them was always known as the Town Warden (MS. Vestry Minutes, Birmingham, Warwickshire, 13th July 1831.) For their history, rights, and duties, see *Injunctions, etc., of Bishop Barnes,* vol. xxii. of Surtees Society, 1850 ; John Ayliffe's *Parergon Juris Canonici Anglicani* (1726) ; *Directions to Churchwardens for the faithful Discharge of their Office,* by Humphrey Prideaux, 1701 ; *Provinciale,* by William Lyndewode, 1679 ; *Codex Juris Ecclesiastici Anglicani,* by Edmund Gibson, 1761 ; *The Parson's Counsellor,* by Sir Simon Degge, 1st edition, 1676 ; 7th edition, 1820 ; and *Ecclesiastical Law of the Church of England,* by Sir Robert Phillimore, 1st edition, 1873 ; 2nd edition, 1895.

[2] The chancel was usually at the charge of the Rector, or other recipient of the great tithes. But in the City of London, Norwich, and "most other cities and large towns," the parishioners, by custom, repaired the whole of the building (*Directions to Churchwardens for the faithful Discharge of their Office,* by Humphrey Prideaux, 1701, pp. 4, 7).

They were bound by oath to inquire at all times, and to report annually to the Ordinary, at the time of his visitation, as to the due performance of duty by the Incumbent and his Curates; as to the state of the church and its furniture, the parsonage and the churchyard; and—most far-reaching of all—as to any moral or religious delinquency of the parishioners.[1] By successive Acts of Parliament[2] they had been jointly associated with the Constables and Surveyors of Highways in the civil business of the parish; and, in the relief of destitution, they were, according to the words of the later Elizabethan statutes, coadjutors with the Overseers of the Poor whom the Justices appointed.[3] But unlike these officers, the Churchwardens were always assumed to be both directly representative of and responsible to their fellow-parishioners. They were, in fact, in a unique sense the popular officers of the parish itself. Their number[4] and the method by which they were chosen depended entirely on the immemorial custom which each particular parish had unconsciously evolved for this purpose. The law courts would uphold practically any proved local usage not involving the compulsory service of persons legally exempted—it might be, as regards any or all of the Churchwardens, service by simple rotation among the parishioners who were liable; it might be service in respect of the tenure of particular lands; it might

[1] " It is well known," writes an ecclesiastical biographer in 1815, " that the Churchwarden is recognised by our laws as a sort of inspector of the morals of the people ; and, in this character, is required to prefer complaints against those of his fellow-parishioners who are disorderly in their conduct. Certain articles of inquiry are tendered to them at every Bishop's visitation, to which an answer is demanded " (*Some Account of the Rev. Thomas Robinson, M.A.; Vicar of St. Mary's, Leicester*, by E. T. Vaughan, 1815, p. 110).

[2] See, for instance, 27 Henry VIII. c. 26 (Vagrancy, 1536); 5 and 6 Edward VI. c. 2 (Poor Relief, 1552); 2 and 3 Philip and Mary, c. 8 (for mending the highways, 1555); 14 Elizabeth, c. 5 (Poor Relief, 1572); 18 Elizabeth, c. 10 (Highways, 1576); 4 James I. c. 5 (for repressing drunkenness, 1606); 3 Charles I. c. 4 (unlicensed ale-houses, 1627); 13 and 14 Charles II. c. 6, and 22 Charles II. c. 12 (election of Surveyors, 1662 and 1670).

[3] 39 Elizabeth, c. 3 (1597), and 43 Elizabeth, c. 2 (1601); followed by 13 and 14 Charles II. c. 12 (1662); 1 James II. c. 17 (1685); and 12 Anne, st. I. c. 18 (1712).

[4] The most common number was apparently two, though in some parts of the country four seems to have been even more frequent, at any rate in the seventeenth century (*Injunctions and other Ecclesiastical Proceedings of Bishop Barnes*, edited by J. Raine, vol. xxii., Surtees Society, 1850). But there might be a custom to choose only one ; in other cases three, five, or six ; or even (as at Leeds) eight.

be appointment at the free choice of an open meeting of all the parishioners; it might be selection by co-option of a close or " select" body; it might be simple nomination by the retiring Churchwardens;[1] it might be appointment by the Incumbent or, as at St. Marylebone, in Middlesex, by the ground landlord and patron of the living,[2] by the Municipal Corporation (as at Arundel and Ruthin), or (as for the Withington and Stretford townships of Manchester), even by the Lord of the Manor;[3] it might be any combination of these methods. Sometimes the Churchwardens would be chosen by or for the parish as a whole; sometimes, on the contrary, one or more would be chosen by or for each of the several townships of the parish, with perhaps an additional one by the Incumbent. In the large parish of Tiverton, in Devonshire, one was chosen for the town and one for the country.[4] In one case, at any rate—that of Brighton—by an ancient custom confirmed by agreement in 1570, different occupations were to be represented, two Churchwardens being always " substantial fishermen," and one a " landsman."[5] No statistics exist as to the relative prevalence of these legal customs. In all the hundred parishes of the City of London, throughout the whole county of Cheshire,[6] and doubtless in many other districts, the Churchwardens were all elected by the Vestry, whether open or close. On the other hand, it was claimed by churchmen that the more ancient and frequent custom was for the Incumbent to choose one and the Vestry the other—a custom which Convocation vainly sought to make universal by embodying it in the Canons of 1604.[7] What the law courts of William and Mary would have held in a parish where no

---

[1] See a case in *The Parish Officer's Complete Guide*, by John Paul, 1793, p. 6.

[2] Confirmed by 8 George III. c. 46 (1767).

[3] MS. Vestry Minutes, Manchester, 4th April 1738 ; so also at Stockport.

[4] *Historical Memoirs of Tiverton*, by Martin Dunsford, 1790, pp. 441-447.

[5] MS. Vestry Minutes, Brighton, Sussex, 9th April 1835. An analogous arrangement, which did not have time to stiffen into a legal custom, was made at Devonport in 1817, when the Vestry agreed "that one-half of the Overseers of the Poor shall be chosen and appointed from amongst persons belonging to the Government departments in this parish, and one Churchwarden alternately elected from the parishioners within the town and parish, and from amongst the persons so employed as before mentioned " (MS. Vestry Minutes, Devonport, Devonshire, 7th April 1817).

[6] *The Parish in History, in Church and State*, by an Hereditary High Churchman, 1871, p. 6.

[7] 89th Canon (*The Ecclesiastical Canons of 1604*, by C. H. Davis, 1869).

local custom could be proved is doubtful: the Incumbent
would have pleaded the Canons of 1604, whilst the inhabitants
would have urged that of a common right " every parish ought
to choose their own Churchwardens." [1]　" The proper and
regular mode " of certifying the election was for the existing
" Churchwardens to return two persons to succeed them," after
they had been chosen according to the local custom, any
election by a Vestry meeting being made by show of hands,
and, if necessary, by polling.[2]

The new Churchwardens had to present themselves to the
Archdeacon on his annual visitation, in order to be sworn in.
But the Archdeacon's function was purely ministerial: he
could not legally refuse to swear a duly-elected person whom
he considered quite unfit—a poor labourer or a servant, a
publican or a sinner, a dissenter [3] or an infidel.　" For the
Churchwarden," said the judges, " is a temporal officer; he has
the property and custody of the parish goods; and as it is at
the peril of the parishioners, so they may choose and trust
whom they think fit, and the Archdeacon has no power to elect
or control their election." [4]　When we remember the financial
responsibilities of the Churchwardens' office, and the distinctly
ecclesiastical and disciplinary character of some of their
functions, this absence of all test of fitness was remarkable, and
led, as we shall see, to some strange results.

The relation between the Churchwardens and the inhabitants, in regard to the expenditure eventually met out of
the Church Rate, was never expressly defined.　This expenditure was neither authorised by any statute nor limited by one.
But by custom and common law, not to say also the Canons of
the Church, certain expenditure was, as we have already

[1] Lord Chief Baron Hale, *Reports of Cases*, etc., by Sir Thomas Hardres,
1693, p. 379 ; a dictum adopted by Chief Justice Holt, *Reports of Cases*, etc.,
by Thomas Carthew, 1728, p. 118 ; see *The Parish*, by J. Toulmin Smith,
1857, p. 81.　In the case of Hubbard v. Sir Henry Penrice, in 1746, as regards
Heston (Middlesex), where the existence of any custom was in dispute, Chief
Justice Lee threw the onus of proof on the plaintiff who urged the democratic
view (*Ecclesiastical Law*, by Sir Robert Phillimore, vol. ii. p. 1481, of edition
of 1895).

[2] *Ibid.* p. 1471.

[3] By 1 William and Mary, c. 18, sec. 7, 1688, a dissenter might, if he chose,
execute the office by deputy.

[4] Morgan v. Archdeacon of Cardigan, *Reports of Cases*, etc., by William
Salkeld, vol. i. p. 165 (Sir Robert Phillimore's *Ecclesiastical Law*, vol. ii. p.
1480 of edition of 1895).

pointed out, obligatory on the Churchwardens,[1] and from the earliest recorded decisions the courts had upheld the right of the parish to sanction other expenditure on public objects. Various sources of income had, in early times, been at their disposal. They were not only the supervisors of the church, and wardens of its ornaments and other possessions, but also, in some senses, general trustees for the parish—to use the celebrated words of Sir Matthew Hale, they were " by the common law a special corporation to take goods or personal things to the use of the parish." [2]   So long, therefore, as their expenditure could be met by the income from " the church stock " or other trust property, customary fees for lights and particular church services, the voluntary offerings of the faithful, and the profits of " churchales," public games and other village sports and feasts, as seems usually to have been the case down to the Reformation, the Churchwardens needed no rate, and it is doubtful whether they could have been compelled to submit their accounts to the inhabitants, as they certainly were neither required nor accustomed to submit them to the Ordinary or to any Justice of the Peace.[3]   But the legal authorities took it for granted that, where these sources were insufficient, a rate—the celebrated Church Rate—could be levied by the Churchwardens on all the parishioners to recoup themselves for their outlay.[4]   When a rate was required the Churchwardens had to submit both their accounts and the

[1] It is noteworthy that Archbishop Thomas Secker, in his *Eight Charges delivered to the Clergy*, 1769, clearly implies that it is the Churchwardens, not the Vestry, who have the power to order repairs.

[2] *Analysis of the Law*, by Sir Matthew Hale, 1713, p. 59.

[3] " The Justices have no power over him *quatenus* Churchwarden " (R. *v.* Peck, in 1663 ; see *Cases in Law wherein Justices of Peace have Jurisdiction*, by S. Blackerby, 1717, p. 178).

[4] The Church Rate was never authorised by statute, except during the Commonwealth, by an Ordinance of the Long Parliament of 9th February 1647 (Scobell's *Acts and Ordinances*, 1658, Part I. p. 139); and by contemporary Local Ordinances like those for Bristol in 1650 and 1656 (Ancient Bristol Documents, by J. R. Bramble, in *Proceedings of Clifton Antiquarian Club*, vol. i. pp. 51-57, 1888). These became void at the Restoration, and although a Bill was introduced in the House of Commons, 18th May 1661, authorising the Churchwardens to make rates for repair of the church fabric, to be signed (like the Poor Rate) by two Justices, this never became law (*Notebook of Sir John Northcote*, by A. Hamilton, 1877, p. 127).   An amendment to enable the Church Rate to be more easily recovered at law was added by the House of Commons in 1692 to a Tithes Bill ; but this eventually became law in 1696 (7 and 8 William III. c. 6) without it (*House of Lords Manuscripts*, vol. i. N.S. 1900).

proposal to make a rate to a meeting of the inhabitants. What exact legal redress the Churchwardens had if the inhabitants refused to sanction the rate remained, right down to the middle of the nineteenth century, a moot question. We may, however, assume that in the halcyon days of the union between Church and State—at any rate for the greater part of the eighteenth century—the ecclesiastical courts would have ordered the Churchwardens to make the rate on their own authority, and the civil courts would have upheld their right to distrain on defaulters, even if the local Justice of the Peace had not, from the outset, arbitrarily backed up the parish officers by issuing his own distress warrants and committing the recalcitrants to gaol.[1]

If we had been describing the parish organisation at the end of the fifteenth instead of the seventeenth century, we

[1] See *Precedents in Causes of Office against Churchwardens and Others*, by W. Hale Hale, 1841 ; and R. *v.* Churchwardens of Lambeth, 1832, in *Reports of Cases*, by R. V. Barnewall and J. L. Adolphus, 1833, vol. ii. pp. 651-654. The Churchwardens had sometimes assistants for particular duties. We do not hear much in parish records of the Sidesmen, or Synodsmen, supposed to have been chosen to represent the parish at the ecclesiastical synods or at visitations of the Ordinary, and in later days becoming general assistants of the Churchwardens for ecclesiastical purposes (see *Injunctions, etc., of Bishop Barnes*, vol. xxii. of Surtees Society, 1850, p. 141 ; Edmund Gibson *Of Visitations*, 1717, pp. 59-61 ; and his *Codex Juris Ecclesiastici Anglicani*). In Stepney there were, in 1580, "appointed and named certain ancient persons in every hamlet to be assistants to the Churchwardens," their principal duty in that extensive parish being to collect the "puage" or seat-rents (*Memorials of Stepney*, by G. W. Hill and W. H. F. Frere, 1890, p. 4). Special assistants of the Churchwardens, appointed annually by them, were the "distributors of the provision for the destruction of noisome fowl and vermin," in pursuance of 24 Henry VIII. c. 10 (1533); 8 Elizabeth, c. 15 (1566); 14 Elizabeth, c. 11 (1572), and 39 Elizabeth, c. 18 (1597). The "collector of all manner of vermin" is mentioned in sixteenth century parish accounts ; that of 1569-1571 at Bishop's Stortford contains an unusually varied selection of vermin destroyed at the expense of the special vermin rate, including hedgehogs, moles, weasels, rats, polecats, mice, crows, magpies, hawks, bullfinches, kingfishers, and starlings (*Records of St. Michael's Parish Church, Bishop's Stortford*, by J. L. Glasscock, 1882, p. 156). How long these officers existed is not clear. A pamphlet of 1611 says the Acts made "so small an allowance . . . that no man made account thereof" (*The Commons' Complaint*, by Arthur Standish, 1611, p. 46). We doubt whether any such special assistants still formed part of the parish economy in 1689, when the Churchwardens seem to have contented themselves with paying by the piece, out of the Church Rate, for vermin brought to them by any one who chose to kill it (*The Exact Constable . . . as also the Office of Churchwarden*, by E. W., 1682, pp. 115-119). The practice did not quite die out until 1860-1870 (see *Dursley and its Neighbourhood*, by J. H. Blunt, 1877, pp. 47-49 ; *History of Torquay*, by J. T. White, 1878, p. 128 ; and the paper "On the Destruction of Vermin in Rural Districts," by T. N. Brushfield, vol. xxix., p. 291, of *Proceedings of the Devonshire Association*, 1897).

should have had, among the parish officers, to give the premier place to the Constable.[1] Down to the latter part of the sixteenth century it is to the Constable and not to the Churchwardens that Parliament entrusts the supervision over beggars, the lodging of the impotent poor, the apprenticing of children, and the general superintendence of the civil economy of the town or village.[2] Even after the famous Elizabethan statutes establishing the Churchwardens, together with specially appointed functionaries called Overseers, as the Poor Law authorities, Parliament continued for another century to designate the Constables as the premier officers in the administration of the Vagrant Acts, the supervision of ale-houses, and the calling of parish meetings.[3] Moreover, the Constable, unlike the other officers, was by common law a " Conservator of the Peace," and was authorised, not only to apprehend any person who had committed a felony, but also, if he saw any minor offence committed, or even a breach of the peace about to take place, to apprehend the offender, and put him in the stocks for safe custody, or detain him in " the cage," where one existed, or in his house, until he could bring

---

[1] The "Petty" Constable of the parish, township, or manor is to be distinguished from the "High" Constable, an officer of the Hundred, appointed normally by the County Justices in Quarter Sessions. The origin and early history of the office is obscure. It is first mentioned in a writ or mandate of 36 Henry III. (1252), but does not get into the Statute Book till 13 Edward I. St. II. c. 6 (Statute of Winchester, 1285), or into literature until its mention in *Piers Ploughman* in 1362. Perhaps the best account of it is still the rare pamphlet, *The Office of Constable*, by Joseph Ritson, 1791 ; see also Bacon's *Office of a Constable*, 1618, vol. vii. pp. 749-754 of Spedding's edition of his *Works* ; *The Commonwealth of England*, by Sir Thomas Smith, 1621 ; *The Exact Constable*, etc., by E. W., 1682 ; the well-known treatises of Lambard, Dalton, and Burn ; "The Office of Constable," by H. B. Simpson, in *English Historical Review*, October 1895 ; and *History of the Criminal Law*, by Sir J. F. Stephen, vol. i. pp. 194-200. The present legal position may be conveniently seen in Shaw's *Parish Law*, edition of 1895, by J. Theodore Dodd, pp. 299-302.

[2] 19 Henry VII. c. 12 (1504) ; 22 Henry VIII. c. 12 (1531) ; 27 Henry VIII. c. 25 (1536) ; 1 Edward VI. c. 3 (1547) ; 3 and 4 Edward VI. c. 16 (1550) ; 14 Elizabeth, c. 5 (1572) ; 27 Elizabeth, c. 13 (1584) ; 39 Elizabeth, c. 4 (1597). In some small towns as distinguished from rural villages, the Constable seems to have continued to be a leading personage throughout the eighteenth century. In 1783 a letter arriving at Olney (Bucks), addressed to "the mayor or other chief magistrate," was opened by the Constable (*Works, Correspondence, etc., of William Cowper*, edited by R. Southey).

[3] 1 James I. c. 7 (1604) ; 7 James I. c. 4 (1609) ; 3 Charles I. c. 4 (1627) ; 13 and 14 Charles II. c. 12 (1662) ; 3 William and Mary, c. 12 (1691) ; 8 and 9 William and Mary, c. 16 (1697) ; 11 and 12 William III. c. 18 (1699).

him before a magistrate. Thus, of all these local officers it
was the Constable who was brought into the closest contact
with the personal rights and liberties of the inhabitants. His
staff of office, sometimes affixed to the door of his house, was a
symbol of real authority. On the other hand, the Constable
had historically little or no connection with the parish as
such. Originally an officer of the manor, or possibly of the
vill or tithing,[1] and never expressly transferred to the parish,
he continued right down to the reign of Victoria, in some
parts of England (especially in the northern counties), to be
appointed at the Court Leet, for an area which was often not
identical with a whole parish. When in the course of the
seventeenth century the Court Leet, over large districts of
England, ceased to be held, or omitted to appoint a Constable,
the choice was by statute transferred, " until the lord of the
leet should hold his court," not to the inhabitants of the
locality, but to any two Justices of the Peace in Petty or
Quarter Sessions.[2] Accustomed by this time to the parish as
the unit of administration, for which they already appointed
Surveyors of Highways and Overseers of the Poor, the Justices
seem to have silently ignored the manor, and, throughout the
South of England at any rate, to have habitually appointed
parish Constables. But whether in the north or in the south,

[1] Officers discharging apparently the same duties as Constables were to
be found in the sixteenth, seventeenth, and eighteenth centuries, under the
names of " headborough," " boroughhead " (which should be " headborh " and
" borhead," or chief pledge), " borsholder " (Kent), " thirdborough " (Warwickshire), and " tithingman,"—frequently, it will be remembered, mentioned in
Shakespeare, and occasionally in such statutes as 28 Henry VIII. c. 10, 20
Henry VI. c. 14, and 2 Edward III. c. 3. These names are all treated by the
legal authorities as synonyms of Constable (see, for instance, *Eirenarcha*, by
William Lambard, 1602, book i. p. 13 ; *Law*, by Sir Henry Finch, 1627 ;
The Country Justice, by Michael Dalton, 1619) ; though the records show
that some of them often acted as assistants to the Constable. Sir Wm. Blackstone suggested that the Constable combined two offices : one ancient, represented by the above archaic titles ; the other dating only from Edward III.
(*Commentaries on the Laws of England*, 1765-1769). To the modern historian,
the titles certainly suggest the possible survival of officers of the English
village, anterior to the systematisation of the manorial courts, if not even to
the ecclesiastical parish. In this connection is significant, not only the persistent popular belief in the right of the inhabitants of each tithing to
nominate their own tithingman, but also the prevalence of the custom of service
by rotation, or in respect of tenure.

[2] 13 and 14 Charles II. c. 12 (1662). Ritson suggests (p. xxiii.) that the
transfer of the Constable from the Manor to the Parish may have been intended
by the writ of 36 Henry III. (1252).

chosen at the Court Leet or appointed by Quarter or Petty
Sessions, the Constable was in all historic times pre-eminently
the Justices' man. He had, under penalty of indictment, to
execute their warrants and obey their orders.[1] He had to
attend them in Petty and Quarter Sessions, and (as we shall
describe in our chapters on the County) make various presentments and returns on his own initiative. Even when the
Justices did not appoint him, they could take upon themselves,
in Quarter Sessions, to excuse him from service. He was, in
fact, the underling of the High Constable, the principal officer
of Quarter Sessions in each Hundred, on whom he had to
attend and for whom he sometimes levied a County Rate. In
spite of no little misapprehension on the part of legal anti-
quarians and literary men [2]—in spite, moreover, of the growth
in some places of a habit of suggesting names to the Justices—
the inhabitants of the parish never acquired any legal right to
interfere with his selection or appointment. Exactly how his
expenses were paid prior to 1778 remains in obscurity.[3] In
many places, especially in the northern counties, the Constable
seems, from time immemorial, to have reimbursed himself by
levying on the manor or tithing a " Constable's Rate," either
by his own authority, or else with the sanction of the Court
Leet or the local Justices.[4] But, in the south of England, this
power appears to have been lost by disuse before the seventeenth century, and we find Parliament in 1662 expressly

---

[1] " He is indictable for refusing to execute a Justice of Peace's warrant "
(Rolle's *Reports*, under date 1619 ; *Cases in Law wherein Justices of Peace have
Jurisdiction*, by S. Blackerby, 1717, p. 56). The best description of the duties
of the Constable as an officer of the Justices is that in the MS. Minutes, Quarter
Sessions, Lancashire, 16th October 1788.

[2] " The parish," said Selden, " makes the Constable, and when the
Constable is made he governs the parish (*Table Talk*, by John Selden). It was
even explicitly argued, in a debate in the House of Commons in 1755, that
Constables were not subordinate to or under the direction of Justices (*Parliamentary History*, 15th January 1755). This, however, only meant that they
had certain legal rights and duties of their own.

[3] In 1778, by 18 George III. c. 19, it was provided that his accounts should
be submitted by the Overseers to a meeting of inhabitants, and paid by the
Overseers out of the Poor Rate.

[4] See the excellent *Constables' Accounts of the Manor of Manchester* (1612-
1776), published by the Manchester Town Council, 1891-1892. The only case
in the South of England in which we have come across evidence of a separate
Constable's Rate in the eighteenth century is that of Lewes, in Sussex (*History
and Antiquities of Lewes*, by T. W. Horsfield 1824-1827), to which we recur in
Book III. Chapter III. " Inchoate Municipalities."

empowering a parish rate, on the lines of the Poor Rate, to be made for the Constable's expenses connected with vagrancy. The Constable exacted certain customary fees, authorised by statute in 1606 and 1754,[1] and was allowed certain expenses by the Justices in or out of sessions, and in our description of the government of the county we shall show that these fees and expenses were sometimes made the excuse for petty extortion.

Besides the Churchwardens and the Constable, every parish possessed certain statutory officers established by Tudor legislation, viz. the Surveyor of Highways and the Overseers of the Poor. Parliament had added these officers to the parish economy apparently as *ad hoc* assistants to the Constables and Churchwardens. In both cases they had acquired, during the seventeenth century, a more independent position, so that, by 1689, we are compelled to treat them as occupying distinct offices. Like their more ancient colleagues, they were annually chosen, unpaid, and compelled to serve under penalty of a fine. In respect of their personal responsibility under the law, subjection to an authority outside the parish, and indeterminate relations to their fellow-parishioners, their position was even more anomalous.

From their establishment by statute of 1555[2] down to 1691, the Surveyors of Highways—otherwise called "overseers" or "supervisors" of the highways, or, more familiarly, "waymen," "waywardens," "boonmasters" (in Lincolnshire), "stonewardens" or "stonemen"—had been chosen by "the Constables and Churchwardens," with more or less participation by some of the other parishioners at their discretion. But by

---

[1] 3 James I. c. 10, sec. 1, and 27 George II. c. 20. Only his vagrancy expenses were to be met by the rate under 13 and 14 Charles II. c. 12 (1662).

[2] By 2 and 3 Philip and Mary, c. 8 ("the statute for mending of the highways"), the "Constables and Churchwardens" were to appoint, after calling together, "a number of the parishioners." By 13 and 14 Charles II. c. 6 (1662), the "Churchwardens and Constables or tythingmen" are to appoint "with the advice and consent of the major part of the inhabitants" present in church at the close of morning prayer. This Act expired in 1670, when, by 22 Charles II. c. 12, the old phraseology was reverted to. The best account of the actual working of the Surveyors of Highways at the end of the seventeenth century is the little book *Of Repairing the Highways*, by William Mather, 1696. For the law, see the well-known works of Lambard, Dalton, and Burn ; the excellent *Digests of the General Highway and Turnpike Acts*, by John Scott, 1778, and *Bibliography of Road-Making and Maintenance*, by S. and B. Webb, 1906.

an amending Act of the latter year,[1] which governed the procedure for three-quarters of a century, thé function of the parish officers and inhabitants was restricted to the submission to the local Justices of the Peace of a list of holders of land, or "most sufficient inhabitants of the parish," from among whom the Justices appointed the Surveyor at their uncontrolled discretion.   It was to the local Justices that the Surveyor had to report upon the state of the roads; it was from them that he received the charge on his appointment; it was to them that he looked for any orders or directions as to the work to be done; and it was to them that he rendered his accounts.   If more money was needed than was supplied by customary sources and casual receipts, it was the Justices in Quarter Sessions who ordered a Highway Rate.[2]   To the inhabitants of the parish the Surveyor was rather in the position of a director and superintendent than in that of a subordinary.   He summoned the substantial inhabitants to send their teams and men, and the cottagers to appear in person, for the performance of the six days' statute duty, at such dates and on such parts of the roads as he chose.   He levied the penalties on the defaulters, and collected commutation money from those who preferred to avoid personal service. He gave peremptory orders for the removal of obstructions from the highways, including the cutting of neighbouring hedges and the scouring of neighbouring ditches.   What remained to the parish was only the common law liability to be presented to Quarter Sessions or the Assizes for failing to keep its highways in repair, and the very real peril of being subjected to a substantial fine, which the Sheriff could legally levy on any inhabitant, but which was collected in practice by the Surveyor of Highways as an unlimited additional rate.

The Overseers of the Poor, definitely established by statute in 1597,[3] were, a hundred years later, nominally as free from

---

[1] 3 and 4 William and Mary, c. 12 (1691).

[2] The Surveyor of Highways could be fined for disobedience to the Justices' orders.   In 1770 the "Overseers of Roads" of a Lancashire parish were even indicted at the Assizes, and convicted, for this offence (*Observations on the General Highway and Turnpike Acts*, by Thomas Butterworth Bayley, 1773, p. 31).

[3] The office of Overseer may be said to have originated in that of the collectors of parish alms or rates, who are mentioned, says Toulmin Smith, in the Year Books (44 Edward III.) and in so early a law book as *Doctor and Student*

the control of their fellow-parishioners, and as much subject
to the Justices of the Peace, as were the Surveyors of Highways. The parishioners had, in their case, by law not even
the opportunity of submitting a list of names. Their appointment rested exclusively with two Justices, who could select
for the office any two, three, or four "substantial householders" of the parish; and they might, by law or custom
(especially in the northern counties named in the statute
of 1662) appoint separate Overseers for distinct townships
of the parish.[1] From the outset it had always been to the
Justices that the Overseers had annually to submit their
accounts for allowance, and their proposed Poor Rate for
signature. Any Justice could order them to relieve a
destitute person, and they had necessarily to be frequently
appearing at Petty and Quarter Sessions as suppliants for the
orders without which paupers could not be removed to their
settlements, bastardy contributions obtained, or destitute
children apprenticed. But in spite of these facts the Overseers of the Poor were, in law as well as in practice, less
subject to the Justices and more dependent on the consent of

(*The Parish*, p. 178). They are expressly authorised in 27 Henry VIII. c. 25
(1536), and 5 and 6 Edward VI. c. 2 (1552). In the Vestry Minutes of Steeple
Ashton (Wilts) we see separate "distributors" appointed in 1573, and again in
1623, in addition to the "collectors for the poor" (*The Parish*, pp. 510, 640).
In 1572 the Act of 14 Elizabeth, c. 5, established a new officer called Overseer,
to be appointed by the Justices to supervise the labour of rogues and vagabonds
who were set to work by Justices' order ; and collectors were also to be appointed
by the Justices. A quarter of a century later these precedents seem to have
been combined in the Act of 39 Elizabeth, c. 3 (1597), to create a new office,
that of Overseer of the Poor, to be appointed by the Justices, both for setting
the poor to work and for collecting the rate. At Bishop's Stortford (Herts) the
collectors went on until 1653, and no Overseer was appointed until 1650 (*The
Records of St. Michael's Parish Church, Bishop's Stortford*, by J. L. Glasscock,
1882, p. 158). At St. John's, Chester, there were no Overseers till 1704, but
merely "collectors of the Poor's Rate," who paid the money to the Churchwardens (*Lectures on the History of St. John Baptist Church and Parish*, by
S. Cooper Scott, 1892, p. 124).

The literature on the office of Overseer of the Poor, including as it does the
whole three centuries of controversy as to the Poor Law, is practically endless.
Beginning with *An Ease for Overseers of the Poore*, 1601, we may cite, in
particular, the well-known works of Lambard, Dalton, and Burn ; Sir Matthew
Hale's *Discourse concerning the Poor*, 1695 ; and *History of the Poor*, by
Thomas Ruggles, 1797.

[1] 13 and 14 Charles II. c. 12. The Justices, we believe, seldom exercised
any real choice, and were only too glad to get any one willing to serve. Even
poor labouring men, temporary inhabitants, and women, were held to be eligible
if no more suitable persons were available. Thus it came about that in most
places the retiring Overseers nominated their successors.

their fellow-parishioners than was the Surveyor of Highways. Once admitted to office, an Overseer—well termed by Sir John Fielding "the father-in-law of the parish"[1]—was liable to be indicted for manslaughter if a destitute inhabitant died of starvation, after having been refused relief. Hence any Overseer was legally entitled to insist on the Poor Rate for reimbursement of all his legal expenditure being signed, whatever the Justices might choose to resolve on the subject. The fact that the Churchwardens were statutorily joined with them as Overseers required all these officers to concur in some of the more important acts of Poor Law administration, and the Churchwardens, as we have seen, were usually popularly elected. Thus the Overseers had to secure at any rate some measure of consent from their fellow-parishioners, even before this consent was rendered necessary for particular purposes by the legislation of 1691-1723.

(c) *The Servants of the Parish*

Besides the unpaid and compulsory serving officers of the parish, who held a definite legal position and were clothed with independent powers, most parishes equipped themselves, at one time or another, with a staff of paid subordinates, who served more or less under the direction of the principal officers, the Incumbent, and the Vestry. Foremost among these in antiquity, if not in importance, was the Parish Clerk, holding an immemorial freehold office half-way between that of a curate or assistant minister and that of a church menial.[2] The law left the appointment either to the Incumbent or to

---

[1] *Extracts from such of the Penal Laws as principally relate to the Police and Good Order of the Metropolis*, by Sir John Fielding, 1761, p. 415.

[2] "In pre-Reformation days they (the Parish Clerks) had ranked among the minor orders of the Church as assistants of the priest" (Abbey and Overton's *English Church in the Eighteenth Century*, 1887, p. 456). In the north it was not unusual, at the beginning of the eighteenth century, for there to be two Parish Clerks ; and two Newcastle parishes deliberately converted one of these places into that of a curate. In 1708 "one of the two Clerks at All Saints dying, it was thought more convenient both for parishioners and minister to have an assistant curate instead" (Vestry Minutes, All Saints, Newcastle, 23rd May 1708, in *Memoirs of the Life of Mr. Ambrose Barnes*, Surtees Society, 1867, pp. 455, 456). So at St. Nicholas, a few years later, "the Upper Clerk dying, it was thought more beneficial to have an assistant curate, paid out of the fees of the clerkship" (Vestry Minutes, St. Nicholas, Newcastle, 1725 ; *ibid.* p. 476). During the eighteenth century the Clerk's office was usually filled by an

the inhabitants in Vestry assembled, according to the custom of each parish, where it became the subject of occasional dispute.[1] Once appointed, the Parish Clerk held office for life, with the right to recover from the individual parishioners, if he could, the customary fees and dues attached to his office.[2] With the Parish Clerk we may name the Sexton (or Sacristan) and Bellringer, usually serving during good behaviour, appointed either by the Vestry, by the Churchwardens, or by the Incumbent, according to local usage.[3] Nor must we forget the Lecturer or Afternoon Preacher, whom the seventeenth and

uneducated layman, who united "the menial duties of a useful church servant" to that of taking a humble part in the performance of Divine Service. "The Clerk is not only to tag the prayers with an Amen, or usher in the sermon with a stave, but he is also the universal father to give away the brides, and the standing god-father to all the newborn bantlings" (*The Connoisseur*, 1756, vol. ii. p. 808). A tradition of clerical learning hung about the office. "A Parish Clerk," said Dr. Johnson in 1781, "should be a man who is able to make a will or write a letter for anybody in the parish" (Birkbeck Hill's edition of Boswell's *Life of Johnson*, vol. iv. p. 125). What he was in a small rural parish may be inferred from the amusing *Memoirs of P. P., Clerk of this Parish*, by Alexander Pope (Roscoe's edition of Pope's *Works*, vol. vii. p. 222, etc.) ; see also *The Antiquary*, vol. ii. p. 95, 1880, for "the office and duty of the Parish Clerk" in a Lincolnshire village in 1713. For his position in the Metropolis, see the anonymous work entitled *London Parishes*, etc., 1824.

[1] As to the conflicting views as to who could appoint the Parish Clerk—which the law left to the custom of each parish—compare John Ayliffe's *Parergon Juris Canonici Anglicani*, 1726, p. 409 ; *Notebook of Sir John Northcote*, by A. H. A. Hamilton, 1877, p. 61 ; *Historical Antiquities of Hertfordshire*, by Sir Henry Chauncey, 1700, p. 85 ; *The English Church Canons of 1604*, by C. H. Davies, 1869, pp. 85-86. When, in 1678, the new parish of St. Anne, Soho, was carved out of that of St. Martin's-in-the-Fields (by 30 Charles II. c. 8), it was expressly enacted that the Parish Clerk was to be chosen by the Rector with the consent of the principal inhabitants. In 1739 it was definitely held that he was a temporal officer, for whom no licence of the Ordinary was required, and who was not entitled to sue in the ecclesiastical courts for his dues or rate (Peake *v.* Bourne, in *Reports of Adjudged Cases*, etc., by Sir John Strange, vol. ii. p. 941 of edition of 1795).

[2] So long as the Parish Clerk was assumed to be a spiritual parson he could sue for these fees and dues in the ecclesiastical courts. But after the Restoration the Judges began to hold that he was a temporal officer, and refused to enforce the jurisdiction of the ecclesiastical courts. An amendment was, in 1692, grafted upon a Tithes Bill, to enable the Parish Clerk to recover his wages ; but the Bill eventually became law without it.

[3] The ecclesiastical authorities made repeated attempts to get these minor church functionaries into their own hands. So long as they were paid from the Church Rate the practical power of the Vestry over them was irresistible. At Greenwich, the Vestry expressly bound the newly-appointed Sexton "not to obtain any licence or faculty from the Bishop or Consistory Court for the holding of his place" (MS. Vestry Minutes, Greenwich, Kent, 3rd January 1812). At Minchinhampton (Glos.) the Parish Clerk was appointed by the Vicar and licensed by the Chancellor of the diocese (MS. Vestry Minutes, 28th April 1824), but the Vestry appointed him to be also Vestry Clerk, and paid his

eighteenth century Vestries in Metropolitan parishes delighted to appoint, in order to supplement—and it may sometimes have been to counteract—the ministrations of the Incumbent, over whose appointment the inhabitants had, as a rule, no control.[1]

Next among the Servants of the Parish we may name an indiscriminate medley of ancient offices, one or other of which we find, in particular parishes, inherited, or silently accreted from the defunct Court Leet. Service in one or other of these offices was often locally regarded as compulsory, though whether the Judges would have endorsed this doctrine, in a parish as distinguished from a manor, is not at all clear. Thus, we may see parish Vestries in the eighteenth century appointing an Aleconner or a Carnival, a Scavenger[2] or a "Town's Husband,"[3] a Bellman or a Town Crier, a Hayward or a "Common Driver,"[4] a Neatherd[4] or a Hogwarden[5]— here and there, as we shall subsequently describe, a Dykereeve or a Wallreeve, or occasionally a Bridgereeve.[6]   More common

---

salary (ibid. 29th June 1825). In the same parish, in 1825, the Sexton was appointed by the Vicar and Churchwardens only (ibid. 29th June 1825), but fourteen years later, the appointment is made by the Vestry itself (ibid. 25th July 1839). It was not unusual for this office to be held by a woman.

[1] The cases in which the advowson of the parish belonged to the inhabitants, though more numerous than is often supposed, were distinctly exceptional. Perhaps the principal instances are those of St. Saviour's, Southwark, where the appointment was in the hands of the Select Vestry ; St. James's, Clerkenwell, where it was in the inhabitants at large ; and St. Peter's at Leeds, where the advowson was vested in trustees for the parish.

[2] As at Royston, Herts, in 1783 ; see Fragments of Two Centuries, by Alfred Kingston, 1893, p. 53.

[3] MS. "Town Book" (1640-1864) of Sheringham, Norfolk, 1687.

[4] Finchley (Middlesex) resolves in 1798 "that Henry Rudd, the present Common Driver, his salary paid by the parish be discontinued for the future" (Vestry Minutes of 10th April 1798, given in Stephens' Parochial Self-Government in Rural Districts, 1893, p. 176). On the other hand, another parish, as late as 1822, "resolved that a Herdsman or Common keeper . . . be appointed by the Churchwardens and Overseers forthwith" (MS. Vestry Minutes, Mitcham, Surrey, 9th April 1822). At St. Margaret's, Leicester, a Neatherd is elected annually between 1793 and 1819 along with the Churchwardens and Sexton (MS. Vestry Minutes, St. Margaret's, Leicester). At Weston Subedge (Worcestershire) two "Fieldsmen" continued to be annually appointed, and the agricultural management of the common fields to be decided on, at a parish meeting which called itself a Vestry (but may have been only a meeting of owners and occupiers under 13 George III. c. 81, 1773), down to the enclosure of the common fields in 1852 (The Last Records of a Cotswold Community, edited by C. R. Ashbee, 1905).

[5] Some Account of the Hamlet of East Burnham, by a late resident (Harriet Grote), 1858, p. 28.

[6] For instance, in the Fens (History of the Drainage of the Great Level of the Fens, by Samuel Wells, 1830, vol. i. pp. 779-780).

than any of these, and perhaps equally archaic, was the Beadman [1] or Beadle, a messenger, often acting as an assistant to the Constable, as also to the other officers of the parish. Another frequent figure was the Dog Whipper, who kept quiet during Divine Service the dogs which the parishioners brought with them to church.[2]

More important than any of these was the Vestry Clerk, who might or might not be the same person as the Parish Clerk, whom we find beginning to be appointed by the Vestries of the more considerable urban parishes. Finally, we have to add to the staff of Servants of the Parish during the eighteenth century, an organist and sometimes other musicians, an organ-blower or "bellows-blower," and not infrequently a pew-opener. All these Servants of the Parish, appointed sometimes by the Incumbent, sometimes by the Churchwardens, with or without the "advice and consent" of a meeting of the inhabitants, and paid either by fees or by salaries from the Church Rate, aided and supplemented the unpaid officers. But although one or two of them, notably the Vestry Clerk, were destined to importance in the administrative development of the eighteenth-century parish, they none of them exercised any independent authority over the inhabitants, or were of consequence in the parish government of 1689.[3]

---

[1] So spelt in MS. Churchwardens' Accounts of Burton Bradstock, Dorsetshire, 6th April 1726, where the appointment by the Vestry is recorded. "Bedemen and bellringers" are mentioned in *The Image of Ipocrysy*, a sixteenth century satire wrongly attributed to John Skelton (*The Poetical Works of John Skelton*, by Alexander Dyce, 1843, vol. ii. p. 440).

[2] The "Dog whipper in Paules" is mentioned in *Pierce Penilesse*, by Thomas Nashe, 1592. He was also called the "knock nobbler," "peace keeper," or "sluggard waker"; and he had a long wand as well as a whip. At Bolton Percy (Yorkshire) "the dogs from the hall were sometimes allowed a special pew and were exempt from the Dog whipper's attentions" (*Lower Wharfedale*, by Harry Speight, 1902, p. 131). Occasionally, at any rate, he was appointed "for the quieting the children during Divine Service," as well as for "whipping out of the dogs" (Vestry Minutes, 9th October 1637, in *History and Antiquities of Richmond* (Surrey), by E. B. Chancellor, 1885, pp. 89-98). At Baslow his whip still hangs up in the Vestry (*History of Derbyshire*, by J. Pendleton, 1886, p. 111; *Old Yorkshire*, by W. Smith, 1881, vol. i. p. 132; *Sheffield in the Eighteenth Century*, by R. E. Leader, 1901, p. 260).

[3] The number and variety of these appointments, and the method of election, differed from parish to parish, and from generation to generation. Thus, in 1797, a Norwich parish was summoned on Easter Monday to elect 2 Churchwardens, 2 Sidesmen, 4 Overseers, 12 Auditors, an Organist, a Clerk, an Upper Sexton, an Under Sexton, a Bellows-blower, and a Pew-opener (MS. Vestry Minutes, St. Peter's, Mancroft, Norwich, Norfolk, April 1797).

(d) The Incumbent

Nor must we omit, from our description of the legal framework of the parish, the Incumbent of the ecclesiastical benefice, whether Rector or Vicar. Originally, it may be, the nucleus on which the whole parish organisation was formed, he had, during the sixteenth and seventeenth centuries, gradually ceased to be charged with definite responsibility for the civic functions which Parliament, by successive statutes, was either newly devolving on the parish, or else making the subject of more precise definition. Thus, for centuries, the parish priest had been the leading figure in the relief of the parish poor, for whom he collected the alms and oblations of his flock; and for the greater part of the sixteenth century he is referred to by Parliament as primarily responsible for the execution of this parish duty.[1] The later Elizabethan statutes on the subject omit all reference to the Incumbent, except as a payer of the new Poor Rate like the other householders. Even in the maintenance of the fabric of the church, and the provision for its services, the actual power and duty passes, either in theory or in practice, out of the Incumbent's hands, when these expenses could no longer be met from voluntary contributions, and the Churchwardens had to levy a rate. But the Incumbent was entitled to be present at the Vestry meetings, though exempt from the Church Rate, and he may even have been legally warranted in assuming the chairmanship,[2] which he frequently,

[1] See 27 Henry VIII. c. 25 (1536), and 5 and 6 Edward VI. c. 2 (1552).

[2] When, in the nineteenth century, his legal right to preside, as of course, at all parish meetings was first seriously questioned (in a case arising out of a parish quarrel in St. Mary Aldermary, City of London), the courts held, with some hesitation, that the custom had been established (at any rate so far as concerned meetings held in the church); see *The Case respecting the Right of Rectors to preside at Vestries* (1819); Wilson v. M'Grath, Barnwall and Alderson's *Reports*, vol. iii. 241; followed in R. v. D'Oyley, Adolphus and Ellis, vol. xii. p. 139. Few authorities can be quoted for the right, though one of these is Dean Prideaux's *Directions to Churchwardens* (p. 92 of 1830 edition). The presidency of the Incumbent whenever present was assumed and implied in 58 George III. c. 69, sec. 2 (1818). On the other hand, Lord Hardwicke had, in 1734, uttered dicta denying the right of the Incumbent to preside *ex officio* (Stoughton v. Reynolds, *Reports of Adjudged Cases*, by Sir John Strange, vol. ii. p. 1044 of edition of 1795; Lee's *Cases*, p. 275; Fortescue's *Reports*, p. 169); for the superior authority of which view Toulmin Smith passionately pleaded (*The Parish*, 2nd edition, 1857, pp. 288-330). See also *The Parish in History, in Church and State*, by an Hereditary High Churchman, 1871, pp. 6, 28.

but by no means universally, held. He was not obliged to attend, and his concurrence was neither required in any action by the Vestry nor in any of the rates levied by the parish officers. Yet he was, in some cases, beginning to be made use of as the authoritative representative of the parish to the outside world. By a statute of 1609 he was to certify in writing to the Justices of the Peace the Constable's account of the vagrants apprehended.[1] "He is to be present," says a legal manual of 1682, "to aid the Constable when rogues are whipped, to register the same, and send a testimonial with them afterwards, on pain of five shillings for every default." He is "to register the testimonial of every servant at his going from his service, for which he may take two pence."[2] From the middle of the sixteenth century he had kept the church register of baptisms, marriages, and burials, and was referred to for certified extracts from these archives. Presently we shall find him expressly authorised by statute to give certificates to persons going to harvest, or leaving their parishes for other work, which will exempt them from apprehension as vagrants.[3] His certificate of good character, with those of a majority of the Churchwardens and Overseers, will enable a man to obtain an ale-house licence.[4] Such a certificate will even be required before a slaughter-house licence will be granted.[5]

(e) *The Parish Vestry*

This sketch of the legal framework of the parish will enable the student to realise how slight was the part assigned at the close of the seventeenth century to the inhabitants at large.[6] At common law, as well usually by local custom, they

---

[1] 7 James I. c. 4 (1609).
[2] *The Exact Constable*, etc., by E. W., 1682, pp. 146, 147.
[3] 13 George II. c. 24 (1740).
[4] 26 George II. c. 31 (1753).   [5] 26 George III. c. 71 (1786).
[6] We leave to others the investigation and discussion of the origin of the parish, of the assumed democratic constitution of the Old English village community, and of its supposed continuance in the meeting of "inhabitants in Vestry assembled." The reader may, however, be warned that Toulmin Smith's passionate assumption of the immemorial antiquity and exclusively civil origin of the parish, the Vestry, and the Churchwardens is, to say the least, unsupported by historical evidence. There appears more authority for the contrary extreme view, stated by Bishop Hobhouse, that "no civil functions

had the right to be summoned at Easter, and at such other times
as might be necessary, to assemble in the church at the tolling

were cast upon them [the Churchwardens] until quite late in the reign of
Henry VIII., when they began to receive orders to provide harness or arms for
soldiers, etc. . . . Henceforth [the parish] passes from an ecclesiastical organisation of churchmen for their own special purposes, to a machinery which, in
addition, could discharge various functions for the civil power. It was used
regularly through the reigns of Elizabeth and James I. for maintenance of army
hospitals, for passing maimed soldiers, for relief of wayfaring Irish and others,
and for equipments of volunteers. Further, as the Hundred and Manor Courts
waned in their active control over the secular interests of the locality, the
Vestry became the chief council of the community, and, having authority to
tax the whole area of the parish, it was able to provide for any dropt duties
and expenses. By successive stages it became the highway board appointing
its waywardens and levying its Highway Rates. The care of the pound, the
appointment of hayward, the repair of the stocks, and appointment of tything-
man often lapsed into its hands" (*Churchwardens' Accounts*, edited by Bishop
Hobhouse, vol iv. p. xv. of the Somerset Record Society, 1890). This is
also the conclusion of Professor Maitland. "After weighing all that has
been said to the contrary by that able and zealous pioneer of history, Mr.
Toulmin Smith, it still seems to me that the Vestry is a pretty modern institution; that we shall hardly trace it beyond the fourteenth century; that it
belongs to the parish, a purely ecclesiastical entity, not to the township; that
it is the outcome of the Church Rate, which in its turn is the outcome of
the appropriation of tithes and the poverty of the parochial clergy; that
the Churchwardens also are pretty modern. Gradually the Vestry may take
upon itself to interfere with many things; the manorial courts are falling into
decay, and the assembly which can impose a Church Rate may easily aspire
to impose other rates; but the germ of the Vestry is an ecclesiastical germ.
The Vestry belongs to the parish; and the temporal law of the thirteenth
century knows nothing of the parish" (The Survival of Archaic Communities,"
by F. W. Maitland, in *Law Quarterly Review*, vol. ix. July 1893, p. 227).
Nor can we draw from it any valid inference as to any previous assemblies.
"To our minds it would be as rash to argue from the Vestries or parishioners'
meetings of the fourteenth and fifteenth centuries to similar assemblies of an
earlier time, as it would be to argue that the commons of the realm were
represented in the Councils of Henry II. because they were represented in the
Parliaments of Edward I. And so with the Churchwardens" (Sir F. Pollock
and F. W. Maitland's *History of English Law*, vol. i. bk. ii. chap. iii. sec. 7,
p. 603). We may add that wherever we have explored the early archives we
have found that the minutes or other records of meetings begin much later
than the accounts of parish officers; and that they usually grow out of these.
It was pointed out in an able *History of the Parish of St. Lawrence Pountney*,
by H. B. Wilson, published in 1831, that the use of the term "Vestry,"
for a meeting of parishioners, belongs almost exclusively to post-Reforma-
tion times. We find it used by Grindal in 1567 in a circular letter to the
London clergy (*History of the Church of England*, by R. W. Dixon, vol. vi.
p. 165), and in a document of 1564, quoted in *Annals of the Reformation*, by
John Strype, vol. i. part ii. p. 132 of 1824 edition. So in the parish accounts
of Steeple Ashton (Wilts), which are continuous from 1542, "the earliest date
at which the parish meeting is called a Vestry in this record is in 1569. From
that date every such meeting is so called" (*The Parish*, by J. Toulmin Smith,
1857, p. 509). In the Churchwardens' accounts of St. Martin's-in-the-Fields,
Westminster, which exist from 1525, the word "Vestry" or "Revestry" does
not occur till 1587; in the MS. Minutes of the same parish it does not occur till

of the bell, as a "town meeting"[1] or "Vestry"; normally
they had to elect one of the Churchwardens, and sometimes
all of them; they were entitled to have submitted for their
allowance the account of the Churchwardens' expenses, and to
decide on the Church Rate; they were, however, compelled by
common law, as well as by the Canons of the Church, to defray
these expenses and to maintain the church and its services
whether they liked them or not. The duly summoned "town
meeting" or Vestry meeting had an undefined right to make
by-laws on matters of parish concern, which were binding on
all the parishioners, whether they consented or not, or whether
or not they were present. It was, indeed, apparently on this
power to make by-laws that rooted the legal right of the parish
to make the Church Rate, to settle the assessment on which
this should be levied, to impose fines for non-acceptance of
parish offices, to administer the pound, the common pasture,
and the wastes of the parish, and generally to perform all
the miscellaneous services of public utility which here and
there it undertook. This by-law making power was warranted
only by immemorial custom, recognised by the law courts
from the earliest times, but beginning, in 1689, in the rare
cases in which it was questioned, to be supported with some
hesitation and dubiety. Nevertheless, whatever may have
been the origin or the antiquity of this power, the fact remains
that, as Gneist pointed out, the open parish Vestry was for
several centuries unique in England, as the only popular
assembly (other than the House of Commons) having the right
to impose compulsory taxation.[2]

To the parish officers the Vestry meeting stood in a
doubtful relation. In the appointment of the Constable and

1576 (*St. Martin's-in-the-Fields; the Accounts of the Churchwardens, 1525-1603*,
by J. V. Kitto, 1901, p. 399). An exceptionally early use of the term is the entry
of 1507 in Dr. Freshfield's *Minutes of the Parish of St. Christopher-le-Stocks*, 1886,
"articles concluded at a Vestry the sixth day of January 1507." The word
does not get into the Statute Book until 1663, when a temporary "Act for the
Regulating of Vestries" (15 Charles II. c. 5) imposed a sacramental test for
members of Select Vestries in the Metropolis.

[1] In many parishes (*e.g.* that of Thornage, Norfolk) the MS. Minutes show
that the term used was always that of "town meeting," the word "Vestry"
being adopted only in our own day. The bell, which was tolled for half an
hour, was known as the mote bell.

[2] *Self-Government, Communalverfassung und Verwaltungsgeschichte*, by R.
von Gneist, 3rd edition, 1871, p. 672.

the Overseers of the Poor, the inhabitants had legally no
share; their statutory participation in that of the Surveyor of
Highways was of the shadowest; whilst over the expenditure
of all these officers, or of the rates which they levied, they had
absolutely no control. Moreover, even where the inhabitants
are mentioned, there apparently lingered in the minds of
legislators and judges, a presumption that such inhabitants
would be only the "principal," the "chiefest and most discreet,"
"the more sufficient," or "the most substantial" of the
parishioners. And if we recollect that the Churchwardens,
the Constable, the Overseers, and the Surveyor of Highways
were clothed with powers over their fellow-parishioners which
we should now deem inconsistent with civil liberty, we can
well understand that, to the poorer folk, the parish government
appeared an uncontrollable parish oligarchy.

(f) *The Parish as a Unit of Obligation*

To the parish officers themselves the parochial organisation
appeared, we may believe, in a different light. The little
farmers or innkeepers, jobbing craftsmen or shopkeepers, who
found themselves arbitrarily called upon to undertake arduous
and complicated duties and financial responsibilities; ordered
about during the year of office by Justices of the Peace;
dictated to by Archdeacon, Incumbent, or squire; at the beck
and call of every inhabitant; losing time and money and
sometimes reputation and health over their work; with no
legal way of obtaining any remuneration for their toil and
pains,—often felt themselves to be, not the rulers, but the
beasts of burden of the parish. The truth is, that the
seventeenth-century parish, as an administrative unit, was
regarded by no one as an organ of autonomous self-government.
It was, if we may coin a new phrase, an organ of local obligation—a many-sided instrument by which the National Government and the Established Church sought to arrange for the
due performance of such collective regulations and common
services as were deemed necessary to the welfare of the State.
And they did this, be it noted, not by the creation of a
salaried hierarchy of government officials, working under the
control of the King, but by the allocation of unpaid offices and

burdensome duties among the ordinary citizens serving more or less in turn; and, as will hereafter abundantly appear in our pages, by the strict subordination of these amateur parish officers to a superior organ of local self-government, the Justices of the Peace of the county or municipal corporation.

CHAPTER II

UNORGANISED PARISH GOVERNMENT

DURING the first years of our researches into the actual working constitution of parish government, we almost despaired of constructing out of the varied and shifting relationships between Churchwardens and Constables, Surveyors and Overseers, the Incumbent and the Lord of the Manor, the parish and the Justices of the Peace, any constitutional picture at once accurate and intelligible. But as we gradually unearthed from the archives the components of parish organisation in one district after another, as we observed the effect of different environments on the relations between these parts, and as we compared the results of our investigation in sparsely populated with those in densely crowded parishes, there emerged from our material a series of definite types, to one or other of which all additional instances seemed to approximate. We classify these types under three main heads. In some places we find the parish business in the hands of a close body apart from the inhabitants at large. With these interesting and unique organisations, usually termed Select Vestries, we shall deal in the last three chapters of this Book.[1] In other parishes there was, between 1689 and 1835, a gradual evolution of what was practically a new working constitution, ultra-democratic in character, and more completely autonomous than anything now existing in the United Kingdom. The successive stages in the development of this Extra-legal Democracy we shall describe in the next chapter of this Book.[2]

[1] Chapter V. The Legality of the Close Vestry ; Chapter VI. Close Vestry Administration ; and Chapter VII. The Reform of the Close Vestry.
[2] Chapter III. An Extra-legal Democracy.

42

But over the larger part of England and Wales, the disjointed and incoherent legal framework that had been provided for the parish resulted in the local government remaining unorganised, most commonly in the hands of a Parish Oligarchy; sometimes administered practically by common consent; occasionally at the mercy of uncontrolled parish officers; less often the prey of a "boss"; and towards the end of the eighteenth century frequently subject only to the vagaries of the turbulent public meeting known as the Open Vestry. It is these various forms of unorganised parish government, changing in particular parishes from decade to decade, that we describe in the present chapter.

(a) *The Parish Oligarchy*

The most widely prevalent and also the simplest form of parish government at the beginning of the eighteenth century was that of the thinly populated rural parish made up of a few dozen families.[1] Here, on Easter Monday or Tuesday, the clergyman would meet the three or four farmers who occupied land in the parish, and who probably formed, with himself and the squire, and possibly the miller, the innkeeper, and a small freeholder or two, the only persons assessed to the rates. Two or three of the farmers would have acted, during the preceding year, as Churchwardens and Overseers of the Poor, and another, or perhaps the innkeeper, as Surveyor of Highways. Rough books, or perhaps only loose papers, in which were entered the rates received and the sums expended on behalf of the parish, would be produced for inspection at this little meeting of parish officers. Such parish account-books, kept by successive Churchwardens or Overseers, and often containing the entries for a whole century, reveal, in inextricable confusion, the multifarious duties of the parish organisation. Items relating to all the different parish functions often appear in one and the same rude account. Payments for the destruction of

---

[1] Even as late as 1831, after a great transformation of rural into urban districts, the parishes having fewer than 300 inhabitants, that is, fewer than 60 families, numbered no less than 6681, or nearly half the total (*First Annual Report of the Poor Law Commissioners*, 1835, p. 9). At the end of the seventeenth century such a population must, we imagine, have characterised four-fifths of all the parishes in England and Wales.

sparrows, hedgehogs, foxes or polecats, or "for dressing the
fields for the crows,"[1] would be mixed up with the cost of the
sacramental wine; a weekly pension to some aged pauper
would be intermingled with occasional items for thatching the
parish cottages, "Guildhall" or "Church house,"[2] "repairing
the stocks," or fitting "irons for the whipping-post";[3] sometimes clothing for a girl going out to service, or "beer for
clerk tolling the bell for Vestry" may appear next to an
annual item of "keeping the book, as usual, one shilling."[4]
There might occur such entries as "Paid the Apparitor for
proclamation,"[5] or "making a parchment levy for the use of
the parish;"[6] whilst with these would alternate "for walking
in the church on the Sunday to keep people from sleeping, and
whipping of the dogs, two and sixpence,"[7] or for whipping
this or that vagrant, "by order of the Rector,"[8] or "gave a
woman big with child to go out of the parish,"[9] or more
benignly, "paid charity to shipwrecked people"[10] or even
"given to four men who had lost their tongues."[11]   Picturesque

[1] MS. Churchwarden's Accounts, Islip (Oxfordshire), 20th October 1701.
(We owe this and other Islip references to the kindness of Mr. Adolphus
Ballard, Town Clerk of Woodstock.)   At Weston-super-Mare, then a lonely
hamlet, no fewer than sixty-four hedgehogs were paid for in 1728; and in 1745 the
principal landowner objected to such an expense "as they seem by this allowance
rather to increase" (*The Sea Board of Mendip*, by F. A. Knight, 1902, p. 101).
At West Lulworth, "chuffs' heads" and hedgehogs were paid for down to 1822,
and sparrows to 1855 (MS. Vestry Minutes, West Lulworth, Dorset).

[2] At Steeple Ashton (Wilts) the accounts show, in 1558, items for "one
dozen of reeds," and "for mending the church house with the same reeds" (*The
Parish*, Toulmin Smith, 1857, p. 508).   At West Lulworth, three centuries
later, we find in 1867, "1½ Hundred of Read Sheaves for Thatching Parish
Houses" (MS. Vestry Minutes, West Lulworth, Dorset).

[3] Parish Accounts, Hutton, Somerset, 1799 and 1823, in *The Sea Board of
Mendip*, by F. A. Knight, 1902, p. 374.

[4] Both in MS. Accounts of West Lulworth (Dorset), 1805-1835.

[5] MS. Vestry Minutes, Holt (Norfolk), 14th November 1741.

[6] MS. Churchwarden's Accounts, Holy Cross, Pershore (Worcestershire), 1st
October 1777.

[7] Almondbury Churchwarden's Accounts, 9th May 1705; see *Annals of the
Parish of Almondbury* (Yorkshire), by C. A. Herbert, 1882, p. 103; "a whip
for the dog whipper, fourpence" (MS. Churchwarden's Accounts, Burnsall,
Yorkshire, 1713, in *Upper Wharfedale*, by Harry Speight, 1900, p. 398);
"paid for one year's walking the Church to Christmas, one pound" (MS.
Churchwarden's Accounts, Holt, Norfolk, 15th January 1781).

[8] Farnham Churchwarden's Accounts, 1699, etc.; see *Records of the Parish
of Farnham Royal* (Bucks), by F. C. Carr Gomm, 1901, p. 64.

[9] MS. Churchwarden's Accounts, Islip (Oxfordshire), 16th December 1791.

[10] MS. Churchwarden's Accounts, Holt (Norfolk), 1721.

[11] MS. Churchwarden's Accounts, Bristow (Norfolk) 1733.

items of poor relief would recur—gifts of shirts and stockings,
coats and breeches, " an iron pot " for this or that poor widow,
a " strike," or bushel, of wheat or barley to some destitute
cottagers, hundredweights of coals and loads of wood for others,
payments to an old lame parishioner " to buy salve for his sore
leg," or " given to Widow Parrie to go to the doctor with her
sore eyes, and for a horse to carry her." [1]   A not infrequent
item is that for postage " For a letter from the Clerk of
Peace, 9d." [2]   " Sixpence for candles " occurs for a pauper
funeral at night, along with a lump sum for " waywarden's
expenses." [3]   Throughout the year there would run items for
" refreshments," termed expenses ; " paid for my dinner and
horse journey, two and sixpence " [4]— it may have been for
attendance at the Archdeacon's visitation, for waiting on the
Justices at Petty Sessions, for going to the Assizes to defend
a " removal " order, or for visiting the neighbouring town to
see masters to whom the parish boys could be apprenticed.[5]
The Surveyor of Highways might oblige his fellow-officers by
showing them his list of commutations and fines in lieu of
statute labour on the roads, or by consulting them as to which
days he should fix for them to send their teams and labourers ;
or might warn them that the squire had declared his intention
of " presenting " the parish to Quarter Sessions for its neglect
to mend the road that led to the Hall.   In this conversation
about accounts some objection might be taken by one of the
officers to this or that payment made by another ; there would
be grumbling at something spent on new church furniture, or

---

[1] All these occur, to give only one case, in the parish accounts of Lapworth,
Warwickshire, between 1688 and 1704 ; see *Memorials of a Warwickshire
Parish*, by Robert Hudson, 1905, pp. 205-208.   An even greater variety may
be found for Kidlington, in Mrs. Bryan Stapleton's *Three Oxfordshire Parishes*,
Oxford Historical Society, 1893, pp. 158-159.

[2] MS. Churchwarden's Accounts, Punknowle, Dorsetshire, 1815.

[3] Overseer's Accounts, Bothenhampton, Somerset, 1679 ; see *Notes and
Queries for Somerset and Dorset*, vol. vii. March 1900, p. 28.

[4] MS. Churchwarden's Accounts, Bristow (Norfolk), 1705.   " Expenses,
man, horse, and turnpikes, 7s. 2d.," occurs in the MS. Churchwarden's Accounts,
Punknowle, Dorset, 1783, along with " Visitation Court fees and Pentecost
Money, 4s. 2½d."

[5] " For going to Halesowen to seek masters for apprentices " occurs, for
instance, in the Lapworth accounts for 1690 (*Memorials of a Warwickshire
Parish*, by Robert Hudson, 1905, p. 207).   Such refreshments were also charged
for at pauper funerals.   " Bread, cheese, and drink at the burial of R. A.
13s. 3d.," is an item in the Puxton parish accounts for 1710 (*The Sea Board of
Mendip*, by F. A. Knight, 1902, p. 227).

at the grant of poor relief to the family of the squire's game-
keeper. But the officer would explain that the Archdeacon
had insisted on the one, and that a neighbouring Justice had
ordered the other.   There might be discussion as to the
wisdom of accepting payment of rates from a new-comer, thereby giving him a "settlement" in the parish, or as to
permitting the continued residence in the parish of a casual
labourer belonging elsewhere ; there would almost certainly be
some talk as to "reputed fathers" and other bastardy business.[1]
There may even be an entry allowing "a pint of sack to the
Minister that officiates the Lord's Day the winter season," [2]
though we have it elsewhere recorded that such a Vestry
strenuously objected to paying for a hood for the clergyman to
officiate in.[3]   But the principal business of the meeting, at
any rate in the eyes of the retiring officers, was to find other
parishioners to relieve them from their onerous and unpaid
duties.   The Vestry might make up a list of persons from
whom the Justices could appoint a new Surveyor of Highways.
The retiring Overseer usually nominated his successor, for the
simple reason that until a successor was found the existing
officer was practically required to continue his service.[4]   " I
Edmund Miller do recommend William Holiday to serve the
office of Overseer for the year ensuing," [5] is a typical entry in
the parish account-book.   The largest farmer would probably
agree to continue for another year as " People's Churchwarden,"
whilst the clergyman would again name the squire's bailiff as

---

[1] " 'Tis agreed by the parishioners present that James Hudson pay into the
hands of the Churchwardens or Overseers the sum of ten pounds for a bastard
child" (MS. Churchwarden's Accounts, Holy Cross, Pershore (Worcestershire),
1st November 1776).

[2] Vestry Minutes, Havering at Bower, Essex, 9th November 1717. See
Notes and Queries, vol. iv. p. 349.

[3] Churchwarden's Accounts, 1746, Bitton (Gloucestershire). See Gloucestershire Notes and Queries, 1890, vol. iv. pp. 93-95.

[4] The statute (43 Eliz. c. 2) required two, three, or four Overseers to be
appointed ; and an order appointing one only (for a township) was eventually
held bad (R. v. Clifton, 1802, 2 East, p. 168). But it is clear that, throughout the eighteenth century at any rate, it was quite frequently the case in
small parishes and townships that only one was appointed ; and when,
occasionally, the matter came before the courts, they displayed great reluctance
to insist on two (see R. v. Harman, 1739, R. v. Bestand, 1746, R. v. Morris,
1792 ; in The Laws Relating to the Poor, by Francis Const, 5th edition,
1807).

[5] Overseer's MS. Account Book of the Parish of Waterperry (Oxfordshire),
1801 to 1817 (in possession of Mr. Henley).

" Rector's Warden." [1]   It would be taken for granted that
" the weaver," [2] the blacksmith, or, in later years, maybe the
master of the charity school, would continue in office as Parish
Clerk for the customary stipend and ancient fees,[3] with an
elderly labourer or woodman as Sexton, whose remuneration
consisted in the customary small fees for bell ringing and
digging the graves.   Formal minute there would be none,
unless the clergyman chose to jot down in a book kept in the
Vestry the names of the Churchwardens among the totals of
the occasional collections made for briefs or on " Communion
Sunday," or unless the Churchwarden thought fit to interpo-
late a memorandum of some decision among the figures in his
cash-book.   At the break up of the meeting the retiring
Overseer would take his cash-book to the Hall, where the
squire and the clergyman, as Justices of the Peace, would
sign the Poor Rate accounts ; whilst the Surveyor of Highways would await notice of the Special Highway Sessions to
make his formal presentments.   Here and there, in a larger
parish, the officers might piously pledge themselves to "meet
at this parish church at the tolling of the bell upon the first
Friday in every month for the settling the affairs and concerns
of the parish, upon the penalty of forfeiting sixpence for every

---

[1] " We in Vestry assembled having examined the above accounts do allow
the sum and nominate M. R. and J. L. Churchwardens for the year ensuing" is
the annual formula in the West Lulworth book (1805-1835), followed by three
to five signatures.   At Farnham Royal the same person was annually chosen
for forty-one years, from 1784 to 1825 (*Records of the Parish of Farnham Royal*,
by F. C. Carr-Gomm, 1901, p. 72).   At Lewes, in the eighteenth century, the
same pair of Churchwardens continued in office for eighteen years, one of them
serving nearly thirty years (*History of Lewes*, by T. W. Horsfield, vol. i. p.
290).

[2] In the Midlands, at the end of the eighteenth century, "in every parish
there was a weaver ; and he was never called by his own name, but ' the weaver,'
which illustrates the origin of some of our surnames.   At Bunny (Notts) the
weaver was the Parish Clerk " (*Autobiographic Recollections of George Pryme*,
1870, p. 20).   Richard Porson's father was a worsted-weaver and Parish Clerk
at East Ruston (Norfolk), in the middle of the century (*Further Memoirs of the
Whig Party*, by Lord Holland, 1905, p. 333).

[3] At West Lulworth (Dorset) it was £2 a year.   In another Dorset village
it was raised from twenty-two to forty shillings a year, on condition that the
Clerk abandoned his former charge of about six shillings for washing the
surplices (MS. Vestry Minutes, Punknowle, Dorsetshire, 4th April 1802).   In
the parish of Tooting (Surrey) the Vestry in 1779 decided to allow him two
guineas a year on condition that he reduced his fee at the "churching" of
women to sixpence only (Vestry Minutes, 1779 ; in *History of Tooting
Graveney*, by W. E. Morden, p. 79).

default." [1]   But in the majority of small rural parishes any further parish business during the ensuing twelve months would be transacted by the several officers as best they could, with a chat among two or three farmers over a pot of beer, or in a chance conversation on the road with the Incumbent or the squire.

The organisation here described may be taken as typical of the parish government of all the strictly rural part of England. There was no formal procedure, no rigid adherence to law, and no regular or systematic outside supervision. The labourers, who included two-thirds of all the heads of families, were not rated, and held no other position in the parish organisation than that of recipients of relief. The so-called "Vestry" was, in fact, in no sense a body representative of the population as a whole. It raised its revenues by direct taxation of its own members, and exercised by its expenditure autocratic power in the details of parish government, but it was, in its turn, subject to a very real, if somewhat spasmodic control at the hands of the squire, the parson, or other neighbouring Justices of the Peace. Moreover, the official relationships between the parties were inextricably woven into the economic relationships that existed between the same individuals in their private capacities. The Justice of the Peace was probably the landlord of the whole of the parish officers; the officers were the employers of the paupers; and even the clergyman, who was in many respects the most independent person in the village, often owed his position to the squire, let his glebe to the Churchwarden, bargained with the Overseer as to the rates on his tithes, and drew these tithes from every occupier of land in the parish. Hence, though there might be grumbling, there could be no effective resistance to the action of the governing group.[2]   On the other hand, though there were no

---

[1] Overseer's Accounts, 31st October 1681 ; see *The Records of St. Michael's Parish Church, Bishop's Stortford* (Essex), by J. L. Glasscock, 1882, p. 165.

[2] Thus in 1788 "the Minister, Churchwardens, and Principal Inhabitants" of Pebmarsh take upon themselves, because of " pernicious effects of fairs in country villages," to prohibit the customary Midsummer assemblage of booths and stalls in the parish, and to direct the Constables to prevent any gathering of people "called a fair" (*Chelmsford Chronicle*, 20th June 1788). Against this, however, may be set the fact, for which *The Times* vouches, of the Vicar, Churchwardens, and Constables of a Derbyshire Parish attending, in 1822, "an

minutes, no printed accounts and no reporters for the newspapers, the persons who paid the rates themselves controlled
every item of expenditure and knew everything that was
going on. Flagrant acts of dishonesty were difficult, and the
public opinion of the whole of the governing class was a real
power. In some cases there would be injustice and favouritism
to individuals outside or beneath the clique, or a silent
encroachment on public rights in common lands, footpaths, or
charitable endowments. But the worst feature of the system
was the total lack of knowledge or capacity to deal with the
problems involved in the government even of the smallest
village. Under the costly parsimony of the rural Vestries the
highways became impassable, and had to be increasingly
transferred to Turnpike Trusts. The unintelligent niggardli-
ness of their treatment of the poor, combined with the lavish
ordering of weekly allowances by the neighbouring Justices of
the Peace, eventually produced a demoralisation of the rural
districts that bade fair to bring the nation to ruin. Yet, so
long as the parish remained strictly rural in character and
fairly stationary in population, there was, generation after
generation, no essential change in its local government.
Right down to 1835, the Vestry, in the vast majority of the
English parishes, retained all its important and multifarious
duties, and continued to be the same little oligarchy of
intimate neighbours, tenants of the squire, and employers of
the paupers, presided over by the clergyman or Senior
Churchwarden, and dominated by the neighbouring Justices of
the Peace.[1]

A more efficient type of parish oligarchy was to be found
lingering on into the eighteenth century in some of the

auction of cattle for the express purpose of purchasing a bull of superior blood
and acknowledged courage to be baited . . . at the approaching feasts"
(*Times*, 18th September 1822).

[1] "I am acquainted," writes Poulett Scrope in 1831, "with parishes where
it has been impossible even to collect three men at a Vestry meeting for the last
six years" (*A Second Letter to the Magistrates of the South of England* (on the
Poor Laws), etc., by G. Poulett Scrope, 1831, p. 27). Arthur Young was so
far from thinking of the Vestry as anything but a little oligarchy that he could
write as follows : " The first attempt towards a Democracy in England would be
the common people demanding an admission and voice in the Vestries, and
voting to themselves whatever rates they thought proper to appropriate ;
which, in fact, would be an agrarian law" (*Travels in France*, p. 336 of
edition of 1892).

corporate municipalities—perhaps confined to those in which the parish happened to be coterminous with the whole borough. Thus, at Leeds, a contemporary diarist gives us illuminating glimpses of the parochial government in the first quarter of the eighteenth century. The extensive parish of Leeds, covering thirty-two square miles, was coterminous with the municipal borough, then including about 13,000 inhabitants, and growing at but a slow rate. The manor had been acquired from the Crown in the preceding century by a group of leading citizens,[1] and its "Great Court" continued to appoint the Constables and perform other public functions. In the first years of the eighteenth century the town was distinguished for its broad-minded and energetic Vicar, its learned and pious Recorder, and a knot of public spirited Aldermen, who served as Justices of the Peace and one of them annually as Mayor, whilst Thoresby, the celebrated and personally charming antiquary, acted on behalf of the Lords of the Manor. This little group of intimate friends and near relations, bound together by evangelical fervour and philanthropic impulses, Whig opinions and scholarly attainments, seem to have dominated alike the Common Council of the borough, the "Great Court" of the manor, and the Vestry of the parish. In the pages of Thoresby's *Diary* we can follow this local oligarchy in their daily administration.[2] We see them pushing forward all good works; building additional churches for the growing population, erecting new markets to compete with the neighbouring county town of Wakefield, maintaining a free school for the children of the townsfolk, and diligently enforcing regulations for suppressing "idleness and debauchery" and "for the more effectually restraining profaneness upon the Lord's Day"—work in which they were warmly supported by the dissenting ministers of the

---

[1] The advowson had been similarly acquired in 1582 in the public interest, and in 1615 it had been definitely vested in twenty-five trustees by decree of Sir Francis Bacon in the Court of Chancery (*Loidis and Elmete*, by T. D. Whitaker, 1816, pp. 24-27).

[2] *The Diary of Ralph Thoresby*, 1677-1724, edited by J. Hunter, 1830, see especially, vol. i. pp. 246, 402, 443 ; vol. ii. pp. 3, 65, 68, 173 ; MS. Vestry Minutes, Leeds (vol. for 1716-1781); *Loidis and Elmete*, by T. D. Whitaker, 1816 ; *Municipal History of Leeds*, by J. Wardell, 1846 ; *Thoresby, his Town and Times*, by D. H. Atkinson, 1885-1887 ; *St. Peter's at Leeds, a History of the Parish Church*, 1896, by J. Rusby and Rev. J. G. Simpson, to the latter of whom we are indebted for suggestions.

town. The Churchwardens, the Constables, the Overseers of the Poor, and the Surveyors of Highways appear as willing subordinates, carrying out the orders which they received from their social superiors. The impression given by Thoresby is borne out by the dry details which still stand recorded in the minute-books of the Vestry. These indicate no interference in parish government by the inhabitants at large. There is no mention of popular election, or even of popular nomination of any parish officers, though some at least of the Church-wardens must have been annually chosen at the Easter Vestry; or of any allowance of accounts or sanction of rates by a public meeting. The minutes of these Vestries are usually signed only by the Vicar, Mayor, and Churchwardens —on one occasion, indeed, also by as many as nine persons, but these were all Aldermen of the borough. These records of parish meetings contain little but church business, the presumption being that the Constables, the Overseers of the Poor, and the Surveyors of Highways dealt exclusively with the Magistrates. In 1726, however, the little oligarchy resolved on the erection, at the parish expense, of a new workhouse in order to set the poor to work; and they then, in successive Vestry meetings, expressly invite to their councils " such other inhabitants as are willing to promote this good work." [1] Even then the management of the institution was given over to a small body of elected trustees, afterwards known as the " Workhouse Board," who for some time renominated themselves from year to year with monoton-ous regularity. During the next ninety years we may trace in the Vestry minutes a slowly growing intervention of the inhabitants, but the Vicar, Mayor, and Recorder still hold their own as the dominating influences in parish affairs. Not till 1819 is this Parish Oligarchy swept on one side by an inrushing democracy—a transformation which we shall describe in a later section of this chapter.

(b) *Government by Consent*

The records of some compact and peaceful parishes reveal the Parish Oligarchy imperceptibly growing into an orderly

[1] MS. Vestry Minutes, Leeds, 26th May 1726.

and harmonious Open Vestry, the administration being carried on by the parish officers with the continuously expressed assent of the ratepayers. "It is most convenient," says a widely read eighteenth century law-book, "that every parish act" done at a Vestry "be entered in the parish book of accounts, and every man's hand consenting to it be set thereto; for then it will be a certain rule for the Churchwardens to go by."[1] "Agreed and consented to by us whose names are hereunto subscribed" is, in fact, a phrase constantly found preceding the lists of signatures by which the "inhabitants in Vestry assembled" were accustomed to authenticate their minutes.[2] And if this duly authenticated assent of all concerned, or at any rate, of "a major part thereof," could be obtained, there seems to have been no limit to the changes in law or custom which a parish Vestry felt itself free to effect. It would, for instance, decide that a bottle of wine for sacramental purposes should, "for ever," be annually given to a particular chapel of ease;[3] or that certain specified sums should be allowed "at the visitation" or "at the perambulation," or for ringing the bells.[4] On the other hand, it would peremptorily suppress any ancient local custom of which it disapproved—ordering, for instance, "that no inhabitant, licensed or unlicensed, or any other person, shall appoint horse-racing, cudgel-play, or any other unlawful gaming"[5]

For litigation it had an unlimited capacity. It would

[1] Shaw's *Parish Law*, p. 55, quoted as authoritative in the early editions of Burn's *Justice of the Peace* (see p. 244, vol. i. of that of 1758). In one case, at least, we find the consent of the inhabitants sought even to the appointment of a new clergyman, though the living was not in their gift. Thus, old minutes of the parish of Bromley St. Leonard (Middlesex) show that the Incumbent appointed by the patron of the benefice (which was a "donative") was in 1678, and again in 1690, "chosen minister . . . with the consent of the parishioners at a Vestry" (*History of the Parish of Bromley St. Leonard*, by James Dunstan, 1862, p. 61).

[2] Thus, at Cromer in 1767, it is recorded that the rate "made by" the Overseers is "with the consent of the inhabitants of the said parish" (Vestry Minutes, 1767, in *Cromer Past and Present*, by Walter Rye, 1889, p. xl.).

[3] "Memorandum that it is agreed upon by the Churchwardens and other principal inhabitants of the parish of Lastingham that the Churchwardens of Lastingham shall yearly for ever after the date hereof give to the Chapelwarden of Ferndale Chapel one bottle of wine against Easter" (MS. Churchwardens' Accounts, Lastingham, N.R. Yorkshire, Easter, 1756).

[4] See, for instance, the agreement of 1709 in *Churchwardens' Accounts of the Parish of Burnsall in Craven*, 1704-1769, by Rev. W. J. Stavert, 1899, p. 1.

[5] Vestry Minutes, Banwell (Somerset), 1727; see *The Sea Board of Mendip*, by F. A. Knight, 1902, p. 446.

resolve, with equal alacrity, to pay out of the rates for the
prosecution of men who deserted their families or of women
guilty of " stealing wood ";[1] of burglars and of those guilty of
the heinous crime of " Sunday fishing "; of vagrants and
strolling players and of local " fence breakers." [2] We find it
deciding " to employ one or more persons immediately to root
up and destroy the Deadly Night Shade throughout this
parish." [3] It would set itself to suppress a plague of cater-
pillars, " dangerous to the parish in general," [4] or a swarm of
mad dogs.[5] What is more remarkable, it would even change
the area of the parish, or alter the legal incidence of local
burdens, not for one year only but for all time. Thus, the
Vestries of Tooting and Streatham, in 1808, in connection
with " beating the bounds " of their respective parishes,
formally agreed by resolutions to exchange certain strips of
land and groups of houses, with apparently no thought that
this matter concerned any one but themselves.[6] In 1804 we
see the Vestry of St. Petrock's, a tiny parish in the very
heart of the City of Exeter, calmly taking upon itself per-

[1] Vestry Minutes, Bampton, Oxfordshire, 1756, 1781, etc., in *History of the
Parish and Town of Bampton*, by Rev. J. A. Giles, 1848, pp. 48-51.

[2] MS. Vestry Minutes, Burton Bradstock, Dorsetshire, between 1758 and
1835.

[3] MS. Vestry Minutes, Minchinhampton (Glos.), 25th June 1823.

[4] As at Camberwell and Hornsey in 1782 ; see *Ye Parish of Camerwell*, by
W. H. Blanch, 1875, p. 7 ; *The Parish*, by J. Toulmin Smith, 1857, p. 236 ;
and *A Short History of the Brown Tail Moth*, by W. Curtis, 1782.

[5] "It is this day agreed, on account of the number of mad dogs lately
appearing in this parish, and of the numbers that are suspected to have been bit,
that every person that shall kill his dog and produce it dead before the Overseer
of the Poor, shall receive of the said Overseer for the same one shilling ; and
that a person be likewise appointed at the parish expense to shoot or destroy all
such dogs as shall be found at large, after notice given to tie them up, for the space
of six weeks, and that the parish shall indemnify such persons employed as above
for doing the same, and that moreover the person so employed shall have one
shilling for every dog he shall shoot or destroy" (Vestry Minutes, Bampton,
Oxfordshire, 28th September 1760 ; in *History of the Parish and Town of
Bampton*, by Rev. J. A. Giles, 1848, p. 48).

[6] Vestry Minutes, 1808, in *History of Tooting Graveney*, by W. E. Morden,
1897, p. 86. The new boundaries so adopted presumably govern the parishes
and the particular ratepayers down to this day. In the following year the
Tooting Vestry refused to make a similar deal with Mitcham, and peremptorily
ordered to be removed the new boundary stones which the latter had set up
(*ibid.* p. 86). In 1713 we see three hamlets of the parish of Devynock in
Breconshire agreeing henceforth to maintain each its own poor, and to become
distinct parishes for the purpose of the Law of Settlement. This agreement
was registered by Quarter Sessions (MS. Minutes, Quarter Sessions, Breconshire, 15th July 1713).

manently to relieve the owners of frontages on its streets from their immemorial legal obligation to maintain the pavement. This momentous resolution was signed by ten persons only as being present, and four of them were deputed " to take this book round to the parishioners who are not present in order to procure their signature hereto." [1] By this decision the burden was thenceforward thrown upon the rates payable by the occupiers.

Such a quasi-voluntary local government is well seen in the records of Minchinhampton, an unincorporated ancient market town and centre of the old-fashioned Gloucestershire woollen industry. The minutes in the latter part of the eighteenth century reveal to us the "Vestry" meeting monthly to relieve the poor, repair the church, and mend the roads. But we gather that, at all these routine meetings, the "Vestry" consists only of the two or three Churchwardens and Overseers, other inhabitants only attending when the business personally concerned them. Thus, the Rector, far from presiding by right of his office, only appears at long intervals, once to protest against a projected removal of the pound, and another time to sign a resolution, along with the principal tithe-payers, by which the parish agreed to exonerate his tithes from rates during his whole life, on condition that he accepted a fixed composition. The half a dozen manufacturers do not bestir themselves to attend at all until the high rates of 1800 incite them to discuss ways and means, and to resist the proposed new assessment of their mills. And here and there, throughout the minute-book, the attendance of this or that substantial ratepayer appears only when he comes to bargain with the parish about the sum he will agree to pay for exoneration from his liability

---

[1] "Whereas," declared the Vestry, "it hath been found by long experience that the obligation to repair the streets and pavements within the said parish, by prescription or by reason of the tenure of lands contiguous to such streets and pavements, is productive of great inconvenience to the public and operates as a discouragement to persons of fortune from residing in this city, we the said inhabitants so assembled as aforesaid, to the public good, and for promoting the welfare and prosperity of the said city as far as in us lies, do hereby consent, agree, ordain, enact, and declare that from and after the date hereof, such obligation as aforesaid shall cease and determine throughout the said parish" (MS. Vestry Minutes, St. Petrock's, Exeter (Devon), 10th October 1804). See "History of the Parish of St. Petrock, Exeter," in *Transactions of the Devon Association for the Advancement of Science*, vol. xiv. 1882 ; *History of Devonshire*, by R. N. Worth, 1895, p. 30.

to maintain a bastard child. What is perhaps more significant is the evidence, during a whole generation, of the constant desire of the parish officers to fortify themselves on every important step, not merely by the legally authoritative resolution of a duly convened Vestry, but by the actual presence and signed agreement of all the principal inhabitants. Whenever the "Vestry" is about to "make, adjust, and finish" a rate, embark on legal proceedings, raise men for the militia, or revise the discipline and dietary of the workhouse, the meeting is habitually adjourned, and "the inhabitants of the parish" are specially summoned to the adjourned meeting, and "earnestly requested to attend so that the general sense of the parish may be known upon the business." On one occasion, when the parish officers were driven to reorganise the whole Poor Law administration of their little kingdom, they plaintively urge, in their notice, that no plan will "succeed" unless "gentlemen of character and ability in the parish so far take an active part in the parochial concerns as to give a regular, constant, and vigorous attention at stated times." [1]

Even so important a parish as Brighton,[2] deemed by Defoe only "a poor fishing town, old built, and on the very shore of the sea," but grown, by the end of the eighteenth century into a watering-place of seven thousand inhabitants, continued down to 1809 to get along on this basis of voluntary agreement. The admirably kept volume of "Minutes of Vestries" holden for the "Town and Parish of Brighthelmstone" makes us intimately acquainted with the "private Vestry," meeting monthly at six o'clock at the different taverns in rotation, and attended only by the three Churchwardens and four Overseers.[3]

[1] MS. Vestry Minutes, Minchinhampton (Gloucestershire). See especially the volume extending from 1786 to 1802.

[2] A Tour through the whole Island of Great Britain, by Daniel Defoe, vol. i. p. 207 of 1748 edition. By the census of 1801 the population was 7339.

[3] MS. Vestry Minutes, Brighthelmstone (now Brighton), Sussex, especially the volume 1799 to 1810 ; History of Brighthelmstone, by John Ackerson Erredge, 1862, chap. ix., which incidentally shows the distinction between the "public Vestry" and the mere meeting of officers to date back to 1727 at least. "In Brighthelmstone," wrote Lord Dudley in 1811, "which, when it is full, contains twelve or fourteen thousand people, there is literally no police at all. There is neither Mayor, Bailiff, Headborough, nor, in short, any vestige of municipal government. The nearest Justice of the Peace lives at Lewes, nine miles off. Yet there is no place so quiet or so completely free from crimes. The doors are

Here they decided all questions of poor relief, managed the workhouse, filled up vacancies in the minor parish offices, and even authorised two of their own number to journey into Lancashire to visit the children lately apprenticed to a mill-owner. But whenever they needed to make a new departure in policy, such as building a new workhouse, alienating parish property, raising men for the militia, making a new assessment for the parish, or getting special constables appointed to prevent theft, we find them summoning what is called a "public Vestry," in order to fortify themselves by an expression of agreement of the inhabitants at large. This happy state of things was broken by the dissensions which arose among different sections of the inhabitants with regard to the constitution and powers of the Street Commissioners, and the provisions of the new Local Act, necessitated by the development of the little fishing village into a fashionable pleasure resort, which we shall describe in a subsequent chapter.[1]

In Mr. Morden's admirable history of the civil administration of Tooting in Surrey,[2] based almost entirely upon the parochial records, we have another instance of intimate and frictionless interaction, extending over a century and a half, among all the elements of parish government. Churchwardens and Overseers, Constables and Surveyors, here work so cordially with each other, with the Court Leet, and with the rest of the principal inhabitants, that no distinction can be traced, either in the minutes or in the accounts, between the public meetings of ratepayers in the church and the private gatherings in the several public-houses, to which in rotation the officers, with the two or three other inhabitants who deigned to attend, regularly adjourned the meeting.[3] Indeed, seeing that one of

all left unbarred, and yet I never heard of anything being stolen" (*Letters to "Ivy" from the first Earl of Dudley*, by S. H. Romilly, 1905, p. 142). By 1831 Brighton had increased in population to 40,634.

[1] Book IV. Chapter V. The Street Commissioners.

[2] *History of Tooting Graveney*, by W. E. Morden, 1897. In 1801 Tooting, made up of one long street, had only 1189 inhabitants.

[3] In 1744 the Vestry resolved "that each public-house do serve wine for the church for one year, and have the Vestries in their turn" (*ibid.* p. 54). A similar custom prevailed, as we have seen, at Brighton, and in many smaller places (*History of the Poor*, by T. Ruggles, 1793, vol. i. pp. 272-273). In Royston (Herts), for instance, "the custom was for the clergyman to announce in church on Sunday the day and hour of meeting of the Vestry, generally on a Monday, and also the subject which was to engage the attention of the Vestry. Monday morning came and with it the tolling of the bell to summon the Vestry,

the leading parish officers was for many years an active Justice of the Peace, it is not easy to distinguish between the action of the magistrates and that of the Vestry itself. The Churchwardens and the Overseers, the Constables and the Surveyors, alike refer for orders to the parish meeting, in which they were themselves the principal figures, on matters which they themselves could legally have decided. We do not hold this parish government up for admiration, as all concerned were too fond of eating and drinking at the public expense,[1] too much addicted to equivocal transactions with the common and the parish lands,[2] and not above sharing the parish charities among themselves as ratepayers,[3] instead of among the poor. What is remarkable in their annals is the perfect agreement that always prevailed between the officers and the inhabitants at large, an agreement which enables the parish between 1812 and 1824 to stand up to the Lord of the Manor and protect the common against his encroachments;[4] to compel in 1747 the absentee Rector to appoint a resident curate;[5] to pass at the Vestry and at the Court Leet identical bylaws suppressing nuisances and protecting the parish against pauper incomers;[6]

but this was only the letter and not the spirit of the local Parliament, which was forthwith adjourned from the church to a more convenient and also more congenial time and place, viz. at six o'clock in the evening 'at the house of William Cobb, at the sign of the Black Swan.' . . . In the seven years, 1776-1782, the Vestry Meetings for Royston, Herts, were held at twenty-two different inns. . . . In this way the tradesmen of the town, or the farmer, the blacksmith and tailor in the village, relieved from the cares of the day, assembled in the evening on the sanded floor of the old inn, and studiously furnished by Boniface with long churchwarden 'clays' puffed away until . . . a little business was sometimes made to go a long way." . . . "Paid at a Vestry at Rogers's for liquor, three shillings" (*Fragments of Two Centuries*, by Alfred Kingston, 1893, pp. 32-33).

[1] See, for instance, the minutes for 1744, 1748, and 1761. "Adjourned to the Castle ; in the same place on Thursday following, by desire of Mr. Arnold, there being nothing to do but drinking a cheerful glass, and depart for good fellowship" (1761, *History of Tooting Graveney*, by W. E. Morden, 1897, pp. 64-65). In 1774, however, it is "ordered that in future there be no money belonging to the parish expended in eating and drinking" (*ibid.* p. 75).

[2] See the transactions of 1752, 1766, 1768, and 1830 (*ibid.* pp. 59, 71, 113).

[3] "No persons shall receive any benefit from the gifts of the parish unless they pay to the rates of the parish" (*ibid.* 1742, p. 54). It will be remembered that in those days no small cottages were rated. A specific case of such sharing out of a small charitable endowment is reported in 1752 (*ibid.* p. 59).

[4] *Ibid.* pp. 89-106.　　　　　[5] *Ibid.* p. 55.

[6] Though the manorial court confined itself usually to business relating to property and rights of common, it ordered, in 1769, that "no person shall, on the penalty of two shillings and sixpence, throw carrion, dogs, cats, or anything offensive into the town ditches, town pond, or other places in the parish, or chamber pots in the evening or night ; that no parishioner shall entertain any

to construct a primitive system of sewers;[1] to look after the water supply;[2] to provide a workhouse; to buy standard weights and measures;[3] and from 1783 onwards even to run, in conjunction with a new Rector, a not inefficient charity school.[4]

In the MS. Minutes of the adjoining parish of Mitcham[5] we can follow the doings of an Open Vestry as peaceful and unanimous as that of Tooting, and characterised by a greater measure of integrity, public spirit, and efficiency. Mitcham, with its papermills on the Wandle, had, in 1801, 3466 inhabitants. To go no farther back than 1793, we see, as at Tooting, the Churchwardens, the Overseers, the Surveyor, the Constable, and the Headborough, with two or three other inhabitants, meeting as an Open Vestry at least once in every month—on Sundays after service in the church, on week-day evenings at one of the public-houses in the village —to manage the parish affairs. Calmly ignoring the exact legal distribution of powers among the officers, and between these and the inhabitants in Vestry assembled, we see the little group deciding questions of policy, or giving executive orders, on all matters indiscriminately, whether it be for church or poor, the administration of the roads or the management of the common, the raising of the parish quota of militiamen or the keeping of the peace. The same meetings serve for the audit and allowance of the Church-wardens', the Overseers', the Surveyors', and the Constables' accounts, and for the making of the Church, Poor, and Highway Rates. With equal unanimity and self-assurance we see them excusing from statute duty on the roads a landowner who concedes a strip for their widening, and permitting another to enclose a part of the waste on payment of half a guinea a year to the Overseers.[6] They unanimously petition the Justices not to grant any additional public-house licences within the parish.[7] We watch them, on the one hand, quite illegally

lodger or lodgers coming with (? without) a certificate without giving notice to the Churchwardens and Overseers of the said parish within three days after his or their first entrance, on penalty of twenty shillings " (*History of Tooting Graveney,* p. 18).

[1] 1765-1783, *ibid.* pp. 70-71, 79, 81-82.   [2] 1821, *ibid.* p. 103.
[3] 1738, *ibid.* p. 52.   [4] *Ibid.* pp. 82-83, 228.
[5] MS. Vestry Minutes, Mitcham, Surrey, 1793-1831.
[6] *Ibid.* 15th February 1795 and 12th March 1797.
[7] *Ibid.* 10th and 14th September 1797.

paying the Beadle fifty guineas a year for acting as Overseer; [1] and on the other bargaining with a stocking manufactory at Cheam to take, as apprentices, "so many of the boys of the workhouse . . . as the Justices shall think proper, at five guineas per boy." They depute the officers "and any other gentlemen that would give their advice . . . to draw up a plan for the workhouse" management.[2] They offer rewards from the parish funds to any person bringing to justice those "who had destroyed the newly erected stocks."[3] In 1801 they make a successful stand against a threatened Parliamentary enclosure of the common, instructing a solicitor to oppose the Bill at the parish expense—moved, it may be remarked, not by any love for open spaces, but believing that the increase in rateable property would not counterbalance "the very serious evils which must be apprehended from suddenly depriving a large number of poor families of their principal means of subsistence."[4] On this emergency the attendance of ratepayers rises from half a dozen to as many as thirty or forty, and the Incumbent begins to take a prominent part. From this time, indeed, the minutes become both elaborate and more formal. Instead of bare entries "at a meeting at the White Hart," we have lengthy preambles, "the parishioners taking into consideration the expediency of . . . do hereby declare their assent." But the expansion of the little group of officers into a well-attended public meeting was accompanied by no loss of unanimity, or disappearance of the note of voluntary agreement. The confidence with which the parish officers were regarded is shown by the fact that, when an inhabitant of the village suddenly died under suspicious circumstances, it was sufficient for the Churchwardens and Overseers, calling to their assistance three local doctors, to hold an inquiry into the circumstances, and to sign a joint report that the death was "from a natural cause," to allay all alarm and save the county the expense of a coroner's inquest.[5] When in 1812 the vicar wishes to expand his Sunday school into a day school "for the education of the infant poor on the principles recommended by the National Society," a largely

---

[1] MS. Vestry Minutes, Mitcham, Surrey, 12th April 1801.
[2] *Ibid.* 16th October 1800.   [3] *Ibid.* 8th April 1804.
[4] *Ibid.* 1st and 19th October 1801.   [5] *Ibid.* 28th January 1811.

attended Vestry meeting agrees to erect a building for the purpose out of voluntary subscriptions.[1]   And when in the following year there is an outbreak of " indecent and outrageous conduct " by the " idle and disorderly young men and boys " of the parish, the parishioners unhesitatingly appeal, not to the Justices of the Peace, but to the Vestry, to put down the disorder.[2]   In 1815 a crowded meeting unanimously decides to revise the parish assessments, hitherto " formed and grounded upon ancient custom and not from the chargeable value of the property."   To make the new assessment, the meeting appoints three outside professional valuers living in Croydon, Reigate, and Cheam respectively, and contentedly leaves the final adjustment to a Committee consisting of the clergy, Church-wardens, Overseers, and principal inhabitants.[3]   Meanwhile, in the bad years between 1811 and 1816, the " unemployed " poor had been starving, and " it was unanimously agreed and ordered " to employ them on the roads at piecework rates. One of the principal inhabitants, dignified by the title of esquire, voluntarily undertook the office of Overseer, in order to carry out a " proper inspection of every case " ; and is, in 1817, publicly thanked by the Vestry for his " unwearied attention to the interests of the parish."[4]   And we may leave this model Open Vestry, quick to take advantage of the Sturges Bourne Act of 1819, unanimously electing, in July of that year, a representative Committee consisting of the Vicar, two curates, five resident landowners, and five substantial tradesmen and farmers, on which all executive powers were immediately devolved.[5]

---

[1] MS. Vestry Minutes, Mitcham, Surrey, 25th August 1812.
[2] *Ibid.* 26th April 1826.   [3] *Ibid.* 20th January 1815.
[4] *Ibid.* 9th December 1812 ; 20th and 27th February, 4th March, 24th December 1816 ; 14th January and 4th February 1817.
[5] *Ibid.* 8th July 1819.   For the Sturges Bourne Act, see Chap. IV. The Strangling of the Parish.   We could describe, from our notes of the parish records, many similar cases of successful "Government by Consent."   We may mention, in particular, the large Dorsetshire village of Burton Bradstock, two miles from Bridport, having a population during the nineteenth century of about 1200, and, during the eighteenth century, possibly nearly as many. Here the extensive mass of miscellaneous archives give us a vision of a well-governed and prosperous little community, administering its affairs by the common agreement of all the substantial householders, who scarcely troubled to attend the Vestry Meetings.

(c) *The Uncontrolled Parish Officers*

So far we have been dealing mainly with old-inhabited parishes, stable in their social and economic relationships, and only slowly increasing in population. But by the end of the eighteenth century there had sprung up another England, presenting new conditions and aggravated problems of local government. Round about the City of London and in the unincorporated mining and manufacturing districts of the northern and midland counties, and even within the walls of some of the old world municipalities, the new industry and the growth of foreign trade were bringing great aggregations of population into ancient parishes. Here the economic and social relations, which went to build up a Parish Oligarchy or a Government by Consent, either had never existed or were in process of rapid disintegration. The powerful tie of landlord and tenant or employer and wage-earner; the strong but intangible link of family relationship or inherited social status, uniting the squire with the clergyman and the country solicitor, the farmer with the handicraftsman and the labourer, and all these with one another, no longer strengthened and supplemented the bare legal relation between the Justice of the Peace and the Overseer, the Incumbent and the people's Churchwarden, the parish officers and the parish ratepayers. The clergyman of the parish, often assumed to be the proper chairman of the Vestry, was frequently an absentee, who had no other secular or religious connection with his parishioners than the delegated exaction of his annual tithes and dues. The Justice of the Peace, whose co-operation was the cornerstone of parish government, without whose signature no Overseer could be appointed, no accounts passed, nor any rate collected, might be a country magnate, living far away from the new urban district; or, what was worse, a partially enriched tradesman with merely commercial traditions, who had, for personal ends, intrigued himself into the Commission of the Peace. Nor was the breakdown in the supervision of Parish Government by the superior classes of society compensated for, in the vast majority of instances, by any increased watchfulness on the part of the ordinary man.

The inhabitants of these new urban districts were unknown to one another; many, as newcomers, were uninterested in the local affairs and unacquainted with the local customs. The actual time, place, and method of appointment of the parish officers, notably the Overseers, the Constable, and the Surveyor of Highways, were, as far as these uninstructed and indifferent citizens were concerned, shrouded in mystery. Respectable householders might find themselves compelled to undertake the onerous duty against their will by the mere fact of their names coming next in the list, and of their being presented by the Vestry or the previous occupants of the offices to the Justices in Petty Sessions, or, in the case of the Constable, to a surviving Court Leet or to Quarter Sessions. When such persons found themselves appointed to act as Constable or Surveyor, Overseer or Churchwarden, they usually did their utmost to escape service. "The imposition of the office" [of Constable], writes Daniel Defoe in 1714, "is an insupportable hardship; it takes up so much of a man's time that his own affairs are frequently totally neglected, too often to his ruin. Yet there is neither profit nor pleasure therein."[1] "It is well known," reports a Poor Law Commissioner in 1833, "that when any person who has received a good education, and whose habits are those of a gentleman, settles in a parish, one of his first objects is to endeavour to exempt himself from parish offices."[2] We see them pleading any possible ground of exemption, and often getting Quarter Sessions to discharge them from office.[3]

If all these efforts failed, they would often pay a heavy fine rather than serve; and in many parishes, especially in and about the Metropolis, there was a customary sum to be

---

[1] *Parochial Tyranny*, by Andrew Moreton [Daniel Defoe], p. 17.

[2] Communication from a J.P. in Codd's Report, p. 53 of Appendix A of First Report of Poor Law Inquiry Commissioners, 1834.

[3] Thus, in April 1694, the Middlesex Justices "upon the petition of J. H. of Shepperton Parish, yeoman," discharge him from his office of Parish Constable, he having served his year. At the same meeting, E. N. of St. James's, Clerkenwell, complains that, "although he is a gentleman and no tradesman," he has been chosen as Scavenger; and he is discharged from the office. A revenue officer appointed Overseer in St. Giles, Cripplegate, is also successful in getting discharged (*Middlesex County Records*, edited by W. J. Hardy, 1905, p. 111). In the following year, two yeomen of Harefield Parish complain that though their year of service as Constables has expired, no Court Leet has been held to appoint their successors, whereupon the Court discharges them and appoints two other Constables and two Headboroughs (*ibid.* p. 149).

paid for such exemption.[1]   Or they would seek to purchase the
" Convict's Certificate " or " Tyburn ticket " already described,
which professional " thieftakers " and active hireling Constables
habitually sold, at a price varying with the onerousness of the
duties in the parish in which the felony was committed, to
some well-to-do citizen who desired to obtain a lifelong
exemption from parochial obligations.[2]   This desire of all the
respectable inhabitants to escape service in the parish offices
was naturally greatest in the new urban districts, where the
duties were most onerous.   When we remember that it was
exactly in these new urban districts that the public business
of the parish was becoming every day more complicated and
difficult, that the mere number of the paupers was becoming
overwhelming; that new buildings by the hundred were
springing up on all sides; that paving, cleansing, lighting,
and watching were all lacking; that the crowding together of
tens of thousands of poverty-stricken persons was creating un-
speakable nuisances; and that the amount of the rates levied
on the inhabitants was at the same time doubling and
trebling, we shall easily understand why, in one parish after
another, the slight legal framework of the parish fell hopelessly
asunder and the situation became almost incredibly bad.

According to all contemporary evidence, whether newspapers or pamphlets, novels or plays, the villains of the piece

[1] Thus, Defoe in 1721 "paid ten pounds to be excused from serving parish
offices" in Stoke Newington, Middlesex (*Memoirs of Daniel Defoe*, by T.
Wilson, 1830, vol. iii. p. 460).   In 1760 a gentleman in Tooting is excused for
a "payment of ten guineas to the Overseers of the Poor for the general use
and benefit of the parish" (Vestry Minutes, in *History of Tooting Graveney*, by
W. E. Morden, 1897, p. 63).   With some of the corrupt Close Vestries in
London, which we describe in the following chapters, the appointment to parish
offices of parishioners known to be willing to pay rather than serve, became an
habitual practice.

[2] "That Mr. T. L. having produced a Convict's Certificate, be excused
serving the office of Overseer" (Vestry Minutes, 1718, in *An Account of the
Church and Parish of St. Giles-without-Cripplegate*, by J. J. Baddeley, 1888, p.
157).   The Tyburn tickets for some parishes became extremely valuable, owing
to the great demand for them.   At Manchester in 1817 we are told that "a
price unknown elsewhere is given for the certificate of exemption, usually called
a Tyburn ticket" (*Charge to the Grand Jury at Preston*, by W. D. Evans,
1817, p. 21) ; "five times more than in any other parish in England," reports
a Parliamentary Committee ; "selling for from two to three hundred pounds"
(Report of House of Lords Committee on the Poor Laws, 1817, p. 153).   An
advertisement for such a ticket may be found in the *Morning Herald* for 17th
March 1802, see *Dawn of the Nineteenth Century in England*, by John
Ashton, 1886, vol. ii. pp. 273-274.

were the unpaid, annually serving, parish officers. The effect
of the common practice of service in rotation was often to
place in office, both in the City of London and in the country,
householders of conspicuous incapacity. " Such persons as
are not fit to govern anything," says one writer ; [1] " persons
scarcely removed from idiotism," says another ; " frequently
those who could neither read nor write, nor are in the least
acquainted with the business," were entrusted with the parish
affairs and the parish funds, merely " because it is the turn of
their farms." [2]   From officers so recruited it was impossible
to expect either zeal or efficiency, or, as it proved, even
common honesty. Uncontrolled by the inhabitants, and in
these places free from any enlightened or systematic supervision by the Justices of the Peace, the average sensual man
who found himself compelled to serve his parish with neither
qualification for the office nor remuneration for his pains,
either wholly neglected his duties or else sought to reward
himself by illegitimate means—by lavish expenses, corrupt
contracts, bribes and blackmail, and sometimes by an even
more sinister indulgence in passion, malice, and spite.

To take the several functionaries one by one, the Churchwardens, we are told, especially after the Toleration Act,
displayed an obdurate " prejudice to the sworn duty of presenting " parishioners guilty of Sabbath-breaking, drunkenness,
and vice ; " for fear," says a bishop of 1720, " of offending
this or that neighbour, or of putting themselves or the parish
to some further trouble." [3]   Their weekly perambulation of

---

[1] From an able letter by Rev. Richard Canning of Ipswich, in *The Christian's
Magazine*, vol. iii. 1763, p. 26.

[2] *Observations on the Abuses and False Interpretations of the Poor Laws*, by
the Earl of Sheffield, 1818, p. 34. "The Courts of Law," adds the indignant
peer, as a climax, " have thought proper to decide that women are eligible
for office ! " A similar devolution of office upon unfit persons, by the effect of
rotation, was described in 1706 in the City of London itself. " Oftentimes,"
says a pamphleteer of that date, " there are persons put into these offices who
are not fit to execute the same, being chosen not for their good qualities or
abilities . . . but in course and order according to the houses they live in"
(*Proposals for Establishing a Charitable Fund for the City of London*, 1706, p. 20).

[3] *Monitions and Advices delivered to the Clergy of the Diocese of Peterborough*,
by Kennett, Bishop of Peterborough, 1720, pp. 28-29. This particular neglect
seems to have become general after 1689. "The Act of Toleration," writes
Dean Prideaux, " hath almost undone us. . . . No Churchwarden or Constable
will present any for not going to church, though they go . . . but to the ale-
house" (*Letters of Humphrey Prideaux to John Ellis* (Camden Society, 1875),
p. 154, under date 1692).

the village ale-houses, bearing their wands of office, to turn out the tipplers during Divine Service, gradually ceased. In the towns, as we shall see, they participated with the Overseers in all the petty perquisites for which the large funds that they administered afforded opportunity. "Nothing is so profitable to these gentlemen," Defoe had pointed out in 1714, "as parish repairs. If the church is new beautified, painted or whitewashed, whip! they come upon you with a Church Rate; and where £200 has been expended, £1200 shall be collected; for Mr. Churchwarden will strive hard, but his daughter shall be a thousand pounds the better. Nay, there are some parishes where Churchwardens, though they went in as poor as rats, have come out too rich ever to be poor again. And yet every booby is willing to eternise his name with an inscription to tell the world in what year he put the parish to an unnecessary charge, so that there is always something to be done to the church to please the vanity of the Church-warden." [1]

But it was the Overseers of the Poor who seem to have excelled in inefficiency, if not in corruption. The wise and learned historian of the Poor Laws, himself an active Justice of the Peace, loses all patience in describing their ineptitude. Their whole idea, he says, is "to maintain their poor as cheap as possibly they can at all events; not to lay out twopence in prospect of any future good, but only to serve the present necessity; to bargain with some sturdy person to take them by the lump, who yet is not intended to take them, but to hang over them *in terrorem* if they shall complain to the Justices for want of maintenance; to send them out into the country a-begging (for why cannot they go as well as others they will mention who are less able in body, and the feebler they are the more profitable will be their peregrination); to bind out poor children apprentice no matter to whom or to what trade, but to take especial care that the master live in another parish; to move heaven and earth if any dispute happens about a settlement, and in that particular to invert

---

[1] *Parochial Tyranny, or the Housekeeper's Complaint*, by Andrew Moreton (*i.e.* Daniel Defoe), 1714, p. 9. This view of the Churchwarden is of old date. "A Churchwarden," said the author of *Hudibras*, "is a public officer entrusted to rob the Church by virtue of his place, as long as he is in it" (*The Genuine Poetical Remains of Samuel Butler*, by R. Thyer, 1827).

the general rule and stick at no expense; to pull down cottages; to drive out as many inhabitants and admit as few as possibly they can, that is to depopulate the parish in order to lessen the Poor Rate." [1] In far too many cases, it is clear, "this petty dictator," as an able critic of 1775 called him,[2] combined negligence with ignorance and cruelty. "The parish officers," said a despairing advocate of the poor in 1775, "are so cruel and insolent that it were better to starve than apply to them for relief." [3] "The whole business of the poor," said a more sympathetic writer in 1799, "hinges upon the duties of the Overseers and the manner in which they are executed, for (except the right of appeal on the part of the pauper to the bench of Justices) there is hardly any check upon their conduct. . . . It is a medley of confidence and of menial duty which has done the mischief. The Overseers, in the first place, have the purse of the parish so completely put into their hands that the statute authorises their calling weekly, if they see proper, for a rate, and without the least limitation with respect to its quantum. . . . There is not a duty, be it ever so menial and degrading, which relates to the poor that is not to be performed personally by the Overseer." [4] The

---

[1] *History of the Poor Laws*, by Richard Burn, 1764, p. 211. It is significant of the state of "enlightened" public opinion at the close of the eighteenth century that one of the publications of the "Cheap Repository for Religious and Moral Tracts," issued in 1797, and republished in many successive editions, is entitled *The Hubbub, or the History of Farmer Russel the hard-hearted Overseer*. Instead of explaining, like Harriet Martineau's *Poor Law Tales* of thirty years later, that the Overseer's parsimony was in the best interests of the poor themselves, the pious tract of 1797 represents the Overseer as a hard-hearted tyrant, who drags a dying man across the parish boundary to avoid having to relieve him, docks the paupers of their weekly allowance whenever any one bestows alms upon them, makes the kind-hearted Justice of the Peace shudder at his cruelty, and finally dies in convulsions by the punishment of Heaven.

[2] *Observations on the Poor Laws, on the Present State of the Poor, and on Houses of Industry*, by R. Potter, 1775, p. 15.

[3] *England's Alarm*, by M. Dawes, 1785, p. 32.

[4] *Observations on the Present State and Influence of the Poor Laws*, by Robert Saunders, 1799, quoted in *Collections Relative to Systematic Relief of the Poor*, London, 1815, p. 161. The practice of rotation of office stood in the way of any sort of efficiency. "Much unnecessary expense," says another observer, "is unavoidably incurred by committing the relief and management of the poor to annual officers. They are obliged to relieve because they cannot employ. Unacquainted, likewise, with their poor, when they enter on their office they are the dupes of their frauds and artifices. And when they begin to acquire a knowledge of their characters and dispositions, they are superseded by others as destitute of this necessary information as they are themselves" (*An Account of the Shrewsbury House of Industry*, by Isaac Wood, 1791, p. 6).

incapacity of these amateur officials was sometimes even pathetic. "I well recollect," said an Assistant Poor Law Commissioner in 1833, "the case of a farmer, who some years since was appointed Overseer of a small parish in the country, who, not being very conversant with the rules of arithmetic, kept his accounts in a pair of boots, putting into one the money he had received, and into the other the acknowledgments for the sums which he expended. When he appeared before the bench of magistrates to swear to his account at the end of his year of office, he stated how he had kept it, and why he was satisfied that it was correct ; and the Bench passed and allowed his account accordingly."[1]

The parish Surveyors were often but little behind their colleagues in inefficiency and corruption. In a subsequent volume on the Administration of Roads we shall give the reader abundant evidence of the malpractices of "those spiritless, ignorant, lazy, sauntering people called Surveyors of the Highways,"[2] and we shall describe the continuance of "the ridiculous farce of appointing one of the parishioners annually (at no salary) to enforce from his relatives, friends, and neighbours a strict performance of a duty which probably he never discharged himself; and from which, by showing lenity to his neighbours, he will expect to be excused in his turn when they shall respectively succeed him in the office of Surveyor."[3] "The greater part of the evils" connected with the road administration, said Macadam, in 1825, "were occasioned by the dishonesty and incapacity of the Surveyors."[4] "Surveyors of roads," said an Assistant Poor Law Commissioner in 1833, "repair those on their own property or which suit their private convenience," and have a "practice of employing regular labourers on the roads during the dull

---

[1] First Report of Poor Law Inquiry Commission, 1834, Appendix A (Codd's Report), p. 99.

[2] *History of the Poor Laws*, by Richard Burn, 1764, p. 239.

[3] *General View of the Agriculture of Herefordshire*, by A. and W. Driver, 1794, p. 55. "The parochial road surveyors," says a later author, "being annually chosen and unpaid, serve the office grudgingly, alike ignorant and incapable of its duties, and with but one object in view, that of getting through their year of forced service with the least possible trouble to themselves " (*Hints on the Expediency of an Improved Divisional Arrangement of England for Administrative Purposes*, 1834, p. 2).

[4] *Observations on the Management of Trusts for the Care of Turnpike Roads*, by J. L. M'Adam, 1825, p. 15.

season of the year as a means of diminishing their own expenses." [1]

Contemporary literature, and even the dry records of Quarter Sessions, abound in testimony to the shortcomings of the Parish Constable. In the little country towns, as distinguished from the purely rural villages, he seems to have continued the traditions of the sixteenth and seventeenth centuries, and to have exercised a Dogberry-like authority. " The Constables," says Cowper in 1783, "are not altogether judicious in the exercise either of their justice or their mercy. Some who seem proper objects of punishment they have released, on a hopeless promise of better behaviour; and others, whose offence had been personal against themselves, though in other respects less guilty, they have set in the stocks." [2] Their sins, it is only fair to remark, were perhaps most usually those of omission. To execute any express orders given by a Justice of the Peace, complains a reformer of 1710, is " the only part of their office that many of them in country villages know anything of: yet even this . . . is not so carefully minded as it ought to be. When we send out warrants . . . I cannot but observe how hardly we are obeyed, how unwillingly the Constable does his office, how long before he sets about it, how many tricks and evasions he makes use of to favour the criminal, and to render his punishment of as little use to his reformation as is possible." [3] " In checking the irregularities of the common people and keeping the publicans in order," writes a despairing reformer in 1788, " much depends upon the Constable, who should be, what I have just reason for believing many are not, respectable housekeepers, of sufficient understanding to know the various and complicated duties of their office, and possessed of property enough to render them superior to temptation." As things are, he finds them " more likely to increase than to lessen the number of offences; to encourage than intimidate offenders by

[1] First Report of Poor Law Inquiry Commission, 1834, Appendix A (Chapman's Report), p. 477.

[2] *Works, Correspondence, etc., of William Cowper,* by R. Southey, 1836, vol. ii. p. 146. We need not quote Shakespeare's opinion of the Constable, as indicated in *Love's Labour Lost, Much Ado About Nothing, Measure for Measure,* and elsewhere.

[3] *A Second Essay upon the Execution of the Laws against Immorality and Profaneness,* by John Disney, 1710, p. xvi.

a participation in their vices."[1]   This laxness on the part of
the Parish Constable continued through the whole century,
with the result, in rural districts, of a gradual spread of
demoralisation and crime.   In the small rural parish, the
office became purely nominal.   "In the far larger proportion
of the agricultural parishes," writes an Assistant Poor Law
Commissioner in 1833, "I was not able to learn that any such"
person as a Constable existed.[2]   But the Parish Constable did
not always confine himself to a masterly inactivity.   In the
proceedings of Quarter Sessions in the different counties, we
come across, throughout the eighteenth and for the first few
decades of the nineteenth centuries, an interminable series of
complaints against Parish Constables, as to their peculations
in the passing of vagrants, their keeping of disorderly ale-
houses or gin-shops, their taking of bribes, and their levying
of blackmail on the publicans[3] and on householders unwilling
to be made to serve in their turn.   When personal service
died out, the office sank to a still lower grade.   In London
and other towns the citizens on whom the service was cast,
habitually shifted the whole of their duties to paid deputies,
"a parcel of loose and mercenary fellows,"[4] whose venality
and ineptitude became a byword.

It was naturally in the new aggregations of population in
the Metropolitan area, or in those springing up about the new
industrial centres of the North and Midlands, that the uncontrolled rule of the parish officers led to the most flagrant
scandals.   The rapidly developing town of Manchester, which
became, even early in the eighteenth century, the largest
manufacturing centre of the kingdom, yields us the most
remarkable provincial example of uncontrolled parish officers.[5]

[1] *Chelmsford Chronicle*, 22nd February 1788.

[2] First Report of Poor Law Inquiry Commission, 1834, Appendix A (Villiers'
Report), p. 71.

[3] "The Constables and Beadles had gone from ale-house to ale-house in
several divisions, extorting money from the victuallers on pretence of carrying
in their licences to be renewed" (Minutes, Quarter Sessions, Middlesex, February
1695, in *Middlesex County Records*, edited by W. J. Hardy, 1905, p. 128).

[4] *The London Spy*, January 1700.

[5] For this account of the parish government of Manchester between 1780
and 1815 we have to rely, partly on the meagre MS. records of the Churchwardens and Overseers which exist from 1664, for access to which we are indebted to the courtesy of Mr. Lings, whose family has been in the service of
the parish for over a century ; on slight references in contemporary local newspapers ; on Sir F. M. Eden's *State of the Poor*, 1797, vol. ii. pp. 342-359 ; on

The local government of Manchester was rendered specially complicated and confused by the distribution of obligations and powers among various conflicting jurisdictions. Throughout the eighteenth century the most important authority in the town was the Court Leet of the Lord of the Manor, and the numerous officers that it appointed; whilst, for the first decades of the nineteenth century, a statutory body of Street Commissioners claims the first place. With the constitution and working of both these authorities, and their intricate relation with each other, and with the parish and its numerous townships, we shall deal in subsequent chapters.[1] But even the parochial government, with which we are here exclusively concerned, was so broken up that it is hard to describe its precise constitution. The great parish of Manchester, which extended over an area of quite 54 square miles, included no fewer than thirty semi-independent townships—one of them bearing like the whole parish the name of Manchester—the exact status and boundaries of which at any particular decade it is now difficult to determine. The maintenance of the ancient Collegiate Church, an obligation resting on the whole

the *Report of the Committee of the Associated Leypayers of the Township of Manchester appointed to inquire into the accounts of the Churchwardens and Overseers, and other matters . . . relative to the . . . poor of the said township* (1794); on the new *Rules for the Government of the Poorhouse in Manchester* (1794); but above all, on the remarkable series of pamphlets by Thomas Battye, between 1796 and 1802, some of which are in the British Museum, some in the Manchester Public Library, and others in possession of Dr. J. Milsom Rhodes, of Didsbury, who kindly placed his copies at our disposal. These comprise *A Disclosure of Parochial Abuse, Artifice, and Peculation in the Town of Manchester which have been the means of burthening the Inhabitants with the present enormous Parish Rates with other existing impositions of office in a variety of facts exhibiting the cruel and inhuman conduct of the hireling officers of the Town towards the poor*, 1796 ; *A Reply to Mr. Unite's Address to the Leypayers of Manchester*, 1796 ; *Reflections on the Subjects of Deputy Constable, Billeting, Beadles, Police Act, Collectors' Accounts, Publicans' Licences, Special Constables, etc.*, 1796 ; *The Red Basil Book, or Parish Register of Arrears for the Maintenance of the unfortunate offspring of illicit amours, with a farther development of most shameful and unprecedented acts of abuse in the Town of Manchester*, 1797 ; *A Concise Exposition of the Tricks and Arts used in the Collection of Easter Dues, with a list of items which compose this Divine Tax*, 1800 ; *Strictures upon the Churchwardens and Overseers of Manchester, etc.*, 1801 ; and *An Address to the Inhabitants of Manchester, etc.*, 1802. Battye is not deserving of implicit credit, but his accusations are supported by other trustworthy evidence, and his incidental allusions tell us much.

[1] Book III. Chap. II. The Court in Ruins, and Book IV. Chap. V. The Street Commissioners. Something of the complications between the parish and the townships may be gathered from the *History of Newton Chapelry*, by H. T. Crofton, Chetham Society, vol. lii. part ii. 1904.

parish, was committed to eight Churchwardens, and at least as many "Assistants" or Sidesmen for the several townships, appointed annually at a Vestry meeting, which was open to all the parishioners. The administration of the Poor Law and the maintenance of the highways were, by local custom, matters for the several townships, for each of which one or more Overseers and Surveyors were appointed by those county Justices who lived in or near them. It was, perhaps, owing to this separation of parochial functions, accentuated by the survival of an active Court Leet, that the Vestry meetings in the parish church never assumed, during the eighteenth century, any control over the Churchwardens of the parish as a whole, or over the Overseers, Surveyors, or Constables of any of the townships, except that of Manchester itself. These meetings were, in fact, until 1818, seldom attended by any one but the retiring officers, with a friend or two.

We may ignore the government of the outlying townships, which still retained their rural character, and apparently remained under the control of the county Justices of the Peace who resided in the neighbourhood. In the township of Manchester itself, which became a densely crowded, insanitary, and disagreeable place of residence, the local administration was apparently left to the inhabitants. Three out of the eight Churchwardens were chosen for this township, and these, together with such Overseers as were presented to the Justices for appointment for the township, had to struggle with the increasing difficulties of the relief of the poor. In 1731, and again in 1763, attempts to get a Local Act, placing the parish government on a better basis, were defeated by the jealousies between the Tory Churchmen, who controlled the Court Leet, and the Whig Dissenters, who claimed a majority in the township.[1] Yet the public business of the township, containing, by 1790, a population of about 60,000, whether relating to street nuisances or to police, poor relief or the collection of the rates, had plainly outgrown the capacity of the annually chosen, unpaid amateur officer. It had therefore become customary for the Court Leet, under the Boroughreeve and Constables, to appoint a paid Deputy

---

[1] *History of the County Palatine of Lancaster*, by Edward Baines, 1836, vol. ii. pp. 293, 306.

Constable, whose salary and expenses were, from 1778 onwards, charged in the township Overseer's accounts. The county Justices who passed these accounts had quietly allowed without objection the payment of remuneration to a rate collector and several salaried Overseers, who were practically appointed by the Churchwardens, but whose legal position must have been derived from their formal appointment by the Justices. At last, in 1790, the then Churchwardens managed to obtain a Local Act [1] to authorise the appointment of more salaried Overseers and to enable a new workhouse to be built for the township, which was placed under the control of the Churchwardens and Overseers of the township, out of a separate township rate.

The exact relation between all these various rates and offices, for parish and township, and the Vestry meeting for the parish as a whole, is not clear. How far separate accounts were kept, as between parish and township, for church and poor and highways and Constables' expenses—how far these were presented "at the parish table," which still stands at the west end of the ancient Collegiate Church—is unknown to us, but we read incidentally of the "Deputy Constable's accounts" being "cursorily read over at the Collegiate Church quarterly, without permission of an inspection afterwards." [2] More important than this quarterly meeting in church, nominally of the inhabitants, was perhaps "the veal pie feast, held monthly at the Bull's Head," when "on . . . the first Sunday in every month, all parties in office, Churchwardens, Overseers, Constables, town and country Sidesmen [*i.e.* the Churchwardens' Assistants for the several townships], etc., a jolly clan, join. At this pious banquet the Churchwardens, who ought to be watchful over the honesty of the [salaried] Overseers, become so familiar with each other, when once fortified with this divine liquor, that all babbling and tale-telling tongues are hushed." Under this system of local government the rates had "increased since the year 1790 from eight thousand to upwards of twenty thousand pounds per annum" four or five years later. In 1794 the Churchwardens

[1] 30 George III. c. 81.
[2] *A Disclosure of Parochial Abuse,* etc., by Thomas Battye, 1796, pp. 53-54, 78, etc.

and Overseers had to make within a few months two successive
rates each of five shillings in the pound.   This seems to have
brought about a crisis.   Charges appeared in the newspapers
accusing the parish and township officers of " ignorance, mismanagement, peculation, and breach of trust." [1]   The Court
Leet authorities—the Boroughreeve and Constables—at last
called a public meeting, which elected a committee of twelve
to inquire into the conduct of the Deputy Constable, who had
recently completed two years' service as salaried Overseer.
About the same time a temporarily formed " association of
leypayers " [2] appointed its own committee " to inquire into the
accounts of the Overseers and other matters . . . relative to
the . . . poor " of the township.   A prolonged investigation
ensued, in the course of which an almost incredible degree of
laxness and negligence was found to prevail in all the unpaid
officers, together with an audacious and long-continued venality
in one or more of their salaried subordinates. [3]   Although
several hundred pounds a week were passing through the
hands of minor officials, no cash-book, journal, or ledger was
kept, and the only accounts were a series of rough memoranda
on odd sheets of notepaper.   No receipts or other vouchers
were produced.   There was no check on the collection of the
parish revenue.   Since the year 1777 the Churchwardens
and Overseers had entrusted this entirely to one Wharmby,
at a salary of £70 a year, who collected not only the " poor's
ley " and the " church ley," but also the " highway ley " and the
voluntary subscriptions to the infirmary, the lending library,
the " lying-in charity," the Literary and Philosophical Institution, and the several associations for the prosecution of
felons, besides several " private stewardships and trusts."
Nothing in the nature of audit was thought of, or would have
been effectively possible with such a medley of duties ; but

[1] *A Disclosure of Parochial Abuse*, etc., by Thomas Battye, 1796,
p. 2.
[2] The word "ley" was used in Lancashire, Cheshire, etc., as the equivalent
of rate ; sometimes (as in Staffordshire) it was written " lune " (*The Borough of
Stoke-upon-Trent*, by J. Ward, 1843, pp. 77, 122, 468, etc.) ; or (perhaps chiefly
in Shropshire) it was " leawn " (*History of Vagrants and Vagrancy*, by C. J.
Ribton Turner, 1887, p. 175).
[3] *A Disclosure of Parochial Abuse*, etc., by Thomas Battye, 1796 ; *A Report
of the Committee of the Associated Leypayers in the Township of Manchester
appointed to inquire into the accounts of the Churchwardens and Overseers*, etc.,
1794.

there was even grosser negligence in the parish officers permitting, for many years in succession, the collector, "in making up the leybook," to adopt simply "the land tax assessment," which continued merely the old valuation of the uncovered land, and omitted most of the new houses altogether, together with all the tolls and such personalty as was legally liable to the Poor Rate.[1]   But even of the properties assessed, many hundreds were allowed to escape payment. "Upon the inspection of the books," the leypayers' committee discovered that at the time of the disposal for a new ley, the uncollected rates and the arrears due to the township "on the bastardy account amounted to ten thousand pounds and upwards."   The expenditure was equally uncontrolled.   The indoor paupers had been moved in 1793 from the wretched old poorhouse to the "superb building" just erected for them, but they were doing practically no work.   "There are," says the Committee, "no rules for the internal government of the house agreeably to the Act of Parliament; and of course no subordination or regularity."   It was not even known how many inmates were being provided for; "the last time the people were counted there were 477, and it is now supposed"—so the Committee reports—"they are about 500."[2]   Nor was the outdoor relief subject to any better check than the workhouse provisioning.   "Clothing and goods," says our contemporary pamphleteer, "have been indiscriminately given to almost every person who made application. . . . Near three thousand pair of shoes given from the workhouse last year."[3]   Enormous sums were paid away in outdoor relief and expenses of removals.   The incredible negligence of the Churchwardens led, it is clear, to extravagance, waste, and peculation among the paid subordinates.   In one case, at any rate, that of Mr. Unite the hired Deputy Constable, who seems also to have

---

[1] *Report of the Committee of the Associated Leypayers of the Township of Manchester*, pp. viii., xviii.-xix.   "I have known," says Battye, "property in the town of Manchester . . . exceeding £600 per annum only rated at £30. The property of a gentleman in the centre of the town, whose rental exceeded £280, was not applied to for Poor Rates for many years, and it was afterwards compromised by Mr. Wharmby for £14, which did not amount to sevenpence in the pound" (*A Disclosure of Parochial Abuse*, etc., by Thomas Battye, 1796, p. 104).

[2] *Report of the Committee of the Associated Leypayers of the Township of Manchester*, 1794, pp. 1-2.

[3] *A Disclosure of Parochial Abuse*, etc., by Thomas Battye, 1796, p. 30.

acted as salaried Overseer, we rise to higher flights than mere peculation.   The duty of billeting soldiers upon the innkeepers of the township was turned into a lucrative source of private revenue.   In order to be favoured in the distribution of billets, each innkeeper was induced to make a series of presents to the all-powerful official.   Thieves and the persons from whom they had stolen were alike laid under contribution, stolen property being impounded, and in many cases converted to private uses.   Even the duty of paying the paupers was made to yield its toll of profit.   A clergyman and magistrate testified to the Deputy Constable having bought £100 worth of "base and counterfeit copper" coin for £40, with which, as Overseer, to pay the outdoor poor their weekly allowance.[1]   His crowning iniquity, at least in the eyes of the respectable inhabitants, was his conversion of the revenue derived from bastardy cases into an all-pervading system of blackmail.   The former Overseer had, in 1786-1787, been regularly collecting and accounting for weekly payments from 614 fathers of illegitimate children.   The "Red Basil Book," in which the names and addresses of these fathers were recorded, was promptly "lost" as soon as the Deputy Constable took office as Overseer, and there was no "regular register of illegitimacy kept from the year 1787 to the year 1790, nor any sum [credited as] received on this account.   If the public are credulous enough to believe that all the children belonging to these 614 fathers, and all the children born since the year 1787, died before the year 1790," this absence of bastardy revenue might be accepted.   Unfortunately it was proved that the Deputy Constable, when acting as salaried Overseer, had been terrifying erring or duped citizens into paying considerable sums for children of whom they were alleged to be the fathers.[2]   Finally, this ingenious official, contriving so

[1] *A Disclosure of Parochial Abuse*, etc., by Thomas Battye, 1796, p. 90. The practice of paying the poor in base coin had been sufficiently frequent to call for express prohibition by Act of Parliament in 1769 (9 George III. c. 37).

[2] *The Red Basil Book*, etc., by Thomas Battye, 1797.   When, on the first of these revelations, an elaborate code was drawn up for the administration of poor relief, one of the regulations, significantly enough, was that "the district Overseers are not to make any agreement to take what is called Hush Money from the reputed fathers of bastard children, but all applications in this respect must be referred to the three Churchwardens" (*Rules for the Government of the Poorhouse in Manchester*, 1794, p. 18).

to use his various powers that each should yield him profit, would at any time oblige a friend or subscriber by apprehending any troublesome person as a vagrant or by locking up a turbulent wife as a lunatic.[1]

How soon the township of Manchester was able to rid itself of this Napoleon of parish officers, we are not able to ascertain. The meetings at the Collegiate Church evidently continued to be formal and perfunctory. The Churchwardens were elected without contest, and the complicated accounts which they presented were passed without complaint. The meagre minutes of the Vestry meetings " at the parish table " indicate an entire absence of public interest, a fact confirmed by the rarity during these years of any allusions to parish business in the local newspapers.[2] The inefficiency of the administration may be judged from the fact that the Churchwardens had, in 1804, to raise a loan of more than £11,000 to make good the defalcations of a tax-collector.[3]

Passing from the new manufacturing centres of the provinces to the rapidly growing parishes around the City of London, we find a similar story of neglect, peculation, and oppression by the uncontrolled parish officers. In a subsequent chapter we shall relate the misdoings of the Close

[1] "It is well known to have been a practice for warrants, for the apprehension of accused individuals, to be signed in blank, and left with the clerk, ready to be filled up, in the absence of the Justice, though they purported to be granted on oath, taken in the presence of the Justice" (*A Disclosure of Parish Abuse*, by Thomas Battye, 1796, p. 64).

[2] See MS. Vestry Minutes, Manchester, in the volume extending from 1766 to 1816; *Manchester Mercury*, 26th April 1808; *Manchester Gazette*, 7th October 1809, 6th May 1813, 16th April 1814, 16th March and 16th November 1816. This or another Deputy Constable of Manchester was reported in 1816 to have amassed a fortune of £20,000 (Home Office Domestic State Papers in Public Record Office, No. 271, 1816). Not until 1808, when the township had a population of 80,000, and was spending nearly £30,000 a year in poor relief, employing altogether sixteen paid officers as "clerks, visiting Overseers, and runners," was any public office rented for the extensive Poor Law business (*Manchester Gazette*, 7th October 1809; MS. Vestry Minutes, 11th and 24th October 1808).

[3] MS. Vestry Minutes, Manchester, 24th October 1804. Even the extreme instance of Manchester could probably almost be paralleled by that of Coventry and Salford, if we had the same amount of information; see, as specimens, the *Report of the Committee appointed at a Town's Meeting held at the Workhouse, Salford, to inspect the late Overseer's Accounts and superintend the collecting of the arrears of leys*, 1811; and the *Report of the Committee appointed to investigate the accounts of the Parish of Foleshill in the County of the City of Coventry*, 1832, giving a history of the misdeeds of the successive Overseers since 1813.

Vestries of the Metropolis. But any careful examination of the records and contemporary literature leaves it an open question whether the maladministration was greatest in those parishes which had Select Vestries, or in those in which the parish officers were nominally subject to an "open" Vestry. Thus, the crowded East End parish of St. Leonard's, Shoreditch (population in 1801, 34,766), was notorious, throughout the eighteenth century, as a hotbed of corruption, the misdeeds of its officers not only becoming the subject of lurid description by contemporary pamphleteers, but also repeatedly coming before the Middlesex Court of Quarter Sessions, where the County Justices strove in vain to check the peculation and oppression.[1] To the south west, the little village of Chelsea was the scene of a century-long series of dishonest enterprises by the parish officers, which the open meetings of inhabitants in Vestry assembled completely failed to prevent. Already in 1723 a Chelsea critic complains of the intolerable licentiousness and corruption of the local parish officers.[2] Throughout the century similar accusations and complaints from time to time appear. In the first years of the nineteenth century, various attempts by the ratepayers to form committees supervising the parish administration were defeated by the Overseers. At last, in 1822, the parish accounts were overhauled by a committee of investigation appointed by an indignant open Vestry meeting, with the result that the parish monies were found to have been running away at all points. Not only did the outdoor relief show "an improvident application of the funds of the parish," with every unsatisfactory feature; the management of the indoor poor was equally wasteful. The provision bills for the workhouse were huge, and "proof can be adduced that the parochial officers meeting at the workhouse were in the regular habit of consuming a portion of these supplies, the quality of which appears, from the prices charged, to have been of the finest description." The bill for three of these dinners amounted

---

[1] *A True State of the Case in respect to the late Disputes in the Parish of St. Leonards, Shoreditch*, by a Parishioner, 1744; MS. Minutes of Quarter Sessions, Middlesex, January 1691 (see *Middlesex County Records*, edited by W. J. Hardy, 1905, p. 29); ditto, April 1743, etc.

[2] *A Dialogue between John Hu-tt and Edward An-on of Ch-a*, by A. B., 1723, p. 18; a revelation of the intrigues and corruption of Chelsea Churchwardens.

to no less than £92. The revenue side of the account was as scandalous as that of the expenditure. The total sums credited to the parish during these years as receipts on account of bastards amounted to no more than £124 for twenty-six cases. The Committee traced back two out of these twenty-six cases and found that, on these two alone, £131 had been paid to the officers; indicating, therefore, a relatively gigantic system of misappropriation of these receipts. Two years later, another committee, suspecting a more obvious form of peculation, began to publish the Poor Rate default lists, whereupon no less than eighty receipts were sent in by ratepayers, who indignantly threatened to prosecute the committee for the libel of publishing their names on the Defaulters' List.[1] It would be easy to multiply examples of corrupt administration by the uncontrolled parish officers of the " open parishes " of the Metropolitan area.

To contemporary observers the source of the evil was obvious. " The mischief," says a workhouse master of 1726, " is caused by the artifice and knavery of some designing men in the parish, who, being tradesmen or shopkeepers, make interest to get into . . . offices of the parish, and particularly into such offices as have the disposal of the parish money." [2] Another writer complains of " the many tricks and cabals " of the lower sort of unsubstantial " householders to get into office." [3] The " tradesmen and mechanics " who, " in large and populous parishes in cities and great towns " generally filled the parish offices,[4] knew how to make neglect and corruption go hand in hand. " Whoever reads what has been done," says the *Gentleman's Magazine* for March 1802, " at Shrewsbury, Hull, and Lewisham [where investigations had recently taken place] will soon be satisfied that parish officers,

---

[1] MS. Vestry Minutes, Chelsea (Middlesex), 20th June 1822, 26th February 1824.

[2] *A Representation of some Mismanagements by Parish Officers, with a proposal for possibly rectifying the same* [by John Marriot, Governor of the Workhouse of St. Giles-in-the-Fields, London],1726, p. 8.

[3] *A Short View of the Frauds, Abuses, and Impositions of Parish Officers*, 1744. This pamphlet was the subject of a review in *Gentleman's Magazine*, December 1744.

[4] *An Inquiry into the Management of the Poor and our usual Polity respecting the Common People*, 1767, p. 4.

particularly Overseers, are vested with a power that cries aloud for abridgment. I shall not be unjust when I say they can pick the pockets of the rich and starve the poor with impunity. Experience warrants this assertion when tradesmen spend, and refuse an account of the expenditure of the money collected by them as Overseers, pretend drunkenness, madness, loss of books, ignorance of the whole matter; and the committee of parish accounts, under whose directions they act, and who have admitted them to their board, and given them contracts to serve the workhouse, sanction their malconduct by their ignorance what to demand of them. . . . The mischief originates from the character and rank of the person so appointed, and from the connivance of his friends of the same rank and character." [1] "Every parish officer," wrote a shrewd London observer in 1796, "thinks he has a right to make a round bill on the parish during his year of power. An apothecary physics the poor; a glazier, first in cleaning, breaks the church windows, and afterwards mends them, or at least charges for it; a painter repairs the commandments, puts new coats on Moses and Aaron, gilds the organ-pipes, and dresses the little Cherubim about the loft as fine as vermilion, Prussian blue, and Dutch gold can make them. The late Churchwardens [of the writer's own London parish] were a silversmith and a woollen draper; the silversmith new fashioned the communion plate, and the draper new clothed the pulpit and put fresh curtains to the windows." [2]

(d) *The Rule of the Boss*

The important parish of Bethnal Green, which practically adjoins the City of London on the north-east, and quickly became, as Francis Place observes, "the residence of an immense number of poor people," presents for half a century a remarkable example of government by what the Americans have since termed a Boss. From the evidence given before various Select Committees of the House of Commons, and other contemporary sources—confirmed by a careful analysis

[1] *Gentleman's Magazine*, March 1802, p. 225. Sir John Hawkins in 1763 was deploring "the practice of electing tradesmen and persons, necessarily dependent and subject to influence, into parish offices."

[2] *The Olio*, by Francis Grose, 1796, pp. 217-218.

of the manuscript Vestry Minutes for the whole period—we get a vivid picture of the skill, persistence, and audacity of the local demagogue who practically ruled the parish, with only a few years' interval, from 1787 until his gradual retirement from active life half a century later—the whole forming a story in which we think the American student will recognise not a few familiar features. The hamlet of Bethnal Green had originally formed an integral part of the immense parish of Stepney. By 1742 its square mile of area had already 15,000 inhabitants, densely crowded in the narrow streets and courts of its southern and western portions; and the Churchwardens and Overseers for the hamlet headed a petition to the House of Commons praying for the constitution of a separate parish.[1] Parliament granted their prayer, and by successive Local Acts, after the manner of the time, equipped the new parish with a Vestry, a body of "Directors of the Poor," a Watch Board, and a Board of Street Commissioners or "Paving Trustees."[2] The Vestry was open to every ratepayer who occupied premises of the value of £15 a year, or, if he had already served as Overseer, even of £10 a year, the former qualification letting in thousands of poor householders, principally, we are told, "journeymen weavers, who live three or four families in a house, and work at home at their looms and reels for the master weavers in Spitalfields."[3] This turbulent democracy, which had, by 1787, increased to some twenty thousand, came about that time completely under the influence of one Joseph Merceron,[4] a local resident of

---

[1] House of Commons Journals, 10th and 25th January, and 31st March 1743; *History of London*, by William Maitland, 1756, vol. ii. p. 1377; *Environs of London*, by D. Lysons, 1792-1811, vol. ii. pp. 27-38; *Stray Leaves from the Past of our Village: a History of Bethnal Green*, by H. G. C. Allgood, 1894-1897; Place to Hobhouse, 2nd April 1828 (Add. MSS. 35148, vol. i. p. 55).

[2] 16 Geo. II. c. 28, 1742; 24 Geo. II. c. 26, 1750; 29 Geo. II. c. 43, 1756; 3 Geo. III. c. 40, 1762; 7 Geo. III. c. 105, 1766; 13 Geo. III. c. 53, 1773; 33 Geo. III. c. 38, 1793.

[3] *Environs of London*, by D. Lysons, vol. ii. pp. 27-38.

[4] We gather that this Joseph Merceron, who lived at Brick Lane, Bethnal Green, was the son or nephew, either of the Joseph Merceron of the same address, whom we find made a Commissioner of the local Court of Requests in 1765, or of the James Merceron, Pawnbroker, likewise of Brick Lane, who frequently attended the Vestry meetings from 1763 onwards, and served as Constable in 1765 (MS. Vestry Minutes, Bethnal Green, 1760-1770). The family was of Huguenot extraction, from Poitou. In the registers of the Huguenot Church of La Patente, Spitalfields, the name frequently occurs.

apparently lower middle class extraction—originally a clerk
to a lottery office-keeper, then assistant to a Poor Rate
collector—who brought business habits and considerable
administrative ability to the management of the now extensive
finances of the parish. First appearing in the parish records
in 1787,[1] he seems at once to have secured the confidence of
the little knot of regular attendants at the Vestry meetings,
by whom the government was carried on; and we find him
within a year or two placed on all the committees, doing
much laborious work for the parish, and undertaking the very
onerous responsibility of keeping its funds—all without salary
or other obvious remuneration. His advent was marked, it is
clear, by a great increase in administrative efficiency; and the
parish government, from slipshod ways and somnolent apathy,
becomes orderly, precise, and business-like. We have no
reason to attribute to Merceron at this period anything more
invidious than the usual English willingness of an ambitious
and public-spirited man of ability to undertake the unpaid
work of local government. Gradually we see him concentrating
all the effective powers of administration in his own hands.
By degrees he made himself not only the leader of the
Vestry, and the dominating influence on its principal standing
committee, the Directors of the Poor, but also the chairman of
the Watch Board and of the Street Commissioners, or Paving
Trustees. What was even more important, he got himself
appointed permanent treasurer of the various parish funds,
whether pavement or poor, " fines " or charities;[2] he became
a leading Commissioner of the Court of Requests (the local
statutory tribunal for the recovery of petty debts), and he
seems presently to have used his influence to get himself
placed by the central government on the local Commissions
for levying the land, income and assessed taxes, on the three
Commissions of Sewers for the Tower Hamlets, Westminster,
and Holborn and Finsbury, and even on the Commissions of
the Peace for Middlesex and the Tower Hamlets.[3] Round

---

[1] MS. Vestry Minutes, Bethnal Green, 9th April 1787.

[2] He was elected by the Vestry as " Treasurer of the Poor " as early as
26th July 1787, and retained that office, with one slight interval, for thirty-one
years (*ibid.* 26th July 1787 ; 23rd March 1818).

[3] We have ascertained from the Government records that he was recommended
to the Home Secretary, for inclusion in the Commission of the Peace, by a Mr.

the power of landlord to that of parish officer and licensing Justice.[1]   Perhaps his first great chance may have come in the great distress of 1800, when Parliament voted a grant in relief of the suffering poor.   The panic-stricken House of Commons could find no better expedient to cope with the increase in the price of food than to shovel out tens of thousands of pounds in aid of the Poor Rate of the East End parishes.[2]   The share of Bethnal Green amounted to no less than £12,165, all of which passed through Merceron's hands, most of it being dribbled away in weekly doles to an uncounted multitude of the destitute.[3]   In 1804 we detect the first evidence of mistrust, in a resolution of the Vestry to appoint a Committee to audit the Treasurer's Accounts, instead of, as heretofore, receiving and passing them with no more scrutiny than is possible on the reading out of figures from a manuscript statement at a public meeting.[4]   Merceron thereupon promptly resigned the appointment.   But some difficulty was found in filling his place, and the following Easter he was unanimously re-elected, and the proposed Audit Committee is heard of no more.[5]   In 1809 the banner of revolt was raised by a new and public-spirited Rector, the Rev. Joshua King, who strove in vain to contest Merceron's control of the Vestry meetings.   Three years later we find the parish in a heated turmoil, over complicated angry controversies which it is now difficult to disentangle.   There was plainly a growing party of respectable inhabitants, headed by the Rector, in revolt against Merceron.   At the same time the Rector was moving for an increase in his inadequate income, and the cessation of the tribute of fees and ecclesiastical dues, Easter offerings, and " small tithes " which Bethnal Green had still to pay to the mother-parish of Stepney.   Moreover, it was becoming clear

---

[1] In 1816, he admitted that he owned eleven public-houses and collected the rents of eleven more, out of a total of ninety in the parish (Report of House of Commons Committee on the Police of the Metropolis, 1816 ; *The Trials at large of Joseph Merceron, Esq.*, by W. B. Gurney, pp. 69-70 of second trial, in edition of 1819).

[2] Fifth Report from the Committee on the High Price of Provisions, 17th December 1800 (Dudley Ryder, Chairman).   Moved by the tales of special distress in Bethnal Green, Spitalfields, and Mile End (which to-day read unconvincing), the Committee recommended an instant vote of twenty to thirty thousand pounds.

[3] MS. Vestry Minutes, Bethnal Green, 19th April 1802.

[4] *Ibid.* 2nd April 1804.   [5] *Ibid.* 15th April 1805.

that further administrative powers were needed for the parish
government. The Vestry, under the influence of Merceron,
together with that of the local Nonconformist minister, refused
to promote a Bill for any of these purposes.[1] A Bill was
nevertheless promoted by the Rector's party, and concurrently
the resolute Rector, who was not to be silenced by what seem
to have been pecuniary offers from Merceron, instituted a
criminal prosecution against him for fraudulent alteration of
the parish assessments in such a way as to favour the tenants
of his own property. This led to attempts at compromise
between the parties, as the result of which the Bill was
amended and passed into law in 1813,[2] though the Rector
refused to give up the prosecution of Merceron. That gentleman managed, however, somehow to get the prosecution
abandoned in court, in a way which the Rector never understood, and thus secured an acquittal, at an expense to himself
of over nine hundred pounds, which he found it inconvenient
to pay. This equivocal triumph was promptly followed by a
fulsome vote of confidence in Merceron's " honour and integrity "
by the Vestry, and, as the minutes declare, by a resolution to
defray all his expenses out of the parish funds.[3] The Merceron
party now carried things with a high hand. It was in vain
that the Rector protested, and appealed in print to all the
inhabitants. By the turbulent mob which filled the church,
his publication was voted " a gross libel," full of " errors and
mis-statements," and only half a dozen hands were held up
against Merceron's re-election.[4] There is reason to suppose
that his triumph made him more overbearing, more audacious,
and more reckless than ever. What with the Sunday dog-
fighting and duck-hunting and the week-day bullock-hunting
through the streets, Bethnal Green became a saturnalia of
turbulent disorder. The public-houses and beer-shops owned
by or subservient to Merceron indulged in the grossest licence,
keeping open on Sundays, and far into the night, harbouring
what were popularly known as " cock and hen clubs " resorted
to by the young weavers of both sexes, and becoming " nurseries

[1] MS. Vestry Minutes, Bethnal Green, 27th February and 16th December
1812.
[2] 53 George III. c. 113.
[3] MS. Vestry Minutes, Bethnal Green, 23rd August 1813.
[4] *Ibid.* 11th April and 4th May 1814.

of depravity and vice" and the centres of "annoying and disgraceful tumults."[1] The state of the parish was at last brought to the notice of the House of Commons Committee then sitting to inquire into the Police of the Metropolis, and the Rector not only gave evidence himself, but also contrived to induce the Vestry Clerk, a local solicitor who had held his office for thirty years, and had not hitherto opposed Merceron, to attend the committee, and describe some of the scenes of disorder that took place.[2] This public exposure to some extent woke up the Constables and Headboroughs of the parish, who began to take proceedings in the police court against some of the publicans, and resolved to "present" to the licensing Sessions, as disorderly, some of Merceron's public-houses—a presentment which Merceron contrived ingeniously to prevent, by promising himself to undertake it, and then quietly relicensing them in defiance of all complaints. In 1816 Merceron's conduct was twice formally brought before the Vestry by a determined group of the respectable inhabitants, who insisted on special meetings being called for the purpose. He was, however, upheld by his usual majority, who passed votes of entire confidence in him, and again re-elected him as Treasurer.[3] But the "Boss" was incensed by the acts of rebellion committed by the Vestry Clerk in supporting the Rector before the House of Commons Committee, and openly threatened this venerable parish officer with dismissal at the next Annual Vestry Meeting. This was, however, too much for endurance. In self-defence the Vestry Clerk co-operated with some of the more respectable inhabitants in instituting a new criminal prosecution against Merceron. Meanwhile the publication of the evidence before the House of Commons Committee, and the discovery that Merceron had actually taken the sum of £925 of the parish funds to defray his own law expenses, without the knowledge of the parish, caused a sudden revulsion of feeling. The Rector and the Vestry Clerk rallied their several forces; the fickle mob "stampeded" with

---

[1] *The Trials at large of Joseph Merceron, Esq.*, by W. B. Gurney, 1819 (see the second trial).

[2] Minutes of Evidence before the Select Committee of the House of Commons on the State of the Police of the Metropolis, 1816.

[3] MS. Vestry Minutes, Bethnal Green, 24th April and 16th May 1816, and 7th April 1817.

dramatic completeness, and the Rector found himself at the head of a triumphant majority. At the Easter Vestry in 1818, when over a thousand persons thronged the church, and the rival parties shouted defiance at each other, the old Vestry Clerk was re-elected, and a new Board of Governors of the Poor was chosen, omitting the prominent Merceronites.[1] The excited Vestry then proceeded to the election of a Treasurer, when the Bank of England was proposed by the reformers, and Merceron, hitherto re-elected virtually unanimously, received only 29 votes. The victorious majority promptly took up, on behalf of the parish, the criminal prosecutions instituted against Merceron, and ordered the business to be carried through to the bitter end by a committee of five of his opponents.[2] When the trials came on in the Court of King's Bench, Merceron was not only found guilty of clandestinely and fraudulently appropriating £925—getting the item secretly entered as having been authorised by the Vestry, entirely unknown either to the meeting or the officers—but also of corruptly renewing the licence of disorderly public-houses in which he was personally interested.[3] Notwithstanding every attempt at compromise—in the course of which he is said to have offered as much as £10,000 to be let off[4]—he was condemned by the full court to the severe sentence of £200 fine and eighteen months' imprisonment. The long reign of misrule seemed at last brought to an end, and all that was respectable in Bethnal Green celebrated the victory by a public dinner.[5] The Rector set up the elementary school which Merceron had hitherto thwarted, and a hundred of the sober householders were sworn in as special constables to suppress the Sunday bullock-hunting and dog-fighting.

[1] MS. Vestry Minutes, Bethnal Green, 19th and 23rd March 1818.

[2] *Ibid.* 29th April 1818.

[3] These trials excited great interest, and two separate reports of them were published ; see *The Trial of Joseph Merceron, Esq. . . . for having fraudulently appropriated . . . certain sums . . . of St. Matthew, Bethnal Green* (1818) ; *The Trial of Joseph Merceron, Esq. . . . for a misdemeanour in procuring certain public-houses . . . to be licensed* (1818) ; and, more authentic, the verbatim report by W. B. Gurney, entitled *The Trials at large of Joseph Merceron, Esq., for fraud as Treasurer of the Poor Rate Funds . . . and also for corrupt conduct as a magistrate in relicensing disorderly public-houses, his property* (published in 1818 in separate parts ; in 1819 under this single title).

[4] *Ibid.* p. xii. of preface to first trial ; *Times,* 25th and 29th May 1818.

[5] *Morning Advertiser,* 22nd May 1818.

" Corruption and delinquency," it was proudly reported a few months later, " have been rooted up. Parochial tyranny and despotism have been destroyed, and this parish now stands decidedly pre-eminent for an economy in the expenditure of the Poor Rate funds, an impartiality of assessment to all the parishioners, a publicity of the parish accounts, and an opportunity on the part of the vestrymen of freely discussing every measure connected with the liberty and general welfare of the parish." [1] But the reign of the reformers was unfortunately of short duration. The parish soon tired of its spasm of virtuous indignation, and a revulsion of feeling set in. Merceron on his liberation from prison published a letter protesting his innocence of any crime. He seems to have been thought to have been very hardly treated; the parish, it was said, had sustained no actual loss, as he had refunded the money ; the new leaders of the Vestry managed matters badly and quickly fell out among themselves.[2] Merceron's friends had continued in possession of the " Watch Board " and the " Pavement Trust," which were permanent statutory bodies, renewing themselves by co-option. In 1820 Merceron's son-in-law is put in nomination for Vestry Clerk, and gets practically half the thousand persons present to vote for him. The election is disputed, and during the rest of the year every meeting opens with the simultaneous reading over of two sets of minutes by the two persons claiming to be Vestry Clerk.[3] For over two years the Vestry meetings are scenes of turbulent disorder, at which the transaction of business is almost impossible. Gradually Merceron reasserts his old power. He is re-elected a Commissioner of the Court of Requests at Easter 1820. In the following year, his son-in-law is definitely elected Vestry Clerk by 1268 votes to 689. From 1820 onward, not only the

---

[1] *Morning Advertiser*, 12th April 1819.

[2] Home Office Domestic State Papers, Nos. 314 and 337, in Public Record Office, 1819, where a leaflet in answer to Merceron's letter is preserved. Another criminal prosecution, ordered by the Vestry in August 1820, against eight leading Merceronites who had given evidence in his favour, had to be abandoned in court, at the instance of the judge, who seems to have regarded it as malignant (MS. Vestry Minutes, Bethnal Green, 20th August 1818 ; *The Trials at large of Joseph Merceron, Esq.*, by W. B. Gurney, 1819).

[3] MS. Minutes, Bethnal Green, 29th March, 3rd, 4th, 21st, and 28th April, 3rd and 4th May, 15th and 28th June, 6th and 21st July, 3rd, 10th, and 17th August 1820, etc., etc.

"Watch Board" and the "Pavement Trust," but also the elected
Directors of the Poor and Commissioners of the Court of
Requests are found to be increasingly made up of his
supporters and dependents. Presently the re-establishment of
Merceron goes so far that we find him even manipulating the
"respectable" party, and co-operating with them in getting a
new Local Act for the abolition of the impracticable Open
Vestry as a governing authority. Against this the more
turbulent frequenters of the Vestry strove their hardest, and
so great was the tumult on one occasion that the Riot Act
was read, and the meeting dispersed by the police.[1] In this
contest Merceron does not appear, and it may be inferred from
various indications that though the Bill was opposed by some
of his followers, it was still more bitterly opposed by some of
his enemies, and that the proposed change was not altogether
distasteful to him. Parliament not unnaturally took sides
against the "government by public meeting," and passed an
Act committing the parish administration to a select body of
the officers for the time being and sixty persons named in the
statute.[2] How this new constitution worked, and how quickly
it came under Merceron's control, we have, unfortunately,
owing to a gap in the archives, been unable to ascertain.[3]
When the records begin again in 1828, we find Merceron

---

[1] We append part of the official record of this meeting from the minute-book:—"The greatest tumult and disorder now began to be manifested in opposition to Dr. Gwynne (who had been elected chairman), the uproar and confusion continued without intermission for more than an hour, when a scene of riot prevailed which became seriously alarming, the obvious intention of several parties present being to compel Dr. Gwynne, by main violence, to quit the chair, many persons getting upon the tables, even over the backs of others, and thus endeavouring to force their way to the top of the room to place Mr. Rennoldson in the chair. The great pressure and suffocating heat added to the vociferation and menacing attitude of various parties, caused the greatest terror and alarm in the Vestry room. A cry of murder was heard, and lives of several vestrymen appearing to be in serious danger, the chairman was requested to disperse the meeting. He thereupon read the Riot Act . . . and . . . ordered the meeting in a legal way to separate . . . whereupon the officers . . . from the Police Department in Worship Street were called in. . . . The meeting was with some difficulty dispersed" (MS. Minutes, Bethnal Green, 6th February 1823).

[2] 4 George IV. c. 10, 1823. The vestrymen, who were to be also the Governors and Directors of the Poor, were to consist of the Rector, Churchwardens, and Overseers, with sixty other persons named in the Act. Of these, ten were to retire annually, and be ineligible for a year. Their successors were to be elected by inhabitant ratepayers assessed at £15 a year and non-resident property-owners of at least £80 a year value in the parish.

[3] The Vestry Minutes for 1823-1828 are missing.

once more in undisputed supremacy. He and another Merceron, probably his son, are leading members of the Select Vestry; he is treasurer both of the "Watch Board" and the "Pavement Trust"; he and his friends are the Commissioners of the Court of Requests; though apparently not reinstated in the Commission of the Peace, he is still by royal appointment a Commissioner for the Land Tax and a Commissioner of Sewers, not only for the Tower Hamlets, but also for Westminster and Holborn and Finsbury; he still owns and controls a quarter of the Bethnal Green public-houses; and his son-in-law continues salaried Vestry Clerk and principal executive officer of the parish. What is even more significant, we find him acting always as the formal spokesman of the Vestry, annually begging permission on the election day "to offer his sincere congratulations to the whole parish for the order, regularity, good-feeling, and satisfaction which had been manifested by every one this day, as indeed had also been manifested by the inhabitants for the last six years in exercising their annual elective franchise under the present Act of Parliament," for members of a Select Vestry, "whose only aim was to watch over the interests of 50,000 individuals by observing the most rigid system of economy and care in the management of our parochial affairs." [1] Nevertheless, when, in 1830, a Parliamentary Committee again inquired into the parish government, all the old complaints of corrupt partiality of assessment, jobbery of the offices, and secret expenditure of the funds were once more made. [2] Yet no reform took place. For at least another decade Merceron, and his son-in-law the Vestry Clerk, go on governing the parish, until at last, from extreme old age, the former gradually ceases to attend to business and dies in the odour of sanctity. His story is forgotten, the scarce reports of his trials are bought up by his family and destroyed, and there is left, so far as we can discover, no other tradition in the parish than that he was an active and public-spirited local administrator, who had suffered harsh treatment from the malignant prosecution of unscrupulous enemies.

[1] MS. Vestry Minutes, Bethnal Green, 2nd March 1830.
[2] *Reports from the House of Commons Committee appointed to inquire into the general operation and effect of the laws and usages under which Select and other Vestries are constituted in England and Wales*, 1830 ; see Stanley v. Dodd, in *Reports of Cases*, by S. Dowling and A. Ryland, 1823, vol. ii. pp. 809-816.

(e) *The Turbulent Open Vestry*

Hitherto we have described types of parish government in which the inhabitants at large took little or no part. This non-intervention in parish affairs, due to the economic subserviency of the labourers in the rural parish, and to the brutish apathy of the new industrial populations, was not universal. It was, as we shall see in a subsequent chapter,[1] the unwelcome intrusion into the parish Vestries of "the meaner sort" that led the principal inhabitants of certain parishes, between the Reformation and the Revolution, to close, by legal or extra-legal devices, the Vestry meetings to all but a select few. After the Revolution this intrusion, as it seemed to the Incumbent and the little clique of past and present parish officers, became more frequent, with results, as must be admitted, which were not always edifying. The Vicar of Codrington, for instance, "gives a curious account of his parish" in the last decade of the seventeenth century. "The people played cards on the communion table; and when they met [in the church] to choose Churchwardens, sat with their hats on, smoking and drinking, the clerk gravely saying, with a pipe in his mouth, that such had been the practice for the last sixty years."[2] In 1734 we hear incidentally of "the clamorous proceedings and irregular behaviour of the great multitude of persons who generally attend the Vestries of the parish of Whitechapel," already a densely crowded part of the Metropolis.[3] "The great are deceived," explains Henry Fielding in 1750, "if they imagine they have appropriated ambition and vanity to themselves. These noble qualities flourish as notably in a country church and churchyard as in the drawing-room or in the closet. Schemes have indeed been laid in the Vestry which would hardly disgrace the Conclave. Here is a ministry and here is an opposition, here are plots and circumventions, parties and factions, equal to those which are to be found in Courts."[4] Such a parish,

---

[1] Chapter V. The Legality of the Close Vestry.

[2] Quoted from the *Gibson Papers*, vol. ix., in C. J. Abbey and J. H. Overton's *English Church in the Eighteenth Century*, 1887, p. 442.

[3] Petition of the Rector, Churchwardens, Overseers, and Principal Inhabitants of St. Mary, Whitechapel, in House of Commons Journals, 22nd February 1734.

[4] *History of Tom Jones*, by H. Fielding, 1750, bk. iv. chap. vii.

we are told by a later writer, became "a kind of republic; and its common business, so far as it is conducted by majorities, is conducted as the business of a republic often is: without system, without consistency, and therefore without the best effect. An individual or two, from constraint or inclination, take the lead; and they are followed by the rest. When these leaders are wearied or disgusted or outvoted, others arise and take the direction of affairs, as their predecessors had done before them, but with different degrees of experience, of judgment, and of integrity: hence arises a want of uniformity of design, of principle, and of proceedings. What is called the sense of the town is usually the opinion of a few individuals. . . . When . . . a Vestry is called, those only assemble who have there some business of their own, some point to carry, some friend to serve, or some foe to combat. . . . Much time is lost in waiting for more attendants, in trifling conversation, or in squabbling about things foreign to the subject for the sake of which the inhabitants were requested to meet; and when business is at last entered upon, want of method, or of time, or of inclination, not only prevents attention to other subjects of equal importance, and which might easily be settled while the inhabitants are together, but often no distinct resolution is formed even upon the particular question about which the meeting was called to deliberate. In many cases the company is much reduced by the departure of one or another before any general opinion can be collected. If a second meeting for the same business should be thought necessary, that meeting is probably attended by a different set of inhabitants, with different information, and different views from that which composed the first meeting; and as in many places the transactions of such meetings are not regularly committed to writing, the business is left, after all, to chance, or to be finally determined by two or three inhabitants who may afterwards happen to meet on the road, at the butcher's shop, at the blacksmith's, or at the shaving house; or the parties concerned are left to judge and act as well as they can for themselves."[1] With such a Vestry there would be, every

[1] *The Select Vestry or Parish Committee*, by the Rev. Hammond Roberson, 1818, pp. 17-19.

now and then, a revolt of the inhabitants against the governing clique, leading to exciting scenes at the meeting. At Greenwich in 1802, we find the Vestry Clerk concluding his record of the proceedings of a meeting as follows:—" And after some altercation and much confusion so that no minutes could possibly be entered at the time, we thought it prudent and necessary to withdraw with this minute-book, lest the same should be defaced and torn." [1] What happened to a Vestry Clerk who failed to withdraw with his minute-book, we may learn from the following resolution of the Vestry of Stoke Damerel (now Devonport). " Resolved, inasmuch as it appears by the report of the Vestry Clerk of this parish that at a meeting of the parishioners held at the workhouse agreeable to order of the Vestry on Wednesday evening last, that the Vestry book was forcibly and in a most outrageous manner taken from him, and the records and resolutions for nearly two years torn out and defaced, and particularly the records and resolutions founded upon the present call of Vestry: it is the opinion of this meeting that the said last-mentioned resolutions, a copy of which is now produced and identified . . . as being a true and perfect copy of the same, be adopted and resolved on by this meeting, . . . and ordered to be entered accordingly." [2] By the year 1818 the Open Vestry meeting—" that many-headed monster"—to use the epithet of the Evangelical Vicar of St. Mary's, Leicester,[3] had in many populous places become a bugbear to quiet and sober folk, with the result that they abstained from parish government. " The meeting at Vestry rooms in the church to settle parish business" was in 1818 declared to be " a great evil, frequently attended with quarrels, and ending in cursing and swearing and abusing each other." [4] " If," writes an Ipswich Incumbent in 1833, " you ask five out of six respectable men you may chance to know, any question relating to parish affairs, the answers you almost invariably get are: ' I know nothing of parish business';

---

[1] MS. Vestry Minutes, Greenwich (Kent), 3rd April 1802.
[2] MS. Vestry Minutes, Stoke Damerel (Devonshire), 24th July 1813.
[3] *Some Account of the Rev. T. Robinson*, by the Rev. E. T. Vaughan, 1815, p. 110.
[4] *A View of the Poor Laws, etc.*, by a Practical Observer, 1818, p. ii.

'I never attend Vestry meetings; they are quite bear-gardens.'[1]

In the troubled political years of 1818-1819, we see this inrushing Democracy submerging the parish government of one provincial town after another, hitherto quietly administered by local oligarchies. In the town of Leeds, for instance, now grown to a population of 75,000,[2] and comprising many townships in a single parish, the Vestry meeting became suddenly transformed into a battlefield of political and religious animosities. The new party, led by the accomplished and wealthy editor of the *Leeds Mercury*[3] and supported by the whole strength of Radicalism and Nonconformity, set itself to bring effectively under the control of the parish meeting the whole of the civil and ecclesiastical administration of the town. In this struggle the Leeds Vestry had certain exceptional advantages. By immemorial custom, no fewer than eight Churchwardens were annually chosen, representing eight several wards, seven of them undoubtedly by the inhabitants, whilst the appointment of the eighth, who served nominally for Kirkgate ward, was claimed by the Vicar. For nearly a century the Vestry had, as we have seen, deputed certain of its members to take part, with the Churchwardens of the parish and the Overseers of the Poor for the central township, in a so-called "Workhouse Board," which managed the whole Poor Law administration of the township, or central part, of Leeds. The Vestry, too, annually elected half of the Board of Street Commissioners, and had the statutory right of auditing the accounts of this important body. But more important than all these customary or statutory powers was the conviction, entertained by every Radical in the borough, that it was the inherent right of the inhabitants, in public meeting assembled, to decide upon every expenditure of public money.

The first step was to establish the control of the Vestry over the accounts of every parish officer. At a Vestry meeting

---

[1] *Remarks and Suggestions relating to the Management of the Poor in Ipswich*, by Rev. Wm. C. Fonnereau, 1833, p. 6.

[2] The population, which was only 17,000 in 1775 and 30,000 in 1801, amounted in 1831 to no fewer than 123,393.

[3] Edward T. (afterwards Sir Edward) Baines; see *Dict. of Nat. Biography*, and *Life of Edward Baines*, by his son, 1851.

in 1819 we find Edward Baines emphatically declaring that
he would " never rest satisfied till a clear and regular account
is rendered to the public of the application of every sum of
money levied by way of parochial rates in this township." [1]
Two years later we find him, in the presence of half the bench
of borough magistrates, without contradiction from them, and
with the unanimous approval of a crowded Vestry meeting,
maintaining as " the popular and just principle of all parish
law . . . that persons who contributed the money should
have the direction of its application and the control over their
officers." [2] It had for some time been customary to appoint
the same man, year after year, as Surveyor of Highways; and
this officer, taking his stand on the statute law, refused to do
more than report his total expenditure. When Michaelmas
came round, the Vestry refused to renominate him, and
submitted to the Justices a list of ten other suitable persons.
The Mayor and Aldermen, as Justices for the borough, ignored
the Vestry's nomination and again appointed the experienced
Surveyor. A great agitation followed, ending in a compromise, by which the Vestry gained a good deal of control.
In the following year we see the Mayor and half the Aldermen attending the Vestry meeting to make peace, promising
to appoint in future from among the Vestry nominees. The
retiring Surveyor apologises for not permitting investigation
into his accounts and promises to do so in future. The
Vestry thereupon gives up its objection to that officer, and
includes him in the new nomination, when he is again
appointed by the borough Justices.[3] Between 1822 and
1834 the Vestry, under the same able leadership, became the
supreme controlling power in Leeds, meeting every few
months in the parish church to nominate parish officers or
elect its representatives on the Workhouse Board and Street
Commissioners, who acted virtually as its executive committee;
to criticise and pass the parish accounts; or to decide, after

---

[1] MS. Vestry Minutes, 11th and 12th April 1819 ; report in *Leeds Mercury*,
4th May 1819.

[2] Report of Vestry meeting to nominate Surveyors of Highways and receive
their accounts, *Leeds Mercury*, 29th September 1821 ; MS. Vestry Minutes,
27th September and 1st October 1821.

[3] *Leeds Mercury*, 29th September 1821 ; see MS. Vestry Minutes, 28th
September 1820 ; 22nd and 27th September and 1st October 1821.

excited debate, such issues of policy as the widening of a
particular street, the assessment of owners of cottage property,
or the support or opposition of Bills in Parliament.[1]   Two
such meetings happen to be described in vivid detail.   In
June 1828 it was determined "at a meeting of the Churchwardens, Overseers, and Guardians of the Poor" to call a
Vestry meeting in the parish church, "for the purpose of
determining the mode in which property shall in future be
rated in this township for the poor's assessment."   The
question had become one of keen popular interest.[2]   The
Vicar was absent, and had sent a curate formally to protest
against the meeting as illegal ; but at twelve noon a Churchwarden was promptly called upon to preside, who "took his
seat to the left of the communion table, there being then
assembled about two thousand parishioners."   Baines led off
the debate in an eloquent speech, which ended in a "unanimous" vote in favour of retaining the old system of assessment.   Next day, there was another Vestry meeting at
10 A.M. to pass the Churchwardens' accounts, which is
described as "one of the most numerous and respectable we
ever witnessed in the town of Leeds, and must have consisted
of from three to five thousand parishioners, including those

---

[1] For all these proceedings see the MS. Minutes of the Vestry and Street
Commissioners ; the *Leeds Mercury,* which was owned and edited by Baines ;
the *Life of Edward Baines,* by his son Edward Baines, 1851 ; the *Leeds
Intelligencer* (Tory organ) ; and contemporary pamphlets such as that entitled
Leeds Vestry Meetings, 1828.   *The Life and Letters of Walter Farquhar Hook,*
by W. R. W. Stephens, 1878, and *St. Peter's at Leeds,* by J. Rusby and Rev.
J. G. Simpson, 1896, describe the Leeds Vestry Meetings in 1837-1838.   See also
*The Parochial System of the Church of England opposed to the present condition of
the Parish of Leeds,* 1842.

[2] The explanation of the keen popular interest in assessment is as follows :—
By the General Vestries Act of 1818 (Sturges Bourne's Act) any poll of the
parish had to be taken on a system of plural voting, according to rateable value,
all occupiers up to £50 having one vote only.   To defeat this plural vote, it
was the custom of the Vestry at Leeds to keep the rateable value down to about
one-sixth of the rack rent, and thus bring practically all occupiers below £50.
The small cottages, from which the collection of a trifling sum was expensive
and troublesome, were either omitted from the assessment or else passed over in
the collection.   To remedy this latter defect the Tories proposed that the owners
should be assessed instead of the occupiers.   This would have had the incidental
result of disfranchising the cottage occupiers, and at the same time of giving
plural votes, under Sturges Bourne's scale, to the owners.   Hence the Radical
objection to all such schemes of "compounding."   See *Leeds Mercury,* 10th
February 1821 and 25th May 1833 ; MS. Vestry Minutes, Leeds, 31st January
1820 and 1st February 1821 ; and articles in *Liverpool Albion,* January 1829,
and *Times,* 22nd January 1829.

from the out-townships." The Radicals maintained a relent-less opposition to passing the accounts. This heated debate was still proceeding, the crowd filling the nave, when " it was announced that prayers had commenced in the choir. The meeting was consequently adjourned till prayers were con-cluded, and the week-day congregation was swelled to a very considerable size. A few minutes before 12, prayers having been concluded, Mr. Musgrave [the Churchwarden] again took the chair." Finally, after two hours more of excited speech-making, the meeting, about 2 o'clock, refused by a large majority to pass the accounts.[1]

This turbulent "government by public meeting" did not go entirely unresisted. The Radicals elected Nonconformist Churchwardens : the Mayor and Aldermen, as Justices of the Peace, retorted by appointing exclusively Tory and Church Overseers.[2] The attempt of these latter officers to take part in the expenditure, even of the Poor Rate, was bitterly resented by the Radical party. "When they first took their seats on the Workhouse Board," one of them afterwards complained, " they were treated with contumely and contempt by what were called the people's representatives. . . . Informa-tion was kept from them, and they were derided as the magistrates' nominees and treated with contumely on all occasions."[3] Driven to bay, the Overseers seem at last to have asserted their legal rights. At a meeting of the Workhouse Board in December 1835, the Overseer members resolved that in future an Overseer should preside ; that no money should be expended except on a vote by a majority of the Overseers ; and that all workhouse officials must be appointed by them alone.[4] The Churchwardens appealed to the Vestry, which denounced " the attempt now making by a

---

[1] *Leeds Vestry Meetings*, 1828 ; *Leeds Mercury*, June 1828 ; MS. Vestry Minutes, 6th March, 20th June, 28th November 1828.

[2] It is one more example of the diversity and confusion of English parish government that in Leeds it appears never to have been the custom for the Vestry to nominate suitable persons to serve as Overseers. These had been, time out of mind, appointed by the Justices without communication with the Vestry, at one time on the nomination of the Constables, and latterly on that of the retiring Overseers. See speech by E. Baines, reported in *Leeds Intelligencer*, 26th March 1836. Moreover, there were never any Sidesmen at Leeds (*St. Peter's at Leeds*, by J. Rusby and Rev. J. G. Simpson, 1896, p. 281).

[3] *Leeds Intelligencer*, 26th March 1836.

[4] MS. Vestry Minutes, 5th December 1835.

majority of the Overseers to . . . exclude the Churchwardens and Trustees from all interference in the appointment of medical and other officers to the town, or the laying of the Poor's Rate, and thus to arrogate to the Overseers themselves the sole power and authority in the management of the poor."[1] The consequent "distracted state of the Workhouse Board" is, throughout 1835, the subject of anxious consideration by the Vestry.[2]   Finally, a few months before the whole organisation was transformed by the advent of the new Board of Guardians, eminent counsel advised that the century-long practice of administering the poor relief of the township of Leeds by a "Workhouse Board" was and had always been illegal, the Churchwardens of the parish of Leeds not being ex-officio Overseers of its component townships, and the so-called Trustees or Guardians appointed by the Vestry being without any lawful authority whatsoever.[3]

Even more disorderly was the experience of Manchester. In spite of the revelations of mismanagement, hideous corruption, and serious oppression, which had been made at the close of the eighteenth century, as described in a previous section, the government seems to have remained, for another score of years, quietly in the hands of the officers of the Court Leet, together with the Churchwardens, incorporated under their Local Act of 1792, and the new body of Street Commissioners.   Suddenly, in 1818 (the year before the so-called "Peterloo Massacre"), we plunge at once into a period of excited democracy.   Manchester was, in the eyes of the Castlereagh and Sidmouth government, a hot-bed of sedition; and some harsh things were done, by Home Office order, during the suspension of the Habeas Corpus Act.   At the Vestry meeting in April 1818 to pass the Constables' accounts, a fierce dispute arose over the expenses incurred in

---

[1] MS. Vestry Minutes, 24th December 1835.

[2] See, for instance, MS. Vestry Minutes, 9th July 1835. The Leeds workhouse and system of poor relief is fully described in the Appendix A to the First Report of the Poor Law Inquiry Commissioners, 1833 (Tweedy's Report), pp. 782-794, where the accounts for 1821 and 1831, and the "Rules and Orders" of 1822 are given at length. The workhouse was used only for the aged, infirm, and children, the able-bodied being always given out-relief.

[3] The opinion was that of Sir Frederick Pollock, and it was obtained by order of the Vestry itself; see MS. Minutes, 24th December 1835, 24th March 1836; *Leeds Intelligencer*, 26th March 1836.

arresting one Ogden.[1]   In 1820 it was the expenses connected
with the Peterloo affair that were objected to, and the local
officers shrank from the ordeal of presenting them.   The
Radicals obtained from the Court of King's Bench a mandamus
against the Churchwardens, requiring them, in their capacity
as Overseers, to lay the Constables' accounts before a public
Vestry.[2]   This took the form of a crowded meeting in the
Collegiate Church (now the Cathedral) at 11.30 A.M., at which
the Radical forces had been gathered by a public handbill.
The items mainly objected to consisted of the cost of the
printing of the circulars by which the Constables had called a
private meeting of the principal inhabitants to pass votes of
thanks to the magistrates, military officers, and the Boroughreeve for their conduct on the field of Peterloo.   The Constable
defended his action in thus summoning only the principal
inhabitants on the ground that in a city of a hundred
thousand people it was impossible to apply the methods
suitable for a small town and invariably call public meetings.
"Manchester," he said, "was a place which within a few years
had increased most rapidly in wealth and population, but
which had not had any corresponding improvements in its
municipal constitution.   He would put it to the candour of
the gentlemen on the other side whether it was possible that
the office of Constable should be served here on the same terms
as in a small country village." [3]   Such scenes reached a climax
during the exciting years of 1830-1835.   When the Churchwardens and Constables appeared in the old Collegiate Church

---

[1] This was the object of Canning's unfortunate gibe, the "revered and
ruptured Ogden" (*Manchester a Hundred Years Ago*, by W. E. A. Axon, 1887,
pp. xv.-xvi. ; *Notes and Queries*, 4th series, vol. iii. p. 431, by C. Ross).   The
Manchester Vestry meeting of this year was thus alluded to by the local poet—

> A bull-ring—Cribb's parlour—a French Chamber sitting—
> Are decorous all when compared to the meeting
> Held in April to settle the quarter's accounts,
> When outrageous disputes about trifling amounts
> As excuse was sufficient, the sum but a farthing,
> To turn God's holy temple into a bear-garden.

"Metrical Records of Manchester," by Joseph Aston, in his *Plays, Poetry, and
Prose*, 1826, p. 65.

[2] This had been required in 1778 by 18 George III. c. 19, but had apparently
seldom been done in Manchester.

[3] See the handbill preserved in the Manchester Public Library (942, 72,
N. 1) ; MS. Vestry Minutes, 8th June 1820 ; and the reports in the *Manchester
Gazette* of 3rd and 10th June 1820.

to pass their accounts, and took their stand by the old " parish
table," they would occasionally have to face a howling mob
of several thousand persons, who filled the whole building,
perched themselves on every coign of vantage, and vigorously
applauded the speeches of their champions.   During the three
years 1831-1833, an open Vestry meeting of this kind was
held in Manchester for one purpose or another nearly every
quarter, at which such popular leaders as John Edward Taylor,
the brothers Thomas, John and Richard Potter, and Archibald
Prentice would make a strenuous fight to elect their own
Churchwardens, to nominate their own Surveyors of Highways ;
to cut down the salary of the Deputy Constable; to disallow
payments made for special constables or partisan handbills :
and in 1833 to resist the imposition of any Church Rate
whatsoever.[1]

By this time the turbulence and incapacity of these
Vestry meetings had seriously discredited the whole system
of government by the ratepayers themselves.   The following
description [2] by a Tory newspaper of the Vestry meeting
which in 1835 rejected the Church Rate, if somewhat
exaggerating the irreverence of the mob, well expresses the
deep disgust felt by the governing classes.   " Excluding Mr.
Hadfield, Mr. Potter, Dr. Johns, and a few other gentlemen

[1] At this poll over 7000 votes were cast, see *Manchester Historical Recorder*,
1874, p. 100.   The *Manchester Guardian*, which was started in 1821 by John
Edward Taylor and the brothers Potter, as the Whig and Radical organ, contains
long reports of these proceedings, especially during 1831-1833, though the active
editor, Garnett, incurred the reproaches of the Radicals for his Whig limitations.
See also *Wheeler's Manchester Chronicle* ; the *Manchester Times*, run by Archibald
Prentice, and the latter's *Historical Sketches and Personal Recollections of
Manchester*, 1851.

[2] The disorder was doubtless greatest in the large towns of the North of England, where political and sectarian animosities were most acute.   But similar
scenes were taking place in other towns.   The leading Plymouth newspaper, for
instance, describes a Vestry meeting in that town in 1834 as follows : " We once
saw a prize fight attended with its usual accompaniments of noise and hubbub,
but to speak truth it scarcely equalled the intemperate display we witnessed "
(*Plymouth Journal*, 3rd April 1834).   Already in 1810, the quarrels of a
proposed addition to the churchyard had made the Stoke Damerel Vestry
meeting " very lively " (*History of Devonport*, by R. N. Worth, p. 58).   " As
to parish meetings," writes a clergyman from Ipswich as early as 1762, " they
are very mobbish assemblies.   At these every contributor to the rates claims an
equal importance with the rest, and the vulgar people, with their noise and their
nonsense, but chiefly by their rude and abusive language, drive away the better
and wiser sort of men " (from an able letter of Rev. Richard Canning of
Ipswich, Suffolk, in *The Christian's Magazine*, vol. iii. 1763, p. 26).

thinly scattered among the mob, the meeting was made up of the lowest scum of the town, the most riotous, disorderly, ill-clad, ill-assorted, and uncivilised portion of the population, who had no capacity to understand the question at issue, who violated all the ordinary rules of decency, and desecrated in a disgusting manner the church it was necessary to hold the meeting in. The scene had literally all the features of a bear-garden. From one to two thousand persons, for the most part unwashed, unshaven, and in rags, had taken possession of all the pews in the church before the proceedings commenced, most of them having their hats on, and the majority standing upon the seats or the backs of the pews; subsequently crowds of these people made their way into the gallery, clambering from seat to seat, and covering with filth the seats and cushions on which they trod." [1] The great Whig organ, the *Manchester Guardian*, was scarcely less outspoken with regard to a Vestry meeting of 1832. It declared that its report utterly failed " in conveying anything like an adequate impression of the disgusting character of the proceedings . . . of the degree of reckless violence, unabashable impudence, and Billingsgate scurrility. . . . We expect that one of the early acts of a reformed Parliament will be to put an end altogether to the necessity of meetings like that of Wednesday. It is utterly preposterous that thirty thousand people (even if the meetings were really confined to leypayers, which notoriously they are not) should be called together for the transaction of parish business. Such assemblies neither have nor can have a deliberative character. They are by their very constitution utterly incapable of the calm and dispassionate consideration of any disputed public question in its various aspects. And we hold it to be utterly impossible that, in the intended

---

[1] *Wheeler's Manchester Chronicle*, 11th July 1835 ; MS. Vestry Minutes, 8th July 1835. In 1827 the Churchwardens had made an attempt to avoid the use of the church for such meetings. "It has," they write, "long been a subject of regret that parish and township meetings are not held in a more appropriate and convenient place than in the Collegiate Church. It is notorious that the tumultuous contests that frequently arise on these occasions are very ill-suited to a place of public worship, and are often the cause of considerable damage being done to the church." They therefore resolve to hold future meetings at the Town Hall, or to begin them *pro forma* at the church and immediately adjourn to the Town Hall. Some doubt seems to have arisen as to the legality of meeting anywhere but in the church, and though some meetings were adjourned to the Town Hall, others continued in the church.

municipal constitutions to be given to the new boroughs, the superseding of these ancient forms, which, however suited to the small towns and sluggish habits of bygone days, are worse than useless among our immense masses of population at the present time, should not form one of the most prominent objects. The representative system must be introduced for the regulation of those expenditures connected with the Poor's Rates, which now come before promiscuous meetings of the leypayers, as well as with those of the other local taxes." [1]

It was, however, in the crowded parishes of the Metropolitan area that the tumult and confusion of this " government by public meeting " and this disposal of the public money by what Whitbread called the votes of " inconsiderable renters " [2] became most notorious. The reformers of London administration found themselves in a dilemma between the corruption of the Close Vestries, to be described in a subsequent chapter,[3] and the incapacity of those that were open to every ratepayer. " Some parishes," said Michael Angelo Taylor in 1816, " were so divided among themselves on almost every occasion that they sat debating like a petty House of Commons, and neglected their most important duties." [4] This continued right down to the end of the period with which we are dealing. " The affairs of the parish," wrote an able observer of the

---

[1] *Manchester Guardian*, 6th October 1832. The local government of Salford (population in 1801, 13,611) closely resembled that of Manchester; see the *Report of the Committee appointed at a Town's Meeting . . . to inspect the late Overseers' Accounts and superintend the Collecting of the Arrears of Leys*, 1811 ; the evidence of J. Brotherton before the *Select Committee of the House of Commons on Select and other Vestries*, second report 1st April 1831 ; and various reports in the *Manchester Guardian*, 1821-1833. The Radicals objected in 1831 to any expenditure from the Church Rate for bell-ringing (*Manchester Guardian*, 28th July 1831), and in a stray newspaper cutting of 16th January 1833 we read, that "in consequence of the town's refusal to pay for bell-ringing, Salford was without for a long time, not even any tolling for church services." It is significant of the uncertainty and confusion of the respective spheres of the Vestry and Court Leet that in 1833 the inhabitants in Vestry assembled transferred the whole management of the Deputy-Constable and Beadles from the Boroughreeve and Constables (who were appointed at the Court Leet) to the Street Commissioners. This was effected by a resolution in May 1833 "that the salaries of the police officers cease to be paid out of the Poor Rate in the month of October next, as provision is made in the Salford Police Act for such establishment" (*Manchester Guardian*, 11th May, 19th and 26th October 1833).

[2] Hansard, vol. viii. p. 896, 1807.
[3] Chapter VI. Close Vestry Administration.
[4] Hansard, vol. xxxiii. p. 18 (7th March 1816).

London parishes in 1836, "necessarily fall into the hands of the jobbers, who are always punctual in their attendance. These gentlemen sometimes push matters too far, and a great commotion is raised by some determined reformer fortunate enough to possess nerves of iron and the lungs of a Stentor, who addresses his fellow-parishioners vehemently for an hour together upon the subject of the parish abuses. The meeting called to pass a motion for a rate is adjourned; another is called, and a thousand persons assemble to rave, storm, wrangle, fight, and perhaps, if they can get through so much business, vote certain strong resolutions against the Church-wardens and Overseers. For a time the jobbers are held in check; but the excitement dies away; each of the ratepayers has his own business to look after; the parish Demosthenes breaks a blood-vessel, or is silenced in some other way; and matters return to their original state." [1]

[1] *Local Government of the Metropolis: A Sketch of the Municipal Institutions of London,* p. 22. (Anon. 1836; reprinted from *Westminster Review,* January 1836.)

CHAPTER III

AN EXTRA-LEGAL DEMOCRACY

In crowded urban districts, with shifting populations and sharp economic religious or political cleavages, the task of creating, out of the disjointed legal framework of parish government, an efficient instrument of democratic government, appeared (as the experience of Bethnal Green, Leeds, and Manchester sufficiently demonstrates) absolutely insuperable. Yet in a few of the populous parishes we see the task accomplished. In some of the crowded towns that were becoming part of the Metropolitan area—still more in the ancient seaport of Liverpool — we watch an energetic and enlightened knot of inhabitants gradually reorganising their parish government, so as to place the whole administration effectively under democratic control, whilst maintaining a continuous and fairly efficient executive policy. This was done by the adoption of constitutional devices for which there was no legal authority. These devices varied in detail from place to place; they were adopted one by one at different periods in different parishes; and only very rarely do we find all of them simultaneously existing in any working constitution. Hence we can best describe the evolution of this Extra-legal Democracy, not by taking the history of any one parish, or by confining ourselves to any one decade, but by dealing separately with each element of the organisation as illustrated by the experience of parishes in different parts of the country between 1689 and 1835.

(a) *The Organisation of the Public Meeting*

The first step in reform was to reduce to order the public meeting of the inhabitants held in the nave (or sometimes at

the west end,[1] or in a side chapel) of the parish church,
though often removed by adjournment to a public-house.
Down to 1818 it was by no means certain—it was at any
rate quite unknown to the Vestries themselves—what the law
provided as to the franchise and the method of voting in
parish matters. The usual assumption was that every
ratepayer in the parish was entitled to a vote.[2] But it
depended practically upon the Churchwardens and Overseers
who should be assessed to the rates. It was customary to
omit from the rate-book all premises of low rental, on the
double ground that the occupiers were themselves poor, and
that the collection was troublesome. And as a settlement in
the parish, and perhaps a right to share in the charities, might
be gained by being rated there, the parish authorities often
used their discretion as to whom they would admit. Early in
the eighteenth century we find the Woolwich Vestry deciding
" that no Churchwarden or Overseer for the Poor do make
any person whatsoever a parishioner of this parish who was
not so before, by receiving of him or her any sum or sums of
money for church or poor, without having first taken the
order and direction of a Vestry to be called for that purpose,
only such qualified by law excepted." [3] The Vestry then
formally resolved from time to time that certain named
inhabitants, " being persons of ability, credit, and reputation,
be and are hereby admitted parishioners of this parish, and
that the Churchwardens and Overseers of the Poor do receive
their several and respective rates." [4] Even those who were

---

[1] At Royston, the Vestry ordered "all meetings to be at the church at toll
of bell, and adjourn as they think proper" (Vestry Minutes, Royston, Herts ;
in *Fragments of Two Centuries*, by Alfred Kingston, 1893, p. 34). At
Manchester the meeting was always "at the parish table," which still stands
under the west window of the Cathedral. At St. Martin's, Leicester, the
parish meeting was formerly held in the spacious side chapel built by the
Corpus Christi Guild. At Birmingham the smallness of the only room available
for town meetings (which were apparently only occasionally held in St. Martin's
Church) has sometimes led to " comic results, such as the division of the
meeting, and the appointment of two chairmen " (*A Picture of Birmingham*,
by James Drake, 1825, p. 79).

[2] There are traces, in the seventeenth century, of restriction to those who
attended Divine Service. Thus, in 1635, the Churchwardens of St. Anne,
Blackfriars, in the City of London, report that their parish has a "Vestry consisting of all sorts of inhabitants that pay scot and lot, and use to come to church,
and are not disorderly or turbulent" (MS. in Lambeth Palace Library, Chartae
Misc. vii. p. 42). [3] MS. Vestry Minutes, Woolwich (Kent), 12th May 1716.

[4] *Ibid.* 5th June 1746, 24th September 1758, and many other entries.

assessed to the rates were not always allowed to vote. The Vestry often made a rule excluding persons in arrear with their payments, and sometimes even fixed an arbitrary minimum of rental value. Thus the St. Pancras Vestry in 1796 passed the following resolution : " Resolved that it is the unanimous opinion of this Vestry that no person ought to vote for a Beadle but housekeepers renting £10 a year and rated to the poor. It is also the opinion of the Vestry that persons being six months in arrear for their Poor Rates ought not to interfere in the election of parish officers of any description, and that the Overseers be requested to be particularly attentive to persons of that description coming forward to vote after the present occasion, that the payment of their rates be enforced." [1]   So, at Kensington in 1806, when a new Sexton was to be elected, the Vestry resolved " that it be observed at this election, and be an established rule and custom of this parish, that no person's vote . . . shall be deemed or allowed to be a good vote, unless he shall be an inhabitant of the parish renting £10 a year at the least, or paying scot or lot therein." [2]   The Vestry of Tooting, more cautious, or perhaps more modest, in 1811 took counsel's opinion as to who was entitled to vote in the election of a new Vestry Clerk.[3]   Whether women ratepayers were entitled to vote was a moot point, often formally decided adversely by resolution.   Thus at St. Pancras, in 1788, " it was decided by the Vestry that ladies should not be admitted to vote for parish officers. " [4]   At Chelsea, on the election of a new lecturer or preacher in the parish church, defaulters in payment of rates and lady ratepayers were alike excluded. " Whereas the lectureship of this parish being vacant upon the death of Mr. Shorthose, and the inhabitants intending tomorrow to proceed to choose another lecturer in his room, it is hereby agreed that no person be allowed to vote until all his taxes be paid. It is also agreed that this Vestry is of opinion that the ladies and gentlewomen, widows and maidens, who pay and stand charged have not a right to vote in this

---

[1] MS. Vestry Minutes, St. Pancras, 1st January 1796.
[2] Ibid. Kensington (Middlesex), 2nd March 1806.
[3] Ibid. Tooting, 15th April 1811 ; History of Tooting Graveney, by W. E. Morden, 1897, p. 187.
[4] Ibid. St. Pancras, 25th March 1788.

election, there being no precedent in this parish for the same." [1]

When the Vestry grew at all large, the procedure of the meeting became of great importance. With regard to the chair, it was commonly assumed, though without explicit authority, that the parish clergyman had a right to preside if he was present. But the Rector or Vicar was often an absentee; and in the populous parishes with which we are here dealing, he seems frequently to have abstained from attending any but the Easter Meeting, at which the Church-wardens were chosen. At other meetings, the senior Church-warden, or the Boroughreeve or Constable usually presided; or the meeting elected (as it possibly had always the right to do) its own chairman. One valuable feature of the procedure was the formal notice given to the parishioners of all the business it was intended to transact. This notice was read out in church, and often specified in detail the subjects to be considered. [2]

Organised parish meetings of this kind regarded them-selves, especially between 1815 and 1832, as channels for the voice of the people, entitled, not merely to deal with parochial affairs, but also to exercise influence on the counsels of the nation. We find such Vestries passing long and argumen-tative resolutions on the political issues of the day, usually on the Radical side: in 1815 denouncing the new Corn Bill by which the importation of corn was forbidden so long as the price of wheat was under eighty shillings per quarter; [3] in 1816 condemning the Property or Income Tax as "partial, odious, oppressive, and inquisitorial"; [4] in 1820 welcoming Queen Caroline and criticising the conduct of the King; [5] and 1831 supporting the Reform Bill [6] and denouncing the assessed

---

[1] Vestry Minutes, 22nd February 1735, quoted in Faulkner's *History of Chelsea*, 1829, p. 89.

[2] For instance, the MS. Vestry Minutes of Chelsea (Middlesex) in the eighteenth century are always prefaced by an exact copy of the notice, with a statement that it had been " read in church." One such notice runs as follows : "The parishioners are desired to meet in Vestry on Wednesday next in order to consider the proper measures to be taken for the removal of the manufactory carried on in Cheyne Walk to the public annoyance" (MS. Vestry Minutes, Chelsea, 11th April 1781).

[3] MS. Vestry Minutes, Greenwich (Kent), 28th February 1815.

[4] *Ibid.* 18th March 1816.   [5] *Ibid.* 10th August 1820.

[6] *Ibid.* Brighton, 18th February 1831.

taxes.[1] Occasionally, too, such a Vestry meeting, under the influence of feeling for the Church, would blame the War Office for breaking the Sabbath by reviewing the troops on a Sunday,[2] or petition against an Insolvent Debtors' Bill as "calculated to deprave the moral character of the people,"[3] or give expression to the dominant Protestantism of the English laity by objecting to Catholic Emancipation,[4] or any other concessions to Roman Catholicism.[5]

The resolutions of the Vestry were decided upon by "show of hands"; but if a division was demanded, or an election contested, the votes were counted in one of two ways. Either the two parties would separate to different sides of the church, or a primitive system of "scratching," as it was termed, would be adopted. On a page of the open minute-book the names of the candidates would be written, each followed by a long line. Each voter would come up to the book in turn and "scratch," that is, make a mark across the line against his candidate's name.[6] But a poll of the parish would often be demanded,

[1] MS. Vestry Minutes, Brighton, 30th August 1831.

[2] *Ibid.* Stoke Damerel, Devonshire, 1st October 1817.

[3] *Ibid.* 27th February 1816.

[4] *Ibid.* St. Martin's, Leicester, 10th March 1825 ; *Ibid.* Bristol, 11th March 1829.

[5] *Ibid.* St. Martin's, Leicester, 7th April 1825 ; *Ibid.* St. Mary's, Leicester, 28th February 1827.

[6] These "scratchings" may be seen in the Minute-Books, to give only a few instances, of St. Pancras and Finchley (Middlesex). The "scratches" are reproduced in the specimen minutes of Finchley Vestry, printed in H. C. Stephen's *Parochial Self-Government in Rural Districts*, 1893, pp. 218, 234. The oldest mention of them known to us is that in Dr. Freshfield's *Minutes of St. Stephen's, Coleman Street*, 1886, where, on the 28th October 1583, the election of a Vestry Clerk is decided by the number of "strokes" set to their names. At a Leicester parish, in 1646, the Vestry elects a minister by "scratching" (*The Accounts of the Churchwardens of St. Martin's, Leicester*, 1489-1844, by Thomas North, 1884, p. 197). In Deptford, in 1738, the meeting "scratches" for a Churchwarden (MS. Vestry Minutes, St. Paul, Deptford, 16th May 1738). R. N. Worth (*History of Plymouth*, p. 296 of 1890 edition) describes this "scratching" as in use there from time immemorial, for the elections of Guardians of the Poor. "A list of the candidates was written on a sheet of paper, and the voter made, or caused to be made 'scratches' opposite the names of those whom he favoured. The oddest feature of the business was that, if a name were passed over, the voter was not allowed to return to it" (that is, to change his mind and place a mark against the name originally passed over). In 1871 an innovating chairman held that there was no legal warrant for this system, and took the vote by show of hands. Next year "scratching" was reverted to, and became the subject of an action at law, when the court held it to be a lawful method of voting. In 1873 the Guardians formally resolved that voters might "try back," or return to a name after they had once passed it by, and with this modification the custom was adhered to

especially for the election of a salaried officer, whether the Vestry Clerk, the Beadle or the Sexton, or in some cases, an Organist or a Curate. The voting would then extend over two days, or sometimes longer, with all the paraphernalia of election addresses, personal canvassing, the circulation of squibs and libels, and no little consumption of liquor. These contests frequently meant no more than the struggle of two or more candidates for what was to them a lucrative office. In some cases, however, particularly between 1829 and 1835, they were pitched battles between political and religious parties. At Wakefield (West Riding), for instance, in 1834, the choice of a Constable was made the occasion of a four days' poll, at which nearly two thousand persons voted, with the result that the Tory and Church candidate was success-ful.[1] The method of election, as well as the franchise, was often settled by agreement among the candidates, with the sanction of the Vestry. At an election to the office of Parish Beadle at St. Pancras, in 1796, the four candidates entered into the following agreement, which was formally ratified by the Vestry : they " do mutually agree to and with each other in the manner following, viz. that the said election shall be by poll, and finally close at four o'clock in the afternoon, and that no person be permitted to vote but such as have £10 a year." [2] Woolwich Vestry adopted, as early as 1754, a complicated system of secret ballot for all parish polls, and in 1762 made elaborate arrangements for eliminating all personal favouritism in filling the important post of organist in the parish church, at a salary of £30 a year. " When the several candidates shall be in the organ loft, and the curtain sewed together, the organ-blower to attend them, and no person whatever to be admitted into the gallery, or any person admitted into the church but those who are parishioners and have a right to ballot." The candidates had to cast lots for precedence in playing, and then each in succession to play a voluntary for about fifteen minutes. When all had played,

---

until 1879, when, under an order of the Local Government Board, election by voting papers was introduced (MS. Minutes, Board of Guardians, Plymouth, 1873-1879).

[1] *Halifax Guardian and Huddersfield and Bradford Advertiser,* 1st November 1834.

[2] MS. Vestry Minutes, St. Pancras, 6th January 1796.

the assembled parishioners (their names being duly recorded) were to declare by secret ballot which playing they preferred, the votes being there and then counted, and the successful performer being declared elected to the post.[1]

The demand for a poll was not restricted to the election of officers. In the more democratic Vestries there grew up the custom of one party or the other appealing, in questions of policy, from a "packed meeting" to a poll of the inhabitants, which habitually lasted for several days, and was often attended by great popular excitement. In Woolwich, for instance, during the nine years 1796-1804, we find it referred to a vote of the inhabitants to decide whether a rate collector should be appointed, whether an Act of Parliament should be applied for, whether the master of the workhouse should have an increase of salary, whether a proposed scale of compounding for rates should be adopted, whether a certain draft bill to give increased powers of regulating the poor should be approved, and whether the organist's salary should be fixed at £30 or at £40 per annum.[2]

(b) *The Control over the Unpaid Officers*

However well the Vestry meeting was organised, and however definitely settled its method of voting, it was

[1] MS. Vestry Minutes, Woolwich, 7th and 21st June 1762 ; see also "The Method for the election of an Organist, 19th September 1754.

"1st. That Ballots be prepared by the Churchwardens, beginning with number 1, and so progressively, according to the number of subscribers ; to be sealed up.

"2nd. That Mr. Crosweller will be pleased to stand in the Vestry Room with the Ballots, and see that each subscriber hath but one ballot, and then turn his back to the subscriber while he puts his ballot into the box for the candidate he ballots for.

"3rd. That each subscriber take a ballot from the whole number, and put into a box marked No. 1, 2, 3, or 4 for the candidate he ballots for.

"4th. That but one subscriber be in the Vestry Room at a time and after he has balloted to return into the church.

"5th. That no subscriber be admitted to ballot by proxy.

"6th. That after the subscribers present have balloted, the boxes to be delivered by Mr. Crosweller to the Churchwardens, and to be by them immediately opened in the presence of the subscribers, and the number contained in each box to be counted, filed, and entered in a book, and the candidate having the greatest number to be declared by the Churchwardens and elected accordingly. THOMAS FLOOD, } Churchwardens."
WILLIAM MATTHEWS. }

[2] MS. Vestry Minutes, Woolwich, Kent, 1796-1804.

dependent, for the actual execution of its public functions, upon the customary parish officers. For, as we have seen in our description of the Legal Framework of the Parish, it was upon the several parish officers in person, not upon the Vestry, that the duty and responsibility of executing the various public functions were cast; and it was these officers alone, not the inhabitants in Vestry assembled, who were clothed with the coercive powers of government. This applied particularly to the statutory powers of the Overseers of the Poor and the Surveyors of Highways, who, as we have described, were appointed by the Justices of the Peace. But the Justices could not themselves conveniently discover suitable persons year by year on whom to impose the office; and in the case of the Surveyors of Highways the legislature had, as we have mentioned, expressly cast upon the parish the duty of annually suggesting names. This custom soon extended to the Overseers and, where the Court Leet no longer made the appointment, also to the Constable. Where the retiring officers had been in the habit of presenting names themselves, this practice was peremptorily stopped by the Vestry's order.[1] Energetic Vestries decided not only the persons, but also how many officers should be appointed, irrespective of statute. In Liverpool, as early as 1733, we see the Vestry electing six "Overseers and Collectors of the Poor's Ley."[2] Birmingham got five Overseers in 1720, six in 1729, and presently twelve, six every half-year, though the Act of 1601 authorises no more than four,[3] and a yearly appointment. "The practice now is," says a writer of 1799, "and probably ever has been, for the parishioners in a Vestry to make a list of persons in their judgment proper for the office, and for the magistrates to nominate the two first in such [parish's] list . . . except cause is shown to them why they should deviate from this

---

[1] "Resolved that the practice recently adopted by the Churchwardens and Overseers of this parish of framing lists of persons eligible and proper to serve the office of Overseers of the Poor for the ensuing year is improper and illegal; and that this meeting do now proceed to frame a list of twelve fit and proper persons from whom the magistrate may appoint to the office" (MS. Vestry Minutes, Brighton, 26th March 1828).

[2] MS. Vestry Minutes, Liverpool, 1733. In 1743 the Vestry elects also eight "leylayors," or assessors.

[3] *History of Birmingham*, by William Hutton, p. 366 of edition of 1835; *A Concise History of Birmingham*, 1817, p. 74.

general course of practice, or that they know those recommended by the Vestry to be ill-qualified for the office." [1] Hence we find, in the proceedings of the more energetic Vestries, at any rate from the latter part of the eighteenth century, the election of Overseers, Surveyor, and Constable made by the Vestry with the same assurance as that of Churchwarden.[2] Presently this came to be so much a matter of course that any deviation in the appointment by the Justices was regarded as an arbitrary exercise of power.[3] When political feeling ran

[1] *The Duties of Overseers of the Poor and the Sufficiency of the Present System of Poor Laws considered*, by James Nasmith, 1799, p. 8. What is here said of Overseers is equally true of the Parish Constable. "Petty Constables," says an authoritative manual of 1829, "though sometimes appointed in Courts Leet according to ancient practice, and occasionally sworn into office either by the lord of such court, or by Justices out of session, are now generally nominated by their respective parishes in Vestry, and sworn into office by the Justices at the Quarter Sessions, which is, on every account, the better and more regular mode" (*A Practical Guide to the Quarter Sessions*, by William Dickinson and T. N. Talfourd, third edition, 1829, p. 60). The "nomination" of Overseers by the Vestry is incidentally referred to in the General Highway Act of 1835 (5 & 6 William IV. c. 50).

[2] One way of doing this, in the case of Overseer or Surveyor, was to submit to the Justices only as many names as there were appointments to be made ; the assumption being that this compelled the acceptance of the Vestry's nominees. At Halifax, in 1833, the Radicals at the Vestry flatly refused to nominate more than four Overseers, the number required, alleging this to have been the local custom (Report of Vestry Meeting in *Halifax and Huddersfield Express*, Easter 1833).

[3] So much was this the case that Toulmin Smith could bring himself to contend, in face of the clear words of the statutes and a complete consensus of legal authorities, that the appointment by the Justices was ministerial only, and that they were legally obliged to appoint the persons elected by the Vestry (*The Parish*, 1857, p. 146). But he could cite no case in which this had been held to be law ; and parish records reveal numerous instances in which the Vestry nomination was ignored.

One such case may be quoted from a contemporary diary for the vision that it gives of local government in Reading in 1818. "It has generally been the custom for the Mayor [as borough Justice of the Peace] to confirm the choice of the parish in its Overseers, *i.e.* to appoint those upon the list who had most votes. Sometimes (though very rarely) this rule has been departed from, when the magistrate, to suit private or party interests, selected whom he pleased from the lists ; but this year—the year in which a general election is expected to take place—His Worship would not leave it even to this partial, this unjust mode ; about a fortnight previous to Ladyday the Mayor held a meeting privately with some of Mr. Weyland's [the M.P.] friends, and with their assistance chose Overseers for the year ensuing ; but still the form of law must be obeyed, the process of going through the Vestry must be submitted to. Accordingly, on the day of election these agents attended with their list of names to be sanctioned by the parishes. Mr. J. Tanner presented the list prepared for St. Mary's, but the meeting rechose their old Overseers, and then wrote to the Mayor requesting him to confirm their choice ; but he was not so easily turned ; the voice of a parish was as nothing to him. He invested with the insignia of office those of

high between the new Democracy of such Vestries as Leeds and Manchester, and the Tory Justices who had to make the appointments, the exercise by the latter of any discretion in the matter was denounced as an unwarrantable inroad upon the rights of the people.[1] By 1828 this spirit of resentment against any intervention on the part of the magistrates has spread to the Metropolis. Thus in Mile End Old Town we find the new Radical Party bitterly complaining that, for many years, " the local magistrates have constantly interfered and appointed persons as Overseers in direct opposition to those nominated by the inhabitants, and, with one or two exceptions, have pursued the same system with the list of names presented for the choice of Surveyors of Highways." [2] The Radical Reformers, said one of their local leaders about this time, " had lately convinced these gentlemen . . . that there was no sympathy between them and the inhabitants, and that the exercise of such powers . . . in the appointment of officers . . . was productive of anything but peace and tranquillity." [3]

The mere nomination of these officers carried with it no legal control over their action, nor, so far as the Overseers, Surveyors, and Constables were concerned, even the right to

his own choice, Messrs. Burnard, Brown, and Trendell ; but this unjust mode of proceeding affronted several even of Mr. Weyland's friends who were not in the secret; therefore His Worship paused before he determined upon the list presented at St. Giles's, where the same farce had been acted by Mr. Law, and their choice thrown very much in the background. At St. Lawrance's the meeting approved His Worship's choice . . . 2nd April [1818]. The Mayor after being out of town for a week, and leaving St. Giles's Parish without Overseers, has at length chosen from the list sent to him from the Vestry, Mr. Boult and Mr. Loscomb, two half-way men, *i.e.* men who vote both for Mr. Weyland and his opponent, and Mr. Robinson, a Weylandite who has served the office twice before " (*Reading Seventy Years Ago*, by P. H. Ditchfield, 1887, pp. 73-74).

[1] Political partisanship was in parish matters, we need hardly say, not unknown at an earlier date. We give an illustrative instance of 1771. "The parish of St. Mary, in Dover, is supposed to contain at least three-fourths of the town, and the business is transacted by the Churchwardens and four Overseers of the Poor. At the election five of these officers were returned in the interests of the Blue Party. . . . Their partiality was so obvious as to be thought a sufficient reason for the magistrates . . . to appoint other officers . . . and four others were placed in their stead " (*Canterbury Journal*, 2nd April 1771). Needless to say, considerable friction ensued between the "blue" Churchwardens and the "yellow" Overseers.

[2] Letter from "An Inhabitant and Reformer," in *Times*, 25th March 1828.

[3] Report of speeches at public dinner in Mile End Old Town, *Times*, 4th June 1827.

approve their accounts.   But the Churchwardens had to
obtain covering sanction, for every item in the expenditure
out of the Church Rate, of the meeting of inhabitants " in
Vestry assembled"; and the active co-operation of these
popularly elected officers was essential to many important acts
of Poor Law administration.   Whilst the parish was small, all
the accounts were, as we have seen, kept together in one rude
cash-book, which was produced as a matter of course at the
Vestry meeting.   When the growth of the parish business and
the differentiation of officers led to separate accounts being
kept and three separate rates made, there was no hard and fast
rule as to which account any particular item should appear in.
The Vestry of Lewes thought nothing of charging a new
parish pump to the Poor Rate, and that of Woolwich a new
watchhouse and stocks.[1]   The relief of the poor was often
divided between the Churchwardens and the Overseers, " the
random poor" being dealt with sometimes by one and sometimes by the other.[2]   The common nuisance caused by hogs
rambling about the streets is ordered, nearly simultaneously,
at the Vestry of Woolwich, to be dealt with by the Surveyor
of Highways; at the Vestry of Camberwell, by the Churchwardens ; at the Vestry of St. Giles's, Cripplegate, by officers
acting under the Lord Mayor's warrant for the benefit of the
Poor Rate ; and at the Vestry of Bradford by the Constable,
through whom it comes in the Overseer's accounts.[3]   Although
the repair of the roads and the prevention of obstructions to
thoroughfares were usually dealt with by the Surveyor of
Highways, we find the Greenwich Vestry in 1808 directing

---

[1] Vestry Minutes, St. Thomas à Becket-in-the-Cliffe, Lewes (Sussex), 3rd
October 1804 ; in *History and Antiquities of Lewes*, by T. W. Horsfield, 1824,
vol. i. p. 292 ; MS. Vestry Minutes, Woolwich (Kent), 16th March 1735.   The
same course was followed at Minchinhampton when the parish fire-engine had
to be repaired (MS. Vestry Minutes, Minchinhampton, Gloucestershire, 20th
April 1778).

[2] Thus the Tooting Vestry resolves in 1743 "that the random poor be
allowed necessary relief by the Churchwardens, who shall have a rate for that
purpose" (Vestry Minutes, 1743, in *History of Tooting Graveney*, by W. E.
Morden, 1897, p. 54).

[3] MS. Vestry Minutes, Woolwich (Kent), 27th September 1798 ; Vestry
Minutes, Camberwell (Surrey), 22nd June 1797, quoted in W. H. Blanch's *Ye
Parish of Camerwell*, p. 7 ; Vestry Minutes, 1763, in *An Account of the Church
and Parish of St. Giles's Without, Cripplegate*, by J. J. Baddeley, 1888, p. 159 ;
Vestry Minutes, Bradford (Yorks), May 1798, quoted in *Historical Notes on the
Bradford Corporation*, by William Cudworth, 1881.

the Churchwardens summarily to pull down certain gates,[1] and
it incidentally appears that in Stoke Damerel Parish in 1815
it was the Overseers who were paying for certain road repairs,[2]
though a Surveyor of Highways had been appointed. If the
Justices, or any other critic, objected to any payment being
charged against the Poor Rate or the Highway Rate, as being
unauthorised by law, all parties would agree to transfer the
item to the Church Rate, which needed no magisterial allowance and had never been limited or restricted by any statute.[3]
Under these circumstances the claim of the Vestry to discuss
indiscriminately all the officers' accounts seemed only reasonable and practically convenient to all parties. Moreover,
though Parliament never brought itself to require the accounts
of the parish officers, as such, to be submitted to the Vestry
for its approval, it did insert clauses, now and again, in various
general statutes between 1691 and 1795, requiring or imply-
ing that this or that parish officer should report to a meeting
of the inhabitants. In these clauses what was apparently in
the mind of the House of Commons was, not so much the
erection of the Vestry meeting into a controlling authority, as
the securing (and that only in a halting and, as it were, a
hesitating manner) of local publicity for the parish officers'
expenditure, and the provision of some means by which the
parishioners could organise a formal appeal to the Justices.[4]

---

[1] MS. Vestry Minutes, Greenwich (Kent), 25th April 1808.

[2] *Ibid.* Stoke Damerel (Devonshire), 18th August 1815.

[3] We have already mentioned, as paid out of the Church Rate, the items for
the destruction of vermin. At Charlton, in 1728, the Vestry "unanimously
agreed to allow the person who serves as Constable of the parish the sum of
thirty shillings per annum for his extraordinary charges, to be paid out of the
Church Rate" (MS. Vestry Minutes, Charlton, Kent, 23rd April 1728). The
rewards offered by Vestries to any person who apprehended a burglar or highway robber were usually paid out of the Church Rate. This is expressly
ordered, for instance in Chelsea in 1793 (MS. Vestry Minutes, Chelsea, Middlesex, 17th December 1793). When, in 1802, the Vestry of an ancient Norwich
parish decided to appoint three additional paid watchmen to assist the Constables
in the nightly protection of property, it expressly added "that these expenses
should come out of the Church Rate" (MS. Vestry Minutes, St. Peter Mancroft,
Norwich, Norfolk, 22nd November 1802).

[4] Thus, by 3 and 4 William & Mary, c. 11 (1691), the Churchwardens and
Overseers were required to keep a book in which to register the names of those
in receipt of regular poor relief, which was to be produced once a year to the
Vestry, when the Vestry was to declare the persons whom it thought "fit . . .
to receive collection." But Quarter Sessions, or any local Justice, might order
relief to others ; and the power and duty of the Overseer to give temporary
relief in urgent cases on his own responsibility was left unimpaired. Further,

But when we remember the natural desire of the unpaid and annually serving officer to avoid trouble during his year of office, and his horror of possible litigation as to his expenditure, which he would have to defend at his own private cost, we can realise how easily a determined and persistent Vestry would acquire control over the whole expenditure of the parish. Thus we find some Open Vestries, throughout the eighteenth century, and even before, exercising more or less authority over the action of all the parish officers, wrangling over objectionable items in their accounts; disallowing outlays previously protested against; and emphatically forbidding particular expenses for the future.[1]   Confining our illustration to our own period, we read, in the minutes of one of the small Exeter parishes, that, in 1701, it was " resolved and agreed that whoever shall succeed Warden to the parish aforesaid, on all occasions which require extraordinary charges above the sum of forty shillings . . . shall by the Clerk summon the Minister, Wardens, and all the parishioners who pay to the poor (and also by toll of the bell half an hour before the appointed time), and to have the approbation of the parishioners then present, or the major part thereof, who shall sign the said

---

by 17 George II. c. 3 (1744), as a check on "the unlimited power of the Churchwardens and Overseers" to make Poor Rates, they were required to give notice in church of every Poor Rate which had been made before they began to collect it, and they were to allow any inhabitant to inspect and take a copy of the rate at a small fee.   But no limit was set to their power of getting a rate, and nothing was said of any prior consultation of the inhabitants.   At a much later date, by 36 George III. c. 23 (1795), the consent of a majority at a Vestry meeting was required before the Overseer could give out relief, otherwise than under Justices' order, or, as we must assume, in case of emergency.   In contrast to the freedom of the Overseer, the Surveyor of Highways was definitely required (though not until 1766, by 7 George III. c. 42) to produce his books and accounts for the inspection (but not for the approval) of the inhabitants at a Vestry fifteen days before he presented them for allowance to the Special Highway Sessions of the Justices.   And the Constable, by 18 George III. c. 19 (1778), had to present his accounts to the Overseers, who were to lay them before a Vestry for express approval, upon which the Overseers were to pay from the Poor Rate the sum due.   But even then nothing was said as to the Overseers presenting the much more important Poor Rate accounts, and with regard to the Constable's expenditure, if the Vestry disallowed any item, the matter had to be referred, as a dispute, to the decision of a Justice of the Peace.

[1] We give one out of many early cases.   "At a meeting of the parishioners of the parish of Thame, it is ordered that if any Churchwarden or Overseer of the poor shall put any person into the collection-book without the consent of the parish at the Stone, that he or they so doing shall pay such person or persons himself" (Vestry Minutes, Thame, Oxfordshire, 8th June 1651; see *The History of Thame and its Hamlets*, by H. Lupton, 1860, p. 96).

order under their hands and enter it on the parish book." [1]
In the minutes of the Vestry of Birmingham, then a town of
only 15,000 inhabitants, but already famous for hardware, it is
recorded, under 7th April 1702, that " it is this day ordered
at a public meeting of the parishioners of Birmingham that
the twenty pence that hath used to be paid to the Churchwardens for the ringing the bell to any funeral shall not be
paid for the future by any person." [2]   The same minute control
over the doings of both Overseers and Churchwardens is
shown by the following quaint record of the Vestry of one of
the parishes of the City of Gloucester.   " At a parish meeting
held in the parish church of St. Michael, the 2nd day of April
1711, it is agreed for the future no Churchwarden or Churchwardens shall lay out or disburse upon the account of the
parish (except for the bread or wine for the sacrament) any
sum or sums of money exceeding twenty shillings without first
having the consent of the parish at the parish meeting under
their hands ; and if any Churchwarden or Churchwardens shall
disburse or lay out upon the account of the parish any sum or
sums of money exceeding twenty shillings as aforesaid, he and
they do hereby acquit and discharge the parishioners from ever
repaying the same to him or them ; and likewise it is agreed that
no Overseer or Overseers shall lay out or disburse for the use of
the poor upon account of the parish any sum or sums exceeding
five shillings without having a legal order from the Mayor or
Justices of the Peace, or the consent of the parishioners for it,
had at a parish meeting under their hands." [3]   In 1735 the
Woolwich Vestry expressly gave to the Churchwardens, whom
it elected and controlled, the direction of practically all the

---

[1] MS. Vestry Minutes, St. Petrock's, Exeter, 21st April 1701.

[2] Two years later, we find it " agreed at a Meeting at the chamber over the
Cross, the Constable, Churchwardens, and Overseers being present, that for the
future no money shall be spent on the public account upon any day of public
rejoicing unless the officer first call a public meeting at the said chamber in
order to have the consent of the inhabitants ; unless particular direction shall
be given by the Deputy-Lieutenant, Justices of the Peace, or others in authority,
for that purpose" (MS. Vestry Minutes, St. Martin's, Birmingham, 7th April 1702
and 19th September 1704 ; see also *Old and New Birmingham*, by R. K. Dent,
section 1, p. 59).

[3] MS. Vestry Minutes, St. Michael's (Gloucester), 2nd April 1711.   The
payments for " visitation " expenses and fees to bellringers are often similarly
fixed ; see, for instance, MS. Vestry Minutes, Minchinhampton (Glos.), 3rd
December 1723.

against at a former Vestry meeting, to be refunded to the present Overseers, in default of which refund an appeal was to be made to Quarter Sessions against the allowance of the accounts by the Justices.[1]   The mere threat of such an appeal was often enough.   Thus in the Vestry minutes of one of the Leicester parishes, we read the following resolution : " That the last Overseers be summoned before the magistrates, and proceeded against, to compel them to pass their accounts." This threat was apparently successful, as there follow a series of adjourned meetings to pass the Overseers' accounts, which are finally allowed by the Vestry.[2]

The power of disallowing items in the accounts which the Vestry possessed in the case of the Churchwardens, and assumed to itself in those of the other officers, enabled it to check peculation, or to stop expenditure of which it disapproved, but it furnished no means by which it could enforce its desires. In order to ensure continuity of policy among these annually changing officers, and still more to obtain control of that policy, it was necessary for the Vestry meeting to lay down definite instructions for the guidance of all who held office in the parish.   Thus many Vestries would in one form or another ordain " that none of the gentlemen hereafter chosen and appointed to the offices of Churchwardens and Overseers of the Poor of this parish shall under any pretence whatever be permitted to serve the workhouse with provisions, or any other article or commodity whatsoever, or send any materials, or do any work either in or about the workhouse, or otherwise on the parish account while in office." [3]   Another typical instruction was " that all repairs, improvements or alterations necessary to be made to the church or workhouse or other building, be done by contract, and that a preference be given in all business of this nature to tradesmen residing in the parish." [4]   Some-

---

[1] MS. Vestry Minutes, Stoke Damerel (Devonshire), 24th July 1813.

[2] *Ibid.* St. Martin's, Leicester, 1st January to 5th March 1805.   Occasionally even a minority of the Vestry would actually appeal to the Justices, and with success, as, for instance, at Liversedge (Yorkshire), in 1808, when the Overseer had a party of his own dominant in the Vestry. The appeal to Petty Sessions failed to get the objectionable items disallowed ; but a further appeal to Quarter Sessions resulted in their being struck out (*The Select Vestry or Parish Committee*, by Rev. Hammond Roberson, 1818, pp. 50-52).

[3] *Ibid.* St. Pancras (Middlesex), 10th April 1787.

[4] Vestry Minutes, Camberwell (Surrey), in *Ye Parish of Camerwell*, by W. H. Blanch, 1875, p. 155.

times they would specifically forbid any expenditure on a particular service, except with the prior consent of the Vestry. Thus St. Pancras objected to its officers' passion for bricks and mortar, and resolved in 1788 " that no article of expenditure be allowed in the accounts of the Churchwardens or Overseers of the Poor of this parish for the year ensuing, for any building, alteration or repair whatsoever, except the same shall have been erected or made by order of a Vestry, expressly called to consider the propriety of such building, alteration or repair, by notice given in the church and chapels of this parish a fortnight at least before the assembly of such Vestry." [1] The Woolwich Vestry continued to tack such resolutions to its passing of the accounts of the Surveyors of Highways, long after it had secured complete control over its poor relief. In 1785 it deferentially requested the Surveyors of Highways to remove a footpath so as to widen a certain roadway.[2] Ten years later it is moved to resolve " that the streets and public roads in this parish are in a very bad state of repair and almost impassable in places, owing in great part to the neglect of the Surveyors of Highways." [3] And, to give one more example of this Vestry control, we may describe the energetic and persistent action of the parishioners of Charlton, by Greenwich, in 1817 and 1818. Not content with the formal " examination and allowance " at a public Vestry, of the accounts of the Overseers and the Surveyors, as well as of the Churchwardens, the Vestry, in 1817, starts on a course of minute investigation. It first refers the Churchwardens' accounts to a committee, whose report leads to both disallowances of past and prohibitions of

---

[1] MS. Vestry Minutes, St. Pancras (Middlesex), 25th March 1788. Deptford had done the same in 1741. " Also it is likewise ordered and agreed that no Churchwarden or Churchwardens for the future have power to lay out and expend any sum or sums of money for the repairing and beautifying the church with any necessaries that shall exceed the sum of £5, without first applying himself or themselves to the Vestry for an order to be made for that purpose, under the penalty of his or their paying such surplus sums out of his or their pockets " (MS. Vestry Minutes, Deptford, Kent, 11th January 1741).

[2] *Ibid.* Woolwich (Kent), 18th November 1785.

[3] *Ibid.* 23rd January 1796. At Stoke Damerel (now Devonport), the Vestry, on passing the accounts of the Surveyors of Highways and agreeing to a rate, resolved : " And the Vestry recommended to the Surveyors of Highways the improvement of the road leading from the Mile House to the parish quarry ; that the following gentlemen be appointed a committee to assist the Surveyors of Highways, in the formation of the above road, as to the best modes of doing it " (MS. Vestry Minutes, Stoke Damerel, Devon, 20th September 1822).

future expenditure. "We whose names are hereunto subscribed, to whom in a Vestry held on the 1st of June last it was referred to inspect the late Churchwardens' accounts from Easter 1816 to Easter 1817, and to report our opinion thereon to the Vestry, do certify that we have accordingly inspected and examined the said account, and are of opinion that with respect to the item charged therein for expenses at the visitation dinner, the sum of 10s. 6d. and no more should be allowed in the future for the dinner of each parish officer attending upon that occasion; that inquiry should be made by what authority the sum of . . . charged in the said accounts to have been paid for the release of . . . Bailey from prison, was paid, before the same be allowed; that inquiry should also be made by what authority the sum of £1:4s., charged to have been expended at the choosing of parish officers, was paid, before the same be allowed; and that the sum charged to have been paid by the late Churchwardens for doing the church duty in the absence of the Rector be disallowed. We are further of opinion that no books for the use of the church be purchased or ordered without the assent and approbation of the general Vestry."[1]   Attention is then given to the Overseers' accounts, by the appointment of a committee to inquire into Poor Rates in arrear, on whose report the parish officers are specifically required to take action against the defaulters.[2]   The Overseers then turned recalcitrant, and managed to slip through the allowance of their accounts by a snatch vote at a thinly attended Vestry meeting on a week-day, which led to the following protest being entered in the minute-book: "We request you will call a Vestry on Sunday, 5th of April, to take into consideration the proceedings of the Churchwardens and Overseers in having convened a Vestry to examine and pass the Overseers' accounts for the last year on Tuesday, 3rd March instant, notwithstanding a notice and protest of several of the parishioners requesting that such Vestry should be held on the Sunday following, according to the ancient usage of the parish, whereby the majority of the parishioners might have been enabled to meet in Vestry and examine those accounts. And also to inspect such accounts and consider the expedience

[1] MS. Vestry Minutes, Charlton (Kent), 27th June 1817.
[2] *Ibid.* 28th December 1817 and 11th January 1818.

of appealing against the allowance thereof by T. Goodenough, Esq., and the Rev. Samuel Watson, Clerk, D.D., two of His Majesty's Justices of the Peace for the County of Kent. And further to consider the necessary measure for establishing a rule that the Vestry for making rates for the relief of the poor, examining and passing the Overseers' accounts, be always held on a Sunday, according to the ancient custom of the parish." When the Sunday Vestry meeting was held in pursuance of this requisition, the requisitionists carried all their proposals triumphantly.[1] Even then the Vestry could not, without various adjournments, get the Surveyor of Highways to produce his account-book, but he presently succumbed, and enabled the Vestry to proceed against those who had failed to pay the Highway Rate.[2] Having at last got the accounts under its control, the Vestry peremptorily forbids any future disobedience to its orders as to expenditure, insists " that no parish officer be employed in repairs or works for the parish, or where there is any benefit arising during the time of his holding office," makes a new and equal assessment of the parish, takes systematic action against persons in arrear with their rates, definitely prohibits the practice of the officers charging interest on the money which they may have to advance out of their own pockets on parish account, and, going with great care through the whole list of our relief, reduces the allowances which it thinks excessive, establishes a maximum of five shillings a week, and stops all gifts of clothes unless by a special vote.[3]

(c) *A Salaried Staff*

So long as the Vestry depended for the carrying out of its orders on unpaid officers, personally responsible to the law for the due execution of Acts of Parliament—even appointed and

---

[1] MS. Vestry Minutes, 5th April 1818. At a subsequent Sunday Vestry, it was, however, agreed as a compromise that future Vestries should be held on Wednesdays, in the evening (*ibid.* 20th April and 3rd May 1818). But in consequence of the previous connivance of the Churchwardens with the Overseers, in thus summoning a Vestry meeting at a time when few of the parishioners could attend, a committee of six parishioners was appointed to act with these officers in calling future Vestry meetings (*ibid.* 13th May 1818).

[2] *Ibid.* 26th and 27th May 1818.

[3] *Ibid.* 1818-1821.

controlled by authorities outside the parish—it was difficult for the meeting of inhabitants to do more than exercise a veto upon policies and actions of which it disapproved. When, however, the parish business outgrew the capacity of unpaid officers, energetic Vestries seized the opportunity to take over the control of parish affairs, by putting them in the hands of paid subordinates, to whom the Vestry itself could give orders, and whom it could dismiss at its pleasure. The most important of these was the Vestry Clerk, a new officer, whose duties were regulated by no statute, who was subject to no external authority, but whose salary was fixed by the Vestry, paid out of the Church Rate, and could be made subject to any conditions which the Vestry might choose to impose.[1] The appointment of such a permanent salaried officer, recording the proceedings and carrying out the wishes of the Vestry, seems to have been restricted, for the greater part of the eighteenth century, to parishes within or adjoining the Metropolitan area; to have gradually extended to the more populous parishes in the South of England; and to have been comparatively rare, right down to 1835, in the Northern Counties.[2]

An early instance of the appointment of a Vestry Clerk is afforded by the extensive parish of Camberwell, in Surrey, now a thickly populated part of the Metropolis. Down to the death of Dr. Parr in 1691, the minutes of the Vestry had been kept by the Vicar. A few years later we find the Vestry appointing a " Clerk to the Vestry . . . during his good behaviour," at the modest stipend of thirty shillings a year, which rose successively to fifty shillings, six pounds, and ten pounds; in 1816 to £105; and in 1828 to two hundred guineas per annum.[3] In the full and interesting manuscript minutes of the Vestry of Woolwich we see this energetic body, as early as 1715, using its Vestry

---

[1] A " Clerk to the Vestry " is mentioned in the records of St. Martin's-in-the-Fields as early as 1620 (MS. Vestry Minutes, St. Martin's-in-the-Fields, Middlesex). Strictly speaking, the appointment was regarded by the law as made only from meeting to meeting. "The office," said Chief Justice Kenyon, " depends entirely on the will of the inhabitants, who may elect a different clerk at each Vestry" (Term Reports, vol. v. p. 714 ; The Parish, by J. Toulmin Smith, 1857, p. 204).

[2] But the exceptionally well-organised parish of Liverpool had one at a very early date.

[3] See the Vestry Minutes printed in Ye Parish of Camerwell, by W. H. Blanch, 1875, p. 123.

Clerk to secure knowledge and control of the doings of all the unpaid officers. The whole secretarial work and keeping of accounts was put into his hands. The Vestry formally ordered him, not only to attend all meetings of the Vestry, but also those of the Churchwardens and Overseers; not only to keep the minutes and draw up orders and documents for signature, but also to transcribe the various rates and assessments, to keep the Churchwardens' accounts, to make copies of those of the Overseers, and even to assist in person at the monthly payment of the poor, when he was required to "take an account of all the monthly pensioners in a book for that purpose, to set down their respective allowance, the time of their admission, their age, and the causes and reasons of such their admission. And at the end of the year he shall likewise enter in the register-book the names of all the parish children put out apprentice, and to whom, the names of such persons who have brought certificates removed by order of Justices, and all bonds and other securities given to the parish." [1] The neighbouring parish of St. Paul, Deptford—created by Act of Parliament in 1730 out of the older St. Nicholas, Deptford—started its separate existence by appointing a Vestry Clerk, who was to make books for the collectors for Poor and Church Rates, to enter up the Churchwardens' and Overseers' accounts, and yearly to present to the Vestry itself "an account of who doth and who doth not pay to the poor." [2] At Greenwich, on the other hand, the Vestry contented itself, down to 1798, with employing a local solicitor for any business it wanted done. In that year, after a discussion about the amount of the charges then incurred, the Vestry appointed a permanent Clerk at £100 a year, with instructions, not only to attend all parish meetings and to advise the Vestry, the workhouse committee, and the parish officers, but also to make out the Poor and Church Rates, keep all the parish accounts, and make whatever attendances were required on behalf of the parish, in order to get done all that the Vestry might direct.[3] In 1816 a Parliamentary inquiry incidentally reveals the presence of Vestry Clerks in practically

[1] MS. Vestry Minutes, Woolwich (Kent), 28th February 1715.

[2] *Ibid.* St. Paul's, Deptford, 10th August 1730.

[3] *Ibid.* Greenwich, 10th April 1798 ; Chelsea, 1783-1802.

all the Metropolitan parishes north of the Thames, who were regularly summoned by the clerk to the stipendiary magistrates to report, whenever a public-house licence was to be granted or transferred, whether "the inhabitants" were satisfied with the character of the incoming tenant.[1] To what extent the practice of these parishes in appointing salaried Vestry Clerks had been copied elsewhere we do not know. But the Vestry minutes of Brighton, Gloucester, Mitcham, Minchinhampton, Stoke Damerel (or Devonport), and Royston reveal the existence of the office in those parishes between 1781 and 1826.[2]

The Parish Beadle, in spite of his proverbial cocked hat, gold lace, and official staff, was a humbler servant of the Vestry than its Clerk; and was employed to take over some of the menial outdoor duties of the unpaid parish officers. No statute had authorised his appointment, or limited his functions, which have, we believe, never been the subject of definition by the law courts.[3] In the records of different Vestries during the eighteenth century, we see the Vestry constantly widening the scope of the office, and assigning all sorts of duties to the person whom it appointed as Beadle. He was to clear the streets of vagrants and beggars for the Constable; to help the Overseers to collect the Poor Rate, carry out the removals of paupers to their settlements, and prevent householders harbouring lodgers from other parishes; to keep order, under the direction of the Churchwardens, in the church and churchyard during Divine Service; on behalf of the Vestry Clerk to "cry" the notices of Vestry meetings and announcements of decisions there arrived at—in short, to be

---

[1] Report of House of Commons Committee on the Police of the Metropolis, 1816; evidence of clerk at the Bow Street police office.

[2] MS. Vestry Minutes, Brighton (Sussex), 5th April 1804; *Ibid.* St. Michael's, Gloucester, 25th November 1813; *Ibid.* Mitcham (Surrey); *Ibid.* Stoke Damerel (Devonshire), 24th July 1813; *Ibid.* Minchinhampton (Gloucestershire); and Vestry Minutes, Royston (Herts), 1781, in *Fragments of Two Centuries*, by Alfred Kingston, 1893, p. 34.

[3] Shakespeare mentions him as a sort of assistant Constable: "Sirrah, go fetch the Beadle hither straight" ("Enter a Beadle with whips)," 2 *Henry VI.* ii. 1. It is chiefly in this character that he has been recognised by the Courts (Lawrence *v.* Hedger, *Reports of Cases*, etc., by W. P. Taunton, vol. iii. p. 14). The Churchwardens' accounts of Bromley St. Leonard (Middlesex) show a Parish Beadle to have been first appointed there in 1658, at £2 a year (*History of the Parish of Bromley St. Leonard*, by James Dunstan, 1862, p. 144).

on hand whenever any superior officer of the parish required an assistant, a messenger, or a porter. When in the early part of the nineteenth century it became necessary to have a salaried officer to relieve the poor, we see some south country Vestries, such as Mitcham and Greenwich, definitely converting their Beadle into this functionary by nominating him to the Justices of the Peace for formal appointment as Overseer.[1] Like the Vestry Clerk, the Beadle was paid for his services—usually out of the Church Rate, but sometimes out of the Poor Rate—such sum as the Vestry chose to fix, varying

[1] Thus, at Tooting (Surrey), in 1742, a person whom we believe to have been the Beadle was ordered by the Vestry "to look after the behaviour of the boys at church, and to look after the beggars about the town as his business will admit" (*Vestry Minutes*, in *History of Tooting Graveney*, by W. E. Morden, 1897, p. 54); the officer being definitely appointed "Headborough, Beadle, and Bellman" in 1784, with a gold-laced hat, coat and collar, and twelve guineas a year (*ibid.* p. 83). In 1795 the Chelsea Vestry instructs its Beadle not only to attend Divine Service, and all meetings of the Vestry and its committees, and to wait upon the parish officers every morning to receive their commands, but also "that he shall endeavour as far as possible to prevent people lodging in the parish who are likely to become chargeable ; and at all times endeavour to keep the parish free from beggars"—for the whole of which he is to be paid £30 a year out of the Poor Rate (MS. Vestry Minutes, Chelsea, Middlesex, 9th July 1795). A Chester Parish Beadle in 1796 has merely "to attend the Overseers" (*Lectures on the History of St. John Baptist Church and Parish in the City of Chester*, by Rev. S. Cooper Scott, 1892, p. 182). At Brighton, in 1800, the Churchwardens and Overseers themselves appoint the "Beadle and Cryer," at £20 a year, "and clothes"; his duties being "to make the poor-book, the church-book, the surveyors'-book, and the town-book. He is also to attend the north and west galleries of the church on Sundays . . . to go round the town with the officers to make the militia list, and is likewise to officiate as Headborough in the town, but not elsewhere, and to be sworn for that purpose" (MS. Vestry Minutes, Brighton, Sussex, 31st March 1800). At Mitcham, in 1801, "it is ordered that the Beadle's name be added to the names of the Overseers, and that he is expected to be aiding them in the collection of the rates, removing of the paupers and vagrants, attending the Bench at Croydon, and to do the usual office of Beadle and Constable ; and that he have a salary of fifty guineas per annum, and to have a coat and hat as usual annually, which he is to wear in the execution of his office" (MS. Vestry Minutes, Mitcham, Surrey, 12th April 1801). The Greenwich Vestry, in 1812, at the request of the workhouse committee, appoint as Beadle an "active, assiduous, and respectable man," at £100 a year, and get him furnished with a warrant as an "Overseer of the Poor" by the Justices, to fulfil all the duties of both offices (MS. Vestry Minutes, Greenwich, Kent, 31st March 1812). The Deptford Beadle is to be appointed a Constable by the Justices (MS. Vestry Minutes, St. Paul, Deptford, 3rd January 1828). Some London parishes had numerous Beadles. We learn incidentally from Maitland that the 143 parishes of the City of London and Westminster had, in 1756, 134 Beadles, of whom about 109 must have been parish Beadles, and 25 those of the Wards of the City of London. The 24 Metropolitan parishes north of the Thames, outside the City and Westminster, had 46 parish Beadles (*History of London*, by Wm. Maitland, 1756, vol. ii. pp. 1381, 1392).

from a mere annual fee of a pound or two, up to a regular
weekly wage of a guinea or thereabouts, or even a salary of
£100 a year—the traditional cocked hat, gold-laced coat, and
staff being always provided in addition. Like the Vestry
Clerk, too, the Beadle seems to have been characteristic of
parishes in the Metropolis and the Southern Counties; and to
have been less frequent, as a parish officer, in the Northern
Counties.[1]

An even greater innovation than the Vestry Clerk and the
Beadle, and one quite unwarranted by law, was the engagement and payment by the Vestries of many of the industrial
parishes of the North and Midlands, of a "standing,"
"stationary," "perpetual," or "hireling" Overseer. The payment of a small fee, at the end of his year of office, to the
compulsorily-serving Overseer was not unknown,[2] but it had
been definitely declared illegal by the law courts. "This
office," said Lord Mansfield, when such a payment was brought
before him in 1785, "is a great burden, but the statute meant
to throw it on the Overseers, and that they should do it
without fee or reward."[3] Notwithstanding this decision,
many Vestries continued year after year calmly to nominate
to the Justices for appointment as Overseers persons expressly
engaged for hire and remunerated out of the Poor Rate,[4] to
undertake all the lawful duties of an Overseer; relieving the
poor, collecting the rates, and even managing the workhouse.
These officers, though nominally responsible only to the
Justices, avowedly took their orders from the Churchwardens,

[1] But see the instance cited in the preceding footnote of a Parish Beadle at
Chester in 1796.

[2] Already, in 1693, we hear of a Welsh Overseer being allowed twenty shillings salary (MS. Minutes, Quarter Sessions, Breconshire, 3rd October 1693).
At Pershore, in 1775, "in case George Washband should be Overseer for
the season ensuing, 'tis agreed that he shall have the sum of seven pounds
seven shillings for his trouble, till Easter next, in 1776" (MS. Churchwardens'
Accounts, Holy Cross, Pershore, Worcestershire). At Mitcham, near London,
in 1797, the Vestry, in nominating six persons to be presented to the Justices
for the office of Overseer, put one person at the head of the list, and voted a
salary of £50 to that person "for his serving the office of Overseer for the year
ensuing" (MS. Vestry Minutes, Mitcham, Surrey, 18th April 1797).

[3] R. v. Welch and Others, 1785 ; The Laws relating to the Poor, by Francis
Const, vol. i. p. 313 of fifth edition, 1807.

[4] Thus, at Chester, from 1800 onwards, there was a "perpetual Overseer"
at £30 a year (Lectures on the History of St. John Baptist Church and Parish in
the City of Chester, by the Rev. S. Cooper Scott, 1892, p. 184).

the Parish Committee, or the inhabitants in Vestry assembled. The Justices, well aware that a salaried officer had become indispensable, had practically no discretion in the choice of persons, as they had no power themselves to order a salary to be paid, and the Vestry would certainly object to any salary being allowed in the accounts to any one but its own nominee. Such an extra-legal arrangement was reported with approval, by a Parliamentary Committee of 1817, to have been "long beneficially adopted in many populous parishes . . . with the unanimous consent of the parishioners." [1]

The payment of a small annual fee to a man who agreed to serve permanently as Constable was never declared illegal, and many parishes adopted this course, in order to bring this officer under control. In towns where the Court Leet still appointed the Constable, the Vestry would sometimes agree to pay wages to him, or his deputy, on condition that he did whatever duties the Vestry imposed upon him.

In the one case in which the law had expressly authorised the appointment of a paid officer, namely, in that of the Surveyor of Highways, it appears to have been less frequently adopted. The Vestry of Camberwell seems to have paid a salary of £50 a year to its Surveyor of Highways from, at least, 1781, the office being held for a whole generation by successive members of two local families.[2] And we have at least one instance in which a large parish,—that of Liversedge, in Yorkshire,—containing many hamlets or townships, each having its own annually-serving and unpaid Surveyor, superseded these in 1811 by getting appointed one permanent paid officer, taking his orders from a Parish Committee.[3]

Finally, it is to be noted that when the parish had a

[1] *The Report from the Select Committee of the House of Commons on the Poor Laws*, etc., 1817, p. 43. Its successful adoption prior to 1770 in a rural parish in Kent is mentioned in *Thoughts on the Present State of the Poor*, 1776, pp. 30, 31.

[2] Vestry Minutes, Camberwell (Surrey), 1781-1820 ; in *Ye Parish of Camerwell*, by W. H. Blanch, 1875, p. 129.

[3] *The Select Vestry, or Parish Committee*, by Rev. Hammond Roberson, 1818, pp. 50-60. Paid subordinates to the parish officers were also appointed, such as Assistant Overseers or Surveyors, Deputy Constables, Assistant Beadles, Watchmen, and Rate Collectors, the appointment being usually made by the Vestry itself. At Brighton, however, in 1808, the public Vestry expressly resolves "that the appointment of Collector of the Poor's Rates be discretionary in the breasts of the Parish Officers to continue or discharge at pleasure" (MS. Vestry Minutes, Brighton, Sussex, 24th April 1808).

workhouse to administer, it necessarily acquired a salaried staff
of officers—a workhouse master and matron, sometimes porters
and servants, occasionally even a surgeon and a chaplain—
appointed during pleasure, and wholly at the disposition of
the Vestry. The master of the workhouse, or even the
contractor by whom it was farmed, might, for convenience,
receive an appointment from the Justices as Overseer or
Constable, and thus further bring these independent parish
offices under popular control.

(d) *The Parish Committee*

The organisation of the Vestry as a democratic governing
body was, however, not complete until it had learned to
appoint a standing executive committee, to control day by
day the salaried staff. The Elizabethan statutes had contemplated that the Churchwardens and Overseers " shall meet
together at least once every month in the church . . . after
service, there to consider of some good course to be taken and
of some meet order to be set down."[1] But where this
" private Vestry " of officers was held with any regularity it
usually developed, as at Manchester and Leeds, not into a
representative executive of the Open Vestry, but into a parish
oligarchy, intent on transacting the necessary parish business,
or serving the interests of its individual members, without
interference by the " inhabitants at large." During the
eighteenth century, however, various developments of parish
government gave energetic Vestries the opportunity of establishing a more representative executive. The movement for
the erection of workhouses in which to employ the poor,
initiated by Local Acts, and greatly furthered by the general
enabling statute of 1723,[2] obliged the Churchwardens and
Overseers to obtain the express consent of the inhabitants in
Vestry assembled to all the preliminary steps. This led to
the election, by the Vestry, of workhouse trustees or com-
mitteemen, who shared with the officers the responsibility of

---

[1] 43 Eliz. c. 2, sec. 2 (1601). A reformer of 1817 wished to revive this
monthly meeting of parish officers, to designate it the Acting Vestry, and to
make it, compulsorily, the only executive of the Vestry Meeting (*The Revised
Parish System*, by a Conciliator, 1817, p. 10).

[2] 9 George I. c. 7.

borrowing money, buying land, erecting buildings, contracting for plant and stores, engaging a salaried staff, or entering into a formal contract to "farm" out the inmates.[1] Thus we see the Woolwich Vestry in 1731 appointing "trustees for this parish for taking down three small tenements belonging to the said parish . . . and in the room and stead thereof" erecting "a proper and convenient workhouse . . . for lodging, maintaining, and employing the poor of the said parish."[2] In the following year, this committee of "the fittest persons in the parish," in co-operation with the Churchwardens and Overseers, submitted to the Open Vestry, for its adoption, twenty-eight extremely judicious "Articles and Orders" for the management of "this House of Piety, Charity, and Industry," under a standing Committee of "Governors of the Poor," who are directed to be "diligent and unanimous in this undertaking, [to] avoid all contradictions and oppositions to one another, and to the rules agreed on among themselves; endeavouring to act with such an exact harmony that, though it be necessary to decide all controversies by the majority, yet, as far as is possible, every single act of each person may have the consent and approbation of the whole number concerned."[3] This extra-legal constitution seems to have worked with such efficiency that it was imitated by adjoining parishes, and eventually embodied in various Local Acts.[4] It

[1] An early instance is that of Kettering, in Northamptonshire, where, without any explicit legal authority, the Vestry in 1717, on agreeing to erect a workhouse, committed all the arrangements to seven persons as "the chief managers of the said business," all their proceedings being subsequently submitted for the Vestry's covering approval (*Sketch of the History of Kettering*, by F. W. Bull, 1891, pp. 55-58).

[2] MS. Vestry Minutes, Woolwich, Kent, 12th August 1731.

[3] *Ibid.* March 1732.

[4] The MS. Minutes of the Vestry of Woolwich (Kent), which exist from 1696, reveal in picturesque detail the working of an interesting democratic government. The greater part of the parish business fell to the principal committee, the "Governors of the Poor." This committee had under its control the parish staff, including a paid "scavenger," a schoolmaster, and a collector of taxes. During the years 1800-1806, the Open Vestry became somewhat rampant in its democracy, and in a subsequent chapter we shall describe the curtailment of its activity by the establishment, under a Local Act, of a body of Street Commissioners, who, though elected by the Vestry, were not subject to its control. In the neighbouring parish of Greenwich a somewhat similar organisation, legalised by a Local Act of 1754, continued until 1855, though the administration of the Poor Law passed to the Board of Guardians on the establishment of the Union in 1837. And when, in 1730, the parish of St. Paul, Deptford, was carved out of that of St. Nicholas

would be easy to multiply from all parts of the kingdom instances of these workhouse committees annually elected by Open Vestries, and frequently helped by the inclusion of a public-spirited Incumbent or philanthropic "esquire." [1] Another representative committee, typical of eighteenth-century Vestries, was one composed of the more literate of the inhabitants, to examine the accounts of the various parish officers.[2] These workhouse and audit committees, recurring year after year, easily merged into a general parish committee. But such a general committee had sometimes an independent origin. At Camberwell the earliest extant Vestry minutes

(by 3 Geo. II. c. 33), the new Vestry started with a constitution similar to that of Woolwich, under which its government was conducted down to the same dates. (For the latter parish, besides the MS. Vestry Minutes, the student should consult an interesting collection of printed documents relating to parish business between 1718 and 1844, preserved in the British Museum as 579. l. 13.)

[1] Thus the able Incumbent of a rural parish in Kent describes how, in 1770, he got his Vestry to appoint a committee of twenty-four to supervise the workhouse, etc. (*Thoughts on the Present State of the Poor*, 1776, pp. 56-58). At Kettering, in Northamptonshire, we read, in 1787, of "the gentlemen voluntarily serving on a committee to manage the poor, whereby great economy was effected" (*Sketch of the History of Kettering*, by F. W. Bull, 1891, p. 61). At Salford in 1796 there was both a "weekly board" and a "general board" meeting once a quarter, acting under the Open Vestry (*Rules for the General Regulation of the Poor of the Township of Salford*, 1796). At Brighton the Vestry, in 1799, "unanimously resolved that a committee be appointed in connection with the Minister and parish officers to take into consideration the present state of the Poor House" (MS. Vestry Minutes, Brighton, Sussex, 8th October 1799). In 1800 the Vestry of Minchinhampton adopted the report of a committee, recommending that "for the management of the parish concerns a General Board should be appointed, consisting of twenty-five gentlemen, which Board should meet at least once a quarter, and the Churchwardens and Overseers for the time being shall be considered as Members of the Board ; at these quarterly meetings they shall audit the accounts, order the payment of bills, confirm or rescind the rules of the weekly and visiting committee hereafter mentioned, and fix the assessment to be levied on the parish" (MS. Vestry Minutes, Minchinhampton, Gloucestershire, 2nd March 1800). The elaborate committee organisation at Bradford (Wiltshire) in 1801 was published as a model for the world in *Parochial Regulations relative to the Management of the Poor of Bradford, Wilts ; with notes tending to promote economy and comfort in the Workhouse*, 1801. From Oldham, in Lancashire, it is reported in 1832 that "the affairs of the poor have long been well managed" by "a species of select Vestry, consisting of a committee of seventeen ratepayers, acting with the Churchwardens and Overseers" (First Report of the Poor Law Inquiry Commissioners, 1834, Appendix A (Henderson's Report), p. 917).

[2] Thus the Vestry of the newly-created Deptford Parish in 1731 appointed eleven persons to audit the accounts of the late Churchwardens and Overseers (MS. Vestry Minutes, St. Paul's, Deptford, 23rd May 1731). A Norwich parish annually elected twelve "auditors" for the same purpose (MS. Minutes, St. Peter's, Mancroft, Norwich, 1700-1800).

record, in 1674, that at "a general meeting of the parishioners
in the parish church . . . a certain number of the constant
inhabitants and parishioners should be nominated, and were
accordingly named and chosen to meet once in every month
(upon notice given) in the parish church, to consult with the
Minister and parish officers about the affairs of the parish,
and to inquire into several gifts and legacies belonging to
the parish, how they are disposed of, and for the better preservation of good order in the parish, and such other matters
as relate to the parish, and accordingly to communicate from
time to time (as occasion shall be) what they have inquired
into and debated of, at such time or times as there shall be
a general meeting of the parishioners at the church upon
notice given." The Incumbent, the three Churchwardens, the
three Overseers, and eighteen parishioners were thereupon
appointed to be the Parish Committee, which continued to
exist down to 1834.[1] At Stockton, in Durham, at the
opening of the nineteenth century, a "general committee,"
selected from the "respectable inhabitants" of the different
districts of the town, met quarterly at the poorhouse "for
general purposes," when they elected a "sub-committee for
the ensuing quarter," to meet weekly, for the closer supervision of the workhouse.[2] So at Chertsey, in Surrey, a few
years later, the parish affairs were committed by the Vestry
to an executive committee "of the parishioners who choose
to go on a Friday evening," which met weekly, directing its
attention primarily to poor relief, and specifying what sum
should be paid by the Overseers to particular applicants.[3]
At Liversedge in 1805, after many scandals, the Vestry
appointed a committee of twelve persons who agreed voluntarily
to manage the parish affairs. "On entering upon the business
of examining the accounts, it appeared that there were four
Overseers of the Poor, thirteen Surveyors of the Highways;
and Churchwardens for four years, whose accounts were still
unclosed," the indebtedness of the parish to these officers
being about £300. The committee met monthly to discuss

[1] Vestry Minutes, 1674 ; in *Ye Parish of Camerwell,* by W. H. Blanch,
1875, p. 98.

[2] *General View of the Agriculture of Durham,* by John Bailey, 1810, p. 318.

[3] Report from the Select Committee of the House of Commons on the Poor
Laws, etc., 1817, evidence of T. Lacoast, p. 163.

all parish business and to give necessary orders to the
"Permanent Overseer" (for whom they got a salary of sixty
guineas a year), deputed three of their number to attend in
rotation at the paying of the poor, reorganised the administration of the highways, and evidently took the whole management of the parish into their own hands. So satisfactory had
the arrangement proved, that in 1818, after thirteen years'
experience, the clergyman wrote a valuable little book com-
mending the example to other parishes.[1] In other large or
populous parishes, the "trustees of the workhouse," "directors
of the poor," or other workhouse committee, would, without
changing their designation, insensibly enlarge their sphere,
and become the standing executive under the Open Vestry for
all parish business,—not only the management of the church
and the levying of rates, but also the suppression of nuisances,
cleansing and lighting the streets, the promoting and opposing
of Bills in Parliament, and even the provision of a "charity
school."[2]

(e) An Organised Democracy

All the constitutional devices described in the foregoing
pages had for their object the securing of some measure of
administrative efficiency, with adequate public control. The
determination of the franchise at the Open Vestry, the organisation of this public meeting of inhabitants, the development of
a salaried staff of servants, the establishment of a representative executive, controlling all the parish servants, but itself
dependent on the periodical meetings of the·parishioners at
large,—all these constitutional devices, taken together, form
an Organised Democracy. But, as we have already observed,
and as our quotations have revealed, it was rare to find a
parish which had secured all these improvements in its
working constitution.

[1] *The Select Vestry, or Parish Committee*, by the Rev. Hammond Roberson,
1818. Already, in 1767, an anonymous pamphleteer had suggested, as the
indispensable instrument of parish reform, a similar elected executive committee,
working under an Open Vestry (*An Inquiry into the Management of the Poor
and our usual Polity respecting the Common People*, 1767, p. 4).

[2] In Lancashire, it was said in 1834, "committees of eight or ten ratepayers
frequently manage the parochial business. This system . . . has long been
extensively established in the country with good effect . . . though without
the sanction of law" (First Report of Poor Law Inquiry Commissioners, 1834,
Appendix A (Henderson's Report), p. 910).

By far the most remarkable example is presented by the great seaport that was growing up on the Mersey.[1] The Parish of Liverpool, which had been formed from the still larger parish of Walton, by Act of 1699, and claimed to be "the most populous undivided parish or single township in the kingdom," [2] being coterminous with the ancient borough, was during the eighteenth century rapidly increasing in wealth and population. As in the somewhat similar parish of Leeds, the Mayor and Aldermen, the clergy and the Church-wardens, had, for the first half of the century, jointly managed all the parish affairs in a sort of friendly governing clique —"the excellent economy among the numerous poor of Liverpool" being in 1752 publicly noticed.[3] But the Liverpool Oligarchy was more successful than that of Leeds in providing for the continuous co-operation of the inhabitants in Vestry assembled, its more distinguished members gradually withdrawing themselves as the Open Vestry found leaders of its own. Perhaps it was for this reason that, in contrast with Leeds, the Liverpool Vestry and Corporation worked right down to 1835, as co-equal authorities, harmoniously together, now and then differing upon such questions as the promotion of a Bill in Parliament, or the liability of the municipal income from dock dues to pay Poor Rate, but never interfering with each other's spheres of government, or coming into conflict over the formal appointment of parish officers. An extra-legal constitution which worked with such smoothness and efficiency merits a somewhat detailed description. The

[1] Though various excellent works have been published upon the history of Liverpool, there exists no systematic account of its parochial organisation, which deserves a monograph. The valuable minutes of the Select Vestry, which extend back to 1681, ought to be printed and published by that body. Besides these MS. Minutes, we may refer to the incidental references in the MS. Minutes of the Town Council and the Lancashire Quarter Sessions, and in the local newspapers ; *Inventory of the Plate, etc. in the two Parish Churches of Liverpool*, by Henry Peet, 1893 ; *An Address to all who are assessed to the Poor's Rate in the Parish of Liverpool*, by the Churchwardens and Parish Committee, 1814, p. 3 ; *Memoir of the Life, Writings, and Correspondence of James Currie of Liverpool*, by W. W. Currie, 1831 ; *The State of the Poor*, by Sir F. M. Eden, 1797, vol. ii. pp. 329, 337 ; First Report of Poor Law Inquiry Commissioners, 1834, Appendix A (Henderson's Report), pp. 912-917 ; *Memorials of Liverpool*, 1875, and *Selections from the Municipal Archives*, 1883, both by Sir T. A. Picton.

[2] *An Address to all who are assessed to the Poor's Rate in the Parish of Liverpool*, by the Churchwardens and Parish Committee, 1814, p. 3.

[3] *A Letter to the Author of Considerations on Several Proposals for the Better Maintenance of the Poor*, 1752, p. 20.

student of the admirably kept and voluminous Minutes of
the Liverpool Vestry, say from 1775 to 1818, finds the
ultimate authority plainly in the hands of "the inhabitants
in Vestry assembled," at their annual gathering on Easter
Tuesday in the old St. Nicholas Church. But this general
meeting never attempted to carry on the executive work of so
vast a parish. This had always been in the hands of a much
smaller body, which, by 1775, had developed into a formally
appointed committee "for managing the affairs of this parish."
This committee, dignified by the designation of "The Gentlemen
of the Parish," organised, with remarkable efficiency, both the
public meetings of inhabitants, from whom it received its
authority, and the permanent paid staff, to which it gave
orders.[1] It persuaded the Vestry to appoint an unusually
large and varied array of paid officials, giving up their whole
time to their duties; from a highly qualified Vestry Clerk
and a salaried Treasurer, down to specialised rate-collectors
and regularly salaried grave-diggers. Under the orders of
the Parish Committee the Vestry Clerk promoted and opposed
Bills, began and concluded litigation,[2] and carried on all the
varied parish business of a large town. The Churchwardens,
whom it annually nominated, attended every morning at the
parish office to sign the numerous documents prepared for
them. Six other members of the Committee were regularly
appointed by the Borough Justices to fill the office of Surveyor
of Highways, and these then acted virtually as a Highways
Sub-Committee, under whose directions the highways were
kept in repair and the commutation money and highway rates
collected by two professional "Assistant Surveyors." The
management of the workhouse, which had 1500 inmates, and
was the largest in the kingdom,[3] was carried out by a paid

---

[1] We have traced this Parish Committee back in the MS. Minutes to 1761,
but it was apparently of earlier origin. In 1775 it assumes a more formal shape,
and includes the Mayor and Aldermen. These officers were omitted after 1806,
when the Committee consisted of the two Rectors, the Churchwardens and
Sidesmen, and thirty-seven other inhabitants. The number of the Committee
varied in different years.

[2] Thus, in 1807, the Vestry Clerk, acting under the directions of the
General Committee, prosecuted, in the name of the Churchwardens and Overseers,
a cotton manufacturer for "withholding the common necessaries of life" from
certain parish apprentices. The manufacturer was convicted and sentenced to
imprisonment (MS. Vestry Minutes, Liverpool, 31st March 1807).

[3] Described in 1797 as exceptionally well managed (*The State of the Poor*,

Governor, assisted by a Deputy-Governor, as well as by a
Master and a Matron, a Surgeon and a Chaplain. The out-
relief was dealt with by two salaried Overseers, charged with
the "bastardy department," and fully occupied in visiting and
paying the five thousand outdoor poor. The rates (and also the
Government's assessed taxes) were got in by four paid Collectors.
The Parish Committee went through the accounts of these
officials month by month, and itself gave the necessary orders
on the details of administration. Elaborate financial statements were printed annually and published in the local
newspapers.[1] But it was in its relations with the Open Vestry
meetings that the Liverpool Committee displayed the greatest
powers of organisation. Far from fearing or resenting the
interference of the popular assembly, the Committee took it
fully into its confidence, and consulted it on every important
occasion. Besides the annual Vestries for appointing officers,
the Parish Committee, whenever a new departure was required,
convened special Vestries, for which detailed agenda were
proclaimed in church; it might be the adoption of silk-
weaving as the employment of the poor, the erection of a
"House of Recovery" or fever hospital, the opposition to a
Bill to establish separate Street Commissioners, or the appointment of additional parish officials. It habitually prepared for
the meetings elaborate and formal reports, bringing forward
the various considerations to be taken into account, and ably
expounding the policy recommended. These reports afford so
complete a vision of the activity of an exceptionally well-
ordered populous parish, that we shall be forgiven for concluding our description by the following lengthy extracts from
one of them :—

"At the Annual Vestry in the parochial chapel of St. Nicholas
and Our Lady, on Easter Tuesday, the 20th April 1802, the
following report from the Parish Committee, stating the various
acts done by them since their appointment, and recommending
others to the notice of their successors, was presented and read
by the Vestry Clerk :—

"Under the impression that the Vestry has a right to expect

---

by Sir F. M. Eden, 1797, vol. ii. pp. 329, 337), and in 1834 earning the rare
praise of the Poor Law Commissioners (First Report of Poor Law Inquiry
Commissioners, 1834, Appendix A (Henderson's Report), pp. 912-917).

[1] *Liverpool Albion*, quoted in *Times*, 22nd January 1829.

from its Committee a particular account of all their transactions, whether the same be materially important to the public, or only of an ordinary nature, and feeling, as the Committee do, a consciousness at least of having intended well, and acted in some things upon their judgments deliberately formed, and in others upon the opinions of gentlemen qualified by their profession to advise, it is their intention, in this their address, to lay open to view the whole of their proceedings, whether in the wisdom of the Vestry they shall be found to merit its approbation, or to bring upon them its censure.

"For the sake of order the Committee will begin with the duty imposed upon them on the day of their appointment, and that will be best done by adverting to the resolutions of the last Annual Vestry. At that Vestry the arguments for and against the rating of shipping by name, and of personal property in general, so as to do equal justice to the inhabitants of every denomination, and give universal satisfaction, ended in the following resolution:—Mr. Leigh moved, 'That it be an instruction to the Churchwardens and Overseers to assess stock in trade, of which ships are a part, after a reasonable rate.' Mr. Stanistreet moved as an amendment, 'That the Churchwardens and Overseers learn from the merchants whether they admit shipping to be rateable, and if so, that the amount of the rate be fixed by arbitration; but if the merchants do not admit the liability of shipping, that the rate be in future laid so as to include shipping, under the opinion of counsel, in order ultimately to enforce the payment'; and the motion, as amended, being seconded by the Rev. Samuel Renshaw, Rector of the Parish, was carried.

"In consequence of this resolution a meeting of the Committee was held on the 28th April, when it was unanimously agreed that a limited number of their body should be deputed to carry it into effect, experience having shown that where a multiplicity of general business is left to be transacted by a numerous body, the whole is greatly accelerated by a division of its members into smaller ones for specific and special purposes, under the control of the body at large. With this view the deputation, and a select number of the merchants, had a conference on the first day of June, when it was not admitted by the merchants that their shipping in the docks, or at the port of Liverpool, were rateable within the parish of Liverpool, and therefore so much of the resolution of the Vestry as directs the amount of the proposed rate on the merchants to be determined by arbitration in the event of their admitting their liability has not been carried into effect. The Committee, having no alternative, immediately adopted the mode of taxation directed by the Vestry, in which, though shipping be not named, yet in the measure of taxation, the profits that arise therefrom, as a species of personal property, are included. In the accomplishment of this rate, on the basis of equal justice between the merchants and the tradesmen, much time was necessarily bestowed by the Committee; and though their meetings on this particular occasion were thirty in number, yet, from the difficulties with which the subject abounded, it was not before the month of November that the rate for the year's service was completed and allowed. The acts of the Committee at each meeting from 28th April to the month of November inclusively, your Committee have caused to be minuted in a book, kept for this purpose only, which is now on the table for inspection.

"The next subject in the order of time which the Committee have to lay before the Vestry, is their proceedings upon another resolution of the last Vestry, founded on the motion of Dr. Currie, in effect that a house for the reception of paupers labouring under fever and other infectious diseases be immediately erected on the open space of ground belonging to the parish, south of the work-house, under the direction of the Parish Committee and the physicians of the Infirmary and Dispensary. . . . Reasons, how-ever, of great weight having since occurred to abandon that situation, your Committee, under the advice of the Faculty, purchased a field to the eastward of the workhouse, and an hospital for the reception of paupers in case of fever, upon an economical plan to answer the end proposed, is now building upon it, under the direction of the Committee and the Faculty of the two institutions. The expense of this building is calculated at £5000, and hitherto has been borne by the rate for the poor, because the use of it is to be confined to persons of that description ; and as upon the whole there will be a very considerable saving to the Parish by the proposed establishment, and as it will also tend to the decrease of fever in the town, the Committee flatter themselves the Vestry will approve the step they have taken in thus departing from the strict letter of the resolution, and by expending the sum of £1200 in the purchase of land, a part only of which is at present necessary for the intended hospital. The minutes of the Committee's proceedings at their meetings on this business are also entered in a book kept for this purpose only, and are now on the table for inspection.[1]

---

[1] For further particulars as to this early experiment of an Isolation Hospital, see *Memoir of the Life, Writings, and Correspondence of James Currie of Liverpool*, by W. W. Currie, 1831, vol. i. pp. 338-343. Dr. Currie describes the Vestry of 1801, when he carried his resolution in a meeting of 2000 persons. The scheme met with much opposition from a certain section of ratepayers, and in their report of 1803 the Parish Committee again revert to the subject: "Your Committee cannot be insensible to the personal interest which every housekeeper in the town must feel in having in times like the present, when

"The Committee having now stated their proceedings upon the acts of the Vestry, it remains for them, in conformity with the sentiments they have already expressed, to lay before the public such other matters as have come under their direction, some of which, they are sorry to be obliged to say, will fall to the lot of their successors in office to be completed. The first is the dispute between the Parish and the Corporation of Liverpool respecting the rates on the dock and town duties, which now amount to a very large sum, no less than £12,000—a sum, however, which the Committee have every reason to hope will shortly be recovered by the judgment of the magistrates, to whom, by the resistance of the Corporation, the Churchwardens have been compelled to apply for redress. The giving judgment upon the application has hitherto been deferred at the request of the solicitor for the Corporation, who was not then armed with sufficient proof to sustain his clients' opposition to the rate, but as the time required for that purpose has now elapsed, it only remains for the magistrates again to meet to form their decision on the claim, a meeting which has hitherto been prevented by the absence of Mr. Dawson.

"The next matter that occurs is the appropriation of a part of the rates in the purchase of ground near the almshouse for a cemetery, or place of interment, the want of which in the Parish is so obvious to every inhabitant as to supersede the necessity of seeking an indemnity from the Vestry for thus well laying out £1400. The present ruinous state of the pavement is an object to which the attention of your Committee has been long directed; and though nothing decisive of the question between the Parish and the Corporation has yet been done, such proceedings have been had under the advice of very able counsel whom some of your Committee have lately had an opportunity of personally consulting, as to afford a reasonable ground of hope of a speedy termination of the dispute ; and that the result will be favourable to the Parish.

"Your Committee, upon mature consideration of the attention and labour necessary to be employed in the well discharging of the duties of the several officers following, and by way of stimulus to each to exert himself the more, have increased their salaries—Mr. Simmon's, from £200 to £210 ; Mr. Lewis's, from £80 to £100 ; the Government Collector's, from £80 to £100 ; the Sextons of the parish churches, £20 each. They have increased the salary

---

disease so fatally prevails, the objects of that disease removed from his neighbourhood—perhaps from his own house. Humanity united with self-interest induces your Committee to press upon the Vestry the necessity of completing the work with all possible despatch " (MS. Vestry Minutes, Liverpool, Easter 1803). For Dr. Currie, see *Further Memoirs of the Whig Party*, by Lord Holland, 1905, p. 377.

of the Rev. Mr. Kidd, the Chaplain of the Workhouse, to 30 guineas per annum.

"On the application of the trustees of the Lunatic Asylum, they have added two shillings per week to the sum allowed by the Parish for the support of these truly unfortunate paupers who are, under the Faculty, attending the institution ; and they look with confidence that these their acts will not only have the approbation of the Vestry, but be confirmed to the respective persons and the charity in future.

"Your Committee have given the necessary order to guard the Parish against any expense that might otherwise be entailed on it by Parliament, on a late application to repeal the Act for building Christ Church ; and on another application to obtain an Act to build a church near the top of Bold Street, and they have also presented a petition to the Honourable the Commons, which has been accepted, for leave to be heard against the Bill, now before Parliament, to equalise the County Rate ; if the same had passed into a law in its present form, a very heavy burden would have been cast upon the Parish at large, by an annual rate for the service of the county on the full annual value of all real property lying within it ; and your Committee are not without hope that, for the reasons to be alleged in support of the petition, a clause of exemption in favour of Liverpool will be introduced in the Bill. In this opposition the Parish has been joined by the Corporation, who have also petitioned against the Bill.

"An application has been made to your Committee to con-tribute out of the rate for the poor the sum of £100 towards expense of plugs in the streets for the use of the public in case of fire, and for the sum of £20 towards the repair of them, on the suggestion of the Company of Proprietors of the Corporation Waterworks, that the like contributions are made in London and other places, and that the giving up of water-carts, which will be a necessary consequence of the present mode of supplying the town, will be an evil only to be cured by the proposed supply ; but your Committee, conceiving this to be an application which should have the previous sanction of the Vestry, have hitherto for that reason declined giving any answer to it. They cannot, however, withhold their opinion that, as the Parish has a great interest at stake in the preservation of its property from which its funds are to arise, the application merits the attention of the Vestry, and they therefore strongly recommend it to its notice.

"The next subject brings the Committee's address nearly to a close, and it is a subject in which, as a body representing the inhabitants out of Vestry, they feel a particular interest. Col-lectively and individually they have seen with satisfaction the exemplary lives and characters of their worthy Rectors ; but while they are thus gratified they cannot help expressing their concern that, comparatively with the income of other Rectors in the vicinity, whose cures bear no proportion to theirs, the salaries and fees annexed to their vocation have, for a series of years, continued to remain so low, in a parish, too, where the rates are under those of every other place in the kingdom. It is upon the conviction of the Committee that the salaries of the Rectors are inadequate to their high situation and deserts, and are no rewards for the pains bestowed by them in the exercise of their religious duties, that they have unanimously resolved to submit to the consideration and justice of the Vestry the following reasonable propositions :—

"1st, That the income of the Reverend the Rectors of Liverpool is inadequate to their services and the duties of their high office.

"2nd, That it be referred to the Committee to be this day appointed to make such a reasonable addition to the income of the Rectors out of the rate to be levied for the churches and clergy, as such Committee shall think proper.

"3rd, That the Committee be authorised to review the Table of Fees and Church Dues, established in 1733, not only as to Rectors, but also as to the Churchwardens, Clerks, and Sextons, and to make therein such reasonable alterations in their favour as the law will warrant and the Committee shall think just between them and the Parish.

"The last subject on which the Committee have to address the Vestry is respecting the rates for the current year ; and they feel a pleasure in having it in their power to say that by the inde-fatigable labour and attention of the Churchwardens and Sidesmen to the making out of the rates for the last year, by their judgment in purchasing provisions and other articles of consumption for the workhouse, and by a watchful eye kept over the Collectors of Rates and the Overseers, in the just distribution of relief, notwithstanding an increase of 250 paupers within doors, and an immense addition in the out-expenditure, yet under these disadvantages there will not be occasion to lay a greater rate for the maintenance and employment of the poor this year than was made for the last. But at the same time that they are assured that a rate of 2s. 9d. in the pound will be fully adequate to the common purposes of a poor's ley, yet with a view to direct and to confine its funds solely to the objects to which by law they are made applicable, viz. ' the maintenance and employment of the poor,' it is the opinion of your Committee that a separate rate should be laid from the book of last year, and immediately be collected for the purpose only of completing the hospital for the sick and the contracts for the land in this address mentioned. It is true the law has vested the power of laying this species of rate in the Churchwardens and Overseers of the Vestry, and it is therefore upon the presumption that they would wish to have their actions, in a matter of such magnitude, sanctioned by the Vestry that the Committee have made this recommendation to the inhabitants at large." [1]

(f) *The Recalcitrant Minority*

The democratic and efficient extra-legal constitution spontaneously worked out, in the course of a century, by some of the more enlightened Open Vestries, of which Liverpool presents so good an example, had, it is clear, an element of weakness, to which the last words of the Liverpool Report significantly point. The constitution had no legal validity. The whole structure depended for its existence on the continued goodwill of two or three different authorities. The salaried staff of Overseers, Surveyors, and Constables might, any year, have been swept away by a hostile bench of magistrates refusing to appoint them to those offices. But this was not all. The Parish Committee could have been rendered absolutely futile by the refusal of the Churchwardens and other unpaid officers to acknowledge its authority. Even if magistrates and parish officers were friendly, it was probably within the power of an obstinate minority of ratepayers to have upset the whole arrangement by an appeal to the law courts. In various parishes the first beginnings of this extra-legal constitution were stamped out by stubborn recalcitrants. Thus, in the great parish of St. Giles, Cripplegate, in 1731, the Overseers flatly refused to be handicapped by any Committee of the Vestry.[2] So at Kensington, in 1776, when a committee had been appointed to "consider the state of the poor," the Vicar refused to attend on the ground of its illegality. The committee thereupon unanimously resolved "that this committee is legally appointed," and elected the Earl of Rosebery to be its chairman. It was supported by three successive meetings of the Open Vestry within one month. But nothing more is heard of it.[3] Similarly, when in the rapidly growing parish

[1] MS. Vestry Minutes, Liverpool, 20th April 1802.
[2] *An Account of the Church and Parish of St. Giles's Without, Cripplegate*, by J. J. Baddeley, 1888, p. 170.
[3] MS. Vestry Minutes, Kensington, Middlesex, 10th and 30th December 1776 ; 8th and 9th January 1777.

CHAPTER IV

THE STRANGLING OF THE PARISH

At this stage in the evolution of English parish government, the Legislature, as we can now see, had a unique opportunity. By a long series of experiments, extending over a whole century, various energetic Open Vestries had spontaneously worked out a new constitution for the administration of their parochial affairs. To have crystallised in a general statute applying to all populous parishes the working constitution, say of Liverpool in 1817, would have gone a long way to democratising English home affairs. The annual election of all officers by the people at large, the frequent public meetings in the church of all rated householders to debate issues of policy and to criticise the accounts, the custom of polling the whole community on disputed questions, together with the extraordinary publicity and free discussion thereby secured, undoubtedly broadened the interests of the ordinary citizen, and educated no small number of persons in the problems of local government. And the conception of local government which the parish had inherited, and to which the new working constitution had been made applicable, was extraordinarily wide and far-reaching. Within the scope and jurisdiction of the inhabitants in Vestry assembled there lay the provision of practically any service, and the enactment of practically any regulation that the majority of the parishioners might think desirable, whether in the management of the church or of the secular institutions of the parish; whether in education, sanitation, or recreation; whether in the relief of the poor, the prevention of crime, or the provision of additional churches and clergy. To carry out any of their objects, the parishioners could not only hold property in trust and receive gifts, but could also levy on all householders a series of rates, unlimited in amount, and varied in incidence so as to include personalty as well as real estate. Such a parish government needed only to be formally set free from the interference of the Lord of the Manor, the Ordinary, and, above all, of the Justices of the Peace; to be confirmed in its free choice and payment of officers; and to have its representative committee, its public meeting, and its polling or referendum, legalised and systematised, to embody all the aspirations of the theoretical democrat, intent on the "restoration" of the free and autonomous English village community. It was for this ideal that Joshua Toulmin Smith, a generation later, explored the archives of the parish, brought to bear all the stores of his great erudition, and devoted the energies of a laborious life. Some such ideal may, even in 1818, have dimly floated before the minds of those who resisted any perversion of the ancient constitution of the parish, from whom, as from Toulmin Smith, its imperfections and shortcomings were hid. Whether a unit of government, varying in area and population from a mere handful of houses up to the thirty-two square miles of Leeds, or the eighty thousand souls of the Liverpool of 1801, could ever have been made suitable for all the multifarious services carried on by the parish, or even for any of them; whether the public meeting and the referendum would have proved as compatible with efficiency of administration as they were conducive to popular interest in it; whether independently elected officers would have long continued loyal subordinates to a representative executive deriving its authority from no higher source, or even loyal colleagues of each other; whether it would have been safe, in the interest of the community as a whole, to say nothing of the protection of local minorities, to have emancipated such a unit as the parish from subordination to, or even supervision by, any superior executive authority; whether, in short, the measure of local contentment and administrative efficiency attained by Minchinhampton and Mitcham, Woolwich and Liverpool, would, under such a constitution, have proved to be the exception or the rule, are questions that will not fail to present themselves to the careful student of parish government between 1689 and 1835.

It is needless to say that no such far-reaching experiment in Local Democracy was attempted, or even imagined, by the Parliament that passed the "Six Acts." An important and, in some sense, an epoch-making measure of reform was passed in the Sturges Bourne Acts of 1818-1819. But though this legislation legalised some of the spontaneous devices of the parish, such as the representative committee, the salaried staff, and even the referendum, it was so ineptly conceived and so unintelligently drafted that its net result was to accelerate the process of strangling the parish, which may be said to have been started by the Local Acts of the eighteenth century, and to have been practically accomplished by the Poor Law Amendment Act of 1834. To understand this series of assaults on the life of the parish as a unit of local government —not deliberately so intended—we must preface our account of the period between 1818 and 1835 by a brief survey of the previous attitude and spasmodic interferences of the Legislature since 1689, the date at which we formerly described the Legal Framework of the Parish.

(a) *Eighteenth-Century Legislation*

Throughout the whole of the eighteenth century, and for the first fifteen years of the nineteenth, neither the Legislature nor the Ministry had shown any concern in the general constitution of the local government of the kingdom. Following the precedents of the sixteenth and seventeenth centuries, the Legislature had, from time to time, increased the local obligations, and used the parish organisation for national ends —whether to provide fire-engines [1] or inspect slaughter-houses,[2] to suppress the hawking of gin [3] or license public-houses,[4] to furnish men for the army and navy, or collect the assessed taxes, to arrange for the billeting of soldiers or transport "His Majesty's baggage." [5] Now and again one of the country gentlemen in the House of Commons, who

[1] 6 Anne, c. 58 (1706) ; 7 Anne, c. 17 (1708).
[2] 26 George III. c. 71 (1786).   [3] 11 George II. c. 26 (1738).
[4] 26 George II. c. 31 (1753).
[5] 3 George III. c. 7 (1762). "His Majesty's baggage" meant, in practice, the baggage of regiments changing quarters.

happened to be an enthusiast for the reform of the Poor Laws or the improvement of the highways, the repression of vagrancy or the prevention of crime and disorder, would get some clause inserted in a general statute, varying the relation between the Vestry and one or other of the parish officers, or between the parish and the Justices of the Peace.[1] The general tendency of these minute and unco-ordinated changes in the legal framework of parish structure was undoubtedly to increase the hold of the Vestry over the parish officers; and, we think, in a slight degree to diminish the arbitrary control of parish administration by individual Justices of the Peace. But it must be noted that each of these small changes affected only a particular function, and thereby even increased tho paralysing uncertainty and complexity of parish law. Certain provisions of general legislation for providing new churches and building workhouses tended also to the dislocation of parish government. Whilst the Church Building Act of 1711[2] permitted the partial division of parishes, the Poor Law Acts of 1723 and 1782 permitted their partial union; with the result, in both cases, that individual Vestries found themselves either specifically restricted to certain parochial functions, or definitely shorn of others. It may, however, be asserted that all this *ad hoc* and permissive legislation made, in the vast majority of parishes, no change in the working constitution of their government. The alterations in the obligatory law either remained unknown or failed to be understood; and, except in a small number of cases, the permissive clauses were not acted upon.

Far more important in its bearing on parish government was the mass of private Bill legislation which forms the most characteristic feature of the Parliamentary activity of the eighteenth

---

[1] The principal changes of this sort were those effected by the Poor Law Acts of 1691 (3 William and Mary, c. 11); 1696 (8 & 9 William III. c. 30); 1723 (9 George I. c. 7); 1782 (22 George III. c. 83); 1795 (35 George III. c. 101); and 1810 (50 George III. c. 49); by the General Highway Acts of 1766 (7 George III. c. 42; 1773 (13 George III. c. 78); and by the Vagrancy Acts of 1699 (11 William III. c. 18); 1702 (1 Anne, St. II. c. 13); 1706 (6 Anne, c. 32); 1713 (13 Anne, c. 26); 1718 (4 George I. c. 11); 1719 (5 George I. c. 8); 1739 (12 George II. c. 29); 1740 (13 George II. c. 24); 1792 (32 George III. c. 45), and 1802 (43 George III. c. 61). The effect of these statutes on the administration of these several services will be dealt with in our subsequent volumes on Poverty and Crime, Health and Convenience, etc.

[2] 10 & 11 Anne, c. 11, 1711.

Act to settle his estate or divorce his wife. This state of general constitutional anarchy was, as regards the parish organisation itself, interfered with by the Sturges Bourne Acts of 1818 and 1819, which, besides slightly amending the Poor Law, for the first time provided, as a matter of national interest, a fixed suffrage and a definite procedure for the meeting of inhabitants in Vestry assembled.

(b) *The Sturges Bourne Acts*

It is easy to trace the causes of this new departure. The parish rates, which had been steadily rising since about 1770, increased in the bad times of 1813-1814 to an alarming extent. The peace of 1815 only momentarily checked the growth of expenditure, and the bad harvests of 1816-1817 sent it up again by leaps and bounds. Whereas the total rates levied in England and Wales in 1785 had been a little over two millions, and in 1802 only five and a third millions, they rose in the bad years, 1817-1819, to more than ten millions, a total that was not again reached for a quarter of a century.[1] To the country gentlemen who then filled the House of Commons, this great increase in the local expenditure, though counterbalanced by an equally rapid growth in the aggregate wealth of the kingdom, seemed destined to absorb the whole rental of their estates. As the greater part of the local expenditure was then defrayed from the Poor Rate, it was upon this that Parliament concentrated its attention. The wasteful and demoralising system of relief, about which Sir William Young, Samuel Whitbread, and others, had vainly striven to interest the House in previous years, suddenly became the favourite topic. Petitions complaining of the rise of rates poured in from rural parishes.[2] Select Committees

[1] See the statistics in *Reports and Speeches on Local Taxation*, by the Rt. Hon. G. J. Goschen, M.P., 1870, pp. 62-64, 66. In the inquiry of 1817 and the contemporary controversy much was made of the case of the parish of Wombridge (Shropshire) which, with a population of 1900, had 620 paupers, and only 33 persons paying rates, the occupiers of 389 houses being left off the rate-book as being too poor. The rates for the past three years had averaged fifteen shillings in the pound on the assessment ; and the current expenditure in 1817 was temporarily at the rate of thirty-three shillings in the pound (*The Report from the Select Committee of the House of Commons on the Poor Laws*, etc., separately published as a book, 1817, pp. 220-222).

[2] Hansard, 7th March 1817, vol. xxxv. p. 907.

on the Police of the Metropolis had drawn attention to scandals in Poor Law administration. In 1817 both Houses of Parliament appointed select committees to consider, not the constitution of parish government, but the working of the Poor Laws. In the references to these committees, in the evidence taken by them, and in their voluminous reports, we see the same lack of concern as to the structure of parish government as a whole, and the same absorption in the narrower question of how to diminish the Poor Rate.[1] But it so happened that the House of Commons Committee, though moved for by Curwen and seconded by Castlereagh, was presided over by Sturges Bourne,[2] who proved to have a fixed idea as to the proper constitution of a parish Vestry. Himself a member of the efficient " select " or Close Vestry of St. George's, Hanover Square, described in a subsequent chapter,[3] and a critical observer of the turbulent Open Vestries of the Metropolitan area, he would have preferred to have introduced the close body into every populous parish. But his particular obsession was the manifest inequity and inexpediency, as he regarded it, of permitting a number of small ratepayers to outvote the large property owners. He appealed to honourable members " whether it was reasonable that one who paid a third or even a half of the Poor Rates should have no more influence in Vestries than one who paid the very lowest sum," and he held up for admiration the contrary principle of the capitalist joint-stock company—such, for instance, as " the proprietors of the East India stock "—who

[1] Report of the House of Lords Committee on the Poor Laws, 10th July 1817 ; First Report from the House of Commons Committee on the Poor Laws, 10th March 1818 ; Second ditto, 28th April 1818 ; Third ditto, 26th May 1818.

[2] The Right Hon. William Sturges Bourne (1769-1845), according to William Cory (*A Guide to Modern English History*, vol. ii. p. 417), was "one of the many thoughtful patriots, who, according to their strength, tried to do good before Reform, to whom modern Liberals do scant justice." He was an active member of Parliament nearly continuously from 1802 to 1831 ; held minor office 1804-1809, and was in the Cabinet 1827-1828 under Canning. See the *Dictionary of National Biography*, and the account given in *Birmingham Journal*, 26th May 1826. The committee of twenty-one included also Curwen, T. Frankland Lewis (destined eighteen years later to be one of the Poor Law Commissioners), Sir Thomas Baring, and Lord Castlereagh ; see *Gentleman's Magazine*, March 1817, giving Curwen's speech in full. Frankland Lewis, writing to his son in 1834, claims that he himself took a great part in the committee's work (*Letters of the Right Hon. Sir G. C. Lewis*, edited by his son, 1870, p. 27) ; and Mr. Mackay states that Lewes, not Sturges Bourne, drafted the report (*History of the English Poor Law*, vol. iii. chap. ii. p. 22).

[3] Chap. VI. Close Vestry Administration.

had votes proportionately to their several holdings.[1] Under the influence of this view he called before the Committee, as witnesses, justices and clergymen, tradesmen and manufacturers, who had suffered from the chaotic inefficiency of Open Vestries, and who had striven in various ways for their reform. Nearly all the witnesses had themselves served as unpaid parish officers, or were otherwise personally acquainted with parish government. The Committee made a long report at the end of the session, explaining the impracticability of such remedies for pauperisation as fixing a maximum Poor Rate, finding remunerative employment for all who applied for it, or reviving the ancient assessment of personalty. Incidentally the Committee recommended a reform of the machinery of poor relief, more especially of the constitution of the Vestry. Sturges Bourne thereupon, in 1818, brought in the two Bills that he had drafted,—one entitled " An Act for the regulation of Parish Vestries," which became law that session, and another, which was not passed until the following year, styled " An Act to amend the Laws for the Relief of the Poor." [2]

The 1818 Act applied compulsorily to the great majority of Vestries, namely, to all such, outside the City of London

---

[1] Speech in House of Commons, reported in *Ipswich Journal*, 9th May 1818.

[2] 58 George III. c. 69 (1818) ; 59 George III. c. 12 (1819). As both Acts deal with Vestry organisation, they are seldom accurately distinguished from each other, and are often referred to, jointly or indiscriminately, as "Sturges Bourne's Act." That the Bills were drafted by Sturges Bourne, then Under Secretary of State for the Home Department, appears from his correspondence with Lord Colchester. The Poor Law Amendment Bill, as introduced, would have removed the irksome limitations of 22 George III. c. 83, 1782, on the power of parishes to acquire farms, on which the poor were to be set to work. Lord Colchester objected to this clause, and got it rejected (*The Diary and Correspondence of Charles Abbot, Lord Colchester*, 1861, vol. iii. pp. 36, 37, 44-47, 50, 51). Both Bills were editorially denounced by the *Times*, and hotly opposed by certain parishes ; and it was in order to silence influential objectors that the City of London and Southwark were excluded from the 1818 Act (*Times*, 13th April and 7th May 1818). The Chelsea Vestry protested strongly (MS. Vestry Minutes, 23rd April 1818) both against plural voting and against the election of a standing chairman, as "contrary to the principles of the constitution of this country." At Reading we read that "meetings were held in St. Lawrence's and St. Mary's Vestries to consider of petitions against two Bills now passing through the House of Commons, called ' The Poor Laws Amendment Bill ' and ' The Parish Vestry Bill ' " (*Reading Seventy Years Ago*, by P. H. Ditchfield, 1887, p. 75). This opposition was reflected in the House of Commons, and led to many postponements and successive recommittals ; see House of Commons Journals, 12th and 13th March ; 6th, 10th, 13th, and 24th April, 7th May, 5th June 1818 ; Hansard, 7th and 25th May 1818, vol. xxxviii., pp. 575, 916 ; *Ipswich Journal*, 9th May 1818 ; *Suffolk Chronicle*, 13th March 1818.

and Southwark, as were not governed by Local Acts or peculiar customs.[1] It expressly enacted rules for the procedure of their meetings, prescribing the notice to be given, the arrangements for chairmanship, the keeping of minutes, and, above all, the franchise. Persons who are not rated, or who had not actually paid their Poor Rates, were excluded even from being present at the meeting. On the other hand, definite provision was made for the presence and voting of new-comers, not yet on the rate-book, and (by amendments in the following session[2]) for joint-stock companies, who were to vote by an agent, and for such non-resident ratepayers as chose to attend. And, most important innovation of all, a scale of plural voting was imposed, so that persons rated at less than £50 should have one vote only, and those rated at or above that sum one vote for every £25, up to a maximum of six.[3] No explanation was, however, vouchsafed in the Act as to how, when, or where these votes were to be counted, it being apparently assumed that there would be no difficulty in taking them at the meeting itself, however large and disorderly.

The Act of 1819 applied nominally to all parishes in England, but was not in any way to interfere with the existing constitution or powers of a Vestry governed by Local Act or established custom. It contained some useful provisions

---

[1] Thus, it did not apply to the Close Vestries, hereafter to be described; nor to those, like Bethnal Green, where the suffrage had already been defined by Local Act. On the other hand, it did apply to those parishes, like Manchester, having Local Acts which defined the position of the parish officers, but which left the Vestry itself unaffected.

[2] 59 George III. c. 12 (1819).

[3] This was the first introduction of plural voting into English public legislation, and it is interesting to see that it was denounced by the *Times* (13th April 1818). It had been suggested by Whitbread in 1807 (see his speech in Hansard, 19th February 1807), and had been adopted in some Local Acts. It was imitated by some of the Local Acts between 1820 and 1830, but was not followed in Hobhouse's Act of 1831, which was put in force in several of the London parishes (but in few others, if any); nor in the Metropolis Management Act of 1855. It was, however, made a feature of the election of Boards of Guardians under the Poor Law Amendment Act of 1834, and continued in force for these elections until 1894. When Local Boards of Health (again under the influence of Chadwick) had to be elected under the Public Health Act of 1848, plural voting again prevailed. It was fiercely denounced as "oligarchical" and "unrighteous" by Toulmin Smith (*Local Self-Government and Centralisation*, 1851, p. 200; and *The Parish*, 1857, pp. 63, 475, 476). Finally, the Local Government Act of 1894 swept it away for all these bodies, substituting everywhere "one man one vote." Plural voting was introduced into Australia, where it still exists in the election of local governing bodies. New Zealand also had it, but abolished it in 1900.

amending the Poor Laws, but its main object seems to have been to legalise, for such parishes as desired it, the extra-legal devices of a representative Parish Committee and a salaried Overseer. The Act provided that any parish might, by resolution passed after due notice, by a majority of the inhabitants in Vestry assembled, nominate, for merely formal appointment by a Justice of the Peace, a Parish Committee, consisting of the Incumbent, the Churchwardens and Overseers, and not less than five, nor more than twenty other parishioners. This Parish Committee, to be annually elected in Open Vestry, in no way superseded that authority; but it was expressly authorised to manage all matters relating to the relief of the poor, laying the minutes of its proceedings, together with a report of its work, before regular meetings of the Open Vestry, to be held at least twice a year. What was specially important was that the Overseers were peremptorily expressly required, in the execution of their office, to conform to the directions of the Committee, and to give only such relief as the Committee might order, except in so far as Justices might command, or as sudden emergency might require. Unfortunately the legislators, oblivious of the inevitable reaction of function on structure, and possessed by the single idea of reforming the Poor Law, failed to recognise how they were dislocating parish government as a whole. The Parish Committee now authorised was not "the General Committee for the Management of the Parish Affairs," such as was successfully governing Liverpool and other places. It was expressly restricted to the business of poor relief,[1] and no provision was made for the multifarious other parish affairs relating to the church, the highways, the pump, the pound, the suppression of nuisances, paving and lighting, and what not. By a confused and intricate clause the Act even tended to a breaking up of the large parishes having separate townships. In these important parishes the popularly elected Church-wardens of the whole parish were apparently ousted from the administration of the Poor Law in each part of it, whilst to the meeting of inhabitants in the ancient parish church, still

---

[1] The Birmingham Vestry was even advised by counsel in 1825 that the Select Vestry could not deal with the Constable's accounts, which the Overseer was bound to pay out of the Poor Rate, after submission to an Open Vestry (MS. Vestry Minutes, Birmingham, 10th December 1825).

retaining its jurisdiction over everything but poor relief, there was added a series of new Vestry meetings for the several townships, each empowered to elect its own committee and to deal only with poor relief. Moreover the Parish Committee, whether in an undivided parish or in a township, had the most insecure tenure. Its institution was made, not only optional, but subject to endorsement by the public meeting year by year, without any protection against overthrow by a mere snatch vote. Finally, this committee was seriously prejudiced at the outset by being given a name—that of Select Vestry—which, as we shall presently describe, was associated in the public mind with exclusiveness, jobbery, and corruption. Under these circumstances it was, perhaps, fortunate that the provision enabling parishes to appoint salaried Poor Law officers could be separately adopted. Whether or not a Select Vestry was appointed, the Open Vestry was given express power to elect one or more Assistant Overseers, and to pay them such salary as it thought fit, the Justices being required formally to appoint them as Overseers.

(c) *The Sturges Bourne Select Vestry*

The first effect of the Sturges Bourne legislation was good. The optional clauses of the Act of 1819 were almost immediately adopted by about two thousand parishes, to which, within the next ten years, nearly a thousand more were added.[1] Orderly Open Vestries, like Mitcham and Charlton, which had already working parish committees, were now able, under the Act, to endow those committees with legal authority both over the distribution of poor relief and over the assessment and collection of the Poor Rate. To describe the case of Charlton, which we believe to have been typical of many others, the MS. minutes of the Select Vestry

---

[1] Already in 1822 the House of Commons was informed that 2006 parishes had chosen "Select Vestries" (Hansard, 10th July 1822, p. 1577). In 1828 the number had risen to 2868 (Hansard, 17th April 1828). The small rural Vestries seem practically to have ignored both the Act of 1818 and that of 1819, the obligatory equally with the permissive sections. Law manuals were published "to enable Vestries to transact the business of their respective parishes" (*A Collection of the Several Points of Sessions Law*, by Rev. Samuel Clapham, 1818, preface, p. vii.).

inform us that "having read that part of the Act of the 31st
of March 1819, for the better regulating the relief of the
poor, the Select Vestry resolved that the Overseers do, the
next day of meeting, produce a list of the persons receiving
relief, stating, as far as they know, the condition and character
of each, also stating each person's weekly relief; secondly, to
produce an account of money in hand, also what further sum is
likely to be wanted; thirdly, to produce a list of defaulters
upon the Poors' Rates." A fortnight later the Select Vestry
summoned all the poor to pass before them, and "having
maturely considered each individual case," they instructed the
Overseers exactly what sums to allow to each pauper. The
result was naturally a quarrel with the "respectable inhabitant"
on whom had been cast the onerous and unpaid office of
Overseer, who eventually resigned, leaving the Select Vestry
obliged temporarily to "pay the poor" with their own hands,
but masters of the situation.[1] What was more remarkable,
some of the Metropolitan Open Vestries were persuaded by
influential members to hand over the management of their
parish assessments and poor relief to elected committees.
Lambeth, Clapham, Rotherhithe, Hammersmith, and Putney,
are all found with Select Vestries in the first few years after
the passing of the Act.[2] Even more unexpected is it to find
the close bodies of "the Four-and-Twenty," which had, "time
out of mind," acted for the parishes of Newcastle, Morpeth,
and Gateshead—Vestries governed by special local customs,
that could have resisted such an innovation—surrendering the
administration of the Poor Law and the levying of the Poor
Rate to committees elected under this Act by open meetings
of the inhabitants.[3] Two of the democratic Vestries of
Leicester found, at least for a time, that the election of a
Parish Committee under the Act gave them more control over
the hostile Overseers whom the Tory Aldermen of the borough

---

[1] MS. Select Vestry Minutes, Report of Select Vestry and Vestry Minutes,
Charlton, (Kent), 1819-1820.

[2] Hammersmith and Rotherhithe retained their Select Vestries down to
their supersession by the Guardians under the Poor Law Amendment Act of
1834 ; see House of Commons Return of Parishes over 10,000 population having
Select Vestries in 1834, 26th March 1841.

[3] MS. Vestry Minutes, St. Nicholas, Newcastle-on-Tyne (Northumberland),
and Gateshead (Durham), 1820-1825 ; for Morpeth, see First Report of Poor Law
Inquiry Commissioners, 1834, Appendix A (Wilson's Report), pp. 119-136.

insisted on appointing.[1] In the great parish of Manchester
the Act seems to have called into being Open Vestry meetings
and representative committees in such townships as Chorlton,
Broughton, Cheetham, Pendleton, and Stretford,[2] where the
Overseers and Surveyors had apparently been previously free
from popular control. At Liverpool the Act came in the nick
of time to prevent the break-up, by rebellious parish officers
such as Dennison, of the elaborate extra-legal constitution
that we have described. The adoption of the 1819 Act put
the Parish Committee on a legal footing as a Select Vestry, so
far, at any rate, as expenditure on poor relief was concerned,
and secured, in practice, its authority in all parish matters.
For about ten years this constitution gave the parish both
peace and efficient administration. From 1821 onward we
see the Select Vestry vigorously overhauling the assessment
of the parish and the collection of the rates (" not one-fourth
of dwelling-houses pay to the Poor Rates . . . whole streets
have been passed over year by year," illegally at the option of
the parish officers [3]) ; we watch their constant struggle to
enforce a wisely stringent limitation of the swollen lists of
the outdoor poor, offering freely the test " of the house " ; we
follow them in their intelligent, if not always successful,
experiments in workhouse administration. Nor did the
Liverpool Select Vestry confine itself to Poor Law business.
Assured of the support of the Open Vestry, to which it
continued elaborately to report, it fought the water company,
the county Justices, and the promoters of the new railways,
to secure better terms for its own parishioners ; it organised a
force of fire-police, and was prompt to initiate a Board of
Health to cope with the threatening cholera epidemic.[4] The
experience of Liverpool was repeated in a less degree in other
parishes. In the first flush of enthusiasm at the working of
the new instrument, we see the new " Select Vestries " all over
the country tightening up their control over the Overseers,

[1] *Leicester Herald*, 30th July 1828 ; 15th April and 6th May 1829.

[2] See the advertisements of and incidental references to such meetings, and
to the Select Vestries of these townships, in *Manchester Guardian*, 26th November
1831, 5th May 1832, and 5th April 1837.

[3] Report of Select Vestry, MS. Vestry Minutes, Liverpool, 25th October
1821.

[4] MS. Vestry Minutes, Liverpool, 1819-1831 ; see also the Place MSS.
(Add. MSS. 35148, vol. i. p. 55).

revising the assessments, overhauling the swollen list of regular pensioners, and adopting administrative reforms. In the parish of Clapham, it was claimed, the amount spent on the poor was reduced in the first four years by no less than one-third, whilst the remaining poor were better treated than ever before.[1] Similar results in the parish of Putney were enthusiastically described in an able letter to Canning by one of the leading inhabitants.[2]

The subsequent experience of the Sturges Bourne Select Vestries was less satisfactory than their start. The fact that the very continuance of the new Select Vestry in any parish depended on a renewed vote of the inhabitants in Open Vestry each year inevitably made for its abandonment. Sometimes a Select Vestry was got rid of because of its merits. At Salford, where the Act was adopted in 1822, the Overseers found the control of the Parish Committee irksome. The ratepayers were apathetic; and in 1824 the Overseers neglected to summon the Open Vestry meeting, at which the Select Vestry should have been chosen. None were thereafter appointed.[3] At Worksop (Notts) the Select Vestry was discontinued because the inhabitants objected to its interference with the Assistant Overseer.[4] In North Wales it is reported that the Select Vestries have been given up in a majority of parishes, partly because the fortnightly meeting was found irksome, but principally because of the restriction which their existence placed upon the jobbery of unpaid Overseers, who were usually shopkeepers, and who compelled the paupers to expend the outdoor relief in buying their wares.[5] At Cambridge the Select Vestry, first elected in

---

[1] Letter in *Times*, 12th April 1828.

[2] *A Letter to the Right Honourable George Canning on the Principle and the Administration of the English Poor Law*, by a Select Vestryman of the Parish of Putney under the 59 Geo. III. c. 12 (1819). The success of the Select Vestry in reducing the Poor Rate in Newport Pagnell (Bucks), Steynton (Pembroke), Winslow (Bucks), and Putney and Wandsworth (Surrey), is described in *The Practical Means of Reducing the Poor's Rate*, by Rev. J. Bosworth, 1824 ; and, generally, in *The Principles of the English Poor Law illustrated and defended*, by Frederick Page, 1829.

[3] See Brotherton's evidence before House of Commons Committee on Select and Other Vestries, in Second Report, 1st April 1830.

[4] First Report of Poor Law Inquiry Commissioners, 1834, Appendix A, p. 118. See also *Ibid.* (Maclean's Report), p. 559.

[5] *Ibid.* (Lewis's Report), p. 667, etc. In the Southern Counties of England many elected Select Vestries "were abandoned at the time of the riotous

1825, began to reform the Poor Law administration, with the result that, at the annual Vestry in 1828, " there was a very numerous attendance of the smaller ratepayers . . . a low mechanic was called to the chair . . . and the elections fell upon a class of persons whose appointment the Justices refused to sign. No appointment of a Select Vestry has since taken place." [1] But even if the new parish committees had all been as good as the best of them, they would not easily have commended themselves to the rising Democracy of the more populous parishes. Thus in the model parish of Mitcham, which is here described as governed down to 1818 by general consent, the Select Committee was tried and abandoned; and after some years again tried and again abandoned, owing, we are told, to " certain dissensions which arose between the occupiers of land and those occupying house property ; it was badly attended by one party ; never by the clergyman ; and considered exclusive by the other." [2] At Lambeth, where the new Select Vestry is said to have reduced the Poor Rates in seven years from five shillings to three and fourpence in the pound, and all that was alleged against it was that its members " quarrelled among themselves very frequently," it had exhausted the patience of the Open Vestry by 1827, when it was discontinued. The inhabitants, it is reported, declared that " they would not have one any longer ; . . . the name of a Select Vestry was odious." [3] The name chosen by Sturges Bourne for his representative executive committee was, indeed, an unfortunate one. The term Select Vestry had been, for more than a hundred and fifty years, applied to close bodies, serving for life and filling vacancies by co-option, by which the government of many London and some provincial parishes had been conducted, with the worst possible reputation for secrecy and corruption. The elected parish committee under the 1819 Act had, said Sturges

proceedings in the winter of 1830-1831, when the lawless and outrageous meetings of the agricultural labourers, and, in some instances, their attacks upon the Vestry, produced . . . intimidation " (First Report of Poor Law Inquiry Commissioners, 1834, Appendix A (Maclean's Report), p. 558).

[1] *Ibid.* (Power's Report), p. 239.

[2] *Ibid.* (Maclean's Report), p. 558.

[3] Report of House of Commons Committee on Select and other Vestries, 1830 ; *Plymouth Herald*, 9th April 1831 ; *History and Antiquities of the Parish of Lambeth*, by Thomas Allen, 1827, p. 441.

Bourne himself in 1831, been constantly confounded with the close body which obtained in these parishes, the principles of which were diametrically opposed to that of the body of the same name authorised by his Act.[1] In many cases, moreover, we find the new Select Vestry got rid of because of its own inefficiency and corruption. It was often found difficult to induce the members to attend. At Stourbridge (Wilts), for instance, the Select Vestrymen attended only when they wished to get outdoor relief given to their own friends or customers; the total amount of poor relief went up; and a reversion to the Open Vestry resulted in a marked improvement. "It is a fact," writes an able observer in 1834, "that parish affairs are greatly injured by the inattention of those chosen [on Select Vestries] for their management. Meetings are frequently adjourned on account of non-attendance, and what is much worse, two or three of the members, generally more punctual than the rest, may be said to have the entire direction of the parish business, instead of twenty or more regulating it."[2]   More sinister accusations were elsewhere made against the new committee. At Morpeth (Northumberland) eleven out of the twenty members in 1831 were publicans or beershop-keepers, the others being small retail shopkeepers, except four who were not householders at all; three of them had their own relations on the pauper roll, one having his wife in the poorhouse; whilst they arbitrarily raised the assessments of the more substantial ratepayers, lowered their own, and ran up the total of outdoor relief to their dependents and customers.[3]   "The common story" told of the Select Vestries under the Sturges Bourne

[1] Letter from Sturges Bourne to Mr. Evans, read at Stonehouse Vestry meeting (*Plymouth, Devonport, and Stonehouse Herald*, 9th April 1831). Even the *Times* was capable of this mistake. In reviewing the Parliamentary Return of 1828, showing that 2868 Select Vestries had been formed under the Act of 1819, it declared these Select Vestries to be "the most opposite to every notion which has hitherto prevailed among Englishmen of what belongs to a free constitution, or ought to be endured by an intelligent people. A Select Vestry is a close corporation," etc. (*Times*, 20th March 1828). Letters protesting against this general misconception appear in the *Times* of 12th April 1828, and 16th May 1829.

[2] *Hints on the Mal-Administration of the Poor Laws: With a Plan for bringing the collection and appropriation of the Poor Rates under the immediate superintendence and control of His Majesty's Government*, 1834, p. 19.

[3] First Report of Poor Law Inquiry Commissioners, 1834, Appendix A (Wilson's Report), p. 129.

Act, summed up by C. P. Villiers in 1833, " was that they had
been useful on their first appointment, as they had checked or
corrected the abuses which led to their establishment, but
that they soon deteriorated, and that, between jobbing and
neglect, parishes derived little permanent advantage from
them." In many cases, perhaps the majority, they fell into
bad hands. " In provincial towns," continued Villiers, " there
is a great disinclination in competent persons to meddle with
parish concerns; they neither ,have the leisure nor is any
adequate motive afforded to them to incur the ill-will of
friends or others by serving the parish. In nearly every
town where they have been established, I find the clergyman
abstaining from attending Vestry meetings, either from the
disrespect which was shown to him by other vestrymen, or
from not wishing to place himself in painful collision with
most of his parishioners among the poor." [1] The new
representative committees were, in fact, as Chadwick reported,
" apt to degenerate into compact combinations of numbers of
tradesmen bound together by mutual local interest." [2] Under
these circumstances it is not surprising to learn that the
number of parishes having Select Vestries under Sturges
Bourne's Act ceased to increase, and even tended to decline.
All those in the Metropolitan area, except two, had discontinued them by 1834; [3] and the total number for England
and Wales, which had reached 2868 in 1828, was only
2392 in 1832. [4]

(d) *The Salaried Overseer*

The appointment of a salaried servant to do the work of
the compulsorily-serving, amateur, and annually-changing

---

[1] First Report of Poor Law Inquiry Commissioners, 1834, Appendix A
(Villier's Report), p. 51 ; see also the memorandum by George Taylor on Select
Vestries in Appendix C, pp. 87-96.

[2] *Ibid.* Appendix A (Chadwick's Report), p. 8 ; see *Observations upon the
Office of a Justice of the Peace*, by A. J. Jellicoe, 1829, p. 40.

[3] House of Commons Return of Parishes over 10,000 population which had
Select Vestries in 1834, 26th March 1841.

[4] Hansard, 17th April 1828, vol. xviii. p. 1526, and First Report of Poor
Law Inquiry Commissioners, 1834. They continued to be prevalent in
Lancashire and Yorkshire. Out of 466 parishes and townships in Lancashire,
202 had Select Vestries in 1830-1831 (*ibid.* Appendix A (Henderson s Report),
p. 910).

Overseer, first generally legalised by the 1819 Act, seems to have proved a more successful experiment than the institution of an annually-elected executive committee of unpaid representatives. It is, of course, easy to pick out instances like that of eighteenth-century Manchester, where the " standing " or " hireling " Overseer proved as incapable, fraudulent, or oppressive as his unpaid brother-officers elsewhere. Thus, in one of the Coventry parishes, where a salaried Overseer had been extra-legally appointed in 1814, and continued under the new legislation, successive holders of the office between 1813 and 1829 " could neither read nor write," failed even to make up their accounts, incurred all sorts of illegal expenditure, were " most slovenly, irregular, and inaccurate," and burnt their books rather than submit them to examination.[1] In this case, however, it is only fair to add that the little farmers, who were the unpaid colleagues of these officers, were distinguishing themselves, not only by gross negligence, but by their own private jobbery. They had, we are told, " an understanding among themselves . . . that when a cow or sheep ' dropped,' the meat should be sent to the workhouse," and charged for at the full price of prime joints.[2] But wherever the Open Vestry or the parish committee bestirred itself in the public interest, the inhabitants secured, by a salaried Overseer, not merely complete control over Poor Law policy, but also a far larger measure of skill, assiduity, and scrupulous exactitude in financial details than could have been exacted from unpaid and compulsorily-serving officers. Thus we find the Vestry of Greenwich in 1820 successfully insisting that its Assistant Overseer should " enter particulars of all outdoor poor in a book," " visit and give particulars of those on pension list," " look after and report upon poor of this parish resident in other parishes, and *vice versa*," " give weekly account of expenditure on outdoor poor," and " make out lists of those liable to serve in the militia."[3] Even more minute were the new rules which the Select Vestry of Liverpool imposed upon its " stipendiary officers," including the prohibition of " any fee, gratuity, or perquisite," of the

---

[1] *Report of the Committee appointed to investigate the Accounts of the Parish of Foleshill in the County of the City of Coventry*, 1832, p. 8.

[2] *Ibid.* p. 16.

[3] MS. Vestry Minutes Greenwich (Kent), 23rd March 1820.

selling or buying anything to or from the parish, and even of the taking of official books or papers to their own homes.[1] The Vestry of St. Margaret's, Leicester, which we find in 1828 denouncing the inhumanity and oppression of the unpaid Overseer appointed by the magistrates, expressly prescribes for its salaried officers in 1833 that " in their intercourse with the poor . . . they will abstain from all abusive or irritating expressions," that they are " to do their duty firmly yet with mildness and moderation, and to bear without retaliation those petulant epithets which the presence of poverty frequently produces." [2] The good results of placing the actual work of dispensing relief in the hands of a professional officer were unmistakable. " As no vote of Parliament," had remarked the wise Sir William Young in 1788, " can immediately alter the dispositions of men, and provide a disinterested zeal and integrity, we must be content with the spirit of zeal and integrity which is not disinterested, but which is roused by a sense of reward and sustained by fear of deprivation." [3] " In the parish of Croydon," we read, " which contains 12,000 persons, it produced a saving of £500 a year to pay an individual £150 annually to devote all his time to the investigation of every claim for parish relief. Every applicant is referred to this officer, who personally examines the party, visits his house, and makes all sorts of inquiries." [4] The Assistant Poor Law Commissioners in 1833 brought back from their tours a unanimous testimony as to the success of this experiment, which had often been continued in parishes that had discarded as unsatisfactory the Select Vestry devised by Sturges Bourne.[5] Whilst the

[1] MS. Vestry Minutes, Liverpool, 19th July 1832.

[2] *Ibid.* St. Margaret's, Leicester, 24th June 1833.

[3] *Observations preliminary to a proposed Amendment of the Poor Laws*, by Sir William Young, 1788, p. 64. The appointment of a salaried Poor Law officer for each Hundred, intermediate between the Justices of the Peace and the parish, had been recommended by Dr. Burn (*History of the Poor Laws*, 1764), as well as by Sir William Young and other able critics. A salaried Poor Law officer for the parish had also been specifically suggested : for instance, in *Remarks on the Poor Law and the Maintenance of the Poor*, by William Blamire, 1800, p. 26.

[4] *Remarks and Suggestions relative to the Management of the Poor in Ipswich*, by Rev. W. C. Fonnereau, 1833, pp. 14, 15.

[5] First Report of the Poor Law Inquiry Commissioners, 1834, Appendix A, *passim*. It was, however, criticised as unsatisfactory in *Observations upon the Office of a Justice of the Peace*, by A. J. Jellicoe, 1829, p. 40.

immediately claimed a poll of the parish; and this had to be granted as a matter of legal right. As the wealthier classes abstained from the public meeting, and, moreover, had most to gain by the strict counting of the plural votes, it was usually the Tories who demanded this Referendum, and the Radicals who objected to it. This unpremeditated experiment in the use of the Referendum—handicapped as it was by every unfavourable circumstance—practically introduced a fatal element of discord into the most smoothly working constitutions of populous parishes. Even at Liverpool, where Toryism and the Church of England dominated the working men as well as the upper classes, we see, from 1828 onward, a constantly increasing number of appeals from the Vestry meeting to the poll. In one year (1832) no fewer than eight of these polls were taken, on such questions as the amount of salary to be paid to an official, the election of Churchwardens and Sidesmen, the assessment of the owners of cottage property, and whether the Churchwardens' accounts should or should not be passed.[1] The active spirits who, in the heated years of the Reform controversy, carried the Open Vestry meetings, were habitually defeated at the poll. They revenged themselves on the Tory party by turning the half-yearly meeting at the old parish church into a pandemonium. "We hardly ever remember," remarks a local newspaper, "to have seen a more numerous or a more stormy meeting of the kind, or one of longer duration. . . . The proceedings commenced a few minutes after six, and during the greater portion of that time the scene of angry bickerings and recriminations presented was one which contrasted strangely with the character of the building in which the meeting was held."[2] The demand for a poll was the signal for redoubled uproar, increased by hissing and cries of "No poll." Though the Liverpool Select Vestry managed to hold its own at these polls, it found them so burdensome that it vainly appealed to the meeting to make them unnecessary, declaring "that the public service of the parish has sustained great inconvenience from the frequency with which the collectors have been taken from their ordinary duties from their attendance being required

---

[1] *Liverpool Chronicle*, April and July 1832.
[2] *Ibid.* 13th April 1833 (an account extending over four columns).

at different polls.[1] We have already described the disorderly
Open Vestries of Manchester and Leeds—to which, as the
reader will now see, the method of voting under Sturges
Bourne's Act largely contributed. At Manchester, in these
years, every Open Vestry became the scene of angry recriminations as to the right of the Boroughreeve, or other chairman,
to declare the meeting adjourned for the purpose of taking a
poll, and as to whether or not the scale of plural voting
applied to a town having such a Local Act as Manchester had
obtained in 1790. At a Vestry meeting in 1832 the demand
for a poll led to something like a riot. "Some of the orators,"
reported the *Manchester Guardian,* " expressed their belief that
one of the first acts of a reformed Parliament would be to
repeal ' Sturges Bourne's infamous Act.' "[2] At Leeds, if the
Nonconformist Radicals carried the election of Churchwardens
at one of the large and turbulent Vestry meetings that we
have described, the Tories insisted on a poll of the parish.
From 1833 onwards, this becomes a regular practice. When
a poll was refused, they obtained a mandamus ordering it to
be conceded. The Tory newspaper, in April 1835, candidly
avowed, that " the only method now left to the friends of
law and order is to appeal from such packed Vestries to the
parish at large. Nor will the appeal be in vain. . . . Rated
females are entitled to vote as well as males. We do not
wish for a gynocracy; but we are sufficiently gallant to
perceive that too many of the wayward lords of creation are
disposed to make a bad world of it; therefore the sooner the
ladies interfere the better."[3] But even this appeal to "the
friends of the Church" was unsuccessful: the poll was kept
open in the White Cloth Hall for no less than eight days;

[1] Report of Select Vestry, MS. Vestry Minutes, Liverpool, 9th April 1833.
One of the Leicester parishes resolved, we imagine quite illegally, "that in consequence of the great expense the parish has sustained of late years in choosing the
Sexton, in future every candidate for that office shall deposit the sum of £10
each in the hands of the Churchwardens before any poll takes place, in order
that the parish may be borne harmless in such contests " (MS. Vestry Minutes,
St. Margaret's Leicester, 21st April 1829).

[2] *Manchester Guardian,* 6th October 1832. The total votes cast at the poll
as to the making of a Church Rate in 1834 were 12,876 (*Manchester Historical
Recorder,* 1874, p. 100). Similar contests were taking place at Wakefield in
1834 (*Halifax Guardian,* 26th July and 1st November 1834 ; *Leeds Mercury,*
18th October 1834).

[3] *Leeds Intelligencer,* 25th April 1835.

and the Nonconformist Churchwardens were again elected by a majority of more than three thousand.[1] The furious indignation of the dominant party boils over in the following angry resolution of the Vestry : " That the late poll was demanded by only two individuals against the all but unanimous sense of one of the largest Vestry meetings ever held in this parish ; that those two individuals professed to represent a party whose name and numbers, however, were not mentioned, and who did not attend the meeting, but sent their deputies to oppose the true and approved servants of the public, and to insist on putting the parish to the expense, trouble, and annoyance of an eight days' poll ; that the poll was kept open by the same party without the smallest chance of success for eight days, to the serious annoyance of the parishioners and interruption of industry and tranquillity ; and that at its close the individuals for whom the poll had been demanded were defeated by a majority of about three thousand votes ; the proceedings were a wanton insult to the Vestry and a factious annoyance to the parish ; and that the least acknowledgment of their improper conduct the parties can make is to pay the whole expense of the poll ; to allow time for this the meeting adjourns to this day year." [2]

---

[1] MS. Vestry Minutes, Leeds, 22nd April and 2nd July 1835.

[2] *Ibid.* 2nd July 1835. An opinion seems to have been obtained from a prominent ecclesiastical lawyer of the period, Dr. L. Addams, to the effect, that those only could vote at a poll who had been present at the original meeting. "For it surely never can be contended that upon a poll demanded on any question and taken by adjournment, all the parishioners, whether present or not at the original Vestry, are to be let in to vote upon the question raised at the original Vestry. This, in effect, would be (especially if, as assumed, a poll must be granted as a matter of right if demanded by any parishioner at any Vestry) to do away with Vestries altogether, and to leave every question on any parochial matter, however slight and insignificant, to be decided upon and determined, not by Vestries (which are meetings of such of the parishioners as choose to attend, after due notice, where and when the major part present bind the whole parish), but of the parishioners at large, upon a polling of the whole parish, the absurdity of which would, I think, be as glaring as the mischief in point of expense, delay, and other palpable inconveniences, would be unfortunate " (*Manchester Times*, 5th April 1834). It was, however, subsequently decided that "the poll is an adjournment of the Vestry, and persons voting in the poll are deemed 'present' in the Vestry in accordance with 58 Geo. III. c. 69, sec. 3" (Elt *v.* St. Mary's, Islington, *Report of Cases*, etc., by E. E. Kay, 1854, vol. i. p. 449 ; Shaw's *Parish Law*, edition of 1895 by J. T. Dodd, p. 184).

(f) *The Death of the Parish*

The death of the parish, as a unit of local government, was now close at hand. For a moment there seemed a ray of hope. Inspired by Sir John Cam Hobhouse and Francis Place, a House of Commons Committee on Select and other Vestries in 1830 led to the passing of an Act in 1831, enabling the inhabitants of any large parish to substitute, for its existing government, a representative body, elected without plural voting on a ratepayer franchise.[1] Two years later another Act, proceeding on entirely different lines, permitted the Open Vestry to appoint a new committee for lighting and watching the parish, out of the proceeds of a new and separate rate.[2] Meanwhile the Whig Ministry, alarmed by the growing absorption of rents in the Poor Rate, no less than by the increasing demoralisation of the rural labourer through the subsidising of his wages—perturbed, moreover, at the insurrectionary democracy that was showing itself in the Open Vestries of London and the great industrial towns, and momentarily inspired by Chadwick's ideal of bureaucratic efficiency—was preparing its celebrated measure of Poor Law Reform. With the long and complicated story of mal-administration that led to this much-needed Poor Law Amendment Act, we shall deal fully in our subsequent historical analysis of the English Local Government between 1689 and 1835 in relation to Poverty and Crime. Here we need only note that, by withdrawing poor relief and the Poor Rate from parochial government, by setting up everywhere a new local authority unconnected with the old organisation, and by the introduction of central executive supervision and control, this Act laid the axe to the root of the most important trunk of the parish structure. There still remained the uncontrolled and unlimited Church Rate, by long tradition applicable to all the other purposes of parochial government, and levied by the popularly elected Churchwardens. It so chanced, however, that, just at this period, the Nonconformist majorities dominating the

---

[1] This Act of 1 and 2 William IV. c. 60 will be dealt with in the next chapter.
[2] 3 and 4 William IV. c. 90 (1833).

Open Vestries in the large industrial towns—forgetting both the past history and the contemporary utility of the parish Vestry and of the powers that it wielded—unwittingly threw away, by steadfastly voting against anything called a Church Rate, the immemorial right of the inhabitants in Vestry assembled to tax themselves for any purpose of public utility ; and incidentally abandoned such public right as existed to the interesting and valuable public buildings which had, from the very beginnings of English history, served as the secular as well as the religious meeting-place of the parish. With the loss both of the Poor Rate and of the Church Rate there departed from the extra-Metropolitan parish all real vitality. For another half century the unpaid parish officers lingered on with annually decreasing functions. The Easter Vestry Meeting was still held, a mere reminiscence of its former self. But though these shadows of the past were finally swept away only in the Local Government Act of 1894, it is not too much to say that, with the passing of the Poor Law Amendment Act of 1834 and the successful "passive resistance" to the levying of the Church Rate, the parish, as a unit of local government in the England outside the Metropolitan area, came virtually to an end.[1]

[1] We shall refer later to the fate of the Metropolitan parishes after 1835.

CHAPTER V

THE LEGALITY OF THE CLOSE VESTRY

WE have reserved for special description one type of parish government, the Close, or, as it was universally termed, the Select Vestry. This peculiar organisation consisted of a body of one or two dozen persons, or occasionally more, serving for life and filling vacancies among themselves by co-option. These Close Vestries had no organic connection with the inhabitants at large, but—together with the Incumbent and the usual parish officers—acted in all respects in their name and on their behalf. In old records they are styled " the masters of the parish," or the " kirkmasters "—sometimes the "ancients" or the " elders "—and frequently the " gentlemen " or the " company " of the " Four-and-Twenty." They annually elected the Churchwarden or Churchwardens; they assessed and collected the rates; they administered the parish property and controlled the parish expenditure; they stood, towards the Overseers, the Surveyors, and the Constables, in exactly the same anomalous position as we have described in the case of the meeting of inhabitants in Vestry assembled; and they found themselves in the same undefined state of subordination to the local Justices of the Peace. The members of these close bodies, as was laconically said by one of them in 1743, " thought [that] they only were intended by the word inhabitants." [1] The Select Vestry was, in fact, a fragment of the parish, which conceived itself to be endowed with all the legal powers of the parish as a whole.

In the absence of any complete or systematic record, we are unable to say in how many parishes this peculiar form of

[1] *Report of [House of Commons] Committee to which the Petition of the Principal Inhabitants of . . . Westminster . . . was referred*, 1743.

government existed between 1689 and 1835. We find it in a considerable number of the small but wealthy parishes in the City of London; in most of those of Westminster; and in some of the other populous parishes that grew to importance outside the area of the old Corporation.[1] The parishes within the old City of Bristol still retain the same organisation.[2] We hear of it in single parishes at Reading and Leicester,[3] and in two of those of Salisbury.[4] Richmond,[5] in Surrey, presents us with an apparently isolated instance, and the tiny village of Hartland,[6] at the extremity of Devonshire, with another. The anomalous government of the Cornish borough and parish of St. Ives[7] was apparently of a similar type. On the other side of England we find it of "ancient usage" at Braintree,[8] in Essex; we have discovered it also in two of the old parishes of the City of Coventry;[9] and the Vestry Minutes of the parish of Great St. Mary, Cambridge, show that it existed there from at least 1504 down to 1738.[10] Throughout Northumberland and Durham[11]—spreading into Yorkshire and Lancashire, Cumberland, and possibly also Westmorland[12]—it may almost be described as the typical form of parish govern-

---

[1] MS. Returns to Court of Star Chamber, 1635 (Chartæ Miscellaneæ, vol. vii.), in Lambeth Palace Library ; *New Remarks of London*, 1732 ; *History of London*, by W. Maitland, 1739 ; *London Parishes*, 1824. We have enumerated between fifty and sixty Metropolitan parishes (out of about two hundred) as having Select Vestries at some time between 1689 and 1835.

[2] See *infra*, pp. 182, 183.

[3] *The Churchwardens' Accounts of the Parish of St. Mary's, Reading*, by F. N. A. and A. G. Garry, 1893 ; *Transactions of the Leicestershire Archæological and Architectural Society*, vols. vi. and vii. 1888, 1890.

[4] *The Churchwardens' Accounts of St. Edmund and St. Thomas, Sarum*, 1443-1702, by H. J. F. Swayne, 1896.

[5] *Richmond and its Inhabitants*, by R. Crisp, 1866 ; *The Richmond Vestry*, by Charles Burt, 1890.

[6] Fifth Report of Hist. MSS. Commission, Appendix, p. 471 ; First Report of Poor Law Inquiry Commission, 1834, Appendix A (Villiers' Report), p. 57. They were called "the twenty-four Governors of the Parish of Hartland."

[7] *History of the Parishes of St. Ives*, etc., by J. H. Matthews, 1892.

[8] MS. Minutes, Quarter Sessions, Essex, 14th April 1713, etc. ; *History . . . of . . . Essex*, by Philip Morant, 1768, vol. ii. pp. 398, 399 ; *New and Complete History of Essex*, by a Gentleman [Peter Muilman], 1770, vol. i. pp. 416, 417 ; *History and Topography of . . . Essex*, by Thomas Wright, 1831-1835, vol. ii. p. 17 ; *People's History of Essex*, by D. W. Coller, 1861, p. 413.

[9] MS. Vestry Minutes, Holy Trinity and St. Michael's, Coventry.

[10] *Ibid.* Great St. Mary's, Cambridge, 1504-1738; *The Churchwardens' Accounts of St. Mary the Great, Cambridge, 1504 to 1635*, by J. E. Foster, 1905.

[11] See *infra*, pp. 179, 181.

[12] In Cumberland we hear incidentally in 1829 of a Poor Rate made at Keswick by a Select Vestry (*Cumberland Pacquet*, 20th January 1829). In

ment in town and country alike. Thus, so far as present
information extends, the Select Vestry seems to have cropped
up, sporadically, over the greater part of England, but to have
been the common form only in the Cities of London, Westminster, and Bristol, and in the Northern Counties. When, in
the course of the eighteenth century, the claim of these close
bodies to govern the parish came to be contested, we find them
basing their authority on three several grounds. Some of them
relied on a local custom, existing time out of mind. Others
had fortified themselves by a faculty, granted by the bishop of
the diocese. Others, again, chiefly in the Metropolitan area,
could definitely explain their origin during the seventeenth,
eighteenth, or nineteenth centuries, in special Acts of Parliament establishing close bodies, either in connection with the
building of new churches and a division of parishes, or on
some reform in the local Poor Law administration. These
three origins are so characteristic of the English Local Government of the period that we willingly devote a few pages to
their examination.

(a) *The Close Vestry by immemorial custom*

We have seen what a large part was played by local
custom in the organisation of the ordinary parish; how the
" ancient usage " of the locality was suffered by the law courts
to modify, and even to contradict, the plain directions of the

---

Yorkshire the cases which came into court reveal Select Vestries at Masham,
Northallerton, and Halifax (see *infra*, p. 181); and the MS. parish records
reveal others at Giggleswick, Dent, Kirby Malham, etc. In Lancashire there were
ancient "Four-and-Twenties" at Lancaster, Poulton, St. Michael's-on-Wyre,
Ribchester, Garstang, and Goosnargh, with a similar body at Kirkham having
a membership of thirty, which was upheld in the ecclesiastical court about
1639. Preston, too, had its Four-and-Twenty, including (as at Lancaster)
representatives of the Municipal Corporation (MS. Vestry Minutes, Preston,
1645-1905; *Records of the Parish Church of Preston*, by T. C. Smith, 1892;
History of the Parish of Ribchester, by T. C. Smith and J. Shortt, 1890; *History
of Lancashire*, by H. Fishwick, 1894, p. 226; *History of Kirkham*, 1874, by
the same; *Lancaster: Town Clerk's Report on Appointment of Sidesmen and
Members of Select Vestry*, 6th January 1904). There seems to have been a
Twenty-Four at Dalton-in-Furness ("A Town ruled by an Oligarchy," by G. A.
Wade, in *English Illustrated Magazine*, August 1901, No. 25, p. 434). At Cartmel, too, we read of the ancient " Society and Fellowship of the Four-and-Twenty,"
found existing as early as 1597, and subsequently termed Sidesmen (*Cartmel-
toniana*, by Rev. William ffolliott, 1854; *The Rural Deanery of Cartmel*,
edited by R. H. Kirby, 1892; *Annals of Cartmel*, by James Stockdale, 1872).

common law and, occasionally, of express statutes; how it could vary the number, method of selection, and area of jurisdiction of all the parish officers, not merely of such old-world functionaries as Constables and Churchwardens, but also of such modern statutory creations as Overseers of the Poor and Surveyors of Highways. It is therefore not surprising to find the close bodies existing in some parishes using the shibboleth of a custom " whereof the memory of man runneth not to the contrary," to justify their substitution for the meeting of inhabitants in Vestry assembled; and including in their claim, not only the ancient ecclesiastical functions of the parish, but also the newer obligations and powers in secular matters which Parliament was perpetually devolving upon it. And it must be admitted that the phraseology of the Tudor statutes relating to these matters of parish government, whilst not distinctly recognising either the open meeting of inhabitants or the close body, points rather to the existence of some sort of oligarchical structure for the English parish, as for the English borough— we need instance only the important part assigned to the various parish officers of the year in the nomination or appointment of those for the ensuing year; the periodical meetings for consultation enjoined upon the parish officers alone; and the significant assumption that, where the inhabitants were to be consulted, a small number of the chiefest or most substantial were to act or answer on behalf of the whole parish.[1]   We

[1] For illustration we need not go so far back as the frequent mediæval representation of the community by an inquest or jury, or to the yet older reeve and four men who spoke for the township—the probiores, honestiores, legaliores, antiquiores, etc., designated in this and other capacities of local administration. But it is at least historically interesting to find that some Somerset parishes had in the sixteenth century a standing committee called "the Four Men" (see for Lydeard St. Lawrence, Notes and Queries for Somerset and Dorset, vol. vii. March 1901, p. 212 ; for Morebath, Bishop Hobhouse's Churchwardens' Accounts, vol. iv. of Somerset Record Society, p. 208). Definite statutory direction was given to similar effect. The early Poor Relief Act of 1555 (2 and 3 Philip and Mary c. 5) allowed "two or three of the chief inhabitants," or the mayor, calling to him "two or three chief parishioners," to certify the existence of more impotent poor than the parish could relieve unaided ; and the mayor "with the assent of two of the most wealthy inhabitants" might persuade a rich parish to contribute. A century later, the Surveyor of Highways is to call in two or three substantial householders to help him in assessing a Highway Rate (14 Charles II. c. 6, 1662). Sixteenth- and even seventeenth-century testators frequently bequeathed money for the poor, or other public objects, to "the Churchwardens and principal inhabitants" (see the numerous wills in History and Antiquities of Hertfordshire, vol. i., by R. Clutterbuck, 1815-1827, e.g. p. 142).
So when, in 1678, Parliament incidentally declared who was to appoint the

have also seen how it was common for the person relinquishing
a parish office to nominate his successor; or for the group of
parish officers, in exact compliance with the statute of 1555,
to "call together a number of the parishioners," chosen at their
discretion, to nominate Surveyors of Highways. And when
this little group of parish officers met, as directed by the
statute of 1601, "to consider of some good course to be taken
and order to be set down," it was, we are told, not infrequent
for them to have an assistance . . . of such only as had
before been Churchwardens and Constables."[1] Thus what
may be called the principle of status and the principle of co-

Parish Clerk of the new parish of St. Anne, Soho, it is to "the principal
inhabitants," in conjunction with the Rector, that the power is given (30
Charles II. c. 8). An old parish account of Edgefield, Norfolk, giving the
receipts and expenditure for 1715-1719, is signed, each half-year, "by the consent of Mr. R. Fish, Churchwarden; Matthew Digby, Nathaniel Fish, *Chief
Inhabitants*; Robert Cubitt, Rector." In a case in 1807, where the advowson
of Painswick (Gloucestershire) had been purchased in the seventeenth century
by trustees for the parish, who were to present such person for appointment "as
the inhabitants and parishioners, or the major part of the chiefest and most
discreet of them, should . . . for that purpose nominate," the appointment was
claimed for the Open Vestry, which agreed upon arrangements for a two days'
poll. Lord Chief Baron M'Donald observed in deciding the case, that "the use
of these words is a strong badge of antiquity. I presume that formerly a few of
the principal people of the parish met and settled the business themselves, and
the rest of the parish was obliged to them for taking the trouble on themselves,
and did not interfere." The Court, whilst admitting that it was not the original
intention of the trust, felt bound, in 1807, to decide in favour of the adult
inhabitant ratepayers (Fearon *v.* Webb, 1807; in *Reports of Cases argued
and determined in the High Court of Chancery*, by Francis Vesey, 1809, vol.
xiv. pp. 13, 24; *History of the Church of St. Mary at Painswick*, by St. Clair
Baddeley, 1902, pp. 43-62).
  There is something to be said for the direct derivation of the Select Vestry
from the inquest or jury of "the sworn men" utilised in the fourteenth century
for the assessment of taxes. (See the Lancaster *Town-Clerk's Report on Appointment of Sidesmen and Members of Select Vestry*, 6th January 1904.) Mr. Hubert
Hall suggests to us that recent researches into Continental analogies (*e.g.* those
made in connection with the Black Book of Bayeux) indicate the possibility of
a certain permanence of local bodies of jurati, whether primarily feudal, or connected with scot and lot, or with the tenmentale, which were also communal. In
the parish any such position of responsibility and representative character would
naturally be connected with the holding of land.
  [1] *Annals of the Reformation*, by John Strype, vol. i. part ii. p. 132 of 1824
edition, quoting a document of 1564; see *The Parish*, by J. Toulmin Smith,
1857, p. 228. It should be noted, however, that this "assistance" in 1564
was described as existing alongside the Open Vestry, and not in substitution for
it. Exactly such a consultative Committee (not, however, leading to a Select
Vestry) we see formed at Mitcham in 1794, when it is recorded that "the Overseers, finding themselves under some difficulties, wish to have the opinion and
advice of the gentlemen who have already executed the said office of Overseer,
and therefore wish to propose as a committee such gentlemen, to meet monthly
at the workhouse" (MS. Vestry Minutes, Mitcham, Surrey, 15th May 1794).

option both existed latent in the legal framework of the parish even without any conscious exclusiveness.   It is easy to imagine that when new-comers settled in the district as handicraftsmen or shopkeepers, the little knot of " principal inhabitants " saw no reason for admitting them into their company, either by summoning them to any consultative meeting or choosing them for the more important parish offices.   Eventually, these outsiders, increasing in wealth, would be brought into " the King's book," as contributors to the subsidy, or subsequently into the assessment to the Land Tax, which was often taken as the basis for the rates, and thus made liable to local taxation.   But by that time the limitation of the Vestry meetings, either to a fixed number, or to those who had served in the unpaid parish offices, had become firmly established in the parish tradition.   It could therefore with some plausibility be argued that " putting the name of the thing out of question, it seems that Select Vestries had obtained by prescription long before Open Vestries were thought of.   These latter appear to have wrested their consequence, such as it is, from a privileged order, which had subsisted in every ancient parish from time immemorial, in the same way as the third estate has of late ages encroached on the two other estates, the lords spiritual and temporal, and even on the monarch himself." [1]   On this view, urged by an exceptionally well-informed parochial historian in 1831, the origin of the local governing body of the parish is to be sought, not in any public meeting of all the inhabitants, but in the more select gatherings of " parochiani nobiliores, parochiani seniores, et honestæ personæ parochiæ "—the chief parishioners, the ancients or the " worshipful men of the parish," of whom we occasionally read in the oldest records.

It was at any rate no detriment to this customary government by the principal inhabitants that the parish was, during the sixteenth and seventeenth centuries, often silently inheriting some of the offices and functions of the decaying manorial courts, with their juries of twelve or twenty-four men, in whose selection the inhabitants had no share.   The enactment of by-laws and even the imposition of a rate, by the local

[1] A History of the Parish of St. Laurence Pountney, by Rev. H. B. Wilson, 1831, chap. xv. p. 167.

officers, assisted only by a select body of the inhabitants, and without submission to any popular vote, was thus no unconstitutional novelty. And it is not without significance in this connection that the most interesting group of examples of a Select Vestry governing by immemorial custom, appears to be historically connected with the occupation or tenure of particular "husbandlands" or farms. In the counties of Northumberland and Durham [1] we find the parish government, for the past three centuries, normally in the hands of a body known as "The Four-and-Twenty" (or occasionally, "The Twelve "),[2] together with the Rector or Vicar, the Churchwardens, and occasionally the Surveyors of Highways for the time being. The "Gentlemen of the Four-and-Twenty," as they are usually termed, habitually comprised the principal occupiers of land in the various townships into which the large Northumberland and Durham parishes are divided. They held office for life, or at any rate so long as they remained occupiers in the parish (no provision being made for their voluntary resignation), and vacancies were filled by co-option. On what grounds the selection of such recruits was made we cannot be sure, but there is some evidence, even as

---

[1] We have gathered much of our information as to these interesting Select Vestries from the MS. Minutes of those at Newcastle, Gateshead, Alnwick, Warkworth, Bamburgh, and Embleton. See also "The Northumbrian Border," by Mandell Creighton, in *Archæological Journal*, vol. xlii., 1885, pp. 41-89 ; *History of Northumberland*, by Rev. J. Hodgson, 1827 (as to Elsdon, p. 92 of vol. ii.) ; *County History of Northumberland*, vols. ii. iv. vi. vii. etc. ; and various papers in *Archæologia Æliana* as to Warkworth (Nov. 1861), Tynemouth (vol. xix. p. 93, 1898), Rothbury (vol. xiii. p. 20, 1900), Hexham and Bywell (vol. xiii. p. 137, 1890), Haltwhistle (vol. xvi. p. 186, 1893). For Morpeth, see R. *v.* Woodman (1821), in *Reports of Cases*, by R. V. Barnewall and E. H. Alderson, vol. iv. pp. 507-510 ; and *Memoirs of Robert Blakey*, edited by Hy. Miller, 1879, p. 33. For those in Durham, see the valuable *Churchwardens' Accounts of Pittington*, etc. (1888), being vol. lxxxiv. of the Surtees Society, mentioning Twenty-Fours at Houghton-le-Spring, St. Oswald, Durham, and St. Nicholas, Durham, and a Twelve at Pittington ; *Memoirs of the Life of Ambrose Barnes*, 1867, being vol. l. of the same ; *History of Durham*, by Robert Surtees (1816-1823), mentioning Twenty-Fours at St. Nicholas, Durham (p. 53, vol. iv.), Houghton-le-Spring (p. 294), and South Shields (p. 100, vol. ii.), and a Twelve at Stainton (p. 66) ; and various papers in the *Archæologia Æliana*, as to Gateshead (vol. viii. p. 228, 1880), and Winston (vol. xvii. p. 101, 1894).

[2] The number twelve seems to have been less usual than twenty-four. It occurs in Durham, at Pittington (*Churchwardens' Accounts*, etc., vol. lxxxiv. of Surtees Society), and Stainton (*History of Durham*, by R. Surtees, 1816-1823, vol. iii. p. 66) ; and in Northumberland, at Haltwhistle ("The Church of Haltwhistle," by C. E. Adamson, in *Archæologia Æliana*, vol. xvi. pp. 177-188) ; and at Bywell St. Andrew (*ibid.* vol. xiii. p. 166).

late as the nineteenth century, of office being connected with the occupation of particular farms. At Embleton, in Northumberland, for instance, in 1828, the Vestry minutes record "the name of William Burrell, Esquire, to be entered in list of the Four-and-Twenty *for lands in Brunton*." [1] In the neighbouring parish of Warkworth, where a "Four-and-Twenty" has existed from time immemorial, we are told that "the list preserved in the Churchwardens' books indicate it to have been a representative body of ratepayers, for every vacancy was filled up by the appointment of another from the same farm or township, and his membership of association with another communion neither rendered him ineligible for, nor relieved him of his duty to serve on the Vestry and as Churchwarden." [2] And when we discover that at Embleton "the Book of Rates," or ancient list of hereditaments liable to pay rates, contained precisely twenty-four assessments; when we trace the same number in various other parishes as the total number of farms; [3] when we find that "this use of the word farm to signify an original unit of land tenure is peculiar to Northumberland," where it was used as equivalent to "husbandland," "living," and "yardland"; [4] and that the "farm" often formed, down to the middle of the nineteenth century, the sole basis of assessment, an equal share in rates and other payments being sometimes traditionally due from

---

[1] MS. Vestry Minutes, Embleton (Northumberland), 8th April 1828.

[2] *County History of Northumberland*, vol. v. p. 194 ; MS. Vestry Minutes, Warkworth, from 1722, and accounts from 1630 ; paper in *Archæologia Æliana*, November 1861.

[3] Thus, the parish of Lesbury was divided into twenty-four "husbandlands" ("The Ancient Farms of Northumberland," by Earl Percy, in *Archæologia Æliana*, vol. xvii. pp. 1-39) ; and that of Ryton into four quarters, one of which has twenty-four "farms" ("The Book of Easter Offerings, etc.," by S. Bailey, in *Archæologia Æliana*, vol. xix. pp. 39-46). Outside Northumberland we may note that the manor of Boldon, in Durham, had exactly twenty-four tenants in the Hatfield Survey ; that of Sedgefield had twenty-four "molmen" tenants (*History of Durham*, by R. Surtees, vol. i. p. 26) ; and that "the parish of Kirkby, in Kendal," comprises twenty-four constablewicks (*History of Westmoreland*, by Joseph Nicholson and Richard Burn, 1777, vol. i. p. 65). See also the significant petition from the "village and hamlet of Cole Aston," in Derbyshire, about 1649, already quoted, as to there being in the village "twenty-four oxgangs of land," the owners or tenants of which had to serve the parish offices in rotation (*Three Centuries of Derbyshire Annals*, by J. C. Cox, 1890, vol. i. p. 108).

[4] "The Ancient Farms of Northumberland," by F. W. Dendy, in *Archæologia Æliana*, vol. xvi., 1893, pp. 121-156.

each " farm " whatever its area or value, we are tempted to speculate, with the late Bishop Creighton, as to whether the " Gentlemen of the Four-and-Twenty " may not represent some common original grouping of the settlers of the parish into twenty-four households.[1] But be this as it may, if we consider together the old-world traditions of the manor and the customary parish procedure under the Elizabethan statutes, it must be admitted that the assertion of the close bodies that they had existed " time out of mind " was not altogether unreasonable. We can accordingly understand how, in the comparatively small number of cases in which the title of a customary Select Vestry was questioned in the law courts during the seventeenth and eighteenth centuries, the lawyers, familiar with the varying customs determining the governing bodies of the manor, the gild, and the municipal corporation, seem easily to have accepted the idea of similar variations of custom determining the constitution of the governing body of the parish.[2]

[1] As to this, see "The Northumbrian Border," by Mandell Creighton, *Archæological Journal*, vol. xlii., 1885, pp. 41-89 ; "The Ancient Farms of Northumberland," by F. W. Dendy, *Archæologia Æliana*, vol. xvi., 1893, pp. 121-156 ; and—most important of all—the further paper with the same title, by Earl Percy, *ibid.* vol. xvii., 1894, pp. 1-39.

[2] The earliest recorded case in which the title of a Close Vestry by prescription was contested in the law courts is that of Masham, in Yorkshire, in 1691 (Batt and Others, late Churchwardens of Masham, *v.* Watkinson). A suit had been begun in the ecclesiastical courts in 1680 to compel the Churchwardens to render accounts. They eventually got a writ of prohibition from the Court of Common Pleas on the ground that they had already rendered their accounts to a body called the Twenty-Four, which had, by immemorial custom, made the rates and administered the property. At last, in 1691, " after several great debates " the Court held that the custom was a legal one (*Reports of the Resolutions of the Court . . . of Common Pleas*, etc., by Sir Edward Lutwyche, 1718, vol. ii. pp. 436, 437). Other instances of customary Select Vestries coming into court are those of Northallerton and Halifax, both in Yorkshire. In the former case (Dent *v.* Coates), the parish had in 1741 a Twenty-Four, who made the Church Rate, and the point at issue was the validity of an alleged custom for the separate levy of " a certain proportion " on one township, Romanby hamlet, by its own Churchwarden. The Court did not uphold this custom owing to its uncertainty (*Reports of adjudged Cases*, by Sir John Strange, vol. ii. pp. 1144-1145 of 3rd edition, 1795). At Halifax the litigation arose in the ecclesiastical court over a faculty for a new organ, to which the Select Vestry had consented, but to which some inhabitants objected. It was pleaded (Butterworth and Barker *v.* Walker and Waterhouse, 1765) " that for twenty, thirty, and forty years it has been usual to collect the sense and consent about all parochial matters at such select meetings or Vestries, and that the whole parish are, and for all the time allegate have been, bound by the acts and consent of such select meetings or Vestries." Lord Raymond doubted whether the consent of the select body could in this case bind the parish, and remarked satirically on the

But the eighteenth-century law courts were not prone to historical research. They were easily persuaded that what had existed for a generation or so had existed time out of mind. We know now that, at any rate in some of the cases in which Close Vestries claimed to have existed from time immemorial, any careful examination of their records would have shattered this pretension once and for all. Hidden away in Churchwardens' accounts and Vestry minutes, the investigator discovers clear evidence of there having been in these parishes during the fifteenth or sixteenth century, public meetings, open to all the inhabitants, to elect the Churchwardens, receive their accounts, and administer the parish property. Sometimes these Open Vestries pass silently into meetings of "the masters of the parish," who are presently alone styled "vestrymen." In all the old parishes of the City of Bristol, for instance, Select Vestries have existed for over three hundred years, maintaining their position and administering their not inconsiderable parish property, on no better ground than the assertion of their immemorial existence as close bodies. To this day, reports a local clergyman, "the normal type of a city Vestry in Bristol is a self-elected body, into which a member is admitted, by election to the office of Junior Warden, the next year he serves as Senior Warden, and continues to be a member so long as he retains an interest, by ownership or occupation, in the parish. He cannot resign. The Incumbent is a member by custom in right of his induction, by which he was admitted to the temporal privileges of his benefice. . . . The new Wardens were chosen by the old Wardens as they are now; custom over-riding the right of election both of the Vicar and the parishioners. The election made by the Vestry is still declared to the people during the service on the Sunday after the Vestry Meeting."[1] Yet no

brevity of the time which it took to establish a custom ecclesiastically. But the Court decided only that a faculty was unnecessary (*Reports of Cases*, by Sir Jas. Burrow, 3rd edition, 1790, vol. iii. pp. 1689-1692). Other cases of litigation will be found subsequently referred to in connection with various Metropolitan parishes.

[1] Rev. C. S. Taylor, in communicating the "Regulations of the Vestry of St. Thomas in 1563," to the *Proceedings of the Clifton Antiquarian Club*, vol. i. 1888, pp. 193-198. This volume contains more information about the Bristol Select Vestries than is elsewhere accessible, as these close bodies, administering to-day considerable endowments, of which they claim to be absolute owners, do

great research into the records of two or three of these bodies shows that they date only from the fifteenth or sixteenth century, prior to which the parish business was done " with the whole assent and consent of the whole parishioners." Thus the oldest existing lease of property granted to the parish of St. Thomas, Bristol, dated 1451, recites that it is made " ex assensu et consensu omnium parochianorum ecclesiæ parochialis St. Thomas." [1] And lest we should imagine that these emphatic phrases are mere legal flourishes, the regulations of the Vestry of St. Stephen, in 1524, expressly provide that the " principal proctor," or Churchwarden, shall produce his accounts in church, on an appointed day, before " the whole parishioners there appearing "; that the minister shall, at Divine Service, " warn all the whole parishioners in general to appear there and then in the said church "; and that they shall at such meeting choose the Churchwarden for the ensuing year.[2] An earlier set of regulations in Latin, " commanded and ordained " for St. Nicholas, Bristol, in 1449, " by the unanimous consent of all the parishioners of the aforesaid church," expressly recites the presence at the meeting, not only of the Vicar, the Bailiff of the city, and six other named persons, but also of " a great many honest, proved, and trustworthy men." [3] There can be little doubt that inquiry into the fifteenth- and sixteenth-century records of other Bristol parishes would give similar results.[4]

not easily permit inspection of their records. They still act as ecclesiastical Vestries, but perform no civil functions. They are briefly referred to in Report of House of Commons Committee on Select and Other Vestries, 1830 ; *Thirty Letters on the Trade of Bristol*, by a Burgess (John Barnett Kingdon), 1836, p. 195 ; First Report of Municipal Corporations Commission, 1835, Appendix, vol. ii. p. 1201 ; *Bristol Past and Present*, by J. F. Nicholls and J. Taylor, 1881-1882, vol. ii. pp. 31, 93 ; vol. iii. p. 268 ; *All Saints, Clifton, Parish Magazine*, vol. xi., 1889-1890, pp. 335-340 ; " Notes on the Accounts of the Procurators or Churchwardens . . . of St. Ewen's, Bristol," by Sir John Maclean, in *Transactions of the Bristol and Gloucester Archæological Society*, vol. xv., 1890-1891, pp. 139-182. We are indebted to Mr. Cuthbert Atchley for some of the above references.

[1] Much the same phrase is used in the fourteenth- and fifteenth-century leases of the Vestry of All Saints, Bristol, see the article by Mr. Cuthbert Atchley in the *Archæological Journal*, vol. lviii., 1901, p. 147.

[2] "Regulations of the Vestry of St. Stephen's," by F. F. Fox, in *Proceedings of the Clifton Antiquarian Club*, vol. i., 1888, pp. 199-206.

[3] "Extracts from an Ancient Vestry Book at St. Nicholas's Church, Bristol," by Cuthbert Atchley, in *All Saints, Clifton, Parish Magazine*, vol. xi., 1889-1890, pp. 335-340.

[4] Mr. Cuthbert Atchley informs us that the MS. Churchwardens' accounts

So in the Metropolis, in the notorious case of St. Martin's-in-the-Fields, where a Select Vestry three times got a judgment that it had existed from time immemorial, the records now published make it clear that, down to March 1546, the Churchwardens had been "chosen by the whole body of the same parish." Between 1547 and 1583 the wording of the record is ambiguous. In December 1583 they are definitely chosen by "the masters," to whom they had accounted every year since 1561. The word "Vestry" or "Revestry" does not occur in these records until 1576, from which date it is used haphazard as an alternative to "the masters" or "the masters of the parish." From 1594 onward "the masters" are referred to as "vestrymen." And from October 1598 we have persons definitely co-opted by "the masters" as new "vestrymen." [1]

In other cases we find recorded the deliberate establishment by the Incumbent, the parish officers, and the principal inhabitants, of a close body or Select Vestry, which suddenly takes the place of the open meeting. Thus the parish of Pittington, in the County of Durham, has from "time immemorial" been governed by a Select Vestry known as the "Twelve Men." Right down to our own day, until superseded successively by the Board of Guardians and the Rural District and Parish Councils, this little oligarchy levied rates on the parish. Yet its origin now stands revealed in the following simple resolution of the Vestry of the year 1584, which had no legal authority at the time, and which could certainly not bind the parish for three hundred years: "Item,

of St. Ewen's, Bristol, during the fifteenth century, show them to be rendered to gatherings described in phrases which do not indicate a close body, and which seem to imply an open meeting of parishioners. In 1497 the phrase is "the parish assembled together to oversee the accounts." See "Notes on the Accounts of the Procurators or Churchwardens of . . . St. Ewen's, Bristol," by Sir John Maclean, in *Transactions of the Bristol and Gloucestershire Archæological Society*, vol. xv., 1890-1891, pp. 139-182.

[1] *The Accounts of the Churchwardens of the Parish of St. Martin's-in-the-Fields*, by John V. Kitto, 1901, Appendix E, pp. 585-586. The return made in 1635 by the Vicar and Churchwardens of this parish, in reply to the inquiry of the Star Chamber, may be significant of one method of origin of the close body. The government of the parish was then declared to be "by the Vicar and Churchwardens . . . twenty of the ancientest parishioners or thereabouts assisting them. . . . The number is supplied successively out of the ancients by the Vicar and Churchwardens" (Chartæ Miscellaneæ, MSS. in Lambeth Palace Library, vol. vii. p. 79).

it is agreed by the consent of the whole parish, to elect and choose out of the same, twelve men to order and define all common causes pertaining to the church, as shall appertain to the profit and commodity of the same without molestation or troubling of the rest of the common people."[1] On the strength of this resolution the "Twelve Men" of Pittington, with the Incumbent and Churchwardens, set about managing the parish flock of sheep, assigned pews in the church, and levied rates, at first for church purposes, and, from 1648 onward, also for the relief of the poor. Their legal authority to act for the parish, and to co-opt their successors, does not appear ever to have been challenged, and right down to the present day they act in all respects as the parish Vestry, now again shrunken to purely ecclesiastical functions. Much the same seems to have been the history of the Select Vestry of Stainton, in the same county, which clearly springs from "the society of twelve honest men, chosen in the parish of Great Stenton for the right ordering of all parochial affairs with the consent of the Minister, 1694," whose election is duly authenticated by the signatures of those who attended.[2]

Similarly, in the parish of St. Mary's, Reading, where a Select Vestry of thirty-three persons governed the parish throughout the eighteenth century on the plea of immemorial custom, its origin can now be traced to no better authority than a resolution of a parish meeting on the 22nd of April 1603, duly recorded in the Churchwardens' book. Prior to that date the outgoing Churchwardens had their account "exoneratur ex assensu parochianorum" and the Parish Clerk was appointed by "all the parishioners present."[3] In 1603,

---

[1] *Churchwardens' Accounts of Pittington and other Parishes in the Diocese of Durham from 1580 to 1700* (Surtees Society, vol. lxxxiv., 1888), p. 12. It is to be noted that it was in practice only "the rest of the common people," who were excluded from participation in parish government. At Pittington and elsewhere we frequently read of "the gentlemen" of the parish being present, though not of "the Twelve" or "the Twenty-Four," when any rate was decided on. The note of agreement is, as usual, strong. Thus at Pittington, in 1615 : "Mem.—That it is agreed upon by the consent of Sir Henry Anderson, Mr. Collingwood, and the twelve men of this parish, that a Cessment of 6d. the pound shall be presently levied for the repairing of the stock of sheep which is decayed, and other necessary uses of the said church" (*ibid.* p. 69). So at Houghton-le-Spring (*ibid.* p. 273 ; and see "Records of Houghton-le-Spring, 1531-1771," by R. W. Ramsay, in *English Historical Review*, Oct. 1905).

[2] *History of Durham*, by R. Surtees, 1816-1823, vol. iii. p. 66.

[3] MS. Churchwardens' Accounts, St. Mary's, Reading, Easter 1571.

as we read, "it was motioned by Mr. Doctor Powell, Vicar of the parish aforesaid, to have a Vestry of the chiefest and ancientest parishioners of the said parish (to the number of three and thirty); to the end that ever after they or the most part of them . . . shall associate themselves together at the church, upon every Good Friday after evening prayer, to see the account finished, and to do then and there all other things as shall be by them there present thought most expedient and necessary for the benefit of the said church. Upon which motion the parishioners that were at this account thought it convenient and fit that the same should take effect, and be finished for good order's sake." The Vicar then nominated the thirty-three, who were directed to fill any vacancies occurring in their number by death or removal out of the parish.[1] It is instructive to discover that the Incumbent of another parish—St. Laurence Pountney, in the City of London—was making a similar attempt in 1615, which was not successful. In the minute-book, under date 1st November 1615, we read: "All those that have set their names hereunto do not consent to have a Vestry, according to one writing tendered to us by Mr. Flowd, our Minister, but do desire to keep our old customs."[2]

[1] *The Churchwardens' Accounts of the Parish of St. Mary, Reading, 1550-1662*, by F. N. A. and A. G. Garry, 1893, p. 90. This body is referred to as "the chief of the parish" in 1616, and as a "Vestry" from 1617 onwards. In 1666 the members formally agree to meet on the first Sunday in the month after evening prayer. In 1680 we find it arranging a general scale of commutation for statute labour on the highways; in 1709 it administers poor relief and fixes the Poor Rate (MS. Vestry Minutes, St. Mary's, Reading). A similar case is that of St. Mary's, Leicester, where the Open Vestry in 1577 agreed that "thirteen of the chief of the parish should be chosen to set order for such things as shall be done for the church behoof." Between 1652 and 1729 the Churchwardens' Accounts show that this body governed the parish and recruited itself by co-option (*Transactions of the Leicestershire Archæological and Architectural Society*, vols. vi. and vii., 1888-1890).

[2] *A History of the Parish of St. Laurence Pountney*, by H. B. Wilson, 1831, p. 167. A similar attempt in St. Michael Royal is mentioned in 1631 (Chartæ Miscellaneæ, vol. vii. p. 17). At Lambeth, too, an attempt was made in 1654 to transform the Open Vestry into a close body, but the usurpation lasted only during that year (*The History and Antiquities of Lambeth*, by John Tanswell, 1858, p. 8). Dr. Killigrew, as Master of the Savoy, is said to have set up a Select Vestry of fourteen persons for that precinct, which was in existence in 1732 (*New Remarks of London*, 1732). But the return made to the Star Chamber in 1635 shows that even at that date the precinct was governed by "the Churchwardens and a selected company of parishioners" (Chartæ Miscellaneæ, vol. vii. p. 73).

It is to be noted that, after the Restoration, we read of Select Vestries being

The most audacious of these usurpations was that of the Select Vestry of St. Saviour's, Southwark, made in 1556, in express defiance of an Act of Parliament only sixteen years old. This close body became, in the course of the next fifty years, " very uneasy to the rest of the parish," being commonly termed " the sharing house," and some of the excluded parishioners petitioned Parliament for a remedy. Their petition of 1608, which John Strype printed in full in the 1720 edition of Stow's *Survey*, tells us very clearly the whole story down to its date. " By Act of Parliament (32 Henry VIII. c. 15, 1540) the parishes of St. Margaret's and St. Mary Magdalen, Southwark, were united and made one ; and the church of the monastery of St. Mary Overy [was] made the parish church and called by the name of St. Saviour's ; the parishioners [were] enabled among themselves yearly to nominate and elect four or six Churchwardens, the Churchwardens [being] made a body corporate and capable in the law. . . . The parishioners did choose Churchwardens sixteen years together, according to the said Act, and did take the Churchwardens' accounts . . . until about 5th March 1556, some of the parishioners, perceiving the revenues and profits of the church to be increased to £300 a year, or thereabout, and being desirous of the rule and sway of the rest, pretended that the assembly of the multitude at the choice of Churchwardens occasioned much confusion, suggesting that the election of the Churchwardens and the dispensation of the revenues and profits of the church were transferred to a selected number, the confusion would be avoided, and all other business better ordered. By which intimation thirty parishioners assumed unto themselves the sole authority to manage the revenues and profits of the church, to exclude the ministers and parishioners for ever from the election, the accounts of the Churchwardens and all other business and privileges belonging unto them ; they choose the thirty themselves, six Churchwardens and four Auditors to take their accounts, out of the thirty. They call themselves Vestrymen,

re-established in their exclusive and irresponsible position by formal votes of open parish meetings ; so, for instance, at St. Giles's, Cripplegate, where an immemorial close body had been temporarily thrown open during the Rebellion (*An Account of the Church and Parish of St. Giles's Without, Cripplegate*, by J. J. Baddeley, 1888, pp. 166-173).

Masters and Governors of the parish. They spend thirty pounds a year or thereabouts in feasting themselves and their wives, upon the revenues of the church. They allow the Churchwardens four pounds a year fees, and their Auditors twenty shillings. They benefit themselves with leases of the church lands, to the great hindrance of the poor. They make by - laws and constitutions. . . . Therefore the parishioners desire that the former Act may be confirmed with these alterations. That the Ministers and subsidymen of three, four, or five pounds may have the election of the Churchwardens and an oversight in all the business belonging to the church and the revenues thereof." [1]   But the petitioners failed to get redress, and the Select Vestry of St. Saviour's, in spite of repeated complaints, continued to rule the parish for more than another century. Not until about 1730 or 1732, and then only by "a kind of parish revolution," was the plain statutory constitution for the parish reverted to, and the meeting of inhabitants in Open Vestry resumed.[2]

Looking back to the whole series of Select Vestries which have claimed to exist merely by prescription, we do not find it easy, in face of the varying decisions of the law courts, to express any useful opinion on their legality. Whatever might be the luck of any particular Select Vestry in making out an immemorial title when challenged in the courts, it is difficult nowadays to resist the presumption against such a claim afforded by historical research. Yet we must not

---

[1] Stow's *Survey of London*, by John Strype, 1720, vol. ii. p. 9. The Act of 32 Henry VIII. (1540) is given in substance in *The History and Antiquities of the Collegiate Church of St. Saviour, Southwark*, by Rev. Canon Thompson, 1904, p. 85.

[2] To the American reader it will be of interest to note that it was by this Select Vestry that John Harvard was elected a Churchwarden. For the whole controversy, see MS. Acts of the Privy Council 22nd July, and 10th and 17th August 1664, when the Close Vestry was restored after the disturbances of the Commonwealth ; House of Commons Journals, February and March 1710 ; the broadside in the British Museum, dated 1729, calling on the parishioners to attend the Easter Vestry ; *The Compleat Parish Officer*, by G[iles] J[acob], 1738, p. 127 ; *New Remarks of London*, 1732 ; *Annals of St. Mary Overy*, by W. Taylor, 1833, pp. 126-129 ; *Lectures on the History of Southwark*, by S. Robertson, 1863 ; *Old Southwark and its People*, by William Rendle, 1878, p. 179 ; *History and Antiquities of the Collegiate Church of St. Saviour, Southwark*, by Rev. Canon Thompson, 1904 ; and *Sketches of Southwark Old and New*, by R. W. Bowers, 1902, pp. 257-296.

conclude that, even by the strictest legal tests, some Select Vestries could not have made good their title. It seems quite possible that a close body, limited in number and co-opting its successors—probably made up of the parish and manorial officers past and present, or of " the sworn men " of the ancient assessment inquest, or of a manorial jury, or even of the feoffees of land or other property belonging to the parish [1] —may have existed, in one or other parish, uninterruptedly from the date of the beginning of legal memory, say the first year of Richard I.[2] But as regards at any rate the great majority of these bodies, the presumption is that they arose from some sort of resolution or agreement of the chief or other parishioners attending the Easter Vestry meeting, some time in the fifteenth or sixteenth century.[3] In all these cases, at least, the Select Vestry must be regarded as merely an extra-legal constitution for the government of the parish—strictly analogous to that of an elective executive committee with a

---

[1] Examples of such feoffees becoming the local governing body for the place are afforded by Melton Mowbray (*An Essay on English Municipal Government*, by James Thompson, 1867 ; see also the papers by Thomas North in *Transactions of the Leicestershire Architectural and Archæological Association*, vol. iii., 1874, pp. 60-79, 180-206) ; and Tetbury, in Gloucestershire (*History of the Town and Parish of Tetbury*, by Rev. A. T. Lee, 1857 ; 57 George III. c. 2) ; although we know of no case in which they can be historically connected with a Select Vestry. It is interesting to find that the lands given in 1692 for the support of a lecturer in Dedham (Essex) were vested in twenty-four feoffees (*New and Complete History of Essex*, by a Gentleman [Peter Muilman], 1770, vol. vi. p. 249) ; and that Oliver Cromwell was a member of a similar set of " Gentlemen of the Twelve," who were feoffees of some charity lands at Ely (Cambridgeshire), which were treated as " the town's money " (*Letters and Speeches of Oliver Cromwell*, by T. Carlyle, vol. iii. pp. 222-224 of edition of 1904).

[2] The oldest historical record of a Select Vestry yet known to us is the mention in 1443 of " masters of the parish "—by which phrase are to be understood the members of a Close Vestry—in the very earliest *Churchwardens' Accounts of St. Edmund and St. Thomas, Sarum*, 1443-1702, by H. J. F. Swayne, 1896, see p. 357.

[3] Instances of such choice of a Select Vestry occur in the City of London (see the returns of St. James Within, Aldgate, and St. Bennet, Gracechurch, to the Star Chamber inquiry of 1635 in Chartæ Miscellaneæ, in Lambeth Palace Library, vol. vii. p. 85). Gibson gives this as the origin of all these Select Vestries : he says they originated "from the practice of choosing a certain number of persons to manage the affairs of the parish for that year, which by degrees became a fixed method ; and the parishioners lost not only their right to concur in the public management . . . but also the right of electing the managers " (*Codex Juris Ecclesiastici Anglicani*, by Edmund Gibson, 1761, p. 219). It was easy to make the assumption of such an originating resolution, but difficult to prove it, especially when access to the old minutes was denied. We know of no case in which a Select Vestry was upheld by the law courts after proof had been given of such an origin.

poll of the ratepayers, of which we have described the eighteenth-century evolution—no more and no less valid in strict law than this latter. It was, in fact, the sixteenth-century analogue of such a constitution, having for that century the advantage of being in consonance, not only with mediæval custom, but also with the Tudor statutes that the parish had to administer.

(b) *The Close Vestry by Bishop's Faculty*

A mere assertion of immemorial custom was sometimes an unconvincing barrier to an indignant crowd of protesting ratepayers. The principal inhabitants naturally sought to get the customary constitution of their Vestry embodied in an authoritative document. Under the Stuart kings, when the diocesan courts expounded the canons of the Church as part of the law of the land, and regarded the parish as an ecclesiastical institution, the first appeal of the close body was to the Church. The Incumbent and Churchwardens of each parish were necessarily in constant communication with the Bishop and the Archdeacon, and were accustomed, in the transaction of church business, to apply for a "faculty" or formal instrument, by which the sanction of "the Ordinary" was conveyed to any alteration in the church or churchyard.[1] The same instrument, it was thought, could be used for determining the constitution of the Vestry. We find therefore a remarkable series of cases between 1590 and 1680 in which a Select Vestry was established or confirmed by bishop's faculty.

The earliest instance that has actually come under our notice of episcopal intervention in Vestry constitutions is that of the small City of London parish of St. Martin's, Ludgate, where "a Vestry of Selected Persons to the number of thirty, besides the parson," is said to have been granted by the Bishop of London in 1591, and to have been formally

---

[1] A faculty is the document by which the sanction of the Ordinary (the Bishop as *judex ordinarius*) is legally conveyed for any alteration of the fabric, utensils, or ornaments of the church, any changes in the churchyard or glebe, or any other matter within his jurisdiction. It is issued by the Bishop's diocesan Court, by his chancellor, vicar-general, or commissary. See *The Ecclesiastical Law of the Church of England*, by Sir Robert Phillimore, edition of 1895, vol. ii. p. 1419.

confirmed by the Bishop in 1600, and by instrument of his
chancellor in 1601.[1] For the vast parish of St. Dunstan's,
Stepney, at that time extending from the Tower of London to
the borders of Essex, we have it noted that "the orders in
Vestry" of the "chief parishioners," establishing some sort of
select body, were "ratified and confirmed" by the commissary of
the Bishop of London, by an entry under his hand in the
Vestry minute-book in 1600.[2] In 1601 the inhabitants
of St. Dunstan's-in-the-West petitioned simultaneously the
Archbishop of Canterbury, the patron of the living, and the
Bishop of London, to give them a Select Vestry of twenty-four
persons, which was accordingly done by faculty. So in 1603,
in the parish of St. Magnus, near London Bridge, at an Open
Vestry meeting at which the Archdeacon of London was
present, it was agreed, with the sanction of that dignitary,
"for avoiding of tumult and future strife," that a Select
Vestry of thirty-two persons should thenceforth govern the
parish.[3] Just at this time, too, the members of the Select
Vestry of St. Saviour's, Southwark, the origin of which we
have described, were claiming that it exercised its powers not
merely by the "consent of the parishioners," to which no
legal validity could possibly be ascribed, but also by force of
a "constitution of the Ordinary," seeing that "there would be
great confusion if the whole parish should be electors"; and
that even "election by three-pound subsidymen will be
popular, and incite the ruder sort to extreme liberty."[4] In
the formal documents of other parishes, both the motive and

[1] Chartæ Miscellaneæ, vol. vii. p. 9 (in Lambeth Palace Library). This
interesting volume contains the original MS. returns made by the Incumbents
and Churchwardens of nearly all the Metropolitan parishes in 1635, to an
inquiry of the Star Chamber as to (1) whether the parish was governed by a
Select Vestry or by all the inhabitants, (2) whether any grant or instrument
had been obtained, (3) what powers were claimed, and (4) what fees were
exacted for burials, etc. These returns are well worth printing and editing, as
they throw some light on the condition of the Metropolis at that date.

[2] Vestry Minutes, Stepney, Middlesex, 22nd May 1600 ; see *Memorials of
Stepney Parish*, by G. W. Hill and W. H. Frere, 1890-1891, p. 35.

[3] Chartæ Miscellaneæ, vol. vii. pp. 4, 104. In St. Bartholomew's the
Great, in 1606, "the parish being much increased by many buildings and the
parishioners finding many inconveniences by a disagreeing multitude, made
complaint to the then Archdeacon of London for a reformation, whose then
official . . . approved of a select number of vestrymen under his handwriting
in our Vestry book" (*ibid.* p. 36).

[4] Petition to Parliament of 1608, in Stow's *Survey of London*, edited by John
Strype, 1720, vol. ii. p. 9.

the occasion of this ecclesiastical intervention are elaborately set forth. Thus, in 1606, we find the Bishop of London issuing a faculty to the parish of St. Botolph Without, Aldersgate, in the City of London, reciting that the Church-wardens and other notable parishioners had petitioned him for such an instrument. The petition had set forth "that through the general admittance of all sorts of parishioners into their vestries there falleth out great disquietness and hindrance to the good proceedings which they desire should be in the said parish, by the dissent of the inferior and meaner sort of the multitude of the inhabitants being greater in number, and thereby more ready to cross the good proceedings for the benefit of the church and parish, than able to further by counsel or otherwise the good."[1] The Bishop thereupon directs that the Dean of Westminster, the Incumbent of the parish, and twenty other persons who are individually named, "of whom the most part have been Constables or Church-wardens, or of the Inquest (as 'tis called)" shall form, what was afterwards termed, a Select Vestry [2] "for the ordering and directing such things belonging to the said church as are to be done by the parish," filling vacancies among their number by co-option. In the course of the next twenty years we have evidence that the Bishop of London granted at least a score of similar faculties to other City of London parishes, using the same formula of "the general admittance of the parishioners into the Vestry," as having produced "great disquietness and hindrance to the good proceedings." The Select Vestries thus created were in full vigour in 1635, when the Court of Star Chamber made an inquiry on the subject, the original MS. answers to which are still preserved in the Lambeth Palace Library.[3] Similarly, at Braintree, in Essex, a

---

[1] This Faculty, mentioned in the parish return of 1635 (Chartæ Miscellaneæ, vol. vii.), is printed in full in *The Report of the Committee appointed by a General Vestry of the Parish of St. Botolph Without, Aldersgate . . . with some Methods proposed to prevent abuses in the future*, etc., 1733). This Vestry was described in 1824 as open ; see *London Parishes*, Anon. (1824), p. 101.

[2] It is noted in the *Hackney Magazine*, 1834, p. 20, that the term Select Vestry is not used in the earlier faculties, but that it appears in that of 1679. The term is, however, used by Sir Henry Spelman in 1641 (*De Sepultura*) ; and "Vestry of selected persons" occurs in the Star Chamber inquiry of 1635 (Chartæ Miscellaneæ, vol. vii.).

[3] Chartæ Miscellaneæ, vol. vii. Among these Select Vestries by faculty may be mentioned (in addition to those named in the text) St. Bartholomew the

thriving little centre of woollen manufacturing, at that time in the London diocese, and shown by the parish records to have been governed since at least 1584 by a close body of twenty-four, referred to as Headboroughs, "Governors of the town," and "Town Magistrates," we find these appealing to the bishop in 1611 to help them to keep out intruders, and for the definite establishment of "a certain number" as the ruling body in the parish. Thereupon the bishop, in 1612, issues a faculty couched in exactly the same phraseology as that for St. Botolph, Aldersgate.[1]   A year later the parish of St. John at Hackney, then just beginning to be affected by the spreading of the Metropolis, makes a similar appeal to the bishop, with a like result. In this case the bishop's faculty of 1613 recites the receipt of a petition from "the better and ancienter sort of the parish," complaining, in an identical formula, of the intrusion of the common people, and again referring to the inconvenience of these forming the majority of the Open Vestry. Therefore the bishop appoints to be vestrymen the Vicar, Curate, and Churchwardens for the time being, together with thirty-two other persons named in the instrument, " of whom the most part have been Constables, Churchwardens, or borne other offices of respect in that parish," and this Select Vestry is to fill vacancies by co-option.[2]   Similar faculties may have been issued in other

Great (1606); St. Margaret, New Fish Street (1611); St. Gabriel, Fenchurch (1612); St. Mary, Mounthaw (1612); St. Michael in Wood Street (1614); Allhallows the Less (1615); St. Mary Aldermary (1617); St. Alphege, near Cripplegate (1619); St. Stephen, Coleman Street (1619); St. Katherine, Creechurch (about 1620); St. Olave, Silver Street (1624); St. Lawrence Jewry (1627, revoked in 1636); and the following as to which the date of faculty is unknown to us :—St. Leonard, Eastcheap ; St. Mary, Somerset ; St. Nicholas, Olave ; St. Mildred, Bread Street, and St. Botolph, Bishopsgate.

[1] *History and Antiquities of the County of Essex*, by Philip Morant, 1768, vol. ii. p. 398 ; *New and Complete History of Essex*, by a Gentleman [Peter Muilman], 1770, vol. i. p. 416 ; *History of the County of Essex*, by Thomas Wright, 1831-1835, vol. ii. p. 17 ; *People's History of Essex*, by D. W. Coller, 1861, p. 413.

[2] *Antiquities of the Parish of Hackney*, by William Robinson, 1842, vol. ii. p. 85. Other faculties creating Select Vestries issued by the Bishop of London about this time were those for St. Mary Matfelon, Whitechapel (1615) ; Christ-church (prior to 1635), and St. Giles-in-the-Fields (1628) ; see the MS. returns in Lambeth Palace Library, Chartæ Miscellaneæ, vol. vii. pp. 43, 50, and 114 ; and (as to the last named) *Account of the Hospital and Parish of St. Giles-in-the-Fields, Middlesex*, by John Parton, 1822 ; and *History of the United Parishes of St. Giles-in-the-Fields and St. George, Bloomsbury*, by Rowland Dobie, 1834. "A faculty Vestry of forty-four persons," in St. Clement Danes, is mentioned in *The History of London*, by W. Maitland, vol. ii. p. 1336 of edition of 1756.

dioceses, but the only one that we have met with is that granted by the Bishop of Winchester in 1614 for the establishment of a Select Vestry at Richmond (Surrey), consisting of the Incumbent, Churchwardens, and twelve persons, renewing themselves by co-option.[1]

There is thus some ground for the remark of a writer of 1733 that "these Select Vestries . . . first sprung up about the time of King James I., and were principally occasioned by the avarice of some who, though they had no notion of the business, yet were fond of being called of the clergy. For the Protestant Religion began to be so well settled as to be thought fashionable."[2]   The same instrument was used after the Restoration to re-establish order in disturbed parishes, and to "purify" the government from those who were disaffected.   Thus, at the Vestry of St. Martin's-in-the-Fields, on the 4th of July 1662, we see "the Churchwarden presenting that a new instrument, or something which he knew not by what name to call, is extant, and in the custody of Mr. Dean, purporting the new ordering or settling of a Vestry." It is thereupon ordered that three of the most distinguished of the vestrymen and the two Churchwardens should wait upon the Dean, "to declare the readiness and great willingness of the Gentlemen of the Vestry that all such members of the said Vestry who are disaffected to the King's Church, or good of the parish, may be removed."[3] The faculty in due course recites "that during the late unhappy times of trouble and disorder within this realm, the public affairs of the said church and parish have been necessitated to be managed by persons not admitted thereunto by the authority of the Diocesan or Ordinary of the place, in whose power alone (as they conceived) the regulation and ordering of business of that nature most properly and peculiarly ought to reside. And that many persons of quality (parishioners of the said parish) very fit to be entrusted with business of that nature and concernment are, notwithstanding, unwilling

---

[1] MS. Vestry Minutes, Richmond (Surrey); *The Richmond Vestry*, by Charles Burt, 1890; as to this, see pp. 219, 362.

[2] *Report of the Committee appointed by a General Vestry of the Parish of St. Botolph Without, Aldersgate*, etc., Appendix, p. 1, 1733.

[3] MS. Vestry Minutes, St. Martin's-in-the-Fields, Middlesex, 4th July 1662.

to act, unless lawfully appointed as aforesaid." [1]   Finally, in St. Dunstan's, Stepney, where, as we have seen, the Bishop of London had already intervened in 1600, and where there had been between 1589 and 1654 more than one attempt to establish some sort of popularly elected parish committee, none of which seems to have long continued, a regular faculty was granted in 1662, in response to a petition which alleged that "by reason of the vast number of inhabitants the public business of the said parish cannot be orderly despatched by general assemblies," and that it is "not possible" for a Vestry "to be chosen by a popular election in so vast a parish." [2]

It is characteristic of the anarchy of English Local Government prior to 1835 that, in spite of the fact that Sir Henry Spelman, the great contemporary authority on ecclesiastical institutions, had, in 1641, expressly declared these faculties to be of no legal authority,[3] the majority of the

---

[1] This lengthy faculty is printed in full in *Acts of Parliament relating to the Parish of St. George's, Hanover Square, with instruments for appointing Vestries,* 1839; and also in R. Dobie's *History of the Parishes of St. Giles-in-the-Fields and St. George, Bloomsbury,* 1834, pp. 274-276.

[2] *Memorials of Stepney Parish,* by G. W. Hill and W. H. F. Frere, 1890-1891, p. 243. Other faculties constituting or confirming Select Vestries about this period are those of 1661 and 1662 to St. Dunstan's-in-the-West (City of London), where, by the way, Isaac Walton was one of the Select Vestry, see *History of Clerkenwell,* by W. J. Pinks, 1881, p. 107; *Historical Account of the Constitution of the Vestry of the Parish of St. Dunstan's-in-the-West,* 1714; and *The Art of being Honest for a little Time, or the Method of making Parish Rates,* etc., 1714; in 1673 another to St. Martin's-in-the-Fields altering the quorum; and in 1679 another to Hackney, printed in the *Hackney Magazine,* 1834, p. 97. We gather that St. Michael's, Cornhill, where "the masters of the parish" are mentioned in 1555, may have had a bishop's faculty about 1662; see Dawson *v.* Fowle, 1664, in *Reports of Cases,* by Sir Thomas Hardres, 1693, p. 379, and *Modern Reports,* vol. i. p. 181; *The Parish Officer's Complete Guide,* by John Paul, 6th edition, 1793, p. 4; and *The Accounts of the Churchwardens of the Parish of St. Michael's, Cornhill, 1456-1608,* by W. H. Overall and A. J. Waterlow, 1869.

[3] Sir Henry Spelman, in *De Sepultura* (1641), says, referring to Vestries (pp. 22, 23): "Let not a dozen or sixteen private persons make orders to bind, like a law, the rest of the parish that consenteth not. What they have used to do time out of mind, I call not to question; but those Vestries that, within these thirty years or thereabouts, have left their ancient form, supported by a lawful prescription, and contrived to themselves a new society, power and jurisdiction over the rest of the parish, countenanced by an instrument from the Ordinary under the seal of his chancellor, and (as new things must have new names) are commonly styled Selected Vestries. I see the bishops' names are used in them; whether with their assents and knowledge I am doubtful. I assure myself their lordships would do nothing against the law; and I understand not by what law they may at this day erect such societies or endow them with such authority as is pretended. But, to deal plainly, I think those instruments confer more

Select Vestries thus constituted proceeded to govern their parishes and arbitrarily to levy rates on all the inhabitants, for generation after generation, and that it was not until 1834 that the last of them was overthrown. When, however, the title of one or other Select Vestry came, in the eighteenth or nineteenth century, to be disputed in the law courts, bishops' faculties proved double-edged instruments, easily turned against their possessors. It was a comparatively minor point that the wording of these faculties contemplated primarily the management of church affairs, and did not purport to convey any authority over the administration of the statutes for mending the highways or relieving the poor. The election of Churchwarden and the making of the general levy called by the name of Church Rate, by this time admittedly partook of the nature both of church and of secular business, and eighteenth-century law courts, however uncritical of prescriptive claims, were totally opposed to the pretensions of ecclesiastical authorities to intermeddle in civil affairs. Select Vestries thus found their precious faculties, as Sir Henry Spelman had predicted, regarded as no more than waste paper.[1] But this was not all. The wording of these instruments or of the petitions which had secured them, usually bore testimony to the existence of an Open Vestry—to the actual participation of "the meaner sort" in the work of parish government. This fact was plainly inconsistent with the claim on the part of the close body to have existed "time out of mind." Powerful Select Vestries, like St. Margaret's, Westminster, accordingly found it convenient to "lose" their faculties, whilst others took care not to produce them in court.

money upon the chancellors than authority upon the Vestries. . . . What have they now for their money ? or more (in effect) than if a private man had granted them as much ? No doubt, many of the wise parishioners do perceive it, and some parishes have renounced it, and are turned back to their ancient Vestry." See J. Toulmin Smith, *The Parish*, 1857, p. 238.

[1] It was, however, not until the nineteenth century that the legal position was definitely and authoritatively stated. In 1827 Lord Tenterden declared (in Golding v. Fenn) that the bishop could, by his faculty, give a Select Vestry no further or better title to exist, or to rate the parish, than it otherwise possessed ; but that the mere grant of a faculty was not in itself a disproof of the claim of the Select Vestry to have existed from time immemorial. In the litigation of 1828-1834 the Select Vestries claimed to have existed before the grant of the faculty, which, it was contended, merely "purified" the pre-existing Select Vestry (see pp. 265-266).

Hence, too, it is not surprising to find that, after the Revolution, aspiring parish oligarchies ceased to apply to the bishops or their chancellors, and turned their attention to other ways of fortifying their position against the parishioners at large.[1]

(c) *The Close Vestry by Church Building Act*

In certain cases, particularly in the Metropolitan area, the Close Vestry is to be traced to ecclesiastical instruments of more undoubted legal authority than a bishop's faculty. The great increase of the Metropolis led, from the latter part of the seventeenth century onward, to the erection of new churches, usually out of public funds of one sort or another, and to the creation of a series of new parishes, which were carved out of those already existing, by the express authority of Parliament. This was effected by the various Church Building Acts, sometimes applying to specified parishes, sometimes to such as might be determined on by an executive commission. Nowadays, when such arrangements are made, the change is confined to the ecclesiastical organisation, the ancient civil parish and governing authority continuing undivided. But in the seventeenth and eighteenth centuries the local organisation of Church and State was still one and the same, and the districts created under these Acts in many cases at once set up for themselves as new and independent local governing authorities, exercising all the prescriptive and statutory functions of the immemorial parish.

The earliest case to which we need refer is that of St. Paul, Covent Garden, where a new church was built, and a new parish created out of that of St. Martin's-in-the-Fields— first by Ordinance of the Long Parliament in 1645, which named thirty-four persons to be " the Governors " of the parish ; and then by Act of 1660, which gave great power to the parish officers, but left it doubtful by whom the Churchwardens were to be elected. From the beginning there seems to have been a close body, which presently took the form of a gathering of

---

[1] An interesting, and, so far as we know, a unique instance of this turning to other authorities is afforded by the Select Vestry of Braintree, to be presently described.

all who had served the office of Churchwarden.[1]   When in
1678 another new parish, that of St. Anne, Soho, was by Act
of Parliament carved out of St. Martin's, no constitution was
expressly provided, and the assumption was evidently that the
parish government would be in the hands of the Incumbent,
the officers, and the "principal inhabitants." Within a few
years, however, some more definite statement was found
necessary, and a new Act of 1685 empowered the bishop to
appoint thirty commissioners to complete the new church, who
were to become "vestrymen" so long as they continued to
reside in the new parish, and who were authorised to fill
vacancies by co-option. Under this somewhat indefinite
statutory provision, the new parish of St. Anne's continued for
half a century to be governed in civil as well as ecclesiastical
affairs by a Close Vestry of thirty persons.[2] The same year
saw another, and, as it proved, a more important precedent
established. By an Act of 1685, the new parish of St. James,
Piccadilly, was set up for all purposes whatsoever, and
was expressly provided with a Select Vestry, practically
identical with that which had been established by the
Bishop of London for the mother parish of St. Martin's-in-
the-Fields.[3]

But it was not until a quarter of a century later that any
systematic attempt was made to provide churches for the
rapidly growing population. Though the author of *Political
Arithmetic* had called attention in 1665 to the vast increase
of some Metropolitan parishes where "the care of about 30,000
souls has been sometimes committed to one minister whose

[1] 12 Charles II. c. 37, 1660 (for the opposition to this Act offered by the
Vestry of the mother parish, see MS. Vestry Minutes, St. Martin's-in-the-
Fields, 25th August 1660); *Some Account of the Formation of the Precinct of Covent
Garden into a Parish* (undated ; about 1828, in a volume of "Gleanings relating
to the Parish of Covent Garden," in British Museum, 1889. a. 20) ; *History of
London*, by W. Maitland, vol. ii. pp. 1347 of edition of 1756 ; *Diary of Thomas
Burton*, by J. T. Rutt, 1828, vol. ii. p, 180 ; *Gentleman's Magazine*, 1789, p. 978.
[2] 30 Charles II. c. 18 (1678) ; 1 James II. c. 20 (1685) ; 8 George II. c.
15 (1735) ; *History of London*, by W. Maitland, vol. ii. p. 1334 of edition of
1756 ; *Autobiography of Sir John Bramston*, 1845, p. 223 ; *Gentleman's Magazine*, vol. i. p. 159, April 1731 ; House of Commons Journals, 28th February
1735, 11th March 1741, 4th and 6th May 1742.
[3] 1 James II. c. 22, 1685.   Evelyn describes his visit to the "elegantly
built" new church in 1684 (*Diary and Correspondence of John Evelyn*, 1859,
vol. ii. p. 211 ; *Handbook for the Parish of St. James's, Westminster*, by Rev.
M. E. C. Walcott, 1850).

church would hardly contain the twentieth part of his flock," it was not until Swift brought the matter forward, in 1709, that it secured sympathetic attention.[1] In a remarkable national spasm of religious fervour, Convocation urged the building of new churches, Queen Anne warmly commended it, and Parliament voted £350,000 without a dissentient vote or outside opposition. The celebrated Act for the erection of fifty new churches, "with towers or steeples to each of them," out of the proceeds of an octroi on coal, created a body of Church Building Commissioners, who were to select the sites, get the buildings erected, and mark off the new parishes. These were to be "distinct" parishes "to all intents and purposes," with the important exception of the levy and expenditure of the Church Rate, the Poor Rate, and the Highway Rate, which remained unaffected unless and until an agreement was arrived at with the authorities of the mother parish. And the Commissioners were expressly directed to name "a convenient number of sufficient inhabitants in each such new parish respectively, to be the vestrymen of such new parish," exercising "the like powers and authorities" . . . as the vestrymen of the mother parish, or "if there be no Select Vestry in such present parish, then as the vestrymen of the parish of St. Martin's-in-the-Fields."[2] Accordingly the Commissioners—the active ones being the Bishops of London and St. Asaph, the Dean of Westminster Robert Nelson and some other church dignitaries—from time to time formulated, at their meetings in Old Palace Yard, Westminster, new and peculiar Vestry constitutions for the eleven new parishes, which were all that got themselves actually established under the Act of 1711. Thus, when in 1724 the parish of St. John was made out of that of St. James's, Clerkenwell, which had an Open Vestry, the new parish was started with a close governing body of the Rector and twenty other persons, owning

---

[1] *Essays on Political Arithmetic*, by Captain Graunt (attributed to Sir William Petty), 1665 ; *A Project for the Advancement of Religion*, by Dean Swift, 1709, p. 22 (p. 105 of vol. viii. of *Works*) ; *The Examiner*, by the same, No. 42, 1710-1711 (pp. 485-489 of vol. iii. of *Works*).

[2] 10 and 11 Anne, c. 11, sec. 20, 1711 ; *Memoirs of . . . Robert Nelson*, by C. F. Secretan, 1860, p. 142 ; *The Church in Danger*, by R. Yates, 1815 ; *Life in the English Church in the Eighteenth Century*, by J. H. Overton, 1887, pp. 163, 428, etc.; *Historical Account of My Own Life*, by Edmund Calamy, 1829-1830, vol. ii., p. 239 ; *Sir Christopher Wren*, by Lucy Phillimore, 1881, p. 307.

no allegiance to the ratepayers.[1] So in 1725 when St. George's, Hanover Square, was separated from St. Martin's-in-the-Fields, it was given a Select Vestry of a hundred and one members "composed," we are told, "of the chief nobility in England."[2] Similarly, in 1728, when the parish of St. John the Evangelist was taken out of that of St. Margaret's, Westminster, the Commissioners nominated a Select Vestry of forty persons, together with the Rector and Churchwardens.[3] These new Vestries were left to find out what were the "powers and authorities" that they possessed, and we see them sending deputations to " attend the Vestry of the said parish of St. Martin's-in-the-Fields to procure a copy of the powers and authorities for ordering and regulating the affairs of the parish "—a request with which St. Martin's apparently complied by supplying copies of the bishop's faculties of 1662 and 1673.[4]

With characteristic incompetence and indifference, Parliament had, as we have seen, left the new Vestries to settle by agreement with the mother parishes whether or not the Church, Poor, and Highway Rates, and the important services to which they related, should be divided.   On this rock the new constitutional vessels were sometimes wrecked. Thus the new Select Vestry of St. John's, Clerkenwell, spent its first fourteen years in a wrangle with the Open Vestry of the mother parish, which steadfastly refused to give up any of its jurisdiction in civil matters.   The antagonistic Vestries levied rival rates, which cautious householders demurred to paying. Surveyors, grave-diggers, and scavengers clamoured for their wages. The Justices and the Court of King's Bench eventually found against the claims of the new Select Vestry, which had, in 1737, perforce to compromise on an agreement to restrict

[1] *A Mid-London Parish: A Short History of . . . St. John's, Clerkenwell*, by W. Dawson, 1885, p. 21.

[2] *New Remarks of London*, 1732, p. 260 ; MS. Vestry Minutes, St. George's, Hanover Square, 1725-1835. The "instrument of the Commissioners . . . for creating a Vestry in the parish " is printed in full in *Acts of Parliament relating to the Parish of St. George's, Hanover Square*, 1839, pp. 19-25. The new Vestry included seven dukes, fourteen earls, two viscounts, seven barons, and twenty-six other persons of title.   The complete independence of the new parish had been enacted in advance by 6 George I. c. 32 (1720).

[3] MS. Vestry Minutes, St. John the Evangelist, Westminster, 1711, 1724, 1729, etc.; *St. John the Evangelist : Parochial Memorials*, by J. E. Smith, 1892, chap. vii. ; *Special and Annual Report of the Vestry of the United Parish of St. Margaret and St. John*, etc., 1889, pp. 76-79.

[4] *A Mid-London Parish*, etc., by William Dawson, 1885, p. 23.

itself to ecclesiastical functions and to the appointment of its own church officers; to allow the election of officers for the whole undivided parish to continue to be held in the open meeting at the mother church; and whilst collecting its own part of the Church Rate by its own Churchwarden, to pay over its quota to the Churchwardens of St. James's.[1] In other cases similar conflicts ended in the compromise of a joint body. Thus the new Select Vestry of St. John's, Westminster, never could agree with that of St. Margaret's as to a division of the civil functions of the parish, though the old Vestry was itself a close body by immemorial custom, and the new offshoot deliberately conducted itself " according to the custom of St. Margaret's." What happened was that, apparently with no legal sanction, a sort of concordat was arrived at. Both bodies went on meeting separately for the business of their respective churches; the new parish levying its own Rector's Rate; each body chose its own Churchwardens and nominated its own Overseers of the Poor; but the members of the two Select Vestries met together for various purposes, including the assessment of the Church, Poor, and Highway Rates, and most of the civil business of the undivided parish, under the title of the " United Vestries of St. Margaret and St. John, Westminster." This extra-legal constitution was gradually ratified by implication in successive statutes— first, as regards a Watch Rate and the appointment of watchmen and beadles in 1736,[2] then by the establishment of a joint-committee of both Vestries, called the Governors and Directors of the Poor, in 1752,[3] and finally, by the well-known series of Westminster Paving Acts.[4]

---

[1] *A Mid-London Parish*, etc., by William Dawson, 1885, p. 28.

[2] 9 George II. c. 17 ; amended by 26 George III. c. 112 (1786).

[3] 25 George II. c. 23.

[4] MS. Vestry Minutes, St. Margaret's, Westminster, 1644-1835 ; *Ibid*. St. John's, 1729-1835 ; MS. Minutes of Watch Committee of the "United Parishes," 1791-1808 ; *Ibid.* of Joint Vestry ; *Ibid.* of Paving Committee ; *St. John the Evangelist : Parochial Memorials*, by J. E. Smith, 1892 ; *History of the Parish Church of St. Margaret*, by M. E. C. Walcott, 1847 ; *A Collection of Acts of Parliament relating to the Local Government of the Parishes of St. Margaret and St. John*, etc., 1837 ; *Special and Annual Report of the United Vestries of St. Margaret and St. John*, etc., 1889, pp. 80-82. In 1797 there was an attempt to bring about a complete amalgamation. In Wilberforce's Diary we read that he "wanted St. Margaret's and St. John's parishes to associate. Vestry meeting. People would not come in to it " (*Life of William Wilberforce*, by R. I. and S. Wilberforce, 1839, vol. ii. p. 222).

After the first flush of enthusiasm of the Church Building Commissioners, the provisions of the 1711 Act as to the government of the new parishes were recognised as anomalous and incomplete; and where additional new churches were built, recourse was usually had to separate Acts of Parliament, more clearly defining the constitution of the new Vestries, and making them the governing authorities for civil as well as ecclesiastical affairs. Sometimes the new Vestries thus created would be close bodies, sometimes not. Thus the great parish of St. Giles's, Cripplegate, partly within and partly without the jurisdiction of the City of London, at the beginning of the eighteenth century probably the most populous single parish in the kingdom, had long been practically divided into two parts for administrative purposes. "The two divisions of the parish (the Freedom and the Lordship)," says a modern chronicler, "each elected its own Churchwardens, Overseers, and Sidesmen, and other parish officers. Each managed the special business belonging to its own district, while for purposes common to both—charities, maintenance of the fabric of the church, etc.—they consulted and voted in one general [Select] Vestry. When from deaths, disqualification by removal out of the parish, or any other cause, the members from one division became fewer than from the other, the general Vestry as a whole elected others resident in that district in which the vacancies occurred to fill the vacant places. The only limit to numbers appears to have been that the one district should not have more representatives than the other. This arrangement for the composition of the Vestry and of its work continued until the creation, in 1732, of the Lordship into a separate parish with its own church of St. Luke, when the general Vestry ceased." The new parish of St. Luke's was then, by Local Act of 1733, equipped with the same constitution as the mother parish had "time out of mind" enjoyed, namely, a Close Vestry of all who had served or fined for parish offices.[1]   But when the great parish of St.

---

[1] *An Account of the Church and Parish of St. Giles's Without, Cripplegate*, by J. J. Baddeley, 1888, p. 163 ; *Records of St. Giles's, Cripplegate*, by Rev. W. Denton, 1883 ; 6 George II. c. 21 (1733); see also Chartæ Miscellaneæ (1635), vol. vii. p. 106 (in Lambeth Palace Library) ; *The State of the Silk and Woollen Manufactures considered . . . likewise the Case of the Parish of St. Giles's, Cripplegate*, etc., 1713 (Bodleian Library) ; *Parish Corrup-*

Dunstan's, Stepney, was at last divided into separate new parishes,[1] although it was itself, as we have seen, governed by a Select Vestry under bishop's faculty, which remained a close body down to 1747 at least, no uniform system was followed. In the new parish of St. Mary, Stratford Bow, established in 1730 out of an autonomous ancient chapelry, the Church Building Commissioners appointed by letters patent a Select Vestry of twelve persons, together with the Incumbent and Churchwardens, the body renewing itself by co-option.[2] The new parish of Christchurch, Spitalfields, on the other hand, was, in 1728, dealt with by a special Act of Parliament, and given a Vestry formed of all who had served in or fined for parish offices, as was the custom in many old parishes in the City of London.[3] Yet, nearly at the same time, the adjoining new parishes of St. George's-in-the-East and St. Ann's, Limehouse, were, by their Local Acts of 1729-1730, given Open Vestries, "of such parishioners" as paid "two shillings a month [in Limehouse twelve shillings a year] and more, towards the relief of the poor, and none else."[4]

tion in part displayed; or a Narrative of some late Transactions in St. Luke's Parish, 1740 ; Place to Hobhouse, 2nd April 1828 (Add. MSS. 35148, vol. i. p. 55); *Times,* 12th January 1829 ; Report of House of Commons Committee on Select and Other Vestries, 1830 ; House of Commons Return of the Churchwardens of the said Parish, etc., 4th August 1832 ; Volume of " Collections as to," in British Museum ; *Proceedings at a Meeting of Parishioners, 1828, on the Subject of Open Vestries,* 1829 ; *Book of the Revelations of St. Luke concerning the Select* [Vestry], 1786.

[1] The division of Stepney into four parishes, viz. Poplar, Limehouse, Stepney, and Spitalfields, had been proposed in 1650 to the Commissioners for inquiring into the state of ecclesiastical benefices, under the Commonwealth ; see *An East End Chronicle,* by R. H. Hadden, 1880, pp. 7, 8 ; *Memorials of Stepney Parish,* by G. W. Hill and W. H. Frere, 1890-1891, p. xi. The MS. Minutes of the mother parish of Stepney are missing from 1747 to 1820.

[2] This constitution lasted until 1829, when it was changed by Local Act, 10 George IV. c. 7, after prolonged local controversy (see *Times,* 27th August, 16th and 26th September 1828, and 11th May 1829).

[3] 2 George II. c. 10; *History of London,* by William Maitland, vol. ii. p. 1350 of edition of 1756 ; Report of House of Commons Committee on the Poor Laws, 1817.

[4] 2 George II. c. 30 (1729) ; 3 George II. c. 17 (1730) ; *History of London,* by William Maitland, vol. ii. pp. 1353, 1361 of edition of 1756 ; *An East End Chronicle : St. George's-in-the-East Parish and Parish Church,* by the Rev. R. H. Hadden, 1880, pp. 14, 15. The reason of this difference of treatment is unknown to us. A petition was presented to Parliament on behalf of the new parishes, objecting to a Select Vestry, and asking to be given an Open Vestry, or at least an elective one. "The inhabitants of the Strand," it continued, " have had a long law-suit about their Church Rate, occasioned by the Select Vestry, doubtless that of St. Mary-le-Strand " (see *The Case of the Inhabitants*

It remains only to be said that when, a century later, Parliament again passed a general Act, and provided large funds, for the building of new churches, the new parishes to be assigned to them by the Commissioners were expressly restricted to ecclesiastical purposes, and the mother parish remained undivided for civil government.[1] These new ecclesiastical Vestries hardly concern the student of local government. Yet it is of interest to note that they were close bodies. The new ecclesiastical districts were each to be furnished with a "Select Vestry . . . appointed by the Commissioners with the advice of the bishop of the diocese, out of the substantial inhabitants of the district . . . for the care and management of the concerns of the church or chapel and all matters and things relating thereto." And as these new ecclesiastical Vestries were expressly empowered to appoint Churchwardens and to levy Church Rates (though litigation arose about the latter point), they could not fail to help the disintegrating influences that were at work on the parish as a unit of rating and civil administration.[2]

(d) *The Close Vestry by Local Act*

The same machinery of a Local Act of Parliament could, of course, be used to create a Close Vestry in an ancient parish, irrespective of any proposal for fission. The most interesting cases in which this device was resorted to, between 1760 and 1820, were those of the extensive parishes of St. Marylebone and St. Pancras, immediately adjoining on the north and north-west those Westminster parishes that we have described as getting bishop's faculties and Church Building Acts during the century before.

of the two new Parishes of Spitalfields and Wapping, in British Museum, vol. 816 m 9 (102). Outside London, Local Acts for providing new parishes with churches sometimes created Statutory Vestries; as at Stockton in 1711 and at Sunderland in 1719, where the Vestry was to be elected triennially by the parishioners (*History and Antiquities of Durham*, by W. Hutchinson, 1794, vol. iii. pp. 129, 523).

[1] 58 George III. c. 45 (1818) and c. 134 (1819); amended by 59 George III. c. 30 (1819); 3 George IV. c. 10 and c. 72 (1822), and 1 and 2 William IV. c. 38 (1831). See *A Digest of the Seven Acts for building . . . Churches*, by G. Bramwell, 1835; and *Ecclesiastical Law of the Church of England*, by Sir Robert Phillimore, edition of 1895.

[2] They were abolished by 14 and 15 Victoria, c. 97 (1851); see *Practical Treatise on Ecclesiastical Law*, by H. W. Cripps, 1886, p. 699.

The ancient parish of St. Marylebone, in 1906 covered with houses, and having 140,000 inhabitants, was, at the close of the seventeenth century, still entirely rural in character; though the thick woods in which Wycliffe's persecuted followers are said to have concealed themselves in 1416 had long since been replaced by pasture fields. Between 1687 and 1708 the total number of persons assessed to the rates was only about 86, and the aggregate rental of the 1473 acres that the parish contains is said to have been no more than £2129 per annum. The minutes and accounts of the Vestry and parish officers, which exist from 1683, show us a parish government of the simplest type, with a group of a couple of dozen farmers, tradesmen, and innkeepers, periodically meeting "in Vestry assembled"; nominating each other annually as Churchwardens and Overseers, Constables and Headboroughs, Surveyors and Scavengers; and levying, on themselves and their neighbours, the twenty or thirty pounds a year that each of the parish officers expended on church or poor, highways or removal of refuse.[1] Gradually the tiny rural "village, about a mile distant from town,"[2] began to be absorbed in the Metropolis. The first considerable outburst of building seems to have taken place about 1716-1720; and even by 1739 there were only 577 houses, with under 4000 inhabitants, on the whole two and a third square miles of the parish. In the next few years, however, the building of new streets and squares proceeded with great rapidity, and the population went up by leaps and bounds. By 1755 the Open Vestry recognised that this growth was far outstripping its feeble powers of government, and it obtained in 1756 a Local Act enabling it to elect a standing Watch Committee, to levy a Watch Rate, to appoint paid watchmen and beadles, to provide lamps, to collect a Lamp Rate, and to arrange for paving, cleansing, and regulating the streets.[3] The ultimate powers of government still rested in

[1] MS. Vestry Minutes and parish accounts, St. Marylebone, 1683-1728; *A Topographical and Historical Account of the Parish of St. Marylebone*, by Thomas Smith, 1833; *Marylebone and St. Pancras*, by George Clinch, 1890; and the authorities cited at pp. 233 and 267.

[2] So described as late as 1760 (*Memoirs of Sir Samuel Romilly*, 1840, vol. i. p. 9).

[3] 29 George II. c. 53 (1756); MS. Vestry Minutes, Marylebone, 1755-1756; House of Commons Journals, 3rd and 15th December 1755, and 18th February

the Open Vestry. For another twelve years the parish muddled on in this way, the little group of attendants at the Vestry meetings, and such of them as annually undertook the duty of the various parish offices, becoming more and more unable to cope with the work. The six amateur Constables, usually publicans or shopkeepers, failed, even with the paid watchmen, to prevent assaults and robberies; the streets went unpaved and uncleansed; the poorer householders would neither put up their own lamps nor pay the Lamp Rate that the Vestry feebly tried to levy; the accounts remained unaudited for years; and in the absence of any public provision for the removal of refuse, the richer inhabitants were reduced to organising a voluntary subscription in order to pay " the person that carries away the ashes." [1] At last the aristocratic proprietors of the new houses could stand it no longer. Quite suddenly, on the 23rd January 1764, we see appearing at the Vestry meeting no fewer than seven peers and four esquires. Under the leadership, apparently, of Lord Foley, this aristocratic irruption dominates the meeting, and carries, then and there, a resolution in favour of an application to Parliament for the establishment of a Select Vestry.[2] The ordinary attendants at the Vestry are furious. For four years the conflict rages between those upholding " the rights of the parishioners paying scot and lot " and those who want more efficient administration than a Marylebone Open Vestry knew how to give. There are petitions to Parliament and counter-petitions. The Vestry·Clerk is summarily dismissed, and a new one appointed after a three days' poll of the parish. In 1764 a Bill for a Select Vestry was defeated, apparently by the influence of the Duke of Portland, the local ground landlord and Whig patron of the living, who refused to co-operate with the predominatingly Tory inhabitants of the large houses. But the Open Vestry was undermined by its own standing " Committee of the Parish," to which it committed the daily administration, and on which several of the

---

1756 ; *Acts of Parliament for regulating the Affairs of the Parish of St. Marylebone*, 1823.

[1] *History of London*, by W. Maitland, vol. ii. p. 1373 of edition of 1756 ; *Marylebone and St. Pancras*, by George Clinch, 1890, p. 110, etc.

[2] MS. Vestry Minutes, Marylebone, 24th January 1764 ; House of Commons Journals, 28th January and 9th February 1764.

aristocratic supporters of a Select Vestry had been elected.[1] At last, in 1767, Parliament passed an Act vesting all the powers of parish government in a close body of the Rector, the two Churchwardens, and a hundred persons named in the Act, among whom the little group of regular attendants at the old Open Vestry were not included, but who were picked apparently from the most distinguished inhabitants, and empowered to fill vacancies by co-option of such "substantial parishioners" as they thought fit.[2]

The development of St. Pancras, which adjoins St. Marylebone on the east, was later and less aristocratic in character. At the close of the seventeenth century, its broad pasture fields had an even smaller population than those of St. Marylebone, and they continued unbuilt on until the very last quarter of the eighteenth century. In 1776 the whole four square miles of the parish had only 600 inhabitants. By 1801 the population had grown with amazing rapidity to no fewer than 31,779, but most of the parish could still be described as a "delightful, luxuriant, and picturesque part of Middlesex."[3] The Vestry Minutes from 1718 onward reveal the usual tiny meeting, regularly adjourning from the old parish church, or "the chapel at Kentish Town," to a neighbouring inn, where money seems to have been freely "spent out of the parish stock for . . . Vestry dinners."[4] They elected the usual parish officers, including a Vestry Clerk at £4 a year, and a Beadle at £5 a year, with coat and staff; and they seem to have managed the affairs of their tiny hamlet in the usual way. But the sudden and over-

---

[1] MS. Vestry Minutes, Marylebone, 1st and 15th February, 19th March, 24th April, 4th and 14th May, and 21st June 1764 ; 17th October and 7th November 1765 ; 10th February 1766 ; 24th February and 8th October, 3rd and 17th November, 11th and 21st December 1767 ; House of Commons Journals, 15th March 1764.

[2] 8 George III. c. 46 (1767) ; MS. Vestry Minutes, Marylebone, 19th January and 5th April 1768 ; *Acts of Parliament for regulating the Affairs of the Parish of St. Marylebone*, 1823.

[3] Tompson's Map, 1804, *St. Pancras Vestry*, 1718-1900, by Walter Brown, 1900, pp. 19-21 ; *Marylebone and St. Pancras*, by George Clinch, 1890.

[4] MS. Vestry Minutes, St. Pancras, 16th July 1718 ; *Some Account of Kentish Town*, 1821, p. 49 ; *St. Pancras Vestry*, 1718-1900, by Walter Brown, 1900, p. 5. In 1635 the Incumbent and Churchwardens reported to the Star Chamber that the parish had, from time immemorial—as they found, from 1575 at any rate—been governed by an Open Vestry (Chartæ Miscellaneæ, vol. vii. p. 108).

whelming increase of population which had set in between 1783 and 1801 had submerged all existing arrangements. From the minutes of this time we see that the Vestry became little more than an active and turbulent crowd, meeting every two or three months in the parish church, to the number of several hundreds, and occasionally exceeding a thousand. At these meetings the inhabitants strove vainly to grapple with the ever-increasing difficulties of assessing and collecting the rates, managing the workhouse, preventing nuisances, maintaining the highways, and furnishing men for the militia. Unlike Liverpool, Greenwich, and Woolwich, it never seems to have occurred to St. Pancras to elect a standing executive committee, or to appoint a staff of salaried officials. The Vestry insisted on doing everything in public meeting, and had apparently no other notion of administration than electing unpaid officers, passing elaborate resolutions, and then appointing committees of audit or inquiry to find out what the last unpaid parish officers had been doing in their year of office. The result was naturally the most scandalous maladministration in every department. The parish business was utterly neglected. The rates remained uncollected. The workhouse was a centre of malversation and inhumanity. Hotly contested elections of Churchwardens and Overseers, accusations of unfairness in the taking of votes, peremptory disallowances of items in the accounts, emphatic resolutions that the Churchwardens should not themselves sell goods to the parish, or incur expenditure not authorised by the Vestry, —all indicate a perpetual state of quarrelling and friction. During the year 1796, the Vestry waged war with the Vicar for not holding enough services. In 1798 it was at loggerheads with the Trustees of the Church Lands for selling a chapel without its permission. In this year there were two sets of Churchwardens, elected by rival Vestry meetings, both admitted, out of prudence, by the timorous Archdeacon, and both appealing to the law courts for confirmation.[1]   At last

[1] MS. Vestry Minutes, St. Pancras, 1783-1800 ; Collection of Papers relating to St. Pancras (made by J. Percival), 2 vols. in British Museum ; *An Address to the Parishioners of St. Pancras from the Trustees of the Church Lands*, 1798 ; *St. Pancras Vestry*, 1718-1900, by Walter Brown, 1900 ; Hansard, vol. iv. p. 510, 30th April 1805 ; *Morning Herald*, 8th April and 10th June 1805 ; *An Act for the Better Government of the Poor of St. Pancras*, 1805 ; 44 George III. c. 47 (1804) ; 45 George III. c. 99 (1805).

the strong man appeared who was to reduce this turbulent democracy to submission. From 1796, if not earlier, one Thomas Rhodes, the great-uncle of Cecil John Rhodes of South African fame, occupied 282 acres of pasture land in the parish, and carried on an extensive business as a cow-keeper and brickmaker. In 1802 we see him getting himself elected Churchwarden, and causing a committee to be appointed to inquire into the scandals of the workhouse and the non-collection of rates. During the next seventeen years we trace, in these interesting Vestry minutes, the machinations of Mr. Rhodes and his party, who, apparently despairing of any reform of the Open Vestry, aimed persistently at its abolition. His first step was to bring before the Vestry a report of his committee to the effect that the parish has become too populous for unpaid officers, and recommending the promotion of a Bill to enable the Vestry to appoint a paid staff. The Vestry is already suspicious of Mr. Rhodes' intentions, but it authorises the preparation of a Bill as suggested, with the significant rider "that this application to Parliament be restricted to this object only, and that the draft of the said Bill be laid before the Vestry previous to the application to Parliament." But this was not enough for Mr. Rhodes. At a subsequent meeting he got the committee reorganised, and obtained authority to include also the building of a new workhouse. The Bill was drafted and formally presented in manuscript to the Vestry, who refused to adopt it without examination, and ordered five hundred copies to be printed and circulated. It was then discovered that the measure was not confined to the modest proposals which the Vestry had approved, but that it contained clauses ousting the Open Vestry from all Poor Law work, in favour of a "Committee of Guardians, elected in perpetuity, and self-continued." The Vestry indignantly refused to sanction such a Bill, as being "subversive in its principles of the most valuable franchises of the parishioners at large," and ordered the Vestry's own solicitor to oppose its further progress. This opposition killed the Bill for that session, but Mr. Rhodes was not to be denied. In the winter there came up a sensational report from his committee on the workhouse. Every possible scandal was shown to exist. Three thousand yards of linen

had been paid for, but the paupers were found destitute of
decent clothing. The expenditure on beer "for nurses sitting
up with the sick" exceeded £200 in one year. The building
habitually contained twice as many inmates as it could
properly accommodate. The committee concluded that at
least one-third of the workhouse expenditure was fraudulent
or illegitimate, and insisted that the management must be
placed in the hands of a permanent committee. The Vestry
gave way so far as to agree to a Bill providing for the
appointment of a body of Directors of the Poor, to be
periodically elected by the Vestry. This compromise was
embodied in a Bill which got through Parliament without
opposition in 1804. But no sooner were the Directors of
the Poor in office under this Act than they themselves
promoted an amending Bill, making themselves members for
life, with power to co-opt their successors, and freeing themselves from any control by the Vestry, except that the Vestry
was to choose seven Auditors out of twenty-one persons to
be submitted by the Directors. This treachery roused the
Vestry to fury, and frequent angry meetings denounced the
iniquitous Bill. But the Vestry had by this time an evil
reputation in Parliament, and Mr. Rhodes got the Bill
through. The Open Vestry was thus stripped of its principal
business, but it still met to elect Churchwardens, Overseers,
and Surveyors of Highways; to pass the accounts; and to
express its opinion on parish and political affairs. This state
of things lasts for ten or twelve years, during which the
parish continues to increase by leaps and bounds. The levies
of the Directors of the Poor rise enormously with the growth
of population and of pauperism, and their secret and irresponsible administration leads to the usual complaints. In
1817 and 1818 an agitation sprang up to get "the Directors'
Act" repealed, as "inimical to the true and genuine interests
of the parish . . . and vesting all authority in the hands of
those who hold their offices for life, are elected by their own
body, and are responsible to no one but themselves." The
Vestry promoted a Bill to abolish the Directors of the Poor,
and these retaliated by one to abolish the Open Vestry. The
Parliament of 1818-1819 was not sympathetic to democratic
ideas; and Mr. Rhodes, who still appeared as the chief

organiser on the unpopular side, was able to score a final victory. In May 1819 an Act was passed completely extinguishing the Open Vestry, expressly forbidding any such body to meet for the future, and transferring all property and powers, both of the Vestry and of the Directors of the Poor, to a Select Vestry of persons named in the Act, and entitled to fill up vacancy by co-option.[1]

(e) *The Constitutions of Close Vestries*

So much for the origin of the Close Vestries. Diverse in their source, they were no less diverse in their size and membership. Along with the one dominating feature of perpetual succession—the renewal of the corporate body by the device of co-option—there went every variety of constitution. Many Select Vestries by immemorial custom—notably those in the old parishes of the cities of London and Bristol—

---

[1] 59 George III. c. 39 (1819). These proceedings can be best followed in the MS. Minutes of the Open Vestry, 1802-1819 ; of the Directors of the Poor, 1806-1819 ; and of the Select Vestry, 1819-1833 ; see also Hansard, 30th April and 10th June 1805, and 15th April 1818 ; Report of Select Committee on Select and Other Vestries, 1830 ; *Case of the Vicar, Churchwardens, and other Inhabitants . . . of St. Pancras* (in support of the 1803 Bill) ; *An Act (1819) for establishing a Select Vestry in the Parish of St. Pancras in the County of Middlesex, and for other purposes relating thereto*, 1836 ; *St. Pancras Vestry, 1718-1900*, by Walter Brown, 1900 ; *A Narrative of certain Statements and Proceedings connected with the Select Vestry of the Parish of St. Pancras*, by E. W. Hamilton, 1831 ; *Substance of a Speech delivered by Henry Revell, Esq., before a Special Board of the Select Vestry of the Parish of St. Pancras*, 1831. Attempts were made in some other parishes to follow the example of St. Pancras. Thus, when in 1821 it was proposed to rebuild the church of St. Mary's, Newington, the very words of the St. Pancras Act of 1819 were inserted in the Bill. This led to excited public meetings in the church, where over 2000 inhabitants denounced the project, which was defeated by the aid of a fund subscribed for the purpose. (See the pamphlets, *St. Molly's in a Hurry, or Scribo Scratchum's Picture of a Select Vestry*, 1821, and others in British Museum, 10350 b. 5, together with the two Reports of the House of Commons Committee on Select and Other Vestries, 1830.) It appears from the minutes of other Vestries that the alarmed inhabitants of Newington sent round printed forms of petition against giving such "unprecedented, arbitrary, and alarming powers" to a close body. The Mitcham Vestry petitioned Parliament against the Bill (MS. Vestry Minutes, Mitcham, Surrey, 16th May 1821. So did that of Christchurch (Surrey), see *Morning Chronicle*, 11th May 1821. In 1823 a Bill was promoted to establish a Select Vestry for Mile End Old Town, but was defeated by the efforts of the Radical inhabitants ; see *Times*, 4th June 1827 and 25th March 1828. The inhabitants of St. Saviour's, Southwark, who had got rid of their old oligarchy about 1730, were warned in 1828 that "a Select Vestry was in preparation" for them (see the handbill in British Museum, 45 h. 13).

were composed, along with the Incumbent and Churchwardens, exclusively of " those who had served or fined " as Church-wardens, or in one or other onerous parish office. In these cases the number of the Select Vestry was undefined, and the inclusion of persons who paid the fine to escape service in the parish offices could be used (since it was the Select Vestry itself that elected) as a means of co-opting to membership any wealthy inhabitant deemed worthy of admission.[1]   Where, as in the other type, the Select Vestry consisted of a definite number of persons, these had often been named in the originating instrument, resolution, or statute, though more frequently the number itself was only traditional.   In either case the body might consist of anything between a dozen and over a hundred members.   In every recorded instance the principle of status brought in a certain *ex officio* element.   The Incumbent of the parish was always a member of the close body; the Churchwardens were nearly always members; the Overseers of the Poor less frequently; [2] whilst here and there the Constable

---

[1] " But, be it observed, no person can fine for an office till he has been put in nomination, and no person can be put in nomination but by one of the Select ; consequently their power of appointing each other is almost as plenary as that enjoyed by those Vestries composed of a limited number" (*Considerations on Select Vestries*, 1828, p. 28).   Such a process of electing and fining we see recorded in the following, from the Vestry Minutes of St. Bartholomew the Great, in 1698.   The parishioner who had been chosen as Churchwarden " was admitted to a fine for Upper Churchwarden, and paid a fine of ten pounds, and Mr. S. R. was chosen Under Churchwarden for the remaining part of the year and paid his fine of ten pounds," and both of them were chosen vestrymen. " Mr. T. D. was chosen Under Churchwarden for the remainder of the year. Mr. T. D. paid his fine of ten pounds and was chosen a vestryman.   And at the same time Mr. T. P. was chosen Under Churchwarden for the remainder part of the year " (MS. Vestry Minutes, St. Bartholomew the Great, City of London, 26th January 1698).   This Close Vestry actually took upon itself in 1783 to alter its composition by offering membership for money.   " This Vestry taking into consideration that by sundry deaths lately happening and removals occasioned by the late dreadful fire in the parish, the number of vestrymen has been so reduced that it is with difficulty a sufficiency can be collected to transact the necessary business of the parish, resolved, that all inhabitants . . . who had served or paid a fine to be excused serving the offices of Constable and Collector of the Consolidated Rate, and are desirous to be excused serving all other parish offices, and shall . . . pay . . . £15, shall be excused thereby and admitted a vestryman " (*ibid.* 20th November 1783).

[2] The Close Vestry of St. Martin's-in-the-Fields not only excluded the Overseers, but tried also to exclude the Churchwardens.   Thus, in 1661, "upon a serious conference whether the Overseers of the Poor ought to be in the Vestry and to have voices in nominating of parish officers . . . decided in the negative " (MS. Vestry Minutes, St. Martin's, 11th April 1661).   In the following year a similar question arose as to the Churchwardens.   But it was shown that

or Surveyor of Highways would also sit as a colleague. In
Northumberland and Durham, as we have seen, there lingered
a shadowy connection with the tenure of land. Occasionally
(as at Morpeth) there would be some traditional division of
the Four-and-Twenty into " town " and " upland " or " country,"
or (as at Lancaster and Preston) a third of the members would
represent the Municipal Corporation. It was a peculiarity of
many of the Metropolitan Close Vestries that they always
included a considerable number of persons of rank and
distinction. The Close Vestry established by bishop's faculty
or under the Church Building Acts occasionally included some
ecclesiastical or other local dignitaries, whilst those established
by Local Acts usually had in their ranks such important
personages as Justices of the Peace or members of Parliament.
The specially aristocratic composition of the Select Vestry of
St. George's, Hanover Square, has been already referred to.
" We have always," said a Marylebone vestryman in 1830,
" made a point of having as many noblemen and members of
Parliament as we could get hold of." [1] The Select Vestry of
St. Margaret's, Westminster, habitually numbered among its
members the Speaker of the House of Commons, a peer or two,
several members of the House of Commons, and a number
of gentry. St. Martin's-in-the-Fields in 1724 had five
noblemen, four baronets or peers' sons, and thirteen esquires,
out of a total of forty-eight.[2] In St. Giles's-in-the-Fields the
Close Vestry included not only peers, but also two Chief
Justices, and two other judges. " The general understanding
has been," it was said in 1830, " that we should have a
mixture of rank and character throughout the parish." [3] This
was systematised by the Select Vestry of St. James's, Piccadilly,
into a primitive " three-class system," under which " the custom
has been to elect one-third noblemen, or thereabout, one-third
gentlemen of rank and members of Parliament, and the other

"anciently the Churchwardens have been sat one on the right hand the other
on the left hand of the Vicar," and on that evidence it was "agreed that the
present Churchwardens do take their places at the Vestry table " (MS. Vestry
Minutes, St. Martin's, 28th August 1662).

[1] First Report of House of Commons Committee on Select and Other Vestries,
1830, p. 32.

[2] MS. Vestry Minutes, St. Martin's-in-the-Fields, 1724.

[3] First Report of House of Commons Committee on Select and Other Vestries,
1830.

third tradesmen, men of business." [1]   The Close Vestries
established by Local Act practically always included *ex officio*
members, and they pass, almost imperceptibly, into the class
of statutory bodies (not called Vestries, and described as
Incorporated Guardians of the Poor or Street Commissioners
in Book IV. of this work), some of which included all persons
of a certain status, whilst others admitted a partial representation of the ratepayers.

---

[1] First Report of House of Commons Committee on Select and Other Vestries,
1830, pp. 135, 136.   The Earl of Bristol notes in 1701 that "I was chosen
into the Vestry of St. James, and took my place there" (*Diary of John Hervey,
First Earl of Bristol*, by S. H. A. Hervey, 1894, p. 34).   When a committee of
parishioners sought, in 1829, to reform this Select Vestry by Act of Parliament,
their proposal was to carry a similar "three-class system" into the election.
The Bill provided that "a meeting of the parishioners rated at or above £30 per
annum should elect by ballot forty-five vestrymen from the following grades of
parishioners, viz. one-third from out of persons rated above £150, one-third
rated from £100 to £150 ; and one-third rated from £50 to £100."

CHAPTER VI

CLOSE VESTRY ADMINISTRATION

THE most interesting question for the student of these Close
Vestries between 1689 and 1835 is the effect, good or evil,
which their characteristic feature, renewal by co-option, had on
their procedure and administration. Our conclusion may seem
paradoxical. It is that these Close Vestries display not only
the utmost variety, but also greater extremes even than may
be found in the parishes in which this peculiar constitution
did not exist. Some are more timid, others more audacious in
the use of their multifarious powers than "the inhabitants in
Vestry assembled." Some are seen to sink permanently to
the lowest depths of venality and maladministration; whilst a
few reach a level of efficiency and honesty not attained by any
other parochial authorities. Without repeating our description
of parish government, we must indicate some of the differences
of the Close Vestries from those with which we dealt in our
last chapter.

(a) *Provincial Close Vestries*

It is characteristic of the Northumberland and Durham
Select Vestries, resting only upon immemorial custom, that
they felt their position to be insecure as regards the levy of
any rate other than the ancient Church Rate, and especially as
regards the administration of eighteenth-century statutes. In
these parishes where the "Twenty-Four" or the "Twelve"
exercised undoubted control over matters relating to the church,
we rarely find them giving much attention to the poor relief
or road maintenance. Such parish business was, we infer,
left in the main to the uncontrolled discretion of the Overseers

and Surveyors whom the Justices appointed.[1]   And we have
evidence that not only was it an invariable custom to give
public notice in church ("from the desk") of every meeting of
the Four-and-Twenty, but also that there were occasional
public meetings open to all the inhabitants for the resolution
of matters of supreme importance.   Thus, in Bywell St. Peter,
Northumberland, where the Twenty-Four have held sway since
the beginning of the earliest records, we find them summoning
meetings of the inhabitants in 1719 to ask the magistrates to
divide the parish into four independent townships for Poor Law
purposes; in 1725 to revolutionise the basis of the parochial
assessment, by changing it from equal lump sums "per plough"
or hereditament, to a regular pound rate on the value thereof;
and in 1781 to decide on a rate for the maintenance of the
families of the militiamen taken from the parish.[2]

The precarious authority of these Northumberland close
bodies over the civil affairs of the parish is well illustrated by
the history of that of St. Michael's, Alnwick.   Here we find the
"Four-and-Twenty," from 1693 to 1798, not only managing
church business, electing Churchwardens and levying the
Church Rate, but also nominating Overseers and Surveyors of
Highways, supervising the list of outdoor paupers, appointing
a "doctor to the poor," ordering the officers to sue on bastardy
bonds, levying a special rate for the cost of bounties to
volunteers for the militia and the navy, and formally deciding
which roads should be kept in repair by the parish.   When,
however, in 1785 they wanted a workhouse, they felt it
necessary—possibly because of the terms of the Act of 1723—
to obtain the authority of "an assembly or public meeting of
the Churchwardens and Overseers of the poor . . . and of the
parishioners or inhabitants," at which, as the minutes carefully
record, "it is consented to and agreed" that the Churchwardens
and Overseers shall buy a house for the poor and contract for
their maintenance.   The workhouse, once started, is evidently
left to the management of the Select Vestry.   But, in 1798,

---

[1] The "Gentlemen of the Four-and-Twenty" did occasionally themselves
levy a Poor Rate ; as at Warkworth in 1729, when they voted "twice and a half
the book of rates for or upon account of the poor for this running year" (MS.
Vestry Minutes, Warkworth, Northumberland, 14th April 1729).

[2] Vestry Minutes, Bywell, Northumberland ; see the paper on "Bywell" by
Rev. A. Johnson, *Archæologia Æliana*, vol. xiii. pp. 89-166.

a year of troubles at home and abroad, the parish of Alnwick had its own little revolution. On the 20th of March 1798, instead of the private gathering of the "Gentlemen of the Four-and-Twenty," we have "a meeting of the Churchwardens, Overseers, and parishioners and inhabitants," a new set of signatures appearing in the minute book. It is "ordered that all meetings in future shall be called for the Churchwardens, Overseers of the Poor, parishioners and inhabitants to meet in the Vestry on business relating to the poor according to the several statutes in that behalf made." This Open Vestry, holding five meetings within seven weeks, itself makes a Poor Rate of twopence in the pound, appoints a committee to prepare a new valuation of the parish, increases the scale of outdoor relief, levies a Church Rate, and takes the precaution to remind the Vestry Clerk to keep possession of the books. In the following year, however, this energetic Open Vestry finds itself defied by the Overseers whom the Justices had appointed, and unable to get in even its Church Rate. By Easter 1800 the revolution is over. The meetings of the old Four-and-Twenty, now for the first time styling themselves a Select Vestry, are quietly resumed, and we hear no more of the reformers. It is, however, significant that all Poor Law business disappears from the Select Vestry minutes, to be managed, we assume, by the Overseers, under supervision of the Justices. When in 1806 it becomes necessary to rebuild part of the workhouse, a public meeting is once more held to give authority to the Churchwardens and Overseers to enter into a contract with the builder.[1]

In the populous town of Gateshead, and still more in the old parish of St. Nicholas, Newcastle-on-Tyne, we find the position of the "Four-and-Twenty" even weaker than at Alnwick. At Gateshead, in the seventeenth century, the Four-and-Twenty ruled the town, and were, indeed, of sufficient importance in 1658 to be summarily removed from office by an Order in Council of Oliver Cromwell himself.[2]

---

[1] See, for all this, MS. Vestry Minutes, Alnwick (Northumberland), 1744 to 1829 ; *History of Alnwick*, by George Tate, vol. ii. 1868, p. 140.

[2] We think this Order worth reprinting :—

"Tuesday, 22 of June 1658.—At the Council at Whitehall. Upon reading a certificate from Robert Fenwick, Henry Ogle, Esq., and John Topping, Governor of Tinmouth, touching the government of Gateside in the County of Durham,

After the Restoration the body was again purged, and fell, we gather, into disrepute. In 1676 it was restored to activity, it having been found that, for lack of such a body, "the rights and privileges of the said town and parish are much weakened and decayed." At the beginning of the nineteenth century we find them still managing the executive business connected with the church, annually electing the Churchwardens, and nominating a list of ten persons for appointment as Overseers. But there are also frequent meetings of the inhabitants, which nominated Surveyors of Highways, and apparently dealt, though only occasionally, with all sorts of parish business. In the old parish of St. Nicholas, Newcastle, much the same organisation existed, though here it seems that the " Four-and-Twenty " did not even elect the parish officers, and considered themselves only as the standing executive of the Open Vestry. We must add that, both at Gateshead and at Newcastle, the distinction between a meeting of the " Four-and-Twenty " and that of the " inhabitants in Vestry assembled " was throughout this whole period only nominal, as the attendance appears always to have been confined to about a dozen of " the principal inhabitants." Both parishes found it convenient to summon open public meetings in order to adopt Sturges Bourne's Act, and to elect at such meetings a representative " Select Vestry," or Parish Committee, for poor law purposes, without abandoning any part of the existing organisation.[1]   Thus,

in pursuance of an Order of the 6th of April last, forasmuch as it appeareth that divers of the Four-and-Twenty of Gateside are persons who, by the Humble Petition and Advice, are disabled from exercising any place or office of public trust, and are guilty of profaneness and divers other crimes, so as they are not fit to be intrusted in that employment, Ordered by his Highness and the Council that the present Four-and-Twenty of Gateside aforesaid be discharged from exercising any power or authority in the said town, and that [24 names] inhabitants of the said town be, and they are hereby nominated to be from henceforth the Four-and-Twenty there, and to exercise the same power and authority, and to do all and every the things in reference to the said town and the inhabitants thereof, and the election of officers, and of such as shall succeed in the place of any of the before named persons dying, as the former Four-and-Twenty might lawfully do and exercise. Henry Scobell, Clerk of the Council" (MS. Vestry Minutes, Gateshead (Durham), June 1658). This Order is also given in *Memoirs of the Life of Mr. Ambrose Barnes*, Surtees Society, vol. l. 1867, p. 384.

[1] In R. *v.* Woodman and others (*Reports of Cases*, etc. by R. V. Barnewall and E. H. Alderson, 1821, vol. iv. pp. 507-510) it was held, about 1821, that Sturges Bourne's Act could be adopted in a parish having a Four-and-Twenty,

between 1820 and 1832, at the time when Leeds and
Manchester were distracted by turbulent mass meetings, and
when even Liverpool's equanimity was shaken by frequent
polls, Newcastle and Gateshead jogged sleepily along in
perfect peace, the ancient "Four-and-Twenty," the new
Select Vestry, and the periodical meetings of the inhabitants
at large, all working harmoniously with each other and with
the Justices of the Peace.

The same uncertainty of footing, with the same concurrent existence of an Open Vestry, is found at an earlier
date in the case of the Close Vestry of Richmond in Surrey,
which was established by the Bishop of Winchester's faculty
in 1614.[1] Notwithstanding this creation of a close body,
serving for life and renewing itself by co-option, the little

but that the meeting to elect the Select Vestry under this Act must be open to
all parishioners, and that the Four-and-Twenty was neither disturbed in its
lawful functions thereby, nor entitled to take any part in the matter. The
Four-and-Twenty of Morpeth parish had from time immemorial been made up of
sixteen from the township of Morpeth, and eight from the farmers in the other
townships of the parish. In 1820 the Churchwardens and Overseers of Morpeth
township, which apparently maintained its own poor, had summoned a meeting
of the sixteen to elect a Select Vestry under Sturges Bourne's Act. This was
held invalid, as the right was in the parishioners at large. (A similar decision
was given in 1831 with regard to an immemorial Close Vestry in a City of
London parish ; see R. *v.* Churchwardens and Overseers of St. Bartholomew the
Great, in *Reports of Cases* by R. V. Barnewall and J. L. Adolphus, 1832, vol.
ii. pp. 506-514.) Morpeth was evidently excited about its case in 1820. In
the *Memoirs of Dr. Robert Blakey*, edited by Rev. Henry Miller, 1879, we
read, "When I came back to Morpeth [about 1820], after six years' absence, I
found the place was full of contention about the poor rates of the parish. They
had got into sad entanglement under the sole management of a self-elected
body. I wrote three pamphlets and many smaller squibs on the disputes in
support of popular rights. The courts of law had ultimately to determine the
contest and gave the award to the people" (p. 33). We have not found copies
of Blakey's pamphlets, nor any other records of the controversy. In 1833 the
Gateshead Open Vestry, with the Rector in the chair, before electing the
members of the Select Vestry under Sturges Bourne's Act, resolved "that it
be an instruction to the Select Vestry to be appointed this day, to request the
Four-and-Twenty of this parish to give up to the parish at large the rights of
election of the parish officers, which they now exercise by virtue of ancient
usage, so far as they can legally do so" (MS. Vestry Minutes, Gateshead,
19th April 1833). Eleven months later we find the Four-and-Twenty, with
the same chairman, resolving, in reply, "that the parish would derive no
benefit by the proposed alteration, and that under the present circumstances it
is not expedient to change the mode of electing the parish officers" (MS.
Minutes, "Four-and-Twenty," Gateshead, 19th March 1834).

[1] The MS. records of Richmond extend, with some gaps, from 1596, but
they do not contain the faculty itself, though it is repeatedly referred to.
Separate volumes record the proceedings of the Close Vestry and of the open
meetings of parishioners.

parish oligarchy, which seems to have met as an Open Vestry
down to that date, went on periodically assembling for various
purposes—to nominate Surveyors of Highways, to audit the
accounts of the Churchwardens, to choose "an afternoon
lecturer," and occasionally to vote a Church Rate for extraordinary repairs.[1]   What was left to the "Gentlemen of the
Vestry," whom the bishop had appointed, was the executive
administration, first of the church, including the allotment of
pews, and then of such mundane affairs as the reassessment
of the parish for the Poor Rate, the keeping out of "strangers"
likely to become chargeable, the supervision of the parish
officers, and the distribution of the parish charities.[2]   But
there was evidently no clear line of demarcation between
their respective powers and duties.   Sometimes a Churchwarden is chosen by "the other Churchwardens and the rest
of the Gentlemen,"[3] sometimes by the open meeting, with
more or less definite confirmation by the close body.[4]   Gradually the meetings of the close body dwindle away.   From
1717 onwards we see the open meeting of parishioners more
and more asserting its supremacy.   By its command a workhouse is built and a separate workhouse committee is elected.
The election of Churchwardens takes place by a regular poll
of the parish.   The meeting arranges with the complacent
Justices that no accounts of parish officers are to be allowed
unless they have first been audited by a committee elected by
the inhabitants, "who conceive that, as subjects of the Crown
of Great Britain, they have a native right to look into the
accounts of the disposal of all such monies as are levied on
them."[5]   From 1717, in short, the "Gentlemen of the Vestry"
seem to have accepted the position of a standing executive
committee for such minor church business as the allocation
of pews, the collection of pew rents and ecclesiastical fees, and
the administration of these funds and some parish charities.
Under the leadership of Charles Selwyn, an undistinguished

[1] MS. Minutes, Open Vestry, Richmond (Surrey), 1st April 1656 ; 28th
March 1665 ; 25th April 1671 ; 26th December 1707, etc.
[2] Ibid. Select Vestry, Richmond, 17th April 1655 ; 24th April 1671 ;
17th October 1714, etc.
[3] Ibid. Open Vestry, Richmond, 30th August 1658.
[4] Ibid. Select Vestry, Richmond, 7th June 1625, etc.
[5] Ibid. Open Vestry, Richmond, 25th October 1725.

member of a distinguished family and an energetic Justice of
the Peace, the open meeting develops into the real governing
authority of what had become an aristocratic residential centre,
apparently managing neither better nor worse than others of
the period. Then comes, in 1734, a gap in the records, and
the next thing we find is the suppression of both open
meeting and Close Vestry by a statutory body of trustees for
poor relief and municipal administration, under Local Acts of
1766 and 1785.[1]

An even more interesting example of administration by
a Close Vestry is afforded by the " Company of the Four-and-
Twenty " of Braintree in Essex, called also " the Headboroughs," the " Townsmen," the " Town Magistrates," and
the " Governors of the Town," who, for at least 150 years,
administered practically all the local authority of a town
described by Defoe as " large, rich, and prosperous, and made
so originally by the bay trade." When or how they arose and
what was their connection with the ancient Manor of Braintree,
long in episcopal hands, is entirely unknown. The parish of
Braintree had been formed out of the larger parish of Rayne
in the twelfth century, and made a market town. Whether
the " Four-and-Twenty " date from this period is perhaps
doubtful. In the sixteenth century we find them actively at
work, renewing themselves by periodical co-option, and forming
a curious body half-way between a gild and a municipal
Court of Aldermen. " When a vacancy occurred, which might
be by ' decay, removal, death, or by becoming scandalous by
drunkenness, whoredom, or other evil life,' the other members
agreed amongst themselves and sent a message to the person
agreed upon, inviting him to become one of ' the Company,' and
to dine with them, which, if he accepted, he was thenceforth
considered as duly placed in his office. Each of them was
' steward ' or head of the Company for one month, and they once
a month dined together." [2] We may infer that their authority

---

[1] 6 George III. c. 72; 25 George III. c. 41 ; *The Richmond Vestry*, by Charles
Burt, 1890 ; *Richmond and its Inhabitants from the Olden Time*, by Richard
Crisp, 1866 ; *Historical Richmond*, by E. B. Chancellor, 1885 ; *History and
Antiquities of Richmond*, by the same, 1894.

[2] Information kindly furnished by Mr. H. S. Cunnington of Braintree, to
whom we are indebted for permitting us access, not only to all the old records
of the Four-and-Twenty, but also to interesting and valuable materials for a
local history as yet unpublished. Brief mention of the Four-and-Twenty is

was, at the outset of the seventeenth century, not altogether un-
questioned, as they found it convenient, in 1612, to strengthen
their position by a faculty from the Bishop of London, in whose
diocese Braintree was then situated, and to whose predecessors
the Manor had belonged down to the Reformation.[1] Fortified
by this authority, these " Four-and-Twenty of the Chief
Inhabitants" were, in 1620, meeting monthly, at ten in
the morning, at each other's houses in turn, appearing, " in
orderly manner in cloaks or gowns," after notice " by the
sexton's tolling of the great bell ten strokes"; taking their
seats round the council table in strict order, "as in their
seniority they shall be placed in the church," and not "removing up and down, in or out," until the business was
done. Each gave counsel in his turn as he sat, the youngest
beginning; and if there was a difference of opinion, the vote
was taken " by putting their balls into the box brought into
the company for that purpose." When the business was
done, the Company, including the Vicar, adjourned, " to the
place where dinner is provided," the meal—limited to " three
dishes, according to the ancient custom, unless it be in
Lent"—being provided by each member in turn, either at
his own house or at one or other of the two principal inns.[2]
On Sunday the " Gentlemen of the Four-and-Twenty " and
their wives proudly occupied eight rows of " stools " in " the
Four-and-Twenty seat," a large pew which we hear of as

made in *History and Antiquities* of . . . Essex, by Philip Morant, 1768, vol.
ii. p. 398 ; *A New and Complete History of Essex*, by a Gentleman (Peter
Muilman), 1770, vol. i. p. 416 ; *History and Topography of* . . . *Essex*, by
Thomas Wright, vol. ii. p. 17 ; *People's History of Essex*, by D. W. Coller,
1861, p. 413 ; and, as hereafter mentioned, in the MS. Minutes, Quarter
Sessions, Essex, 1680 and 1713.

[1] The faculty, dated 24th September 1612, is printed in *History and
Antiquities of* . . . *Essex*, by Philip Morant, 1770, vol. ii. pp. 398, 399. It
refers in the usual terms to "the general admittance of all sorts of parishioners
into their Vestries "; and this common form,cannot be taken as evidence of
fact. But it is definitely stated in a local history that the custom was
temporarily broken in 1611 (*New and Complete History of Essex*, by a Gentleman
[Peter Muilman], vol. i. pp. 416, 417), and restored by the faculty. It is not
without significance that, in the old minute book containing the records of the
annual choosing of parish officers, the form of entry changes in 1611, and that
it is from that date that the term " Vestry " is used in it.

[2] MS. Standing Orders of the Four-and-Twenty, 1620, countersigned as
approved by the Lord of the Manor (Earl of Warwick). The Lenten exception
to the maximum number of dishes implies that this Puritan " Company " so far
observed Lent as to restrict itself to fewer than three dishes during that season.

constructed in 1577, and which is still standing in the south aisle of the old parish church. From various entries in a volume of Churchwardens' accounts extending from 1581 to 1719, we infer that open meetings of parishioners were also held—at any rate after 1611—and that these were called Vestries. Exactly how the parish officers were chosen is not clear. The open meeting and the Four-and-Twenty each had a hand in it, one "confirming" the other's choice. But we gather that, in practice, the offices were, without competition, filled by the members of the Four-and-Twenty serving in rotation. Only very occasionally do we find the open meeting passing any resolution, and then only on such matters as keeping order in church and the scale of fees levied for burials. It was at the monthly meetings of the Four-and-Twenty that all the town's business was done. We see these so-called Headboroughs or Town Magistrates, in the first half of the seventeenth century, keeping a close supervision of all the poorer inhabitants, putting children out as apprentices, peremptorily finding service for "masterless" men and women, and sternly banishing unauthorised "inmates" from the town.[1] The rulers of Braintree evidently took the Poor Law of the time very seriously. Case after case of a man or a woman "who has no service" is disposed of by commitment to the House of Correction, apparently without any need for the warrant of a Justice of the Peace. By an agreement with the adjoining township of Bocking, a mutual prohibition of migration from the one place to the other was made, the intention being evidently a reciprocal exclusion of "undesirables."[2] It is interesting to find—in close analogy to the allocation of the Aldermen of London, Norwich, and Bristol to particular wards—that each two members of the Twenty-Four of Braintree had their own "walk" or district of the town, for which they were made personally responsible, being constantly called upon jointly to "survey" their "walk," report the number of households, discover what "inmates" they had, bring up the names of "journeymen that live in the town contrary to law, find out such persons as absent themselves from church," and detect any cases of unlicensed

---

[1] MS. Vestry Minutes, Braintree (Essex), 1619-1630.
[2] *Ibid.* 2nd August 1630.

selling of ale. It is even agreed, in 1634, "that every one of the Company shall walk his particular circuit and collect the gratuity of the town, and shall take notice of the poor, and take their names." [1] In 1667 they have to "look after . . . disorders that shall be committed upon Lord's Days," and to perambulate their precincts for this purpose, with the constables, "at least twice" on every Sunday. [2] Unlike most Close Vestries, the Four-and-Twenty of Braintree—perhaps thus indicating a manorial origin—seem not to have recruited themselves by choosing outsiders to serve or fine as Churchwardens, and then admitting them to membership of the close body, but to have kept all the parish offices in the hands of those who were already members, who had thus to serve in turn as Constables, Churchwardens, Overseers, and Surveyors. [3] This plan, it may be observed, made the Four-and-Twenty more than usually independent of the other ratepayers, but at the cost of rendering onerous personal service to the town. The only other local authority was, in fact, the Court Leet ; and of this, as we have ascertained, the Jury, at any rate in the seventeenth century, habitually consisted, for the most part, of the members of the Four-and-Twenty. The Court Leet appointed as Constables the members whom the Four-and-Twenty had selected, and also Ale-tasters, Flesh-tasters, and Sealers of Leather, but it left the work of government practically to the Four-and-Twenty. [4] All parish accounts were rendered to them ; and they took it in turns to serve as Auditors, according to the stools on which they sat in church, and the little rota of Auditors for the time being decided, there and then, what new rate was required. [5] The Churchwardens and Overseers, like the Con-

---

[1] MS. Vestry Minutes, Braintree (Essex), 1st December 1634.

[2] *Ibid.* 1st July 1667.

[3] "It's now agreed that Constables, Churchwardens, and Overseers . . . shall be yearly elected out of the company" (*ibid.* 13th April 1629). "It is agreed that there shall be a Surveyor chosen, being one of the company, every year as it falls to every one by turn" (*ibid.* 7th April 1634).

[4] MS. Minutes, Court Leet, Braintree, 1616-1830.

[5] "Mr. Burnett's seat and that beyond it are to take in the Overseers' account. Mr. Daniel Waller's seat and that beyond it are to take in the Churchwarden's account. Mr. John Debnam's stool and that beyond it are to take in the Constable's account. Mr. Jeffrey's seat and that beyond it are to take in the Surveyor's account" (MS. Vestry Minutes, Braintree, 4th May 1635).

stables and Surveyors, acted, in fact, as the executive officers of the governing council. Nor did they confine themselves to Poor Law business. In 1619 they ordered "the chief street of this town to be cleaner kept, for all the country speak shame of it."[1] They repaired the town pump[2] and the church steeple;[3] they ordered a drain to be constructed;[4] they made good the timberwork on "the bridge to London Road";[5] they had the town fire buckets put in order and renewed,[6] and they "scavenged the streets."[7] They were enterprising enough in 1632 to buy "an engine, . . . such an one as is in use in London . . . for the common good of the parish, to quench any fires that may befall."[8] They appointed a Bellman, a Beadle, and a "Keeper of the Cross and Market Bushel."[9] They were diligent in enforcing the licensing laws, and in taking care that the number of licensed houses was not increased. From first to last we see no trace of corruption, partiality, or jobbery. The members of the Four-and-Twenty, as we have seen, even paid out of their own pockets for their monthly dinners, and were evidently always subscribing money for charitable objects. At no little expense of time and money to themselves, this little company of "ancients" fulfilled what they doubtless felt as their obligation to give both deliberative and executive service in the administration of their community. But the end of their authority was at hand. In 1682 the number of "the Company" was not complete. The trade of the town was in decay, and several vacancies had remained unfilled. The Court Leet Jury was apparently no longer made up of the members of the Company. Some sort of local rebellion took place. The four Constables whom the Court Leet had appointed refused to render their accounts to the audit committee, on the plea that they had already rendered them to other persons—presumably to an Open Vestry meeting. The Four-and-Twenty appealed to Quarter Sessions to sustain

---

[1] MS. Vestry Minutes, Braintree, 12th July 1619 ; 25th July 1625.
[2] *Ibid.* 3rd April 1620.   [3] *Ibid.*
[4] *Ibid.* 3rd September 1621.   [5] *Ibid.* 4th December 1626.
[6] *Ibid.* 7th January 1621 ; 2nd December 1633.
[7] *Ibid.* 25th July 1625.   [8] *Ibid.* 1st October 1632.
[9] *Ibid.* 3rd January 1625 ; 7th December 1629 ; 2nd December 1639 ; 4th May 1691.

the authority consecrated by "ancient usage," and the Justices made an order to this effect, qualifying it, however, by providing that "any other inhabitants" might, if they chose, be present at the yearly rendering of accounts, "so as they do not give disturbance to the persons nominated to take the accounts."[1]   This decision maintained the position of the Select Vestry for another generation.   New standing orders were agreed to, and "the Company" filled up its vacancies and pulled itself together to fulfil its administrative duties. Presently, however, the power again broke in its hands.   In 1711 the four Constables of the year once more refused to account to the Select Vestry, which again had recourse to Quarter Sessions.   After a long and careful hearing, in which counsel appeared for both sides, and a local magistrate gave evidence as to the virtues of the Four-and-Twenty, the assembled Justices, apparently, were unable to bring themselves to sanction a continuance of the close body.   They therefore brought about a compromise, which they embodied in an authoritative order of 14th April 1713.   By this the Court directed that "the ancient usage and custom ought to be observed," but "for quieting the minds of the parishioners and prevention of future differences," the existing vacancies in "the Company" are to be filled by popular election, all resident owners and occupiers paying scot and lot to have votes.   Moreover, future vacancies, as they occurred, were to be similarly filled by popular election.[2]   In fact, the Essex Justices, in Quarter Sessions assembled, took upon themselves, without any sort of legal authority, to frame a new constitution for the parish of Braintree on the basis of a popularly elected committee—a constitution, to say the least of it, as entirely "extra-legal" as that of the quaint old "Company of the Four-and-Twenty" which it was to supersede.

This pouring of the new wine of Whiggish doctrine into old Tory bottles was not a success.   For a few months "the Company"—reinforced, we must assume, by the elected members—meets monthly as before, and dines at the accustomed village inns.   But the old savour of company member-

---

[1] Order of Quarter Sessions, Essex, 13th July 1680.
[2] MS. Minutes, Quarter Sessions, Essex, 14th April 1713; MS. Vestry Minutes, Braintree, July 1713.

ship, the mild romance of exclusiveness, the subtle sense of historic continuity, had all been lost. The "cameraderie" among the Four-and-Twenty, fostered by a hundred and fifty years of unbroken succession by gradual co-option, could not long survive the chilling effect of intrusion by popular election. The dinners which had formed the central feature of the old Company quickly became irregular, and (as members continued to have to pay for themselves) presently ceased. Within a year the mere attraction of service on the Four-and-Twenty seems to have failed to secure the members' attendance at meetings. From 1716 onwards all trace of their existence disappears, and the minute books record the meetings and transactions of a Vestry of the normal type, nominally open to all ratepayers, but in practice attended only by a little handful of past and present parish officers, whose activities are restricted to the barest minimum.

(b) *Metropolitan Close Vestries*

Surveying all the examples that we have studied, we may say generally that, in the provincial Close Vestries resting their claim on immemorial custom or bishop's faculty, there was, between 1689 and 1835, a shrinkage in the functions of the close body, and in some cases its partial or complete supersession by an open meeting or representative committee. This was not the tendency in the Metropolis. In the small but wealthy parishes within the City of London, the immemorial Close Vestries, equally with those having open meetings of inhabitants, occupied themselves (as did the very similar bodies within the City of Bristol) mainly with the election of Churchwardens, the management and repair of the church, the payment of a lecturer or curate, the levying of a Church Rate, and the distribution of the parish charities. Within the jurisdiction of the Lord Mayor and Court of Aldermen, many of the civil functions of the parish, especially those relating to the thoroughfares and to the police, were dealt with, as we subsequently describe, by wardmote or Precinct meeting. Close Vestries outside the City boundaries were often in much the same state. For one reason or another, many of them had little or nothing to do with poor relief. The great highways were often in the hands of Turnpike Trusts, whilst the new streets springing up on all sides would frequently be managed by estate trustees, or by Street Commissioners for paving, lighting, and watching, to be subsequently described. On the other hand, some of the Close Vestries within the so-called City of Westminster (which never acquired as a city any effective municipal organisation), together with those of Marylebone and St. Pancras, united in their grasp powers of administration and taxation that make the contemporary Open Vestries of Chelsea and Kensington seem by comparison mere village debating societies, and even put into the shade the considerable achievements of the well-organised representative Vestries of Woolwich and Greenwich. It is true that in many, perhaps in nearly all, the Metropolitan parishes there existed, side by side with the Close Vestry, a sort of latent power to call an open meeting of the inhabitants, which we find, now and again, at long intervals, voting on such matters as the choice of a lecturer or afternoon preacher, the election of this or that parish officer, or the reassessment of the parish —usually, as we understand it, by way of fortifying the position taken up by the close body. This very occasional intervention of a public meeting was of small account, and did not seriously interfere with the continuous administration of the autocratic Close Vestry. In other cases the powers were curiously shared between the close body and the inhabitants at large. Thus, in St. Mary-le-Strand in 1732, the Vestry is described as " Select, but the parish choose one Churchwarden." [1] So, at the same date, it was said of St. Leonard's, Shoreditch, that its vestry was " Select, unless for rating of books or choosing of parish officers, which is done by the whole parish."

[1] *New Remarks of London*, 1732. In St. Stephen, Coleman Street, and St. Martin, Ludgate Hill, the Vestry is described as " general in most cases " or " Select in some cases." The extensive collection of MS. records of City Vestries in the Guildhall Library affords other instances. In Hackney, covering five square miles to the north-east of the City of London, we find a curious dual government. The earliest parish archives, in the latter part of the sixteenth century, indicate the existence of a purely rural Open Vestry of the ordinary type. In 1613, as already mentioned, we have the establishment of a Close Vestry by bishop's faculty, and when this had been disturbed, " by reason of the late rebellion," a new faculty was granted in 1679. During the eighteenth century the parish had been, Maitland tells us, " deserted by the nobility, yet it so greatly abounds with merchants and other persons of distinction, that it excels all other villages in the kingdom, and probably upon earth, in the riches and opulency of its inhabitants, as may be judged from the great number of persons

No consistent line of division between the functions of the close body and that of the public meeting can be detected, except that the details of routine church administration fell always to the close body. Thus, at St. Giles's-in-the-Fields, where a bishop's faculty of 1628 had created or confirmed a Select Vestry, it was reported to the Star Chamber in 1635 "that our parish business of greatest moment, as for building and finishing of our church, and fencing in our churchyard . . . are propounded, debated, and ordered by a meeting of all the who keep coaches therein" (*History of London*, by Wm. Maitland, vol. ii. p. 1366 of edition of 1756). These opulent merchants were not excluded from parish affairs. Alongside the Select Vestry, and apparently always on the best of terms with it, there was a continuous series of open "parish meetings," usually held every few months, presided over by a Churchwarden, assisted by the Vestry Clerk, and sometimes attended by several score of people, including some of the Select Vestry. It was these Parish Meetings that nominated to the Justices, the Surveyors of Highways, and voted the Church Rates. Down to 1764 they even made the Poor Rate. They chose the lecturer or afternoon preacher ; they audited the accounts of the Churchwardens and Surveyors ; they even regulated the election of the Parish Clerk. They were specially active in resisting encroachments on the commonable lands, and, after 1800, they carried on a long feud with the Rhodes family (of whom we have already heard in connection with St. Pancras), who had obtained the sanction of the Lord of the Manor to extensive enclosures for brick-making and building purposes. A private Bill to exempt their estate from the Highway Rate, and enable it to provide its own paving, etc. was stopped by the Parish Meeting in 1823. The Select Vestry—sometimes referred to as "gentlemen of the parish"—went on acting as a sort of standing executive committee, presently joined in this position by what were virtually other standing committees formed by Local Acts (the "Poor Board," under Acts of 1763 and 1810 ; the "Lamp Board," under that of 1763 ; and the "Church Trust," under those of 1790, 1795, and 1803). The Parish Meeting even disposed of "the unappropriated funds" of the parish, by which was meant the proceeds of the fines exacted by the Select Vestry from persons who refused to serve the parish offices. In these circumstances, it is scarcely surprising that when, in 1833, the Close Vestry was seriously attacked, and pronounced by counsel to be unlawful, it ceded its position without resistance, and both Parish Meeting and Select Vestry were merged in an Open Vestry. See MS. Vestry Minutes, St. John, Hackney (Middlesex), containing the records of both Parish Meetings and Select Vestries, 1762-1833 ; the Local Acts 4 George III. c. 43 (1763) ; 30 George III. c. 71 (1790) ; 35 George III. c. 70 (1795) ; 43 George III. c. 102 (1803) ; 50 George III. c. 93 (1810) ; 54 George III. c. 91 (1814) ; House of Commons Journals, 4th May 1713 ; Hansard, vol. xxvii. p. 325, 30th March 1814 ; *Times*, 20th February 1830 ; *Customs and Privileges of the Manors of Stepney and Hackney*, 1736 ; *A Statement of Facts showing the Abuses that exist in the Management of the Affairs of that Parish*, by William Cotton, 1830 ; a MS. "History and Antiquities of the Parish of Hackney," by John Thomas, 1830 (in Tyssen Library, Hackney) ; *The Hackney Magazine and Parish Recorder*, 1833-1836 ; *Ideal Horsewhipping, Facts relating to . . . Vestry Clerk of Hackney*, etc., by Chas. Green, 1834 ; *Collectanea Geographica, Historica, Biographica, Litteraria, Generalogia, Heraldica et Miscellanea de Hackney*, by Caleb Thomas, 1842 ; *History and Antiquities of Hackney*, by Wm. Robinson, 1842-1843 ; *The Hackney Journal*, 1842 ; *The Healthiness of the Hackney District*, by Samuel Roper, 1842.

parishioners in general, but the ordinary business of smaller moment, as assessments for the poor, highways, choice of yearly officers, 'and such other like business, are ordered by a select assembly of the parson, churchwardens, and other ancient inhabitants of the parish, which hath, time out of mind, been called the Vestry." A directly opposite division was made in St. Magnus, near London Bridge, where " the business of the greatest importance," such as the selling and letting of land, was done by the close body ; and such matters as choosing officers were left to the public meeting. On the other hand, at St. Botolph, Aldersgate, where a close body had been established by faculty in 1606, the Select Vestry claimed, in 1635, only " the matters of the church," and reported that " the other public affairs of the parish touching the choosing of Scavengers, Constables, and Questmen, and such like . . . have beyond memory used to be ordered by the parishioners at their meetings in their several precincts, with the assistance of the alderman of the ward for the time being, or his deputy." [1]

A greater constitutional innovation was the practical absorption by the close body, not only of the powers of all the parish officers and of the inhabitants in Vestry assembled, but frequently also of those of the Justices of the Peace. Thus, in the records of St. Martin's-in-the-Fields, Westminster, we watch the close body and its little committees sitting alternately as a Select Vestry and as a Petty Sessions of the Westminster Justices. Evidence was given before a Committee of the House of Commons in 1742 " that the Vestry give notice to the Justices and order them to attend when there is to be a day of appeal, but that the Vestry attend likewise, and the business is done in a Vestry ; that the Justices give a sanction to it, but that they are mere cyphers, and that the Vestry govern and manage all these matters; and that there are generally eight or ten vestrymen present and sometimes two Justices, sometimes one, and sometimes none at all; and that the Vestry do what they will in everything." [2] This

---

[1] MSS. in Lambeth Palace Library, Chartæ Miscellaneæ, vol. vii. St. Olave, Hart Street ; St. Michael, Crooked Lane ; Allhallows the Less ; St. Alban's, Wood Street ; St. John Baptist upon Walbrook ; St. Stephen, Coleman Street, and St. Mary, Aldermary, also report this double constitution in 1635 (*ibid.* pp. 5, 18, 19, 28, 41, 80, 109).

[2] *Report of the Committee to whom the Petition of the Principal Inhabitants of*

enabled the Vestry, by its own members, not only to appoint
any Overseers, Surveyors, and Constables that it chose, and
to pass their accounts, but also to make any orders it chose in
bastardy cases and removals of paupers, to issue its own distress
warrants on non-payment of rates, and even to hear and decide
the appeals against its own assessments.   The result was to
place the close body in a position of complete uncontrolled
authority, and to deprive the inhabitants of all opportunity of
appealing against its action, except such as might be afforded
by the expensive and dilatory machinery of appeal to Quarter
Sessions or the Court of King's Bench.   And it was at any
rate no disadvantage to the Select Vestries, whenever their
action and their title were thus questioned in the law courts,
that so many of the judges should themselves be Select
Vestrymen.[1]

These indirect and illegitimate powers of the Metropolitan

... *Westminster (so far as it relates to* ... *St. Martin's*) ... *was referred,* 1742,
p. 8.   This practice seems to have grown up between 1723 and 1742.   In 1723
the Vestry is still in the position of passing a resolution asking " the Justices of
the Peace of this parish " to make the Scavengers account to the Vestry (MS.
Vestry Minutes, St. Martin's-in-the-Fields, 23rd April 1723).   In 1728-1729 two
Justices in succession are co-opted into the Vestry (*ibid.* 13th September and
3rd October 1728 ; 25th March 1729).   In 1729 we hear already of "Petty
Sessions Vestries," of which the Vestry Clerk keeps the minutes.   Thus it is
" ordered that no Overseers of the Poor of this Parish shall (except upon sudden
and emergent occasions) relieve out of the moneys collected for the relief of the
poor of this parish, any person but what are and shall be agreed to at *a Petty
Sessions Vestry,* or a committee thereof, or by particular order from a Justice of
the Peace " (*ibid.* 4th March 1729).   Between 1772 and 1789 the minute
books record the frequent meetings of Justices in Petty Sessions ; those attending being always members of the Select Vestry, and meeting either in the Vestry
Room or in a committee room at the workhouse.   In 1793 the Vestry formally
thanks two Justices for their frequent attendance (*ibid.* 1st February 1793).
In 1833 additional magistrates are asked for, expressly "to do the ordinary
business of the parish" (Home Office Domestic Entry Book, 11th March 1833).
The business consisted principally of appeals against the Poor Rate, the enforcement of the rates against defaulters, and the audit of the Overseers' accounts.
For the Report of such a Court of Petty Sessions, held in the St. Martin's Vestry
Room by Sir Rd. Birnie, the well-known police magistrate, and himself a member
of the Select Vestry, see *Times,* 5th January 1827.

[1] The sessions of these parochial Justices were expressly recognised by 32
George III. c. 53 (1792), and the fees to be taken by the Vestry Clerk as clerk
to such Justices were specially allowed (when all other fees outside the public
police offices were abolished) in proceedings before such Justices acting within
the parishes in which they reside in enforcing parish taxes or assessments, or
the provisions of Local Acts.   In 1805 and 1818 we see such Close Vestries as
those of St. Margaret's, Westminster, and St. Andrew's, Holborn, suggesting
the names of parishioners to the Home Secretary for appointment as Justices,
expressly to do the parish business (Home Office Domestic Entry Book in
Public Record Office, vols. xli. and liii.).

Close Vestries were, in these parishes, often consolidated and supplemented by statutory enactments. When Parliament granted additional powers of parish government by Local Act, it was disposed to entrust more to the close body than to the meeting of inhabitants in Vestry assembled. The close body had, in fact, a great advantage over the Open Vestry in the promotion and passing of private Bills. The drafting and "lobbying" could be undertaken in secrecy. It was easy for the close body to engage and pay the best professional assistance, including the clerks of the House of Commons itself, who in those days acted as Parliamentary Agents. The important Select Vestries of the Metropolitan Parishes, freely co-opting peers and members of the House of Commons, could always appeal for support to their own members in either House. Thus, when about the year 1788 a committee of the inhabitants of St. George's, Hanover Square, opposed a Bill which the Select Vestry of that parish was promoting, "they found a very thin attendance of the House, but a very large attendance of such members as are of the Vestry, of which there are a great number." [1] And if any watchful member objected to the grant of new powers to irresponsible bodies, he could always be met by production of the names of the eminent and representative personages who figured among the vestrymen. "When you look at the list of the Vestry," said a vestryman of St. Giles's to one objector, "and see Lord Tenterden, Chief Justice Best and the judges, and such respectable persons on the Vestry, how can you imagine anything can be going on wrong?" [2] These potent personages might themselves neglect to attend Vestry meetings, but they were singularly helpful to those who did attend.

The extent and variety of the statutory powers thus secured would excite the envy of the most ambitious of modern municipalities. The great parish of St. Marylebone, for instance, the rise of which we have already noticed, further doubled its population between 1800 and 1835.[3] Its

[1] *Case of the Inhabitants of St. George's, Hanover Square* (n.d. ? 1789), p. 2.
[2] Report of House of Commons Committee on Select and Other Vestries, 1830, p. 20.
[3] Population in 1801, 63,982 ; in 1831, 122,206. In 1901 it was only 133,301, so that already by 1835 it must have been nearly as fully populated as it is at present.

Select Vestry of 123 members, established, as we have seen, by Local Act of 1768, met in secret, published (until after 1820) absolutely no accounts, and autocratically ruled the parish. By virtue of no fewer than eight successive Acts of Parliament, it had accumulated in its own hands an amazing array of governmental powers. It assumed to itself, to begin with, all the large and indefinite powers of the parish and all the parish officers, who became themselves mere subordinates. It appointed a committee which managed the poor and distributed relief by its own officers, independently of any appointment or audit by the Justices. It fixed the assessments absolutely without appeal, and levied, without limit or control, no fewer than four distinct rates. Under its series of Local Acts it paved, cleansed, and lighted the streets, carried out improvements, maintained a force of paid watchmen, administered the parish charities, and regulated the personal conduct of the inhabitants by innumerable clauses prohibiting specific nuisances. When we add to all this that it built new churches, and paid the salaries of a whole staff of parish clergymen, we need not be surprised to find that it had, by the year 1828, piled up a parish debt amounting to nearly a quarter of a million sterling.[1]

Passing from the extent of the powers of these Vestries to the way in which they exercised whatever powers they had, we find the same extreme diversity. If, indeed, we were to believe even one-half of the evil ascribed to Close Vestries, from Daniel Defoe in 1714 down to Francis Place in 1830, we should dismiss their activity as one continuous series of ' gross abuses, impositions, and oppressions.[2] " Select Vestries," said a blunt critic in 1754, " are select companies of rogues." [3]

[1] The well-kept MS. minutes of the Marylebone Vestry, which are unusually full and detailed, afford abundant materials for its history ; see also the authorities cited at pp. 205 and 267 ; the incidental references in the *Times*, 7th and 19th June 1828 ; 3rd March 1829 ; 17th February and 1st April 1830 ; and *Sunday Times*, 13th April 1828 ; the volume of accounts entitled *Receipts and Expenditure of the Parish of St. Marylebone, 1798 to 1819-1820* ; *The Acts of Parliament for Regulating the Affairs of the Parish of St. Marylebone; printed by Order of the Vestry*, 1823, 459 pages ; the subsequent edition of 1832 of 491 pages, set up by a different local printer ; and the Report and Evidence of the House of Commons Committee on Select and Other Vestries, 1830.

[2] See *The Vestry laid Open; or, a full and plain detection of the many Gross Abuses, Impositions, and Oppressions of Select Vestries*, by Joseph Phipps, 1739.

[3] *The Constitutional*, quoted in the abusive reply written on behalf of the Select Vestry of St. Paul, Covent Garden, *The Select Vestry justified*, 1754, p. 14.

But any careful student of the minutes and other records of
the different types of these close bodies will arrive at a more
discriminating conclusion.   We must, in the first place,
distinguish between the Select Vestries of London and those
elsewhere; and we ought, moreover, to compare them, not
with a well-organised modern municipality, but with such
contemporary Open Vestries as those of Liverpool or Greenwich,
Leeds or Chelsea.

The first point that strikes the investigator is naturally
the superior continuity of the Select Vestry : for years
together these little committees pursue the same policy in
guiding or controlling the annually-changing parish officers.
How far this continuity was advantageous depended, it is
obvious, on whether the policy suited the needs of the parish,
and whether it was honestly carried out.   The close bodies of
the Northumberland and Durham parishes seem to have
differed in no way from the typical Parish Oligarchy of
similar districts.   The more self-assured close bodies which
ruled the little manufacturing town of Braintree (down to
1713), and the ancient parish of St. Mary's, Reading (during
the eighteenth century), seem to have added to the advantages
of continuity and superior control over the parish officers a
somewhat larger measure of honesty and enlightenment than
was possessed by the parochial administrators of the majority
of the smaller urban districts of the time.   On the other
hand, there can be no doubt that a large majority of the
Select Vestries in the Metropolitan area during the eighteenth
century sank to the lowest depths of venality and peculation,
accompanied not infrequently by positive cruelty and oppression.   We need not describe in detail the innumerable
"venison dinners" and other Gargantuan repasts ; the guzzling
at every meeting ; the frequent drives "in glass coaches" to
inspect the paupers, children, or lunatics in the suburban
institutions, and the other petty perquisites of the London
vestryman of this period.   More serious was the arrangement
by which all the supplies for the workhouse, and all the work
done for the parish, was shared among the little knot of
shopkeepers and contractors who formed the acting body of
the vestry, and who complacently allowed each other to charge
the parish the most extravagant prices for goods short in

weight and adulterated in quality. "These Select Vestries," it was said in 1828, "are a focus of jobbing: the draper supplies the blankets and linen; the carpenter finds the church pews constantly out of repair; the painter's brushes are never dry; the plumber is always busy with his solder; and thus the public money is plundered and consumed. . . . If the honest Overseers visit a few pauper lunatics at Bethnal Green, the journey is so long and their nerves so shaken that adjournment to a tavern is indispensable, and the evening closes with a flaming supper. Another visit to the distant town of Greenwich to catechise the nurses of some pauper children is wound up by a glorious dinner."[1] Every department of the parish administration was distorted by the same corrupt partiality. The streets in which the vestrymen lived were often the only ones that were paved or cleaned or lighted. Their assessments were usually scandalously lower than those of ordinary parishioners, and in some places it was an understood thing that the collectors should never call for their rates. And parish after parish would, like St. Sepulchre's, or Christchurch, Spitalfields, go in for an extravagant building or repairing of churches, often, as the evidence clearly shows, with the express object of securing for individual members of the Vestry a series of profitable contracts at the parish expense. In short, the administration of the majority of Metropolitan Close Vestries, throughout the latter part of the eighteenth century and often well into the nineteenth, had all the characteristics that we have described in our section on the Uncontrolled Parish Officers, with the significant difference that in the case of the Close Vestries the mal-administration and peculation were continuous, far more free from any control by the Justices of the Peace, and wholly exempt from the spasmodic interruptions or partial ameliorations brought about by the appearance, in the meetings of inhabitants in Vestry assembled, of knots of more or less determined reformers.

But even among Metropolitan Close Vestries there were exceptions to this continuous pandemonium of peculation and jobbery. Sometimes a powerful Select Vestry would begin

---

[1] *Sunday Times*, 1828, quoted in *Considerations on Select Vestries*, 1828, p. 49. Rowlandson, in 1806, had a caricature of vestrymen guzzling, which, as a matter of course, he entitles "A Select Vestry."

well, gradually deteriorate, and end badly.   Thus in St. Martin's-in-the-Fields the succession of gentlemen—colonels, knights, and baronets—whom we find attending the Close Vestry for fifty years after the Restoration, seem, from the records, to have managed the affairs of this great parish with wisdom and integrity.   They effectively controlled the expenditure of the Churchwardens and Overseers; they viewed the highways and levied a money rate for their repair; they consulted Sir Christopher Wren as to the repairing and furnishing of their church; for the lax pension-list of the Overseers they substituted a workhouse; they engaged a doctor to visit the sick poor; they set up a school in which poor children were maintained and taught; when the Scavengers fraudulently collected excessive rates, and the Beadles neglected their duty, these officers found themselves promptly prosecuted.[1]   It is therefore not surprising that St. Martin's had, in 1714, the reputation of being the best-governed parish in Westminster.   But, as a matter of fact, the rot had already set in.   From the very beginning of the eighteenth century the attendances of "the gentlemen" fall off.   Gradually we perceive that their place has been taken by a clique of local shopkeepers.   Sinister reports now get about, and a House of Commons Committee in 1716 reports considerable laxity in the accounts, exposes apparent neglect in the collection of the large rates that are levied, and hints at collusion between the Vestry Clerk and the collectors. The failure of the Parliament of 1716 to effect any reform, and, still more, the successful resistance of the Select Vestry in 1742 to an attempt to assert the rights of the inhabitants at large, seem to have encouraged the vestrymen in their corrupt practices.   It was in vain that the House of Commons in 1743, as we shall presently describe, exposed the gross partiality òf the parish assessments; the excessive expenditure on sacramental wine, and the flagrant overcharges of the vestryman glazier who repaired the broken windows, and the vestryman candlemaker who supplied the candles for the watchmen's lanterns.   Meanwhile the Vestry was obtaining

[1] We may note that, until his murder in 1678, Sir Edmund Bury Godfrey, the most active of the Westminster Justices, was a member of this Vestry; he was, in fact, known as "the mouth of the Vestry" (*Brief History of the Times*, by Sir Roger L'Estrange, 1688, vol. iii. pp. 381/4).

from Parliament new powers of taxation and government to enable it to deal with the growing needs of the parish; and the miasma of corruption quickly spread from the church and the workhouse to the newer services of paving, lighting, and cleansing the streets. In 1773 a public-spirited Justice of the Peace, Robert, afterwards Sir Robert, Taylor,[1] becomes a member of the Vestry, and we watch, for a dozen years, his persistent efforts to reform and reorganise what by this time had become a powerful municipal body. Resolutions prohibiting the taking of parish contracts by vestrymen or parish officers, peremptorily forbidding public expenditure on eating and drinking, and insisting on paid officers residing in the district and giving their whole time to their work, are passed and repassed with wearisome iteration. Disorderly public-houses are now regularly reported to the Justices' Sessions, unlicensed "dram-shops" are hunted out and prosecuted, and Sunday closing is enforced. Unfortunately, on Taylor's death in 1789 the other vestrymen quickly slip back to their old bad habits. In policy the Vestry continues vigorous enough, levying and spending an ever-growing revenue. But no student of the contemporary evidence can doubt that, between 1800 and 1835 at any rate, the secret and irresponsible administration of the little gang of local tradesmen who wielded this large revenue covered every kind of petty jobbery, corrupt partiality, and reckless waste.

The administrative career of the United Vestries of St. Margaret's and St. John's, Westminster, shows alternations of honesty and corruption. Beginning the eighteenth century well, and displaying throughout energy and continuity of policy, these two Vestries gradually lose the attendance of their better members, and sink into the same morass of squalid corruption as did the neighbouring parish of St. Martin's-in-the-Fields. In 1814 "a great proportion" of the vestrymen and Directors of the Poor "hold contracts for supplying the workhouse." One vestryman had enjoyed for many years the lucrative privilege of supplying all the bread required for the army of paupers, at the price which he himself fixed, without

---

[1] Sir Robert Taylor (1714-1788), perhaps the leading architect of his day, was knighted in 1783 on serving as Sheriff. He was the father of Michael Angelo Taylor, whom we shall hereafter have occasion to mention, and the founder of the Taylorian endowment for modern languages at Oxford.

even the pretence of competition. " An opinion seems to have been entertained," we learn, " that the parish officers were not assessed to the rates for the relief of the poor," but this, it is explained, " is erroneous, for these persons are actually rated the same as other inhabitants, but, fortunately for them, their rates are never collected ! " [1] But the Close Vestries of St. Margaret's and St. John's were capable of reform, and the exposures of 1814 seem to have led to some permanent improvement in honesty. In 1830 the most hostile of critics, the Radical tailor, Francis Place,[2] admits that their vestrymen, being " well known and respected, secure a better administration than is usual." [3]

[1] *Thoughts on the late Inquiry into the System of Parochial Government of the United Parishes of St. Margaret and St. John*, 1814, pp. 12, 24, etc. It was an ancient custom that those who collected the Royal taxes should be exempted from contributing in return for their services. It was therefore natural that the parish collectors should assert a similar privilege. But there was no legal warrant for it.

[2] Place to Hobhouse, 2nd April 1830 (Add. MSS. 35148, p. 35). For the history of this parish see the MS. Vestry Minutes ; its petition in House of Commons Journals, 28th February 1696, vol. xi. ; the report of a committee of inquiry in 1742, *ibid.* vol. xxiv. p. 250 ; the investigation made by a parochial committee about 1814, reported in *Thoughts on the late Inquiry into the System of Parochial Government of the United Parishes of St. Margaret and St. John*, 1814. See also *A Collection of Acts of Parliament relating to the Local Government of the Parishes of St. Margaret and St. John*, etc. 1837 ; Report and Evidence of the Committee on Select and Other Vestries, 1830 ; *St. John the Evangelist, Westminster, Parochial Memorials*, by J. E. Smith, 1892 ; Special and Annual Report of the Vestry of the United Parish of St. Margaret and St. John, etc. 1889.

[3] The ancient parish of St. Bartholomew the Great in the City of London, governed from 1606 onwards by a Close Vestry of those who had served or fined as "Upper Churchwardens," seems—from its well-kept records from 1662 and from the paucity of hostile criticism—to furnish another example of relatively honest administration. Here the close body, at any rate for a very long period of its existence, welcomed into its ranks any respectable inhabitant who was willing to serve the parish offices, or pay the customary fine, and we are inclined to think that it was justified in its resolution, in response to Sir John Cam Hobhouse's letter of inquiry, to the effect that "this Vestry, conscious of its own integrity, anxiously invites Parliamentary inquiry" (MS. Vestry Minutes, St. Bartholomew the Great, 15th May 1829). The worst that could be said of it in 1830 was that it kept its accounts secret, indulged in "Vestry suppers," and had not made all the assessments equal. (See its return to the Star Chamber inquiry in 1635, Chartæ Miscellaneæ, vol. vii. p. 36 ; MS. Vestry Minutes 1662 to 1835 ; *Times*, 4th March 1830 ; Report of House of Commons Committee on Select and Other Vestries, 1830 ; House of Commons Journals, 15th January 1755 ; 28 George II. c. 39 (Lighting and Watching Act, 1755) ; 9 George III. c. 23 (ditto, 1768) ; R. *v.* Brain, 1829-1832, in *Reports of Cases*, by R. V. Barnewall and C. Cresswell, 1832, vol. i. pp. 614-627 ; R. *v.* Churchwardens and Overseers of St. Bartholomew, 1831, in *Reports of Cases*, by R. V. Barnewall and J. L. Adolphus, 1832, vol. ii. pp. 506-514).

In the newer parish of Marylebone, of which we have already described the early history, the Close Vestry, between its establishment by Local Act in 1768, and its abolition in 1834, ran up the rates and indulged in no little administrative extravagance, but it does not seem to have been either inefficient or dishonest. Here the nobility and gentry of the neighbourhood were continuously represented on the " Committee of Management." This body met weekly, and from time to time displayed considerable energy and foresight in parish affairs. It put the paving, scavenging, and lighting out to contract, but exercised constant supervision over the contractors, and certainly did not, in these services, fall below the standard of the time. It had a little police force of its own, which increased between 1800 and 1829 from about one hundred to over three hundred, composed of superintending constables appointed by the Justices, sergeants armed with muskets and cutlasses, and watchmen carrying ash staves. The public-house keepers were supervised with strictness, and often reprimanded or prosecuted for the usual offences. There were active inspectors of weights and measures. A sharp look-out was kept on Parliamentary proceedings likely to affect the parish, and one of the clerks of the House of Commons was paid a retaining fee to keep the Vestry informed on the subject. In 1812 and following years we find the Vestry vigilant in protecting the public interests against the promoters of Bills entrusting large powers to canal and water companies ; in 1815 it energetically opposed in Parliament the severe Corn Law, excluding all importation of corn so long as wheat was under eighty shillings per quarter ; in 1808-1812 it found brick earth on its land, and used it, through a contractor, for manufacturing all the bricks required for parish work ; it sank its own wells for water ; and in 1819 it even made an ineffectual attempt to obtain Parliamentary power to supply the whole parish in competition with the water companies— action which resulted at least in its getting the companies' charges greatly reduced.[1]

There was, indeed, one Close Vestry which attained a

---

[1] MS. Vestry Minutes, Marylebone, between 1800 and 1834 ; see the argumentative summary of grievances, and the Vestry's reply in *Sunday Times*, 13th April 1828.

higher level of efficiency and integrity than any other contemporary local authority, and enjoyed a remarkable freedom from adverse criticism of either policy or administration. In all the attacks made on the Metropolitan Close Vestries between 1731 and 1743 we do not find it suggested that the noblemen and gentlemen of St. George's, Hanover Square, levied rates illegally, imposed offices with partiality, made uneven assessments, committed acts of petty jobbery, wasted the public money in dinners, or used any effort to escape publicity. The minutes and other records of this parish from 1725 onward, reveal the Select Vestry as a little knot of public-spirited peers and gentry who governed this great and wealthy parish with consistent honesty, and, relatively to the standards of the time, with exceptional efficiency. From the outset we see the Vestry taking complete control of all the parish business, and, with the assent of the local Justices of the Peace, placing the Overseers of the Poor in the position of subordinate officers acting under a systematic code of instructions.[1] They promptly organised a salaried police force, to the astonishment of some of the inhabitants, who preferred the older system of voluntary watch and ward.[2] In the great Parliamentary inquiry of 1742 this Close Vestry was subjected to severe scrutiny, but no allegations of corruption were made against it, and the committee reported that it had conducted affairs to the benefit and advantage of the parish. "Inhabitants of figure," observed Lord Kames in 1770, "not excepting men of the highest rank, take it in turn to be Churchwardens, which has reduced the Poor Rate in that parish to a trifle."[3] In later years the Select Vestry, strengthened

---

[1] MS. Vestry Minutes, St. George's, Hanover Square (Middlesex), 1st February 1727.

[2] "In 1727 the Vestry of St. George's, Hanover Square, for example, established a force of thirty-two watchmen and four beadles for that parish; several of the inhabitants, however, refused to pay the Watch Rate, and set up an opposition establishment which they called 'the inhabitant watch,' consisting of some sixteen persons, who repudiated the authority of the existing Constables, and on one occasion flatly refused to arrest certain offenders even when required to do so by the High Constable" (History of Police in England, by W. L. Melville Lee, 1902, p. 150).

[3] Sketches of the History of Man, by Henry Home (Lord Kames), vol. ii. p. 200 of 1819 edition. "The Churchwardens," we read in 1732, "have hitherto been persons of distinction; the two first were the Right Honourable Lord Carpenter and the Right Honourable General William Stuart, who gave

by successive Local Acts, paved, watched, and lighted the streets and squares; carried out a certain amount of scavenging and put down nuisances; systematised the assessment and collection of rates and put a stop to illegal exemptions; and, in the administration of the Poor Law, voluntarily anticipated by several years many of the reforms of 1834. No evidence of mal-administration was produced against these vestrymen at the House of Commons Inquiry in 1829; and when, in 1832, the inhabitants had the opportunity of electing a new Vestry, they contented themselves with unanimously choosing their old governors. Our own impression is that, during the eighteenth century and the first quarter of the nineteenth, St. George's, Hanover Square, was, under its Select Vestry, by far the best-governed parish in the Metropolitan area.[1]

(c) *Close Vestry Exclusiveness*

We have left to the last a feature in which the Metropolitan Close Vestries differed from the open meetings of inhabitants, and resembled the contemporary borough councils, namely, their partisanship and exclusiveness. It was alleged against the Close Vestries of St. Saviour's, Southwark, and St. Botolph's, Bishopsgate, shortly before the hotly contested Parliamentary election of 1710, that they had made " Scot

the ground whereon the church was built, and bequeathed by his will £4000 to be laid out in erecting a charity school" (*New Remarks of London*, 1732, p. 260).

[1] This Select Vestry included among its members Sturges Bourne, who probably derived from it the name which he gave to the elective Parish Committees, established by his Act of 1819; and also Sir James Graham, described by Hobhouse in 1830 as "a reformer who will go all lengths with me" (Hobhouse to Place, 23rd March 1830, Add. MSS. 35148, p. 49). It is interesting that, whilst no tradesman was co-opted to the Vestry itself, the three important committees which it annually appointed (for poor relief, watch, and paving respectively) included, to the extent of about one-third, persons who were not members of the Vestry, and who were, in fact, local tradesmen. See MS. Vestry Minutes from 1726; *Acts of Parliament relating to the Parish of St. George, Hanover Square, with Instruments for appointing Vestries*; House of Commons Journals, May 1742 (vol. xxiv. pp. 250-256); *Case of the Parishioners of St. George's, Hanover Square* (complaint of the proposed basis of assessment), 1789; Report and Evidence of the Committee on Select and Other Vestries, 1830; *A Practical Illustration of the Principles upon which the Poor Law Amendment Act is founded as exhibited in the administration of the Poor Rates in the Parish of St. George, Hanover Square*, etc., by John Leslie, 1835; *Further Illustrations of the Principles upon which a Metropolitan Poor Rate is administered in the Parish of St. George, Hanover Square*, by John Leslie, 1836.

and lot men [and therefore Parliamentary voters] of whom
they chose," and that they used the influence of their parochial
office on the electors.[1]   More conspicuous during the reign
of Queen Anne was the active participation of these Close
Vestries in the wave of High Church Toryism that then
prevailed in certain social strata.[2]   It was the support
which the Metropolitan Close Vestries thus gave to the High
Church party, that, more than anything else, earned for them
the repeated hostile criticism of the Whigs in the House of
Commons, the prejudiced statements of such contemporaries as
Oldmixon and Calamy, and the ironical approval of Daniel
Defoe.   After the French Revolution the Metropolitan Close
Vestries everywhere formed a part of the wall of resistance to
political and other reforms against which the Radicals so long
beat in vain.[3]

As we might expect, the spirit of religious exclusiveness
was even more characteristic of these close bodies—and that
from an earlier period—than mere political partisanship.
This seems to have risen to its greatest height in the
Metropolis.   Already, in 1635, we find it reported to the Star
Chamber that St. Andrew's, Holborn, had " a Selected Vestry
of twelve persons, grave and ancient inhabitants, men of
approved, honest, and good discretion, and (which is ever
regarded in their choice) men that are known to be well addicted
to the rites and ceremonies of the Church of England, and no
way prone to faction."[4]   In 1663 an Act of Parliament (which
expired in 1670) had temporarily closed the Metropolitan
Select Vestries to all who would not take the sacramental
test; and the same spirit, in most parishes, kept the Close
Vestry, right down to 1834, predominatingly, if not exclusively,
Anglican.   In St. Martin's-in-the-Fields a formal resolution
was passed, definitely excluding Nonconformists from becoming
either Churchwardens or vestrymen, and other Select Vestries
adhered to the same policy without public announcement of
it.   This fact did not prevent the Vestries from choosing well-

---

[1] House of Commons Journals, 16th February 1710 (vol. xvi. p. 315).

[2] See *Transactions of Royal Historical Society*, N.S. 1900, vol. xiv. p. 90.

[3] The Bristol Select Vestries were notorious for their active political partisanship. From the latter part of the eighteenth century, down to 1835, they were, in fact, Tory electioneering clubs, in shameless electoral alliance with the Corporation.

[4] MS. in Lambeth Palace Library, Chartæ Miscellaneæ, vol. vii. p. 57.

to-do Nonconformists for the lower and more burdensome
parish offices, and then letting off their victims on payment
of a substantial fine. What was perhaps of more consequence
to the ordinary ratepayer was the lavish and, in some cases,
grossly extravagant expenditure in church furniture and
church repairs, the rebuilding of the old parish church and
the erection of new " chapels of ease " in different parts of the
parish, when the population grew manifestly too large to be
accommodated at one centre. Nor was this at first unpopular.
Throughout the eighteenth century the building or rebuilding
of churches out of the rates frequently received—as at Hackney
and St. Pancras—the sanction of public meetings of the
inhabitants. And besides the general measures of 1711 and
1818, when public funds were freely granted for new churches,[1]
it is to be noticed that the Close Vestry of St. Margaret's,
Westminster, found no difficulty in getting direct government
grants for rebuilding its parish church. But the extravagant
contracts for the repair and redecoration of St. Sepulchre's,[2]
Christchurch, Spitalfields, and St. Mary, Stratford Bow; and
the reckless new building operations involved in the new
churches of Marylebone and St. Pancras between 1815 and
1830, were carried out by the Close Vestries at the ratepayers'
expense in defiance of the repeated and passionate protests of
what was apparently a majority of the inhabitants.

(d) *The Worst and the Best*

We can now sum up our comparison of the Close Vestries
with the ordinary government of the parish. Those in rural
districts do not seem to have differed essentially from the
usual informal parish oligarchy, except perhaps by a tendency
to leave to the statutory parish officers and to the local
Justices of the Peace the uncontrolled administration of such
statutory services as poor relief and road maintenance. In
ancient urban parishes, especially in the City of London, the

[1] So strong a Nonconformist as Calamy admits that the grant of £350,000
by the House of Commons in 1712 for building new churches "was a very
popular thing" (*Historical Account of My Own Life*, by Edward Calamy, 1829,
vol. ii. p. 239 ; *The English Church in the Eighteenth Century*, by J. H. Overton,
1887, p. 428).

[2] *Local Government in the Metropolis*, 1836, p. 23 ; *Westminster Review*,
January 1836.

Close Vestry became the instrument of petty jobbery, corrupt waste, and extreme partiality in the assessment and collection of rates; to which was sometimes added, especially latterly in Bristol, gross political partisanship. In the populous parishes of the Metropolitan area, the close body, strengthened by influential membership and successive Local Acts, often excelled all other contemporary local authorities in independence, variety of functions, and extent of powers. In most cases their administration of these powers and functions was more continuously corrupt and more extravagantly wasteful than that of the Open Vestries. In two or three of these Metropolitan close bodies the policy was exceptionally efficient and public-spirited, and the administration not less honest than that of other parishes. In one great parish under a Close Vestry, both policy and administration were, as we have seen, markedly superior to those of any other parish government of the period.

The paradox of so extreme a divergence in administrative results between bodies practically identical in the form of their government is capable of explanation. In the rural parishes of Northumberland and Durham the Close Vestry was composed of all the principal occupiers of land—exactly the same persons who would have formed the governing clique on an Open Vestry—and was subject to the same influence of the parson and squire. They were, in practice, no more secret in the one case than in the other, and they were equally dependent on the effective public opinion of the village. In the crowded life of a big city, on the other hand, the absence of publicity, the lack of any independent audit, and of any external control, laid the parish open to be plundered by the Select Vestry, if the vestrymen were in the least inclined to avail themselves of their opportunities. In the majority of these parishes the close body fell into the hands of the small shopkeepers and builders, to whom the opportunities for eating, drinking, and making excursions at the public expense, and the larger gains of extending their little businesses by parish work, offered an irresistible temptation. The Vestry came more and more to attract the unscrupulous and to repel the refined members of this class, whilst the filling of vacancies by co-option tended inevitably to make the whole body homogeneous in its low standard of public morality. "As the old ones drop off," Defoe had remarked in 1714, "they are sure to choose none in their room but those whom they have marked for their purpose beforehand; so rogue succeeds rogue, and the same scene of villainy is still carried on, to the terror of the poor parishioners. . . . Whilst the election is in themselves we have no hopes of amendment. If they happen to be mistaken in their man, and by chance choose an honest man among them, he must either absent himself or come into their measures; otherwise he is like an owl among the birds. So that it may be said of a Select Vestry, as of the Mint, let a man go in never so honest, he's sure not to come out so."[1] On the other hand, in St. George's, Hanover Square, the Select Vestry was composed, from its origin, exclusively of persons unconnected with trade, and moving in a different sphere. The "noblemen and gentlemen" of the West End squares were, as a class, quite as unscrupulous as the shopkeepers of Spitalfields, in obtaining pay without work, at the public expense. But the opportunities of this class for plunder and jobbery—for the most scandalous public sinecures and pensions, and bribes from the secret-service money—lay in another direction. Feeding and driving in carriages at the parish expense was no temptation to them. The supply of groceries to the workhouse, or the repainting of the parish church, offered them no chance of profit. Hence this Vestry attracted to itself, not the unscrupulous and avaricious members of its class, but those who took an interest, as owners, occupiers, or philanthropists, in the good government of their parish. And here, equally, the practice of co-option tended constantly to a homogeneousness of motives and morals. In Marylebone, as also in St. Margaret's and St. John's, Westminster, the composition of the Select Vestry was mixed. In practice, the routine administration fell into the hands of the shopkeepers, but the direction of the policy and the final control seem to have remained with the small set of persons of higher status. To this we ascribe the mixture of vigorous and straightforward policy with extravagant and wasteful administration.

---

[1] *Parochial Tyranny; or the Housekeeper's Complaint against the Insupportable Exactions and Partial Assessments of Select Vestries*, etc., by Andrew Moreton [*i.e.* Daniel Defoe], 1714 (?), p. 10.

But what excited the long campaign against these Close
Vestries, which we shall presently describe, and what finally
brought their rule to an end, was neither their extravagance
nor their corruption.   In fact, such merits as they had were
apt to be counted against them as crimes.   Their continuity
and efficiency of policy lacked the indispensable element of
popular consent.   All public expenditure, even on such socially
advantageous services as paving and cleansing, lighting and
watching, was resented, during the eighteenth and early
nineteenth centuries, by the bulk of the lower middle class
ratepayers.   When it took the form of increasing the provision
for public worship, it was deemed unnecessary by the majority
of the people, and it became at length supremely distasteful to
an energetic and growing minority.   And all the objections to
public expenditure and rising rates were swollen into an
irresistible torrent by the spreading conviction—by 1832
reaching almost to fanaticism—of the indissoluble connection
between taxation and direct popular election.[1]   Even if all
the Close Vestries had remained passive in the domain of
religion, and had become, in secular matters, as actively
efficient as that of Marylebone itself—even if they had all
been as scrupulously honest in their administration as the
gentlemen of St. George's, Hanover Square—so indispensable
to good government is, in modern England, the sentiment of
popular consent that they would nevertheless have found
themselves, after 1815, enveloped in an atmosphere of suspicion
and hostility, in which their continuance would have been
positively detrimental to the community.

[1] "We object," said the organ of the Hackney reformers in 1833, "to
money being drawn from our pockets to be placed at the control of those about
whom we know nothing.   The money may be spent, every farthing of it, as it
ought to be spent. . . . Still . . . we are competent to select for ourselves. . . .
If a ten-pound householder be qualified to judge of the merits of a member of
Parliament, he is surely as well qualified to select proper persons to attend to
his interest in the parish Vestry " (*Hackney Magazine*, November 1833).

CHAPTER VII

THE REFORM OF CLOSE VESTRIES

THE evil results of Close Vestries in the populous parishes of the Metropolitan area had, even before the end of the seventeenth century, excited the attention of reformers. The movement for their abolition extended over a period little short of a century and a half. It falls, as we shall see, into three distinct epochs, to which we may give the following designations. We have first a Whig and anti-ecclesiastical movement from 1693 to 1743. The dominant characteristic of this period, as regards the Close Vestries, was the almost constant willingness and desire of the House of Commons for their drastic reform, coupled with a curious inability—due partly to the absence of governmental action or authoritative leadership, but also, as we think, to the intermixture of anti-Church prejudice—to surmount the difficulties that stood in the way. The collapse of this movement after 1743 was followed by a couple of decades of apathy and indifference. From the peace of 1763 to that of 1815 was an epoch of piecemeal attempts at functional reform, which only incidentally affected the Close Vestry along with other bodies, whilst constitutional structure was left to be dealt with in Local Acts, to be described in a subsequent chapter,[1] in which we trace a total absence of objection to a close body or to the principle of co-option. From 1819 onward we have a rising tide of Radical reform, dealing mainly with structure, which led, after a dozen years of agitation, to the final supersession of the close body..

[1] Book IV. Chap. II. Local Acts of Parliament.

247

(a) *The Assaults that Failed*

The earliest case of revolt against the Close Vestry—not considering here the popular " usurpations" during the Commonwealth—appears to have been that made in St. Margaret's, Westminster, in 1667. For the sake of its interesting description of procedure we give in full the quaint entry in the minute-book of 1669. " The Churchwardens," records the scribe, " are chosen, according to the ancient custom of the said parish time out of mind, the Thursday before Whit Sunday at 2 of the clock in manner following: There is a bell appointed to be tolled, by which the parishioners have notice, and thereupon do repair to the Church to see the Churchwardens who be going forth of their office deliver up their accounts and balance moneys, and also to understand who be chosen Churchwardens for the year ensuing. Then they have a table set in the chancel at which the Doctor or Minister of the parish and the rest of the Vestry do sit. And thither the Churchwardens in being bring their accounts fairly engrossed and bound up in vellum, together with the balance moneys, the ancient vestrymen at the upper end of the table receiving them, and inspecting at least the total sums of what hath been received, what paid and what remains to adjust the said Churchwardens' account. Then they order and appoint some that have already executed the same office of Churchwarden to audit the said account and within one month to make report thereof. This being done, the vestrymen adjourn from thence into the vestryroom, and there take out of the records of the names of former Overseers of the Poor the names of eight or ten persons, and set them down in this manner :

A. B..............................

C. D.............................

always setting down the younger of the present Churchwardens first. Then they debate the fittest man for that office, and every one crossing those whom they judge the meetest for it, he that hath the most crosses stands Churchwarden for the year. As soon as this is done they give the paper into the

249

hands of the Reader, who immediately goeth therewith into
the reading pew, and then in the open church and audience of
the parishioners present publisheth and declareth the name of
the persons elected for Churchwardens, to the end they may
have notice of the same. After this the Churchwardens
expired do use to invite the Doctor or Minister together with
the vestrymen and other ancient inhabitants of the parish to
a supper at the charge of the said Churchwardens." In 1667,
however, after the vestrymen had withdrawn as usual to make
the election, two other parishioners " having a mind and
longing desire for the office of Churchwardens, believing (as
well they might) that the vestrymen would not now choose
them, procured these few that were remaining in the chancel
when the Minister and vestrymen withdrew themselves " to
elect them Churchwardens for the year 1667. The case
between the rival sets of Churchwardens was tried first in the
Court of the Dean of Westminster; subsequently, on appeal,
by a special Court of Delegates appointed by the King; and
ultimately by the Court of King's Bench, the decision in each
case being in favour of the Select Vestry.[1]

The first serious attempt to deal with the Close Vestries
by legislation may probably have been the Bill introduced by
Sir John Guise in 1693, "for the better governing and
regulating of Vestries." This Bill, of which we do not know
the origin or purport, was read a second time by the House
of Commons, but not further proceeded with.[2] Three years
later we learn that " a petition of divers gentlemen and others,

[1] MS. Vestry Minutes, St. Margaret's, Westminster, 1669; *History of the
Parish Church of St. Margaret's, Westminster*, by Rev. M. E. C. Walcott, 1847,
pp. 76-79. It was in 1680 that the quarrel began with the Select Vestry of
Masham (Yorkshire), which, ending in 1691 in a reported legal decision in
favour of the close body, gave it an authoritative position (Batt and Others *v.*
Watkinson, *Reports of the Resolutions of the Court . . . of Common Pleas*, by
Sir Edward Lutwyche, 1718, vol. ii. pp. 436, 437).

[2] House of Commons Journals, 10th and 13th February 1693 (vol. x. pp.
809, 811). The records of the Middlesex Justices contain, between 1690 and
1693, frequent complaints by inhabitants against the corruption and oppression
of their Vestries, notably against the Close Vestries of St. Giles-in-the-Fields;
St. Andrew, Holborn; St. Botolph, Aldersgate; St. Anne, Soho; and St.
Clement Danes (*Middlesex Quarter Sessions Records*, edited by W. J. Hardy,
1905). It may be added that the dummy bill which is introduced every session
into the House of Lords, as an assertion of its right to debate before the King's
Speech is read, is entitled " A Bill to reform Select Vestries." This is believed
to date from a couple of centuries back. It is mentioned in the *Further Memoirs
of the Whig Party*, by Lord Holland, 1905, p. 250.

substantial inhabitants in several parishes within the weekly
Bills of Mortality, was presented to the House, and read,
setting forth that the petitioners are very uneasy under the
heavy burden of parochial taxes which are imposed in a most
unequal manner by a few persons who assume to themselves
the name of Ancients, in pretended Vestries; and who audit
the Churchwardens' and Overseers' books in a private
manner."[1] This petition was in support of a Bill brought
in by Mr. Manly, "to regulate abuses in Select Vestries,"
which also got read a second time.   It was, however, met by
a swarm of petitions from the Select Vestries, who protested
that "popular elections were dangerous"; that "the peace of
the inhabitants would be broken"; that "the election of
vestrymen would end in a mutiny if the methods prescribed
by the Bill . . . should be established by law"; and even that
"it would endanger the starving of the poor before they can
be relieved by the intended new constitution."[2]   The result
was that the Bill was not further proceeded with.   But we
may perhaps infer its purport from the drastic clause which
some valiant peer attempted to insert in the Poor Law
Amendment Bill sent up by the House of Commons in 1697.
After a graphic recital of the evils of Select Vestries,[3] this

---

[1] House of Commons Journals, 6th April 1696.

[2] See the Petitions from St. George the Martyr, Southwark; St. Olave's,
Southwark; St. Dunstan's, Stepney; St. Margaret's, Westminster; St. James's,
Piccadilly; and St. Martin's-in-the-Fields, in House of Commons Journals, 18th,
28th, and 29th February and 2nd March 1696 (vol. xi, pp. 391, 439, 448,
453, 469, 474, 477, 481, 490); *History of the Parish Church of St. Margaret's,
Westminster*, by Rev. M. E. C. Walcott, 1847, p. 93.

[3] "Whereas in many parishes, especially in the Cities of London and
Westminster and the weekly Bills of Mortality, and in other cities, boroughs,
corporations and places in the kingdom of England and dominions of Wales,
manifest great evils and abuses do frequently happen and arise by and from
Select Vestries or pretended Select Vestries, divers private persons under colour
and pretence thereof, and without consent of the greater part of the most able
and sufficient inhabitants of such parishes, usurping to themselves the sole
power and disposal of the public moneys and stock, and of the yearly revenues,
rates, taxes, incomes, and profits belonging and appertaining to the same
parishes . . . such Select Vestrymen or pretended Select Vestrymen . . .
wrongfully and unjustly applying the said monies . . . in extravagant and
unnecessary feastings and other eating and drinking, to the great loss and
prejudice of such parishes . . . Select Vestrymen make public rates . . .
partial, unequal, and oppressive . . . refuse and omit to give due and just
account . . . for the sake of their private lucre and gain the said Select Vestrymen by indirect methods and practices, impose and continue themselves in the
said place and office of Vestrymen for divers years together."

clause proposed to place the complete control of the parish officers and parish funds, "where there is or hath been Select Vestries," in a representative body of "the chief and most discreet and able men," to be elected annually by all the rate-payers occupying premises above a certain value (the amount being left blank); the Incumbent and Churchwardens to be members *ex officio,* and the former (or his curate) to preside. This clause, endorsed "a clause to prevent the poor's being cheated," was actually moved in the House of Lords, but had to be withdrawn, and the Bill became law without any reference to Select Vestries.[1]   Early in 1710, when the Whig majority in the House of Commons was at the height of its power, we find another Bill ordered by the House itself,[2] at the instance of the inhabitants of St. Botolph's, Bishopsgate, in the City of London, where it was alleged "twenty-seven persons have for several years past, under the name of a Select Vestry, assembled themselves, and by an arbitrary power raise money upon the inhabitants . . . and clandestinely apply part of it amongst themselves, as they think fit; and take upon themselves to choose into and dispose of the parish offices without any regard to order or common justice, by which means they influence the electors for Parliament as experience has shown; and in time may tend to the utter subversion of the petitioners' liberty, and is a notorious oppression and grievance upon them."   Other petitions against Select Vestries were presented from the inhabitants of St. Saviour's, Southwark, and St. Dunstan's, Stepney, with contrary petitions from Select Vestries reciting the great advantages of such institutions.[3]   Meanwhile the ill-judged impeachment of Dr. Sacheverell was shattering the power of the Whig majority.   Every day it was becoming more clear that public opinion had turned against them.   The bewildered House could find no better expedient than repeatedly to put off considering the Select Vestry Bill which it had itself ordered, until the measure was lost by the Dissolution of Parliament[4] that led to so crushing a defeat of the Whigs at the polls.

---

[1] 8 and 9 William III. c. 30 (1697); MS. Archives of House of Lords, 1697.
[2] House of Commons Journals, 16th February 1710 (vol. xvi. p. 315). The Bill was ordered by 140 votes to 83, Harley telling for the minority.
[3] *Ibid.* vol. xvi. pp. 312, 315, 347.
[4] *Ibid.* vol. xvi. pp. 368, 374, 380.

But the agitation was not allowed to sleep. In 1714 we find Daniel Defoe publishing in the name of Andrew Moreton a scathing denunciation under the title of *Parochial Tyranny, or the Housekeeper's complaint against the insupportable exactions and partial assessments of Select Vestries*, in which he vehemently asserted that "there is not a greater abuse in the world than that of Select Vestries." [1] Defoe's pamphlet gave abundant evidence of the need for reform in the details of parish administration, but, as we have mentioned, we suspect that part, at least, of his fury is to be ascribed to the fact that the Select Vestries of the Metropolis were, just in these very years, among the strongest outposts of the Tory, Church, and Jacobite party. "At this time," writes the Whig historian, Oldmixon, "there was a very great complaint against the corrupt and base management of the Select Vestries . . . and particularly of their disaffection to the Government, of which the choosing Joseph Trapp, M.A., Lecturer of St. Martin's-in-the-Fields, was reckoned an undoubted instance." [2] With the Whig triumph of 1714-1715 in the undisputed accession of George I. and the defeat of the Pretender, the question again came to the front in Parliament. The discomfort and misery of the exceptionally severe winter of 1715-1716,—when the Thames was frozen for three months, and such vast quantities of snow fell that great numbers of the poor labourers were unemployed, and members of Parliament complained of "the great annoyance and obstructions which are at this present season in the streets by reason of the great heaps of dirt, ice, and snow,"—led to the appointment of a committee to inspect the accounts of the Poor Rates and Scavengers' Rates in all the Metropolitan parishes, in order to discover why, when so much money was raised, the poor were starving and the streets unswept.[3] The members of this committee, under the direction of their chairman, Molesworth,

---

[1] The same year saw also the publication of an *Historical Account of the Constitution of the Vestry of the Parish of St. Dunstan's-in-the-West*, revealing the origin of a Close Vestry by bishop's faculty ; and also a curious pamphlet relating to the same parish, entitled *The Art of being Honest for a little time, or the Method of making Parish Rates to chastise the inhabitants demonstrated, in the Assessments made for the Scavengers of St. Dunstan's-in-the-West, London, for the year 1713 and 1712*.

[2] *History of England*, by John Oldmixon, 1735, p. 633.

[3] House of Commons Journals, 21st January 1716 (vol. xviii. p. 345).

soon found the task an impossible one, and decided to confine their examination to the Select Vestry of St. Martin's-in-the-Fields, on the ground, as reported, that it was "represented to them as the most free from frauds and abuses"; but, also, as we may suspect, because it had been conspicuous in its Church and Tory partisanship.[1] The lengthy and detailed report presented by the Committee revealed an inextricable confusion of the parish accounts, a complete absence of adequate checks on malversation, and no little extravagance in "sacramental" wine and Vestry dinners. "Whatever is wanting for the use of the church," declared the Committee, "is bought at the worst hand, and paid for at extravagant rates, because the persons who furnish the goods or the work are for the most part such as have been Churchwardens and vestrymen." Whilst not proving any specific case of embezzlement, or more than a few instances of jobbery, the Committee prophetically pointed out, what more than a century of costly experience was to demonstrate, that the effect of renewal by co-option and self-audit would be "that should once any corruption get in, 'tis scarce possible it can be otherwise remedied than by the authority of this House." The House of Commons was so incensed at the revelations—again, as we may suspect, not without political bias—that, within two months, it had ordered, passed through all its stages, and transmitted to the House of Lords, a drastic Bill "regulating" all the Close Vestries within the Metropolitan area.[2] By this measure all the Close Vestries in the Metropolitan area were to be peremptorily set aside. A day was to be fixed by Quarter Sessions on which, in each parish, in the presence of designated Justices of the Peace, all the inhabitants qualified by the ownership of real or personal property worth £300, were to elect for a three years' term a body of between fifteen

---

[1] Report of Committee, in House of Commons Journals, 8th March 1716 (vol. xviii. pp. 392-397); *History of Vagrants and Vagrancy*, by C. J. Ribton-Turner, 1887, p. 183; *History of England*, by J. Oldmixon, 1735, p. 633. The Committee led to a breach of privilege. One of its Whig witnesses, a Justice of the Peace, was grossly insulted for his testimony by a Select Vestryman of St. Martin's, who was brought to the bar of the House, committed to custody, and only released on his humble apology, a severe reprimand, and payment of fees (House of Commons Journals, 10th, 17th, and 18th February 1716, vol. xviii. pp. 371, 378, 382).

[2] House of Commons Journals, 8th March and 25th April to 24th May 1716 (vol. xviii. pp. 392, 434, 436, 438, 439, 445, 449).

and forty vestrymen, who were to be persons worth at least £1000. Churchwardens and Overseers, and all who had served these offices within the preceding three years, were declared ineligible as vestrymen; and after each three years' term, not more than one-third of those who had been vestrymen were to be eligible for re-election. These representative Vestries were to have great power. Besides all the authority of the old Vestries, they were to have the unrestricted appointment of Beadles and other Poor Law officers (except Overseers); they were to control and audit the accounts of all parish officers; and they alone were to pass bills for payment. Stringent provisions forbade all eating and drinking at the public expense; prohibited vestrymen or their sons from taking parish contracts or being appointed to paid offices by the Vestry; required separate accounts to be kept for Poor Rate and Church Rate respectively; insisted that rates should be levied at per pound on a proper assessment, and stipulated that whilst the Overseers should collect the Poor Rate, the Churchwardens themselves were to collect the Church Rate, and that under no circumstances were these offices to be held by the same persons. Many of these provisions were made applicable to all the Metropolitan parishes, whether governed by Close or Open Vestries, so that the measure really amounted to a laudably early attempt at the reform of the local government of the Metropolis.[1] Unfortunately, as it seems to us, the dominant Whig majority in the House of Commons was really more concerned to attack the power and

---

[1] As this Bill seems to exist only in the MS. parchment copy which was transmitted to the House of Lords, and now in the archives of that House, we transcribe its humane preamble: " Whereas, notwithstanding the many good laws of the realm, frequent and great abuses have been of late and are still committed in the collection and distributing of the money for the maintenance of the poor within the Cities of London and Westminster and the other parishes within the Bills of Mortality . . . money collected for the poor diverted from that goodly intent and spent at riotous feasts and other unnecessary expenses and meetings of Churchwardens and of parish officers, and turned to the private profit of persons who ought in a more special manner to have had the interests of the poor in their mind, to the great dishonour of Almighty God and scandal of all charitable Christians, and the starving of great numbers of poor men, women, and children who have miserably perished, and do daily perish for want . . . the poor rather increased than diminished, and great numbers of idle vagabonds, men and women, are permitted daily to beg in the streets through the carelessness and corruption of beadles and others . . . to the great annoyance . . . and the spreading of infectious distempers within these populous cities," etc.

influence of the Church than to bring about a reform of
parish administration. Under cover of "regulating" the
Vestries, it sought virtually to disestablish the clergyman
from his immemorial participation in local government, to
place in a completely subordinate position the Churchwardens
who were the most ancient officers of the parish, and practically to confiscate, merely because they were under church
influence, the voluntary charity schools which were a feature
of the philanthropy of the period. The Incumbent and even
the Churchwardens were no longer to be members of the
Vestry, which was to choose its own chairman at each
meeting. This entirely lay body, elected by the substantial
householders, was to appoint, for each church, the lecturer or
afternoon preacher. The elected vestrymen were themselves
to collect the "sacrament money," or offertory in church,
which was to be counted in public. Finally, this purely
elective public authority was to have the sole right of appointing the masters and mistresses of any voluntary charity schools
that might be carried on within its parish, and of selecting
the children to be admitted to such schools. Whatever may
be said in favour of these anti-ecclesiastical clauses in themselves, it was clearly a mistake in tactics to mix them up
with the reform of parochial government. Against so sweeping a measure the Church made a desperate resistance. The
clergy of London and Westminster petitioned the House of
Lords that the Bill "cast a reflection upon their body which
they trust they have no way merited; that it will divest
them of those legal privileges which they have reason to
think secured to them by the Act of Uniformity; that it will
introduce innovations into the Church which they fear may
prove dangerous and which they hope are unnecessary; that
it will apparently weaken the episcopal authority, and diminish
the charity of well-disposed people."[1] The trustees of charity
schools, in which nearly 5000 poor children were being
educated and clothed, represented forcibly that these schools
were not maintained by the parishes, but were "chiefly
supported by voluntary subscriptions," and that the greater
part of the subscribers contributed because they thereby

[1] MS. Petition of the Clergy of London and Westminster, 1716 (in House of
Lords archives).

secured the right of appointing the schoolmasters and nominating the children to be admitted. To hand these powers over to an elected body would certainly check the flow of subscriptions, and would, in fact, " tend to discourage, if not totally dissolve, the said schools." [1]   Meanwhile the Close Vestries themselves had used all their influence in defence of their privileges.[2]   When the Bill came on in the House of Lords, " it was opposed," as the Nonconformist Calamy complains, " by the Archbishop of Canterbury, who made a set speech against it.   Not a peer having the courage to speak for it afterwards, it was thrown out by a considerable majority.   This action of the Archbishop was generally applauded by the clergy." [3]

The rejection of the Bill of 1716 seems to have given the Close Vestries twenty years' undisturbed possession of their powers.[4]   From 1731 onwards we watch approaching a new storm, heralded by occasional references in the pamphlets and journalism of the time.[5]   The publication in 1733 of an able

---

[1] MS. Petition of Trustees of Charity Schools in London and Westminster, 1716 (in House of Lords archives).

[2] In one case, at least, they were not above paying money to the clerks of the House of Commons ''for the great trouble they were put unto upon the proceedings of Parliament against this parish " (MS. Vestry Minutes, St. Martin's-in-the-Fields, 1st November 1716).

[3] *Historical Account of My Own Life*, by Edward Calamy, 1829, vol. ii. pp. 352, 353 ; House of Lords Journals, 25th and 26th May, 1st and 5th June 1716 (vol. xx. pp. 365, 366, 368, 372). " All the bishops voted against it," says the Whig historian, "chiefly because it gave laymen an authority over the masters of the charity schools " (*History of England*, by John Oldmixon, 1735, vol. ii. p. 633).

[4] We have noted only one publication during these years—a "merry poem " entitled *Parish Guttlers, or the Humours of a Vestry*, 1722, describing a close body which may perhaps have been the Vestry of St. Botolph, Bishopsgate.   In 1720 some of the inhabitants of St. Bartholomew the Great seem to have resisted their Select Vestry, and appointed Churchwardens at a public meeting in their fine Norman Church, at which the members of the Select Vestry refused to attend.   This led to proceedings, first in the ecclesiastical court, and then in the Court of Common Pleas, where the jury, whilst holding that the immemorial existence of a close body had been proved, found that the particular custom alleged had not been completely made out (Lock v. Hyett, Michaelmas term, 1720 ; apparently not reported).   On this inconclusive verdict, both parties chose Constables and Scavengers of their own.   On appeal to the Lord Mayor and Court of Aldermen, an order was made upholding the Select Vestry and appointing its nominees.   We hear no more of resistance (MS. Vestry Minutes, St. Bartholomew the Great, 4th May and 3rd November 1720, 9th March 1721).

[5] See *Gentleman's Magazine*, April 1731 ; *Grub Street Journal*, 22nd April 1731 ; *Daily Post*, 9th December 1737 ; *Exactions and Impositions of Parish Fees*, by Francis Sadler, 1738 (which went through six editions by 1771) ;

report on the constitution of the Close Vestry of St. Botolph, Aldersgate, where a rebellious Churchwarden overthrew the local oligarchy, must have done something to reveal to those concerned the uncertain legal position of the bishop's faculty Vestries.[1] At Great St. Mary's, Cambridge, governed for 250 years by a close body, the inhabitants in 1738 seem to have insisted on holding an Open Vestry, at which they formally resolved that as " such Select Vestries have of late times been found to be ill-grounded, and the illegal custom of supporting the same ridiculed and despised," the government should henceforth be by open meeting and freely elected Churchwardens.[2] In London the attack begins in an attempt to overthrow the Close Vestry of St. Martin's-in-the-Fields. At Easter 1741 a gathering of some two hundred inhabitants, summoned by the reform party, attempted to enter the Vestry for the choice of Churchwardens, and when they were shut out, held a meeting of their own and elected a Churchwarden, in opposition to the election made by the Select Vestry. When their nominee was not admitted by the Archdeacon, they applied to the Court of King's Bench for a mandamus. The Court seems, however, to have been easily convinced that the close body had existed time out of mind, and upheld its authority.[3] Meanwhile the attack on the Select Vestries had developed into a formidable petition to the House of Commons from the inhabitants of the five great Westminster parishes, alleging "that a particular number of men in each of the said parishes, by wresting the sense of some laws now in being and taking advantage of the ambiguity of others, have assumed to themselves under the title of Select Vestrymen the various powers and authorities of assessing all

Parish Corruption in part displayed ; or a Narrative of some late Transactions in St. Luke's Parish, 1740 ; and above all, *The Vestry laid Open ; or a full and plain detection of the many Gross Abuses, Impositions, and Oppressions of Select Vestries,* by Joseph Phipps, 1739, in which the above are cited.

[1] *The Report of the Committee appointed by a General Vestry of . . . St. Botolph Without, Aldersgate, . . . with some Methods proposed to prevent abuses in the future,* 1733 ; *Daily Journal.* 25th April and 4th October 1733 ; *Daily Courant,* 15th May 1733.

[2] MS. Vestry Minutes, Great St. Mary's, Cambridge, Easter Tuesday, 1738.

[3] This judgment (Kendal *versus* Penrice), in Trinity Term, 1741, was produced in the trial of Berry *v.* Banner in 1792, and in that of Golding *v.* Fenn in 1827, and is referred to in the reports of these cases (*Cases at Nisi Prius,* by Thomas Peake, pp. 156-160 of edition of 1810 ; *Reports of Cases,* by R. V. Barnewall and C. Cresswell, 1828, vol. vii. pp. 765-783).

or most of the parochial rates . . . of electing and appointing Churchwardens, Overseers, etc. . . . and in general of managing the affairs of the said parishes, exclusive of and without the knowledge and concurrence of the rest of the inhabitants."[1]   Unlike most petitions, this one was followed up by energetic action.   When it was referred to a committee, counsel appeared in support of its allegations, which were regularly proved, for parish after parish, by a series of credible witnesses, and the production of the actual parochial documents and accounts.   In a succession of long and detailed reports, Lord Perceval, who acted as chairman, brought all the facts before the House, and reported that the allegations of the petitioners were amply proved as regards four of the parishes, whilst in the case of St. George's, Hanover Square, it was not shown that the Close Vestry was either corrupt, extravagant, or addicted to any undue secrecy.   On the other hand, in the parish of St. Martin's the corruption, as had been predicted by the committee of 1716, had risen to a great height.   The large expenditure on " sacramental wine " now included not only " sack, hock, and white wine ordered in pints and single bottles," in a manner which " seemed not to be for the service of the church," but also " oranges, sugar, and butter," which can hardly have been used in the communion service.   The vestrymen shopkeepers grossly overcharged the parish for everything that it had to buy.   The prices for repairs charged by the vestryman glazier were proved to be exactly twice those charged by the King's glazier.   Since the vestryman candle-maker had supplied the watchmen's candles, the yearly cost had just doubled.   The accounts were in the most hopeless confusion.   The assessment and collection of rates were both scandalously partial, the Vestrymen being either rated at nominal sums or not at all, and such rates as were due from them being often left uncollected.   What was new in the revelations was the extent to which these Close Vestries had concentrated in their own hands all the powers of other local authorities.   They had everywhere assumed the powers of the parish officers, reducing the Churchwardens, Overseers, and Scavengers to mere subordinates.   The House of Commons heard with indignation that they had even taken to themselves,

[1] House of Commons Journals, vol. xxiv. p. 118, 11th March 1742.

by means of docile Justices among the vestrymen, the powers
of the magistrates in Petty Sessions, themselves making all the
rates, appointing Overseers, and hearing appeals. If the
members of Parliament ever troubled to read the forty
foolscap pages of detailed reports which Lord Perceval presented in four successive batches during the month of May
1742, it must, we think, have seemed to them that there was
scarcely any limit to the autocratic authority secretly and
corruptly exercised by these close bodies. Yet so strong were
the allies of the Select Vestries, and so incapable was the
House of Commons of that date of any effective legislation
without government leadership, that the consideration of these
reports was indefinitely postponed, and leave to bring in a Bill
to reform the Select Vestries was refused by 160 votes to 132.[1]
On this failure, the inhabitants of St. Martin's attempted
once more to remedy their own grievances. In May of the
same year when " the Gentlemen of the Vestry met in their
Vestry Room " they were, as the minutes record, " interrupted
by several inhabitants from proceeding to business " and
"were obliged to retire to the Library, they not being able
to retire to the Church on account of the prayers that were
being read there." This interruption, so decorously recorded,
was the prelude to an action in which the right of the Select
Vestry was, in 1744-1745, again tried in the Court of King's
Bench. But the Vestry kept its early records secret, and
though we know now the baselessness of the contention that
the close body had existed from time immemorial, the plaintiffs
could not disprove it, with the result that the Court for
the second time upheld the ruling clique.[2] The inhabitants.
of the neighbouring parish of St. Anne's, Soho, taking the
law into their own hands against a weaker Vestry, were
more successful. Obtaining counsel's opinion to the effect
that the inhabitants had not lost their right to attend the

[1] House of Commons Journals, 4th, 6th, 10th, 18th, 25th, 28th May 1742
(vol. xxiv. pp. 118, 196-211, 220, 232-244, 250, 256, 261). These proceedings
attracted the attention of *The Champion*, which had an article on 3rd June 1742,
entitled "Fraudulent Practices of Select Vestries" (reprinted in the *Gentleman's
Magazine*, June 1742, vol. xii. p. 303). See also the *Report of the Committee to
whom the Petition of the principal inhabitants of* . . . *Westminster so far as it
relates to* . . . *St. Martin's was referred*, etc., 1742.

[2] Ferrers *v.* Nind, 1744 (MS. Vestry Minutes, St. Martin's-in-the-Fields,
10th May 1744).

Vestry meetings, the reformers forcibly "entered the Vestry Room and turned out the gentlemen who were acting as Select Vestrymen and burned the books."[1]   The Select Vestry gave up the contest, and the parish was henceforth governed by an Open Vestry.   With this merely fragmentary success the Whig Movement for the reform of the Close Vestries may be said to have come to an end.[2]

We need not here concern ourselves with the successive attempts at the functional reform of parish government that marked the period between 1763 and 1815, as they did not deal particularly with the Close Vestries, and they will be described in our subsequent volumes upon the several services of Poor Law, Road Maintenance, etc.   During this period the House of Commons was so far from manifesting any objection in principle to close bodies, renewing themselves by co-option, that this was the form which it most frequently gave to the new statutory bodies created by Local Acts.[3]   Between 1790 and 1792 a third attempt was made to upset the Close Vestry of St. Martin's-in-the-Fields.   An influential body of local ratepayers approached the Vestry to get its co-operation in seeking a Local Act to put the government of the parish on a representative basis.   When this request was treated with contempt, the solicitor for the petitioners applied in vain for access to the parish archives.   The inhabitants then claimed

[1] Report of House of Commons Committee on Select and Other Vestries, 1830.   For the character of this Close Vestry see the letter in the *Grub Street Journal*, 22nd April 1731, quoted in the *Gentleman's Magazine*, April 1731, p. 159 ; House of Commons Journals, May 1742 (vol. xxiv. p. 204).

[2] With the following insignificant exception, we know of no pamphlet or journalistic attack on the Close Vestries between 1743 and 1794—a remarkable contrast with the preceding half-century.   In 1754 we find a scurrilous and worthless pamphlet, vaguely alluding to St. Paul's, Covent Garden, entitled *The Select Vestry justified, in answer to a pamphlet entitled " The Constitutional."*

[3] In 1783, when the Select Vestry of St. James's, Piccadilly, was promoting a Bill to free itself from the control of the Westminster Paving Commissioners, twenty-three inhabitants petitioned against it on the ground that the Vestry was a close body.   The House of Commons considered petitions and counter-petitions, heard counsel, and made some inquiries, but finding that the Close Vestry was supported by over 1600 petitioners, passed its Bill unaltered (House of Commons Journals, 3rd and 8th April, 9th May, 13th and 16th June 1783 ; vol. xxxix. pp. 354, 359, 413, 478, 486).   In 1775 some of the parishioners of St. Giles's, Cripplegate, strove to dethrone their Select Vestry.   An open meeting elected Churchwardens, but when the case came into court, Lord Mansfield nonsuited them, as they could not prove that the election had ever been made in that parish by an open meeting (*An Account of the Church and Parish of St. Giles's Without, Cripplegate*, by J. J. Baddeley, 1888, p. 172).

admission to the Vestry meeting—only to be sternly refused by the Select Vestry. The Vicar vainly attempted to mediate between the parties. The matter was at last brought to an issue by a public meeting electing its own Churchwardens, who claimed, by a suit in the Ecclesiastical Court, the privilege of using the Churchwardens' pew in the parish church. The rival Churchwardens got a writ of prohibition from the Court of King's Bench, and, on Lord Kenyon's direction, a jury for the third time upheld the right of the Close Vestry to govern this great parish.[1] But there was no public agitation against the Select Vestries—perhaps because the helpless Metropolitan ratepayer thought them no worse, and no more free from his practical control, than the parish government, where the Vestry meetings were nominally open to all comers.[2] Right down to 1820, the few members of the House of Commons who were interested in the improvement of local government were more concerned to get rid of the turbulent ineptitude of the Open Vestry, with its unpaid and uncontrolled parish officers, than to get democratic institutions for the great London parishes. Sturges Bourne, himself, as we have mentioned, an active member of the Select Vestry of St. George's, Hanover Square,

---

[1] MS. Vestry Minutes, St. Martin's-in-the-Fields, 18th February, 11th and 17th March, 1st and 5th April, 14th and 21st May 1790 ; 4th and 17th February and 16th March 1791 ; and the general "Report of the Committee for conducting the case," 1st February 1793. The legal report is Berry *v.* Banner, in *Cases at Nisi Prius*, by Thomas Peake, pp. 156-160 of edition of 1810. The first volume of the Vestry minutes was, it is now known, "kept out of sight during the hearing of the cause of Berry *v.* Banner in 1792, and its non-production secured a victory for the self-elected vestrymen who then ruled the parish." The volume was afterwards found in the roof of the church ! (*Catalogue of Books and Documents belonging to the Parish of St. Martin's*, by Thomas Mason, pp. 36, 37 ; based on Vestry minutes, 6th November 1834). "The entries upon which the verdict was obtained," reported the indignant Open Vestry of 1834, "are evidently the work of an interpolator, and it is quite clear . . . that the then parties obtained that verdict by fraud " (MS. Vestry Minutes, 6th November 1834).

[2] The *Times* (23rd December 1794) reported that, in connection with a reform of the Poor Law, a Bill was in preparation "to abolish, *in toto*, the practice of Select Vestries, and to direct that whenever a Vestry is intended to be held, all the inhabitant housekeepers shall be summoned by written notices, delivered at their respective houses. In short, parochial smuggling is to be totally abolished. Something of this kind is requisite, for the people are now even more parish-ridden than law-ridden. But this may easily be accounted for, as there is always a parish lawyer at the head of a parish feast or parish job. It is a well-known fact, and Mr. Gilbert brought in proof, that seven-eighths of the parish taxes were either idly expended by the parish officers, or sunk into their pockets as parochial perquisites."

not only omitted, at his Poor Law Committee of 1817, to
call any evidence about the manifold iniquities of the Select
Vestries, but actually adopted the same designation for the
elective parish committee which in 1819 he carried into law.[1]
And when we add that it was in the same year—the year of
the " Six Acts "—that the Open Vestry of St. Pancras was, as
we have described, peremptorily extinguished by an Act of
Parliament, and superseded by a close body, we may realise
how little the House of Commons of that date was inclined to
democracy in local affairs.

(b) A London Movement

It will be remembered that the year 1820 was marked by
an outburst of democratic feeling at Manchester and other
towns in the North of England, which found expression in
the meetings of the Open Vestry.   The minutes of the Open
Vestries in London reveal no similar movement.   Such
popular feeling and political excitement as existed among
the working classes in London was just then taking the form
of cheering Queen Caroline.   During the next few years we
find a few reformers at work in particular parishes.   The
financial collapse of 1825-1826 produced great distress among
London householders, and led to a great increase in pauperism.[2]
The rapid rise in the local rates, which was taking place in
every London parish, almost compelled the more energetic and
public-spirited of the inhabitants to look into their parochial
affairs.[3]   Where the parish was governed by an Open Vestry,

---

[1] Sturges Bourne repented in after years.   In 1831 we find him expressing
to the parochial reformers of Stonehouse (Devon) his regret that his legislation
of 1819 was commonly called "the Select Vestry Act," as this caused the
elective parish committee which he advocated, to be confused with self-chosen
Select Vestries which had become notorious in certain London parishes.   (See
Plymouth, Devonport, and Stonehouse Herald, 9th April 1831.)

[2] Cobbett notes that "in the suburbs of London during the distress of 1825
and 1826" there were "thousands of houses" to let (Rural Rides, p. 174,
vol. i. of 1885 edition).

[3] It may be mentioned that in 1825 Sir J. Newport brought before the
House of Commons the malpractices of the parish Vestries in Ireland, which
(owing partly to the exclusion of all Roman Catholics) had shrunk to very small
bodies, and had committed every kind of extravagance.   See Hansard, 1825,
p. 617, etc.   This speech was quoted in some detail in Considerations on Select
Vestries, 1828, p. 19, but it does not appear that the Irish Vestries were avowedly
close bodies.

the reformers strove, as at Bethnal Green, Chelsea, Paddington, and Islington, for an Act of Parliament which should place the government in the hands of a limited number of vestrymen, to be elected annually by all the ratepayers assessed at a certain amount. This dislike of government by public meeting, and preference for representative institutions, together with the high qualification for electors and representatives that usually characterised these proposals, are in remarkable contrast with the Radical claims of Manchester and Leeds. Parish reform in London was, in fact, almost entirely a movement in favour of economy and efficiency, promoted by the well-to-do ratepayers, often including the clergyman of the parish. Similar causes led to agitations for reform in some of the parishes governed by Close Vestries. A series of confused and inconclusive campaigns took place between the Close Vestries on the one hand and the discontented ratepayers on the other. Sometimes, as in St. Giles's-in-the-Fields and St. George's, Bloomsbury, the necessary instrument of reform was found in a Churchwarden of popular sympathies, who insisted on summoning an Open Vestry, which promptly took steps to test the validity of the Select Vestry. After repeated and inconclusive litigation in this case, the Select Vestry, in 1830, itself promoted a Bill constituting a joint Vestry for the two parishes, elected by £30 occupiers. This measure, which Hume and Hobhouse strenuously resisted on account of its restricted franchise, was successfully piloted through Parliament by Lord John Russell.[1] In St. Paul's, Covent Garden, where, as we have mentioned, a Close Vestry had existed for a century and a half without specific legal authority, one energetic parishioner named Corder took action in 1826, and had sufficient popular backing to extort from the reluctant vestrymen a verdict by consent, so that the court declared in favour of the right of the inhabitants to participate in the

[1] See the parish histories by John Parton (1822), Rowland Dobie (1834), and Walter Blott (1892); *Considerations on Select Vestries*, etc., 1828, pp. 16, 17 ; *Refutations of Charges against the Select Vestry made in several printed Papers* . . . 1828, 1829 ; *Times*, 23rd April 1829 ; Report and Evidence of the House of Commons Committee on Select and Other Vestries, 1830 ; *St. Giles-in-the-Fields and St. George's, Bloomsbury, Vestry Bill—Explanation of the Objects of the Bill*, 1830 ; Hansard, vol. xxiii. pp. 378, 1126, March and April 1830 ; the papers in British Museum, vols. 816 m 9, and 579 l 7 ; and *Life and Times of Thomas Wakley*, by S. Squire Sprigge, 1897, pp. 239-245.

Vestry meeting. He was therefore able to get a public meeting of an Open Vestry, which adopted Sturges Bourne's Act, defeated an attempt to reintroduce a self-electing body by a new Bill, and finally, in 1829, got passed a Local Act empowering the £20 occupiers to elect by ballot a standing committee in which all parochial authority was vested.[1] In Hackney a considerable agitation was begun in 1830 against the old Select Vestry, established, as we have seen, by bishop's faculty in 1613. Here the Select Vestry was supposed to have existed from time immemorial; but, as we have noted, parish meetings continued to be held for certain purposes, leaving, however, the bulk of the actual administration in the hands of the Select Vestry. The parish reformers went energetically to work, found references to the existence of a faculty, and finally discovered a copy of it among the diocesan records in St. Paul's Cathedral. On its being submitted to counsel (Serjeant Coleridge) he advised that such a faculty could give no legal validity to a Select Vestry. That body thereupon, after some hesitation, abandoned its claim and made way for an Open Vestry, which accordingly, on the 19th of November 1833, after over two centuries of acquiescence, resumed the government of the parish.[2] Other parishes were less successful. In St. James's, Piccadilly, where the Select Vestry rested on Local Acts of 1685 and 1735, a committee of parishioners promoted a Bill in 1829, to establish an elective body. In spite of the efforts of Sir J. C. Hobhouse, this measure was rejected by the House of Commons.[3] In

---

[1] See *Times*, 8th March 1827; 19th January, 27th March, 9th, 10th, and 13th April, and 26th September 1828; 6th January 1829; and 20th February 1830; *Some Account of the Formation of the Precinct of Covent Garden into a Parish*; Place to Hobhouse, 2nd April 1828 (Add. MSS. 35148, vol. i. p. 55); Report and Evidence of House of Commons Committee on Select and Other Vestries, 1830; *Considerations on Select Vestries*, etc., 1828, p. 14; *Reports of the Sub-Committee appointed by the Committee of Management of the Parish of St. Paul, Covent Garden, for the Revision of their Workhouse*, etc., 1831.

[2] MS. Vestry Minutes, St. John, Hackney (Middlesex), 1834. Much the same had happened at Allhallows, Barking, in 1808 (*Modern History of the City of London*, by C. Welch, 1896, p. 129).

[3] *Times*, 18th February and 25th December 1828; Hansard, 21st May 1829, and 16th December 1830; see for this Vestry the Report and Evidence of the House of Commons Committee on Select and Other Vestries, 1830; also House of Commons Journals, vol. xxiv. p. 250; vol. xxxix. pp. 354-478, and the interesting *Sketch of the Present State of all the Poor in January 1797*, reprinted from *Annals of Agriculture*, vol. xxviii., and ably reviewed in *Gentleman's Magazine*, June 1797, p. 492; also Prebendary Kempe's letter in *Times*, 9th March 1901.

Christchurch, Spitalfields, where a Select Vestry, composed exclusively of past Churchwardens, had been established by Act of Parliament in 1727, the most scandalous jobbery and malversation of public funds were found to exist. The Select Vestry had incurred an expenditure of £7000 in repairing and redecorating the church, much of it paid to vestrymen for work done, and nearly the whole of it borrowed from other vestrymen at five per cent interest. A special Church Rate was made to defray this outlay, but many of the ratepayers refused payment. The attempts to enforce it extended over several years, and were, owing to this delay, largely unsuccessful. It was a further grievance that the assessments were grossly unequal, some householders being assessed up to the hilt, whilst the colossal brewery of Messrs. Truman, Hanbury, Buxton and Company, that dominated the parish, supposed to have cost between two and three hundred thousand pounds, was rated only at one thousand. A little committee of reformers kept up the agitation for over a year, holding public meetings every few weeks, which were reported in the Radical newspapers.[1] The legal position of the parish authorities proved, however, unassailable, and the agitation died away without accomplishing any result. In St. Pancras, now become a parish of over 100,000 inhabitants, the Select Vestry, which, as we have seen, was established by Act of Parliament in 1819, was the object of widespread denunciation. The total rates of the parish had risen from little over £10,000 in 1802 to over £44,000 in 1828. Over a hundred thousand pounds had been expended, during recent years, on building a new parish church and certain "chapels of ease." A "parochial committee" was formed in 1829, which kept up an agitation for two years, but failed to secure any change in the parish constitution.[2] In St. Martin's-in-the-Fields the claim of the Select Vestry to rate the parish,

---

[1] See *Weekly Despatch*, May, June, and 8th October 1826 ; *Times*, February 1827, April 1828 ; *Public Ledger*, May 1826 ; *Representative*, July 1826 ; *Considerations on Select Vestries*, 1828, p. 119 ; Report and Evidence of the House of Commons Committee on Select and Other Vestries, 1830.

[2] *A Narrative of certain Statements and Proceedings connected with the Select Vestry of the Parish of St. Pancras*, by E. W. Hamilton, Hon. Sec. to the Parochial Committee, 1831, p. 6 ; *The Substance of a Speech delivered by Henry Revell, Esq., before a special Board of the Select Vestry of the Parish of St. Pancras*, 1831, p. 6.

three times, as we have seen, upheld by the law courts, was again challenged, this time by a public-spirited inhabitant named Fenn, who began his agitation about 1822,[1] and did not shrink from expensive litigation, in which he received the powerful assistance of Brougham and Scarlett, the first lawyers of the time, and of Francis Place of Charing Cross, the most energetic and resourceful of Radicals.   During the year 1826 Fenn and Place were constantly in consultation, and their elaborate researches into parish history made them confident of success.   However, when the case came on in May 1827, it was tried before Chief Justice Abbott (afterwards Lord Tenterden), himself a Select Vestryman of St. Giles-in-the-Fields, who had, says Place, " shown his teeth at us from the first," and who certainly summed up in such a way as to make it difficult for the jury to do otherwise than find a verdict in favour of the Select Vestry.[2]   But the case which secured most attention, and was often brought before the House of Commons, was that of the large and rapidly increasing parish of Marylebone, in which the total expenditure had

---

[1] Place records in a memorandum of 1829, that " Mr. Fenn's pertinacity in his proceedings against the self-appointed Vestry of St. Martin's-in-the-Fields during the last seven years had roused the attention of many other parishes, had exposed many corruptions and abuses, and led to many amendments. Many persons came to me from different parishes, and in some cases it became requisite for me to take much pains to reconcile differences amongst those whose object was reformation of parish proceedings " (Add. MSS. 35146, p. 99).

[2] See for all this, Place's Diary, Add. MSS. 35146 ; *Times*, 5th January 1827 ; 4th, 5th, 7th, and 8th April 1828 ; 18th February and 2nd July 1829 ; MS. Vestry Minutes, St. Martin's-in-the-Fields, 3rd July and 11th August 1823 ; 19th April and 23rd November 1824 ; 14th and 23rd May 1827, and 14th February 1828.   The heavy expenses of the Vestry were paid from the Church Rate (*ibid.* 19th March 1829 and 6th November 1834).   On 18th October 1826, Place writes in his Diary : "Found a petition of Vicar and Churchwardens of St. Martin's" (House of Commons Journals), " anno 8 William III., in which they claim to be a Select Vestry in consequence of a faculty obtained from the Bishop of London in 1662, and confirmed in 1673.   This will put them out of court " (Add. MSS. 35146).   The case (Golding *v.* Fenn) was elaborately gone into in 1827 (fully reported in *Reports of Cases*, by R. V. Barnewall and C. Cresswell, 1828, vol. vii. pp. 765-783 ; also in *Reports of Cases*, by J. Manning and A. Ryland, 1828, vol. i. pp. 647-662), and though, by bias of the judge, the Select Vestry was again successful, it seems to have been felt by lawyers that what was virtually Chief Justice Abbott's decision could not be maintained.   In May 1834 the issue was again tried before Lord Denman, when Vestry minutes right back to 1525 were produced, with the result that, after prolonged deliberation, they gave a verdict against the Select Vestry (Simpson *v.* Holroyd, *Times*, 13th and 14th May 1834 ; MS. Vestry Minutes, 6th November 1834 ; *Our Parish*, by H. B. Simpson, 1836 ; see also the earlier case in 1832, R. *v.* St. Martin's, *Reports of Cases*, by R. V. Barnewall and E. H. Alderson, vol. iii. p. 907).

risen from less than £50,000 at the beginning of the century to over £145,000 in 1833. The fact that the parishioners had been for a century and a half entirely excluded from any share in or control over their local affairs had never excited any popular indignation. When, however, the rates rose from 2s. 6d. in 1824 to 3s. 11d. in 1827, the middle-class rate-payers began to protest. The Select Vestry—which indulged largely in Parliamentary expenses—happened to be promoting two Bills in 1827, one as to new churches, and the other consolidating all the parish law. Both these were opposed and eventually abandoned. The latter Bill was taken up in the following year by a committee of the parishioners, who put in clauses providing for an elective Vestry, but failed to induce the House of Commons to pass the measure. Then followed petition and counter-petition, with desultory discussions in Parliament from time to time, but without resulting in any reform of the Vestry constitution.[1]

By this time the agitation in particular parishes had developed into a general London movement for the total abolition of Select Vestries. " These nefarious and uncon-stitutional bodies," we are told in a powerful pamphlet of 1828, "have now become so intolerable a curse upon the parishes where they exist," [2] that a committee is formed to work for their defeat all over the Metropolis. What this committee did, or how long it lasted, we do not know. We hear of meetings of delegates from different parishes, represent-ing an aggregate population of half a million, which decided to petition Parliament and to recommend a general refusal to pay rates.[3] The *Times* gave the movement its support. During

---

[1] *Times*, 7th and 19th June 1828, 3rd March 1829 ; *An Account of the Church and Parish of St. Giles's Without, Cripplegate*, by J. J. Baddeley, 1888, p. 171 ; *Reply to a Circular recently issued by a Self-appointed Association formed in this parish for the purpose of opposing Mr. Hobhouse's Bill for the Abolition of Self-elected Vestries, 1831* ; a *Topographical and Historical Account of the Parish of St. Marylebone*, by Thomas Smith, 1833 ; a good description in the *Hackney Magazine*, March 1836 ; and a remarkable work scurrilously denouncing the reformers, entitled *The Democrats of Marylebone*, by James Williamson Brooke, 1839.

[2] *Considerations on Select Vestries ; showing from the oppressions and corrupt practices now prevailing in the different parishes where they exist, the necessity of their abolition, and the expediency of restoring to the parishioners at large a legitimate interference and control in the management of parochial business*, by One of the Non-Select, 1828, p. 3.

[3] *The Substance of a Speech delivered by Henry Revell, Esq., before a special Board of the Select Vestry of the Parish of St. Pancras*, 1831, p. 6.

the years 1827-1830 it frequently contained notices of public
meetings, agitations, and petitions promoted in different parts
of London, with the object of throwing open all the Select
Vestries.[1]   In St. Martin's parish the indefatigable Fenn continued year by year to protest against the exclusion of the
ratepayers from the Easter Vestry, holding meetings outside
the barred door, and attending before Petty Sessions to make
vain objection to the allowance of the Overseers' accounts.[2]
The agitation might possibly have died away, as others had
done before, had not the reform of the parish been taken up by
the little knot of Radicals in and about the House of Commons,
as part of their general crusade for the establishment of
representative institutions in every branch of government.
The "rotten boroughs" in the provinces, against which these
Radicals were always declaiming, attracted, because so many of
them elected members of Parliament, more public attention
than the London Select Vestries.   But the close corporations
of the provincial municipalities usually took little part in the
services that now make up most of local government, and in
the majority of cases they lived on their property, with its
ancient adjuncts of fees and tolls, and levied no direct taxation
on the householder.   The "self-elected" Vestries of the London
parishes, on the other hand, were wielding large and apparently
unlimited powers of government; they came at every turn in
contact with the daily life of each household; and they levied,

---

[1] See, for instance, 5th January and 4th June 1827; 18th February, 20th, 22nd,
and 25th March, 4th, 5th, 7th, 8th, 9th, and 30th April, 27th August, 16th
and 20th September, and 25th December 1828 ; 12th and 14th January, 18th
February, 30th April, 11th and 16th May, and 2nd July 1829 ; 17th February
and 1st April 1830.   The following is from a leading article of 20th March 1828 :
"A Select Vestry is a close corporation self-elected so often as vacancies occur,
and responsible to no power but itself ; and possessing, what the House of
Commons does not, unbounded control over the fortunes of the public. . . .
Whatever rate the Select Vestry please to impose upon their parish they may
enforce : there is none to gainsay them.   Whatever abuse or corruption it thinks
fit to ordain or tolerate, in employment of the revenue thus wrung from the
people, there is none to question.   It is the most terrible prerogative committed
to the most unassailable of agents ; a rotten borough erected in the heart of
each parish, exercising a sway at once unbounded and irresponsible.   Parliament,
we are sure, if it listen to the voice of the people from Marylebone to Penzance,
will revise and cut away this modern excrescence upon the constitution of the
country."
[2] *Times*, 4th, 5th, 7th, and 8th April 1828 ; 18th February and 2nd July
1829 ; MS. Vestry Minutes, St. Martin's-in-the-Fields, 13th March, 7th April
7th November 1828.

without limit or control, a constantly increasing taxation, in many parishes already exceeding in amount the direct demands of the national government itself.[1] To those Radicals who were Nonconformists in religion, it was an added grievance that this parochial taxation included the maintenance and extension of the services of the Church of England.

(c) *Opening the Close Vestry*

The scandals of local administration in London had long attracted the notice of Francis Place, the tailor of Charing Cross to whose consummate organising skill and unwearied energy so many legislative reforms are to be ascribed.[2] On his initiative, the question was at length taken up in Parliament by John Cam Hobhouse (afterwards Lord Broughton), then one of the Radical members for Westminster, a constituency governed almost entirely by Select Vestries. Working in close association with Place, Hobhouse began in 1828 to worry the House of Commons with the scandals of London local government. The Parliamentary reports for this period unfortunately paid little attention to so dull a subject as Vestry reform; but the occasional references in Hansard and the newspapers, supplemented by Place's own letters and manuscripts, give us a vision of Hobhouse presenting petitions against the Close Vestries, opposing any Bills which they promoted, and doing his best, with the aid of Sir Francis Burdett and Joseph Hume, to compel Parliament to take the matter up. With Place always at his elbow with facts and

---

[1] The leading parish reformer in St. Pancras thus expressed this feeling: "A great city, under the denomination of a parish, containing 120,000 inhabitants, raising a revenue sufficient to have enabled England to have conquered the ancient Kings of France; a parish equal in population, knowledge, and wealth to many first-rate cities in the realm, and which even send members to Parliament,—this great parish is under the direction of a board in the appointment of which the inhabitants have no voice nor control whatever. What, sir, we want is that the principle of Election should be adopted in the appointment of those by whom we are governed: that those who are invested with offices of trust should be subject to responsibility" (*The Substance of a Speech delivered by Henry Revell, Esq., before a special Board of the Select Vestry of the Parish of St. Pancras*, 1831, p. 17).

[2] See *The Life of Francis Place*, by Graham Wallas, 1898; *History of Trade Unionism*, by S. and B. Webb, 1894, chap. ii., and the many manuscript volumes of Place's Autobiography, Diary, Letters, etc., in British Museum, here referred to as Add. MSS.

arguments, and aided by the agitation in Marylebone, St. James's, and St. Martin's, where many members resided, Hobhouse at last got his way.[1] In April 1829, in a speech of considerable power, he moved for a Select Committee to inquire into the constitution and administration of Select and other Vestries, which was assented to by the Ministry.[2] In the management of this committee, which included Sturges Bourne, Sir James Graham, and Daniel O'Connell, Hobhouse was not sufficiently bold to gain the approval of Place, who was a hard taskmaster.[3] But the committee had, by the end of the session, heard evidence about twenty-six urban Vestries, twenty in London and six in other towns. Hobhouse, having gathered a convincing mass of facts about the London parishes, decided to close the inquiry, and report to the House in general terms early in 1830 in favour of elective Vestries.[4] Upon this

---

[1] Place records, in 1829, that "Mr. Hobhouse had said in the House of Commons that, early in the session of 1829, he should introduce a Bill to regulate Parish Vestries in the Metropolis. As the meeting of Parliament drew near, people came to me from many parishes to learn if possible what the provisions of Mr. Hobhouse's Bill were to be, and to suggest such matters as they thought should be introduced into it." Place knew that Hobhouse had no Bill ready, and "had not at all considered either the matter of which it should be composed, or the extent of the trouble he was likely to bring upon himself." Place, in consultation with Mr. Dennison, M.P., a friend of Hobhouse, advised "that the best way for him to proceed would be a motion for a Select Committee to take evidence" (Add. MSS. 35146, p. 99).

[2] Hansard, vol. xxi. pp. 890-905, 28th April 1829 ; House of Commons Journals, vol. lxxxiv. p. 244, 28th April 1829.

[3] To quote Place again : "Mr. Hobhouse trifled in the Committee on Parish Vestries. He was overpowered and subdued by Sturges Bourne, and did not push his examination of witnesses to the extent he ought to have done. When the report was to be made he received, as I afterwards discovered, a request from the Speaker that he would not move that the minutes be printed, so he went out of town and the minutes were simply laid on the table." It will be remembered that the Speaker was himself a member of the Select Vestry of St. Margaret's. Place continues as follows : "Mr. Hobhouse's conduct gave great offence and put his seat in jeopardy. . . . Mr. Hobhouse soon discovered that he had made many enemies and no friends, and he therefore promised to have the report printed, and the committee renewed, as soon as the session commenced" (Add. MSS. 35146, p. 102 ; see also Place to Colonel Jones of Marylebone, 5th November 1829, in Add. MSS. 35148, p. 37).

[4] See the two *Reports from the Select Committee appointed to inquire into the general operation and effect of the laws and usages under which Select and Other Vestries are constituted in England and Wales* ; 10th February and 1st April 1830, vol. iv. of Session 1830, p. 427 ; and the interesting, but very biassed, commentary on this evidence by Francis Place in Add. MSS. 35148, p. 44, etc. The biographer of Sir James Graham states that he devoted great attention to his work on this committee (see *Life and Times of Sir James Graham*, by T. M'Cullagh Torrens, 1863, vol. i. p. 238).

report he founded a Bill, into which he put as much democracy as he could venture to bring before an unreformed House of Commons. We see Place, as usual, eager to prompt the legislator. "If they who have the power," he writes to Hobhouse on the 22nd March 1830, "had the requisite knowledge, they would at once pass an Act giving to every parish both the right and the power to elect their own Vestries annually, giving to each Vestry the power to originate and control all parish matters in every department ; compelling them, however, to proceed in one uniform way all over the country, doing everything openly, and publishing their audited accounts every three months. It is objected that if men are elected for short periods they will have no time to acquire the necessary experience, but will be continually displaced by others, who will proceed in the same course. The very reverse is the fact, and always will be so where the elections are really free and the periods short, and accountability as perfect as it can be made. . . . Annual election is election for life if the representative do his duty in a becoming manner."[1] After some further correspondence, Hobhouse, in his letter to Place of 16th April 1830, gives us the first draft of his Bill. "I am now doing my best to prepare that Bill, but I find myself a good deal embarrassed with technical difficulties, as also with the necessity of making the provisions apply to all parishes, small as well as large, rural as well as metropolitan. It is also very much against my own inclination, that for the sake of doing some good, I find myself compelled to give up the great principle of giving to every ratepayer one vote and no more. If, however, I restrict the right of voting to persons rated at a certain sum, I shall endeavour to prevent more than one vote being given to any man whatever may be his property. In this great effort I shall probably be defeated, but I will do all I can to get all they will let me have. I will have no open polling at all. Votes shall be given by writing and by lists which shall be examined by sworn inspectors. All the executive officers of every parish shall be elected. The government shall be in a Committee of Vestry, not less than twelve and not more than twenty (?), which shall

[1] Place to Hobhouse, 22nd March 1830 (Add. MSS. 35148 ; see also *Life of Francis Place*, by Graham Wallas, 1898, p. 155).

be chosen annually. The two Churchwardens shall be chosen annually. Eight Overseers chosen annually, and of these, two elected by Justices. Three Auditors of Accounts chosen annually. Five inspectors of elections chosen annually. All parish servants, such as clerks, collectors, treasurers, church beadles, etc., to be chosen by the Committee of Vestry, and such [parish servants] as have funds entrusted to their hands to give adequate security. And all these elections to take place on the same day and in the same form, that is, by list as above mentioned. The Bill is not to apply to any parish except at the desire of a majority of the ratepayers. The machinery of this adoption of the Act in populous parishes I find very difficult to construct, and I wish much to have some talk with you on that and many other provisions of my statute. If what I have told you suggests any hints pray be so good as to favour me with them. The penalties are a hard chapter. I do not like them, but must have them. Oaths, too, I fear I must have them."[1] But although this Bill was supported by Francis Place, and those who were eager for increased honesty and efficiency of administration in the great London parishes, it was far from pleasing the Radicals of the North of England. At Leeds and Manchester they clung fondly to government by the Open Vestry meeting, in which every ratepayer could take part. They regarded the establishment of an administrative body, even though elective, as a falling away from democratic principles, all the more so because it was commonly understood that Parliament always insisted on a high qualification. Besides, the fact that the concentration of duties must necessarily lead to the actual work of the parish being done by a salaried staff was the reverse of attractive to these early democrats. Thus Hobhouse found his Bill resisted by the Tories, and not strongly supported—even sometimes opposed—by popular Radicalism.[2]

[1] For all these transactions, see the Place Manuscripts in the British Museum, Add. MSS., especially 35146 and 35148 ; briefly noticed in Graham Wallas's *Life of Francis Place*, 1898, pp. 154, 155 ; and Hansard, especially vol. xxi. p. 890, 28th April 1829 ; vols. v. and vii. of 3rd series, 30th June, 25th July, and 30th September 1831.

[2] The Leeds Vestry opposed the Bill by a petition containing the following interesting arguments :—

"It would not secure its chief object, economical administration of parish monies : it is complicated in its details and abundantly prolific in stipendiary

Moreover, the Bill in its first form seems to have proposed to repeal all Local Acts inconsistent with its provisions, and thus to have virtually compelled the application of the new parish constitution throughout the whole country. This brought up to London the solicitor of the Plymouth Street Commissioners, and doubtless many others, in hot alarm lest such bodies should be interfered with.[1] Nevertheless Hobhouse persevered, and the Bill slipped through second reading. It was, however, so emasculated by the Tories in committee, that its author lost interest in its progress, and was not sorry when the King's death, on the 26th June 1830, brought the Parliament prematurely to an end.[2] The new House contained an unusually large proportion of new members, and under the influence of the successful " July revolution " in Paris, the Whigs began to take heart. Then followed the dramatic collapse of the Government, the first Ministry of Earl Grey, the defeat of the Reform Bill in Committee, and the sudden dissolution. The new Parliament which met in June 1831 contained a majority of over a hundred who were for " the Bill, the whole Bill, and nothing but the Bill," and who could just then think of little else. The first session lasted only for four exciting months, during which the Reform Bill was fought with the utmost bitterness and obstruction, and the momentous political crisis that was approaching filled everyone's thoughts. Under cover of this excitement Hobhouse reintroduced his Vestry Bill in an amended form; slipped it through its various stages; and after some mutilations from Lord Althorp, saw it passed into law just as the House of

---

appointments. Complication would be caused by mixing the duties of Overseers, Churchwardens, and Improvement Commissioners, and by merging all townships in parishes. Township divisions are generally to be preferred to parish divisions. The Bill would give the Committee of Vestry absolute power for their year of service, and whatever might be their misrule or malversation there could be no public or Open Vestry, nor could the inhabitants of the parish individually or collectively call them to account. It would subvert the principle on which Vestries have hitherto been conducted, as it would deprive three-fourths, at least, of the ratepayers of any control over parish affairs " (MS. Vestry Minutes, Leeds, Yorkshire, 3rd June 1830).

[1] MS. Minutes, Street Commissioners, Plymouth (Devon), 13th April and 8th June 1830.

[2] The amendment to which Hobhouse and his friends most strongly objected was that which introduced the Sturges Bourne system of plural voting. Hobhouse evidently refused to reintroduce the Bill in the following session unless he was allowed to omit this clause.

Lords, by throwing out the Reform Bill, was bringing the country to the verge of armed revolt.[1]

"Hobhouse's Act," as this measure was called, differed radically from the legislation of Sturges Bourne. It included among parochial electors every person, male or female, who paid rates, however low the assessment. It gave every ratepayer one vote only. It even introduced annual elections and vote by ballot. It adopted the system of voting, since known as *scrutin de liste*, under which each elector voted for a list of candidates, and himself deposited this list in the ballot-box. On the other hand, here again differing from Sturges Bourne's Act, it restricted the choice of the electors to persons having a rating qualification so high as to exclude the great majority of the population.[2] And it introduced, doubtless with the object of securing continuity of administration, a system by which one-third only of the elected representatives retired each year. Other important innovations were the annual election, by the ratepayers, of independent auditors empowered to audit all parish accounts; the requirement that the Vestry should publish annually a complete statement of the parish property and the parish charities; and the throwing open to public inspection of the minutes and accounts. The elected Vestry was not restricted to the management of the poor, or to any other particular function, but became at once the general administrative body for all the business of the old Vestry. And most important of all, the Act, unlike that of Sturges Bourne, entirely superseded the "meeting of inhabitants in Vestry assembled," giving all its powers to the elected body, and accordingly making this the supreme governing authority, with all the powers, customary or statutory, that the previous Vestry had possessed. Thus the Act was not only, to use the words of M'Cullagh Torrens, "the first legislative attempt to apply the principle of municipal self-government to the inorganic masses of population and property

---

[1] 1 and 2 William IV. c. 60, "An Act for the better regulation of Vestries and for the appointment of Auditors of Accounts in certain parishes of England and Wales." The Royal Assent was given 20th October 1831, the day on which Parliament was prorogued.

[2] The qualifications for vestrymen in all parishes within the Metropolitan Police District, and in others having 3000 rated householders, was the occupation of premises within the parish rated at £40 or upwards; in other parishes, £10 or upwards.

forming the modern additions to London," [1] but was also the
first instalment of the legislative revolution which has since
placed the whole of English local government uniformly upon
the basis of representative institutions.

But in one respect the Act followed the precedent of
1819. Unlike the subsequent reforms of 1834 and 1835,
it did not compulsorily impose the new constitution upon any
parish. It was left to one-fifth of the ratepayers to call upon
the Churchwardens to take a poll of the parish, and the Act
was not adopted unless an actual majority of all the ratepayers took the trouble to vote, and unless two-thirds of those
voting were in favour of the change. Moreover, though
Hobhouse contemplated no such limitation,[2] and though the
Act expressly states that it is applicable to "any parish or
parishes in England and Wales," having eight hundred rated
inhabitants, it was commonly understood to concern only
those parishes which were governed by close bodies. For
this and other reasons, it was only adopted in a comparatively
few parishes; principally, if not entirely, those having Select
Vestries in the Metropolitan area.[3]

Meanwhile, as we have described in a preceding chapter,
the life of the parish itself was being brought to an end by
the withdrawal from it of the administration of the Poor Law
and the gradual cessation of the Church Rate. To this
strangling of the Parish, as we have described it, there was
destined to be one great exception. By a curious irony it

---

[1] *Life and Times of Sir James Graham*, by T. M'Cullagh Torrens, 1863,
vol. i. p. 239.

[2] Toulmin Smith says "it was, no doubt, introduced more immediately to
meet the cases of close Select Vestries. But it was not the idea of Sir John
Hobhouse (Lord Broughton) who introduced it, that it should be limited in
operation to those cases only. I speak here from the written statement, which
I have seen, of Lord Broughton, to that effect" (*The Parish*, 1857, p. 240).

[3] As the adoption of the Act was not compulsory, it did not repeal Sturges
Bourne's Acts of 1818-1819, nor any of the Local Acts affecting particular parishes.
The purely optional character of the Act was felt as a grave drawback. "This,"
says a critic of 1833, "is the first and only instance in the statute-book which
gives an option to the people to act upon or reject a law as they may please"
(*A Letter to the Ratepayers of Great Britain on the Repeal of the Poor Law*, by
J. Sedgwick, 1833, p. 41). Two local newspapers were started in London, one
for and the other against the adoption of the Act in Marylebone and St. Pancras,
see *The New Vestryman*, 1833-1834, and *The True Vestryman, or Borough of
Marylebone Gazette*, 1833-1834, from each of which many glimpses of the contemporary local government may be obtained. Another journal, *The Vestryman,
and Metropolitan Parochial Gazette*, started in 1834, lived only for a few weeks.

was the Metropolitan Vestries, which had proved on the whole so corrupt, and not the purer bodies of the provincial parishes, that were destined to continue as important local governing authorities. The London Vestries were, however, to undergo a change in function. They, like the provincial Vestries, lost the administration of poor relief, which, under the Act of 1834, gradually passed to elected Boards of Guardians. They, too, by refusing to vote anything called a Church Rate, threw away their immemorial autonomy and their unrestricted power of undertaking any service that the common good required and that the parishioners desired. Nevertheless, unlike all other Vestries, the work of those within the metropolitan area, but outside the City of London, was destined, not to shrinkage but to enormous enlargement. The effect of the absence of any organised municipalities in the great parishes of the metropolitan area was to throw into the hands of their Vestries during the reign of Queen Victoria the administration of many of the new services of urban life. Partially reformed under Hobhouse's Act, and further re-organised by the Metropolis Management Act of 1855, it was to these Vestries that Parliament was driven to commit more and more powers of sanitation and control, until at last, in 1900, they were, with some little rearrangement of their areas and powers, raised to the dignity of Metropolitan Borough Councils, sharing with the London County Council the whole municipal government of the greatest city in the world.

BOOK II

THE COUNTY

INTRODUCTION

To any member of the governing class at the time of the Revolution, the notion of beginning the present volume with an elaborate description of the Parish and its Vestry would have seemed preposterous. In their eyes, the government of the various parts of England and Wales rested, under King and Parliament, with the official dignitaries of the County [1]—

---

[1] No convenient treatise on County government is known to us. Much information is, as usual, afforded by the various works of Rudolph von Gneist (especially *Self-Government Communalverfassung und Verwaltungsgechichte in England*, 3rd edition, 1871); which may be supplemented by the earlier sketch, *Darstellung der inneren Verwaltung Grosbritanniens*, by F. L. W. P. von Vincke, 1815; by a convenient French manual, *Le Gouvernement Local de l'Angleterre*, by Maurice Vauthier, 1895; by the scholarly treatise, *Le Developpement de la Constitution et de la Société Anglaise*, by E. Boutmy, 1887; and by an able work of recent date, *Englische Local Verwaltung*, by Dr. S. Redlich, 1901; translated and revised as *Local Government in England*, by Dr. S. Redlich and F. W. Hirst, 1903. For English books, see the footnotes to the subsequent pages. Whilst making great use of contemporary pamphlets, charges, speeches, newspapers, novels, plays, and even sermons, we have had to construct our account in the main from the statutes, the law text-books, and the judges' decisions on the one hand, and, on the other, from the MS. minutes and orders of Quarter Sessions from 1689 to 1835, which we have explored in about two-thirds of the English counties. These county records are only now beginning to be printed, and that only imperfectly, and in a few counties; but they afford most valuable material for contemporary social history. The principal of these publications are *The Middlesex County Records*, 1550-1709, edited first by J. C. Jeaffreson and then by W. J. Hardy, 5 vols. 1888-1905; *The Worcestershire County Records*, edited by J. C. Willis Bund, 1899; the *West Riding Sessions Rolls*, 1597-1602, edited by J. Lister, 1888; the *North Riding Quarter Sessions Records*, 1578-1778, edited by J. C. Atkinson and T. Turton, 10 vols. 1884-1904; the *Shropshire County Records*, in 10 parts, edited by Sir Offley Wakeman, Bart., Rev. L. S. Lee, and R. G. Venables, and a printed volume of miscellaneous documents of the Justices of Hertfordshire. Unfortunately hardly any of them at present extend much beyond the seventeenth century. Extracts from the records of Wiltshire (1591-1744) and Worcestershire (1577-1696) will be found in the Report of the Historical Manuscripts Commission (Cd.-784), 1901, vol. i. pp. 65-176, 282-326. Two books founded on such documents, *Three Centuries of Derbyshire Annals*, by J. C. Cox, 2 vols. 1890; and *Quarter*

the Lord-Lieutenant, the High Sheriff, and the Justices of the Peace. They would, of course, have been aware that the City of London was wholly exempt from county control and that, up and down the land, there existed many cities, boroughs, franchises, and liberties which successfully claimed to exclude this or that particular county jurisdiction. But the suggestion that there existed any kind of lawful autonomy in the ten or fifteen thousand parishes and townships would have appeared to the country gentleman, at the end of the seventeenth century, an absurd and dangerous innovation. The Constables, the Overseers of the Poor, and the Surveyors of the Highways held their appointments from the Justices, and had to obey the Justices' orders, whilst even the Churchwardens seemed to act partly as colleagues of the Overseers, and partly as ecclesiastical officers, under the direction of the Incumbent and the Archdeacon. The little meeting of inhabitants in Vestry assembled appeared only as a convenient device for communicating to the Justices the names of those on whom the onerous parish offices might be cast, for bringing to light any dereliction of duty on the part of these officers, and for promulgating the amount of the rate and other decisions for which the Justices were legally responsible. And if, excluding the management of the parish church and its semi-voluntary revenue, we were to confine our attention strictly to the legal framework of the constitution, or even to its working in the rural and stationary parts of the country, we might admit the substantial accuracy of the Justices' view. Looking back to our preceding chapters, it will be seen that the practical autonomy of the parish manifested itself chiefly in the extra-legal developments made necessary by the growth of the urban population of the New England of the Industrial Revolution.

It will be convenient here to draw attention to a shortcoming in our work, not apparent in our treatment of the Parish, but radically affecting both the following description of the County and the succeeding volume on Seignorial Franchises and Municipal Corporations. We have restricted ourselves to a description of local institutions as organs of

Sessions from Queen Elizabeth to Queen Anne, by A. H. A. Hamilton, 1878, also afford valuable material. *The Story of Some English Shires*, by Mandell Creighton, 1897, gives, in popular form, much historical information as to nearly half the counties.

Local Government as the latter phrase is at present understood : we do not aim at displaying their working as subordinate parts of the national machinery for the administration of justice. Local Government, as we nowadays interpret it, is concerned always with the organisation of public services for existing and future needs. The execution of justice, now the only function of the courts of law, deals with the application of previously enacted rules of law to cases of individual conduct, usually of the past. When a modern local authority passes a resolution to license a public-house or repair a bridge, its action is nowadays clearly distinguished from the order of a judicial tribunal condemning a person to fine or imprisonment, or to the payment of compensation or damages. But in the reign of William and Mary, whether the Justices in Quarter Sessions assembled ordered a highwayman to be transported or a road to be mended—whether the Petty or Divisional Sessions licensed an ale-house or committed a murderer to stand his trial at the Assizes—whether an individual Justice directed some destitute person to be relieved or sentenced him as a vagabond to be whipped, no distinction was made, either by the Justices themselves or by the text-book writers, between the two classes of cases. All these decisions had, according to constitutional theory, to be arrived at upon the evidence and in strict accordance with pre-existing obligations imposed by the law of the land.[1]

In practice, however, even seventeenth century Justices

[1] Even down to the nineteenth century the administrative and judicial functions of the Justices were so intermingled that most writers give up the attempt to distinguish between them. We are told that " it is not easy to fix any rule for distinguishing, in the abstract, between what things are the subject of orders of Justices, and what of convictions by them. Before the Statute of 4 Geo. II. convictions were always recorded in Latin, whereas orders were returned in English ; and we find this circumstance referred to as a criterion. . . . Perhaps the only criterion that can be furnished for distinguishing when penal proceedings are to be considered as orders, and when as convictions, is that alluded to by Lord Hardwicke in R. *v.* Bissex, viz. whether they be so denominated by the statute which gives the Justices jurisdiction to make them " (Burn's *Justice of the Peace*, vol. v. p. 287 of edition of 1845). Yet the distinction was of more than theoretical importance. An order by one or more Justices out of sessions could usually be appealed against to Quarter Sessions under the general jurisdiction given by the Commission of the Peace. A conviction by two or more Justices could only be made the subject of appeal to Quarter Sessions if such appeal had been expressly provided for by the statute enabling the offence to be dealt with summarily (*The Introduction of a Justice of the Peace to the Court of Quarter Sessions*, by W. Robinson, 1836, p. 350).

felt themselves much more free to exercise their discretion in the relief of destitution, in the maintenance of roads and bridges, in the regulation of wages and prices, in the licensing of ale-houses, and in the establishment and administration of Houses of Correction, than they did in punishing theft or suppressing a riot.　Gradually this distinction between the administration of local affairs and the execution of national justice becomes more and more marked, both in practice and in the language of the statute book.　This widening cleavage between the old and the new conception of Local Government led, as we shall see, to the spontaneous and largely unconscious development of a constitution for the County that was unknown to the law.　But in 1689 the distinction had hardly begun to be characteristic, and we necessarily find ourselves describing machinery which was devoted, in the main, to the execution of justice.　We shall, however, focus our attention principally on the working of this machinery in so far as it dealt with services coming under the modern definition of Local Government.　We leave to students qualified by practical experience of judicial procedure the fascinating but intricate task of describing and valuing the County, the Manor, and the Municipal Corporation in so far as they furnished the lower members of a series of courts for the administration of civil and criminal justice, culminating in the House of Lords or the King in Council.

CHAPTER I

THE LEGAL CONSTITUTION OF THE COUNTY

WE begin our description of county government between 1689 and 1835 with a sketch of the legal framework of the county organisation, as we think it would have been determined by the law courts of William and Mary.

(a) *The Area and Divisions of the County*

To take first the geography, we see at once that the shire or county differed from the parish in comprising a wide but definitely ascertained area, varying from the 150 square miles of Rutland, with a population in 1689 probably of less than 15,000, to the 2600 square miles of Devonshire, with a population that cannot have been less than 300,000, whilst Middlesex must have had twice that number.[1] Though some of the fifty-two counties into which, since the reign of Henry the Eighth, England and Wales had been definitely divided, had, at the Revolution, and indeed, down to our own day, many detached outliers of territory interspersed with that of neighbouring counties, the limits of jurisdiction of each county were accurately known, and the county boundary was, nearly everywhere, the deepest and most enduring of English divisions. The parish, as we have seen, not infrequently extended across the county boundary, but the jurisdiction of the county officers, high or low, was rigidly confined to their own shire. " If a parish lies in two

---

[1] We estimate, however, that about half the geographical counties of England had, in 1689, fairly even populations of somewhere about 100,000 as a mean. Those of Wales were mostly under 20,000 each.

counties," says a statute of 1601, "or if part is within a town corporate and part without," then the respective Justices are to concern themselves only with that part of the parish which is within their jurisdiction.[1] With the exception of Berwick-on-Tweed (which was not legally included in England) there soon came to be, even if there was not already in 1689, from one end of the country to the other, no "extra-comitial" place.[2] The City of London, it is true, was not only a county in itself, but, unlike other "counties corporate," even had its own Commission of Lieutenancy excluding the authority of the Lord-Lieutenant of Middlesex, the "county at large" in which it is geographically situated. The little town and "county in itself" of Haverfordwest, lying geographically in Pembrokeshire, had its own independent Lord-Lieutenant and Custos Rotulorum. The Lord Warden of the Cinque Ports and the Constable of the Tower of London might continue to claim an independent status. But all the other cities and boroughs that were and are "counties corporate," and all the liberties, franchises, boroughs, and cities that were exempt from this or that county jurisdiction, were nevertheless presently regarded, if not already so regarded in 1689, as falling, in respect at least of the military jurisdiction of the Lord-Lieutenant, within one or other of the "counties at large."

Within the county the principal division was the Hundred, Wapentake, Ward, Lathe or Rape,[3] an adminis-

---

[1] 43 Eliz. c. 2 (1601). About eighty-five parishes extended into more counties than one.

[2] We refer, in an appendix to this section, to the difficulty of deciding what constitutes a county, and to the peculiar position of the "counties corporate," the "Counties Palatine," and certain ecclesiastical Liberties.

[3] In Wales, the ancient division analogous to the Hundred was the Cantrev. This, with its subdivisions of Commote, Maenol, Trev, and Gavel, largely determined the modern county divisions (*The Welsh People*, by John Rhys, 1900 ; *Kalendars of Gwynedd*, etc., by Edward Breese, 1873 ; *Cambrian Register*, 1795-1796, etc.). The term Hundred, used principally in the Anglian part of England, has tended to become dominant. Wards are found only in Northumberland, Durham, Cumberland, and Westmorland, when the defensive border warfare left its mark on the local organisation. Wapentakes exist in Yorkshire, Lincolnshire, Derbyshire, Nottinghamshire, Northampton-shire, Leicestershire, and Rutland. Lathes and Rapes are found in Kent and Sussex respectively (*Self-Government*, etc., by R. von Gneist, part ii. ch. ii.). The origin and history of these divisions of the county have given rise to much discussion ; see *History of Taxation and Taxes in England*, by S. Dowell, 1888, vol. i. book i. ; *History of English Law*, by Sir F. Pollock and F. W. Maitland

trative unit of unknown origin or purpose, but of great antiquity, which served, in 1689, together with the various cities, boroughs, liberties, and franchises, as convenient local subdivisions for most county purposes. Compared with the complicated network of parish government, different in each locality, and perpetually changing, the government of the county was, at the close of the seventeenth century, from one end of England to the other, simple, uniform, and stable. If the parish authorities resemble the dense and tangled undergrowth of a primæval forest, the administrators of the county stand out, in contrast, like the forest trees, enduring in their stately growth from generation to generation, each individual remaining true to one or other of a relatively small number of clearly defined species.

(b) *The Custos Rotulorum*

At the head of each county was the great personage, usually a peer or a great local landowner, whom we find, from the Revolution onwards, nearly always combining in himself the civil office of Custos Rotulorum, or keeper of the records of the county, and the military post of Lord-Lieutenant, in command for the King of all the armed forces of the county.[1]

1895, vol. i. p. 543 ; *Feudal England*, by J. H. Round, 1895, p. 97, etc., and *The Growth of the Manor*, by P. Vinogradoff, 1905, p. 144 ; together with the references there cited. The Hundreds, which were in mediæval times often connected with the bailiwicks into which the county was divided under the High Sheriff, and in later years with the Petty Sessional Divisions of the Justices, varied enormously in area, population, and compactness. "So irregular is this distribution of territory, that while some of the southern Hundreds do not exceed 2 square miles . . . the Hundreds of Lancashire average at 300 square miles in area" (Population Abstract, Census of 1831, vol. i. p. xv.). See also House of Commons Return, No. 235 of 1856. Dorsetshire had no fewer than 100 Hundreds or Demi-Hundreds ; Kent 72, Sussex 70, and Somerset 42 ; whilst Durham had only 4, Cumberland 6, Westmorland 4, and Northumberland 9. The total for England and Wales, including the equivalent Liberties and Franchises, was about 900 ; now readjusted into about 675 Petty Sessional Divisions.

[1] For the offices of Custos Rotulorum and Lord-Lieutenant, see 37 Henry VIII. c. 1 (1545) ; 3 and 4 Edward VI. c. 1 (1550) ; 13 and 14 Charles I. c. 3 (1661), and 1 William and Mary c. 21 (1688) ; Harding *v.* Pollock, 1829, in *Reports of Cases*, etc., by P. Bingham, vol. vi. p. 25 ; *Eirenarcha*, by W. Lambard, 1602, book iv. ch. iii. p. 369; Hallam's *Constitutional History*, 1827, vol. x. ch. ix. ; *Rise and Progress of the English Constitution*, by Sir Edward Creasy ; *Military Forces of the Crown*, by C. M. Clode, 1869, vol. ii. ; *Self-Government*, by R. von Gneist, part ii. ch. i. sec. 9 ; *War Office Manual of Military Law*, 1894 ; *Law and Custom of the Constitution*, by Sir W. R. Anson, 1896, vol. ii.

From at least the beginning of the sixteenth century onwards it had been customary for the Crown, as we learn from the statute of 37 Henry VIII., to designate in the Commission of the Peace, as Custos Rotulorum, or "keeper of the rolls of the peace," one of the leading justices of the county, "a man," says Lambard, "especially picked out either for wisdom, countenance, or credit."[1] The military office of Lieutenant of the county dates only from the middle of the sixteenth century, and was at first a temporary appointment unconnected with the civil administration; often held, in fact, by one trusted officer for several counties.[2] From the reign of William and Mary, however, we find the two offices usually united (though always by separate and generally not quite simultaneous appointments, the one under Letters Patent, the other by writ of Privy Seal) in the same person,[3] who came to be regarded as the representative in the county of the Monarch himself. With the disuse of the ancient "musters" of the county, and of the commissions of array, the military duties of the Lord - Lieutenant had, at the Revolution, shrunk to little more than patronage and ceremonial. He still appointed Deputy - Lieutenants[4] for

pp. 156, 245, 356, 450; *Three Centuries of Derbyshire Annals*, by J. C. Cox, 1890, vol. i. sec. 2; Report of Royal Commission on Amalgamation of the City and County of London, 1893; and *The Lord-Lieutenant and the High Sheriff*, by C. G. Y., 1860. Lists of the Custodes Rotulorum and Lord-Lieutenants for nearly a century are given in *Magna Britanniæ Notitia, or the Present State of Great Britain*, by E., and then J., Chamberlayne; the last edition being 1755.

[1] *Eirenarcha*, by W. Lambard, 1602, book iv. ch. iii. p. 371; 37 Henry VIII. cap. 1 (1546).

[2] In 1687 ten great peers held over twenty lieutenancies among them. There are still common Lord-Lieutenants for Cambridgeshire and Huntingdonshire, and Cumberland and Westmorland respectively.

[3] But in 1755, the two offices were held by different persons in Durham, the North Riding, and Herefordshire. Moreover, there was a Custos Rotulorum for the soke of Peterborough, appointed 1727, but no Lord-Lieutenant (Home Office Domestic Entry Book, vol. x., 18th October 1727, in Public Record Office; *Magna Britanniæ Notitia, or the Present State of Great Britain*, by J. Chamberlayne, 1755, book iii. pp. 54-56).

[4] The office of Deputy-Lieutenant, now a mere social distinction, carrying the right to wear a gorgeous military uniform, was, in the eighteenth century, part of the organisation for national defence. The Home Office Domestic State Papers for 1745 in the Public Record Office show us the Deputy-Lieutenants in each county actively engaged, under the Lord - Lieutenant, in the details of military organisation. On the reorganisation of the militia under the Act of 1756, such duties fell rather to the officers of the newly raised militia regiments, whom the Lord-Lieutenant equally appointed; and we assume that it was then that the office of Deputy-Lieutenant became one of

the county and all the officers of the county militia, and took command, in any emergency, of all the local forces of the county in its fullest geographical sense, including, to use the words of his commission, "all cities, boroughs, liberties, places incorporated and privileged, and other places whatsoever within the said county and the limits and precincts of the same." Of his legal functions as Custos Rotulorum, that of presiding at the General Sessions of the Justices was seldom exercised, and the most important had come to be that of filling, once in a generation, a vacancy in the life office of Clerk of the Peace, who had originally been merely his deputy, and whose appointment remained down to 1888 exclusively in his gift.[1]

(c) *The Sheriff and his Court*

Next in dignity to the Lord-Lieutenant—in strict law not even to him—and far superior in antiquity, was the Sheriff of the county, often called the High Sheriff, who was appointed, like the Lord-Lieutenant, directly by the Crown, but, unlike him, only for a single year. His office, too, had, by 1689, greatly shrunk in actual importance from the time when he was "the governor of the shire, the captain of its forces, the president of its court, a distinctively royal officer." [2]

purely social dignity (see *The Military Forces of the Crown*, by C. M. Clode, 1869, p. 134). In 1843 the total number of Deputy-Lieutenants in England and Wales (excluding the City of London, where there is, instead, a numerous "Commission of Lieutenancy") was 3012, of whom 2545 were at the same time Justices of the Peace. The number varied from 5 in Rutland to 118 in Lancashire, 122 in Lincolnshire, 124 in Devonshire, 130 in Essex, 138 in Norfolk, and 161 in the West Riding (Dodd's *Manual of Dignities*, 1843, quoted in Gneist's *Self-Government*, chap. vi.).

[1] For the legal constitution of the ancient office of Clerk of the Peace, see 12 Rich. II. c. 10, 1388 ; 37 Henry VIII. c. 1, 1545 ; 3 and 4 Edward VI. c. 1, 1549 ; 1 William and Mary, st. 1, c. 21, 1688, and c. 23 sec. 4, 1688 ; 57 George III. c. 91, 1817, and 3 George IV. c. 46, 1822 ; and 27 and 28 Victoria, c. 65, 1864. See also Parliamentary Papers, No. 605 of 1844 ; Nos. 75 and 224 of 1845 ; No. 520 of 1861, and No. 276 of 1866, and the important case of Fox *v.* Harcourt in 1693, referred to in *House of Lords' Manuscripts*, 1900, vol. i. (N.S.), pp. xxv. 8 ; and reported most fully in Sir B. Shower's *Reports of Cases*, etc., 1794, vol. i. pp. 429, 506, 516. But, as has been aptly said, "all the learning on the office of Clerk of the Peace may be found collected in the judgments delivered in the case of Harding *v.* Pollock, 6 Bingham's Reports, 25 " (*Oxfordshire Annals*, by J. M. Davenport, 1869, p. 121).

[2] *History of English Law*, by Sir F. Pollock and F. W. Maitland, 1895, vol. i. p. 519. For the office of Sheriff at various dates, see the Sheriffs' Act, 1887 (50 and 51 Vic. c. 55), which gives the present law ; *History and*

We need not remind the historical student of the magnitude
and importance of the place that he once filled as the King's
fiscal and judicial representative in the county, or of the
narrow escapes that England had, first from an hereditary,
and then from an elective shrievalty.[1]   Even in 1689 his

Antiquities of the Exchequer, by Thomas Madox, 1769 ; *The Authority*, etc., *of
County Courts . . . Sheriffs*, etc., by W. Greenwood, ninth edition, 1730 ;
Officium Vicicomitum, by Michael Dalton, 1628 ; The Complete Sheriff, 1727 ;
The Complete Practical Under-Sheriff, by George Skirrow, 1811 ; *The Office of
Sheriff*, by John Impey, 1786 ; Reports of House of Commons Committees on
the office of Sheriff, 1830 and 1888, and that of the House of Lords' Committee,
1893-1894 ; *Commentaries on the Laws of England*, by Sir W. Blackstone,
book i. ch. ix. ; *Constitutional History of England*, by W. Stubbs, 1875-
1878 ; *Self-Government*, etc., by R. von Gneist, 1871 ; *Local Government*, by
M. D. Chalmers, 1883, pp. 94, 95 ; *Three Centuries of Derbyshire Annals*, by
J. C. Cox, 1890, vol. i. pp. 50-66 ; *Practical Treatise on Sheriff Law*, by
George Atkinson, 1839 ; *Practical Treatise on the Office of Sheriff*, by W. H.
Watson, 1827 and 1848 ; *Treatise on the Law of Sheriff*, by R. C. Sewell,
1842 ; *Compendium of Sheriff and Execution Law*, by Philip Mather, second
edition, 1903 ; *The Lord-Lieutenant and High Sheriff*, by C. G. Y., 1860 ; and
the amusing reference to the respective precedency of these two dignitaries in
Lord Beaconsfield's *Lothair*, 1870, vol. ii. pp. 135, 139.

[1] See 28 Edward I. c. 8 (1300) ; *Constitutional History of England*, by W.
Stubbs, 1880, vol. i. p. 314 ; vol. ii. p. 225 ; *History of English Law*, by Sir
F. Pollock and F. W. Maitland, 1895, vol. i. p. 519. The shrievalty of
Westmorland remained hereditary in the family of the Earl of Thanet until
1850 (13 and 14 Vic. c. 30). This office had, in past times, descended to and
been executed by a woman. "Ann, Countess of Pembroke, had the office of
hereditary Sheriff of Westmorland, and exercised it in person. At the assizes
of Appleby she sat with the judges on the bench" (Hargrave's notes to Coke's
Institutes, 1832, p. 326 ; *Commentaries on the Laws of England*, by Sir W.
Blackstone, book i. ch. ix., vol. i. p. 339 of 1809 edition). The shrievalties
of Berkshire and Oxfordshire were united until 1566 (8 Elizabeth, c. 16, made
perpetual by 13 Elizabeth, c. 22, 1571). Those of Cambridgeshire and Huntingdonshire continue to be held by the same person (50 and 51 Vic. c. 55, sec. 32,
1887), who is appointed in turn from each county and from the Isle of Ely.
The office of Sheriff of Middlesex was purchased from the Crown in the twelfth
century by the Corporation of the City of London, and was for at least six hundred
years held by the two Sheriffs of the City for the time being. "For the City
there were two Sheriffs ; for Middlesex they acted as one, dividing the individual
appointment between them, and putting their plural signature to documents
written in the signature, as by the Sheriff of Middlesex" (*Compendium of Sheriff
and Execution Law*, by Philip E. Mather, 1903, p. 3). In opposition to Stubbs
and Freeman, Mr. Round takes the view that this transaction represented the
purchase, by the largest town within the county, of the shrievalty of the county
as a whole, and that no distinct Sheriff of the City of London had previously
existed. "There never was but one ferm and never but one shrievalty" ("The
Early Administration of London," in *Geoffrey of Mandeville*, by J. H. Round,
1892, pp. 347-373 ; *The Commune of London*, by the same, 1889, pp. 219-260).
Separate Under-Sheriffs and bailiffs were appointed for London and Middlesex
respectively, and separate courts held. By 51 and 52 Vic. c. 41 (1888) this
ancient arrangement was ended, and separate Sheriffs are now appointed for
both London (outside the City) and Middlesex (Report of Royal Commission
on Amalgamation of City and County of London, 1893). In the Counties

legal powers and official dignity still remained of great importance in the practical administration of the county. To him, to use the formal words of his royal warrant of appointment, was still entrusted " the custody and charge of the county." " As a judicial officer," says an old law book, " the Sheriff has the administration of justice in the County Court ; as a ministerial officer he has the execution of all process, whether civil or criminal, mesne or final. Besides which it is his duty to preserve the peace, and for that purpose he may raise the posse comitatus, and arrest felons, etc." [1] At the end of the seventeenth century he was still " the chief sworn officer of the county . . . trusted with the execution of all writs and processes of law, and with the power of the county to suppress all violence, unlawful routs, riots, and rebellions." [2] But these functions were discharged by deputy. The Sheriff always appointed for his year of office a professional Under-Sheriff, almost invariably the same person as had served his predecessor, in whom was merged the ancient post of County Clerk, and who performed all but the ceremonial duties of the Sheriff. Responsible to the Sheriff, and usually appointed by him (but often by the " lord of the Hundred" or other owner of a Franchise) were the High Bailiffs of Hundreds, Franchises, or Liberties." [3] An indefinite number of underlings, called " foot " bailiffs, " bound bailiffs," or deputies, appointed by the Sheriff or Under-Sheriff as required, served both to carry messages and to execute the processes of justice.[4]

Palatine the Sheriff is appointed by the Lord, and thus the Sheriff of Cornwall continues to be appointed by the Prince of Wales as Duke of Cornwall ; and that of Lancashire by the King as Duke of Lancaster—in both cases separately from the Sheriffs of the other counties.

[1] *The Office of Sheriff*, by John Impey, 1786, preface. He was not a Justice of the Peace, but was a Conservator of the Peace, entitled to commit any person to prison for breach of the peace or felony (*The Compleat Sheriff*, 1696, p. 4).

[2] *The Security of Englishmen's Lives, or the Trust and Duty of the Grand Juries of England* (supposed to have been written by Lord Somers), 1716, p. 8.

[3] A learned *Treatise on the Office of High Bailiff of a Liberty*, by J. Ritson, 1811, is mentioned, but we have found no copy. In the thirteenth century "those Hundreds which had not fallen into private hands were in the King's hands. The Sheriff seems usually to have let them at farm to bailiffs ; the bailiff presided in the court, and after paying his rent made what gain he could from fees and amercements " (*History of English Law*, by Sir F. Pollock and F. W. Maitland, 1895, vol. i. p. 544).

[4] These officers, says Blackstone, are "employed by the Sheriffs on

We must here mention the County Court, the immemorial assembly of the county out of which, it may be inferred, all its other institutions historically sprang. The County Court was still in full existence in 1689, though most of its ancient functions had long been superseded by the newer machinery of the Commission of the Peace, that we shall presently describe. It was still held nominally by the Sheriff—really by the Under-Sheriff—almost entirely as a Court for the recovery of civil debts under forty shillings, to which sum a statute of 1278 had limited its jurisdiction. For such small amounts, it had become dilatory and expensive, often leading to extortion and oppression by unscrupulous litigants and attornies. It was in this Court that the antiquated proceedings in outlawry had still to be taken.[1] It was nominally as holding this Court that the Sheriff made his return to the Lord Chancellor's order for the election of a Coroner, and even to the King's Writ requiring the election of two Knights of the Shire to serve in Parliament. And it was by a Jury summoned as part of the machinery of this Court that the Sheriff assessed the amount of the compensation due in certain cases from the Hundred, or the sum to be paid by the County for taking land to widen the road.[2] It is significant of the

account only of their adroitness and dexterity in hunting and seizing their prey. The Sheriff being answerable for the misdemeanours of these bailiffs, they are therefore usually bound in an obligation with sureties for the due execution of their office and thence are called bound-bailiffs ; which the common people have corrupted into a much more homely appellation " (*Commentaries on the Laws of England*, by Sir W. Blackstone, book i. ch. ix., vol. i. p. 345 of 1809 edition).

[1] Thus, as is often stated, Wilkes was outlawed, in the County Court of Middlesex held, on this occasion, "at the Three Tuns in Brook Street near Holborn," by the Under-Sheriff (Burrows' *Reports of Cases*, etc., vol. iv. p. 2530 ; see *A Series of Letters of the First Earl of Malmesbury*, 1870, vol. i. p. 156, for a contemporary account). The procedure of the Middlesex County Court had been somewhat simplified by 23 George II. c. 33 (1750) ; passed on the petition of the Grand Jury in 1749.

For a full description of the proceedings in outlawry, see R. *v.* Yandell, 1792, Durnford and East's *Term Reports*, 1817, vol. iv. p. 521. Though abolished in 1879 in civil cases, outlawry may still be resorted to, in the case of a person against whom a true bill has been found on an indictment. No person has, however, been outlawed for forty years. (For the last case, see Ex parte Stoffel, *Law Reports, Chancery*, vol. iii. p. 240 ; *Encyclopedia of the Laws of England*, by A. W. Renton, vol. iii. pp. 527, 528, vol. xi. p. 532.)

[2] We have found little information as to the actual existence of the County Court in or after 1689. The Sheriff's Officers contrived to remove the Berkshire County Court from Abingdon to Reading in 1687, which the Privy Council remedied (MS. Acts of Privy Council, 17th February 1688). The day of meeting

way that history has been studied that there is less known about the actual working of the English County Court in 1689 than of the Vehmgericht or the Court of the Praetor Peregrinus.

(d) *The High Constable*

By 1689 the Sheriff's Bailiwick was in some parts of the

was altered from Monday to Wednesday by 7 and 8 William III. c. 25 (1696). For its history see *The History of English Law*, by Sir F. Pollock and F. W. Maitland, 1895, vol. i. pp. 521-543 ; *Self Government*, etc., by R. von Gneist, 1871 ; *Justice and Police*, by F. W. Maitland, 1885, pp. 22, 23, 139 ; *A Short Treatise of the History, Antiquities, and Jurisdiction of all the Courts of Law*, by H. Aldridge, 1835, pp. 207-213 ; *Local Government*, by M. D. Chalmers, 1883, p. 91 ; *Local Government*, by W. Blake Odgers, 1899, pp. 193, 194 ; *The Authority*, etc., *of County Courts*, by W. Greenwood, 9th edition, 1730 ; *Encyclopedia of the Laws of England*, by A. W. Renton, vol. iii. pp. 527, 528, vol. xi. p. 532. Various manuals of practice exist, giving tables of fees, from Judge David Jenkins' *Pacis Consultum*, 1657, to G. B. Rogers' *Practice of the Sheriff's Court of Cornwall*, 1824 ; ditto *of Devon*, 1824 ; R. H. Anderson's *Law and Practice of County Courts* (Yorkshire), 1830 ; G. B. Mansel's *Practice by Justices and Plaint in the County Court*, 1834 ; and Joseph Sweet's *Practice in the County Court*, 1835. These give us, however, little vision as to its real operation, and we should be almost without evidence of its active existence were it not for the rare work, *An Address to the Country Gentlemen of England and Wales*, by James Bland Burges, M.P. (afterwards Sir James Lamb), 1789. In this work, the County Court is denounced as "an engine of the most nefarious oppression," leading frequently to "the necessary ruin" of one or both litigants, and the profit of rapacious attornies, in collusion with one of their number acting as Under-Sheriff, aided by venal jurymen, serving for the shilling fee. The cases cited appear to support this indictment. But Burges became a permanent civil servant, and dropped the Bill he had contemplated. We find no movement for reform until Lord Althorp, in 1820-1821, attempted by a Bill, as Lord Shelburne had suggested in 1785, the adaptation of this court, "to the increased exigencies of the times." But the lawyers in Parliament in those days successfully opposed any development of local tribunals (*Life of William Earl of Shelburne*, by Lord Edmond Fitzmaurice, 1875-1876, vol. iii. p. 436 ; *Memoir of Earl Spencer*, by Sir Denis Le Marchant, 1876, p. 190). Between 1824 and 1835 there was evidently an increase in the business of this ancient court in its unreformed state. It was even said in 1833 to be "much resorted to" in Brecknockshire (First Report of Municipal Corporation Commissioners, 1835, Appendix, vol. i. p. 180). Its civil jurisdiction (except in Durham, where it was expressly abolished by 6 and 7 William IV. c. 19, 1836) lasted until 1846, when the new statutory county courts were created. But it was even then not abolished, and the Sheriff's Act, 1887 (50 and 51 Vic. c. 55, sec. 18), still continues its existence for (besides outlawry) the assessment of compensation under the Lands Clauses Acts, etc., and the return to a writ of inquiry as to damages, etc. "The statute book authorises the modern county voter to believe, if he can, that when in strictest secrecy he is dropping his voting paper into the ballot box, he is attending a county court of the old type held by the Sheriff" (*Justice and Police*, by F. W. Maitland, 1885, pp. 22, 23). "In theory it is still the duty of the Sheriff to proclaim in the county court all new Acts passed by the Legislature" (*Local Government*, by M. D. Chalmers, 1883, p. 92 ; ditto, by W. Blake Odgers, 1899, p. 194).

country becoming obsolete, and we hear usually of Hundreds, Wapentakes, or Wards, at the head of each of which (as of those Liberties and Franchises that were equivalent divisions) there stood one or two officers, more directly responsible to the Justices of the Peace than were the Sheriffs' High Bailiffs, and known as Head, Chief, or High Constables. These officers, mentioned, though not established, by the Statute of Winchester in 1285, had formerly been appointed for one year at the Court Leet of the Hundred, Liberty, or Franchise ; but by 1689 these Hundred Courts had become in nearly all cases disused, and the appointment was made by Quarter Sessions, usually, in form, for one year only. The High Constables had, in the sixteenth century, exercised some of the powers of a Justice of the Peace, especially in issuing peremptory instructions to the Petty Constables, and in sentencing vagrants to be whipped.[1] But their most important duties had, by 1689, come to be the new functions imposed on them by the growth of the modern administration of the County that we shall presently describe, including especially the levying of the County Rate, or, as we should now say, the enforcement of the precepts by which the requirements of Quarter Sessions were apportioned among the several Hundreds, and subdivided among the parishes and townships of each Hundred. The High Constable had to get the prescribed sums from the Petty Constables—sometimes from the Churchwardens or Overseers—of the several parishes and townships, and hand over his collections to the Clerk of the Peace or County Treasurer.

(e) *The Coroner*

There remain to be mentioned the Coroners, from two to ten or twelve for each county, somewhat anomalous officers of great antiquity, who had formerly " kept the pleas of the crown," [2] from which their authority had been derived.   Their

---

[1] 22 Henry VIII. c. 12 (1531) ; we have not found any copy of *The Duty and Office of High Constables of Hundreds*, by a Mr. Brown, 1677. The best authority is still *The Office of Constable*, by J. Ritson, 1791.

[2] For the Office of Coroner see the Coroners' Act, 1887 (50 and 51 Vic. c. 71) which, with secs. 5 and 114 of the Local Government Act, 1888 (51 and 52 Vic. c. 41), gives the present law ; 3 Edw. I. c. 10, the Statute of

distribution was anomalous; some counties would have only two or three, others as many as eleven.[1] By 1689 their work had become practically restricted to the holding of inquests in cases of death under circumstances of suspicion, and the committing for trial at the assizes of persons against whom the Jury at such inquests had returned a verdict of murder or manslaughter. Very occasionally they might have to hold an inquest to determine the ownership of " treasure trove ": we may ignore their analogous and already obsolete duties with regard to deodands and wrecks. Alone among county officers, the Coroners were elected by the freeholders of the county,[2] though with many exceptions for particular Honours, Liberties or Franchises, in which the appointment was, by ancient royal grant or immemorial custom, vested in some individual or corporate owner or lessee.[3] The office was held

Westminster (1275); 4 Edw. I. c. 7 (1276); 3 Henry VII. c. 1 (1488); *Select Cases from the Coroners' Rolls*, by C. Gross (Selden Society, 1896); *History of English Law*, by Sir F. Pollock and F. W. Maitland, 1895, vol. i. p. 519; *Local Government*, by M. D. Chalmers, 1883, pp. 95-98; *The Early History of the Office of the Coroner*, by C. Gross, 1892; the speeches reported in Hansard, vol. 230, p. 1301, 1876; Reginald Bray's *Concise Directions for Obtaining the Lord Chancellor's Orders for the Election and Removal of Coroners and of Verderers and Regarders of Forests*, 1831; Jardine's *Remarks on the Coroner's Inquest*, 1846; R. Clarke Sewell's *Treatise on the Law of Coroners*, 1843 and 1854; *The Office and Duties of Coroners*, by Sir John Jervis, 4th edition, 1880, and *The Coroners' Act*, 1887, by the same. The Home Office return of June 1895 gives a useful list of the existing Coroners' jurisdictions, whilst the successive annual reports of the Coroners' Society afford much insight into practical administration.

Other ancient officers—for instance, the Escheator—connected with the seignorial interests of the Crown, play an important part in the history of county organisation, but had, by 1689, generally ceased to exist, or at any rate to influence Local Government. An Escheator is mentioned as existing in Pembrokeshire in 1796 (*Cambrian Register*, 1799, vol. ii. p. 172).

[1] Thus Dorsetshire has eleven (Hansard, vol. 230, p. 1301).

[2] The election of a Coroner occasionally gave rise to keen contests. Thus, of Preston, in 1832, we read that "the town presented a lively bustling appearance; vehicles of all descriptions constantly arriving from various parts of the county, laden inside and out with voters for the respective candidates, whilst groups of sturdy yeomen, with dusty shoes and stout sticks, were seen striding along the entrances of the town, their zeal for their favourite candidates having apparently brought them many miles from their little freeholds." On the first day's poll the "blue" candidate had 552 votes, to 427 for the "pink." But the winning candidate, "on seeing that the contest, if persisted in by both parties, would cost each of them more than the office was worth, agreed to withdraw from it on the condition that his expenses should be paid by his opponent." This contest cost between four and five thousand pounds. (*Manchester Guardian*, 4th August 1832.)

[3] Thus, in the Liberty of St. Peter, York, the Dean of York appointed two Coroners; in the Liberty of the Tower of London the appointment lay with the

for life, though it could be terminated by a special royal writ for certain specified reasons.

(f) *The Commission of the Peace*

In spite of the antiquity and official dignity of these county officers, they had, by 1689, become actually less concerned with the civil administration of the county than the noblemen and gentlemen whom the king had appointed— to use the formal words of the document addressed to them —"jointly and severally, and every one of you, our Justices to keep our peace" in the particular county. "Under the Tudors and Stuarts," says Mr. Maitland, "the Justices, their number always increasing, gradually became rulers of the county, acting under the supervision of the King's Council and the King's Bench, and carrying into effect, both judicially and administratively, the many detailed statutes relating to police and social economy. The practice of committing to them all the affairs of the shire" had, in fact, by 1689 become "habitual."[1] The "Commission of the Peace" has always been regarded by Continental writers as amongst the most unique and distinctive features of the English Constitution. The Englishman takes it for granted, but to him it has the additional charm of antiquity and quite exceptional stability of form. Though the functions of the Justices of the Peace have from time to time necessarily been adjusted to changes in the law of the land, five centuries have passed without any essential change in the constitution of the office or its procedure. From the first Commissions of the Peace issued on the definite settlement of the office by Edward III., to those renewed on the accession of Edward VII., we have the same formal appointment by the monarch of certain noblemen and gentlemen in each county "to keep and cause to be

Constable of the Tower. "In one franchise in Cheshire the office is said to go with an hereditary horn. In a manor in Essex the tenants appoint . . . The number of these Franchise Coroners, as they are called, is said to be fifty-five" (*Local Government*, by M. D. Chalmers, 1883, p. 96). In Shropshire (Halesowen) and Worcestershire (Dudley), as well as in Yorkshire (three Ridings), the Coroner was elected by the freeholders for part of a county (*Concise Directions for obtaining the Lord Chancellor's Orders for the Election and Removal of Coroners of Counties*, by Reginald Bray, 1831, p. 5).

[1] *Justice and Police*, by F. W. Maitland, 1885, p. 80.

kept all ordinances and statutes for the good of our peace " and " to chastise and punish all persons that offend against the form " of those ordinances and statutes.[1] The wording of the stately document commissioning the Justices of each county, definitely settled by the Elizabethan statesmen of 1590,[2] and handed down almost unchanged from reign to reign, implies, if it does not assert, that the Justices are to act in three separate ways according to the matter in hand— severally as individual magistrates sitting alone; jointly with one or more of their colleagues in a particular Division; and collectively, as a General Sessions of the whole county, at a publicly convened assembly, when the Sheriff is charged to provide the whole machinery of a court of justice. This threefold division of the Justices' work, expressed or implied in the commission, extended and refined by successive statutes, Privy Council orders, and decisions of the Judges, had already by 1689 become a sort of legal constitution, to be learned by every acting Justice from carefully prepared legal manuals,

---

[1] The best account of the Justices of the Peace is to be found in the works of Vincke, Gneist, and Redlich already referred to, and in such English manuals as *Justice and Police*, by F. W. Maitland, 1885. *Quarter Sessions from Queen Elizabeth to Queen Anne*, by A. H. A. Hamilton, 1878, is also an informing book ; whilst *Three Centuries of Derbyshire Annals*, by J. C. Cox, 2 vols., 1890, gives, on the whole, the best picture of their activity. The historical information is given in *The History of English Law*, by J. Reeves, 1783-1829, vol. ii. p. 468, vol. iii. pp. 216, 242, 290, vol. iv. p. 154 ; and in the useful monograph, *The Office of Justice of the Peace in England*, by C. A. Beard, 1904. Of the books purporting to deal with the office and duties of a Justice of the Peace—of which several dozens might be cited, appearing in literally more than a hundred different editions, from Sir Antoine Fitzherbert's *L'Office et Auctoritie de Justices de Peace* (1514), through Lambard's *Eirenarcha* (1581) and Dalton's *Country Justice* (1618), and such followers as Archbold, Barlow, Barry, Blackerby, Bond, Browne, Burn (30 editions, 1755-1869), Chamberlain, Collins, Deacon, Eagle, Fleetwood, Glasse, Harvey, Higges, Jacob, Keeble, Kilburne, L'Estrange, Nelson, Paley (7 editions), Pearce, Rastall (or Dickinson), Raynes, Robinson, Shaw, Sheppard, Toone, Lord Ward, Williams, and Young, down to John Stone's *Practice of the Petty Sessions*, of which nine editions have appeared (1836-1882), Samuel Stone's *Justice's Manual* (36 editions, 1842-1904), and G. C. Oke's *Synopsis of Summary Convictions*, which runs to fourteen editions (1848-1893)—it cannot be said that they are more than unscientific (usually alphabetic) statements of the law prepared for the assistance of the Justices and their clerks, in dealing with any case that can come before them. The nearest approach to a description of the actual work of a Justice (and that only on its magisterial or judicial side) is afforded by the unpretentious *Handybook for a Justice of the Peace*, by a Devonshire Magistrate, 1877. For records of the proceedings of Justices in Sessions see the footnote to p. 279.

[2] The Commission will be found in full in *Select Statutes and other Constitutional Documents*, by G. W. Prothero, 1898, pp. 144-149 ; *History of English Law*, by J. Reeves, 1829, vol. v. p. 227.

into successive editions of which were fitted the innumerable new functions which the eighteenth and nineteenth centuries saw piled on the already overburdened shoulders of the gentlemen magistrates.

At the General Sessions of the Peace for the county, which had to be held at least four times a year, all the Justices of the county were summoned to form a Court, the well-known Court of Quarter Sessions, which was, in 1689, the supreme county authority.   At this Court the whole county was supposed to appear.   The Custos Rotulorum was assumed to preside, but the law made no provision for the chairmanship, and in any case it was the Justices themselves who collectively gave judgment, any chairman acting only as the spokesman of the whole bench.   The Sheriff and his High Bailiffs, the High Constables of Hundreds and Franchises, together with the Coroners, and even the Petty Constables of manors or parishes or townships, had all to be in attendance, with the obligation of reporting such offences or derelictions of duty as had occurred within their respective jurisdictions.   But this was not all.   The Court had to be assisted in its inquiries at various stages by Juries of sworn men, each at least twelve in number ; and the High Bailiff of each Hundred and Franchise had therefore to summon a sufficient number of its residents, to furnish the local Juries of inquiry, whilst the Sheriff had himself to summon from the county at large, not only a Grand Jury of the leading gentlemen, but also a sufficient number of ten-pound freeholders or copyholders [1] of the county to furnish the so-called Petty Juries, "Traverse Juries," or "Felon's Juries," by whom the issues of fact in criminal trials were ultimately decided.   With the elaborate procedure of Quarter Sessions as a court of criminal jurisdiction—which differed in no way from that of the Assizes—we are not concerned.[2]   But inextricably intermingled with this criminal jurisdiction there had, by 1689, come to be carried on at Quarter Sessions the bulk of the civil administration of the county. The repairing of bridges, the maintenance of the King's gaols,

---

[1] 4 William and Mary, c. 24, 1692.

[2] An elaborate account of the procedure at both Quarter Sessions and Assizes is to be found in *The Office of the Clerk of Assize . . . together with the Office of the Clerk of the Peace, showing the true manner and form of the Proceedings at the Court of Quarter Sessions of the Peace* (1682).

THE COMMISSION OF THE PEACE 297

the building and management of the newer Houses of Correction, the fixing of wages, prices and rates of land carriage, the licensing of various kinds of traders, the suppression of disorderly houses, the sanctioning of special levies for various parish needs, the confirmation or disallowance of the orders of individual Justices or pairs of Justices on every conceivable subject, were among the multifarious civil functions of Quarter Sessions. This civil business, already noticed as important by Lambard, Dalton, and Sir Thomas Smith, had, after the Restoration, steadily increased.[1] Moreover, we must not forget that, in 1689, Quarter Sessions still possessed, as an administrative court of first instance, in practically all cases, civil powers concurrent with those of one or two Justices—powers which were gradually withdrawn as the activities of individual Justices increased and the need for a separate tribunal of appeal from their orders became more apparent.

Besides meeting in these Quarter Sessions, and such other General Sessions as might be held for the business of the whole county, the Justices had been expressly directed by certain sixteenth and seventeenth century statutes and Privy Council orders to group themselves by local Divisions—usually coinciding with the Hundreds—so "that fit Justices of the Peace be assigned to have the special charge and care of every such Division," who were to assemble "at some convenient place" in each Division, at what gradually became known as "private sessions or monthly meetings," and eventually as Special Sessions.[2] At these local sessions, held at stated times

[1] *Eirenarcha*, by W. Lambard, 1602; *The Country Justice*, by M. Dalton, 1618; *The Commonwealth of England*, by Sir Thomas Smith, 1581; see *Local Government in England*, by J. Redlich and F. W. Hirst, 1903, vol. ii. p. 57.

[2] The early history of these Divisional Sessions has not yet been explored. Though some early attempts in this direction were of short duration (11 Henry VII. c. 3, repealed by 1 Henry VIII. c. 6; 33 Henry VIII. c. 10, repealed by 37 Henry VIII. c. 7; *The Law and Practice of Summary Conviction on Penal Statutes by Justices of the Peace*, by W. Paley, 1814, pp. xix.-xxv.), certain statutes of the sixteenth century had directed the Justices of each county to group themselves by local divisions for dealing with vagrancy, poor relief, and various offences (22 Henry VIII. c. 12, 1531; 14 Eliz. c. 5, 1572), and Lambard describes the habit of some counties to hold four, eight, or more sessions at which only the local Justices were summoned (*Eirenarcha*, by W. Lambard, 1602, p. 558; *Office of a Justice of the Peace in England*, by O. A. Beard, 1904, p. 163). In 1605 an elaborate Privy Council order directed a similar grouping for practically all the functions of the Justices, with four Divisional Sessions annually, apparently transacting all business not requiring Juries. (This important order is printed in full in *Three Centuries of Derbyshire*

and places, only those Justices resident in the Division were summoned, together with the local Hundred and parish officers. If we may judge from the Privy Council Order of 1605, there was nothing that these Divisional Sessions were not competent to deal with, except the actual trial of offences requiring a Jury, and such orders for expenditure as needed presentment by the Grand Inquest, or appertained to the county as a whole. But by 1689 another kind of " Privy " or " Petty " Sessions had come into existence, as a result of the various statutes by which duties had been imposed on two or more Justices. Under the Poor Law Acts, from 1597 onwards, two Justices had annually to meet in each locality to appoint the Overseers of the Poor for the neighbouring parishes, and to pass their accounts. Moreover, although the great mass of what we now call summary jurisdiction had not then begun, so that the smallest charges of petty larceny or assault could be disposed of only at Quarter Sessions or the Assizes, various statutes already empowered any two Justices of the Peace, sitting together, to try and sentence certain offenders,[1] or to give

---

Annals, by J. C. Cox, 1890, vol. i. pp. 4-5, and in *Quarter Sessions from Queen Elizabeth to Queen Anne*, by A. H. A. Hamilton, 1878, pp. 67-71). Four years later we have these Divisional Sessions made use of for the repression of vagrancy (7 James I. c. 4, 1609). We are not aware of any minutes or other actual records of these "private sessions" or "monthly meetings," as they were then called ; but they are frequently referred to (under the name of "Justices' assemblies ") during the first ten years of the reign of James I. as being held in Middlesex (*Middlesex County Records*, by J. C. Jeaffreson, vol. ii. pp. 230-231) ; about the same time also in Worcestershire (*Worcestershire County Records*, by J. W. Willis Bund, 1900, vol. i. p. 31) ; and after the Restoration in Derbyshire (*Three Centuries of Derbyshire Annals*, by J. C. Cox, 1890, vol. i. p. 7). In 1665 Lord Clarendon officially urged the Justices to be diligent in "keeping up their monthly meetings " (*The Justice of the Peace, his Calling and Qualification*, by Edmund Bohun, 1693, preface). In 1689 we see the Breconshire Quarter Sessions directing that "the poor of the parish of D. are to be settled at the next monthly meeting of the Justices" (MS. Minutes, Quarter Sessions, Breconshire, 1st July 1689). In 1696 the Privy Council directs them to be held for consultation as to how the poor can best be relieved (MS. Acts of Privy Council, 2nd July 1696). After 1691 (as "Highway Sessions") they were made the occasion for the annual appointment of Surveyors of the Highways and the passing of their accounts (3 William and Mary, c. 12, 1691) ; and after 1729 (as "Brewster Sessions") for the licensing of ale-houses. But the old form still continued. The Shropshire Quarter Sessions in 1728 directed the Justices to "meet in their several Divisions a fortnight at least before every Quarter Sessions," to organise a "Privy Search" for vagrants (*Shropshire County Records*, Part III., edited by Sir Offley Wakeman, p. 66).

[1] Thus (besides the earlier jurisdiction over forcible entries, 12 Ric. II. c. 2 ; and riots, 13 Henry IV. c. 7), an unlicensed ale-house-keeper persisting in supplying drink might be committed to prison and fined (5 and 6 Edward VI. c. 25,

orders to parochial officials in matters of Poor Law and high-way administration.[1] Hence, there existed in 1689, alongside of the Quarter Sessions and the Divisional Sessions, a rough and ready organisation of Petty Sessions or Privy Sessions—informal meetings of two or three Justices at the village inn, or even in their own parlours—to appoint Overseers of the Poor and Surveyors of Highways, to allow their accounts, to sanction the parish Poor Rate, to make orders for the removal of paupers to their place of settlement, to order the maintenance of a bastard child by its reputed father, to commit to the House of Correction parish officers who neglected to account for their expenditure or parents who refused to support their children, as well as to try, convict, and sentence persons guilty of various minor offences, or to hear and commit for trial at Quarter Sessions those accused of assault, petty larceny, and graver offences against the law of the land.   It was an anomaly that, for all these purposes, any two Justices of the county would suffice, whether or not they resided in the particular Division concerned, or even both in the same Division, so that it was theoretically possible for various pairs of Justices to deal with the same case and to deal with it differently.[2]

sec. 4-5) ; the reputed father and mother of a bastard child becoming chargeable to the parish might both be ordered to be whipped, and made to pay for its maintenance, under penalty of imprisonment (18 Eliz. c. 3) ; the mother might in the alternative be sentenced to a year's imprisonment in the House of Correction (7 James I. c. 4) ; the goods of the runaway parents of a bastard child might be confiscated (13 and 14 Car. II. c. 12, sec. 19) ; any servant leaving his or her employment before the expiry of its term might be fined and sent to gaol (5 Eliz. c. 4) ; any woman between twelve and forty living idly might be peremptorily sent to service, or put in prison for refusal (5 Eliz. c. 4) ; any person killing game or taking eggs might be committed to prison for three months or fined (1 James I. c. 27 ; 7 James I. c. 11)—all by any two Justices of the county, meeting without notice at any place whatsoever, and with no more formality or publicity than was necessarily involved in the hearing of one or two witnesses in the presence of the defendant.   Three Justices so meeting might even sentence a person to seven years' transportation, for the offence of rickburning, if the accused, to avoid the risk of a death penalty, elected to be dealt with summarily (22 and 23 Car. II. ć. 7).

[1] In 1555 any " Bailiff or Head Constable " refusing to account, might be brought before two Justices (2 and 3 Philip and Mary, c. 8).   The Poor Laws of 1563, 1572, and 1575 made use of a similar tribunal (5 Eliz. c. 3 ; 14 Eliz. c. 5 ; and 18 Eliz. c. 3), though in some cases requiring the presence of three Justices.   Two Justices became the regular authority in the seventeenth century under the Acts of 1597, 1601, and 1662 (39 Eliz. c. 4 ; 43 Eliz. c. 2 ; and 13 and 14 Car. II. c. 12).

[2] Occasionally the statutes required cases to be dealt with by the "next" Justices, or by those "dwelling in or near the parish or Division" (43 Eliz. c. 2, sec. 1), without defining more particularly who were to act, and thus

Finally, we have to add that, as the Commission directed the Justices severally as well as jointly to keep the King's peace, any one Justice could not only issue a summons requiring a person to appear at the next Sessions, or direct by warrant the arrest of any suspected offender, and commit him for safe custody to the county gaol, but was also empowered to order any suspected person to find sureties for his good behaviour, or be committed to prison in default; and summarily to commit any person obstructing the course of justice by flagrant contempt of his authority in his presence in the course of his magisterial duties. Nor were the judicial powers of a single Justice limited to mere commitment to the county gaol to await trial. If he heard a profane oath, discovered any person tippling in an ale-house, or saw a man drunk, he could, "on his own view," and without further evidence or formality, then and there sentence the offender to pay a fine, commit him to prison in default of payment, or order him to be put in the stocks for four hours. Any person not attending church might similarly, by a single Justice, be fined a shilling. The labourer daring to attend a bull-baiting or other similar sport on Sunday might also be thus fined or set in the stocks, whilst heavier penalties were incurred by any carrier conveying goods, any butcher killing beasts or selling meat, and any other person pursuing his accustomed avocation on the Lord's Day.[1] "Our prudent legislators," said a contemporary moralist, "foreseeing how hardly the greatest part of our magistrates would be got to execute such laws, have left it in the power of any one Justice of the Peace that has a sense of religion and his duty, to act in these things, that he might not be wind-bound by the vicious negligence of his brethren."[2] But the greatest authority of a single Justice was seen in his dealing with the undefined and elusive offence of vagrancy. If, after hearing the evidence of the village Constable, or other witness, he chose to consider any person, male or female, guilty

without preventing any within the county from acting. The Settlement Act, 1662 (14 Car. II. c. 12), directs that one of the two Justices ordering a removal must be "of the Division" that the subject of the order inhabits. Upon this, Dorsetshire was declared to contain five Divisions (MS. Minutes, Quarter Sessions, Dorsetshire, 11th July 1705).

[1] 3 James I. c. 4 ; 1 Car. I. c. 1 ; 3 Car. I. c. 3 ; 29 Car. II. c. 7.

[2] *An Essay upon the Execution of the Laws against Immorality and Profaneness*, by John Disney, 1710, p. 137.

of any act of vagrancy, he might condemn such person to the stocks, order him to be stripped from the middle up and soundly whipped in public "until his back be bloody," and then despatch him with an ignominious pass to his last place of settlement.[1] Besides all this authority as Conservator of the Peace, the individual Justice had, by a long series of statutes, to which we have already referred in our chapter on the Legal Framework of the Parish, been given wide powers of supervising and supplementing the activities of the parish officers in the relief of the poor and the maintenance of highways. And it was to the individual Justice, as much as to High and Petty Constables, that Quarter Sessions looked for the presentment, "on his own view," of parishes and parish officers, for defaults in fulfilling their legal obligations—a presentment which carried the same weight as if made by a Jury of twelve sworn men. It was, indeed, not to be wondered at that Blackstone should declare the English country gentlemen "of all men, next to common lawyers, indispensably obliged to apply themselves seriously to the study of our municipal law." When we survey all the manifold powers and duties which the unpaid, untrained country gentleman was, already in 1689, required to exercise and fulfil as a Justice of the Peace, we may well exclaim with Coke that "it is such a form of subordinate government for the tranquillity and quiet of the realm as no part of the Christian world hath the like, if the same be duly exercised."[2]

(g) County Service

We may now consider what provision had been made in law for securing that all the Rulers of the County should be

---

[1] 22 Henry VIII. c. 12 (1531); 27 Henry VIII. c. 12 (1536); 14 Eliz. c. 5 (1572); 39 Eliz. c. 4 (1597); see the *History of Vagrants and Vagrancy*, by C. J. Ribton-Turner, 1887, p. 73. For a case of the misuse of these vagrancy powers in order to prevent the delivery of a sermon by an outside clergyman, see *London in the Jacobite Times*, by Dr. Doran, 1877, vol. i. p. 331.

[2] *Institutes of the Laws of England*, by Sir E. Coke, 1797 ed., vol. iv. p. 170. We may see how it strikes a scholarly Frenchman two centuries later: "Non seulement l'administrateur et le juge se confondent dans le magistrat anglais, mais tous nos fonctionnaires et nos corps locaux : préfet, sous-préfet, conseil de préfecture, conseil général, conseil d'arrondissement, juge de paix, juge d'instruction, commissaire de police, maire, se retrouvent plus ou moins en lui par telles ou telles de leurs attributions" (*Le Developpement de la Constitution Anglaise*, by E. Boutmy, 1887, p. 268).

qualified for their high duties, and induced to fulfil them. Though John had promised, by Magna Carta, that he "would not make any Justice, Constables, Sheriffs, or Bailiffs but of such as know the law of the realm and mean duly to observe it,"[1] we cannot say that, in 1689, there existed much law on the subject. To begin with the Lord-Lieutenant, we find no kind of qualification required beyond the King's favour. The Custos Rotulorum was legally only one of the Justices of the Peace. The Sheriff did not need even to be a Justice, and required, by law, no qualification by residence and no very definite qualification by estate. The Coroner had, it was said, to be a freeholder of the county for which he acted, but the amount of the necessary interest was never defined, and it has been held that the mere ownership of a share in a freehold grave is legally sufficient to warrant his assumption of the office.[2] Only in the case of the Justice of the Peace was any qualification fixed by statute. They were nominally required, in 1689, to be "of the most sufficient knights, esquires and gentlemen of the law" resident within the county, and possessing an estate therein of not less than £20 a year; unless, indeed, there should not be in the county sufficient persons of position who were expert in law and administration, when the Lord Chancellor was authorised to add persons of legal experience who had not the necessary estate.[3] The statutory assumption that some knowledge of law and administration was required for the proper fulfilment of the duties of a Justice had led, for over three centuries, to the well-known "quorum" clause in the commission. At the point at which powers were entrusted to two Justices, words were added signifying "of whom we will that A. B. or C. D. etc. should be one." (quorum aliquem vestrum . . . unum

---

[1] Magna Carta, 45th clause.

[2] *Local Government*, by M. D. Chalmers, 1883, p. 96.

[3] 13 Richard II. st. 1, c. 7 (1389); 2 Henry V. st. 1, c. 4, and st. 2, c. 1 (1413, 1414); 18 Henry VI. c. 11, secs. 1 and 2 (1439). The latter statute, it was somewhat bitterly said in 1832, "is remarkable as being the first Act of the legislature that fixes any precise amount of property as a qualification, and the last which recognises the necessity of intellectual and moral fitness for the office of a county magistrate" (*Letter to Lord Brougham and Vaux on the subject of the Magistracy of England*, 1832, pp. 4-5). In 1700 the Privy Council ordered "that where father and son live together in the same house," only one should be regarded as eligible for the Commission (MS. Acts of Privy Council, 20th June 1700).

esse volumus). The Justices so named were those assumed to
possess the qualification of a knowledge of law, and were
popularly said to be "of the quorum." By 1689, however,
the clause had become a mere form, as the practice was to
name, in each commission, all the Justices as of the quorum.
Practically the only qualification that remained, beyond the
£20 a year of freehold property, was the necessity, imposed on
all but the humblest public officers, of receiving, within three
months, the "sacrament according to the usage of the Church
of England in some public church on the Lord's Day"; the
production and authentication by two witnesses of a certificate
signed by the minister and Churchwarden that it had been taken;
the formal taking of the oaths of allegiance and supremacy;
and subscribing the declaration against transubstantiation.[1]

Unlike the parochial offices, those of the county were, in
1689, practically not obligatory on the ordinary citizen. No
one was compelled to serve as Lord-Lieutenant or Custos
Rotulorum, nor to accept the office of Coroner. It may be
doubtful whether a duly qualified county resident could legally
take any steps to disburden himself from having his name
included in the Commission of the Peace, and if so included,
he was presumably required by law to obey the King's command.[2] But before a Justice of the Peace could act in that
capacity, he had to "take out his Dedimus Potestatem"—to
journey to the county town, present himself to the Clerk of
the Peace, take the prescribed oaths and pay fees to the amount
of about £4 [3]—a series of ceremonies which, often neglected,

---

[1] 25 Car. II. c. 2 (1672); 30 Car. II. st. 2, c. 1 (1678). Another oath,
that of abjuration, was added by 1 George I. st. 2, c. 13 (1714); see as to these
requirements, 5 George II. c. 18 (1732), and 18 George II. c. 20 (1745).

[2] In the fifteenth and sixteenth centuries, service was sometimes avoided by
obtaining special patents of exemption; for example, see *Calendar of Patent Rolls*,
1476-1485, p. 55; *Calendar of State Papers, Domestic*, 1594-1597, p. 48; and
The Office of a Justice of the Peace in England, by C. A. Beard, 1904, p. 141.

[3] Here is the account of a Wiltshire Justice in 1743:—

Imprimis, paid for a certificate of my receiving the Sacrament	0	1	6
Paid for my Dedimus Potestatem	3	13	6
Gave Mr. Salmon for his trouble in taking it out	0	10	6
Paid the Clerk of the Peace for being sworn in Court	0	2	0
Paid my Colt Ale for my first acting	0	10	6
Spent at Devizes Quarter Sessions over our pay of four shillings a day	0	7	6

(MS. Diary of William Hunt, 1743-1744, in library of Wiltshire Archæo-

were never enforced. We may therefore say that the only really obligatory county offices were those of Sheriff and High Constable. Service as High Constable was, in 1689, by common law nominally compulsory[1] on any person whom Quarter Sessions chose to appoint to this office. The office of Sheriff had to be borne for one year by any adult male inhabitant of the county who "had lands sufficient in the county to answer the King and his people,"[2] and whose name had been "pricked" by the King on the list of names of the eligible gentlemen in each county, annually presented for this purpose "on the Morrow of All Souls" by certain high legal and official dignitaries.[3]

As little legal provision existed for the payment of the rulers of the county as for their qualification and compulsory service. To none of them was any salary assigned. There was never any question of remuneration of such local dignitaries as the Custos Rotulorum and Lord-Lieutenant. The Clerk of the Peace had his customary fees of office, including two shillings for each day of sessions, unalterable during his life tenure of his post, except by his own consent. The Sheriff had his own fees, which were numerous and substantial enough to provide the necessary remuneration for the Under-Sheriff and the whole staff of horse, foot, and bound bailiffs. The Coroners were, in 1689, avowedly professional officers, serving for the fees which they earned for every inquest held. The High Constables got either nothing or whatever might be allowed by Quarter Sessions—sometimes a customary payment for their expenses. All these fees were payable partly by individuals, for acts in which they were specially concerned, partly out of the general funds of the county, for

logical Society at Devizes.) The Privy Council in 1700, when making great changes in the Commissions, ordered that no fees should, on that occasion, be exacted (MS. Acts of Privy Council, 26th September 1700).

[1] With the same exemptions as for Petty Constable (see Book I. Chapter I. The Legal Framework of the Parish).

[2] 9 Edward II. st. 2 (1315) ; 2 Edward III. c. 3 (1328) ; 13 and 14 Car. II. c. 21 (1661), sec. 7 ; *Commentaries on the Laws of England*, by Sir W. Blackstone, book i. ch. ix., vol i. p. 345 of 1809 edition.

[3] 14 Edward III. c. 7, 1340 ; 24 George II. c. 48, sec. 12, 1746. In 1818 a Sheriff who wished to be relieved of the office in order to become a candidate for Parliament, was informed that there was no precedent for such a release (Home Office Domestic Entry Book, 12th June 1818, vol. liii. in Public Record Office). For the actual process of selection, see p. 484.

acts done at the command of Quarter Sessions itself. In the case of the Sheriff, however, whose duties in the execution of justice extended to the judgments of the King's judges as well as to those of Quarter Sessions, a bill for certain fees and expenses incurred was annually to be presented to the Exchequer, and these "Sheriff's Cravings," as they were called, were allowed, from the twelfth century down to the twentieth, in their accounting to the King for the fines and amerciaments which they had received on his behalf. The legal position of the Justices with regard to remuneration was obscure. By definite provisions in two statutes of the fourteenth century which were not repealed until 1854, it had been provided that they should have wages at the rate of four shillings a day for their attendance at the Sessions, but the number so paid was limited to eight in each county, and Justices who were peers of the realm were excluded from the payment.[1] The Sheriff could take credit for the "Justices' wages," as also for those of the Clerk of the Peace, in his annual bill of "cravings" to the Exchequer; and the Justices could always have recovered their dues from him.[2]

(h) *An Organ of National Government*

The student will note that, with the unimportant exception of the Coroners, all the Rulers of the County were

---

[1] 12 Ric. II. c. 10 (1388), and 14 Ric. II. c. 11 (1390). It seems to have been assumed that each county would have only eight Justices. When Wales was divided into counties this number was made a statutory maximum, which had to be repealed in 1693 (34 and 35 Henry VIII. c. 26, 1544; 5 William and Mary, c. 4, 1693; House of Lords Journals, 30th Dec. 1693, vol. xv. p. 330). The Statute of Labourers (5 Eliz. c. 4, sec. 31, 1562) provided that the Justices should have five shillings per day, payable out of the fines imposed, when sitting in execution of the Act. A few early statutes had also provided trifling perquisites of office; thus an Act of 1531 gave them a part of the goods seized in possession of "Egyptians" (22 Henry VIII. c. 10), and the first Licensing Act accorded them half the shilling fee charged on the recognisance of an ale-house keeper (5 Edward VI. c. 25, 1551). See further as to Justices' emoluments at pp. 409, 413, 423, and 438.

[2] The shrievalty was, in 1689, only just ceasing to be an office of profit. Sir John Reresby relates that when in 1667 he was Sheriff of Yorkshire, "the gaoler gave me £160 to have the custody of the gaol. I had the same sum presented to me for the county court, and I made off the bailiwicks about £145; in all, about £465, besides the profits of the seal, which made the whole near £1200. But the charges of both assizes, salaries to officers, liveries, and equipages took off so much that I cannot say I saved clear £200, all charges considered"

appointed by the King, and removable at his pleasure. The Lord-Lieutenant and the Sheriff were avowedly his representatives, and acted on the instructions of his ministers. The Justices of the Peace, whether acting in General Sessions, or by ones and twos "administering justice indifferently" in ale-house or private parlour, were subject to the control of the Court of King's Bench. The King's Judges could summarily remove any case from the Justices' jurisdiction, could quash their proceedings when they made a mistake of law, could peremptorily order them to proceed when they had refrained from taking action, and could try and determine all accusations against them of venal, malicious, or merely mistaken decisions. All the civil functionaries of the county — the Custos Rotulorum, the Sheriff, the Justices of the Peace, the High Bailiffs and the High Constables, the Grand and Petty Juries, and even the Petty Constables of manors or townships, were by law required to appear before the King's Judges when they visited the county in their periodical Assizes, in order to report to them as to the keeping of the King's peace and the due execution of the laws of the realm. The Justices of the Peace were, moreover, expressly directed, by their Commission, not themselves to give judgment in any case of difficulty, but to reserve it until it could be dealt with by one of the King's Judges. Finally, the King's Privy Council could, either through the Judges on their periodical Assizes, or directly through the Custos Rotulorum, at any time issue peremptory instructions for the execution—and even for the supplementing—of the statutes and common law in whatever way the public welfare made necessary.

In the eye of the law the county was not, in fact, any more than the parish, an organisation of local self-government. Like the parish, but on a higher plane, it was a unit of obligation. Its officers and its Courts were so many devices by which the National Government sought to exact the fulfilment of its quota of service to the State, whether this took the form of soldiers, taxes, the maintenance of peace, or the

(*Memoirs and Travels of Sir John Reresby, Bart.*, edited by A. Ivatt, 1904, p. xvii.). The diminishing revenues of the office, attributed to "the granting of Liberties . . . and erecting and enlarging of inferior Courts and jurisdictions," had led the Privy Council in 1677 to endeavour to reduce the expenses (MS. Acts of Privy Council, 10th Nov. 1676 and 26th January 1677).

performance of specific duties. For it was on the county itself, not on the individual officers, that rested the immemorial obligation of furnishing an armed force, whether, as the *posse comitatus*, to put down any resistance to the keeping of the peace, or, in the form of the ancient militia, to contribute to the defence of the nation. It was to the county as a whole, and to the Hundreds as divisions of the county, that the King looked for the collection of aids and subsidies, land tax, and even "ship money." Upon the county lay the duty of maintaining the principal bridges, keeping the King's gaols, and providing proper Courts for the King's Assize Judges. For any failure to fulfil these obligations the county as a whole could be indicted and fined, and the fine could be levied, in need, by execution against the goods of any inhabitant thereof.[1] From the standpoint of constitutional law the officers of the county were but instruments to secure the keeping of the King's peace, the due execution of the King's writs and of the decisions and sentences of the King's Judges, the exact and punctual payment of the King's revenues, the safe keeping of the King's gaols, the accommodation of the King's Judges, and the maintenance of the great bridges without which there could be no safe passage along the King's highways.

This theory of obligation on which the whole of English local government was, at the Revolution, still legally based, explains why the bulk of county administration was cast in what seems at first sight the anomalous forms of presentment and indictment, trial and sentence. Among the "presentments" which the various officers, the Juries for the Hundreds, and the "Grand Inquest" or Grand Jury for the county as a whole, were "charged" to make to the Court, were not only the ordinary breaches of the law by private individuals, but also the shortcomings of parochial and manorial officers, the failure of parishes to keep up their stocks and their pounds, their highways and their minor bridges; the neglect of

---

[1] The "inhabitants of the county" of Shropshire were fined £2000 in 1783 by the Judges of Assize, "for not providing a proper place to hold the Courts in "; though the fine was subsequently discharged on Quarter Sessions showing that a Local Act had been obtained, and that new premises were about to be built (*Shropshire County Records*, part ix., edited by Sir Offley Wakeman, p. 3).

Hundreds and Franchises to keep the peace, whereby damage had been caused,[1] or to maintain in good order the bridges and gaols belonging to them; and even the derelictions of duty of the county itself in failing to keep in repair the county bridges and the county gaol. The consideration of these presentments followed the ordinary judicial forms. The officer or locality "presented" might be formally indicted; if the Grand Jury found the indictment a "true bill" (or itself made the presentment), the defendant person or locality might either submit or "traverse" the indictment: if traversed, the indictment was tried by the Court, with or without a Petty Jury; and if found guilty, the defendant, whether officer or parish, Hundred or manor, or even the county itself, would be fined in a greater or less sum, which the Sheriff had to levy as best he could. It is, indeed, not too much to say that, at the Assizes and Quarter Sessions, the county, the Hundred, and the parish, together with most of the unpaid and compulsory serving officers, were, one or other of them, always in the dock as defendants to criminal indictments, on which they were perpetually being fined. From this judicial procedure there had, by 1689, already developed, so far as the obligations of the county were concerned, both the civil administration by the Justices of the so-called "county business" and the imposition of the County Rate. If a county bridge was presented as being out of repair, the Justices in Quarter Sessions then and there examined witnesses as to what work was required, ordered some person to execute it, and directed the necessary sum of money to be levied upon the county, each High Constable or High Bailiff of a Franchise or Liberty being required to collect the quota falling upon his district from the officers of the various parishes, according to an immemorial assessment, or scheme of repartition of a given sum among the several divisions of the county. A similar course was taken whenever it occurred to the "Grand Inquest"

---

[1] The Hundred was "amerced" if any person guilty of homicide escaped; and it had to "make good the damages in the cases of robbery, cutting banks, cutting hop binds, burning houses, barns, outhouses, hovels, cocks, mows or stacks of corn, straw, hay or wood, mines or pits of coal, destroying granaries or corn intended for exportation, destroying turnpikes or works of navigable rivers and the like" (*The Justice of the Peace*, by R. Burn, 1758, vol. ii.). Its liability for damage caused by riot lasted until 49 and 50 Vic. c. 38 (1886).

to present the county gaol as out of repair. And though, under particular statutes, individual Justices or pairs of Justices could appoint parish officers, allow their accounts, authorise rates, direct the mending of founderous roads, order relief to a destitute person, command a father to pay a weekly sum for the maintenance of a bastard, apprentice a poor child, or remove a pauper to his place of settlement, the fact that there was in all these cases a right of appeal to the superior Court of Quarter Sessions indicates that, in the eye of the law " our county rulers have been, not prefects controlled by a bureau, but Justices controlled by a Court of Law ";[1] that even their apparently executive duties had to be done " with judicial forms and in a judicial spirit "; and that their most discretional orders partook of the nature of judicial decisions, to be given only upon evidence, and " according to the straight rule and course of the law." [2]

The foregoing survey of the legal framework of county government might lead the student who confined his reading to statutes and law books to conclusions involving the non-existence of anything that could properly be called local administration. He might infer, first, that the whole internal government of England and Wales was, in 1689, so strictly centralised as to leave no place for local autonomy; and, secondly, that it consisted, not in decisions as to policy and discretional acts, but in a series of judicial awards and sentences as to the obligations of persons, and bodies of persons, according to the law of the land. When, however, we leave the legal constitution, and seek to discover what actually happened in the county, we find ourselves driven to a diametrically opposite conclusion. In spite of all forms and appearances, the Rulers of the English County felt themselves at liberty to administer the local affairs as they thought fit. If we were asked to name a period in English history during which the county possessed the largest measure of self-government, when its local administrators were most effectively free from superior control, either by the National Executive, Parliament, or the Law Courts, we should suggest the years between 1689 and 1835, or, more precisely, the century that

---

[1] *Justice and Police*, by F. W. Maitland, 1885, p. 85.
[2] *Eirenarcha*, by W. Lambard, 1581, p. 46.

elapsed between the accession of the House of Hanover and the close of the Napoleonic wars. In order to appreciate the nature and extent of this practical autonomy of the Rulers of the County, the student must be asked to follow us in an examination of the actual working of county administration between 1689 and 1835.

APPENDIX TO CHAPTER I

ON SOME ANOMALOUS COUNTY JURISDICTIONS, INCLUDING THE COUNTIES PALATINE

It is not easy to determine exactly what constituted a county jurisdiction, nor how many counties there were. By statute and in common parlance there were, of course, forty counties in England, and (since 27 Henry VIII. c. 24, 1536) twelve in Wales. In many respects the Sheriff was the officer most characteristic of the county. Each of the fifty-two geographical counties had, down to 1888, but one Sheriff,[1] even if (like Yorkshire and Lincolnshire) it was legally divided into three distinct Ridings or Parts, or (like Suffolk, Sussex, Hampshire, and other counties) practically divided into two or more districts, each having a distinct county administration. On the other hand, there were, within such counties, not a few places entirely exempt from the jurisdiction of the County Sheriff, and entitled to have Sheriffs or equivalent officers of their own. Such were, for instance, the "counties corporate," or cities and boroughs that were "counties in themselves," having been granted by royal charter exceptionally large immunities from the jurisdiction of the "counties at large" in which they were geographically situated. Such "counties corporate" were, in 1689, 19 in number, viz., Bristol, Canterbury, Carmarthen, Chester, Coventry, Exeter, Gloucester, Haverfordwest, Hull, Lichfield, Lincoln, London, Newcastle, Norwich, Nottingham, Poole, Southampton, Worcester, and York.[2] In former times there had been other boroughs claiming a similar immunity, such, for instance, as

---

[1] The office of Sheriff of Middlesex was (until 1888) filled jointly by the two persons who were Sheriffs for London.

[2] *An Inquiry into the Elective Franchise of . . . the Corporate Counties*, by Uvedale Corbett, 1826; First and Second Reports of Municipal Corporation Commissioners, 1835; 3 George II. c. 15 and c. 16 (schedules). Nine of them had one Sheriff each, but ten of them had two; reduced to one in 1835 for all but the City of London. Oxford has a Sheriff without being a county corporate,

Lewes, in Sussex,[1] and (as mentioned below) Stamford in Lincoln-shire.

We are, however, prevented from classifying as counties all places having a separate shrievalty, because of the complicated inconsistencies into which we should thereby be led. Thus, Yorkshire, having only one Sheriff, might have to be regarded as one county ; but there was and is no Custos Rotulorum or Lord-Lieutenant for Yorkshire, nor any Commission of the Peace, Quarter Sessions, Grand Jury, County Rate, or civil administra-tion for the geographical county. In all these respects the three Ridings are separate counties. The same is true of the three Parts of Lincolnshire, except that these have a common Custos Rotulorum and Lord-Lieutenant, as well as a common Sheriff. On the other hand, the City of Oxford, as we have mentioned, has always had a Sheriff, without being in any sense a county. There is, at first sight, more to be said for taking as the mark of a county the existence of a separate Custos Rotulorum or Lord-Lieutenant. Thus, the "counties corporate" nearly all fall within, at least, the military jurisdiction of the Lord-Lieutenant of the county at large. The City of London, with its inde-pendent commission of lieutenancy, and the Borough of Haver-fordwest, with a Lord-Lieutenant of its own, seem alone to rank among the counties. Unfortunately there seems to have been no consistency in the practice of the Government during the seventeenth and eighteenth centuries as to which places should enjoy the dignity or advantage of having their own Custos Rotulorum and Lord-Lieutenant, or either of these. The irregu-larities of the public lists reflect an equal irregularity in the Patent Rolls.[2] During the Commonwealth the Assessment Acts treated some corporate counties, such as Poole and Lichfield, as separate counties ; and others, such as York and Coventry, as part of the geographical counties at large. The Privy Council during the eighteenth century would not infrequently address the com-munications that it sent to Lords-Lieutenant of counties, not only to the Lord Mayor of London, but also to the Lord Warden of the Cinque Ports and to the Constable (or Custos Rotulorum) of the Tower of London,—thus treating these districts as if they were counties,—and occasionally even to the Custos Rotulorum of

or specifically exempt from the jurisdiction of the Sheriff of the county. This was confirmed by the Municipal Corporation Acts of 1835 and 1882. Coventry ceased to be a county corporate by 5 and 6 Vic. c. 110, sec. 1 (1842).
    [1] *Ancient and Modern History of Lewes*, by William Lee, 1795 ; *History and Antiquities of Lewes*, by T. W. Horsfield, 1824-1827; Report of Municipal Corporation Commissioners, 1880. Perhaps it was the Rape, not the borough, which kept out the Sheriff.
    [2] Thus the lists for 1687 give, for Essex, two Lords-Lieutenant simul-taneously holding the office (*Angliæ Notitia*, by Edward Chamberlayne, 1687, part ii. p. 155). "Wales and the Marches" also had one (*ibid.*).

Westminster.[1] Yet the Tower Hamlets were certainly within the jurisdiction of the Sheriffs of London and Middlesex. Moreover, in a list of Lords-Lieutenant given in 1687 we find such officers named for Bristol and Southwark, and even for the Isle of Purbeck in Dorsetshire.[2] Now Southwark was certainly part of the county of Surrey, and the Isle of Purbeck of that of Dorset. In the corresponding list for 1755 these disappear, only Haverfordwest and the Tower Hamlets standing beside the normal counties. Even then, however, the list of Custodes Rotulorum gives such an officer also for the Soke of Peterborough, whilst the great peer who was Custos Rotulorum for both the West and North Ridings is stated to be also Custos Rotulorum for the City of York, as if that city had one of its own.[3]

Moreover, one place which was certainly not even a county corporate had yet been free from the interference of the Lord-Lieutenant of the county at large. Thus, the Borough of Stamford, in the Parts of Kesteven (Lincolnshire), whilst not claiming to be a county in itself, nevertheless asserted that it was exempt from all county control. "They boast in this town," wrote Defoe, "of very great privileges . . . such as being 'freed from the Sheriff's jurisdiction, and from being empannelled on Juries out of the town; to have the return of all writs, to be freed from all Lords-Lieutenant, and from their musters, and for having the militia of the town commanded by their own officers, the Mayor being the King's Lord-Lieutenant, and immediately under his Majesty's command, and to be esteemed (within the Liberties and jurisdiction of the town) the second man in the Kingdom.'"[4] This claim, founded on a charter of 1461, and perhaps implicitly recognised by 15 Car. II. c. 4, 1663 (which

---

[1] MS. Acts of Privy Council, George II., vol. vi. p. 599; vol. xv. p. 532; vol. xvi. p. 461. The Cinque Ports are treated as a distinct county by 15 Car. II. c. 4, sec. 19 (1663), and are ranked as if they formed a county corporate in the schedule to 3 George II. c. 16, as to payment of the Sheriff's expenses. The twenty-one hamlets within the jurisdiction of the Constable of the Tower—then including Hackney and Bethnal Green as well as what would now be called the Tower Hamlets—were expressly declared to be free from the jurisdiction of the Lord-Lieutenant of Middlesex, in 13 and 14 Car. II. c. 3 (1662); see Stow's *Survey of London*, vol. i. p. 77 of Strype's edition of 1720. There was a separate Quarter Sessions for what was often called "His Majesty's Royalty of the Tower," but the Sheriff of Middlesex acted for it (*History* . . . *of the Tower of London*, by J. Bayley, 1825, vol. ii. sec. ii.).

[2] *Angliæ Notitia, or Present State of England*, by Edward Chamberlayne, edition of 1687, part ii. pp. 155-157. We have not come across any separate Commission of the Peace for either place. The independence of the Lord-Lieutenant of the Isle of Purbeck was expressly recognised by 13 and 14 Car. II. c. 3, sec. 22 (1662).

[3] *Magna Britanniæ Notitia, or Present State of Great Britain*, by John Chamberlayne, edition of 1755, Book III. pp. 54-56.

[4] *Tour through the whole Island of Great Britain*, by Daniel Defoe, vol. iii. p. 37 of edition of 1748.

places a certain suburb of Stamford under the Lord-Lieutenant of
the county), was, we think, not effectively sustained after 1689.
The words giving exemption from the jurisdiction of the Lord-
Lieutenant had, in fact, been omitted from the charter of 1688.[1]

The counties of Lancaster, Chester, and Durham, the Isle of
Ely, Pembrokeshire, and Hexhamshire, are described as being, at
one period or another, "Counties Palatine," in which the prerogative vested elsewhere by the Crown was claimed by a great earl
or bishop on whom this "regality" had been conferred. We
cannot here enter into the history of these exceptional jurisdictions, the importance of which had by 1689 greatly diminished.
We must not, however, pass them by without a brief notice, in
the framing of which we have had the advantage of the kind
assistance of Mr. Hubert Hall.

We may practically ignore the so called palatinates of Hexhamshire and Pembrokeshire, which were never of any great consequence, and which in the sixteenth century found their franchises
in conflict with the new personal government of the Crown.[2] By
that time the great Counties Palatine of Lancaster and Chester
were permanently annexed to the Crown, and though remaining
independent regalities, ceased to be in any position of rivalry to
the royal authority. In Durham, the palatine jurisdiction of the
Bishop, which included, it must be remembered, the important
detached districts of Norhamshire, Islandshire, Bedlingtonshire, and

---

[1] *Antiquities of Stamford*, by W. Harrod, 1785 ; *History of Stamford*, by
J. Drakard, 1822 ; First Report of the Municipal Corporation Commissioners,
1835, Appendix, vol. iv. p. 2527.

[2] Hexham or Hexhamshire seems to have been carved out of the ancient
kingdom or earldom of Northumbria as a Liberty possessing all the attributes
of a palatinate which was claimed in turn by the Sees of York and Lindisfarne
before the Norman Conquest. From the twelfth century onwards this regality
was vested in the Archbishop of York, and it was occasionally referred to in
statutes as equivalent to a county jurisdiction (see, for instance, 8 Edward IV.
c. 2, 1468), but its position scarcely differed from that of neighbouring Liberties
like those of Tynemouth and Tynedale. The latter was incorporated in the county
of Northumberland by Henry VII., and in the next reign the Crown, taking
advantage of the election of a new bishop, acquired Hexhamshire by exchange.
Owing, however, to the enhanced importance of the few remaining Liberties in
private hands, Hexhamshire seems to have acquired about this time the reputed
status of a County Palatine, and, as such, proved an obstacle to the effective
administration of the county of Northumberland after the Northern Rebellion.
For this reason the reputed palatinate was abolished by the 14 Eliz. c. 13 (1572),
and was reduced to the position of a private Franchise of the Crown within the
county of Northumberland.

Pembrokeshire was *ipso facto* reduced to the position of an ordinary county
by the 27 Henry VIII. c. 24 (1536), which delimited a new county in the
place of the old palatinate and its component lordships. Already some doubts
seem to have existed as to the exact status of this palatinate, but its existence
was to some extent recognised by the withdrawal of the town of Haverfordwest
from the county of Pembroke as a distinct administrative county under the Act
of 34 and 35 Henry VIII. c. 26 (1543).

Craikshire, was doubtless, to some extent, overshadowed by the activities of the Council of the North and the Wardens of the Border Marches, and was much weakened after the abortive rebellion of "the Pilgrimage of Grace." The Isle of Ely, whatever its peculiarities, seems never to have been truly in the position of a separate county. Though exempt from all jurisdiction of the county of Cambridge, it had no Sheriff, all the duties being performed by the Chief Bailiff, or Temporal Steward, who was appointed by the Bishop for life, and did not account to the Exchequer.[1]

Thus we find the four palatine areas of Lancashire, Cheshire, and Durham—to some extent also the Isle of Ely—holding in the sixteenth century a position essentially different from that of the ordinary county. The lord palatine appointed his own administrative officers, his own Sheriff, his own Coroner, his own Justices of the Peace, and (to mention here an office to be subsequently described), as lately as 1629 and 1640, his own Commissioners or Justices of Sewers. The office of Lord-Lieutenant often remained unfilled, and, in the case of Lancaster at least, may have been replaced by that of Steward. The office of Custos Rotulorum in these palatinates is mentioned in a *Liber Pacis* of 1577 and other official compilations, but it is clear from the final Acts of resumption for Durham and Ely that the office did not continue in the hands of the Crown. Now a large territorial division to which the term county is only loosely applicable, which bears the distinctive name of County Palatine, which differs from the ordinary county in respect of the status of its essential officers, the custody of its records, and its judicial procedure, and to some extent its taxation, cannot simply be classed with the ordinary counties.

It is not easy to ascertain or to estimate how far the surviving palatine divisions retained their separate attributes during the period 1689-1835, with which alone we have to deal. The tendency in favour of the gradual assertion of the supremacy of the Crown was strong and continuous, especially in matters of military defence and national taxation, which came more and more to be carried out uniformly throughout the whole country. To this we have to add the continuous effect of several statutes of total or partial resumption (27 Henry VIII. c. 24, 1536; 5 Eliz. c. 26, sec. 1, 1563; 13 Eliz. c. 16, 1571; 27 Eliz. c. 9, 1585, and 25 Car. II. c. 9, 1673), the intention of which seems to have been to assimilate the position of the palatinates still remaining in private hands to that of other counties.[2]

---

[1] But the Isle of Ely was occasionally actually described in statutes as a County Palatine, along with Lancashire, Cheshire, and Durham; see, for instance, 5 Eliz. c. 23, sec. 9 (1563).

[2] The Act of 27 Henry VIII. c. 24 (1536) appears to be a declaratory measure, and is chiefly important as paving the way for subsequent encroachments upon

Nevertheless, the distinction between the Counties Palatine and ordinary counties continued strong in men's minds. The legal writers interpreted the Acts of incorporation or resumption in a merely declaratory sense. Compilers of official lists of Sheriffs and Justices of the Peace of the seventeenth and eighteenth centuries frequently omitted to mention among the counties some or all the palatine areas, especially Lancashire and Durham. When the freeholders or the inhabitants of these areas petition the Crown, they are found, either priding themselves on their peculiar position as compared with that of the denizens of an ordinary county, or else airing their grievances in that respect, according to their interests or inclinations. On the other hand, the attitude of the Crown towards the palatine jurisdictions obviously differed according to their ownership. Thus, whilst the Franchises in private hands were being forcibly assimilated in certain respects with the general scheme of county government, the immemorial privileges of the inhabitants of Lancaster and Chester were carefully preserved and readily confirmed on demand.

Of these four areas, the principality of Chester lost much of its distinctive position as a County Palatine through its natural association with the greater principality of Wales. It returned members to Parliament from the reign of Edward VI. Its Lords-Lieutenant date from the reign of Elizabeth, and there was also a Custos Rotulorum, side by side with the distinctive palatine officials. The city of Chester was created a separate county by Letters Patent in the twenty-first year of Henry VII.[1] We find the inhabitants of the palatinate petitioning for the confirmation of their distinctive position in the reign of Elizabeth, and this was conceded in 1568 with the approval of the English Judges. The palatinate was still a flourishing jurisdiction in 1656, when it was described by Smith in his *Vale Royal*, and it was clearly recognised in the statute-book in 1689. After that date, though the county continued to have a Chief Justice to itself, and was not included in the ordinary circuits of the English Assize Judges, it is difficult in

private franchisements which might prove antagonistic to the royal jurisdiction. Thus the Act of 13 Eliz. c. 16 (1571) deprived the Bishop of Durham of his vested interest in the forfeitures of the northern rebels, whilst the Act of 25 Charles II. c. 9 (1672) was intended to diminish the power of the palatine see by supporting the claims of its inhabitants to parliamentary representation. Probably the Act of 1 Eliz. c. 19 (1558), authorising the Crown to annex the territories of any see on voidance, in exchange for an equivalent revenue, was intended to carry out the line of policy initiated by Henry VIII. in the case of Hexhamshire, as well as to prevent alienations of the property of the see, such as were attributed to Cox, Bishop of Ely, in this reign. The Acts of 1563 and 1585 extended to these counties the common practice as to enrolments and as to conveyances by fine.

[1] The Lord-Lieutenant might even be described as for "Cheshire and the City of Chester" (*Angliæ Notitia, or the Present State of England*, by Edward Chamberlayne, edition of 1687, part ii. p. 155).

practice to distinguish its constitutional position from that of an ordinary county.[1]

The Bishoprics of Durham and Ely nominally retained their regalities throughout the whole period, though a Lord-Lieutenant for Durham—distinct from the Bishop as Custos Rotulorum—existed from Bishop Tunstall's death down to 1687, when Bishop Crewe was appointed. From 1689 to 1721 there was again a lay Lord-Lieutenant, but Bishop Talbot served from 1721 to 1754. From 1755 onward there was a layman.[2] In theory the Bishop could still issue charters and incorporate gilds and municipalities. He could preside in any of the Courts of the county. He took all the forfeitures and fines, whilst the judicial officers drew their salaries from him. On the other hand, the Commissions of the Peace for both Durham and the Isle of Ely were, by the end of the eighteenth century at any rate, issued by the Crown, not by any palatine lord; and they may have been so issued from a much earlier date. For judicial purposes, however, both Durham and the Isle of Ely continued to be separately organised under their own Chief Justices until 1836 and 1837 respectively, all appointments to judicial offices (other than the Commission of the Peace) being made by the Bishop.[3] Even then their regalities were

---

[1] Its Sheriff was allowed fees at a slightly different rate from other Sheriffs; and, along with the Sheriff for Lancashire, accounted to the Auditors for the County, and not to the Clerk of the Pipe (3 George II. c. 15 and c. 16; *The Authority, etc., of the County Courts and . . . of Sheriffs*, by William Greenwood, 9th edition, 1730, pp. 189, 221). Moreover, he was not required (nor were the Sheriffs of the Welsh counties) to take the new oath prescribed by 3 George I. c. 16, 1717, secs. 18-20. The palatinate included Flint.

[2] *Magna Britanniæ Notitia, or the Present State of Great Britain*, by John Chamberlayne, edition of 1755, book iii. pp. 54-56; *Historical . . . View of the County Palatine of Durham*, by E. Mackenzie and M. Ross, 1834, p. xcv. On the accession of George II., for instance, the Bishop of Durham was appointed by Letters Patent to be Custos Rotulorum of his own county.

[3] 6 and 7 William IV. c. 6 (1836); 7 William IV. c. 53 (1837).

We may here mention three other great ecclesiastical Liberties which may once have been on a footing not very dissimilar from that of the Bishopric of Ely, though we do not know that they were considered palatine jurisdictions. The Liberties of the Abbot of St. Edmunds were in many respects administratively distinct from the rest of the county of Suffolk, having not only a separate meeting of Quarter Sessions, an independent Grand Jury, and, by prescription at least, a distinct County Rate—though never, so far as we are aware, a separate Custos Rotulorum, Lord-Lieutenant, or Commission of the Peace. Their ancient position has left a trace in the fact that West Suffolk, always practically divided from East Suffolk, became an entirely separate administrative county under the Local Government Act of 1888. The Soke of Peterborough, long under the special jurisdiction of the Bishop of Peterborough, had its own Custos Rotulorum, who was not the same person as for Northamptonshire, though there was not, so far as we know, any Lord-Lieutenant for the Soke. It, too, has had its position recognised by being made an entirely separate administrative county under the Local Government Act, 1888. With these we must mention the Liberty of Southwell in Nottinghamshire, where the Archbishop of York

not actually abolished, but merely transferred to the Crown as independent Franchises—a distinction which has been generally forgotten. Traces of their ancient distinction may still be found in
the circumstance that the ancient records of the county are still in
the custody of the Bishop of Durham ; in the existence of the Court
of Pleas of Durham, reorganised on the lines of a modern County
Court ; and in the fact that the Isle of Ely was made, in 1888, a
separate administrative county, still has a separate Commission
of the Peace, and supplies, by custom, the High Sheriff of Cambridgeshire and Huntingdonshire every third year.

In the case of Lancashire nothing was abolished in form,
but the practical difference became of the slightest. Throughout the eighteenth century the Custos Rotulorum and Lord-
Lieutenant, the High Sheriff, and the Justices of the Peace continued to be appointed by the Duke of Lancaster under the seal
of the Duchy—meaning, in fact, by the King's minister who was
Chancellor of the Duchy of Lancaster, instead of by him who was
Secretary of State or Lord Chancellor. The High Sheriff did not
account to the Clerk of the Pipe. The Palatine Court of Common
Pleas continued to sit at Lancaster, and the Palatine Chancery
Court at Manchester administered civil justice throughout the
county, whilst the Court of the Duchy at Westminster dealt with
revenue cases. Down to the Judicature Act, 1873, appeals were
still made from the Vice-Chancellor's Palatine Court to the

had one of his palaces. "The civil government of the jurisdiction of
Southwell," say Defoe, though how far accurately we have not been able to
ascertain, "is distinct from the county at large. It is called the 'Soke of
Southwell cum Scrooby,' which is another town in this county. There are
about twenty towns subject to this jurisdiction. The Custos Rotulorum and
the J.P.'s are nominated by the Archbishop of York, and constituted by a
Commission under the Great Seal of England, who hold their Session both at
Southwell and Scrooby, and perform all other Justiciary Acts distinct from the
county. The late Lord Lexington, whose ancestors were great benefactors to
this Church, bore the office of Custos Rotulorum" (*Tour through the whole
Island of Great Britain*, by Daniel Defoe, edition of 1748, vol. iii. p. 68).
That great immunities had been granted to the chapter of canons of Southwell is
clear. They were a corporation by prescription,—even, to the confusion of the
lawyers, a corporation without a head,—and they may well have formed, in
practice, "an independent self-governing republic," free from the jurisdiction
of either King or (except by way of appeal) Archbishop (*Visitations and
Memorials of Southwell Minster*, by A. F. Leach, 1891, Camden Society, N.S.
vol. 48). It is, however, not clear to us whether this area was, after the
surrender of the collegiate church and all its possessions in 1540, and its
subsequent new foundation in 1543-1585, ever in practice exempt from the Lord-
Lieutenant of Nottinghamshire, so far, at any rate, as concerned musters and
the militia. We have come across nothing to confirm Defoe's account of its
status at the beginning of the eighteenth century, and we do not find any trace of a
commission under the Great Seal during the reign of George I. (Compare *The
History and Antiquities of Southwell*, by William Rastall, afterwards Dickinson,
1819 ; Twelfth Report of Historical Manuscripts Commission, part ix., 1891,
p. 539.)

Chancellor of the Duchy, himself a layman. They were heard by him, as Childers relates of 1872, sitting in the Duchy Office in London, with two Lords Justices (*Life and Correspondence of the Right Hon. Hugh C. E. Childers*, by S. Childers, 1901, vol. i. p. 213). We know of no other practical distinction between Lancashire and other counties.[1]

[1] These separate jurisdictions deserve further study, especially as regards the later period. For their history and constitutional position the student should consult *The County Palatine of Durham*, by G. T. Lapsley, 1900, which contains an elaborate bibliography ; " Some Remarks on the Northumbrian Palatinates and Regalities," by William Page, in *Archæologia*, li. p. 143 ; *An Enquiry into the Ancient and Present State of the County Palatine of Durham*, by S. Spearman, 1729 ; *History and Antiquities of the County Palatine of Durham*, by Wm. Hutchinson, 1785-1794 ; *Historical . . . View of the County Palatine of Durham*, by E. Mackenzie and M. Ross, 1834 ; *History of Northumberland* (Northumberland County History Committee), 1893-1899 ; *History of the County Palatine and City of Chester*, by G. Ormerod, 1882, vol. i. (which includes excerpts from *The Vale Royal of England*, published in 1656 by Wm. Smith and Wm. Webb) ; *Chester in the Plantagenet and Tudor Periods*, by Rupert H. Morris, 1893 ; *The Description of Pembrokeshire*, by George Owen, edited by Henry Owen, vol. i., 1892 ; "Haverfordwest," by Rev. James Phillips in *Archæologia Cambrensis*, Series V. vol. xv., 1898 ; "The Laws of Wales and the Marches," by Henry Owen, in *Y Cymmrodor* XIV. ; "The Welsh Shires," by T. F. Tout, in *Y Cymmrodor* IX. 201 ; *Mediæval Manchester and the Beginnings of Lancashire*, by James Tait, 1904 ; *John of Gaunt*, by Sidney Armitage - Smith, 1904 ; *The Lancashire Lieutenancy under the Tudors and Stuarts*, by J. Harland, 1859 (Chetham Society, vols. xlix. and l.) ; *Lancashire and Cheshire Records preserved in the Public Record Office*, by W. D. Selby, 1882-3 (vols. 7 and 8 of Record Society for . . . Lancashire and Cheshire); *A Brief View of Ecclesiastical Jurisdiction*, by W. Bohun, 1733 ; *History and Antiquities of the Cathedral Church of Ely*, by James Bentham, 1817 ; *Historical Account of the Ancient Town of Wisbech*, by W. Watson, 1827 ; *History of English Law*, by Sir F. Pollock and F. W. Maitland, vol. i., 1895 ; "Hereditary Revenues of the Crown and the Civil List," by G. Percival, in *Fortnightly Review*, March 1901 ; and such Parliamentary Papers as the First and Second Reports on the Courts of the County Palatine of Lancaster, 1836 ; and the Report of the Committee on the Auditor of the Duchy of Lancaster, 1857.

CHAPTER II

THE RULERS OF THE COUNTY

OUR survey of the legal constitution of the county brings out
the fact that the whole administration of county affairs, as
well as the ultimate authority in parish business, rested with
a limited class of persons—the Justices of the Peace, the
High Sheriff, and the Lord-Lieutenant,—unpaid gentlemen,
appointed, at any rate in form, by the Crown. These Rulers
of the County acted both as isolated individuals, on their own
initiative, and collectively, in Petty, Special, and Quarter
Sessions. Before we describe the actual working of this collective organisation, and its development between 1689 and
1835, it is desirable to give some description of the persons
themselves—of their number and distribution throughout the
country, of their social status and characteristics as judges
and administrators, and of the actual process, as distinguished
from the official form, of their selection and appointment.

(a) *Number and Distribution of Justices*

It is characteristic, both of the lack of system of English
Local Government and of absence of any serious investigation
into the subject, that neither the number nor the local distribution of these Rulers of the County can be stated with
accuracy or completeness. There was no fixed number of places
for which separate Commissions might be issued, apart from the
county, no fixed area over which each of them might extend, and
no definite number of Justices assigned for each district. All
these varied from generation to generation according to acci-

dent, courtly design, or the idiosyncrasy of the Lord Keeper or
Lord Chancellor for the time being. Besides the fifty undivided
counties and the six " Ridings " or " Parts " of two more, which
always had their own Commissions of greater or smaller size,
there seem to have been nearly thirty " Liberties," cities, or
towns to which, for some reason or another, separate Commissions were occasionally issued.[1] The seventy to eighty Commissions thus in force at any one time each contained the
names from half-a-dozen to more than a hundred Justices, the
total number commissioned for England and Wales (deducting
duplicates) having been in 1650 about 2500.[2] As the number
was steadily increasing, we may assume that by 1689 it had
reached 3000.

How these 3000 magistrates were distributed over the
country cannot be precisely ascertained. Doubtless the Lord-
Lieutenant of each county, and the Judges who visited it on
their circuits, would attempt to secure that there should be at
least one or two resident Justices in each large natural division.
But their ability to do so would depend on circumstances
beyond their control. An active Justice of the Peace grew,
could not be made, and was not always to be found. Where
a whole tract was owned by great magnates living in London,
or by small yeomen unfit for magisterial duties, or by Roman
Catholic or disaffected families, it was frequently impossible,
over desolate areas of more than one or two hundred square
miles, to discover any fit resident on whom to cast the office.
And when such a person was found, though the Crown might
appoint him, it did not follow that he would consent to enter
upon an employment that, to quote a contemporary, was " but
a little unprofitable honour attended with much envy "; an
office, in fact, that would " occasion him much loss of time,
some expense, and many enemies, and, after all, will afford him

---

[1] Between 1689 and 1835 the records in the Crown Office show these to
have been the Isle of Ely, the Soke of Peterborough ; the Liberties of Ripon,
Cawood, St. Albans, Otley, Southwell, St. Peter at York, and the Tower of
London ; the cities of Westminster and Oxford ; the Cinque Ports ; the
boroughs or vills of Haverfordwest, Cambridge, and St. Albans (distinct from
the Liberty) ; and, more occasionally, those of Buckingham, Saffron Walden,
Sudbury, Bedford, Taunton, Macclesfield, Poole, Thetford, New Woodstock,
and Malden.

[2] *The Names of the Justices of Peace in England and Wales as they stand
in Commission in their several Counties this Michaelmas term*, 1650.

little or nothing towards bearing these inconveniences."[1] It is therefore not surprising to find Lord Clarendon complaining in 1665 that many persons named in the Commissions of the Peace had neglected to "take out a Dedimus," and remained thus unqualified to perform a single act of duty. It was in vain that he threatened them with proceedings at the instance of the Attorney-General for ignoring the King's Commission. No such proceedings were, we believe, ever taken, and for a whole generation successive Judges in their charges at the Assizes went on calling attention to the same neglect.[2] Thus, of the 2500 to 3000 Justices in the Commission between 1650 and 1700, though absolutely no records exist on the subject, we doubt whether more than half would have qualified to perform the duties of their office; and of those who had qualified, not more than half can have habitually devoted themselves to the work,—giving, as we might speculate, to each of the 700 or 800 active magistrates an average district of more than seventy square miles, and, omitting the corporate boroughs, a population which must have exceeded 5000. Unfortunately, any such averages, at best merely hypothetical, entirely misstate the position. The 700 or 800 active magistrates, whom we imagine to have existed, found themselves distributed, it is scarcely too much to say, inversely as the need for their presence. The pleasant counties of southeastern England had many resident Justices. They were fewest in the districts lacking in residential amenity, such as the desolate wastes and moorlands remote from the metropolis; among the peasant occupiers of the Fenland; or on the dreary upland wastes in which worked the lead-miners of Derbyshire or Cleveland.[3]

(b) *The Justice of Mean Degree*

When we analyse the different types of Justice to be met

---

[1] *The Justice of the Peace, his Calling and Qualification*, by Edmund Bohun, 1693, p. 14.

[2] *Ibid.* Thus, Evelyn, who was in the Commission for Surrey, "most industriously avoided" qualifying to act, notwithstanding the personal solicitation of Charles II., because of "the perpetual trouble thereof in these numerous [*i.e.* populous] parishes" (*Diary and Correspondence of John Evelyn*, 11th April 1666, vol. ii. p. 4 of 1859 edition).

[3] For the statistics of a century later, see the last section of this chapter; and Chapter VI., The Reaction against the Rulers of the County, pp. 383, 581.

with in the eighteenth century we find that this same absence
of a governing class in certain districts, coupled with the disqualification of the old families as recusants or as disaffected
persons, and the desire to give influence to others specially
zealous for the Government, had begun, already in the seventeenth century, to lead to the introduction into the Commission
of the Peace of "the Justice of Mean Degree." From
statutory preambles and incidental complaints we may infer
that some men of humble station had, almost from the first,
crept into the Commission of the Peace. After the Restoration,
however, this type of Justice multiplied rapidly. The party
struggles of the succeeding years led to many successive
removals from the Commission of influential personages un-
friendly to the dominant faction of the time being.[1] At the
end of the seventeenth century this courtly manipulation of
the Commission became the subject of severe animadversion
in Parliament. Smollett describes how, "boiling still with
indignation against the Lord Chancellor, who had turned many
disaffected persons out of the Commission of the Peace, the
House ordered a bill to be prepared for qualifying Justices of
the Peace, and appointed a committee to inspect the Commission.
This reporting that many dissenters, and men of small fortunes
depending on the Court, were put into those places, the
Commons declared in an address, that it would much conduce
to the service of His Majesty, and the good of this kingdom,
that gentlemen of quality and good estates should be restored
and put into the Commissions of the Peace and Lieutenancy,
and that men of small estates be neither continued nor put

---

[1] "None," notes Bishop Burnet in 1691, "were left, either on the bench
or in the militia, that did not with zeal go into the humour of the Court"
(*History of My Own Times*, by G. Burnet, vol. ii. p. 285 of 1833 edition).
"Several of our factious Justices," writes Dean Prideaux in 1681, "were left
out of the Commission . . . which is a great affliction to them" (*Letters of
Humphrey Prideaux to John Ellis*, 1875, p. 89). In Duvall *v.* Price, 1694-1695,
we have a case reported that arose out of a Justice being removed from the
Commission merely because a neighbour had reported him to be "disaffected to
the Government" (*House of Lords Manuscripts*, vol. i. N.S., 1900, pp. xxxvii.
397). In 1696 sixteen were put out of the Gloucestershire Commission (MS.
Acts of Privy Council, 9th July 1696). *The Letter Books of John Hervey, first
Earl of Bristol*, 1894, contain contemporary references to the removals of 1702-
1710 (*e.g.* vol. i. p. 220), which were occasionally ordered by the Privy Council
(MS. Acts of Privy Council, William III., April to June 1700, and, Anne,
vol. iii. p. 419), or by the Secretary of State (Home Office Entry Books, in Public
Record Office, vol. i. p. 207, 31st March 1708 ; p. 322, 15th June 1708).

into the said Commissions. The King assured them he was of the same opinion, and that he would give directions accordingly. They were so mollified by this instance of his condescension, that they thanked him in a body for his gracious answer."[1] The Whig House of Lords, a few years later, had its own view of the changes that had been made. "The chief objection made . . . in the House of Lords," in 1704, as Bishop Burnet incidentally tells us, "was that the Justices of the Peace had been put in and put out in so strange a manner ever since Wright had the Great Seal, that they did not deserve so great a power. . . . Many gentlemen of good estates and ancient families had been of late put out of the Commission for no other visible reason but because they had gone in heartily to the Revolution, and had continued zealous for the late King. . . . At the same time, men of no worth nor estate, and known to be ill-affected to the Queen's title and to the Protestant succession, were put in, to the great encouragement of ill-designing men; all was managed by secret accusations and characters that were very partially given."[2] To some extent, we may infer, both these complaints arose from nothing more valid than a social prejudice against newly-enriched tradesmen, in which the legislators but shared the common feeling of the country gentlemen. Hence the hostility of the

---

[1] *History of England*, by T. Smollett, vol. i. p. 312 of 1848 edition; see House of Commons Journals, 28th November and 18th December 1699; 4th and 9th January, 4th and 26th March, and 1st April, 1700; 8th, 10th, and 11th March, 15th April, 7th, 9th, 13th, and 15th May, 10th, 13th, 14th, 15th June, 1701; and MS. Acts of Privy Council, 18th, 25th, and 29th April, and 20th and 27th June, 1700. For Sir Nathan Wright, appointed Lord Keeper in 1702, on the dismissal of Somers, see *Diary and Correspondence of John Evelyn*, 1862, vol. ii. pp. 372-373. In 1702 a large number of Justices were removed from the Middlesex Commission, and thirty-four Tory and High Church adherents added (*History of England*, by John Oldmixon, 1735, p. 293). This, however, may have been partly due to the removal of Justices who had proved themselves unfit. A contemporary poem seems to have so interpreted this or the similar removal of seventy-five in 1700 :—

> "Full seventy-five turned out! A handsome drench,
> Though much too late. Sure this will purge the Bench,
> Informers may now find th' employment bad,
> And justice may from Justices be had.
> So sorely did the trading harpies waste us,
> We suffered less from Spanish guarda costas.
> O Liberty! defend these harassed nations
> From foreign and domestic depredations."

(Quoted in *A Handybook for Justices of the Peace*, by a Devonshire Justice, 1877.)
[2] *History of My Own Times*, by G. Burnet, vol. v. p. 137 of 1833 edition.

old-standing Justices of the Peace to the new-comers did not
spare even public-spirited and well-qualified persons who
happened to be outside the clique of county society. " I
remember," said Oldmixon, " a West Country baronet, distinguished alike by his fiery face and fiery zeal, being opposed
on the bench by a Justice who had the reason on his side,
said in answer to his reason, ' Fine times, indeed, when gentlemen must be taken up by Blue Apron men,' alluding to his
brother Justice having been a shopkeeper. The latter retorted,
' Whatever the Blue Apron man has is his own,' alluding to
a very heavy incumbrance which the baronet could never clear
his estate of." [1] " The great men," complains a learned Suffolk
Justice of small possessions in 1693, " will neither do the duties
of their places themselves, nor suffer the meaner but more active
to do it for them." The gentlemen of smaller estates, on whom
the work fell, found, we are told, " combinations made amongst
the rest to cross and quash whatever they shall propose, be it
never so just and reasonable, and nothing alleged for it but
that they are mean, proud, busy people, and will perk up too
much above their betters, if they be not thus mortified and
kept under." [2] But elsewhere the animadversions upon the
magistrates of humble station were better justified, though the
remedy was not so easily discovered. In the urban parishes,
especially in the metropolis, "no person of distinction or family "
would, we are told,[3] discharge the onerous and disagreeable
duty of a magistrate. " In places inhabited by the scum and
dregs of the people and the most profligate class of life, gentlemen of any great figure or fortune," writes a contemporary
journalist, " will not take such drudgery upon them. . . . If
[the qualification] were higher, proper persons would not be
found in such places for the Commission." [4] Successive Lord

---

[1] *History of England*, by John Oldmixon, 1735, pp. 192-193.

[2] *The Justice of Peace, his Calling and Qualification*, by Edmund Bohun, 1693.

[3] Rigby's Speech, in *Parliamentary History*, 8th May 1780, vol. xxi. p. 592 ;
see Place MSS. in Add. MSS. 27826, p. 141.

[4] *Applebee's Journal*, 19th August 1732, quoted in *Gentleman's Magazine*,
August 1732, p. 910. Even when, by 5 George II. c. 18 (1731), and 18 George
II. c. 20 (1744), the qualification was raised to the possession of landed property
worth £100 a year, persons of mean degree contrived to get appointed. There
was no provision for ensuring that every Justice should actually possess the
statutory qualification. And £100 a year, it was pointed out in 1732, " is but
a small estate to live upon in town, as such a magistrate ought to do, and may
be evaded before the Act takes place." Moreover, it was observed, some kinds

Chancellors found themselves, especially in Middlesex, driven
to fill the Commission with small professionals and tradesmen
who, as it was said, " had picked up a little knowledge by
attending on special juries, and thought themselves lawyers." [1]
This lowering of the social status of the Commission was
spasmodically resisted. We see, for instance, Lord Hardwicke
in 1744 making a stand against appointing an organist
whom a great peer was pressing on him.[2] But in Middlesex
and Westminster it proved quite impossible to maintain the
social status of a magistrate. "The Justices of Middlesex,"
said Burke without contradiction in 1780, "were generally
the scum of the earth—carpenters, brickmakers, and shoemakers; some of whom were notoriously men of such infamous
characters that they were unworthy of any employ whatever,
and others so ignorant that they could scarcely write their
own names." [3] But whether the motive was political partisanship, personal jobbery, or mere inability to find more substantial candidates, the placing of impecunious men in the
Commission of the Peace had, throughout the eighteenth
century, most disastrous results. Honourable men who were
dependent for their livelihood on their daily exertions could
not afford to undertake what had become an onerous unpaid
office, which entailed great loss of time, some out-of-pocket

of freehold land, such as cottage property at weekly rents, might "be bought
in the City for four or five years' purchase," and this, even if mortgaged, would
"serve all the purposes of a qualification" (*Gentleman's Magazine*, August
1732, p. 892).

[1] *Memoirs, etc., of Lætitia Matilda Hawkins*, 1824, vol. i. p. 18.

[2] "The true and real reason why I have not yet put him into the Commission
for Westminster is the low employment of organist of St. James's Church which
he is now in the actual possession of. This has made some persons of that parish
who are Justices of the Peace object against him—they consider him only as
their organist, and, whether from a certain hauteur or other considerations,
think it improper that he should be brought upon the Bench with them.
Neither can I find that any person in that situation has ever been put into the
Commission" (Lord Hardwicke to Lord Orford, 4th August 1744, in *Life of
Lord Chancellor Hardwicke*, by George Harris, 1847, vol. ii. p. 96).

[3] Burke's Speech, in *Parliamentary History*, 8th May 1780, vol. xxi. p. 592;
see Place MSS. in Add. MSS. 27826, p. 141. "It used to be said," recounts the
garrulous daughter of Sir John Hawkins, "of one of them, whose name was
David, and who had been a bricklayer at the east end of the town, where, by
prescription, these Justices were of the lowest order, that he never wrote more
of his baptismal name than the two first letters, having a doubt in his mind as
to one of the subsequent ones." "There are two generals, the soliciting general
and the returning general," is a saying ascribed to another of these Justices
(*Memoirs, etc., of Lætitia Matilda Hawkins*, 1824, vol. i. p. 19).

expenses, and, as we shall see, not a little pecuniary risk. The class of needy adventurers who pushed or intrigued themselves into some of the Commissions were, to use an American expression, "not there for their health." Thus, we find, up and down the country, but especially in Middlesex, Westminster, the Tower Hamlets, and the Metropolitan parts of Surrey, a particular type of Justice, who gained, in the documents and literature of the eighteenth century, an infamous notoriety under the appellation of a "Basket" or "Trading Justice."[1]

(c) The Trading Justice

The Trading Justice was not necessarily corrupt, in the sense of accepting bribes or giving venal decisions. He was the product of the system which aimed at making the administration of justice self-supporting by exacting a fee for every act that was performed. These fees were individually small in amount, and they could only be made to yield an income to magistrate and clerk by a perpetual flow of business which it thus became the interest of both of them to promote. As early as 1616, James I. had complained to the Star Chamber

[1] The best known and most accessible references to the Trading Justices are to be found in Samuel Butler's *Hudibras*, and in the works of Gay, Fielding, and Smollett ; see also Newcastle MSS. in Add. MSS. 33053, and Place MSS. in Add. MSS. 27826 ; the Home Office archives in Public Record Office ; *A Vindication of a Certain Middlesex Justice and the Rest of the Gentlemen in the Commission of the Peace*, 1718 ; *A True State of the Case in respect of the late Disputes in the Parish of St. Leonard's, Shoreditch, concerning the Pound Rates*, by a Parishioner, 1744 ; *Memoirs of the Life and Times of Sir Thomas de Veil*, 1747 ; *Considerations on Several Proposals lately made for the Better Maintenance of the Poor*, 1751 [by Charles Gray, M.P. for Colchester] ; *Gentleman's Magazine*, December 1769, p. 539 ; the debate in the House of Commons, 8th May 1780, see *Parliamentary History*, vol. xxi. p. 592 ; *Morning Chronicle*, 5th June 1780 ; *Observations on the Police or Civil Government of Westminster*, by Edward Sayer, 1784 ; *Considerations on the Authority of the Magistrate, commonly called the Police*, by Joseph Cawthorne, 1788 ; *Essay on the Means of Preventing Crimes and Amending Criminals*, by Sir W. Blizard, 1785 ; *Memoirs of Laetitia Matilda Hawkins*, 1824 ; R. v. Spiller in *Times*, 7th February 1797 ; *History and Survey of London*, by B. Lambert, 1806, vol. iii. p. 522 ; *Londiniana*, by E. W. Brayley, vol. ii. p. 287, 1829 ; *Life of Fielding*, by Wm. Watson, 1808 ; *Treatise on the Police and Crimes of the Metropolis*, by the Editor of the *Cabinet Lawyer*, 1829, p. 56 ; *Annual Register*, vol. xxxiv. p. 157 ; *Life of Lord Chancellor Hardwicke*, by George Harris, 1847, vol. i. p. 390 ; *Life of Henry Fielding*, by Frederick Lawrence, 1855 ; *Revelations of Prison Life*, by G. L. Chesterton, 1856, vol. i. p. 17 ; *History of Clerkenwell*, by W. J. Pinks, 1865, p. 629 ; *London and Westminster*, by John Timbs, 1868, vol. ii. pp. 1-8 ; *Fielding*, by H. Austin Dobson, 1883 and 1890 ; *Calendar of Home Office Papers*, vols. i.-iii.

that among the Justices there were some " busy bodies who
did so much, embracing many businesses for the enlargement
of their private gain and profits." [1] With the multiplication
of Justices of Mean Degree, we find repeated references in
contemporary literature to those who made their office " a
trade for maintenance," [2] and, in the words of Samuel Butler,
" used two equal ways of gaining, by hindering justice or maintaining." [3] " Persons engaged in a troublesome employment,"
said the Solicitor-General in the House of Commons a century
later, " would inevitably contrive some means of paying themselves," and the method of the Middlesex magistrates, he
explained, was to divide with the clerk the fees allowed by
law. [4] " A mercenary magistrate," the gentle Oliver Goldsmith
reminds us, " who is rewarded in proportion not to his
integrity, but to the number he convicts, must be a person of
the most unblemished character, or he will lean on the side of
cruelty. . . . A corrupt magistrate may be considered a human
hyena." [5] The more prominent members of the confraternity
of Trading Justices had, however, something to say in extenua-
tion of their profession. They were, as the biographer of one
of them declares, " a sort of people that have never stood in a
very fair light, either with their superiors or inferiors ; by the
former they are generally considered as low, needy, and
mercenary tools who subsist on their Commissions. On the
other hand they are hated and dreaded by the common people,
who fancy they have greater powers than they really have."
Such magistrates, it was urged, " are a kind of necessary evil ;
for though the part they act is low, and very frequently
oppressive and injurious, yet if there were not such little
magistrates the laws could not be well put in execution, or

---

[1] *The King's Speech in the Star Chamber*, taken by Ned Wakeman, 1616 ;
see *History of Political Literature*, by R. Blakey, 1855, vol. ii. p. 89.

[2] *Tatler*, 12th May 1709. A subsequent pamphleteer mentions the "mean
and low persons who have nothing to live upon but their trades, or who are
made Justices of the Peace on purpose to get a livelihood " (*Serious Thoughts
in Regard to the Public Disorders*, by a Country Justice of the Peace, p. 50, n.d.
? 1770). "Many of those who exercised this species of magistracy within the
bills of mortality were," writes a contemporary historian, "to the reproach of
government, men of profligate lives, needy, mean, ignorant, and rapacious, and
often acted from the most scandalous principles of selfish avarice " (*History of
England*, by T. Smollett, ch. xxii. vol. iii. p. 81 of 1848 edition).

[3] *Hudibras*, by Samuel Butler, 1674-1676, Part III. Canto iii.

[4] *Morning Chronicle*, 24th June 1785.

[5] *The Citizen of the World*, by Oliver Goldsmith, 1760.

the common sort of people kept within any bounds in regard to their superiors or to one another."[1]

The transition from "encouraging business" to a corrupt or oppressive use of the magisterial authority in order to extort fees or levy blackmail was, to a Trading Justice, seldom perceptible.[2] He "who makes it his object to create business for his own emolument," it was observed, "turns the exercise of his authority into an iniquitous traffic, and encourages and shares the extortions and scandalous profits of his agents."[3] It was in the purlieus of the large towns that the corruption of the Trading Justice had its most hideous side. "There is one abuse in this town," writes Dean Swift, in 1709, "which wonderfully contributes to the promotion of vice; that such men are often put into the Commission of Peace whose interest it is that virtue should be utterly banished from among us; who maintain, or at least enrich themselves by encouraging the grossest immoralities; to whom all the bawds of the ward pay contribution for shelter and protection from the laws. Thus these worthy magistrates, instead of lessening enormities, are the occasions of just twice as much as there would be without them. For these infamous women are forced upon doubling their work and industry to answer double charges of paying the Justice and supporting themselves."[4] In the very same year Sir Richard Steele corroborates the testimony of Swift. "It grew a phrase," says the *Tatler*, "who would do justice on the Justices." One of them "never spared a pickpocket, but was a companion to cheats." Another would "make compliments to wenches of quality, but certainly commit poor ones." "If a poor rogue wanted a

---

[1] *Memoirs of Sir Thomas De Veil*, 1748, p. 18.

[2] It was a comparatively small matter that the mercenary Justice could, in practice, usually retain for himself the shilling fine for an oath, which he could impose summarily, without trial, whenever and wherever he heard any one swear. These fines were, according to the statute, to be paid over to the Churchwardens and Overseers in aid of the Poor Rate. Frequent receipts from this source are found in parish accounts. But it is clear that much was never paid over. Thus the Westminster Justices, in 1719, found that one of their number had levied thirty shillings in this way within eight days; and they had to take special steps to get the sum credited to the parish (MS. Minutes, Westminster Petty Sessions, 6th August 1719).

[3] *An Enquiry into the Duties of Men*, by Thomas Gisborne, 1794, vol. i. p. 289.

[4] *A Project for the Advancement of Religion and the Reformation of Manners*, by Jonathan Swift, 1709, p. 15 ; pp. 94-95 of vol. viii. of *Works*, edition of 1883.

lodging," such a Justice " sent him to gaol for a thief. . . . If
a poor whore went only with one thin petticoat," he " would
imprison her for being loose in her dress." [1] The plays of
Gay and Fielding, and the novels of Fielding and Smollett,[2]
abound in vivid and scarcely quotable scenes, in which the
Trading Justice commits acts of turpitude which would be
incredible if these romances could not be authenticated by
official documents and contemporary descriptions of actual
cases. Laconic *dossiers* of particular Justices prepared for the
Lord Chancellor, and soberly worded summaries laid before
the Prime Minister, help to convince us that the worst of the
Trading Justices of Middlesex and Westminster were quite as
bad as the contemporary novelists and dramatists have
pictured them.[3] Half-a-dozen times or more, in the course of

[1] *Tatler*, 12th May 1709. The Trading Justice became the butt of the contemporary dramatists. "An old fellow," says a forgotten farce of 1717,
"qualified with ill-nature and avarice, by the help of a little money and some
interest, gets into the Commission. He entertains a clerk, some broken
attorney (for they make the best clerks) . . . and for their honesty they are
generally on a par. The fees are divided into four parts ; the Justice has two,
the clerk one, and the favourite constable the other" (*The Per-juror : a farce*,
1717 ; see *A Vindication of a certain Middlesex Justice*, 1718, pp. 6-7).

[2] See, for instance, the doings of "Mr. Justice Thrasher" in Fielding's
Amelia, and of "Mr. Justice Squeezum" in his *Coffee-House Politician, or the
Justice caught in his own Trap* ; and the confession of Jourdin, the Middlesex
Justice, in *The Debauchees*. These may be compared with Smollett's "Justice
Gobble" in *The Adventures of Sir Launcelot Greaves*, 1762 (chap. xi. "Descrip-
tion of a Modern Magistrate"), and "Justice Buzzard" in *The Expedition of
Humphrey Clinker*, 1771.

[3] Thus, a confidential report headed "A True Account of some Justices of the
Peace," written about 1737-1738 for the then Lord Chancellor, contains the following among other character sketches : "One Sax, a Justice near Wapping ; very
poor and scandalous ; lately a prisoner in the King's Bench for debt ; now
skulks about in blind alehouses for debt about Tower Hill and Wapping, and
takes affidavits at a little alehouse near the Victualling Office. . . . Anthony
Wroth had formerly an estate in Suffolk, but has ruined himself by gaming.
Was lately a prisoner in the Fleet for debt. Since he came out of prison he has
lived in several populous parts of the town most proper for a Trading Justice,
and at last has opened a shop in Red Lion Street, Clerkenwell, having hired a
house of Justice Mitchell's, whose tool he is. The Justice uses the ground floor
for his business ; the rest of the house his worship lets out in lodgings, and a
woman of very ill-fame lodges one pair of stairs" (Hardwicke MSS. ; see *Life
of Lord Chancellor Hardwicke*, by George Harris, 1847, vol. i. pp. 390-391). A
paper laid before the Duke of Newcastle in 1758 describes the Middlesex
Justices as follows : "They are no sooner appointed than some of them open shops,
contiguous to their trade and employment, for the distribution of justice. The
poorer sort that have dealt with them in their various ways of traffic . . .
upon all occasions apply to their different law shops where justice is retailed.
. . . Those gentlemen have for the sake of their two employments scouts and
spies of observation either to inform or [to] find out the poor wretches that . . .

the eighteenth century, the Middlesex Quarter Sessions is driven to make formal representations to the Lord Chancellor as to particularly gross cases of misconduct and oppression, when the offenders were removed from the Commission. Thus, in 1750, we have an elaborate representation of the iniquities of Sir Samuel Gower, Knight, an active Justice of the Tower Hamlets division, who insisted on protecting certain keepers of disorderly houses, from whom alehouse licences had been withdrawn, doing his utmost to persuade another magistrate to join in relicensing them, and finally granting them "permissive licences" over his own signature only. He was himself the landlord of "a notorious house, the Goodman's Fields Wells . . . wherein plays, interludes, and other disorders are often acted, and . . . wine, punch, ale, and spirituous liquors are constantly sold at exorbitant prices." This disorderly house he refused to join in suppressing, and persisted in encouraging in every way. He employed "as his clerk one Winstone, victualler, who lately was a Whitechapel bailiff, and now keeps an alehouse in the Tower Liberty, near half a mile distant from the said Justice; to whom, at his own alehouse, all persons applying to the said Justice for a warrant are to go; and he, the said Winstone, when at leisure, is to take their informations and examinations, and there to make out warrants."

In 1769 Quarter Sessions makes a formal representation, asking for the removal from the Commission of one John Sherratt, whose name had been inserted in it eight years before. He was, they represented, "originally a hatter, and,

are threatened with immediate ruin. However, this is palliated by dealing with them; and by that means they live undisturbed; so long as they continue customers by buying of them at ten and twenty per cent dearer than of any other . . . the keeper of brothels and stews escapes. The purlieus in and about Covent Garden by known fame were once divided between —— and —— who were in partnership, and the spoils of the miserable, being not equally divided, occasioned a dissolution of that partnership. . . . In the taking up of a number of the poor prostitutes, those of them which can pay the expense of discharging the warrant and other incidental fees . . . then become reputable objects. . . . Those, on the other hand, who from miserable poverty are committed and continued in prison . . . are bereft of every necessary of life. . . . The reason for committing those sort of prostitutes, or supposed such, indiscriminately is most frequently for the sake of the different gaolers, and they in their turn are as obliging to the Justices. For whoever are to be bailed out of their cells they carry to their respective favourites" (Newcastle MSS. in Add. MSS. 33053, p. 223). See also *Calendar of Home Office Papers*, 1878, p. 383.

from the course of his education and the nature of his business, can hardly be supposed capable of exercising the office of a magistrate with any degree of credit to the Commission or benefit to the public. That from the time of his first appearance in the world the said John Sherratt hath been shifting about from one occupation to another. That he hath been at different times a broker, a proprietor of a place of public resort called Marylebone Gardens, an agent for the proprietor of a private ship of war, and is now, as he pretends, a notary, but without employment or any visible means of subsistence." He had been, since 1745, twice declared a bankrupt, and was again so much in debt that, to avoid arrest, he had " procured his name to be inserted in a list of the servants of Foreign Ministers as one of the servants of . . . the Envoy Extraordinary . . . of Bavaria ; " and that, in short, " he is a disgrace to the Commission."[1] Of the actual conduct of this particular magistrate we have no information. But those students who have moved about among the contemporary records and daily literature of eighteenth century London, necessarily become familiar with these Justices of low degree and unscrupulous character—small shopkeepers, alehouse keepers, little builders, ex-bailiffs or brokers, discharged army officers, administering " their functions in their own houses, and so unblushingly " making a living from the fees as to win " for their residences the by-word of justice shops " ;[2] several of them on Clerkenwell Green, in the streets behind Holborn, or beyond Whitechapel High Street ; usually in close contiguity with their other trading establishment if they had one ; often combining the retailing of justice with the sale of groceries or the execution of house repairs. Round these centres would cluster their " barkers," men employed to inveigle customers

---

[1] MS. Minutes, Quarter Sessions, Middlesex, 23rd February 1751 and May 1769. In 1773 we have a glimpse of another magistrate's venal collusion with the riotous coalheavers (*Calendar of Home Office Papers of the Reign of George III.* vol. iv. p. 39). Four years later, Quarter Sessions appoints a Committee to inquire into the cases of " certain acting Magistrates within this county" who " have grossly misbehaved themselves in the execution of their office " ; and the report reveals scandalous cruelty and judicial oppression by two Justices, one of whom died, and the other was presently removed from the Commission (MS. Minutes, Quarter Sessions, Middlesex, December 1777, 15th January, 13th March, and 30th April 1778).

[2] *Revelations of Prison Life*, by G. L. Chesterton, 1856, vol. i. p. 17, giving the recollections of a Middlesex magistrate.

for warrants and summonses, exactly like those engaged by
touting shopkeepers for the sale of their wares;[1] to them
would report their "runners," or scouts and spies, bringing
information of poor wretches who might profitably be arrested
for petty offences; and from them would, at nightfall, be
despatched their hireling constables with orders to "haul the
dragnet," or make a complete sweep of the streets, arresting
indiscriminately, on the slightest of pretexts, all the pedes-
trians from whom at least a bail fee could be extorted.[2] The
circumstances of the time, it must be admitted, played into
the hands of such Trading Justices. The general relaxation
of manners and morals—the incessant disorders of the London
streets, the blasphemies and indecencies, the rows and riots,
the universal gambling, drunkenness, and debauchery—brought
numberless individuals of all classes within the letter of the
law. Statute after statute had endowed the Justices with the
widest discretionary power of arrest and commitment,[3] and
the right to exact the cost of these proceedings from the
defendants themselves, whether innocent or guilty. The state
of the gaols—their filth, overcrowding, and promiscuity, the
tyranny and extortions both of the gaoler and of the other
prisoners, not to mention the enormous mortality from the
"gaol distemper"—was such that a mere remand in custody,

---

[1] "They would . . . occasionally give credit for warrants to encourage
litigation and promote the obtaining of fees" (*Londiniana*, by E. W. Brayley,
1829, vol. ii. p. 287 ; *History of Clerkenwell*, by W. J. Pinks, 1865, p. 628).

[2] "It was," relates Townsend, the well-known "Bow Street runner," of the
time prior to 1792, "all a trading business. . . . The plan used to be to issue
out warrants and take up all the poor devils in the streets, and then there was
a bailing out at two and fourpence each. . . . They sent none to gaol, for the
bailing them was so much better" (Report of House of Commons Committee on
the State of the Police of the Metropolis, 1816, p. 140). Francis Place, com-
menting on this evidence, observes that "the periods when these things occurred
were irregular, and depended on the cupidity of the magistrate. I have known
nearly a hundred women of the town to be shut up in one watch-house. A
sweep was made early in the evening and another late at night. This was what
was called 'general search nights' ; partial sweeps were made occasionally of a
street or two" (Add. MSS. 27826, p. 142).

[3] Eighteenth century moralists noticed what American experience has since
abundantly demonstrated, viz. that the more numerous and more severe the
laws, the greater is the opportunity which they afford for corruption. "A
weak, vicious, but above all . . . a mercenary magistrate," said Goldsmith in
1760, "desires to see penal laws increased, since he too frequently has it in his
power to turn them into instruments of extortion ; in such hands, the more laws
the wider means, not of satisfying justice, but of satiating avarice" (*The Citizen
of the World*, by Oliver Goldsmith, 1760).

or commitment for non-payment of a fee, was more to be
dreaded than the actual sentence inflicted on a convicted
criminal at the present day. The ordinary citizen, unlucky
enough to fall into the clutches of such a Trading Justice,
practically could not avoid the payment of whatever money
forfeit was within his means. Now and again, it is true, a
pugnacious or public-spirited person—more usually, a crafty
attorney intent on his own blackmail—would sue a magistrate
for damages in the Court of King's Bench for some exceeding
of his power or irregularity of proceeding.[1] But long-continued practice had generally taught the Trading Justices
how far they could go with impunity; and we watch them
bargaining with the keepers of disorderly houses for the
quarterly payment of blackmail; we see them sometimes
levying a regular amercement on the prostitutes plying in the
thoroughfares, and the publicans carrying on illicit practices
within the reach of their venal constables; we may note their
careful avoidance of interference with the gaming houses
frequented by the rich,[2] or with any offenders likely to give
them trouble instead of yield them fees and blackmail; we
trace them generally continuing their careers unchecked, in

[1] An exceptional instance of a criminal information being filed against a
Justice for malpractices is reported in *The Times* of 7th February 1797 (Court of
King's Bench, R. *v.* Spiller). A London Trading Justice before whom the
examination of a thief was conducted, had said that he should like the conduct
of the case to be given to a certain attorney, who acted as his clerk. The
prosecutors, a canal company, preferred to employ their own solicitors. The
Justice thereupon deliberately neglected to produce the necessary documents at
the trial, with the result that the prisoner had to be acquitted. This "gross
and abominable prostitution of the situation" that he held, "for the purpose of
defeating a public prosecution," was committed for "this reason only, that it
was not carried on by the instrumentality of an attorney who was his worship's
clerk. . . . There was too frequently in such places an animal in the character
of a solicitor, recommended by the magistrate, and perhaps . . . in a sort of
partnership with the magistrate in the business that was carried on there."

[2] "The laws are turnstiles," remarks a Trading Justice, "only made to stop
people who walk on foot, and not to interrupt those who drive through them in
their coaches" (*The Coffee-House Politician; or, the Justice caught in his own
Trap*, by Henry Fielding). "There were two coaches with coronets on them at
the door, so we thought it proper not to go in," reported the hireling constable
to the Trading Justice in the same play. The Trading Justice, it was said in
1785, "will have his office and his runners . . . the neighbourhood will be
made tributary . . . every abuse in public-houses will be connived at and their
number increased . . . public stews will be hunted out—for pay (he will suppress none) . . . petty offences will be permitted; his myrmidons will only
attend to a reward; everything private or public in its nature will remain
unnoticed unless some gain may repay his labour" (*Morning Chronicle*, 27th
August 1785).

some cases, indeed, abandoning the most evil of their practices
as they advanced in wealth, and even ending up in the respecta-
bility of a knighthood and a reputation for public work.[1]

The more sensational iniquities of these "guardians of our
laws and liberties" were connected with their criminal jurisdiction, which it does not fall within the scope of this work
further to examine.   But some of the Trading Justices found,
in the performance of their administrative duties, larger and
less disreputable opportunities of personal gain.   In their
obligation to oversee the practical administration of the Poor
Law and Highway Acts, to audit the accounts, or sanction
the arrangements of paving, cleansing, lighting, and watching
committees or Boards of Trustees ; and, above all, in the
assessment of the rates and the licensing of public-houses,
unscrupulous magistrates discovered lucrative sources of
income.   We have already described the collusion between
"Select Justices" and the corrupt Select Vestries of the
metropolitan parishes, and the long-continued financial
manipulations open to such a magistrate as Joseph Merceron
of Bethnal Green.[2]   During the first half of the eighteenth
century, the Justices of the Peace residing in the crowded
industrial parish of St. Leonard's, Shoreditch (which adjoins
Bethnal Green on the south-west), displayed so much corrupt
connivance in the allowance of parish accounts, and so much
venal partiality in the assessment of the parish rates (which
they themselves evaded), that the Middlesex Quarter Sessions
had repeatedly to intervene, and had in the end to depute the
magisterial control of the parish to six Justices living outside
its limits.[3]   We shall have occasion later to describe the
extended operations at Brewster Sessions and elsewhere of
such more distinguished Justices as Sir Daniel Williams of the
Tower Hamlets Division, the friend and ally of Merceron, and
himself, we suspect, a successful practitioner in the higher
flights of remunerative use of the manifold powers of a Justice
of the Peace.

[1] See, for instance, the edifying end of one of the most notorious of the
Clerkenwell Green Trading Justices, in E. W. Brayley's *Londiniana*, 1829, vol. ii.
p. 287, and *The History of Clerkenwell*, by W. J. Pinks, 1865, pp. 51, 629.

[2] Book I. Chap. IV., The Rule of the Boss.

[3] See MS. Minutes, Quarter Sessions, Middlesex, 26th June 1744 ; *A True
State of the Case in respect to the late Disputes in the Parish of St. Leonard,
Shoreditch, concerning the Pound Rate*, by a Parishioner, 1744.

One of the worst results of the mercenary activities of the Trading Justices was the discouragement which it produced among honest magistrates who valued their reputation or clung to their ease. For no sooner did any zealous Justice of the Peace begin to exert himself to curb the thefts and disorders of the common people, than there was spread abroad the accusation that he was merely covering mercenary activities by a hypocritical concern about the morals of his neighbours. Among the lower grades of Trading Justices there were doubtless to be found sanctimonious rascals, such as he who is described as ordering his clerk to "tell the cook to boil the leg of mutton I took from the butcher last Sunday morning, and to put the beef in salt against next week," [1] when he had been setting in force the Act of Charles II. penalising the sale of meat on the Lord's Day. And what between a genuine sympathy with the pléasures of the average sensual man, a horror of being associated in reputation with the Trading Justices, and a fear of provoking reprisals, the gentlemen in the Commission of the Peace seem to have given up all attempt to stem the swelling tide of licentiousness and crime. It was in vain that the pious Queen Mary and the decorous Queen Anne successively gave their patronage to Societies for the Reformation of Manners, and allowed proclamations to be made and circular letters to be issued, enjoining the magistrates to put in operation the laws against swearing, profanation of the Lord's Day, drunkenness, vice, and immorality. Equally inefficacious were the charges to Grand Juries of Judges of Assize and Chairmen of Quarter Sessions, urging Justices and Constables to " the glorious enterprise of suppressing the public gaming-houses," and "extirpating vice and wickedness in general." [2] The popular prejudice against a compulsory reformation of manners, of which we frequently read,[3] was, throughout the first half of the eighteenth century, too strong to be overcome by such means. When any pious Justice tried to act on these injunctions he often found even

---

[1] *The Per-juror*, a farce acted in 1717 ; quoted in *A Vindication of a Certain Middlesex Justice*, etc. 1818, p. 15.

[2] See, for instance, *The Third Charge of Whitelock Bulstrode, Esq.*, 1718, p. 2 ; and *The Charge of Sir Daniel Dolins, Knight*, 1725.

[3] See, for instance, *An Essay upon the Execution of the Laws against Immorality and Profaneness*, by John Disney, 1710, p. 134.

his colleagues on the bench taking sides against him.[1]   "The state of magistracy," declared Sir John Hawkins in 1763, is "a painful pre-eminence, in which a man becomes odious by doing good, and he whose public spirit would induce him to take upon himself the trouble of procuring obedience to the laws of his country, must relinquish the endeavour if he has not fortitude enough to despise the secret malevolence of those who have formed an erroneous judgment of the extent of civil liberty and the clamorous invectives of others who consider the slandering and traducing the characters of all in authority as the birthright of an Englishman."[2]   What was perhaps more depressing was the grave risk he ran of having to bear law costs and possibly pay damages.   A pamphleteer of 1736 puts this danger very graphically.   "When a Justice of the Peace, inspired with a true public spirit, meets with inferior officers of courage and intrepidity, and sets about a reformation of the unlicensed houses, he finds himself surrounded with numbers of pettifogging attorneys and solicitors, who watch his steps, and if there happens to be the least flaw in the method of drawing up and managing the proceedings, he finds himself obliged to attend a certiorari in the King's Bench, where, failing in some circumstances, the whole proceedings are quashed, and the magistrate, who has been at great expense, has the mortification to see the impudent fellow triumph over him and increase his iniquitous trade."[3]   Thus it was that Henry Fielding, deploring "the increase of robberies" and "the impatience of discipline and corruption of morals," asserts that the Justice of the Peace has become helpless now that "every riotous independent butcher or baker with two or three thousand pounds in his pocket laughs at his power, and every pettifogger makes him tremble."[4]

---

[1] When in 1691 Sir Robert Bulkeley, Bart., and another Middlesex Justice "set up an office in Lincoln's Inn," from which they carried on a campaign against tippling and Sunday trading, the Middlesex Quarter Sessions blamed their "rash and unadvised actings . . . pretending great zeal," and appointed a committee to scrutinise their proceedings, which deprecated their indiscretions (*Middlesex County Records*, 1689-1709, by W. J. Hardy, 1905, pp. 57, 64, etc.).

[2] *Observations on the State of the Highways*, by [Sir] John Hawkins, J.P. for Middlesex, 1763, p. 58.

[3] *Distilled Liquors the Bane of the Nation*, etc. 1736 ; a powerful pamphlet attributed to Rev. Thomas Wilson, D.D. (1703-1784) ; a copy preserved in Place MSS. 27825, p. 178.

[4] *Inquiry into the Causes of the late Increase of Robberies*, by Henry Fielding,

" The neglect of the Justices," declared a subsequent Chairman of the Middlesex Quarter Sessions in 1785, " is the principal cause of all the robberies and daring offences which happen every night and day." [1]

(d) *The Court Justice*

Out of the corruption and disorder of the Middlesex Trading Justices there gradually emerges, in the precincts of the Court, a semi-official magistracy, acting under the orders of the Ministry of the day, in which we may recognise the germ of the Metropolitan Police Magistrate of the present time. Early in the eighteenth century, if not before, it became recognised that there existed what was called " the Court Justice "—one of the Justices of the Peace for the Metropolitan area, to whom the Government gave instructions, and on whom it relied for prompt and obedient action in any emergency. Such a personage, it is suggested, had existed at any rate from the sixteenth century, though he was not always recognised as a government officer. The maintenance of order in the capital city, the protection of the Court, the management of the spies and secret agents on which all Governments rely, and the importance of being able quietly to secure the arrest of suspected persons, would naturally lead to confidential communications between the national government and one or other of the local magistrates. " It is certainly to the interest of every administration," it was remarked in 1748, " to have such a magistrate in the County of Middlesex, if it be possible, because he is very capable by the character he bears, and the influence he must necessarily obtain, of freeing them from abundance of trouble, as well as doing them continual, useful, and acceptable pieces of service.

1784, vol. x. p. 333 of *Works*. The Chairman of the Westminster Sessions and other Justices petitioned the Government for protection against actions brought against their peace officers by " the Covent Garden gang," and asked that the Treasury solicitor might defend such actions at the expense of the Crown, as had been done on former occasions when gaming houses were suppressed (MS. records in Public Record Office, Home Office, State Papers Domestic, George II., bundle 59, No. 64).

[1] Mainwaring's Charge to the Grand Jury at Middlesex Quarter Sessions, September 1785 ; see *A Defence of the Police Bill in answer to a Charge delivered by W. Mainwaring, Esq.*, etc., 1786, p. 10.

. . . The public reaps very great benefit therefrom, and the very reputation of such a magistrate is a great security to their property, and more effectual for intimidating rogues than a double watch."[1]   Queen Elizabeth, it was remembered, and Lord Burleigh had frequently made use of Sir William Fleetwood (1535-1594), the Recorder of the City of London. Sir Francis Mitchell, a creature of the Duke of Buckingham, had been active as a Middlesex magistrate under James I. in the execution of the orders of the Court.   After the Commonwealth, when a separate Commission of the Peace was issued for the City and Liberties of Westminster—partly, we suspect, with the object of easily creating Justices subservient to the Court[2]—we find Sir Edmund Bury Godfrey, a timber and coal merchant, and member of the Select Vestry of St. Martin's-in-the-Fields, living in Hartshorn Lane (now Northumberland Street), close to Whitehall, and taking a specially energetic part, alike in the administration of the sewers, the government of the parish, and the execution of justice.   "He had the courage," relates Bishop Burnet, "to stay in London and keep things in order during the plague, which gained him much reputation, and upon which he was knighted.   He was esteemed the best Justice of the Peace in England, and kept the quarter where he lived in very good order.   He was entering upon a great design of taking up all beggars and putting them to work,"[3] when he met his death in 1678, under the mysterious circumstances of which our histories make so much.[4]   Godfrey was apparently succeeded as the Court Justice by Sir John Reresby, a Yorkshire baronet of many adventures, who had specially applied himself, as he tells us, " to the study and exercise of the office of Justice of the Peace,"[5] and who was, in 1681, rather exceptionally added to the Commissions for Middlesex and Westminster. After his removal to York and his death in 1689, we fail to

---

[1] *Memoirs of Sir Thomas De Veil*, 1748, pp. 66-67.

[2] This is hinted in *Observations upon the Police and Civil Government of Westminster*, by Edward Sayer, 1784, p. 10.   The separate Commission had apparently been started by Cromwell.

[3] *History of My Own Time*, by G. Burnet, vol. ii. p. 154 of edition of 1833.

[4] *Who killed Sir Edmund Bury Godfrey?* by Alfred Marks, 1905 ; see also Book IV. Chap. I. The Court of Sewers.

[5] *Memoirs and Travels of Sir John Reresby, Bart.*, by A. Ivatt, 1904, p. xvii.

trace the succession for forty years or so. There may, of course, have been no such succession, though we may be sure that the governments of both William III. and Anne, not to mention Sir Robert Walpole, were at least as well served as those of the Stuarts. From 1729 to 1747 the post was evidently filled by Sir Thomas De Veil, an adventurer of courage and resource. The son of a poor Huguenot minister from Lorraine, whom Archbishop Tillotson appointed librarian at Lambeth Palace, he was successively apprentice to a bankrupt London mercer; a private soldier in William's army in Flanders; and ensign and captain of an infantry regiment that was sent to Portugal. Retired on half-pay at the Peace of Utrecht, he picked up a livelihood by drafting petitions and soliciting favours for officers like himself, eventually keeping an office in Scotland Yard for this business. In 1729 he was put in the Commission of the Peace, when he quickly drove so extensive a trade in justice at his new offices, first in Leicester Fields and then at Thrift Street (now Frith Street), Soho, that he excited the jealousy of the other Trading Justices, and drew upon himself the attention of the Ministry. Within five years we find him getting a Treasury grant of £250 for his services. For seventeen years he seems to have been the leading Metropolitan magistrate. In 1738 he was appointed Inspector - General of Imports and Exports, an office that enabled him to direct innumerable prosecutions for frauds on the revenue. To facilitate his work he was made a Justice for no fewer than four counties, besides being in the Commissions for Westminster and the Tower Hamlets. " In all emergencies where a man of his capacity could be useful, no other man was thought of." When it was sought to put in force the hated Gin Act of 1736, it was to De Veil that the task was entrusted. If any riot or tumult was appre-hended or reported, it was he who was sent for. " Though he did not preside, all the court was paid to him at Quarter Sessions; he sat by the Judge at the Old Bailey [Assizes], and he sat like a judge at his own office," which was now transferred (thus beginning a memorable local habitation that has ever since endured) to Bow Street, Covent Garden.[1]

[1] *Memoirs of the Life and Times of Sir Thomas De Veil*, 1748 ; a con-temporary picture of the successful Trading Justice which is full of interest.

Two years after De Veil's death, the Ministry asked Henry
Fielding, when that great novelist was more than usually in
low water, to fill what was then becoming recognised as the
distinct office of "the First Magistrate for Westminster." [1]
For four years, he tells us, he toiled at the duties, avoiding,
as we may well believe, the corruptions and extortions which
De Veil had not disdained, and giving to the office both a
dignity and a utility that it never again wholly lost. " A
predecessor of mine," he relates, "used to boast that he made
one thousand pounds a year in his office. . . . A man must
be a rogue to make a very little this way. . . . The truth is
the fees are so very low, when any are due, and so much is
done for nothing, that if a single Justice of Peace had business
enough to employ twenty clerks, neither he nor they would
get much by their labour. . . . I had not plundered the
public or the poor . . . on the contrary, by composing instead
of inflaming the quarrels of porters and beggars (which I

See also *Observations on the Practice of a Justice of the Peace*, by Sir Thomas De
Veil, 1747, which is naturally much less candid.   De Veil, who is not included
in the Dictionary of National Biography, is referred to in *The Huguenots*, by
Samuel Smiles, 1867, p. 506.   He was appointed Ensign in Toby Caulfield's
regiment, 14th February 1706, and Captain of Foot, 28th February 1708 (at
Lisbon) ; see War Office Commission books in Public Record Office.   The MS.
Treasury books and papers in the Public Record Office contain many references
to his career.   On his petition (Treasury Money Book, vol. xxxvii. p. 376),
praying for an allowance as compensation for having been stabbed through the
body and constantly molested by bad characters owing to his magisterial
activity, a grant of £250 was made to him, 11th September 1734 (Treasury
Minute Book, vol. xxvii. p. 286).   His appointment as Inspector-General of
Imports and Exports follows on 14th February 1738, at a salary of £500 a year,
with £280 for clerks (Treasury Customs Book, 1738).   This was probably in
reward of his services connected with the Gin Act, and in his hands must have
been indirectly an office of great profit, though it has been held as a sinecure by
Horace Walpole himself, and was afterwards given to Henry Pelham (*The State of
Great Britain*, by J. Chamberlayne).   In February 1740, on De Veil's petition,
the Treasury made a further grant to him of £100 for his extraordinary charges
in executing with great diligence and application his office of Justice (Treasury
Board Papers, vol. cccii. No. 23 ; Minute Book, vol. xxviii. p. 195 ; Letter
Book of 1740, p. 525) ; and in 1744 an additional sum of £400 (with £38 : 6 : 6
for fees) out of the Royal Bounty item of the Civil List (Treasury King's
Warrant Book, vol. xxxv. p. 422).   By this time he was officially styled
Colonel (*ibid.* vol. xxvii. p. 286), we believe, of the Westminster Militia.   He
was knighted in 1744 and continued in office until his death in 1747.

[1] The phrase is that of his first biographer, A. Murphy, in the "Essay on
the Life and Genius of Henry Fielding," prefixed to the 1775 edition of his
Works.   Fielding himself speaks of his office as that of "a principal Justice of
the Peace in Westminster" (*Voyage to Lisbon*).   There was, of course, legally
no such office ; in form he was merely a Justice for Westminster and for
Middlesex, like any other member of the Commission of the Peace.

blush to say hath not been universally practised), and by
refusing to take a shilling from a man who most undoubtedly
would not have had another left, I had reduced an income of
about five hundred pounds of the dirtiest money on earth to
little more than three hundred pounds, a considerable proportion of which remained with my clerk."[1]   The predecessors
of De Veil and Fielding had possibly received from the
Court only titles and favours, and had sufficiently paid themselves by exactions from their victims.[2]   From Fielding's
time onward, however, with a constant increase of work and
a growing preference for honesty, there seems always to have
been one or more salaries of £200 a year paid from the Secret
Service money, or other funds at the disposal of the Ministry,
to particular Middlesex or Westminster magistrates in aug-
mentation of the income to be derived from fees.[3]   After
Henry Fielding's death in 1753, we see sitting regularly at
the Bow Street Police Office his half-brother and quondam
assistant in the work, the blind Sir John Fielding; and also
Saunders Welch (1710-1784), the friend of Dr. Johnson,
both of whom were certainly in receipt of government salaries,
together with Sir John Hawkins, Johnson's first biographer,
who became a magistrate in 1761 and chairman of the
Middlesex Quarter Sessions in 1765.[4]   With the valuable

---

[1] *Journal of a Voyage to Lisbon*, by H. Fielding, vol. xii. p. 230, of 1775
edition of *Works*.

[2] We cannot, however, be sure how soon there began to be the "secret
salaries" mentioned in *Observations on the Police or Civil Government of
Westminster*, by Edward Sayer, 1784, p. 10. "No person of distinction or
family would undertake it, and therefore it was right to give douceurs to those
who did," said Rigby in the House of Commons in 1780 (*Parliamentary History*,
8th May 1780, vol. xxi. p. 592). The emoluments may have been hidden under
other names. We have seen that Sir Thomas De Veil was appointed Inspector
of Imports and Exports. Sir John Fielding got £20 a year from the War
Office for looking after deserters (War Office Records, Secretary of State,
Miscellanies 1763, in Public Record Office).

[3] As to Henry Fielding's magistracy (1749-1753), see his *Journal of a
Voyage to Lisbon*, introduction; in vol. xii. of the 1775 edition and vol. x. of
the 1784 edition of his *Works*, p. 185; the poor "Essay on the Life and
Genius of Henry Fielding," by A. Murphy, prefixed to the 1775 edition of his
Works; *Life of Fielding*, by W. Watson, 1808; *Life of Henry Fielding*, by
Frederick Lawrence, 1855; Dr. Birkbeck Hill's edition of Boswell's *Life of
Johnson*, vol. iii. pp. 216-217.

[4] For Sir John Fielding (who became a Justice in 1754, was knighted in
1761, and died in 1780) and his plans, see his *Extracts from Such of the Penal
Laws as relate to the Peace and Good Order of the Metropolis*, 1761; *My Own
Life and Times*, by Dr. Thomas Somerville, 1861, pp. 179-182; *Calendar of*

suggestions and successful experiments of both the Fieldings in connection with the prevention of crime we shall deal in another volume. It was under their administration, continued by Saunders Welch and Sir John Hawkins, that the Bow Street Police Office gradually became the centre of the police administration, not only of the Metropolis, but, to some extent, also of the whole country. "By means of the late friendly attention to the police of His Grace the Duke of Grafton," explains Sir John Fielding in 1768, " one magistrate at least attends daily in Bow Street from ten to two, and from five to nine; and on every Wednesday three or more Justices sit there from ten to three, in order to re-examine all such prisoners as have been committed in the preceding week, that they may have time to send for friends and witnesses to show their innocence, and to prevent their being unwarrantably precipitated into trials for fraud or felony; and also to transact such public business relative to nuisances, apprentices, and the wages of artificers as requires the presence of more than one Justice, to execute which is a singular convenience to this Metropolis." [1]   There seems to have been at this time a rough division into districts, Sir John Fielding at the Bow Street Office taking special cognisance of the immediately surrounding neighbourhood, including Covent Garden; whilst Saunders Welch, from his office in Litchfield Street, Soho, dealt particularly with the district west of St. Martin's Lane, including " Marylebone Fields." To the further development of the Court Justice, or " First Magistrate for Westminster," into an official stipendiary magistracy, and the final supersession of the Trading Justices, we shall recur in the concluding chapter of this book.

Home Office Papers in the Reign of George III., vol. iii. p. 562, vol. iv. pp. 10, 12, 65, 80 ; Home Office Domestic Entry Books, vols. xxiv. and xxv. ; Place MSS. in Add. MSS., 27826 ; *London and Westminster*, by John Timbs, 1868, vol. ii. pp. 1-3. For Saunders Welch, see Dr. Birkbeck Hill's edition of Boswell's *Life of Johnson*, vol. iii. pp. 216-217. For Sir John Hawkins (1719-1789), see note on page 561.

[1] *Extracts from Such of the Penal Laws*, etc. by Sir John Fielding, 1769, p. 7. "The magistrates of Westminster, for the better securing of their persons, and to procure a more ready obedience to the laws, had his Majesty's permission to wear the arms of Westminster, with the emblems of magistracy, on a gold shield, fastened to a ribbon hanging down the breast" (*London and Westminster*, by John Timbs, 1868, vol. ii. p. 3). The Justices petitioned for this distinction, which was graciously accorded to them (Home Office Domestic State Papers, in Public Record Office).

(e) *The Sycophant Justice and Rural Tyrant*

The Court Justice and his successor, the Stipendiary
Magistrate, were peculiar to the City of Westminster and the
adjoining parishes. The Trading Justice was, in the eighteenth
century, typical only of those parts of Middlesex and Surrey
that were being overrun by the mean streets, shops, and warehouses of the Metropolis.[1] This absence of the grosser forms
of corruption had not always characterised the rural magistracy. " It was a sharp reflection that was made on them in
Parliament in the forty-fourth year of the reign of Queen
Elizabeth," said Bohun in 1693, "when one said a Justice
of Peace was a living creature that for half a dozen chickens
would dispense with a whole dozen of penal statutes." And
even after the Revolution, though the rural Justice was no
longer open to so simple a bribe as " a couple of capons,"
there was room for more subtle forms of corruption. It was
" impossible to enumerate them all; sometimes the wife, the
children, the clerk are purchased underhand to recommend
the case to the Justice. . . . Another method is to offer their
services as labourers at small or no wages, upon urgent
occasions, and then these days' work are chalked up upon the
dorman, or behind the door."[2] But, by the middle of the
eighteenth century, the evidence before us indicates that a
distinguished Essex landowner and member of Parliament
was right when he asserted that "mean, low Trading Justices
are not much heard of in the country."[3] When such a
mercenary did creep into the Commission, he was, we are
told, forced by the paucity of business to travel to " distant
towns in the county, where at fairs and other public meetings
he expects a demand for his warrants."[4] This does not mean

---

[1] We shall recur, in Book III., Seignorial Franchises and Municipal
Corporations, in our account of some of the worst of the Municipalities, to
another class of Trading Justices.

[2] *The Justice of Peace, his Calling and Qualification*, by Edmund Bohun,
1693, pp. 118-119.

[3] *Considerations on Several Proposals lately made for the Better Maintenance
of the Poor*, 1751 [by Charles Gray, M.P. for Colchester], p. 24.

[4] *Gentleman's Magazine*, December 1769, p. 539 : "I have known a Trading
Justice boast," continues the writer, "that he grants not less than forty
warrants a week, makes them all special that the fees may be double, and by
his management in the hearing, contrives to bind the parties over to the Sessions

that there were no miscreants in the rural Commissions of the
Peace. The place of the Trading Justice, subsisting on his
fees of office, was, in the country, taken by the Sycophant
Justice, edging himself, by venal subserviency, into the favour
of the magnates of the county; or by the Rural Tyrant
brutally enjoying the oppression of all who ran counter to his
party bias, class interest, or personal egotisms. We can well
believe the substantial accuracy of Smollett's inimitable
portrait of " a modern magistrate " in a rural county. " Mr.
Justice Gobble " was, he tells us, a London tradesman,
" sycophant to a nobleman in the neighbourhood who had a
post at court." Marrying a rich widow, he had retired from
business to live genteelly in the country, and had compounded
a loan to his lordly patron at the price of his admission to the
county bench. This man did not attempt to make money out
of his justiceship, but used his office to minister to his pompous
self-importance, an inordinate vanity, some malice, and an
incipient cruelty. At Vestry and Sessions, as well as in the
parlour that he used as a " Justice room," he " took all opportunities of holding forth " on his own consequence and the
defects of the humbler folk around him. Merely to spite a
publican who had voted contrary to his wish in the election
of a Vestry Clerk, he got suppressed the local fair, and
eventually even the alehouse itself. The local House of
Correction he filled with the miserable objects of his severity,
not scrupling to commit any powerless person whom he
happened to dislike.[1] In Fielding's " Mr. Justice Frolic " we
have another variety of the sycophant type. When Lady
Booby desires to punish the disdainful Joseph Andrews, the
low country attorney that she consults immediately suggests
applying to the Justice to commit him to prison as a vagabond. " I know," he said, " some Justices who make as much
of committing a man to Bridewell, as his lordship at 'size
would of hanging him; but it would do a man good to see
his worship, our Justice, commit a fellow to Bridewell, he takes

for the sake of unbinding them again, and then dismisses them as an act of
grace, taking only ten shillings for his trouble." But he admits that such a
person is rare in the rural districts; "a trading country Justice," he says,
"viz. one who makes a trade of his office, has been hitherto, I believe, unnoticed."

[1] *Sir Lancelot Greaves*, by Tobias Smollett, 1762, chap. xi. vol. v. pp. 99-
109 of 1790 edition of his *Works*.

so much pleasure in it; and when once we ha' um there we seldom hear any more o' um. He's either starved or eat up by vermin in a month's time." [1]

A more common variety of the rural Justice at the beginning of the eighteenth century was the sensual and ignorant small squire, dividing his life between field sports, sexual irregularities, and the pleasures of the table. The multifarious and extensive powers vested in every Justice of the Peace, unchecked by any systematic criticism from above, or by any publicity, led to the growth in this common variety of rural magistrate of some ugly features. It is these Justices whom Swift describes as " oppressing their tenants, tyrannising over the neighbourhood, cheating the vicar, talking nonsense, and getting drunk at sessions." [2] Into the dining-room of such a magistrate it was, " in the height of his mirth and his cups," and surrounded by his boon companions, that Fielding drags Parson Adams, in order to let us see him subjected to the ignorant revilings of this dispenser of justice ; whilst the " company " enjoy the sport and crack indecent jokes at the expense of the unhappy Fanny. And in the pages of *Tom Jones* we watch Squire Western not merely recklessly committing to the horrors of the county gaol every labourer suspected of poaching, but also only prevented from sending thither the serving-maid of his disobedient daughter by the prudent remonstrance of his clerk, who reminded him that " he had already two informations exhibited against him in the King's Bench for grossly abusing his magisterial powers." [3] As in the case of the Trading Justices of Middlesex, the portraits of the lower types of rural magistrates presented by Fielding and Smollett are corroborated by more authoritative evidence. We owe to Daniel Defoe a vivid picture of the " ignorance, folly, and tyranny " of two Kentish Justices, in committing to prison as a beggar and vagabond a hapless clergyman whom they seem to have disliked as a Jacobite.[4] The carelessness with which Justices

---

[1] *The Adventures of Joseph Andrews*, by Henry Fielding, book iv. chap. iii.

[2] *A Letter to a Young Clergyman*, by Dean Swift, 1721, p. 27 ; in vol. viii. p. 217 of his *Works*.

[3] *The History of Tom Jones*, by Henry Fielding, 1750, vol. ii. p. 119.

[4] *Charity still a Christian Virtue*, by Daniel Defoe, 1719 ; *Memoirs of Daniel Defoe*, by Thomas Wilson, 1830, pp. 345-350 ; *London in the Jacobite Times*, by Dr. Doran, 1877, vol. i. p. 331.

were appointed by the Lord Chancellor and the Lords-Lieutenant—already complained of by Coke and Spelman—
became, by the middle of the eighteenth century, the subject
of serious concern. " In this kingdom," writes an indignant
pamphleteer of 1748, " any booby is invested with the
ensigns of magistracy, provided he has as many acres of land
as are necessary to qualify him under the Act. . . . Thus,
they are nominated by dint of estate or ministerial influence,
without any regard to their knowledge, virtue, or integrity. . . .
After this manner in every county we have ignorant petty
tyrants constituted to lord it over us, instead of honourable,
ingenuous, upright, conscientious, learned, and judicious magistrates." [1] " To be able to bluster (and sometimes more than
bluster) at a poacher ; to keep their own parish under their
own government, and to prevent other persons from exercising
authority there," were, we are told in 1751, the principal
motives of the lower type of country Justice.[2] We may
conclude with the following graphic description of those lower
types by a contributor to the *Gentleman's Magazine*, as late as
1788. " If," says this writer, " his Majesty's lieutenants of
counties are not more attentive to the birth, parentage,
and education, as well as the lives, fortune, character, and
behaviour of those who apply to have their names inserted
in the Commission, in a very few years it will be found
difficult to prevail upon men of fortune and abilities to
act. . . . The little property I have is in two remote parts
of England. In the first place the neighbouring Justice is
a well-meaning man, with some share of parochial knowledge.
But alas ! all his good qualities are rendered useless by
passions ungovernably furious, a fantastic whimsical wife, and
a penchant for strictly enforcing the game laws. . . . Without
any Justice in the neighbourhood of property or importance
sufficient to withstand his outrages, he is degenerated into
that worst of all despots, a judicial tyrant. . . . In the other
parish the principal Justice is a good-natured fox-hunter, who
spends his days on horseback and his evenings in eating and
drinking. He regularly attends the Justices' meeting, and

---

[1] Pamphlet of 1748, quoted in *Morning Chronicle*, 3rd December 1824.
[2] *Considerations on Several Proposals lately made for the Better Maintenance
of the Poor*, 1715, p. 25, by Charles Gray, M.P. for Colchester.

when business begins pouring in, he opens as follows, first
taking out his watch. ' Well, gentlemen, you are better
acquainted with Burn and Blackstone than I am; you will
recollect that dinner is to be ready at four.' He then retires
to an adjoining room, which he devotes to a more pleasing
amusement with the landlord's daughter ; his humble brethren
are too well bred to break in on his pleasures. Thus, though
naturally a good kind of man, he gives up his neighbours to
pettifoggers and half-gentlemen, who torture the laws to base
purposes of petty quarrels, low prejudices, and mercenary
cabal." [1]

(f) *The Mouthpiece of the Clerk*

The corrupt Trading Justice, the Sycophant, and the Rural
Tyrant were all, on the face of it, bad men, prostituting the
great powers of a magistrate to personal ends. From the
evidence before us, we infer that these evilly disposed Rulers
of the County were, even in Middlesex, a minority of the
whole, whilst in other counties they were certainly merely
exceptional. The bulk of the local squirarchy who were in
the Commission of the Peace were " average sensual men," too
well off to care to make a trade of justice, too pugnaciously
independent to serve the caprices of powerful neighbours, too
anxious to live in peace and enjoy their sporting privileges
unimpaired to wish to act in ways that would seem arbitrary
or oppressive to their tenants and labourers. Their motives
for undertaking the unremunerated and troublesome office of
Justice of the Peace were, for the most part, quite ordinary ;
their fathers had done so before them ; it was convenient to
themselves and their fellow-parishioners to have a Justice
near by ; they instinctively disliked the intervention of any
other person in the village that they dominated or over the
estate that they owned. Their worst characteristics were
indolence and ignorance. " A man just arrived at the age
of maturity," exclaims a polemical writer of 1832, " having
left the University where a common degree requiring some
knowledge, some examination . . . presents insurmountable
difficulties to a mind absorbed in the sole consideration of

[1] *Gentleman's Magazine*, April 1788, p. 315.

dogs and horses . . . comes to reside in the family mansion —applies to the Lord-Lieutenant of the County to be put in the Commission of the Peace, and takes out his Dedimus to punish and imprison his fellowmen as a companion to his certificate to kill game—attends the next Quarter Sessions, and makes the declaration that he will not upset the pure and reformed established religion of which he perhaps knows as little—takes his seat on the Bench with the perhaps equally wise Justice. This . . . is the very common English education for a Justice of the Peace." [1]   Such a Justice became, in too many cases, merely the mouthpiece of his clerk. The intolerable toil of taking down depositions, making out warrants, issuing summonses—not to mention the mental strain of coming to any decision as to the facts and law of each case—induced him, with his standing apprehension of being cited to appear for any mistake in the Court of King's Bench, to have always by his side a Justice's Clerk, on whom he came implicitly to rely. Some sort of "hedge-lawyer,"—it might be the village attorney, the schoolmaster,[2] or the Parish Clerk, sometimes a bailiff or a butler—with sufficient penmanship to write out depositions and copy precedents—would learn up one of the numerous alphabetical manuals of the Justice's powers, and make it his business not only to be perpetually at the beck and call of the squire, but also to be always on hand when there was any Justice's duty to be done. Such an assistant might, of course, be no less ignorant of the law than was his master. "A Justice and his Clerk," writes an elegant satirist in the middle of the eighteenth century, "is now little more than a blind man and his dog. The profound ignorance of the former, together with the canine impudence of the latter, will, but rarely, be found wanting to vindicate the comparison. The principal part of the similitude will appear obvious to every one; I mean the Justice is as

---

[1] *Letter to the Right Honourable Lord Brougham and Vaux on the Subject of the Magistracy of England*, 1832, p. 5.

[2] As early as 1720 we note that "Mr. Wainwright, Schoolmaster of Bunny," was "clerk to Sir Thomas Parkyns, Bart." (*A Method proposed for the Hiring and Recording of Servants*, by Sir Thomas Parkyns, Bart.). Sometimes, we may believe, the Justice had recourse to his steward or agent, who may have had experience in presiding over the Manorial Court. As early as 1660 we find mentioned a legal manual written expressly for the Justice's Clerk (*The Justice of the Peace's Clerk's Cabinet*, by William Sheppard, 1660).

much dependent on his clerk for superior insight and implicit guidance, as the blind fellow on his cur that leads him in a string. Add to this that the offer of a crust will seduce the conductors of either to drag their masters into a kennel." [1] On the other hand, as practice brings expertness, we may well accept as typical Fielding's lifelike description of Squire Western's Clerk, as sufficiently qualified by "some understanding in the law of this realm," to save his master from "informations exhibited against him in the King's Bench." [2] Moreover, the Clerk would occasionally be a man of some education. Samuel Butler, the author of *Hudibras,* was a Justice's Clerk. But whether or not the Clerk knew the law, such a relationship between Justice and Clerk could hardly fail to lead to a multiplication of the legal formalities and processes by which alone the Clerk was paid. It necessarily became one of the objects of the Clerk to multiply these fees —"to get money," as it was bluntly put by a rude critic, "the Clerk being of the willow kind, ingratiates himself into a position of influence; gets summonses and warrants ready signed; issues them whenever required"; even sells them, it is alleged, at so much the dozen "ready signed, a blank being left only for the name and cause of complaint." [3] Without the check of social responsibility or publicity, such an arrangement, moreover, opened the door to petty corruption, personal favouritism, and the indulgence of malice.[4] The ignorant magistrate, in short, not infrequently degenerated "into a passive and mischievous instrument in the hands of a rapacious attorney, or some discarded underling of the law." [5]

[1] *Essays on Men and Manners,* by William Shenstone, 1764, p. 61 ; vol. ii. p. 216 of his *Works.*

[2] *The History of Tom Jones,* by Henry Fielding, book vii. chap. ix. In the Metropolis, we are told, he was often "some broken attorney (for they make the best clerks)" (*The Per-juror,* a farce, 1717 ; see *A Vindication of a Certain Middlesex Justice,* 1718, pp. 6-7).

[3] *Letter to the Rt. Hon. Lord Brougham and Vaux on the Subject of the Magistracy of England,* 1832, p. 5.

[4] Sometimes, it seems, the Justice left the business of hearing complaints to the Clerk alone—

> Nor leave thy venal clerk empowered to hear,
> The voice of want is sacred to thy ear ;
> He where no fees his sordid pen invite,
> Sports with their tears, too indolent to write.

(*The Country Justice,* a poem, by John Langhorne, 1774-1777, part ii. p. 11.)

[5] *Enquiry into the Duties of Men,* by Thomas Gisborne, 1794, p. 288.

" The Clerk," sums up our critic of 1832, " has become a greater man than the Justice himself." [1]

(g) *The Clerical Justice*

For practical purposes we may count the clerical Justice of the Peace as an innovation of the eighteenth century. It is true that, already in the sixteenth century, bishops had sometimes been put in the Commission,[2] and in the early part of the seventeenth century some clergymen had been made magistrates, but public opinion was at the latter date against their appointment,[3] and after the Rebellion the practice seems, for half a century, to have been for the most part abandoned. For this exclusion from the Commission the Whigs found a complete justification in the contemporary persecution of the recusants and nonconformists, in which, unfortunately, the clergy were not to be trusted to preserve even a modicum of fairness.[4] It may have been with some surprise that the governing class heard Swift's suggestion that the rural magistracy might be improved " by receiving into their number some of the most eminent clergy." As the century wore on, however, the necessity of greatly increasing the number of magistrates, and the desire to find suitable residents, qualified

---

[1] *Letter to the Rt. Hon. Lord Brougham and Vaux on the Subject of the Magistracy of England*, 1832, p. 5. We recur in the next chapter to the position and remuneration of the Clerk.

[2] *Quarter Sessions from Queen Elizabeth to Queen Anne*, by A. H. A. Hamilton, 1878, p. 331. In Middlesex it was usual to put the Archbishops of Canterbury and York, and the Bishop of London, at the head of the Commission (see, for instance, House of Commons Return, No. 110 of 1856).

[3] House of Commons Journals, 11th March 1640 ; see *History of the English Church during the Civil Wars*, etc., by W. A. Shaw, 1900, vol. i. pp. 47-52.

[4] Until 1689 the clergy seem to have striven spasmodically to enforce, by penalties, universal attendance at the parish church. An Archdeacon ;in 1674 complains of his inability to cure the evil of non-attendance " by the ordinary ecclesiastical proceedings as Archdeacon, those being too long and slow," and asks the Secretary of State whether he had not better take proceedings as a magistrate under the Conventicle Act (*Memoirs of Ambrose Barnes*, Surtees Society, vol. l. 1867, p. 141). A vision of malicious persecution by a clerical magistrate is given in Daniel Defoe's *The Experiment, or the Shortest Way with the Dissenters exemplified, being the case of Mr. Abraham Gill, a Dissenting Minister, in the Isle of Ely ; and a full account of his being sent for a soldier by Mr. Fern, an ecclesiastical justice of peace, and other conspirators*, 1705 ; see also *Memoirs of De Foe*, by W. Wilson, 1830, vol. ii. pp. 345-350. This, however, is alleged to have been a journalistic invention of Defoe's ; see the *Answer*, etc., by Rev. Hugh James, 1707 ; and *Fenland Notes and Queries*, vol. i. pp. 108-110.

by freehold possessions, in every ten or twelve square miles of the whole country, led, in many counties, to the placing in the Commission of the principal clerical owners of glebe and tithe, and latterly, even, as was with some exaggeration complained in 1833, adding "almost every clergyman in a county." [1] In the contemporary records of sessions, as well as in eighteenth century memoirs, we may easily trace the way in which the Clerical Justice was distinguished from the ordinary country squire.

One unexpected feature was, speaking generally, the greater knowledge of English law possessed by the beneficed clergyman who was made a magistrate, than was usual on the eighteenth-century benches. In county after county we find the rectors and prebendaries coming to the front as competent Chairmen of Quarter Sessions,[2] ably fulfilling the duty of "charging" the Grand Jury, and guiding the Court amid the intricacies of settlement cases and the criminal law. In the diary of a Gloucestershire clergyman between 1715 and 1756, we have a graphic picture of his almost constant work as village Justice, issuing warrants, orders, and "mittimuses" (or commitments to gaol) at his unaided discretion; composing differences and deciding points of controversy among all sorts and conditions of men, dealing strictly but not unsympathetically with innumerable cases of assault, bastardy, disputes as to wages, hedge-breaking and wood-stealing, profane swearing and "haunting alehouses with lewd fellows." He is diligent in attendance at Quarter Sessions and Assizes, following the intricate legal arguments with keen interest and noting in his diary those turning on nice points of law. We see him disputing with the Chairman of Quarter Sessions as to whether the grasping Keeper of the County Gaol had any legal right to require all prisoners to be committed to him, and thus made

---

[1] First Report of Poor Law Inquiry Commission, 1834, Appendix C. p. 375. In Cardiganshire there were in 1775 only two clerical Justices in a Bench of 99 ; in 1816 there were no fewer than 25 in a Bench of 160 (MS. Sessions Rolls, Cardiganshire, 1775, 1816).

[2] Among distinguished clerical chairmen of Quarter Sessions whose charges have come down to us, we may mention the Rev. Samuel Partridge, of Holland, Lincolnshire (*Seven Charges given to Grand Juries at the General Quarter Sessions of the Peace*, etc., 1809) ; the Rev. John Foley, who ably presided over the Gloucestershire Quarter Sessions (*Charges delivered to the Grand Jury at the General Quarter Sessions*, etc., 1804) ; whilst many clergymen habitually managed their Petty Sessions.

subject to his fees, instead of to the better regulated House of Correction. " I had," he records, " a long dispute with our Chairman, who presently began to be warm for the gaoler without understanding the case. It seems he knew nothing (nor indeed any Justice on the Bench but myself) of the Act (6th, I think) of King George the First to empower Justices for small crimes to commit either to gaol or bridewell. 'Twas a good while before I could make him believe there was any such law, or that the smallest felons could be detained anywhere but in gaol. At last I found the Act and read it to him, and made him sensible of his mistake." This amateur of the law did not even shrink from disputing at the Assizes the hasty dicta of His Majesty's judges. " Judge Montague," he notes, " was very angry about the highway that leads from Crickley Hill to Gloucester, and examined the Surveyors [of Highways] in court whether they had done their work, and presented to the Justices in Petty Sessions the condition of their ways. He said two things which are contrary to common practice, and we had some discourse with him about. The one was that subsidymen (which he said [were such] as have 40s. a year lands or £5 in goods, etc.) are to find two men to work at the highways. The other, that £50 a year being generally considered a ploughland, for which a man is liable to find a team to the highway, he that has £100 a year, being two ploughlands, must find two teams. This, I think, is never done, unless he keeps two teams. " [1]

So, in the North of England, when Paley became rector of Bishop Wearmouth, he was expressly asked by the Bishop of Durham, then the Custos Rotulorum, " to act in the Commission of the Peace, for which," we are told, " he was equally

[1] Unfortunately we have been unable to trace this manuscript vellum-bound diary, which seems to have contained, in parallel columns, a record of forty years' magisterial work in and out of sessions respectively. It was kept by the Rev. Francis Welles, rector of Prestbury, near Cheltenham, who was an active member of the Gloucestershire Bench from 1715 until his death in 1756. Our knowledge of its contents is derived from three long articles in the *Law Magazine* of 1861-1862, Nos. xxi. xxii. and xxiii. pp. 125-142, 247-291, 99-126. These were reviewed in the *Gloucester Journal* by J. J. Powell (see his *Gloucesteriana*, 1890) ; and it is there stated that they were written by Conway Whithorn Lovesy, J.P., an active practising barrister, colonial official and legal writer, who died at Cheltenham in 1885 (Boase, *Contemporary Biography*). We mention these details, as it would be very desirable that this valuable old diary, for which we have in vain inquired, but which was evidently existing in 1861, should be discovered and published.

well qualified by his talents for close investigation, and by his knowledge of the criminal law. . . . Whenever he attended the Quarter Sessions . . . his opinions commanded deference and respect. His penetration and sagacity there acquired a wider field of action; and his marked, though somewhat singular questions at times produced an answer which at once involved the issue of the cause." It is perhaps not surprising to learn that his behaviour when acting as examining magistrate in his own parlour was criticised as "being hasty and irascible"; his quick appreciation of the "evidences" for unusual occurrences making him impatient "when engaged in the examination of petty causes, which the folly, the ignorance, or the knavery of the parties or their witnesses, alone render difficult or complex." [1] Nor were the Clerical Justices less assiduous in learning up the important precedents as to repair of bridges or mastering the complicated details of assessment and rating than in acquiring a knowledge of the criminal law. To cite one instance out of many, the Gloucestershire Justices, in 1805, were moved to pass a special vote of thanks to the clerical chairman of their Special Committee on the County Records, "for his laborious exertion in searching the several records, for arranging the several subjects and forming an index thereof, and for the critical exactness with which he has corrected the table of parochial assessments to County Rate from the earliest recorded authorities." [2]

This partiality and capacity for the practice of the law, for which the eighteenth-century Clerical Justices were distinguished, enables us to understand why they were so often found filling the important position of Chairman of Quarter Sessions, and thus acting virtually as the presiding judges in grave criminal cases, questioning witnesses, determining points of legal procedure, keeping counsel in order, and finally delivering sentences reaching up to transportation for life. When the Justices of the important county of Lancashire found the criminal business of the Salford Hundred (including Manchester and many South-East Lancashire industrial centres) growing beyond their capacity, it was to a clerical member of the Bench, the Rev. W. R. Hay,

---

[1] *Memoirs of William Paley*, by G. W. Meadley, 1810, pp. 190-193.
[2] MS. Minutes, Quarter Sessions, Gloucestershire, January 1805.

that they turned to conduct their Parliamentary proceedings
in obtaining power to appoint a salaried chairman. And when
the necessary Act was obtained, it was this reverend gentleman,
formerly the chaplain to the Salford House of Correction, that
they appointed to be the first judge of what was, in effect, one
of the most important of local criminal courts.[1] The same
widespread study of the law by the Clerical Justices explains
also the various legal text-books written by the clergymen of
this period. If the worthless parish priest spent his time in
sport, when he was not drinking with the squire,[2] the refined
and accomplished incumbents seem to have found a no less
keen enjoyment in poring over statutes and compiling elaborate
books of precedents from the judges' decisions. The most
famous of these law books by clerics is, of course, *The Justice
of the Peace and Parish Officer*, by the Rev. Richard Burn
(1709-1785), Vicar of Orton in Westmoreland, Chancellor of
the Diocese of Carlisle, the learned historian of his county,
and its most active Justice of the Peace. The practical
accuracy, great learning, and convenient arrangement of this
book made it, from its first appearance in 1755, the standard
work of reference for magistrates and overseers; and led to
the issue of no fewer than thirty editions, extending over
more than a century. Nor is it merely a legal text-book.
The terseness, modesty, humour, and shrewd criticism of
contemporary institutions which characterise its prefaces, notes,
and concluding observations must, we think, always endear it
to the student of the eighteenth-century literary style and
social philosophy.[3]

[1] 45 Geo. III. c. 59 (1805); MS. Minutes, Quarter Sessions, Lancashire,
4th February 1805. The Rev. W. R. Hay, who had been called to the Bar,
filled this onerous and responsible office until 1823 apparently without drawing
the salary authorised by the Act (*An Account of the Expenditure of the County
Palatine of Lancaster*, by Robert Hindle, 1843, p. 197 ; *Abstract of the Accounts
of the County Treasurer . . . of Lancaster*, by James Rushton, 1885).

[2] The *Connoisseur*, a forgotten journal of 1756, describes for us one clergyman,
the Rev. Jack Quickset, a brother of the Squire, who held "a deputation from
him as lord of the manor, consigning the game to his care, and empowering him
to take away all guns, nets, and dogs from persons not duly qualified. Jack is
more proud of this office than many other country clergymen are of being in the
Commission for the Peace. Poaching is in his eyes the most heinous crime in the
two Tables, nor does the cure of souls appear to him half so important as the
preservation of the game" (No. 105 of *The Connoisseur*, 1756).

[3] For Burn's life, see *Worthies of Westmoreland*, by Atkinson, vol. ii. pp.
119-132. The 30th edition of *Burn's Justice*, swollen to five stout volumes,

No less to the credit of many of the Clerical Justices is the fact that we find them among the foremost to recognise that the magistrate had duty in protecting the helpless, and in raising the Standard of Life of the people. At a time when no ordinary Justice dreamt of visiting the fever-haunted prisons—ten years before John Howard set a memorable example to the world—we find the Rev. George Botts, a Suffolk Justice, representing to Quarter Sessions that the House of Correction at Botesdale was in a shocking state, getting himself formally deputed to report what steps should be taken, and inducing his fellow-justices not only to provide materials on which to set the prisoners to work, but also to pay an increased salary to the keeper, on condition that he abandoned the taking of fees.[1] A few years later, in the adjoining county of Essex, we see another Clerical Justice, Rev. John Tindel, exercised about the filthy state of the County gaol at Chelmsford; and obtaining the authority of Quarter Sessions " to give directions that the wards . . . be cleaned and the joints of the floors caulked, for rendering the same more wholesome, in such manner as he shall think fit, at the charge of the . . . county." [2] And among the most devoted of Howard's disciples in prison reform were such typical Clerical Justices as the Rev. Henry Zouch, Chairman of the Quarter Sessions of the West Riding of Yorkshire, to whom was due the complete re-organisation of the county gaol at Wakefield; [3] and the Rev. Samuel Glasse, who not only

---

was published as lately as 1869. We may quote a rule laid down in the author's original preface, with which we too have endeavoured to conform. " He hath made it an invariable rule upon all occasions to cite his authorities whatsoever they be ; and in all material instances, in the very words of the original authors ; that so, what may be of good authority in itself, shall not be rendered less so by his handling of it."

Among other law books by clergymen may be mentioned *The Magistrate's Assistant,* by a magistrate [Rev. Samuel Glasse], 1784, and *A Collection of the Several Points of Sessions Law alphabetically arranged,* by Rev. Samuel Clapham, two vols. 1818.

[1] MS. Minutes, Quarter Sessions, Suffolk, 13th January 1764 ; 19th July 1765.

[2] MS. Minutes, Quarter Sessions, Essex, 12th April 1768. He also obtained authority " to employ a proper surveyor and get an estimate of the expense of lining the walls in the men's workroom in the House of Correction at Chelmsford . . . with plank, so as to render the same more secure from the escape of prisoners "—thereby, it may be explained, making it possible for the ironing and chaining the prisoners to be dispensed with.

The Rev. Henry Zouch, rector of Swillington and Tankersley, and chaplain

published a small legal handbook for Justices, but may be said to have spent the greater part of his life in the unthankful task of inducing the Middlesex magistrates to introduce the principles of classification, non-intercourse, and employment into their scandalous prisons. It is noticeable that, when it became customary for Quarter Sessions to appoint regular visitors of the county prisons, the bulk of the work fell to the clerical members of the bench.

When the rise in rates and the stress of famine prices brought the administration of the Poor Law before every county bench, we find the Clerical Justices taking a leading part, both in expounding principles and in introducing practical reforms. Between 1794 and 1834, when the rain of pamphlets was thickest, at least forty were by clergymen, most of whom were Justices of the Peace. It was a Clerical Justice of Hampshire—the Rev. Edmund Poulter—who drew up the able and elaborate report on the whole question of the labourer's position, which the assembled Justices of that county adopted in 1795.[1]   Among the local reformers, whose practical recognition of fundamental principles and rare administrative skill made possible the successful experiments on which the New Poor Law was subsequently based, no one stands higher than Whately of Cookham, Lowe of Bingham, and Becher of Southwell, all three clerical Justices of the Peace.

There was, however, in the characteristics of the Clerical Justice, a more equivocal feature.   In the remarkable national movement " for the Reformation of the Manners of the Lower Orders," which swept through all the county benches between 1786 and 1800, it was the clergymen among the magistrates

to the Marchioness of Rockingham, was for many years the most active and influential of the West Riding Justices. His pamphlet, *Hints respecting the Public Police*, 1786, marked by good sense and ability, seems to have had a wide circulation. He was deputed to go to London in 1790, as delegate for the West Riding to the national convention of magistrates, to confer with the Proclamation Society as to means of improving the prisons and police (*Leeds Intelligencer*, 21st July 1789). On his death in 1795, it was said that he "displayed an accurate and comprehensive knowledge of the laws of England ; an unbiassed integrity in the administration of justice, and a most condescending attention to the complaints of the lower classes of society" (*Leeds Intelligencer*, 29th June 1795).

[1] MS. Minutes, Quarter Sessions, Hampshire, 14th July 1795 ; *Enquiry into the State of the Poor*, by Rev. Edmund Poulter, 1795.

who took the lead. This movement, which we shall describe in another volume,[1] took, in the main, the form of suppressing dram-shops and unnecessary alehouses, prohibiting Sunday trading and Sunday drinking, meting out stern treatment to all sorts of vagrants, and persistently discouraging, if not preventing, all kinds of amusement or even assemblages of the common people that were deemed by their social superiors brutalising, disorderly, and seditious. It was the clerical Chairman of the West Riding Quarter Sessions, the Rev. Henry Zouch, who, together with William Wilberforce, M.P., was the most powerful influence in this crusade. The spirit with which the Clerical Justices threw themselves into this movement may be judged from the following extracts from Zouch's writings. "It is found by long experience," he said, "that when the common people are drawn together upon any public occasion, a variety of mischiefs are certain to ensue ; allured by unlawful pastimes, or even by vulgar amusements only, they wantonly waste their time and money to their own great loss and that of their employers. Nay, a whole neighbourhood becomes unhinged for many days, quarrels are too often promoted, and the young and inexperienced are initiated into every species of immorality." In fact, what the reverend author aimed at was that all these "preparatory stages and inlets for gaming and debauchery" should be "not only regulated but also greatly reduced in numbers." [2] With many of the practical results of this movement, such as the reduction of the number of alehouses, the prohibitions of "cockings, bull-baitings, and bear-baitings," and the stemming of the evil tide of subsidised vagrancy, the modern student finds himself in sympathy. But it never entered into the head of Zouch or his fellow-magistrates to provide for the people any superior forms of recreation, or even the alternative of education.

---

[1] *English Local Government in relation to Poverty and Crime.*

[2] Quoted with approval in *Leeds Intelligencer*, 20th June 1786. "It is interesting to find the zealous Zouch specially reprobating in this connection, 'the practices of performing oratorios in country churches for money,' as being 'very exceptionable, not only by the indecencies committed therein, but by giving occasion for great numbers of persons of all kinds to be brought together, so that the adjoining villages do often become scenes of drunkenness, disorder, and riot.' The Archbishop of York has disapproved of 'introducing sacred music in this way'" (*Hints respecting the Public Police*, by the Rev. H. Zouch, J.P., 1786, p. 7).

There is, to our mind, something unpleasant in the combination of luxurious living, which the wealthy Evangelicals of the end of the eighteenth century themselves indulged in, and the wholesale prescription for the lower orders of an abstinence from all sensual indulgences. The Parliamentary Radicals between 1815 and 1832 are found objecting, with equal vehemence, to both the spirit and the practical outcome of this characteristic development of the Clerical Justices of this period. As we shall show in subsequent parts of this work, the Radical spokesmen in the press and in Parliament, in the keenness of their pursuit of political liberty, systematically objected to any authoritative interference with the habits of the people, or to any governmental modification of their environment. It was an additional ground for objection when this interference was undertaken by a non-elective magistrate and a beneficed clergyman. Remembering the brutality, the drunkenness, and the disorder of English street scenes and village life of 1828, it is nowadays scarcely to be credited that Brougham was always to be found denouncing what he considered to be the excessive activity of the magistrates, and condemning the Clerical Justice as specially guilty of "this very high magisterial offence."[1] In the eyes of the Parliamentary Radicals of this period, the superior knowledge of law for which the Clerical Justices were distinguished, their greater philanthropy and, we think we may add, their higher standard of integrity,[2] were outweighed by the objection to their political Toryism and their inclination towards increasing

---

[1] Most of the magistrates distinguished for over-activity "are," he said, "clergymen" (*Hansard*, 1828, vol. 18 (N.S.) p. 161). Windham was reported to have said "that he did not know a more noxious species of vermin than an active Justice of the Peace" (*A Letter to the Right Honourable Lord Brougham and Vaux on the Magistracy of England*, 1832, p. 24).

[2] We have, in an extensive survey, come across no case in which a Clerical Justice was accused of any departure from integrity. In one instance, in 1767, we have a clergyman acting up to a higher standard than was usual at the time. When the property of certain London cheesemongers had been endangered by riots in Derbyshire, and had been saved by "the prudence of a worthy magistrate, the Rev. Mr. Taylor of Ashbourne," the owners presented him with a silver cup, in testimony of their gratitude. This Clerical Justice refused to accept the gift, stating—"I think all acceptance of presents by a magistrate of so dangerous example [that] though I am highly gratified by the honourable notice you have taken of my conduct, I must refuse so valuable a testimony, unless you will appoint some agent to receive the price to be distributed in charity" (*Manchester Mercury*, 10th February 1767).

collective regulation. When, in 1816, it was suggested by one zealous cleric that, in order to enforce the laws against drunkenness, all beneficed clergymen should be given the powers of magistrates, it called forth indignant protests, and evoked a demand for the exclusion of all clergymen from the Commission of the Peace.[1] "It is now almost universally agreed," wrote the *Examiner* of 1826, "that clergymen make bad magistrates; experience has fully established this fact, and the cause alone allows of dispute. . . . Their errors . . . are seldom on the side of indulgence."[2]

In this description of the Clerical Justice, we have left on one side the larger question of the expediency, from the standpoint of the Church itself, of allowing so many of the ablest and most public-spirited of its ministers to be absorbed in judicial and administrative work, which necessarily brought them into direct collision with some members of their flocks. Brougham had some justification for thinking that, in that combination, the magistrate went far to spoil the clergyman. It cannot, we think, have been to the advantage of religion or the Church that Cobbett should have found, in 1826, the incumbents everywhere much better "known as Justices of the Peace than as clergymen."[3] The same view was taken by Bishop Blomfield, the most statesmanlike of contemporary ecclesiastics, who, himself an active Justice when a parish priest, afterwards persistently discouraged the clergy of his diocese from undertaking any civil duties.[4] When the

---

[1] *Times*, 29th November 1816.

[2] *Examiner*, 1826, quoted in *Chester Courant*, 15th August 1826. We have no record of the extent to which Clerical Justices may have used their power as magistrates to put down "enthusiasm" and other revivalist tendencies of which they disapproved. We get glimpses of this, not only in Wesley's *Journal*, but also in the *Memoirs of the Life and Correspondence of Hannah More*, by W. Roberts. Though she had opened her school at Blagden at the earnest request of the local curate, who was also a Justice of the Peace, the latter came near proceeding against the schoolmaster for "enthusiasm."

[3] *Rural Rides*, by W. Cobbett, vol. ii. p. 168 of 1885 edition.

[4] We get a glimpse of the clergyman as county administrator in the *Memoir of Bishop Blomfield* by his son, Alfred Blomfield. In 1813 the future bishop, then rector of Dunton (Bucks), and at the same time instructing private pupils and contributing articles to the reviews, writes to a friend as follows: "My time will be somewhat more occupied than formerly, as I am now a commissioner of turnpikes (there's for you!) and a Justice of the Peace; and the county business will never get on without me. I must study Burn with diligence before I can 'indifferently minister justice.' (By the way, that's a very awkward expression in the Liturgy.) I shall, moreover, probably be a commissioner of

beneficed clergyman was the only person of education and
social position in a parish; working harmoniously with the
absentee landowner and his law agent or steward; and
combining in his own person, or through his clerk, various
local offices, he must often have been in a position of
uncontrolled power, which could not fail to impair his pastoral
influence.[1]

(h) *The Leader of the Parish*

The Clerical Justice, though far better than his reputation
among the reformers of 1832, was, in our opinion, not the
most admirable type among the Rulers of the County. It is
among the simple country gentlemen that we find some of the
best combinations of integrity, kindliness, and breadth of view,
of zeal and devotion to the public interest, with no small
degree of practical statesmanship. Even in the avowedly
satirical novels of Fielding and Smollett, we are introduced to
such wholly beneficent characters as Squire Allworthy and Sir
Lancelot Greaves, both estimable Justices of the Peace.[2]   And

property tax—all which offices will a little interfere with Greek." His biographer
tells us that "he used to ride to the Petty Sessions at the neighbouring town of
Wing, equipped in yellow overalls to protect him from the mud of the
Buckinghamshire lanes. . . . In later life, as a bishop, he disapproved of such
union [of duties], saying that 'the secular duties would be likely to interfere too
much with the spiritual'" (pp. 38, 39). An interesting MS. pamphlet by
George Coles, preserved among the Home Office Domestic State Papers for 1830
in Public Record Office, makes the suggestion that no clergyman should be made
a magistrate without the consent of his Bishop.

[1] "Would it not be advisable," writes a correspondent of the *Liverpool
Mercury*, in 1831, "particularly in large towns like Liverpool and Manchester,
to call public meetings for the purpose of petitioning Government to dispense
with the assistance of clerical magistrates, on the ground that their characters
as civil officers and spiritual teachers are incompatible with each other, and
frequently render them obnoxious to their congregations? For instance, in this
little place (Ormskirk), favoured as it is with a Vicar and a curate, the former
might, if he were not determined to steer the path of virtue and to avoid any
interference which is not in strict keeping with his office . . . be a very terror
to all around him, and in this way. He is . . . a juror at the Court Leet held
in this town; his magisterial clerk is the law agent of the Lord of the Manor,
and may summon such men to serve on the Jury as he thinks proper. . . . To
show how his power would be by this means increased, I may state that this
Jury (or rather himself) appoints the head civil officer of the town; the
Constable, Bailiffs, market brokers, and official underlings of several descriptions;
so that the Vicar has the command of the civil department of the town, and
over these also presides as Justice; of the church because it is his freehold; and
over the Warden because the latter is merely an agent or tool for him"
(*Liverpool Mercury*, 11th November 1831).

[2] Fielding gives us even an honest Middlesex Magistrate in Justice Worthy.

if we turn away from the too complete virtue of Fielding's model squire and the ridiculous Don Quixotism of Smollett's errant knight, we may find relief in Addison's charming portrait from life that he calls Sir Roger de Coverley. Here we see the plain country gentleman of the reign of Queen Anne acting as the benevolent autocrat of the parish, and fully living up to Blackstone's subsequent ideal of a rural magistrate, " maintaining good order in his neighbourhood by punishing the dissolute and the idle, by protecting the peaceable and industrious, above all, by healing petty differences and preventing vexatious prosecutions." [1] And we delight in Sir Roger de Coverley as much for his little foibles of permitting no one to sleep through the Sunday service save himself, and orating somewhat inconsequently at Quarter Sessions, as for his gentlemanly dislike for " the mischief that parties do in the country; how they spoil good neighbourhood and make honest gentlemen hate one another," and disturb the good fellowship of Quarter Sessions by " innumerable curses, frowns, and whispers . . . besides that they manifestly tend to the prejudice of the Land Tax and the destruction of game."   Leaving mere romance, we may quote Burke's stately epitaph on an eminent Whig statesman who, for half a century, served his country as a Justice of the Peace. " Immersed in the greatest affairs, he never lost the ancient native generous English character of a country gentleman. Disdaining and neglecting no office in life, he was an ancient municipal magistrate; with great care and clear judgment administering justice, maintaining the police, relieving the distresses and regulating the manners of the people in his neighbourhood." [2] And those who have explored the Vestry minutes of little towns and the larger rural parishes cannot fail to have met with numerous instances in which a local squire, or other resident Justice, has quietly and benevolently become the unofficial leader of his parish; attending the meetings of the Open Vestry; suggesting decisions and even

---

[1] *Commentaries on the Laws of England*, by Sir William Blackstone, 1765. Sir Roger de Coverley has been supposed to have been sketched from a Wiltshire Justice whom Addison had known in youth (*Reminiscences of the Oxford Movement*, by Rev. T. Mozley, vol. i. p. 326).

[2] Burke's epitaph on the Right Hon. W. Dowdeswell, M.P. for Worcester, in *Correspondence of Edmund Burke*, 1844, vol. i. p. 141.

drafting reports; providing the small piece of land, or the little capital required for such departures as erecting a workhouse or paving the streets; acting as a channel of communication between the Vestry and Petty or Quarter Sessions, and sometimes himself undertaking the onerous duties of Churchwarden, Overseer of the Poor or Surveyor of Highways, in order to carry into execution some particular reform. Thus, at Richmond, in Surrey, we see Charles Selwyn, an undistinguished member of an eminent family, and an active Justice of the Peace, helping to reorganise, between 1717 and 1730, all the government of that rising suburban resort. He is diligent in attending the Open Vestry; he encourages his neighbours to shake themselves free from the usurpation of "the Gentlemen of the Four and Twenty"; he suggests their insisting on the old and "laudable" custom, which the parish officers had "discontinued," "to have yearly accounts laid before the inhabitants"; he persuades his fellow-magistrates to join with him in ordering the compliance with this request; he accepts the position of "People's Church-warden" in order to preside over parish meetings and Vestry committees; gradually leading the Vestry to adopt such new administrative devices as a fire-engine; a workhouse, to be used as a test of destitution; the setting apart of "four tenements . . . for the lodging and dieting" of the sick poor, where they would be attended by a head nurse "and her assistants," and prescribed for by a medical practitioner; and the engagement of a salaried Constable, to save the inhabitants from the inconvenience of personal service.[1] In the vast majority of cases this beneficent public service has gone unrecorded.[2] Occasionally, we get a glimpse of it in such

[1] MS. Vestry minutes, Richmond (Surrey), 25th October, 15th November 1725; 12th April, 21st November, 12th, 19th, and 26th December 1726; 17th September 1729; 11th and 25th May 1730; 27th December 1731.

[2] No records exist, for instance, of the long parish leadership of William Hay (1695-1755), who might indeed claim also county and even national importance. Succeeding as an orphan to a small landed estate in Sussex, he was educated at Oxford, called to the Bar, and formed by foreign travel. He published various scholarly works; sat in the House of Commons from 1733; held various minor offices (including the keepership of the Records of the Tower of London); and came near to carrying a comprehensive reform of the Poor Laws, with which we shall deal in our future volume on Poverty and Crime. For the moment he is of interest to us as a pattern Justice of the Peace. "His diligent study of the law in the early part of his life fitted him to act as

lives as that of Lloyd Baker, the Gloucestershire Justice and squire, whose successful " dispauperisation " of the demoralised parish of Uley in 1830 attracted the attention of Poor Law reformers. We see this gentleman regular in attendance at the Vestry meetings of his parish; perplexed at the " fifteen rates each of twentypence in the pound," on nearly the rack rental of the land, which did not suffice to meet the parish expenses between Lady-day 1829 and Lady-day 1830 ; buying all the books and pamphlets on the Poor Law that he could obtain, and diligently seeking some device to save himself and his neighbours from ruin ; arriving by reflection at the idea of what we shall hereafter describe as the Test by Regimen ; persuading the Vestry to let him put his system into operation ; personally organising the administration of the new workhouse, and patiently overcoming all the difficulties ; and, finally, when he had most effectually reformed his own parish, taking the unusual trouble of publishing his experiences for the benefit of his fellow-magistrates.[1] It is, indeed, to the initiative and patient administrative zeal of magistrates of this type—and with them some of the Clerical Justices—that we owe most of the experiments in Poor Law administration tried between 1825 and 1833, out of which sprang the great reforms of the New Poor Law. Even Edwin Chadwick himself, strongly prejudiced as he was against the unpaid Justice of the Peace, has expressly to admit that " the majority of the persons who have dispauperised parishes and introduced those beneficial amendments of the mode of administering relief, which the Legislature will probably extend to all parts of the country, and render permanent, are magistrates," and

magistrate. He thought it of importance to the country that gentlemen of fortune and knowledge should take the trouble to act in the Commission of the Peace. . . . For near thirty years he acted in it himself, and constantly attended all its meetings in the district to which he belonged. He never refused to see those persons who applied to him as a magistrate, though their numbers often made this fatiguing to him ; his meals, or his company, were left by him that he might not keep those waiting who came from a distance ; nor did he suffer any, even the smallest, fee to be taken in his house. His activity did not stop here, for he was many years Chairman of the Quarter Sessions for the Eastern Division of the county " [of Sussex] (*Works* of William Hay, 1794, vol. i. preface, p. 9).

[1] As to all this, see First Report of Poor Law Enquiry Commission 1834, Appendix A. (Cowell's Report) pp. 619, 634, 650-652 ; (Bishop's Report) pp. 885, 886 ; *A Letter to the Rev. George Cooke, D.D., Chairman of Quarter Sessions for the County of Gloucester,* by T. J. L. Baker, 1830.

it is interesting to find him adding that "these amendments . . . were not effected by them in their capacity of magistrates, but in the capacity of vestrymen. I do not recollect having met with an instance of one important improvement effected by these same gentlemen by active interference from the bench."[1] This preference for persuasion and dislike of giving authoritative orders was, we think, characteristic of the best type of English country gentleman when acting as Justice of the Peace, and runs all through his participation in civil administration. We cannot imagine the continental prefects or subordinate officials condescending, as the English Justices frequently did, to get resolutions passed and reports adopted by open meetings of their social inferiors, when they might have given peremptory orders. "If I should be asked," said one of Pitt's Ministry in 1805, "why I do not interpose as a magistrate . . . my answer would be that I have hitherto confined myself to remonstrances and persuasion, by which I have sometimes, though with difficulty, succeeded; thinking that it is, on the whole, more for the interest of the poor, as well as more consonant to my own feelings, to avoid the other course till the last extremity."[2]

(i) *Leaders of the County*

Among these beneficent magistrates were some who progressed from the unostentatious government of their own parishes to a position of leadership in their counties. This progress is especially to be noticed between 1760 and 1820. In contrast with the sullen torpor of the Jacobite sympathisers, and the cynical acquiescence in evil of the Walpolean Whigs, the country gentlemen, with the accession of George the Third, awakened to a heightened sense of their responsibility for the social condition of their counties. The impassable quagmire into which the roads had got, the increase of robberies, the prevalence of drunkenness and public gambling, the danger of riots, the scandalous cruelties and dangerous fevers of the

[1] First Report of Poor Law Enquiry Commission, 1834, Appendix A. (Chadwick's Report) p. 167.

[2] *Observations on the Poor Laws and on the Management of the Poor*, by the Right Hon. George Rose, 1805, p. 35.

prisons, the rapid growth of the Poor Rate, and the semi-starvation to which the labourers were presently reduced—all these typical circumstances of the latter half of the eighteenth century united in stimulating the more enlightened and public spirited of the Rulers of the County to apply their minds to civil government. Hence we see, now in one county, now in another, a Chairman of Quarter Sessions or a simple Justice of the Peace—occasionally a High Sheriff or a Lord-Lieutenant—fixing his attention on one of these evils; observing facts and considering remedies; becoming in course of years a sort of amateur specialist in some particular branch of administration. We watch him acquiring influence among his colleagues, and gradually persuading them to adopt his proposals; we find him publishing pamphlets and corresponding with magistrates in other counties as to his hobby; sometimes from his seat in the House of Commons getting a committee appointed; and occasionally even embodying his administrative reforms in a permissive or compulsory statute applicable to the whole country. These leaders of county reform were, be it observed, not drawn exclusively from any one social grade, any one political party or any one religious denomination. Prominent among them were, as we have already noted, clergymen of the Church of England. Others were great noblemen or baronets of large estate. Others were old-fashioned squires of small account. A few—including, as it happens, the most heroically self-devoted and the most technically efficient of them all—sprang directly from the commercial or manufacturing class, and were Nonconformist by creed or inclination. Such a one was John Howard, the son of a wealthy London tradesman, who had left him, early in life, a considerable fortune. After a period of desultory travel, he bought a small estate in Bedfordshire and quickly endeared himself to his neighbours by his modest but persistent attempts to raise the moral standard and improve the material condition of his dependants and fellow-parishioners. We do not gather that his name was ever included in the Commission of the Peace. But by happy chance he was, in 1773, " pricked " for the office of High Sheriff of Bedfordshire, thus becoming, during his year of office, legally and formally responsible for the administration of the County Gaol. We shall describe, in a subsequent volume,[1] Howard's patient heroism and scientific investigation into prison organisation and the reforms which he inaugurated. What concerns us here is to emphasise the ease and rapidity with which this tradesman's son and fervent Nonconformist acquired a position of influence among the Rulers of the County, passing, indeed, within a few years, beyond the sphere of county administration into the arena of Parliamentary committees, and eventually into the counsels of Foreign Courts.

In the career of Thomas Butterworth Bayley (1744-1802) we have a less abnormal instance of the rise to county leadership of a wealthy magistrate of Nonconformist extraction. The son of a rich and influential Dissenter,[2] Bayley was sent by his father to Edinburgh University, and advised to study law, with the deliberate purpose of becoming, as a country gentleman, an active Justice of the Peace. Owing to the prevalence of Roman Catholicism among the old families and sturdy Nonconformity among the recruits which the new manufacturing industry might otherwise have furnished to the land-owning class, the Commission of the Peace for Lancashire was, in the middle of the eighteenth century, in a parlous state. At the same time the growth of a disorderly and turbulent population, whilst it necessitated an increase in the number of Justices, disinclined gentlemen from accepting the office. There seems, at any rate, to have been no difficulty in getting young Bayley, now an "occasional conformist,"[3] placed in the Commission at the age of twenty-two, immediately on his return from the University. In 1768, at the age of twenty-four, we find him acting as High Sheriff, whilst in a few more years he became standing Chairman of Quarter Sessions of this important county. It must have needed all

---

[1] *English Local Government in Relation to Poverty and Crime.*

[2] For the life of Bayley (1744-1802), see *Dictionary of National Biography*; the occasional references to his work in the MS. Minutes of the Lancashire Quarter Sessions and in the *Manchester Mercury* and other contemporary newspapers; *The Family of Bayley*, by Ernest Axon, 1894, pp. 13-19; *Gentleman's Magazine*, 1802, vol. lxxii. p. 777; *Biographical Memories of the late Thomas Butterworth Bayley*, by Dr. Thomas Percival, 1802, also included in his *Works*, 1807, vol. ii. pp. 289-305; *Observations on the General Highway and Turnpike Acts*, by T. B. Bayley, 1773.

[3] An "occasional conformist" was, of course, one who, whilst retaining his own religious opinions and practices, went once or twice a year to the Anglican Church to take the sacrament.

his knowledge of the law, all his untiring industry, all his cultivated tolerance of all religious creeds and political opinions, all his tact and benevolence, to counteract the ignorance and indifference, the brutality and partiality of many of his colleagues. Unlike most of our class of Leaders of the County, he seems to have had no one hobby, but to have devoted himself equally to all the branches of county government. It is recorded of him that "he was sedulously watchful over the parochial workhouses under his jurisdiction, which he frequently visited that he might make the strictest scrutiny into their domestic regulations, their comforts, salubrity, and the proper distribution of labour." [1] By diligently presenting founderous ways he brought the highways of his county, once the terror of every traveller, by the end of the century into a state of relatively good repair. We see him exercising even-handed justice between a particularly grinding class of employers and a brutalised and disorderly population of mill hands. He sets himself to track out and punish the incessant pilfering of material from workshop and warehouse, whilst objecting to sanction the wholesale apprenticeship of pauper children to the mill-owners, and giving persistent and public support to all proposals for regulating the hours and sanitary conditions of the cotton factories. He steadfastly refused to call in aid the troops for the repression of every little riot, as he was importuned to do, preferring, we are told, "by temperate firmness and authority mixed with conciliation . . . to disperse the mobs without the effusion of blood. . . . He has been known to ride into the midst of an enraged multitude armed with stones and bludgeons, and when exhortations and threats availed not, has assisted personally in the seizure of their ringleaders." [2] For the public service of the town of Manchester he set on foot a magistrate's office, and organised a rota of county Justices who undertook to maintain an attendance twice a week. From 1780 onward, we find him in frequent correspondence with the Home Secretary in regard to crime, the state of the prisons, and the necessity for transportation. [3]

---

[1] *Biographical Memoirs of the late Thomas Butterworth Bayley*, F.R.S., by Dr. T. Percival, 1802, p. 4.   [2] *Ibid.* p. 9.

[3] MS. Domestic State Papers in Public Record Office, 1st and 26th January 1785, and 7th February 1787.

He was the principal correspondent in the Manchester district for William Wilberforce, contributing freely both time and money to the movement for the Abolition of the Slave Trade.[1] Along with his friend Dr. Percival, he got a local Board of Health established in 1796, over which he presided until his death, and which rendered diligent service in introducing the rudiments of house and street sanitation and providing a voluntary fever hospital. In 1801 we find him vainly trying to get the law as to county bridges improved.[2] But perhaps his most considerable achievement was persuading Quarter Sessions to erect and maintain, on the principles of John Howard, the " New Bailey " prison at Salford, which is said to have been called after his name.[3] All this varied administrative work was carried on unremittingly for over thirty years, without any suggestion of personal profit or the slightest accusation of class partiality or political or religious favouritism. We cannot discover in him even the ordinary leaning towards self-aggrandisement or an officious use of power. We gather that he found his reward in a quiet enjoyment of the daily routine of public administration; in stimulating intercourse with like-minded persons in the Metropolis and in other counties; and in a gratification of his benevolent and public-spirited impulses.

Sir George Onesiphorus Paul (1746-1820), Justice of the Peace for Gloucestershire, affords us another type of the Leaders of the County. Belonging to the aristocratic manufacturing class of the West of England clothiers, a baronet of good estate, educated at Oxford, formed by ten years' continental travel, he had, on his return home at the age of thirty-four, immediately taken an active part in the work of the county bench. Sheriff in 1780, Foreman of the Grand Jury in 1783, he was in the latter year moved by the propaganda of John Howard to attempt the reformation of the fever-stricken seminaries of vice which served as the Gloucestershire county prisons. In the minutes of Quarter Sessions and the contemporary local newspapers we watch him unre-

---

[1] *Life of William Wilberforce*, by R. I. and S. W. Wilberforce, 1838, vol. i. p. 152.

[2] MS. Minutes, Quarter Sessions, West Riding, 3rd December 1801.

[3] *Biographical Memoirs of the late Thomas Butterworth Bayley*, by Dr. T. Percival, 1802, p. 4 ; but see *Gentleman's Magazine*, 1819, vol. ii. pp. 224, 386.

mittingly pursuing his task, organising to this end all
the machinery of the county, preparing resolutions for the
bench and presentments for the Grand Jury, delivering fervent
orations at the Sessions, speaking at every local assembly,
publishing reports and pamphlets, and overcoming, step by
step, the indifference and inertia of his colleagues. After
thirty years of unsparing personal toil, Paul brought the
management of the Gloucestershire County Gaol and Houses
of Correction to "the highest pitch of perfection in polity"[1]
then known. This success, it is clear, was the work of Paul,
and of Paul alone; the co-operation of his fellow-magistrates
consisting chiefly in suffering patiently his interminable
admonitions in the form of charges, speeches, reports, and
pamphlets, and eventually learning to pass with effusion
portentous resolutions—we suspect, drafted by himself—
thanking him for his zeal in carrying out his own policy. If
we were estimating Paul as a man, or even as a prison
reformer, we should need to inquire to what extent his
exuberant public spirit, useful initiative, and pure administration were damaged by doctrinaire views, pompous disciplin-
arianism and an almost childlike delight in self-advertisement.
But among his fellow-Justices he stands out, for a whole
generation, as an energetic and beneficent Leader of the
County.

In the neighbouring county of Somerset, during the
latter part of Paul's career, we watch the rise to local
influence, and eventually to national importance, of another
Justice of the Peace and amateur specialist in local government—not in the management of prisons but in the maintenance of roads. John Loudon M'Adam, a Scotchman of small
independent means, settled himself in the closing years of the
eighteenth century, as Victualling Agent for the Admiralty,
in the neighbourhood of Bristol. Placed in the Commission
of the Peace, he brought his Scotch experience as a Commissioner of Turnpike Trusts to bear on the abominable highways
of the south-western counties. For the next twenty years he
drudged at County administration, varied with tours of

---

[1] *State of the Prisons*, by James Neild, 1812, p. 249. For Paul's life, see
Dictionary of National Biography, and the works there cited. But the main
source must always be the MS. Minutes of the Gloucestershire Quarter Sessions,
1783-1820.

observation all over England. In subsequent parts of our
work we shall describe his career as the inventor of a new
technique of road-making and the reformer of highway
administration. In this place it suffices to mention the ease
and rapidity with which this socially undistinguished specialist
in a tiresome subject became the recognised Leader of his
County on all questions of road administration.

We have dwelt on the intellectual leadership in county
government of Howard, Bayley, Paul, and M'Adam, because
their intervention was continuous over a long period, and produced relatively good results. More commonly, the leadership
of a particular magistrate would be confined, not merely to
one department of county administration, but also to a short
space of time. Thus, it was the distinguished and refined
Whig magnate and friend of Burke, the Duke of Richmond,
who, as Lord-Lieutenant of Sussex, bestirred himself, immediately after Howard's first visit to his county, to get new county
prisons built at Petworth and Horsham.[1] Half a century
later, it was the Duke of Buckingham who, as Lord-Lieutenant
of his county, induced his fellow-magistrates, in the somewhat
peremptory communications which he had read at Quarter
Sessions, to resolve on the abandonment of the evil system of
using the Poor Rate in aid of wages.[2] When such potentates
chose to take the lead in their counties, Quarter Sessions
obsequiously followed — at least as far as the passing of
resolutions was concerned. Not that the new departures
initiated by Leaders of the County were always in the right
direction. The deliberate adoption in 1795 and following
years of the famous "Speenhamland Scale" of outdoor relief
for the able-bodied labourer, and its enforcement by the
Justices on parish authorities, can be traced, in one county
after another, to one or two public-spirited and benevolent
Justices, keenly realising the semi-starvation to which the
agricultural labourers were reduced, and refusing to use the

---

[1] MS. Minutes, Quarter Sessions, Sussex. In 1790 the Lord-Lieutenant of
Essex (Lord Howard and Braybrooke), apparently concerned about the increase
of vagrancy and petty disorders, sends the Clerk of the Peace a pamphlet
entitled *The Duties of Constables*, published by Robert Raikes of Gloucester,
which he suggests that the justices should distribute to every parish constable,
to incite them to discharge their functions more zealously (MS. Minutes, Quarter
Sessions, Essex, 13th April 1790).

[2] MS. Minutes, Quarter Sessions, Buckinghamshire, January 1830.

overcrowded, insanitary, and vicious contemporary workhouse, which seemed to them the only alternative method of relief. Similarly, the amazing policy of compelling untried prisoners, innocent and guilty alike, to labour on the newly invented treadmill, exactly as if they were convicted felons, was introduced in 1819 into the North Riding County Gaol by a high-minded zealot for prison reform. This Chairman of Quarter Sessions was so enamoured of his regimen that he induced his fellow-magistrates obstinately to persist in it, not only against the indignant ridicule of public opinion,[1] but also against the condemnation of the House of Commons; and gave way only to the express prohibition that had to be inserted in a subsequent Act.[2] Sometimes, however, a magistrate of position and reputation would lose the lead, owing to his striking the wrong note. Thus, Sir Thomas Beevor, a Norfolk baronet of good family, carried his county with him in the reform of prisons by the skill and success with which he administered the new House of Correction at Wymondham, where, putting in practice the ideas of Howard, he combined a separate cellular system with profitable employment of the prisoners. But only three years later, when, in 1787, he put himself at the Quarter Sessions into violent opposition to the national movement, started by Zouch and Wilberforce, for the suppression of ale-houses and the reformation of manners of the lower orders, his witty and forcible speech found no supporter. It was in vain that he pointed out the unfairness of confining all the restrictions to the amusements of the poor; and the absurdity of Justices, themselves notoriously intemperate, trying " to deprive the poor of a great part of that scanty pittance of happiness which their lot in life can afford." Quarter Sessions nevertheless resolved, with no other dissentient vote than his own, " to

[1] This Leader of the County was scarified by Sydney Smith in the *Edinburgh Review*, for his treatment of untried prisoners, in order " that a prison-fancying Justice may bring his friend into the prisons and say, ' Look, what a spectacle of order, silence, and decorum we have established here, no idleness, all grinding !— We produce a penny roll every second. Our prison is supposed to be the best regulated prison in England ' " (*Works*, by Sydney Smith, 1854, vol. ii. p. 361).

[2] See *A Letter to the Right Hon. Robert Peel . . . on Prison Labour*, by John Headlam, 1823 ; *A Second Letter to the Right Hon. Robert Peel . . . on Prison Labour*, 1824 ; Hansard, 5th March 1824, N.S. vol. x. p. 755.

exert their utmost endeavours" to reform the manners of the common people.[1]

We could, from our storehouse of material, multiply examples of Justices rising, for a longer or shorter period, into our class of Leaders of the County. With endless minor variations in antecedents, character, and career, these specially prominent Rulers of the County agree in certain important characteristics. They are all, not merely legally honest, but absolutely distinguished for integrity and personal honour. Throughout our researches into the local government of nearly every county of England, for the whole period from the Revolution to the Municipal Corporations Act, we have failed in the English county at large to discover a single example of anything approaching to "the Rule of the Boss." This high standard was, as we have seen, not always characteristic of the government of the parish, whether this was in the hands of a Justice of the Peace or of an uncontrolled parish officer. Nor was such a standard maintained, as we shall presently relate, in the contemporary municipal corporations. It was, as we have seen, very far from being invariable in the Commission of the Peace itself. But it is distinctive of the county at large, as contrasted with the parish or the municipal corporation, that the corrupt Justice never rose to a position of leadership. Even in the demoralised county of Middlesex, with its long-continued array of Trading Justices, it can hardly be said that the Quarter Sessions, or the county as a whole, fell under their sway except perhaps for the generation 1781-1815. In this, as in other counties, decade might follow decade without the appearance of any leader to raise the level of efficiency or curb the oppression and peculation of individual magistrates. In nearly all cases, the squires and clergymen who filled the Commission seem to have had an instinct for choosing, as chairmen and trusted administrators, men of remarkable incorruptibility and public spirit.

The second characteristic of all this praiseworthy, voluntary effort was its casual, we might almost say anarchic, character.

---

[1] See the report in *Leeds Intelligencer*, 4th September 1787. "How can a Justice of the Peace," it had been asked a century before, "send a man to the stocks for drunkenness when he is hardly well recovered of his last debauch, or punish a man for profane swearing with forty oaths in his mouth?" (*The Justice of Peace, his calling and qualification*, by Edmund Bohun, 1693, p. 21).

Now and again a country gentleman of leisure, instigated by his experiences as a Justice of the Peace, would begin to ponder over workhouses, prisons, roads, bridges, or vagrants, exactly as he did over the rotation of crops, breeding stock or planting trees — not on account of any special fitness or training for the task, or even from any special need or opportunity, but merely because he happened to have his interest excited in one or other subject by some local accident or contemporary publication.   And whether he tired quickly of the subject, or followed it as a lifelong hobby, depended, again, not on any external direction or imperative demand, but merely on whether he happened to be flighty or persistent, versatile or monomaniac, or whether his domestic circumstances discouraged or promoted this particular form of activity.   But perhaps the most equivocal quality of this amateur leadership was the absence of any kind of guarantee of the wisdom of the leader.   The ruck of Justices who formed what may be called the constituencies of these leaders, without whose acquiescence the use of the machinery of county government could not be obtained, were, as regards intellectual criticism, a negligible quantity.   They had an instinct for an honest man, but no conception of a wise one.   Thus it does not seem to have been difficult for any worthy and assiduous Justice, with a strong conviction in any department of county business, however narrow-minded or impracticable it was—if he had the advantage either of considerable social position or merely of patient industry and zeal—to impose such ideas as he had on the administration of his county.

(j) *The Lord-Lieutenant and the High Sheriff*

We have incidentally mentioned two figures officially distinguished from the other Rulers of the County—the Lord-Lieutenant presiding over the whole county, normally for life, and the High Sheriff, who served it for a single year. Between 1689 and 1835 it seems to have been usual for the one to have been far superior in social status to the bulk of the magistrates, and for the other to have been somewhat their inferior, or at least their junior.   The combined office of Custos Rotulorum and Lord-Lieutenant formed an object of desire to almost every territorial magnate. It entailed little expense and few duties; carried with it no little patronage of an honorary kind ; placed a man on a pedestal in his county, and brought him frequently into official contact with the Court and its Ministers. Hence we find it usually filled by one of the greatest noblemen owning land within the county. Once appointed, the great personage normally held office for life; though in not a few instances an act of political rebellion, or some special malice at Court, led either to a peremptory dismissal or to an omission to reappoint on the demise of the Crown.[1] Of the characteristics of these great personages in

[1] Although commonly asserted to have been an innovation of Henry Fox's in 1763, such removal of a Lord-Lieutenant from office had not been unknown in the seventeenth century. Charles II. dismissed the Duke of Buckingham from the East Riding in 1667 (*Life and Letters of Sir George Savile, First Marquis of Halifax*, by H. C. Foxcroft, 1898, vol. i. p. 47). James II. dismissed, as Macaulay puts it, "half the Lord-Lieutenants of England" when, in 1687, they refused to interrogate their Justices, and carry out the orders of the new Board of Regulators (*History of England*, by Lord Macaulay, vol. ii. p. 77 of 1864 edition). William III. greatly changed the membership of the Commission of Lieutenancy of the City of London in 1689-1690 (*History of My Own Times*, by G. Burnet, 1833). The office terminated on the demise of the Crown, and the appointments made by James II. in 1687 were not renewed by William and Mary. So on the accession of Anne, Lord Wharton and other extreme Whigs lost their Lieutenancies (*Quarter Sessions from Queen Elizabeth to Queen Anne*, by A. H. A. Hamilton, 1878, p. 275). In 1711 the Duke of Devonshire was dismissed from the Lord-Lieutenancy of Derbyshire (*Three Centuries of Derbyshire Annals*, by J. C. Cox, 1890, vol. i. p. 25). On the other hand, on the accession of George I. some of the Tory Lord-Lieutenants lost their places in favour of Whig peers (*ibid.*). The practice of removal had, however, died out when Fox revived it. "Strip the Duke of Newcastle of his three Lieutenancies immediately," wrote Fox to Bute, November 1762, "I'll answer for the good effect of it, and then go on to the general rout, but let this beginning be made immediately" (*Life of William, Earl of Shelburne*, by Lord Edmond Fitzmaurice, 1875-1876, vol. i. p. 179). This was done in 1763, when the Duke of Grafton and the Marquis of Rockingham were also deprived of their counties ; whereupon the Duke of Devonshire resigned his (*History of England in the Eighteenth Century*, by W. E. H. Lecky, 1887, vol. iii. p. 57, and the references there cited ; *Early History of Charles James Fox*, by Sir G. O. Trevelyan, 1880, p. 33). This was deemed by Lord Shelburne an innovation. "When . . . the Lord-Lieutenants of Counties were dismissed, not only was the course new, but no real argument could be found to justify it" (*Life*, p, 181). "Lord Temple," in the same year, as the Earl of Malmesbury notes, "was himself removed from the Lord-Lieutenancy of Bucks," for his sympathy with John Wilkes (*A Series of Letters of the First Earl of Malmesbury*, 1870, vol. i. p. 101 ; *Political History of England*, 1760-1801, by Rev. W. Hunt, 1905, p. 47). The Duke of Bolton was not actually dismissed from the Lieutenancy of Hampshire, but he was led abruptly to resign that office in 1763, on the dismissal of Lord Temple (see his letter of May 1763, in *Calendar of Home Office Papers*, *1760-1765* (1878), p. 279). Perhaps the most sensational case was that of the Duke of Leeds (then Lord Carmarthen), dismissed from the Lieutenancy in 1780, along with the Duke of Richmond and Lord Pembroke. The House

the capacity of Rulers of the County little need be said. Except in organising the militia after 1756, and, as we shall presently see, in nominating Justices of the Peace, they intervened only spasmodically in county administration. " There are few," complains Sir William Blizard, in 1785, " who seem to consider their office in any other view than as conducive to their own aggrandisement and Parliamentary interest in the counties over which they preside." [1] We see them, towards the close of the eighteenth century, beginning to preside a little more frequently at Quarter Sessions or county meetings; and volunteering, personally or by letter, benevolent advice on the knotty problems of prison administration or Poor Law relief.

The High Sheriff, on the other hand, was, at any rate during the first half of the eighteenth century, often a gentleman standing somewhat below the social grade of the typical country Justice of the Peace. He had during his year of office to fulfil somewhat arduous ceremonial duties in attendance on the Judges of Assize; [2] he had to incur

of Lords negatived by 56 to 31 Lord Shelburne's motion of protest (*Political Memoranda of Francis, Fifth Duke of Leeds*, by Oscar Browning, Camden Society, N.S. vol. xxxiv., 1884; *Parliamentary History*, vol. xxi. p. 226; *Military Forces of the Crown*, by C. M. Clode, 1869, vol. ii. p. 122; *Life of William, Earl of Shelburne*, by Lord Edmond Fitzmaurice, 1875-1876, vol. iii. p. 72). But the Whigs soon had their revenge. In 1782, when Lord Carlisle was recalled from Ireland, he was simultaneously dismissed by Lord Rockingham's Ministry from the Lord-Lieutenancy of the East Riding of Yorkshire, to which Lord Carmarthen was now restored (*ibid.* p. 140 ; also i. p. 183) ; whilst Lord Chesterfield was dismissed from Buckinghamshire in order that Lord Temple might be appointed (*Political Memoranda of Francis, Fifth Duke of Leeds*, p. 65). In 1798 the Duke of Norfolk was dismissed from the Lord-Lieutenancy of the West Riding of Yorkshire for proposing a Whig toast at a banquet (*History of England*, by J. Adolphus, vol. vi. p. 691 ; *Life of Pitt*, by Lord Stanhope ; *Political History of England*, by Rev. W. Hunt, 1905, p. 402). His successor, Earl Fitzwilliam, was himself dismissed in 1819, to the surprise and alarm of the Whigs, for his public protest against "The Massacre of Peterloo" (Home Office Domestic Entry Book, 21st Oct. 1819, vol. lv. in Public Record Office ; *History of England*, by Spencer Walpole, 1879, vol. i. pp. 514, 515). Gneist says that the Lord-Lieutenant of Nottinghamshire was removed from office in 1832 (*Communal Verfassung oder das Self-Government*, vol. i. p. 563 of edition of 1863), but this seems to be an error. He was rebuked, and even warned, by Lord John Russell, for his outrageous Toryism (see *Dictionary of National Biography*), but both the published lists and the Patent Rolls in the Public Record Office give Clinton Henry, fourth Duke of Newcastle, as holding the office continuously for the whole decade, 1830-1840.

[1] *Essay on the Means of Preventing Crimes and Amending Criminals*, by (Sir) William Blizard, 1785, p. 73.

[2] "Now in the Assizes in all the Counties of England the Sheriff . . .

considerable expense ; he was ordered about by Judges and Justices alike ; he found himself responsible for the mistakes and possible oppressions of a host of subordinates, whom he inherited from his predecessor and over whom he had no practical control. Hence there was a sort of tacit conspiracy to let the office fall either on the minor gentry, or on a young man who had succeeded early to his father's estate, or else on a commercial gentleman recently settled in the county, who in this way "paid his footing." [1] Thus, we have already mentioned T. B. Bayley, at the very outset of his career, as serving as High Sheriff for Lancashire at the early age of twenty-four,[2] and John Howard, chosen to the same office for Bedfordshire, though this Nonconformist and City tradesman's son was not thought of for the Commission of the Peace. A

comes to the edge of the county and receives the judge from the hand of the Sheriff of the next county, and conducts him to the county town, attended with the gentry, and there is a large house in the town hired . . . for the judge, and all the Sheriff's officers attend him, and he in person : also he sends the judge a present, the first night, of meat and wine, and gives him one dinner " (*Through England on a Side-Saddle in the Reign of William and Mary : being the Diary of Celia Fiennes*, edited by the Hon. Mrs. Griffiths, 1888, pp. 263-266). There is a good description of it in *Rural Life in England*, by William Howitt, 1838, vol. i. pp. 116-120.

[1] An annalist of 1748 remarks that "it is very common of late years to put on rich yeomen or farmers" for this office (*Magnæ Britanniæ Notitia, or the Present State of Great Britain*, by John Chamberlayne, edition of 1748, p. 125). This is borne out by the lists of Sheriffs for Derbyshire, where six out of the seven who served between 1743 and 1749 never became Justices of the Peace (*Three Centuries of Derbyshire Annals*, by J. C. Cox, 1890, vol. i. p. 62). The "unpolished High Sheriff" of the eighteenth century is mentioned in the *Literary and Miscellaneous Memoirs* of J. Cradock, 1828, vol. i. p. 85. "The following homely notes," says Cox, " are the comments of the Derbyshire Antiquary, John Reynolds, written in 1780, on the various County High Sheriffs of his recollection " (Add. MSS. 6700):—

1745. " A substantial farmer of £100 to £120 per annum, I am told."
1747. "His father was a common carrier."
1757. "His father was a working blacksmith."
1763. "His father was a maltster, as he himself was till about ten years before his death : his estates were but small."
1767. "His father was a footman."
1771. "His grandfather was a farmer and millstone drawer, and got the principal part of his fortune by that employment."
1776. "His grandfather was a footman."
1777. "Was a gentleman farmer, but had no arms." (*Three Centuries of Derbyshire Annals*, by J. C. Cox, 1890, vol. i. p. 62.)

[2] A Leicestershire gentleman observes that "having no shelter in a profession I was, soon after my marriage, obliged to serve as High Sheriff," at the age of twenty-five (*Literary and Miscellaneous Memoirs*, by J. Cradock, 1828, vol. i. pp. xvi. 71). Addison makes Sir Roger de Coverley serve as High Sheriff at the age of twenty-two. Davies Giddy, afterwards Gilbert, and M.P., F.R.S., was High Sheriff of Cornwall, in 1792, at the age of twenty-five.

contemporary essayist gives us a portrait, evidently from life, of " Sir Theodore Thimble," son of an " eminent tailor in the precincts of St. Clement's," who " purchased an estate in Essex, with a fine old mansion. Theodore set out upon a new establishment and figured off as the first gentleman of his family: he served as Sheriff of the County, and acquired great reputation in that high office by the elegant and well-cut liveries which he exhibited at the Assizes; a lucky address from the county gave him a title." [1] It is perhaps of a piece with these examples that we find Buckinghamshire having as Sheriff in 1754 the London distiller's son, John Wilkes, then only twenty-seven years of age ; and, a generation later, the amiable ex-jeweller, John Neild, whose philanthropic prison explorations rank second only to those of Howard. We note, towards the end of the eighteenth century, an upward tendency in the status of the office. [2] The growing interest in county administration—especially the vogue of the example set by Howard—seems to have somewhat checked the evasion of service as Sheriff by gentlemen of ancient family and good estate.

Our description of the different types of Justice of the Peace as they successively appear in contemporary documents and literature will, we think, have left on the student's mind impressions of a continuous rise in the standard of honour, legal attainments, and social status of these Rulers of the County. These impressions are, we believe, borne out by the facts. [3] The

---

[1] *The Observer*, by Richard Cumberland, in vol. xxvi. of *The British Essayists*, 1827, p. 16.

[2] In Derbyshire, in the half century from 1780 to 1830, at least thirty-five out of the fifty High Sheriffs seem to have been furnished by the fifty families which have supplied nearly half of all the Justices who have ever been in the Commission for that county. See the lists in *Three Centuries of Derbyshire Annals*, by J. C. Cox, 1890, vol. i. pp. 62-64.

[3] Especially towards the close of the eighteenth century does there seem to have been an attempt to let die out of the Commission "every man who is dependent, whose time and attention are engaged in business, who is ignorant, who lives by granting warrants, who is suspected "; and to " invite and animate to exertion men of probity, fortune, learning, and spirit " (*Essay on the Means of Preventing Crimes and Amending Criminals*, by (Sir) William Blizard, 1785, p. 74). There arose a demand for more attention " to the birth, parentage, and education of aspirants to the Bench " (*Gentleman's Magazine*, April 1788, p. 315). Unfortunately, as a contemporary journalist observed, "property and politics are the qualifications looked for. Legal knowledge, mixed with philanthropy, sometimes proves attendant, but the case happens too seldom" (*Morning Chronicle*, 27th August 1785).

baser kind of Trading Justice, pilloried by Gay, Fielding, and Smollett, seems, after the close of the eighteenth century, wholly to have disappeared, even from the Metropolis.[1] The worst type of Sycophant Justice and Rural Tyrant, such as Justice Gobble and Squire Western, had by 1820 become inconceivable, even to Radical politicians avid for evidence against the institution of a non-elective magistracy. The advent of the Clerical Justice, and the legal text-books which he so diligently wrote and circulated, may account for the closer attention to legal requirements which we notice in the execution of justice in Petty and Quarter Sessions. The growth of social compunction and zeal for the public interest, which distinguished the age of Wilberforce from that of Walpole, was fully reflected in the county magistracy. On the other hand, this rising standard of integrity, knowledge, and public spirit among the Rulers of the County, was, as we shall presently recount, marred by an increasing aloofness of their class from those whom they considered their social inferiors—an aloofness which led to social exclusiveness, a selfish " class policy," and no little prejudice in dealing with offences against the Game Laws. Coincidently with these changes in the mental characteristics of the County Justices, we watch a steady rise in the social status of those who actually took part in the routine administration of the county business. In our perusal of the Quarter Sessions records of many counties we have been struck by the absence, during the first half of the eighteenth century, of the names of the more distinguished county families. Whoever may have figured in the Commission of the Peace, the actual work of Petty and Quarter Sessions was at that time practically always left to half a dozen of the smaller squirarchy.[2] After

---

[1] "The Duke of Northumberland," it was said in 1784, "as Lord-Lieutenant of Middlesex and Westminster, has taken every precaution in his power to prevent improper persons from being in the Commission of the Peace. . . . The present Justices are more respectable, perhaps, than they were ever known to be" (*Observations on the Police or Civil Government of Westminster*, by Edward Sayer, 1784, p. iv.). The Duke declared that he "intended to have no magistrates but men of great property"; and accordingly appointed thirty-five wealthy men at a batch. These, however, would not put themselves to the trouble of doing the work (*Considerations on the Authority of the Magistrate*, by Joseph Cawthorne, pp. 19-21; a rare pamphlet, of which a copy happens to have been preserved among the Home Office MS. archives in the Public Record Office).

[2] This was noted by Bohun in 1693. Though the great personages of the

the accession of George the Third, we watch dropping into the lists of those present at the Sessions, not only the "clerks" and Doctors of Divinity, but also an occasional baronet, an "honourable," the holder of a courtesy title, or even a peer of the realm. Yet "how few," exclaims T. B. Bayley in 1773, "amongst the great number of noblemen and gentlemen of knowledge, fortune, and independence, who áre in the Commission of the Peace in every county . . . have patriotism or activity sufficient to induce them to act under it."[1] Towards the end of the eighteenth century, the larger country gentlemen and clerical magistrates are always to the front as Chairmen of Quarter Sessions and draftsmen of the reports of the various committees, whilst in the opening decades of the nineteenth century, it is not unusual to find an earl, a marquis, or a duke condescending to take part in the proceedings.[2]

It may not be unconnected with these changes in the County Benches that the method of selection of Justices of the Peace itself underwent a subtle change. The legal appointment remained, from first to last, in the Crown. What was of greater practical importance was at whose instance and with what objects the Royal Prerogative was exercised. Down to the Rebellion, we gather that the Judges of Assize

realm, he says, were named "in all the Commissions, yet the persons who reside in the several counties and do actually execute the office are for the most part" ordinary country gentlemen, "the great men" not doing "the duties of their places" (*The Justice of Peace, his Calling and Qualifications*, by Edmund Bohun, 1693, p. 6). Derbyshire seems always to have had an exceptionally homogeneous Bench. In a complete list of its Justices from 1594 to 1889 we see that, out of a total of about 1320 names, no fewer than 535 are those of one or other of the 50 principal families of the county, there being 30 Wilmots, 29 Cavendishes, and 25 Cokes. But we notice among those of the eighteenth century only eight peers in the course of a hundred years (*Three Centuries of Derbyshire Annals*, by J. C. Cox, 1890, vol. i. pp. 37-50).

[1] *Observations on the General Highway and Turnpike Acts*, by T. B. Bayley, 1773, p. 5.

[2] We may cite the well-known devotion to their duties of Chairman of Quarter Sessions of Northamptonshire both of the Earl Spencer, who as Lord Althorp had led the House of Commons, and also of his father (*Memoirs of Earl Spencer*, by Sir Dennis le Marchant, 1876). We do not attribute much of the rise of the general level of social status of the magistracy to the change in the legal property qualification. But it should be noted that this, which had been £20 a year in lands within the county since 18 Henry VI. c. 11, was raised in 1731 and 1744 to £100 a year in lands within the county, or £300 a year in reversion (5 Geo. II. c. 18; 18 Geo. II. c. 20), except for peers, their eldest sons and heirs, and the eldest sons and heirs of persons owning £600 a year in lands.

were expected by the Privy Council to pick out suitable persons to administer each county under their supervision.[1] After the Restoration, we infer that the nomination of Justices by the Assize Judges came to an end with their supervision of county business, though they continued, as they do down to the present day, to suggest the names of suitable persons for appointment as High Sheriffs. In regard to Justices there ensued at first a period of courtly manipulation of the Commissions of the Peace throughout the country. This manipulation, which consisted of spasmodic removals from and additions to the ranks of the Justices according as they were disaffected or subservient, had no reference to local government; and resulted, as we have seen, in a multiplication of "Justices of Mean Degree." A few years after the accession of George I. this courtly manipulation gradually ceased. The power of removal was silently disused. After the first quarter of the eighteenth century, it became extremely rare for any Justice to be removed from the Commission, or to have his name omitted on the issue of a new Commission.[2] It was, in fact, laid down as a rule by Lord Eldon, and acted on by him during his long tenure of the office of Lord Chancellor, as it has virtually been ever since, "that however unfit a magistrate might be for his office, either from private

[1] In 1601 a member of the House of Commons, in declaiming against Justices of low birth and mean condition, "Basket Justices" who made money out of their office, explained how such persons crept into the Commission. "When any desireth to be a Justice, he [they] getteth a certificate from divers Justices of the Peace in the county, to the Justices of Assize, certifying them of their sufficiency and ability. And they again make their Certificate (believing the former) to the Lord Keeper, who at the next Assizes puts them into Commission. And thus is the Lord Keeper abused, and the Justices of Assize abused, and the country troubled with a corrupt Justice put in authority" (*Historical Collections*, by Heywood Townshend, 1680, pp. 268-328).

[2] No complete or systematic record exists of the Commissions of the Peace that were issued between 1689 and 1835, or of the persons whose names were added, removed, or omitted. Our impression (from examination of the scanty MS. archives of the Crown Office, and the incidental references in the MS. books and papers of the Home Office) is that the last removals on political grounds, apart from isolated individual cases, took place under George I. or George II. But the Home Secretary, in 1820, asks the Lord Chancellor to erase Sir Charles Wolseley's name from all Commissions (Home Office Domestic Entry Book, 17th May 1820, in Public Record Office). The actual recorded removals from the Commissions for Middlesex and Westminster between 1730 and 1835 (done by "fiat" of the Lord Chancellor—in fact, a bare order written on any half-sheet of letter paper) do not seem to have exceeded a score; and though no cause or motive for these removals is recorded, we think that they can be accounted for by actual misconduct.

misconduct or party feeling, he would never strike that magistrate off the list until he had been convicted of some offence by the verdict of a Court of Record. . . . As the magistrates gave their services gratis they ought to be protected." [1] Ministerial interference with appointments to the Commission continued spasmodically to be exercised. Sir Robert Walpole and his successors used their own discretion in getting added to the Commission any one whom they wished to favour, or any one who was backed by any influential personage, whether or not connected with the county concerned. Gradually the practice seems to have grown up of leaving it (except in the Counties Palatine of Lancashire and Durham) to the Lord-Lieutenant of each county to recommend additions to the Commission, though the Lord Chancellor never abandoned the right of adding names without such nomination, or even in direct defiance of the Lord-Lieutenant's advice.[2]

By the end of the eighteenth century the way to the Commission of the Peace in the counties other than Lancashire [3] had thus come to be almost exclusively through the Lord-Lieutenant. It became so unusual for any person to be added except on his recommendation, that aspirants for the honour were referred to him as a matter of course.[4] This practical transfer of the power of selection to the leader of each county put a stop to the appointment of Justices of

[1] Brougham's Speech, in Hansard, 7th Feb. 1828, vol. xviii. N.S. p. 161.

[2] See the discussions in the House of Commons, Hansard, 7th Dec. 1819 (when Lord Eldon's letter defining the position was read), 7th Feb. 1828, and 29th Nov. 1830. This Royal Prerogative is still maintained. "There are many instances in which the Crown has made the appointment without any such recommendation, and in some cases even contrary to the wish of the Lord-Lieutenant" (Renton's *Law Encyclopædia*, article "Justices," vol. vii. p. 162). Especially in Middlesex did the Ministers continue to add their own nominees. The lack of care with which the Middlesex Justices were appointed was commented on in 1815 (*An Address to the Magistracy of the County of Middlesex*, etc., 1815, p. 4). It was, moreover, always open to the Lord Chancellor to issue a separate Commission for a particular Borough or Liberty, and in such cases (of which Westminster and the Tower Hamlets were the most important) we do not find that any one recommendation was exclusively acted upon.

[3] The County Palatine of Lancaster (Lancashire), as we have already noted, has always remained nominally in charge of the King as Duke of Lancaster, and being presided over by the King's Minister (Chancellor of the Duchy of Lancaster), who is now usually a member of the Cabinet. The Chancellor of the Duchy performs the duties elsewhere devolving on the Lord-Lieutenant and Custos Rotulorum (including the appointment of Clerk of the Peace); and himself issues the Commission of the Peace for the county.

[4] "Such a thing is hardly ever known," said Brougham in 1828, "as any

Mean Degree. Exercising this honorary patronage under the close supervision of influential local opinion, the Lord-Lieutenant quickly fell into the habit of recommending no one whose admission would be likely to be unwelcome to the existing magistrates. In some counties, at any rate, he relied largely on the suggestions of the Clerk of the Peace.[1] In any case of doubt he consulted informally the Chairman of Quarter Sessions and other leading Justices; and to their opinion he seems almost invariably to have deferred.[2]

(k) *Class Exclusiveness*

Under this system the County Benches were, at any rate

interference with respect to these nominations by the Lord Chancellor. He looks to the Lord-Lieutenant, or rather to the Custos Rotulorum, for the names of proper persons. The Lord-Lieutenant, therefore, as Custos Rotulorum, absolutely appoints all the Justices of the Peace in his county at his sole will and pleasure" (Hansard, 7th Feb. 1828; vol. xviii. N.S. p. 161, etc.). The Home Office Domestic Entry Books in the Public Record Office show that (as in a case on 24th July 1830, vol. lxiv.) Sir Robert Peel "invariably declines making any recommendations of the names of gentlemen for the Commission of the Peace."

[1] In a memorandum book of the Clerk of the Peace for Merionethshire in 1821 will be found copies of his letters to Sir W. W. Wynn, the Lord-Lieutenant, discussing the eligibility of particular aspirants to the honour, including a recent High Sheriff, whom one of the Justices strongly objects to. In this county it was the Clerk of the Peace who habitually brought the names before the Lord-Lieutenant at suitable dates.

[2] A case of formal consultation occurs in the Minutes of Quarter Sessions of Derbyshire (Epiphany 1807):—

"His Grace the Duke of Devonshire, the Lord-Lieutenant of the County, having, with his usual attention to the Magistracy, referred to the present Bench, through the Clerk of the Peace, the question of introducing Mr. Thomas Hassall into the Commission of the Peace; the Justices now assembled, in obedience to His Grace's request to receive their opinions in writing, find it their duty to state that, though the good sense and unexceptional character of Mr. Hassall are fully acknowledged by some of them who have had opportunities of knowing him, his situation in life does not seem to entitle him to a place in the Commission of the Peace of this county conformably to those regulations under which His Grace's consideration has supplied and guarded it. They hold that any departure from them in any instance, however unexceptionable in itself, would unavoidably open the way to others which might not be so, to the injury of that weight and consequence of the Magistracy in the public mind on which its efficacy so materially depends. They recollect similar objections to similar applications; and they cannot consistently with precedent, or with their deliberate judgment on a review of the rules and usages hitherto observed here, recommend the admission of Mr. Hassall into the Commission of the Peace. In thus submitting their unanimous opinion they beg leave to offer to His Grace the Lord-Lieutenant their respectful acknowledgments of that confidence with which he has honoured them and his obliging consideration of their wishes and satisfaction" (Cox's *Three Centuries of Derbyshire Annals*, vol. ii. p. 301). Mr. Hassall was never made a J.P.

from the beginning of the nineteenth century, normally recruited by what practically amounted to co-option. The result was, notwithstanding a rapid and continuous increase in the number of Justices,[1] a quickly developing homogeneity in social status and political opinions of the members of the Commissions of the Peace for the counties at large. With this we may in fairness connect the rise in the average standard of conduct and personal character, to which we have already alluded. Against it must, however, be set the social exclusiveness which a system of co-option engendered. The country gentlemen set their faces against the admission of any person engaged in trade, manufacture, or commerce;[2] they were prejudiced against any unconventionality in opinions, tastes, or conduct even in men of their own class; they resented any expression of Radical or even of Whig politics, and they extremely

---

[1] Already, in 1781, a Leicestershire Justice deprecates "filling the Commissions so prodigiously as of late" (*The Irenarch, or the Justice of Peace's Manual,* by Ralph Heathcote, 1781, p. 174). The number of "acting Justices," qualified by "taking out their Dedimus"—estimated, as we have mentioned in the first section of this chapter, in 1700 at 1500—was ascertained in 1796 to be 2656, without counting those for Lancashire (Report of House of Commons Committee on the Distribution of the Statutes, 1796). In 1818 it was estimated that they numbered in all, excluding duplicates, about 4000 (*A Collection of the Several Points of Sessions Law,* by Rev. S. Clapham, 1818). By 1831 they had increased to 4842. In 1832 the total number was given in Parliamentary Paper No. 39 as 5371, of whom 1354 were clergymen. The statistics sometimes include and sometimes exclude Lancashire.

The number habitually attending Sessions, which we put at seven or eight hundred for 1700, was estimated by a competent authority in 1832 at about 2200 (*Administration of the Poor Laws,* 1832, a privately printed pamphlet without author's name, which was by John Rickman).

[2] Thus it is specifically stated that "a rule had been established by the Chancellor of the Duchy of Lancaster that no manufacturer should receive the Commission of the Peace, consequently the magistrates were either landowners or clergymen. The Lancashire squires viewed the manufacturing population with a jealousy which may have been unreasonable, but certainly was not unnatural" (*Life and Times of Sir Robert Peel,* by W. Cooke Taylor, 1851, p. 120). The existence of this rule was referred to in the House of Commons in 1813; see Hansard, 12th May 1813. When the Ministry defended it, Bathurst, speaking in reply to Sir S. Romilly, said "he had no objection . . . to introduce into the Commission of the Peace for Manchester (meaning Lancashire) wealthy and respectable persons engaged in trade, but not in manufactures. . . . As a great part of the business of the magistrates in Manchester consisted in settling disputes of masters with their workmen, a magistrate who was himself engaged in manufacture might be suspected by some persons as not impartial." On the other hand, in Derbyshire, we have Richard Arkwright, the cotton-spinner, in the Commission from 1793, and his son from 1815; whilst three of the Strutts, the great Derbyshire mill-owners, were admitted together in 1827 (*Three Centuries of Derbyshire Annals,* by J. C. Cox, 1890, vol. i. pp. 37, 48). But the Arkwrights and Strutts had become millionaires.

disliked any active association with the Methodists or other Dissenters. "Some Lord-Lieutenants," it was said, "appoint men for their political opinions, some for activity as partisans in local contests, some are so far influenced as to keep out all who take a decided part against themselves in matters where all men should be free to act as their conscience dictates."[1] In some counties, such as Derbyshire, Kent, and Sussex, they made it a rule to exclude also Anglican clergymen.[2] To such an extent was this exclusiveness carried by the Lord-Lieutenants that even the Tory Lord Chancellor of 1830 felt obliged publicly to warn them in the House of Lords that they must not omit from their nominations those persons "whose powers, whose activity, and whose character would make them desirable accessories to the present force of the magistracy." "If they do so," he said, "he would exercise his right to insert their names in the Commission." Even Lord Eldon agreed in this hint, adding that in the event of wrongful omission, it was both within the power and within the duty of the Lord Chancellor to correct the list supplied by the Lord-Lieutenant.[3] Yet at the very end of the period with which we deal, when

---

[1] Brougham's Speech, 7th February 1828, Hansard, vol. xviii. (N.S.) p. 163.

[2] Brougham, in 1828, declared that there were "some Lord-Lieutenants" who made "it a rule never to appoint a clergyman to the magistracy" (Hansard, 7th February 1828, vol. xviii. (N.S.) p. 161). On the other hand, the total number of clergymen who were Justices was, in 1832, no fewer than 1354, or one-fourth of the whole. The clergymen, too, attended with more than average regularity. We note, for instance, at a Quarter Sessions for the West Riding, out of six Justices on the Bench four were clergymen (MS. Minutes, Quarter Sessions, West Riding, 8th October 1799). At an important meeting of the Breconshire Quarter Sessions there were present eight laymen and ten Clerical Justices (MS. Minutes, Breconshire, 11th October 1826). There were in 1821 for the East Riding of Yorkshire forty-one acting magistrates, of whom seventeen were clergymen. At the Quarter Sessions at which certain important standing orders were made on 10th July 1821, there were present sixteen Justices, of whom no fewer than ten were clergymen ; see *The Names of the Acting Magistrates and Public Officers of the East Riding of the County of York, with several matters relating to the Practice and Proceedings of the Court of Quarter Sessions,* 1824. In Buckinghamshire it was noted in 1826 by a Radical newspaper that "out of thirty-eight magistrates on the Bench at the opening of the late Aylesbury Quarter Sessions, seventeen were clergymen" (*Chester Courant,* 14th November 1826). The counties in which there were, in 1832, the largest proportion of Clerical Justices were stated to be Cornwall, Hereford, Lincoln, Norfolk, Somerset, Brecon, Denbigh, and Glamorgan, in all of which they made up more than one-half of the acting Justices (*Liverpool Chronicle,* 11th February 1832), and therefore probably a positive majority of those usually attending Sessions.

[3] Hansard, 29th November 1830, 3rd ser. vol. i. p. 678.

the new Whig Government was supposed to wish to break down the social ascendancy of the County Justices, this spirit of class exclusiveness manifested itself more keenly than ever. In Merionethshire in 1833, for instance, the county magistrates actually "went on strike" for a time, in their resentment of the appointment of a wealthy local landowner who had, within their recollection, kept a retail shop, and who belonged to the Wesleyan Methodist denomination. The strike of the Merionethshire magistrates, it was officially reported, "arose solely on account of a person who had been put into the Commission of the Peace contrary to their wishes. They objected to this individual, not so much on account of religious differences,.which might possibly be overlooked, but because his origin, his education, his connections, his early habits, occupations, and station were not such as could entitle him to be the familiar associate of gentlemen. . . . In answer to a remonstrance, it was alleged by the Lord-Lieutenant that the person objected to having served the office of Sheriff, it was impossible to refuse to put him into the Commission of the Peace." And the Commissioner from whose report we quote—Thomas Jefferson Hogg, afterwards the biographer of Shelley—fully justified this early example of Merionethshire passive resistance. "The refusal of the County Magistrates," he reported, "to act with a man who has been a grocer and is a Methodist is the dictate of genuine patriotism ; the spirit of aristocracy in the county magistracy is the salt which alone preserves the whole mass from inevitable corruption. The power, which is almost irresponsible, could not have been endured if it were not controlled by the sense of private honour. . . . Unless some condition of gentility (as, for example, the very slight one that the County Justice be at least the son of a person who was not himself unfitted by education and manners for the magistracy) be speedily imposed, tacitly or otherwise, and enforced with much strictness, it will unquestionably be necessary to contrive without delay some sufficient substitute for the subsisting administration of the counties of England and Wales." [1] It was in this spirit

---

[1] Report on Certain Boroughs (Municipal Corporations Inquiry Commission), drawn by T. S. Hogg, Esq., H.C., No. 686 of 1838, p. 5. A local witness assigns an interesting subsidiary reason for the strike. "These gentlemen have lately ceased to act because they had sentenced to transportation for fourteen years two

that Quarter Sessions was, during the first quarter of the nineteenth century, invariably recruited.[1] We accordingly leave the County Benches in 1835 composed (with either no clergymen or else a considerable proportion of them) almost exclusively of the principal landed proprietors within the county, whose fathers and grandfathers had held their estates before them; nearly all men of high standing and personal honour according to their own social code, but narrowly conventional in opinions and prejudices; and—with the exception of the members of the old Whig families of the governing class who could not decently have been kept out—exclusively Tory in politics.[2]

women for receiving stolen goods, and the sentence had been remitted by the Secretary of State without consulting them. They ceased to act in consequence of this remission, and because a person qualified lately who is a Calvinistic Methodist. Several other magistrates have resigned also for the same cause" (*ibid.* p. 4).

[1] The following observation, made in 1850, is curious, but we have not been able to verify it. " I was remarking," writes Frederick Hill, ". . . on the youthful appearance of most of the county magistrates at the [Lincoln] meeting last week (1850), and was surprised to hear . . . that most of them had been put into the Commission of the Peace when they were mere infants, and that till lately this was a common practice, just as children used to have commissions in the army and navy" (*Autobiography of Frederick Hill*, 1894, p. 270). So far as we have noticed, Justices were not appointed under age, but, if eldest sons, not infrequently soon after twenty-one.

[2] This complete ascendancy of the Tory party led to gross political partisanship. In 1821 the Buckinghamshire Justices refused to give any of the county advertisements to the Aylesbury newspaper, though the principal one in the county, because it was an "Opposition" organ. The Whig Justices signed a protest against this action (*Letters of Lord Althorp*, privately printed, p. 116).

CHAPTER III

THE full and varied authority conferred in each county upon the Justices by the Commission of the Peace was exercisable either by these Justices collectively, or by them individually or in pairs. "At certain days and places" the High Sheriff was commanded to assist them by summoning Juries, and by constituting the well-known Court of Quarter Sessions, with which, as the principal and supreme authority in the county, we shall presently deal. But apart from these "General Sessions of the Peace," the King, in addressing the magistrates by his Commission, expressly assigns to "any of you," and to "any two or more of you," great powers and duties, which were thus exercisable, as it was said, "out of Sessions." We find accordingly no small share of county administration devolving upon the individual magistrates, singly or in pairs, or upon the meetings of local groups of magistrates, which (though in later times called Sessions) were not "General Sessions of the Peace" for the county as a whole, and were thus technically "out of Sessions."

(a) *The " Single Justice "*

We begin with the Justice acting alone. To the house of the country gentleman of the eighteenth century, who had "taken out his Dedimus" as a magistrate, there came, from time to time, a succession of cases of every imaginable description. In the interesting advice given to Justices by Edmund Bohun in 1693 for "the private hearing in the hall," we get a vision of this side of the magistrate's work. When a complaint is brought to him he is warned that he must first consider whether the matter falls within his jurisdiction; for "some men have a custom to extend their power beyond the just bounds of it, that they may have the more business, and others will not do what they might and ought, either out of fear or ignorance."[1] Whenever the Justice issues a summons, grants a warrant, takes a recognisance, or makes an order, he should invariably enter in a book the names of the parties, the subject-matter, and a copy of the instrument itself. The same book should record all appearances of parties before him, the substance of their evidence, and an exact statement of any judgment or determination arrived at by him. Bohun, like other writers for Justices,[2] lays great stress on the importance of each magistrate keeping this notebook of his proceedings. "And if," he wisely counsels, "just upon a Sessions, they be all read over, he shall have a prospect of all he has done that quarter, which will be of great use."

Such a notebook, intermittently kept by three successive magistrates of Lancashire belonging to the Mosley family, between 1616 and 1739, is now in the Manchester Public Library.[3] In its faded and discoloured pages the student finds, roughly entered and interspersed with other memoranda, many of the day-by-day proceedings of a Justice in the seventeenth century. He issues a precept to the Constables of Failsworth and Gorton to appear at the next Quarter Sessions "to answer their default . . . in not paying in the bridge money." The same day he grants two warrants, at the instance of two separate complainants, for the apprehension of those who had wronged them by theft or assault. Two days later

---

[1] *The Justice of Peace, his Calling and Qualifications,* by Edmund Bohun, 1693, p. 149. Bohun mentions the "Justice Book" that he himself kept as an active magistrate for Suffolk from 1675 to 1694, but this has not come down to us (*Diary and Autobiography of Edmond Bohun,* by S. Wilton Rix, 1853, p. 64).

[2] The keeping of careful records was enjoined on the Justices by Michael Dalton in 1618 (*The Country Justice,* c. 115, p. 6) and by Dr. Richard Burn (*The Justice of the Peace,* vol. v. p. 71 of edition of 1756).

[3] The first part has been published, with editorial notes by Ernest Axon, by the Record Society for . . . Lancashire and Yorkshire, as *Manchester Sessions: Notes of Proceedings before Oswald Mosley . . . and other Magistrates,* vol. i. 1616-1623 (1901). In MS. the notes cease with the year 1672, and there is a gap of sixty years, terminated by a few more notes of work done between 1734 and 1739.

he has a couple of cases of petty crime, in which he binds over the defendants, with two sureties each, to appear at the next Quarter Sessions. Sometimes he has four or five cases to deal with in a single day; sometimes, though whether from lack of business, neglect to record it, or absence from home is not specified, there is no entry for months. Another such Diary, that of William Hunt, a Justice of the County of Wilts, is preserved for the years 1743-1748. We see him doing something every two or three days, granting warrants and summonses, signing parish accounts, swearing persons to affidavits, issuing certificates and passes of one sort or another, disposing of petty cases of bastardy, assault, "hedge-pulling," and non-payment of wages; and holding frequent Petty or Special Sessions with one or two more Justices for Highway and Licensing business.[1] We imagine that the work of most active Justices in the eighteenth century was equally varied, and certainly not less continuous. To the house of such a Justice the Parish Constable would bring the men or women whom he had arrested as vagrants, reputed poachers, suspected thieves, or merely as participants in a drunken brawl. Any such defendants the Justice would have to examine—it might be in the presence of a crowd of curious or excited villagers who had swarmed in with the Constable and his prisoners—taking down himself, as best he could, if he had no clerk, the nature of the accusation, the statements of the witnesses and the defendants' replies; and deciding whether or not to order them summarily to pay a fine, to be set in the stocks, to be whipped, to be bound over, with sureties, to appear at Quarter Sessions or the Assizes, to be committed to the House of Correction or County Gaol, to be set free with a vagrant pass, or to be simply discharged. When the individual magistrate, sitting in his own parlour, happened to have to deal with pugnacious prosecutors or defendants, and failed to write up his notebook fully and correctly, he might easily find himself in a difficulty when called upon to justify his action in the Court of King's Bench. Thus, an unfortunate young cleric describes in a pamphlet of 1809 how he had been worried against his better

---

[1] MS. Diary of William Hunt, 1743-1748, in the collection of the Wiltshire Archæological Society at Devizes ; see there also the MS. Diary of Edward Poore, J.P., 1784. The Diary of Thomas Smith, in the *Wilts Archæological Magazine*, vol. xi., gives details as to the passing of parish accounts in 1721-1722.

judgment, by a malicious prosecutor, into hearing an accusation against the local miller for selling corn by false measure; and had been induced, against the weight of the legally admissible evidence (as was asserted on behalf of the miller), to impose the heavy cumulative fine authorised by the statute. " I regret," he says, " that I kept only loose minutes of what passed before me at the hearing, instead of taking down the evidence fully and correctly, as ought always to be done. For this inattention I have to plead that I was but little conversant with the details of business; and, secondly, the interruption and distraction occasioned by the clamour and contention of the parties completely bothered me." [1]

These purely judicial hearings, perhaps fortunately for the ordinary magistrate, did not constitute the bulk of his work. As a rule, he was giving decisions which, though often judicial in form, were assumed to be determined by his own views of social expediency. The Surveyor of Highways would consult him as to the roads to be mended, or seek his order for the enforcement of the Statute Labour on some recalcitrant cottager or negligent farmer. "" Justices of the Peace," had written an early Poor Law reformer, " are emphatically, or more eminently, the Overseers of the Poor of the county (all others being their

---

[1] *The Case of the King against the Rev. T. Hornsby*, 1809, p. 59. This is an able and elaborate defence by the Clerical Justice of his proceedings. The case brought before him was a complicated one. The young magistrate was completely puzzled by the evidence, and endeavoured to avoid dealing with the case, referring the prosecutor to Quarter Sessions. The prosecutor, however, proved to him that he must adjudicate, and threatened him with a mandamus. After nine months, the harassed Justice yielded to this importunity, heard the case, and did his best to unravel the evidence. Notwithstanding all that this Clerical Justice could do to assuage the dispute, the prosecutor insisted on the utmost rigour of the law, with the result that the defendant got the case removed by certiorari to the Court of King's Bench, where the conviction was quashed, but the Justice absolved from blame. The modest attitude of Mr. Hornsby was, we fear, not usually characteristic of the Justice's parlour. "The individuals who are brought before him," remarks Gisborne, "are almost invariably his inferiors, and commonly in the lowest ranks of society. The principal share of his business is transacted in his own house, before few spectators, and those in general indigent and illiterate. Hence he is liable to become dictatorial, browbeating, consequential, and ill-humoured ; domineering in his inclinations, dogmatic in his opinions, and arbitrary in his decisions. He knows, indeed, that most of his decisions may be subjected to revisal at the Sessions ; but he may easily learn to flatter himself that he shall meet with no severe censure from his friends and brethren on the bench for what they will probably consider an oversight, or at most as an error easily remedied, and therefore of little importance " (*The Duties of Men*, by Thomas Gisborne, 1794, chap. v. "The Duties of a Justice of the Peace," p. 285).

substitutes and acting by their orders)." [1]   When an Overseer
gave less relief than the pauper considered reasonable, the
disappointed applicant appealed to the Squire. "Whoever
thinks himself neglected," wrote Arthur Young in 1767, "has
nothing to do but take a walk to the first Justice of the Peace
and make his complaint." [2]   The country gentleman, it was
said, "consults only those feelings which give him pleasure, and
which Nature has taught us to admire," [3] and forthwith
orders the hard-hearted Overseer to give the relief asked for.
The country Justice of the Peace was, in fact, if he chose, the
source of all local authority.   "In parochial administration,"
sums up an eighteenth-century observer of rural local government, "the ostensible minister, the nominal Overseer, is sometimes a person of inferior rank; but the King of the Parish
still acts behind the scene, and the Overseer dares not alter
his arrangements.   Happy is the parish that has a good
King!" [4]

The work of the individual Justice was not confined to
dealing with such cases as were brought before him.   The law
enabled, and in some cases positively enjoined, him to go out
into the highways and byways to discover cases in which parish
officers were neglecting their duties, and to hunt out the crimes
and misdemeanours of private persons.   "More especially are
they bound," says a writer of 1700, "to have a strict regard
to . . . ale-houses, masters, servants, and the poor." [5]   Now
and again we see magistrates breaking out into what may almost
be regarded as a crusade against one or other class of offences.
Between 1689 and 1714, for instance, we find them, "goaded
on by the Societies for the Reformation of Manners, . . . very
active in putting down Sunday desecration," [6] gaming-houses,
profane swearing, and "vice and immorality"—a spasm of
activity in which, we are told, "many worthy gentlemen in

---

[1] *A Plain and Easy Method showing how the Office of Overseer of the Poor
may be managed*, etc., by Richard Dunning, 1686, p. 24.

[2] *The Farmer's Letters to the People of England*, by Arthur Young, 1767,
p. 162.

[3] *Observations on the Various Plans offered to the Public for the Relief of the
Poor*, by Rev. J. Townsend, 1788, p. 7.

[4] *Observations on the Present State of the Parochial and Vagrant Poor*, by
John Scott, 1773, p. 50.

[5] *Campania Felix*, by Timothy Nourse, 1700, chap. xv. "Of Justices of the
Peace," p. 255.

[6] *Life in the English Church, 1660-1714*, by J. H. Overton, 1885, p. 320.

the Commission of the Peace laid out their time an
A more normal form of activity was the rural
general supervision of the roads and bridges of his
hood, to which we shall presently recur.[2]

(b) *The " Double Justice "*

Throughout the whole period, from 1689 or
notice the Justice of the Peace struggling with
increasing volume of business. But, as we ha
described in our chapter on the Legal Constitut
County, there were many cases, both judicial and adm
in which the law had imposed upon him a collea
work. We have therefore the institution of wha
temporary lawyers' slang, was known as the " Doub
It is for this reason that we find, throughout the wl
with which we are dealing, one country gentleman
another, in order to constitute with him the necessa
to settle such matters as the making of the Poor Rate, the
appointment of Surveyors of Highways and Overseers of the
Poor, and the allowance of their accounts; and, down to
1729, the grant of a licence to the keeper of an ale-house.
As the century wore on, and Parliament attempted to deal
with the growing nuisances of urban life, the business of the
" Double Justice " in many districts increased, so as to constitute this pair of gentlemen an important criminal court—a
court without legal assistance; held at no stated time, but
fortuitously whenever two magistrates of the county happened
to meet; often in the hall or parlour of one of them, or any
other private place; without public announcement, or even
the admission of any one except the parties immediately
concerned.

It was a further anomaly of this remarkable jurisdiction
that neither the individual Justice nor the pair of Justices
had any definite geographical area smaller than the county
within which alone they could function. Every Justice of
the Peace of the county had full and unrestricted jurisdiction

---

[1] *The Third Charge of Whitelocke Bulstrode . . . to the Grand Jury of Middlesex*, 1722, p. 2.
[2] Chapter IV. The Court of Quarter Sessions.

anywhere within the county. Hence there was nothing to prevent any magistrate from being importuned by any suitor, from hearing any applicant, or from dealing with any business, administrative or judicial, arising in or relating to quite another part of the county from that in which he resided; and nothing to hinder his taking action, wittingly or unwittingly, in cases which some other magistrate of the county had already disposed of—it might be in a contrary sense. It is true that, as we have mentioned, the earlier statutes frequently implied, and sometimes expressly provided, that the jurisdiction which they conferred upon the county magistracy should be exercised by the "next Justice," or by those "residing near the place," or by those "dwelling in or near the parish or Division."[1] These phrases were, however, too vague to make it clear in all cases which Justice of the Peace was thereby designated; and they were too indefinite to derogate from the general authority given by the Commission of the Peace throughout the county. The result was that we not infrequently see one pair of Justices formally appointing Overseers, allowing their accounts, or making a Poor Rate for a particular parish, only to discover presently that another pair of Justices had already conferred the appointment, made the rate, or allowed the accounts for that same parish.[2] Apparently, in such dilemmas, the Courts

---

[1] See Chapter I. The Legal Constitution of the County, p. 299.

[2] Thus in 1713, after three Overseers had been properly appointed for Honiton by one set of Justices, "in a private house and in a very private manner, and without any presentment or recommendation of the old Overseers for that purpose . . . Sir Edmond Prideaux and Sir William Pole" were led to appoint four other persons to be Overseers for the same parish, antedating their warrant, "for some private purpose," by three days. Both sets of Overseers claiming to act, an appeal is made to Quarter Sessions. It is explained that the second appointment was obtained "by surprise," the confidence of Sir Edmond Prideaux and Sir William Pole having been "abused." The appointment by them, though purporting to be prior in date, is thereupon quashed (MS. Minutes, Quarter Sessions, Devonshire, Easter 1713). In a Middlesex case in 1708, four Overseers for St. Andrew's, Holborn, were appointed by the Justices at the Court House in Bloomsbury on the 7th of April, and officially "proclaimed in the parish church," only to find that four others had been appointed on the previous day by the Justices "at the King's Head in Holborn." On appeal to Quarter Sessions, the earlier appointment was confirmed (*Middlesex County Records, 1689-1709*, by W. J. Hardy, 1905, p. 327). Sometimes a tithing or township of a parish would get appointed separate Surveyors of Highways for its little area, after such officers had already been appointed by another set of Justices for the entire parish. Such a case came before the Hampshire Quarter Sessions at Easter 1742, in which Wigley and

held, with some doubt in cases where both acts had been
performed on the same day, that the first alone was valid,
by whatsoever Justices of the county it had been done.[1]
More serious than such duplicate orders, and, we imagine,
more common, was the habit of picking and choosing among
the Justices, in order to obtain lenient, partial, or merely
careless decisions.   Thus, in 1715, the four Overseers of
St. James's, Clerkenwell, fearing some objection, refused to
submit their accounts to the two magistrates living near
the parish, who had been accustomed to deal with this
business, and presented them to two other Justices of the
county, who were " surprised into allowing the said accounts."
On proof to Quarter Sessions that the allowance " was gained
by surprise," the order of the chosen Justices was quashed,
and the Overseers were ordered to submit their accounts to
the local magistrates.[2]   Still greater difficulty was found in
the licensing of ale-houses, which remained, down to 1729, in
the power of any two Justices of the county.   In Gloucestershire, in 1707, the Quarter Sessions feels compelled to
" recommend " to all the Justices " that they license no ale-
houses out of their own Division." [3]   The evil was naturally
seen at its worst in the unorganised agglomeration of houses
that already made up so much of the County of Middlesex.
In that county there were, in 1716, many magistrates quite
ready, as Quarter Sessions complained, " to grant licences to
persons who live out of their parishes and Divisions, . . . and
for want of a due knowledge and character of such persons
obtaining such licences several persons disaffected to His
Majesty's person and Government and of lewd and debauched

Cadnam sought thus to escape their contributions to the highways of the parish
of Eling, to which they belonged.   Quarter Sessions upheld the parish as a
whole (MS. Minutes, Quarter Sessions, Hampshire, 27th April 1742).

[1] R. v. Searle, 1714 ; R. v. Merchant and Allen, 1769 ; *A Collection of
Decisions of the King's Bench upon the Poor Laws*, by Francis Const, 1800, vol. i.
pp. 21, 25.   " Jurisdiction in any particular case attaches in the first set of
Justices duly authorised who have possession and cognisance of the fact, to the
exclusion of the separate jurisdiction of all others.   So that the acts of any
other, except in conjunction with the first, are not only void, but such a breach
of the law as subjects them to indictment" (*Law and Practice of Summary Conviction*, by W. Paley, 1814, p. 11 ; R. v. Sainsbury, *Term Reports*, vol. iv.
p. 456).

[2] MS. Minutes, Quarter Sessions, Middlesex, 28th April 1715.
[3] MS. Minutes, Quarter Sessions, Gloucestershire, Trinity 1707.

lives"[1] were keeping ale-houses. It was indeed "no uncommon occurrence for an individual whose licence had been suppressed to obtain surreptitiously, or by surprise, a renewal of that licence from a magistrate in some distant part of the county."[2] Even when offenders had been committed to gaol by some Justices, other magistrates of the county, "living at a great distance from the Justices who committed them, have, by false suggestions and misinformation, been prevailed upon, without the knowledge or privity of such Justices, . . . and without sending to know what information had been given against such offenders, to take insufficient bail for, or discharge and set at liberty, such offenders."[3] This concurrent jurisdiction and lack of definite areas was felt to be so paralysing to administration that the Middlesex Quarter Sessions adopted in 1716 elaborate "Rules and Directions" —which we doubt whether they could have enforced— insisting on all the Justices of the county restricting their action in granting licences, passing Overseers' accounts, making rates, or ordering poor relief, strictly to the parishes in which they actually resided, together with such parishes having no resident Justice as immediately adjoined their own. They were enjoined to refer other applicants to Justices residing in the parishes to which such applicants belonged, or, failing any, to those of parishes immediately adjoining them. They were urged "that for avoiding oppression by informers and other great inconveniences in putting in execution the laws against such persons who sell drink on Sundays, or [use] short or unsealed measures, or neglect to set up lights, and in all other offences of the like nature, they do confine themselves to the respective parishes wherein they dwell." Above all, they were abjured not to grant licences, even in their own parishes, "to any whose licence hath been taken away or suppressed or refused to be renewed by any other Justice"; and in no case to grant bail or to discharge

---

[1] MS. Minutes, Quarter Sessions, Middlesex, 6th December 1716. In Devonshire also we read of improper persons obtaining ale-house licences from two Justices "by surreptitious practices," and such licences are quashed by Quarter Sessions (MS. Minutes, Quarter Sessions, Devonshire, Michaelmas 1712).

[2] *Middlesex County Records, 1689-1709*, edited by W. J. Hardy, 1905, p. xv.

[3] *Ibid.*

offenders committed by other magistrates without sending to such magistrates for a full account of the alleged offence.[1]

(c) *The Special Sessions*

In spite of the assumption, by the whole Court of Quarter Sessions, of the minutest details of the Justice's work, and of the extensive powers accorded to the "Single Justice" and the "Double Justice," the magistrates residing in the several parts of the county were, as we have already mentioned, from the sixteenth century onward, encouraged, and even enjoined, by Royal Proclamations and judicial orders, to meet together at regular intervals for the systematic super- vision of the affairs of their particular districts. For this purpose the counties had been divided, as we have described, into geographical divisions, in many counties normally corresponding with the Hundreds. With what regularity and frequency the particular "private sessions" or "monthly meetings" referred to in the proclamations and injunctions of the earlier Stuarts were continued after the Civil War is not clear. After the Revolution, however, these general Divisional Sessions developed, under a series of statutes, into what eventually came to be known as "Special Sessions,"[2] held at stated times for particular kinds of county business. Thus, under the Act of 1691, all the Justices of each Division

---

[1] MS. Order of Middlesex Quarter Sessions, 6th December 1716. We gather that in some other counties the Court of Quarter Sessions determined the area of jurisdiction of individual magistrates. Thus, upon petition from the inhabitants of Yate in the Hundred of Henbury, the Gloucestershire Quarter Sessions made an order "allowing them for the future to apply themselves to the J.P.'s of the Hundred of Grombald's Ash" for the despatch of their parish and other business. Similar orders were made for other parishes (MS. Minutes, Gloucestershire Quarter Sessions, Epiphany 1726).

[2] These Divisional Sessions had at first no name. An order of the Hamp- shire Quarter Sessions in 1746 refers to "the Justices of the Peace who usually meet at Ringwood" (MS. Minutes, Quarter Sessions, Hampshire, 8th April 1746). As late as 1808 they are referred to only as "subdivision meetings" (MS. Minutes, Quarter Sessions, Cardiganshire, 27th April 1808). The term "Special Sessions" seems to have been only gradually adopted, and to have needed judicial definition. "A Special Sessions," said Mr. Justice Bayley, "means a sitting convened by reasonable notice to the other Justices of the Division" (R. *v.* The Justices of Worcestershire, *Reports of Cases*, etc., by R. V. Barnewall and E. H. Alderson, vol. ii. p. 233 ; Burn's *Justice of the Peace*, vol. v. p. 215 of 1820 edition). The term had originally been used for any Sessions of the Justices of the county as a whole for a special branch of their work (*Pleas of the Crown*, by W. Hawkins, vol. i. p. 42).

were periodically summoned for highway purposes to certain divisional meetings known as " Highway Sessions." Though the duties were, we fear, often perfunctorily performed, we must visualise " the Justices of each Division," as one of them tells us in 1767, holding, at the inn in the largest village, a "special Sessions once in four months, to receive from Surveyors an account of the state of the roads within their district, and to give directions for the amendment thereof; to examine, upon oath, into the application of money raised for the repairs, to punish the neglects of Surveyors, and to levy penalties upon defaulters." [1]

Gradually the device of special Divisional Sessions was made use of for other purposes. Thus, during the wars of the Spanish Succession we find the Justices for each Division sitting to superintend the enlisting of recruits for the army.[2] In 1745, when the Jacobites were invading England, we see Quarter Sessions appointing meetings of the Justices of each Division, to be held monthly during the ensuing half-year, "for enlisting soldiers pursuant to the late Order in Council."[3] But by far the most important of these ever-increasing divisional meetings were those held, from 1729 onwards, for the licensing of public-houses, when this power was taken out of the hands of any two Justices meeting when and where they chose. At these " Brewster Sessions " we see (to use a phrase of Sydney Smith) " the little clumps of squires and parsons gathered together in ale-houses in the month of September, so portentous to publicans," [4] in the " sessions room " at the village inn, which would be thronged with the ale-house keepers of the whole Division attending to answer complaints, to get their annual licences renewed, and to sign, with their sureties, the formal recognisances binding them to good behaviour. For the most part, we imagine, the Justices during the first half-century of "Brewster Sessions" granted and renewed ale-house licences with the greatest laxity, though we cannot say how far the following lively satire on a licensing sessions in 1754 may be accepted as typical. At " the Brewster

---

[1] *An Enquiry into the Means of Preserving and Improving the Public Roads,* by Henry Homer, 1767, p. 15.

[2] *Middlesex County Records, 1689-1714,* by W. J. Hardy, 1905, p. 301.

[3] So in MS. Minutes, Quarter Sessions, Suffolk, 24th April 1745.

[4] *Edinburgh Review,* September 1826.

Sessions at Bray in Northungria," five Justices are represented as being present. "Mrs. Drab" comes in to apply for a renewal of her licence; she brings a certificate signed by some of her neighbours, certifying that "Mrs. Drab, of the Round O, keeps a very regular and orderly house; and that we have been often entertained there with much pleasure, wit, and humour; and desire that her licence may be renewed; for we cannot live without her and hers."

Sir John Bear: "The Round O lies in my neighbourhood. I wish there was never a Round O near me; it debauches my servants. I could give many reasons why she ought not to have a licence." Mr. J. Lock then refers to "irregularities committed at the house in April," and "shameful doings in May and June," and "infamous revels in August." Other objections are made.

The Chairman: "Hem! hem! There are two Justices required to the granting every licence by the statute. Brother Friar, you and I must sign it. The woman must not be undone, nor the excise diminished. The house draws a great deal of ale, and pays a round sum into the office." (They sign the licence.) [1]

Down to 1786, at any rate, the remissness of the Justices in neglecting their powers of control was as complete and universal as their laxness in granting licences. The recognisances and surety bonds and certificates became mere meaningless formalities. In one county, at any rate—that of Durham—the "practice . . . had long prevailed of signing blank licences, and leaving them to be filled up at the discretion of the Clerk of the Peace." [2] Towards the latter

---

[1] *Gentleman's Magazine*, October 1754, vol. xxiv. p. 461.

[2] Paley, when Rector of Bishop Wearmouth and a Justice of the Peace for the County of Durham, induced his fellow-magistrates to abandon this lax practice (*Memoirs of William Paley, D.D.*, by G. W. Meadley, 1810, p. 192). The Justices seem to have allowed the recognisances to become a mere formality. Here is a description of the latter part of the eighteenth century: "On every day of licensing the Clerk of the Peace or his deputy attends the meeting of the Justices of the Peace, and upon a large roll takes a recognisance of the ale-house keeper, who produces any sureties without inquiry being made into their circumstances upon oath (which I admit the statute doth not empower the Justices to do), and for this he, the Clerk of the Peace, receives twelve pence (which I am sorry to say is the only advantage arises to any one from these recognisances), and then the roll is carried to the Clerk of the Peace's office and never heard of after. . . . And hereby is the statute of King Edward VI. evaded" (*Serious Thoughts in Regard to the Publick Disorders*, by a County

part of the century, as we have elsewhere described, the " Brewster Sessions " came to take its regulative duties more seriously. Sometimes one of the Justices, vain of his eloquence, would formally " charge " the motley assembly, reciting the duties of innkeepers and beer retailers, and admonishing them to obey the law. Thus, in 1819, we see the veteran Sir George Onesiphorus Paul proudly referring to his " forty years' participation in the execution of this duty in this Division," addressing a long and eloquent harangue to the company assembled at the " Brewster Sessions " at Horsley in Gloucestershire, and concluding with a warning against giving any encouragement to the seditious passions that unhappily prevailed " throughout the northern manufacturing districts." [1] Occasionally there would be presented petitions from the respectable inhabitants of particular parishes asking for the withdrawal of licences. " At the Petty Sessions held here," we read of Gloucester in 1786, " a petition was presented to the Justices by the principal inhabitants of the parish of Pitchcombe, stating that their Poor's Rates before the licensing an ale-house in the parish were two shillings in the pound, but since two ale-houses had been opened the common people have become idle, drunken, and profligate, and have spent their wages in the public-houses, leaving their families to be supported by the parish ; by which means the rates have lately risen to eight shillings in the pound." Upon this representation the Justices suppressed both the ale-houses.[2] There might even come a formal recommendation from the Vestry itself. Thus at Marylebone, in 1800, " the Vestry having been informed that application had been again made to the magistrates acting for the Holborn Division for the renewal of the licence to the public-house called the ' Wheatsheaf' in Callmel Buildings in this parish, which had been refused last year on account of the many irregularities committed in the said house by gamblers and other persons of the most abandoned characters, resolved unanimously, that in consideration of the advantages already derived to the peace-

Justice of the Peace, n.d. pp. 14, 15). The certificates also became formalities ; see *Seven Charges given to Grand Juries*, by Rev. Samuel Partridge, 1809, pp. 23-30, as regards the practice in Lincolnshire.

[1] *Bristol Journal*, 25th September 1819.

[2] *Leeds Intelligencer*, 26th September 1786.

able inhabitants of that neighbourhood, and of those likely to
accrue to them in future should the licence be refused, it be
recommended to the magistrates at their adjourned meeting
not to renew the said licence." [1] In 1816 the dominant idea
in the minds of the Justices at " Brewster Sessions " was the
iniquity of the brewers in creating " tied houses " and the
badness of their beer. At the " Brewster Sessions " at Christchurch, Hampshire, in 1816, the Justices, we read, " animadverted very strongly on the exorbitant price and improper
quality of beer sold at ale-houses under the control of public
brewers, and expressed their decided determination to enforce
the duty of ale-tasters on their district . . . apprising the
innkeepers that they would, . . . next year, provided any
complaints were made and sufficiently substantiated, of the
brewers of whom they rented their houses having sold them
beer of bad or improper quality, grant to such innkeepers
licences for houses of their own, so as to free them from the
control of such brewers." [2]

(d) *Petty Sessions*

The " Special Sessions " convened for highway or liquor-
licensing purposes left untouched the powers of individual
Justices or pairs of Justices in all other matters. Gradually,
however, the inconvenience of transacting magisterial business
in a private house, at all hours, without a regular clerk—
together with the necessity in many cases for the presence of
two Justices—led from the early part of the eighteenth
century to the regular holding of other divisional meetings,
which—apparently in imitation of the old Sessions held by
the High Constable of each Hundred—became universally
known as Petty Sessions.

This new organisation for the transaction of county
business arose sometimes on the initiative of individual
magistrates, sometimes at the express desire of Quarter
Sessions. In some counties, at any rate, the magistrates of
each Division seem voluntarily to have agreed to meet—or to
arrange for at least two among their number to meet—

---

[1] MS. Vestry Minutes, Marylebone (Middlesex), 13th September 1800.
[2] *Times*, 24th September 1816.

regularly, between the days appointed for " Special Sessions," at
the largest inn in one of the villages, or at the local market
town (if this had not corporation magistrates of its own), in
order to transact, in a formal Petty Sessions, such business as
required the concurrence of two Justices, or more legal
knowledge than they had individually at their command.[1]
The " Single Justice " sitting in his own parlour was thus, to a
large extent, spontaneously and, so to speak, extra-legally,
replaced by Divisional Sessional Courts. Naturally, the
counties differed as to the date and also as to the extent of
this supersession. It was in the County of Middlesex, with
its enormous urban population, that this development of Petty
Sessions first took place, and in that county it had certain
exceptional features. The lack of any efficient municipal
government outside the City of London, and the extraordinarily
disorganised state of the densely peopled Metropolitan
parishes, led to the spasmodic assumption by the Middlesex
Justices of more than the usual magisterial duties of interference in parochial affairs. This interference was exercised
not so much by casual pairs of Justices as by regular
Divisional Sessions, held at stated times and in public places.
Already, in 1705, we find Quarter Sessions insisting on this
reform. The Court "having information that Petty Sessions
are held in several places in the Holborn Division, and that
parish officers are frequently summoned to attend at several
places at one and the same time, is of opinion that the Petty
Sessions should be held at the known and usual place in each
Division, and that no such Sessions should be held during
General or Quarter Sessions." [2] But the work was too heavy,

---

[1] In the important unincorporated towns of Manchester and Birmingham,
there came to be established, by the end of the eighteenth century, a
"magistrate's office," at which a couple of county magistrates arranged to
attend, in rotation, once a week, or even more frequently. The Surrey Justices,
early in the nineteenth century, established what they called "the Rotation
Office" in Southwark, which they attended in turns as a public police court, in
order practically to oust both certain "Trading Justices" in their own Commission and the jurisdiction which the Aldermen of the City of London
attempted to exercise there.

[2] Order of April 1705 in *Middlesex County Records, 1689-1710*, by W. J.
Hardy, p. 287. In 1801 there was rivalry between the Justices of the Divisions
of Tavistock and Roborough in Devonshire, as to which of them should license
public-houses at Plymouth Dock. It had been generally agreed that the total
for the town should be limited to fifty, but each insisted on licensing as many as
it chose (Home Office Domestic Entry Book, vols. xxxviii. and xxxix., March to

and the interference too minute, to be done by the Justices meeting for the large Hundreds of the county, which were only six in number. One of these Hundreds, in fact, that of Ossulston, included much more than the whole of the Metropolitan area outside the City, Westminster, and the Tower Hamlets, and extended from the Brent on the west to the Lea on the east.[1] Hence we find created such subsidiary Divisions as Finsbury, Holborn, and Kensington alongside of Westminster and the Tower Hamlets. Moreover, within such Divisions, extensive and populous parishes, such as St. Martin's-in-the-Fields, St. Marylebone, and St. George's, Hanover Square, came, in the eighteenth century, to have regular Sessions of their own, at which not only was the highway and licensing business done, but also the whole parochial administration supervised and directed. Thus, in 1720, when the plague was raging in Marseilles and was daily expected to reach London, we see the Middlesex Quarter Sessions directing all the Justices of the county in their respective parishes to "hold a Petty Sessions one day at least in every week (except in such week in which the Quarter or General Sessions shall be held), to receive any informations that may be brought against parish officers or inhabitants," for breach of the hastily improvised sanitary regulations which they issued. They recommended also that the Justices in every parish "do once within the year (at least) take a view of all the wards, districts, or divisions in the said parish, and punish all persons offending."[2] Two years later we watch, in the lively pages of a contemporary narrative, the "Justices of Covent Garden," in response "to the commands

October, 1801, in Public Record Office). As late as 1826 we hear of two rival Petty Sessions of Kent Justices in the parish of Deptford, one set of four magistrates insisting on meeting weekly at "The Centurion" public-house, whilst another set had, since 1813, assembled weekly at another public-house in the parish. The Chairman of the Justices of the Division appealed for the intervention of the Home Secretary, but the dispute was eventually settled amicably (Home Office Magistrates' Book, in Public Record Office, 1826).

[1] "The Hundreds of Middlesex," in *London and Middlesex Notebook*, by W. P. W. Phillimore, 1892, p. 9. Even the Divisions so created within the County of Middlesex became inconveniently extensive. In 1801-1821 their population is given as follows :—Westminster, 1801, 153,272 ; 1821, 182,085 : Finsbury, 1801, 73,268 ; 1821, 119,802 : Holborn, 1801, 175,820 ; 1821, 276,630 : Kensington, 1801, 40,642 ; 1821, 70,808 : Tower Hamlets, 1801, 189,293 ; 1821, 291,650 (Home Office Magistrates' Book, Public Record Office).

[2] MS. Minutes, Quarter Sessions, Middlesex, 6th December 1720.

they received from Lord Townshend," holding no fewer than twenty Petty Sessions in the course of six weeks—sometimes sitting formally in the vestry of St. Paul's Church, sometimes meeting " by surprise " in one of the taverns of the Strand—in order " to rout out or at least check " the demoralising and licentious practices of the gambling-dens and disorderly houses for which their neighbourhood was becoming shamefully notorious. Finding that, in spite of all precautions, the keepers of the houses got wind of their projected raids, we see the more determined of the reforming Justices agreeing to being privately summoned by their chairman, or by one another, so as to exclude from their counsels such of their own body as were in league with the offenders.[1] Again, in 1730, when assaults and robberies in the streets were specially common, Quarter Sessions recommends the Justices " to meet and hold Petty Sessions once a week or oftener in their respective parishes or divisions, so long as occasion shall require, for the discovery, apprehending, and bringing to justice offenders who have committed . . . street robberies, etc. and to suppress persons who keep disorderly houses, and to give strict orders to the Constable to apprehend vagrants, and to proceed against persons who sell spirits and suffer tippling, according to law ; and to call before them the respective Parish Constables and watchmen of every parish, hamlet, and place, and to see that there be a sufficient number of proper and able watchmen for the guard and security of their several parishes, and that their stands and walks be duly regulated." [2] In 1746 the Justices were recommended to " hold their Petty Sessions twice in every week." [3]

That the Middlesex Justices held Petty Sessions in and for particular parishes—often at the Vestry Hall itself—and constantly intervened in the civil administration of the parish, at any rate during the first half of the eighteenth century, is clearly proved, though from the paucity of Petty Sessional records comparatively few examples can be cited. Thus in 1712, as we find by the accidental preservation of a single document, the Justices of St. Giles-in-the-Fields, in

---

[1] *An Account of the Endeavours that have been used to suppress Gaming-Houses,* 1722 ; see Home Office Domestic State Papers in Public Record Office, 1721-1722.

[2] MS. Minutes, Quarter Sessions, Middlesex, 3rd December 1730.

[3] *Ibid.* 10th December 1746.

Petty Sessions assembled, made a series of detailed orders on the occasion of some parochial upheaval. They declare in a preamble that "divers sums of money have been of late years unnecessarily expended in this parish," and "for preventing thereof in future . . . and that the present and succeeding Churchwardens, Overseers, paymasters of the poor, and other officers concerned, may have due notice and govern themselves accordingly," they resolve and order on a dozen different points of financial administration. They direct "that no money be allowed to any Churchwarden for any expenses at his election," and "that no allowance or payment be made to or for any vestryman's expenses at any meeting of the Vestry." They limit the expenses for Vestry dinners to £17 a year, and order the perambulation of the bounds to take place only triennially. They cut down the bell-ringing and the ringer's fees; they deprive the Parish Clerk of the charges he has been making for writing out lists of pauper funerals and for stationery; they even try to limit the number of inquests and the Coroner's fees. They declare that "if any of the collectors of the parish rates, without leave from two Justices, take less of any of the inhabitants than what is charged in their books, they shall be accountable for the whole sum charged." Finally, they give a series of directions as to the rudiments of parish book-keeping, and specially order that no bills exceeding forty shillings be paid unless they have been signed and allowed by three vestrymen or by two or more Justices in Petty Sessions.[1] So, at a Petty Sessions for St. George's, Hanover Square, in 1738, we read that the Justices, on allowing the Overseers' accounts, came to the following decision, which is entered as an order of Petty Sessions: "That the present Overseers of the Poor have notice given them by the Clerk that they do not disburse

---

[1] St. Giles-in-the-Fields (Middlesex), Order of 5th August 1712, by two Justices in Petty Sessions, a printed broadsheet in the British Museum (816 m. 9, 74). See also Home Office Domestic State Papers, 19th September 1720. We find similar regulations, by the Justices in Petty Sessions, for the parish of St. Marylebone between 1730 and 1775, sanctioning the conditions under which the poor were "farmed," regulating the use of the badge for all paupers, ordering the Overseers not to appoint any person as "apothecary" except after election by the Vestry, and (in 1745) giving detailed instructions to the Overseers as to the method of relief. Similar orders appear in 1738 as to the work of the Surveyor of Highways (MS. Minutes, Petty Sessions, Marylebone, 1730-1775).

or give away any monies to casual poor except upon extraordinary occasions, or by the consent of some magistrate of
this parish signified by writing under his hand; and that
they do not send any poor into the workhouse except upon
urgent occasion. It appearing by the butcher's bill in
the late Overseers' accounts that a great quantity of mutton
is used in the house, which we are of opinion is unnecessary,
and occasions a greater number of people to come and continue
therein, it is hereby ordered that the Master of the Workhouse have notice to send for less mutton, and that only when
the doctor directs it, by thinking it absolutely necessary for
sick patients." In the following month we find the same
Justices, on passing the accounts of the Surveyor of Highways, peremptorily forbidding the provision of strong beer for
the labourers on the roads.[1] In the adjoining parish of St.
Margaret's, Westminster, there are fortunately preserved the
detailed minutes of proceedings of the Justices in Petty
Sessions for nearly a century.[2] From 1708, at least, we find
the "Justices for the Parish" attending "at the Vestry room"
once or twice a month, between two and six at a time, to give
orders for poor relief and to issue directions to the Overseers,
the Scavengers, and the Constables, whilst they occasionally
"suppressed" an ale-house and dealt with any other local
business that needed their authority. We see them formulating elaborate Standing Orders for the government of the
Overseers in the assessment and collection of the rates,[3]
commanding a "privy search" for vagrants,[4] deciding what
relief should be given to particular paupers,[5] insisting that
the paupers should be made to wear the statutory badge,[6]
summoning all the Scavengers to attend before them,[7] dis-

---

[1] MS. Minutes of Petty Sessions for St. George's, Hanover Square (Middlesex), 10th July and 5th August 1738. These meetings of the magistrates
resident within each parish served also as Special Sessions. In 1816 it was
given in evidence that "in the parishes in Westminster the public-houses are
licensed by the parochial magistrates in each parish" (Report of House of
Commons Committee on the State of the Police of the Metropolis, 1816, p. 77).

[2] These MS. Minutes of the "Westminster Petty Sessions," beginning in
1708, are in the custody of the Westminster City Council. After the middle
of the century the meetings cease gradually to deal with poor relief, and
become evidently those of the "Vestry Justices" described in Book I. Chap.
VI. Close Vestry Administration.

[3] MS. Minutes, Westminster Petty Sessions, 1708.

[4] *Ibid.* 22nd July 1712.   [5] *Ibid.* 5th May 1716.

[6] *Ibid.* 28th May 1719.   [7] *Ibid.* 10th August 1721.

charging Constables from office for neglect of duty,[1] deciding
which poor persons should be put "on the Collection," and
forbidding all other regular doles;[2] systematically overhauling this list of standing pensioners,[3] and enforcing on
recalcitrant householders in some cases a total prohibition,
and in others a limitation in the number, of "inmates."[4]

In the ordinary rural county the work of the Justices did
not need so elaborate an organisation as that of the Metropolitan parishes. We see that Overseers continued to be
appointed, rates to be signed, and accounts to be allowed by
casual pairs of Justices meeting when and where they chose.
Similarly the country Justice long continued in his own house
to deal with every offender whom the Parish Constable brought
into his "justice-room." But the wiser and more experienced
magistrates, who in most counties formed the governing cliques
of the Quarter Sessions of the close of the eighteenth century,
persistently discouraged this anarchic jurisdiction, and advised
the institution of regular divisional meetings at stated times
and places. Already in 1770 we find the Essex Quarter
Sessions supplying one set of the statutes for the common use
of the magistrates of each Division of the county, and in 1786,
also a copy of Burn's *Justice of the Peace.*[5] Presently we have
definite recommendations. In 1782 the Middlesex magistrates
formally agreed in general meeting, that they "should meet in
their several Divisions, and then subdivide themselves, for the
purpose of" drastically suppressing rogues and vagabonds.[6] In
1786, at the beginning of the movement for a "reformation of
manners" that we elsewhere describe, we see the West Riding
Justices resolving that it would "be of great public benefit if
all Justices of the Peace would please to hold a Special

---

[1] MS. Minutes, Westminster Petty Sessions, 9th November 1719.
[2] *Ibid.* 3rd August 1721.   [3] *Ibid.* 10th August 1721.
[4] *Ibid.* 9th and 23rd November 1721. The Justices insisted that all orders
for removal should be dealt with at their Petty Sessional meetings ; and even
resolved that no parish rates or accounts "shall be allowed or signed except
in Petty Sessions" (*Ibid.* 15th September 1720). So in Chelsea in 1748, we
find a Middlesex Justice, after consulting the Chairman of Quarter Sessions,
absolutely declining to allow a rate "out of sessions" (MS. Vestry Minutes,
Chelsea, 27th October 1748).

[5] MS. Minutes, Quarter Sessions, Essex, 2nd October 1770, 11th July
1786.

[6] Home Office Domestic State Papers in Public Record Office, 8th November
1782.

Sessions in the several districts once a fortnight (as it is already done in several parts of this Riding) or even oftener, at least for some time, if they find occasion for so doing."[1] So in Gloucestershire in 1787, stimulated by the Royal Proclamation against vice and immorality, Quarter Sessions declares it to be "essentially necessary to the carrying any useful system into effect that regular periodical Sessions should be held in each district for the transacting such business as demands two Justices." The Magistrates are accordingly requested to "confer with each other, and establish certain periodical Sessions to be held as frequently as is consistent with their convenience."[2] The adjoining county of Somerset followed suit. At the next ensuing Sessions, they definitely attribute much of the debauchery, petty crime, and disorder, to which the Home Secretary had called their attention, to "the want of fixed periodical Petty Sessions to be held in each district for the superintendence and regulation of the conduct of the officers of the public peace and economy." They accordingly "recommend to the magistrates of the county to establish fixed and periodical Petty Sessions in their respective districts, so regulated that the gentry and clergy of the neighbourhood may be induced to attend them." . . . And whereas "it appears, from the reports made to this bench, that many parts of this county must be deprived of the benefit of such Petty Sessions, from a deficiency of acting Justices to undertake the duty; whilst many gentlemen whose names are in the Commission of the Peace reside in the district without qualifying themselves to act as magistrates," these are urged to take out their Dedimus.[3] As such regular Petty Sessions became general they were, for the most part, merely inter-

---

[1] Resolution of Justices at Quarter Sessions, West Riding, 24th April, 1786 ; in *Leeds Intelligencer*, 16th May.

[2] MS. Minutes, Quarter Sessions, Gloucestershire, Michaelmas, 1787. Contemporaneously a Durham Justice reports to the Home Secretary that "We have a respectable meeting of Justices every fortnight at Durham" (John Eden, 17th October 1787, in Home Office Domestic Papers in Public Record Office). In 1812, three Warwickshire Justices reported from Aston, near Birmingham, "We hold a Petty Sessions at this place regularly every Wednesday, where we transact the business of an extensive district, and not a little that arises in the town of Birmingham cn those days that the magistrates acting for that town do not sit" (*Ibid.* No. 237, 1812).

[3] Orders of the General Quarter Sessions at Bridgewater, Somerset, Epiphany, 1788 ; see *Bristol Gazette*, 24th January 1788.

calated with the statutory Special Sessions, the like summonses
being issued for them to all the acting Justices of the Division.
By the end of the first quarter of the nineteenth century,
regular Divisional Sessions of this kind, monthly, fortnightly,
or weekly, had become practically universal. We are told, in
1827, that " in most large market towns Special Sessions for
licensing ale-houses, appointing parish officers, etc. are held at
the principal inn ; and as on these occasions such business as
requires two or more Justices is generally brought forward, it
has become the general practice for the neighbouring Justices
to meet sometimes once a fortnight, sometimes every market
day, to transact the business of a Petty Sessions." [1]   At these
Divisional Sessions, Sydney Smith describes the little group of
country gentlemen and clergy as " overwhelmed with all the
monthly business of the Hundred " [2] turning alternately to
one or the other side of their work without consciousness of
distinction between them.   More generally, the judicial work
was done " in open court," whilst the local government work
was transacted in private.   Thus, at the Aylesbury Petty
Sessions, in April 1829, " the magistrates divided, one-half of
them remaining in the room usually devoted to the Petty
Sessions business to audit and pass Overseers' accounts, the
others adjourning to the Clerk's office, to hear and examine
criminal charges." [3]   At these Divisional Sessions, too, took
place whatever effective administration there was of the
statutes against false weights and measures ; and we see
occasionally all the Chief Constables of Hundreds and Liberties
summoned to attend, bringing with them the reports of the
special inspection and examination that they were supposed to
make of " the weights and measures of all shopkeepers, inn-
holders, victuallers, and all housekeepers within their respective
Hundreds and Liberties." [4]   Occasionally we find the Justices

---

[1] *Summary of the Duties of a Justice of the Peace out of Session*, by Henry
James Pye, 4th edition, 1810, p. 13.

[2] *Edinburgh Review*, 1820 ; *Works*, vôl. ii. p. 138 of 1854 edition.

[3] *Bucks Gazette*, 4th April 1829.

[4] See, for instance, the notice for the Petty Sessional Division of Basingstoke,
Hampshire, in *Reading Mercury*, 6th August 1787.   At such meetings the
social dinner of the Justices was evidently a prominent feature.   " A Trading
Justice," says the *Gentleman's Magazine* in 1769, "when it is his turn to
appoint the monthly meeting, puts it up to auction, and the dinner is ordered
to be got at the house of the best bidder (oftentimes some paltry ale-house),
where we fare very ill and pay very high, or the poor ale-house keeper would be

using their divisional meetings as an opportunity for consulting the leading citizens of the parishes within their Division ;
as when, in 1800, the magistrates for Basingstoke by public
advertisement formally requested " the attendance of the
parish officer and principal inhabitants . . . to take into
consideration the expediency of lessening the consumption of
wheat flour." [1] More usually the Justices took the opportunity
of announcing their own opinion as to the parochial administration. We learn by chance that the Justices of the Petty
Sessional Division of Ploughley, in Oxfordshire, at the close of
the year 1818 were, on the supremely important question of
the " rate in aid of wages," talking wisely but acting weakly—
a course which we suspect was widely followed by many, if not
all the benches in the Southern counties. At this obscure
Petty Sessions, in December 1818, " It was resolved that the
practice of permitting the labouring poor to be paid wages for
their labour, partly by those who employ them and partly out
of the Poor's Rate, is most mischievous and unjust ; that it
not only destroys all the power of the master over the servant,
and all the respect of the servant for the master, but that it
tends to the waste of half the time that ought to be applied to
labour, and one-half of the money received by the labouring
poor. The magistrates, therefore, are determined to do everything in their power to put an end to that practice, and for
that purpose they declare that they will not hereafter pass or
sign any Overseer's account unless such Overseer shall make
oath that since the first day of December 1818 no money has
been paid out of the poor's book to make up the wages of such
labourer who shall have worked for any other person." But
in spite of this grandiloquent protest, the Justices weakened
in their resolve, and at the very meeting at which it was

a loser by the bargain " (*Gentleman's Magazine*, December 1769, p. 539). In
the Tower Hamlets Division of Middlesex in 1727 there seems to have been " a
subscription of the Justices . . . towards the support of the Justices' dinner
. . . during the first three days of every Sessions " held for that important
Division (MS. Minutes, Quarter Sessions, Middlesex, 1st July 1727). Sometimes, it is clear, the dinner at Special Sessions was paid for out of the fees. In
1692, in an elaborate order providing for a division of the fees for ale-house
licences among the justices' clerks and the Clerk of the Peace, the West Riding
Quarter Sessions orders the latter first to deduct " the necessary charges of the
Justices who shall respectively act " (MS. Minutes, Quarter Sessions, West
Riding, 5th April 1692).

[1] *Reading Mercury*, 6th January 1800.

made, they concluded by agreeing that the wages of married couples might be made up to 7s. 6d. per week, with 1s. 6d. extra for each child under ten.[1] At a Berkshire bench of magistrates in 1828, Dr Mitford is reported as announcing that " the magistrates are determined to enforce the provisions of the law in every respect. They will not allow one shilling hereafter for any foolish parish feasting and drinking; no such accounts will be passed, and if parish officers choose to indulge in feasting they shall pay every farthing themselves." [2] In the hard times of 1829-1830, when the growth of pauperism in the agricultural counties of the south of England has become both a danger and a scandal, we get, from a local newspaper, many glimpses of the sayings and doings of the Justices at the Aylesbury Petty Sessions. At every meeting they discuss the " heavy complaints " of the poor. On one occasion the contractor for the poor, who " farmed" them at a fixed sum, is complained of as having reduced the weekly allowance to the aged in order to recoup the loss he had sustained during the summer.[3] Another time, the Overseer " appearing in the chamber on parish business," receives from the chairman a series of impracticable proposals to " set the poor to work " on the land.[4] The orders of the Justices varied, indeed, according to the idiosyncrasies of those who happened to attend. At one meeting we find the chairman definitely advising that the parish authorities should " propose to the agriculturalists to employ all the surplus labour at full price, one-half or one-third of their wages being made up from the rates." [5] But only five weeks later, at the same Petty Sessions, when the Overseer of another parish attended to get his rate allowed, another Justice acting as chairman refuses his application, on the ground that the magistrates had decided to refuse to " pass the Overseer's accounts where the practice existed of paying farmers' labourers from the funds collected

---

[1] *Globe*, 3rd December 1818, quoted in *Thoughts on Poverty and the Poor Laws*, by the Rev. Robert Walker, 1819.

[2] *Morning Herald* some time during 1828, quoted in *Considerations on Select Vestries*, p. 27.

[3] *Bucks Gazette*, 14th November and 26th December 1820. By the Act, 45 George III. c. 54 (1805), all contracts for farming the poor required the sanction of two Justices (Sir George Nicholls' *History of the English Poor Law*, ii. 147).

[4] *Ibid.* 23rd January 1830.   [5] *Ibid.* 26th December 1829.

for the relief of the poor." [1]   On another occasion we hear of
an Overseer's book being handed back unsigned, because the
magistrates insisted on the old rate being collected before a
new one was levied.[2]   But perhaps the most extraordinary
case is that of the "poor of Haddenham," who are reported as
coming to the Petty Sessions to make "their accustomed complaint that the Overseers were in arrear with their weekly
stipends.   To one man eight weeks' money was due, and others
had arrears for five, four, and three weeks owing to them."
The magistrates ordered the money to be paid.   The Overseer
replied that he could not collect the rates, much land being
unoccupied.   The magistrates thereupon advised him to borrow
money for the use of the parish, but the Overseer retorted that
"no one will lend on the security of the rates." [3]   Finally, we
even have the Justices in Petty Sessions acting as a court of
appeal against the Overseers' decisions in the grant of relief.
Thus, ten paupers appeared on one occasion to complain that
they had not been paid.   The Overseer explained that, before
they had completed their task of work, they had, without permission, "gone to the St. Albans' races, where they said they
could earn more money than off the parish by holding gentlemen's horses."   The bench nevertheless ordered the Overseer
to pay the amount claimed.   Another time a pauper appeared
to complain that the Overseer allowed him only 1s. 6d. a
week.   The Overseer explained that this was because the
pauper was in receipt of 8s. a week from his club or friendly
society.   The magistrates ordered the allowance to be increased
to 3s. 6d. a week, one of them, a clergyman, observing that if
parishes acted in this way no one would subscribe to clubs.
And to cite one more decision, when a crowd of paupers
appeared, with clamorous demand for relief, and the Overseer
explained to the bench that it had been suspended because the
paupers had been out gleaning, "which would enable them to
support themselves," the humane Justices decided that "there
ought not to be any deduction on that account.   Gleaning
existed from time immemorial, and the trifling benefit the poor
derived from it they were allowed to enjoy as a boon and a
blessing." [4]

---

[1] *Bucks Gazette*, 30th January 1830. [2] *Ibid.* 9th January 1830.
[3] *Ibid.* 9th January 1830. [4] *Ibid.* 1829-1830.

(e) *The Servants of the Justices*

For all the multifarious business falling upon the " Single Justice " or the " Double Justice," or transacted at Special or Petty Sessions, the legal constitution of the county provided no salaried assistance of any kind. There were, it was true, the parish officers—the Overseers, the Surveyors of Highways and the Petty Constables—all nominally obliged, in their several parishes and in their own branches of work, to receive the orders and carry out the instructions of the Justices of the Peace. But these parish officers, during the whole of the eighteenth century, and, in rural parishes, also during the nineteenth century, were unpaid citizens, annually elected; serving under compulsion; belonging to the small profit-making or wage-earning class; and, even if they happened to have zeal and capacity, unable to give more than a fraction of their time to public business. When it became customary for urban parishes to appoint " hireling " or stipendiary Overseers, Watchmen, or Surveyors, these officers, as we have described in our chapters on the Parish, naturally took their orders from their paymasters, the Parish Vestries, and considered themselves less than ever as the servants of the Justices.[1] Moreover, much of the work that fell upon the Justices was not within the legal duties of any parish officer; and in the majority of cases, no such officer was even in attendance. The Justices had, therefore, to look for assistance elsewhere than to the local officers recognised by the law.

For the payment of any new subordinate, otherwise than out of the Justices' own pockets, there was one source, and one source only, namely, the fees of which legal custom authorised the exaction from practically every person who

---

[1] Such stipendiary parish officers were, it is true, still subject to the orders of the Justices in all that concerned the legal obligations of the parish in their several departments, and they could be proceeded against and fined for any act of disobedience. But, if such officers were supported by their Vestries, the cost of their defence, and even their fines, might be defrayed out of the parish funds; whilst the prosecuting Justices would find themselves mulcted in time, temper, and expenses. Thus, in effect, it was exactly in these parishes, as we have demonstrated, that the Justices exercised the least control over the parish business.

sought the help of the Justice, or was brought before him. Whether, and to what extent these fees had ever been taken by the Justices themselves—apart from those who in Middlesex and occasionally elsewhere earned the epithet of "Trading Justices"—remains uncertain. In the eighteenth century, at any rate, such a practice was repudiated by reputable magistrates. "I know," said an enthusiastic and newly-appointed Leicestershire Justice, "that the fees accustomed and costs limited by statute are mentioned and allowed of in the oath of office, but, gentlemen, as far as yourselves are concerned, touch them not, make an open, a solemn, an absolute renunciation of them all, and avoid as much as possible not only the crime, but even the very suspicion of gain." [1] But though

---

[1] *The Justice of the Peace's Manual*, by a Gentleman of the Commission, 1771, p. 42. The words of the oath are : "You shall take nothing for your office of Justice of the Peace to be done, but of the King, and fees accustomed, and costs limited by statute" (*Justice of the Peace*, by R. Burn, vol. ii. p. 88 of 1756 edition ; *Select Statutes and other Constitutional Documents*, by G. W. Prothero, 1898, p. 149). That those Middlesex Justices who attended the Westminster Petty Sessions in 1717 took the recognisance and other fees for themselves personally, is clear from a case recorded in their minutes, in which a rebellious citizen who objected to the payment of a salary to the Clerk out of the parish rates, was expressly told that the Justices kept all the fees they exacted (MS. Minutes, Westminster Petty Sessions, 24th July 1724). In 1721 a correspondent of the Home Office in Devonshire states that the Justices share the licensing fees with their own clerks (Home Office Domestic State Papers in Public Record Office, 17th November 1721). We have already mentioned that an equitable sharing of these fees among all the Justices' Clerks of the county, together with the Clerk of the Peace, was ordered in 1692 by the West Riding Quarter Sessions. "Whereas . . . some Justices of Peace Clerks have at these Special Sessions received three times the advantage of others whose masters have acted as much as any in the service of their Majesties' country ; and whereas . . . every Justice . . . within this Riding hath equally power to act at the Special Sessions as well within any other Division in this Riding as in that wherein he is resident, notwithstanding several differences have been occasioned . . . ; for the preventing, therefore, of the same for the future it is ordered that the Clerk of the Peace for this Riding shall receive all the moneys arising for ale-house licences at the several Special Sessions, . . . and that at the end of every such Sessions . . . the said Clerk of the Peace shall first out of the same moneys defray the necessary charges of the Justices . . . and of himself, and such Justices' Clerks, and shall then draw up an account . . . The said Clerk of the Peace shall keep for his own use one moiety of all the said moneys (such charges as aforesaid first deducted), and shall distribute the other moiety amongst the respective Clerks of such Justices as shall have acted, . . . share and share alike ; and no Justice's Clerk to have more than one share even though his master signed such account in two or more Divisions" (MS. Minutes, Quarter Sessions, West Riding, 5th April 1692). The emoluments so derived by the Clerks gave them, it is clear, a direct interest in multiplying ale-houses. "The fees allowed to Justices' Clerks at the Brewster Sessions," writes the Foreman of the Grand Jury of York in 1787, "are the occasion for many improper or superfluous houses being licensed ; . . . it is an object essentially

these fees were foregone as emoluments by the Justices themselves, they furnished a means of remunerating the clerical labour which the country gentlemen were frequently neither willing nor competent themselves to undertake. Hence we see emerging, already in the seventeenth century, a new official, unknown to the legal constitution of the county, in the Justice's Clerk.

We have already referred, in the preceding chapter, to the Justice's Clerk in his relation to the magistrate acting in his own house. When the Justices met at Divisional Sessions, they seem, during the first half of the eighteenth century, to have taken with them their personal clerks, who shared the fees among themselves. " I was at a Sessions for licensing ale-houses held at a trading town in Wilts," writes a correspondent to the *Gentleman's Magazine* in 1739, " where there were seven Justices sitting, one of whose clerks told me with an air of gladness that his share came to between three and four pounds." [1] But the plan of each magistrate having his own clerical menial seldom provided him with any trustworthy legal advice, and opened the door to many abuses. To avoid these abuses, " some few Justices of the Peace in different parts of the County of Gloucester," we read in 1788, " have made a practice of officiating as their own clerks, and from motives of liberality declining to take the customary fees; but this has been found to have an unfavourable tendency by promoting applications to the magistrates on matters extremely frivolous. These gentlemen have therefore resolved to take the fees and bestow them on the objects of the Sunday Institution." [2] Gisborne, too, in 1794, notes that benevolent magistrates sometimes remit all fees, but warns them that this has been found undesirable, as leading to unnecessary litigation. [3] A way out of this dilemma was meanwhile being found in another direction.

worth the attention of Government " (Thomas Frankland to Home Secretary, 19th March 1787 ; No. 108 in MS. Domestic State Papers in Public Record Office). [1] *Gentleman's Magazine*, January 1739, p. 8.

[2] *Bristol Journal*, 1st March 1788.

[3] *The Duties of Men*, by Thomas Gisborne, 1794, p. 290. It was recorded of William Hay, M.P., Chairman of the East Sussex Quarter Sessions, and for thirty years an active magistrate, that he did not "suffer any, even the smallest, fee to be taken in his house" (*Works*, of William Hay, M.P., 1794, vol. i. preface, p. ix.).

With the growing importance and frequency of Special
Sessions, and the upgrowth of regularly-held Petty Sessions,
it became possible for the Justices collectively to obtain
the assistance of a local attorney, not, it is true, at their
own houses, but at their meetings in the little towns or
villages where these Divisional Sessions were held. There
was no legal provision for the appointment of any officer
by or for the Divisional Sessions itself. What seems to
have happened is that the Justices of the Division all
agreed, expressly or tacitly, to make use, as their clerk,
of the same local attorney, and to let him receive all the fees.
The Justice's Clerk, attending or residing at the private
house of the country gentleman, in this way gradually
ceased to exist. When any person importuned a magistrate at his private house on any business requiring a
warrant or other instrument, he was generally referred to
the office of the attorney in the market town, who took
the fee and prepared the necessary document to be signed
by the magistrate when he rode in to attend the Divisional
Sessions.[1] In cases of emergency the Justice might sometimes act on his own responsibility when he charged no fee,
leaving it, however, open to the Clerk to the Petty Sessions
to add to it anything due on subsequent proceedings. Under
such an arrangement the work was doubtless better done, and
the public had the convenience of an office to which they
could resort at any time for the transaction of preliminary
formalities. But when every item of business came to be
part of a solicitor's bill, the fees exacted evidently increased
in magnitude and variety. Every Constable who had to be
sworn in, every Surveyor of Highways or Overseer of the Poor
on whom office was cast, every parish officer who wanted his
accounts allowed or rate sanctioned, was mulcted in a fee of
from one to ten shillings.[2] Similar fees were levied for

---

[1] So described for Gloucestershire by Charles Bathurst, J.P. to Home Office,
23rd September 1836 (in Home Office Magistrates Book in Public Record
Office). It was objected in 1830 that magistrates were assuming "that there is
no occasion for their acting on any other day, making themselves weekly
magistrates only" (Home Office Domestic State Papers, No. 4, March 1830).

[2] In Devonshire, in 1769, the Justices' Clerks had to be expressly forbidden
to exact a fee on the mere swearing to the correctness of the bills for work done
on the county bridges (MS. Minutes, Quarter Sessions, Devonshire, Easter,
1769).

every document prepared by the Clerk, whether summons, warrant, certificate, recognisance, licence, or pass. The defendant committed to gaol or admitted to bail, the witness bound over to give evidence, the householder forced to take a pauper boy as apprentice, the farmer compounding for Statute Duty on the highways, the reputed father charged for the keep of a bastard, even the pauper obtaining an order for relief, or the vagrant sentenced to be whipped—all had to pay the customary fee. This inevitably led to a shameless heaping up of fees, amounting, in the worst cases, to positive oppression.[1] This we find the Justices trying to check by fixing tables of authorised fees. Thus, the Gloucestershire Quarter Sessions in 1718, reciting that the Justices' Clerks in many parts of the county often do not know what fees they may properly take, enact an elaborate schedule of the fees that may alone be taken on each item of business. This table is to be printed and everywhere placed on record in "the parish books," so that the parish officers may not in future be overcharged. A similar table was settled by the Devonshire Quarter Sessions in 1737.[2] To ensure similar protection in all counties, Parliament, in 1753, required Quarter Sessions everywhere to make a table of Justices' Clerks' fees, confirm it at a subsequent sessions, and submit it for approval to the Assize Judges.[3] But such tables were

---

[1] In one case, at any rate, the amount of the fees exacted by Justices or their Clerks became the subject of formal presentment by the Grand Jury. At the Essex Quarter Sessions in 1698 the Grand Jury reports as under :— "We also present Francis Stern, Clerk, for demanding and taking extortive fees, viz. five shillings for one pair of apprentices indentured for binding our parish children. We also present Robert Aylett, Clerk, for the like ; and also present Henry Foxwell, Clerk, for the like offence. We also present the said Francis Stern, Robert Aylett, and Henry Foxwell for taking two shillings and sixpence for confirmation of the Poor's Rate. We also present Robert Aylett aforesaid for taking one shilling from one Robert Gitley for being [word obscure] an office about births and burials. We also present Edmond Butler, jur., for taking one shilling for a printed warrant and directions about the Capitation Act. We also present John Sharpe, Robert Berryman, and Robert Brooks for the like offence " (Presentment of Grand Jury at Chelmsford, 11th January 1698 ; in Sessions Bundle 8, among Essex Quarter Sessions Archives).

[2] MS. Minutes, Quarter Sessions, Gloucestershire, Epiphany, 1718 ; *ibid.* Devonshire, Michaelmas, 1737. The Shropshire Justices in 1718 ordered "an inquiry to be made whether Justices' Clerks take any fees not allowed by the table " (*Shropshire County Records*, part ii., edited by Sir Offley Wakeman, pp. vi., 33).

[3] 26 Geo. II. c. 14 (1753), and, as to Middlesex, 27 Geo. II. c. 16, sec. 4 (1754). For examples of such tables see MS. Minutes, Quarter Sessions,

seldom known to the poor wretches of offenders, and seldom
regarded by the parish officers, from whom the fees were
exacted. "The Clerk," we are told in 1832, "makes out a
long bill of fees, totally disregarding all allowed tables of
fees; no common suitor of a Petty Sessions daring to dispute
the authority of the Clerk to charge what he pleases." The
Clerk, it was alleged, even got "summonses and warrants
ready signed" in blank, to issue as required. "I may
positively state," declares this critic, "they have been sold at
so much the dozen ready signed, a blank being left for the
name and cause of complaint."[1] It was an incidental result
of such an origin of the office, and such a method of remuneration, that the Clerk to the Petty and Special Sessions
inevitably came to regard himself merely as registrar of the
Court, and legal adviser to the individual Justices, rather
than executive officer or secretary to an administrative
committee; and it is to this habit of mind that we attribute
the fact that official records of these important local authorities
appear to have been seldom either made or preserved.[2]

Dorsetshire, 1st May 1753 ; *ibid.* Surrey, 18th July 1753 ; *ibid.* Breconshire,
10th July 1753 ; *ibid.* Cardiganshire, 17th July 1765 ; *ibid.* Devonshire,
Easter and Midsummer, 1806 ; *ibid.* Buckinghamshire, Michaelmas, 1811 ; *ibid.*
Gloucestershire, Easter, 1835. When the Assize Judges at York had, in 1827,
rejected the table of fees submitted by the West Riding Quarter Sessions as unnecessarily liberal, the Home Secretary refused to act as a Court of Appeal (Home
Office Domestic Entry Book, 25th October 1827). It was successfully argued in
the Court of King's Bench in 1826 that the office of Clerk to the Divisional
Sessions was not a "public and responsible office, and known to the law, . . .
but [its holder was] merely the private assistant of the magistrates, and no way
responsible to the public for his acts or omissions" (R. *v.* Justices of Surrey,
1826, in *Reports of Cases relating to the Duty and Office of Magistrates*, by
J. Dowling and A. Ryland, 1831, vol. iv. p. 9). The office was often combined
with that of Clerk to the Court of Sewers, to the Land Tax Commission, or to
the Court of Requests. It is interesting to find that the Westminster Parochial
Justices not only had their own clerk, but that they also used him as an executive officer to control the Overseers and the Constables, and to investigate their
administration exactly as we have described such Vestries as Woolwich doing
with their Vestry Clerks. They even awarded him a definite salary, payable,
not out of any funds of their own,—such fees as they exacted they evidently
kept for themselves (MS. Minutes, Westminster Petty Sessions, 24th July 1717,
6th August 1719, 10th and 17th August, and 9th November 1721),—but out of
the Parochial rates, the item being allowed by the Close Vestry : "Ordered that
it be recommended to the next Vestry to allow J. F., Clerk attending this Board,
the salary of eleven guineas, viz. six guineas out of the Watch Rate and five
guineas out of the Poor Rate" (*ibid.* 28th September 1747).

[1] *A Letter to the Rt. Hon. Lord Brougham and Vaux on the Magistracy of
England*, 1832 ; with regard to such blank warrants, see p. 76.

[2] Though the evils resulting from the Clerk having an interest in multiplying

(f) The Sphere of Justices "Out of Sessions"

We spare the student any detailed catalogue of the powers and duties of the Justices of the Peace otherwise than in Quarter Sessions assembled. Their criminal jurisdiction ranged from the smallest misdemeanour penalised by a shilling fine, such as the utterance of an oath[1] or the commission of a trivial statutory nuisance, up to the grave offences of incorrigible vagabondage,[2] rick-burning,[3] or the killing of game,[4] for which severe corporal punishment, a long term of imprisonment, or even, in one case, seven years' transportation could be inflicted. In what would now be considered the sphere of local administration, we find them charged with the supervision of practically all the affairs of the parish, whether poor relief, maintenance of highways, the appointment of officers, the making of rates, or the allowance of accounts. The licensing of ale-houses was entirely within their discretion. Moreover, in the latter half of the eighteenth century, and particularly in the early years of the nineteenth, Parliament tended to transfer from Quarter Sessions to the Justices out of Sessions such "county business" as the inspection of weights and measures,[5] and the diversion or closing of footpaths;[6] whilst Quarter Sessions itself, as we shall presently see, spontaneously devolved some of its work in the repairing of bridges and the supervision of prisons on one or more local magistrates, or on all "the Justices of the Division." The exact distribution of these old and new duties between the "Single Justice," the "Double Justice," "Petty Sessions," and "Special Sessions," varied from decade to decade, and seems to have been based upon no definite or consistent plan. Parliament and Quarter Sessions alike were almost as willing to trust both criminal

---

fees were often pointed out (see, for instance, Home Office Domestic State Papers, No. 271 of 1816), not until 1851 was the payment from county funds of a salary to the Clerk to Petty and Special Sessions allowed, or the office expressly recognised by statute (14 & 15 Vic. c. 55); and even at the present day payment by salary in lieu of fees, though general, is not invariable.

[1] 22 Henry VIII. c. 12 (1531); 39 Elizabeth, c. 4 (1597); 17 George II. c. 5 (1744); 27 George III. c. 11 (1787); 32 George III. c. 45 (1792).

[2] 1 James I. c. 27 (1603); 7 James I. c. 11 (1610).

[3] 22 & 23 Car. II. c. 7 (1670).   [4] 19 George II. c. 21 (1746).

[5] 37 George III. c. 143 (1797).   [6] 55 George III. c. 68 (1815).

jurisdiction and local administration to any pair of magistrates, fortuitously met together, as to a specially convened assembly of all the Justices of a particular Division at a stated time and place.

In this multifarious work of the Justices, " out of Sessions," we note common features significant to the student of constitutional development. Neither the individual magistrate nor the Divisional Sessions made any distinction between (i.) a judicial decision as to the criminality of the past conduct of particular individuals; (ii.) an administrative order to be obeyed by officials; and (iii.) a legislative resolution enunciating a new rule of conduct to be observed for the future by all concerned. All alike were, in theory, judicial acts. Though many of these orders were plainly discretional, and determined only by the Justices' views of social expediency, they were all assumed to be based upon evidence of fact, and done in strict accordance with law. Yet there was no provision for any trial by jury or for the publicity of an open court.[1] Even in prosecutions under such drastic penal statutes as those relating to vagrancy and the preservation of game, the "Single Justice" or the "Double Justice" heard the case wherever he chose, without necessarily admitting the public, or even the defendant's attorney;[2] took whatever evidence he deemed necessary; and himself decided both law and fact. It is true that practically all cases dealt with by Justices—like those before other subordinate jurisdictions—might, if the persons concerned were prompt enough and wealthy enough, be removed, by writ of certiorari, to the Court of King's Bench at Westminster.[3] But

---

[1] Though it was held that natural justice required the defendant to have been duly summoned to appear, he might even be tried and sentenced in his absence if he did not appear after due notice (R. v. Simpson, *Treatise on Convictions on Penal Statutes*, by W. Boscawen, 1792, p. 60 ; *Reports of Cases*, etc., by J. Strange, 1795, p. 44 ; *Treatise on Summary Convictions*, by W. Paley, p. 21).

[2] The Court of King's Bench refused to interfere in a case in which two Justices had excluded the defendant's attorney (R. v. A. & B., Justices of Staffordshire, *Reports of Cases*, by Chitty, vol. i. p. 217). As late as 1836 we find a complaint by the editor of a local newspaper that his reporter had been refused admission to a trial of an assault case by Justices in Petty Sessions at Ipswich (MS. Home Office Magistrates Book in Public Record Office).

[3] "A certiorari is an original writ, issuing out of the Court of Chancery or the King's Bench, directed in the King's name to the judges or officers of inferior courts, commanding them to certify or to return the records of a cause depending before them, to the end that the party may have the more sure and

the only practical resource against the mistake or tyranny of the Justices out of Sessions was the almost universal right of the aggrieved party to appeal to the Court of Quarter Sessions. Hence we find, from the early years of the eighteenth century, an ever-growing mass of appeals, from every part of the county, to the whole body of magistrates in Quarter Sessions assembled. In these multifarious appeals from the decisions of the Justices we see represented every branch of their work. Their sometimes savage sentences in summary criminal jurisdiction were seldom brought up for revision—the "incorrigible rogue" had suffered his whipping, and the poacher was safe in gaol. The relatively well-to-do householder who felt aggrieved at the amount of his rate assessment, at the imposition upon him of a pauper apprentice, or at having to serve a public office out of his turn, would not infrequently seek relief at Quarter Sessions. Still more often would "reputed fathers" dispute the equity of orders made against them for the maintenance of illegitimate children. But, as might have been expected, it was those whose expenses were defrayed from public funds who most frequently invoked the aid of the Court. Of all the appeals four-fifths—we hazard the estimate —were those instituted by one parish against another, in the incessant litigation as to the settlement and the removal of the ever-increasing army of paupers."[1]

speedy justice before the King or such Justices as he shall assign to determine the cause" (*Abridgment of the Law*, by Matthew Bacon, vol. i. p. 559). Such a writ lay in all cases of judicial nature, even where by statute they were to be "finally" decided by some particular tribunal, unless Parliament had by express words directed that it should not lie. By 5 George II. c. 19 (1731), a recognisance had to be given, with sufficient sureties, in the sum of £50 before the case was removed. By 16 George III. c. 30 (1776), dealing with deer-stealing, etc. this sum was raised to £100.

[1] "The few pages which contain the Pauper Settlement Laws have been the main employment of the Quarter Sessions since the Revolution, at the expense of litigation estimated at ten millions" (*Administration of the Poor Laws*, 1832, an anonymous and privately printed pamphlet by John Rickman). "It is notorious," William Hay had said a century before, "that half the business of every Quarter Sessions consists in deciding appeals on orders of removal" (*Remarks on the Laws relating to the Poor*, by William Hay, 1735 ; included in his *Works*, 1794, vol. i. p. 121). The student of the minutes of the proceedings of Quarter Sessions often finds the bare entries of settlement appeal cases occupying more space than all the rest of the business.

CHAPTER IV

THE COURT OF QUARTER SESSIONS

IT would be easy to put together from the legal text-books of the seventeenth century an imposing description of the pageantry and ceremonial of the ancient Court of Quarter Sessions—the formal summons by the High Sheriff, besides the Justices, of practically all the county to attend; the elaborate empanelling not only of a Jury of gentlemen to serve as the "Grand Inquest" for the county, but also of separate Juries representing each Hundred, and an ample panel of petty jurors from which to draw the various "Traverse Juries" or "Felons' Juries" that were required for the criminal business; the gathering of this extensive company at the county town; the formal procession through the town, to the Shire Hall or Moot Hall, of the magistrates in their gold-laced coats, full-bottomed wigs, and three-cornered hats, preceded by the Under-Sheriff, "with his bailiffs two by two with their white wands in their hands";[1] the Justices taking their seats on the bench with their hats on—perhaps to signify that they represented the King, and had in this Court no superiors; the formal opening of the Court by the Clerk of the Peace or his deputy solemnly reading the Commission of the Peace and the Royal Proclamation for the Suppression of Vice and Immorality; the tedious swearing in of the jurors and the delivery to them by the Chairman of a lengthy oration or "charge"; the presentation by the High Sheriff of his interminable parchment lists of Hundred and Parish Officers who were required to be in attendance; the loud calling over of these names, with the

---

[1] *The Office of the Clerk of Assize . . . together with the Office of the Clerk of the Peace, showing the true manner and form of the Proceedings at the Court of Quarter Sessions*, 1682, p. 107.

quaint warning of the Cryer, "Answer to your names, every
man at the first call, and save your fines"; the crowding and
jostling of "the Tithing men with their presentments"; the
Headboroughs and the Constables, and their monotonous
answering as the names of the Hundreds and Parishes· are
called;[1] and then the adjournment of the Court for dinner,
with the same elaborate procession of gold-laced Justices,
Bailiffs, Constables, long staves, white wands, and all the rest
of it.

In prosaic fact, we imagine, the gathering of the Justices
every three months at the somnolent little towns and moulder-
ing villages of the end of the seventeenth century presented a
very different aspect.   In the great majority of cases neither
Custos Rotulorum nor High Sheriff deigned to put in an
appearance.   The High Constables and High Bailiffs of the
Hundreds or Liberties would, some of them, neglect to attend.
Probably the majority of Parish Constables risked the chance
of an uncertain fine rather than incur the loss of time and the
expense involved in a journey to the county town.   So far
from the whole county taking part in the proceedings, even
the Justices themselves did not trouble to come.   "I have
known," said the experienced Dr. Burn, "many a Quarter
Sessions where not above two or three Justices attended—
many adjournments of a Sessions which were never attended
at all."[2]   Right down to the last quarter of the eighteenth
century it was evidently unusual for the bench at Quarter
Sessions to consist of more than three or four magistrates.
When for authorising certain action under the Highway Acts
Parliament proposed to make the quorum as many as five, it
was vehemently objected[3] that this number was excessive.

---

[1] "In each county," says a lady who saw the Court as it was in 1695,
"they have quarterly Sessions, to which all Constables of that precinct repair,
and the Tithingmen with their presentments, and complaints to punish and
relieve in petty matters, which the Justices of the Peace are judges of"
(*Through England on a Side-Saddle in the Reign of William and Mary . . .
Diary of Celia Fiennes*, edited by the Hon. Mrs. Griffiths, 1888, p. 264).

[2] *Observations on the Bill . . . for the Better Relief and Employment of the
Poor*, by Richard Burn, 1776, p. 30.

[3] *Observations on the General Highway and Turnpike Acts*, by Thomas
Butterworth Bayley, 1773, p. 29.   In reading through the MS. Minutes of the
Northumberland Quarter Sessions at the end of the eighteenth century, to give
only one instance, we noted that frequently only two Justices were in attendance.   The bill of the Clerk of the Peace for Dorsetshire in 1752 contains
numerous items for messengers despatched on horseback to Justice after Justice

"Where," said the able Chairman of the Lancashire Quarter Sessions "(except in Middlesex and some southern counties in the neighbourhood of London), is there a Quarter Sessions that can commonly produce a number of magistrates sufficient to form such a majority as this?"[1] All the evidence, in fact,

in his endeavours to get even two together to hold the Quarter Sessions (MS. Sessions Rolls, Quarter Sessions, Dorsetshire, 14th July 1752)

[1] The practice with regard to "Justice's wages" is obscure. The payment provided for by the two statutes of 1388 and 1390 was at the substantial rate of four shillings for each day's attendance at Quarter Sessions, equal to about sixteen times the contemporary wages of a day labourer. This sum, limited to eight Justices per county, continued to be allowed by the Exchequer to the High Sheriff in his "bill of cravings." Thus, the bill of cravings of the Sheriff for Yorkshire in 1749 contains the item, "Paid the Justices their wages at the East Riding . . . £12:18:0" (Treasury Misc. Var. 167 in Public Record Office). "In practice," says Mr. Cox, "the wages came to be paid to the eight senior Justices who were not ennobled." In the latter part of the seventeenth century the Derbyshire Justices complained that the High Sheriff, whilst receiving the money, had neglected to pay it to the Justices, who insisted on their rights (MS. Minutes, Quarter Sessions, Derbyshire, Michaelmas 1679; *Three Centuries of Derbyshire Annals*, by J. C. Cox, 1890, vol. i. p. 31). So in Devonshire in 1717, we see the Justices directing their County Treasurer to inspect the Sheriff's accounts in order to discover "what is charged to be paid to the Justices of the Peace . . . for their attendance at the General Sessions for this County" for the past years (MS. Minutes, Quarter Sessions, Devonshire, Epiphany 1717). On the other hand, in other counties the magistrates evidently took care to draw their stipends, which, even at the close of the seventeenth century, amounted to five or six times a labourer's pay. We read in 1693, in the work of a Suffolk magistrate, of Justices "who come and take the King's wages, and before half the business is done betake themselves to the tavern, leaving two or three to finish and conclude the business" (*The Justice of Peace: his Calling and Qualifications*, by Edmund Bohun, 1693, p. 166). And in the Diary of a Wiltshire Justice, in 1744, we find him carefully recording, after every attendance at Quarter Sessions, how much he spent "over our pay of four shillings a day," or, "more than my wages of four shillings a day" (MS. Diary of William Hunt, 1743-44, in library of Wiltshire Archæological Society). Our impression is that, in many counties at any rate, the Justices' wages were not taken by any individual, but formed a fund out of which was paid the cost of the Justices' Sessional dinners. At the Durham Quarter Sessions, in 1690, "the Justices resolved to give their wages towards procuring a plate or plates to be run for upon Durham Moor" (*History of Durham*, by R. Surtees, vol. iv. 1840, p. 88). We find, however, the Northumberland Justices ordering, in 1804, "that the Clerk of the Peace do collect from and receive from the Sheriff . . . the wages due to the respective Justices of this County for attending the respective Sessions from Epiphany Sessions last" (MS. Minutes, Quarter Sessions, Northumberland, 12th January 1804). In 1810 a great storm arose among the Worcestershire Justices about the disposal of these "Justices' wages," and a formal committee of investigation was appointed. It appears to have long been the custom for the Chairman of Quarter Sessions to draw the whole sum, and to use the amount to provide refreshments for the Justices (*Worcestershire in the Nineteenth Century*, by T. C. Turberville, 1852, p: 93). In Sussex in 1819, we read:—"It having been suggested by E. R. Curtois, Esq., the propriety of the magistrates within this county obtaining the allowance to which

goes to show that the assembly was neither large nor imposing. The surroundings of the Court were not usually conducive to its dignity. In 1689, at any rate, few of the numerous towns and villages in which the Sessions were held possessed a "Shire Hall" or other public building belonging to the county in which to hold the Court; whilst the convivial habits of the time made the Justices even prefer—at any rate for their deliberations on "county business"—the accommodation of the largest inn. "In these places it is," says a lively critic of 1700, "where the Divans, or (as I may say) the States Provincial of a county are held with great solemnity. In these petty conventions 'tis, where all matters relating to their office are with great judgment and silence agitated and determined amidst the smoking of pipes, the cluttering of pots and all the noise and ordure of a narrow room infested with drinking and a throng. . . . 'Twould be much more suitable to the gravity of a Court of Justice were it kept in some town-house or market-house." [1]

they are entitled of four shillings a day for attending the Quarter Sessions, and of applying the same to some charitable purposes, it is ordered by this Court that the same be submitted to the magistrates assembled at the next Western Sessions, and also at the General Adjourned Sessions intended to be holden on the day after the next assizes" (MS. Minutes, Quarter Sessions, Sussex, 23rd April 1819). In Berkshire, too, we see the Justices in 1828 inquiring what became of the money (MS. Minutes, Quarter Sessions, Berkshire, 11th April 1828). In Middlesex, where the Commission was exceptionally numerous, the Treasury seems, in the seventeenth century, to have sanctioned payment of the allowance to as many as eighteen Justices. In 1692, Quarter Sessions successfully petitioned that this number might be raised to twenty-four (*Middlesex County Records, 1689-1709*, by W. J. Hardy, 1905, p. 37). Nearly a century later, when it was said that "a much greater number . . . do usually attend the Sessions . . . than before ever were accustomed to do"—on an average forty-six, half of whom were daily in attendance—Quarter Sessions appointed a Committee (on which it is interesting to see that Jeremy Bentham sat) to consider how the increasing cost of the Justices' dinner could be met ; and, on its report, decided to ask the Treasury to allow fees for thirty Justices (MS. Minutes, Quarter Sessions, Middlesex, 10th December 1778, January and February 1782). By 1833 the ordinary counties seem to have been drawing £48 a year for Justices' wages, and the claim of Middlesex had reached £435 : 11s. At this the Treasury revolted, and refused to allow more than £200. In August 1835 it issued an order rigidly confining the allowance for the future in all counties alike (including Middlesex) to four shillings for each day's attendance at Quarter Sessions up to a maximum of eight Justices on any one day (Burn's *Justice of the Peace*, vol. v. p. 984, of edition of 1845). The provisions relating to Justices' wages in the statute of 1388 and 1390 were repealed by 18 & 19 Vic. c. 126, sec. 1 (1854), when we assume that the payment ceased.

[1] *Campania Felix*, by Timothy Nourse, 1700, chap. xii., "Of Inns and Ale-houses," p. 166.

(a) *The Time and Place of Meeting.*

The ceremonial pageant set out in the law books, and the squalid crowd described by the satirists, represent extremes between which ranged the actual proceedings of the Court of Quarter Sessions in different counties and at different dates. It is probable that when Quarter Sessions were held at the capital city of an important populous county, on specially notable occasions—perhaps when the Custos Rotulorum had signified his intention of honouring the Easter Sessions with his presence, or when the High Sheriff for the year chose to display either his knowledge of constitutional forms or his wealth — something like an elaborate pageant might be attempted. On the other hand, the two or three Justices who struggled through the mire or snow of the infamously bad roads of the period to the mid - winter " Hilary " or "Epiphany " Sessions in some sleepy little market town in a remote corner of a desolate county, would content themselves with the slovenly ways of the ale-house parlour in which they met, and shorten the formalities that delayed their dinner. County differed from county in the details of its actual procedure and in the extent of its ceremonial, partly, no doubt, according to size and importance, but chiefly, we believe, according to whether the Quarter Sessions was really held for the shire as a whole, or only for a fragment of it. For though, by law, every Court of Quarter Sessions was held for the entire county, and the entire county was summoned to attend, the practice was, in many shires, exactly the opposite. In the absence of speedy means of communication, it was neither easy nor cheap to travel to the county town, and many counties fell into the habit of holding the four quarterly gatherings at different towns in the county, so as to give the different parts of it equal opportunities of attending. In Merionethshire, for instance, the General Sessions of the Peace were habitually held alternately at Bala and Dolgelly ; in Berkshire, at Reading, Abingdon, Newbury, and Wallingford ; in Surrey, at Kingston, Croydon, Reigate, Epsom, Guildford, and Dorking ; in Cardiganshire at Aberystwyth, Cardigan, Tregaron, and Lampeter ; in Derbyshire at Derby, Chesterfield,

Bakewell, and Wirksworth;[1] in the North Riding at Richmond, New Malton, and Northallerton,[2] in a more or less regular rotation, in which the county town sometimes had a double turn.[3] A further stage in disintegration was reached in those counties which, by the device of adjournment, contrived to hold each Quarter Sessions three or four times over, at as many different towns or villages, in the different parts of the county.[4] At each of these meetings all the paraphernalia of the Court would nominally be found, but the business was confined to that of the particular Division in which it was held, and only those magistrates, bailiffs, constables, and jurors residing in the Division were supposed to attend. Thus in the West Riding of Yorkshire, between 1689 and 1835, whilst the Easter Sessions was held only at Pontefract, each of the three others was held by successive adjournments at a different set of three towns, thus providing one Sessions a year in ten different towns.[5] In Lancashire, so inconvenient was it on the roads of the period to reach any one centre from Salford on the south and Cartmel in the north, that we find every

---

[1] In 1796 a riot at Bakewell about the militia balloting caused the Justices to substitute Derby for Bakewell for their future sittings. In 1827 it was proposed to hold all four Sessions at Derby, but this was strenuously resisted by Chesterfield, and the change was not made until 1859, since which date Derby has been the only place of meeting. "Adjourned" Sessions were occasionally held at other towns, and down to 1787 sometimes even at private houses (*Three Centuries of Derbyshire Annals*, by J. C. Cox, 1890, vol. i. pp. 9-11).

[2] *The Names of the Noblemen, Gentlemen, and Clergymen in the Commission of the Peace for the North Riding of the County of York*, etc. 1802.

[3] The reverse process is seen, by exception, in Merionethshire, where the Quarter Sessions in the sixteenth century having met at different places, was fixed in 1608 at Harlech, by Ralph, Lord Eure, then President of Wales, at the urgent request of the Justices and other inhabitants, who gave him a present of £30 to secure his assent (*Kalendars of Gwynedd*, by Edward Breese, 1873, p. 18). There might even be a disorderly struggle among the Justices as to where the Sessions should be held. In Cardiganshire in 1741, two Justices sent the High Sheriff a precept to summon the Midsummer Quarter Sessions at Lampeter, whilst two others sent him one requiring the Sessions to be at Tregaron. Rival Sessions were, in fact, held (MS. Minutes, Quarter Sessions, Cardiganshire, 16th July 1741).

[4] Norfolk had the custom of always opening the Quarter Sessions at Norwich, and then repeating it by adjournment at two other towns, chosen in a complicated rotation from King's Lynn, Holt, Little Walsingham, and Swaffham, so that the first named usually had three turns for every one of the last named (MS. Minutes, Quarter Sessions, Norfolk, 1791-1799).

[5] MS. Minutes, Quarter Sessions, West Riding, 1730; *ibid.*, 13th April 1801. The Sessions towns were Pontefract, Skipton, Bradford, Rotherham, Knaresborough, Leeds, Sheffield, Wetherby, Wakefield, and Doncaster. In 1597-1602 Barnsley and Halifax had held the places of Sheffield and Bradford (*West Riding Sessions Rolls*, edited by J. Lister, 1888, p. 40).

Quarter Sessions habitually transferred by adjournment from Lancaster, successively to Preston, Wigan, Kirkdale or Ormskirk, and Manchester or Salford, each place having, practically, though not legally, a separate jurisdiction and distinct business.[1] In the counties of Suffolk and Sussex, each nowadays legally divided into two, but having during the eighteenth century but one Custos Rotulorum and Lord-Lieutenant, one Clerk of the Peace, one High Sheriff, one Commission of the Peace, and, so far as the law knew, one County Rate, we find the shire divided, " time out of mind," into four separate parts, each having its own group of Justices and its own Court of Quarter Sessions, each trying its own prisoners, repairing its own bridges, maintaining its own House of Correction, levying its own differential rates on its own parishes, making its own orders as to pensions and poor relief, and only occasionally recognising the supremacy of the Courts held at Ipswich and Bury, or at Chichester and Lewes, as representing the two halves into which these counties were, each of them, eventually legally divided; and still less that at Ipswich or Lewes as representing either county as a whole.[2] In such practically

---

[1] On one occasion we find an adjournment " to the house of Mrs. Dean in Chorley," there being fever in Preston (MS. Minutes, Quarter Sessions, Lancashire, 16th October 1783). In Shropshire " the Court sometimes sat by adjournment at Bridgnorth, Bishop's Castle, and Oswestry ; and in April 1713 the strange course was taken of adjourning the hearing of an appeal between the parishes of Round Acton and Barrow to Muckley Cross, on the road between Wenlock and Bridgnorth, to hear witnesses ! " (*Shropshire County Records*, part ii., edited by Sir Offley Wakeman, p. 14). For the convenience of persons desiring to take the oaths of the period, Quarter Sessions was often formally adjourned to, and nominally held at many small places, sometimes even particular private houses. Thus in Shropshire, in 1723, the " Sessions adjourned to seventeen named places, besides every Wednesday and Saturday at Shrewsbury up to 5th December, for the convenience of persons taking the oaths." And in Essex, where the Sessions were nearly always at Chelmsford, we find in 1722, adjournments into the various divisions of the county " for the ease of persons required to take the oaths " (MS. Minutes, Quarter Sessions, Essex, 16th July 1722).

[2] In Suffolk the liberty of St. Edmund (West Suffolk) had its own Grand Jury until 1839 (*History and Antiquities of Suffolk*, by Rev. A. Suckling, 1846, p. 13). The four County Rates, so Charles Austin advised, were good by prescription (*Suffolk in the Nineteenth Century*, by John Glyde, p. 30). In Westmoreland, a dispute between the two halves of the county as to the place of meeting was referred to the arbitration of Lord Keeper North in 1676. He suggested the holding of Sessions " on both sides of the county by adjournment, as is done in Suffolk and other large counties. But then they were so weak as to hold double Sessions, independent of each other, which is not legal, because the quarterly Sessions is defined by statute and can be but one " (*Autobiography of the Hon. Roger North*, edited by A. Jessopp, 1887, par. 171,

divided counties the Court of Quarter Sessions naturally
suffered both in dignity and in importance. Whilst it was
necessarily at all times distinguished by the attendance of at
any rate a dozen of the smaller gentry or principal tenant
farmers, to form the Grand Jury,[1] and at least a dozen other

p. 137 ; see *Life of the Lord Keeper North*, par. 209). The practical division
of Sussex into East and West Sussex was expressly declared by Lord Kenyon,
in 1792, to be unwarranted by law (Evans *v.* Stevens, King's Bench, Midsummer,
1792). It was partially recognised by Local Act, 45 George III. c. 100
(1805) ; and by that of 58 & 59 Victoria, c. 86 (1895). The similar
partial division of Kent into East and West Kent (though for certain
purposes endorsed by Local Act, 9 George II. c. 12) was equally held to be
unlawful by the same judge. "There are no legal subdivisions of the county,
though very convenient arrangements have taken place" (R. *v.* Buston,
11th January 1798). Time out of mind East and West Kent (though with
one Commission of the Peace, one Custos Rotulorum and Lord-Lieutenant, and
one High Sheriff) had held distinct Quarter Sessions at Canterbury and Maidstone respectively—originally admittedly by adjournment, but since the early
part of the eighteenth century without even this legal fiction—attended by
different magistrates, presided over by different chairmen, served by different
Grand and Petty Juries, and making separate County Rates. The business was
entirely localised, even the county militia forming two distinct regiments,
except that there was only one debtor's prison. The new gaol at Maidstone was
built in 1746 by West Kent, and in 1793 an agitation was begun to get the cost
of its maintenance borne by the county as a whole. After much controversy
and some actual litigation the two Divisions referred the matter to arbitration,
the result of which was the repeal of the Act of 1732 by 43 Geo. III. c. 58 of
1803, and a new apportionment of the common expenses, against which West
Kent presently protested. A third Local Act, 47 Geo. III. c. 34 (1807),
maintained the formal unity of the county, and empowered the Justices to
"make a fair and equitable County Rate for the said county," but left West
Kent charged with three-fourths of the common charges, and the amount of the
rate was differentiated accordingly. For the heated controversy between East
and West Kent on the subject, see MS. Minutes, Quarter Sessions, Kent, 6th
August 1792, 17th January and 17th July 1793, 15th July and 26th December
1794, 11th January and 17th April 1798, 15th March 1800, 6th and 19th
October 1801, 14th January and 19th July 1802, 26th June and 25th July
1805, 16th January 1806, 12th January, 4th October, and 13th December
1808, 12th, 18th, 27th, and 30th January, and 17th February and 14th April
1809.

[1] These Quarter Sessions, held by adjournment in different towns remote
from each other on successive days, certainly tried felonies and inflicted
sentences. We assume, therefore, that there must have been a Grand Jury at
each to find true bills. There is no trace of all the indictments to be preferred
at all these adjourned Sessions being referred in advance to the Grand Jury at
any one of the towns. The Grand Jury of the county, representing the county
as a whole, cannot have attended all these adjourned Sessions. Only in the
case of West Suffolk, as the old Liberty of St. Edmund, do we understand that
there was a separate Grand Jury (*Suffolk in the Nineteenth Century*, by John
Glyde, p. 30). Yet it is not easy to understand how the High Sheriff could
have brought himself, as we believe he must have done, in some or all of the
cases at any rate, to summon a separate "Grand Inquest for the body of the
County" for each adjournment to a different town. From the MS. Minutes and
Sessions Rolls of the West Riding of Yorkshire in the eighteenth century we

persons to form the "Felon's Jury," without both of which the
Court could not transact its criminal business, the little knot
of Justices, jurors, and officials who met at Beccles or Woodbridge, Horsham or Petworth, must in fact, both numerically
and in dignity of procedure, have often been inferior to the
fortnightly or monthly Petty Sessions of a market town at the
beginning of the twentieth century.[1]

The difference of practice in this respect led to more than
a difference in dignity and formality.   It resulted, we believe,
in marked difference in efficiency between one county and
another.   In Gloucestershire the Quarter Sessions were all
held at the same town, we notice from the minutes that they
were habitually attended by the same little knot of Justices.
In such a case the close personal intimacy and detailed

infer that there, at any rate, there seems to have been empanelled for each
Quarter Sessions a Grand Jury of forty-eight, but this was in form only.   What
happened was that at the opening of the Sessions, and upon each adjournment
to a different town, about fifteen persons out of the forty-eight were specially
summoned to attend, largely according to their propinquity to the particular
town.   Thus, instead of a Grand Inquest representing the whole Riding, there
were practically several Grand Inquests of local residents.   "This is the mode
now pursued," say the Glamorganshire Justices in 1831, "in selecting Juries for
the Quarter Sessions which are held in four different towns in the county ; and
to every one in the habit of attending the Quarter Sessions it must be obvious
that the arrangement is attended by very injurious consequences to the impartial
administration of justice.   Juries thus selected bring their minds full of all they
have heard and felt before the trial to the consideration of the question at issue,
whilst Juries selected indiscriminately from the county at large have some of
their members freed from local prejudices (Home Office Magistrates Book in
Public Record Office).

[1] In Hampshire, which legally included the Isle of Wight, separate Quarter
Sessions were held, by adjournment, at West Cowes, at which only the Justices,
Constables, jurors, etc. residing on the Island attended, and at which the whole
civil and criminal business of the Island was dealt with.   When funds were
required for bridges or other purposes, a separate County Rate was made by and
for the Island alone.   Thus, in 1718 we find that the Hants Quarter Sessions at
Winchester expressly "refers the matter of taxing the inhabitants of the several
parishes, etc. within the Isle of Wight for the passing, conveying, or maintaining of rogues, vagabonds, etc." under the Act of 12 Anne, c. 18 "to the good
judgment and consideration of His Majesty's Justices . . . residing within the
said Isle . . . that shall . . . be assembled at the adjournment of this present Sessions at . . . 'The Feathers,' in West Cowes" (MS. Minutes, Quarter
Sessions, Hampshire, 7th October 1718).   The Island maintained its own
bridges and House of Correction, and had entirely distinct Poor Law and
highway administrations (see the interesting pamphlet, *The Isle of Wight
System of Roads and System of Guardians of the Poor, not a model, but a warning
to the Legislature*, 1845).   It became in effect, extra-legally, a separate administrative county, to such an extent that even the minutes of its Quarter Sessions
are not among those of the Court at Winchester.   It was legally made a separate
administrative county by the Local Government Act 1888.

acquaintance with the business of all the members of the real governing body can hardly have failed to produce continuity of policy, whilst they offered, at any rate, the opportunity for active and capable administration. To this may be due the fact that the Gloucestershire Quarter Sessions, as we shall see in the course of this work, was distinguished for the efficiency with which its county business was carried on. A great contrast is presented by the adjoining county of Wiltshire. There the aim seems to have been to have the Quarter Sessions in as many different towns as possible, so as to give equal facilities for attendance to all the Justices, in whatever part of the county they resided. The four quarterly Sessions were accordingly, not only each opened at a different town,— Devizes, Salisbury, Warminster, or Marlborough,— but they were each of them also habitually transferred by adjournment to other towns. Thus the Easter Quarter Sessions for Wiltshire in 1809 was opened at New Sarum (Salisbury); then adjourned to the County Gaol at Fisherton Anger, where a new chairman was chosen ; then further to the " King's Head " at Melksham, where an entirely different set of magistrates were present ; and, finally, to the " Boar Inn " at Devizes, where, under the same chairman, yet another set of magistrates attended.[1] At other times the Sessions were opened at or adjourned to Malmesbury, Christian Malford, and other decaying boroughs or even small villages, the Magistrates in attendance being different on every occasion.[2] As it was customary in Wiltshire to gather the sense of the Justices on any important new departure in county policy from resolutions passed by four quarterly Courts in succession, so as to give every corner of the county an opportunity of being heard, it always took a year before any decision could be arrived at. As a matter of fact, the minutes show that the Wiltshire Justices found it almost impossible to introduce any fundamental reforms in county administration, as the various little knots of acting magistrates discussing the questions separately at quarterly intervals, naturally failed to arrive at any identical resolution.

[1] MS. Minutes, Quarter Sessions, Wiltshire, 12th-14th April 1809.
[2] During the seventeenth and eighteenth centuries the Oxfordshire Quarter Sessions were adjourned to such small places as Sarsden, Burford, Chipping Norton, Bicester, and Witney (*Oxfordshire Annals*, by J. M. Davenport, 1869, p. 106).

And, if we may cite another case, we see the Surrey Quarter Sessions, in 1751-52, passing backwards and forwards in successive resolutions of the Court, upon the state of the Gaol and House of Correction at Southwark, according as the Justices met at Epsom, Guildford, or, by adjournment in Southwark itself, with the result that nothing was done to get a new building, and gaol distemper raged unchecked for another generation.[1]

The inefficiency resulting from the practical division of the county was sometimes mitigated by an understanding that all questions of general county policy, and especially matters of county finance, should be dealt with only at the Easter, or at some other Quarter Sessions, held always at the county town. We note, for instance, that in Hertfordshire, in the middle of the eighteenth century, it is only at the Easter Sessions that Earl Cowper and about a dozen of the leading gentlemen of the county ever troubled to attend. At the other Quarter Sessions only two or three Justices of humbler station put in an appearance.[2] In the extensive county of Lancashire, where the four Quarter Sessions, as we have mentioned, were multiplied, by the device of adjournment, into sixteen or twenty separate meetings in the course of the year, it had been the custom, so it was asserted, near the end of the eighteenth century, " in ancient times and down to a very late period, for the Justices to assemble at the General Session of Assize held at Lancaster, at a meeting convened by the Sheriff, called the Sheriff's Board, for the special purpose of communing together and transacting all business relating to the county at large, and particularly that of nominating public officers ; and where, with the advice and assistance of the Gentlemen of the Grand Jury and others of the county, they have almost invariably been nominated so long as such meetings continued to be held." From the middle of the

---

[1] MS. Minutes, Quarter Sessions, Surrey, Easter, Michaelmas 1751, 14th January, 18th February, 7th April, 26th May, 18th June, 14th July 1752. The evil continued down to our own day. " When the Quarter Sessions of a county," said an influential local magnate in 1836, "are held at different places, different sets of magistrates attend ; and this is ill-suited to any systematic attention to the duties of the pecuniary administration imposed on them " (Report of House of Commons Committee on the County Rate, etc., 1834 ; *A Treatise on the Magistracy of England*, by Edward Mullins, 1836, p. 76).

[2] MS. Minutes, Quarter Sessions, Herts, 1741, and following years.

eighteenth century onward, the business of the Assizes gradually became so heavy and, as we may infer, the work so much more strenuous, that it interfered with these pleasant gatherings of Justices and Grand Jury. It "became difficult during the hurry of an Assizes to apportion sufficient time to the above purposes, and the Sheriff's Board was very ill attended, and at last so totally neglected," that, as we infer, somewhere about 1785, it ceased to be held.[1] But the evil results of divided counsels soon made themselves felt. In 1787 the Lancashire Quarter Sessions declared it to be "the unanimous sentiment of this Court," that an annual General Sessions should be held at "Preston, a central place in the county, . . . for the special purpose of transacting" all business relating to the county at large.[2] This resolution did not, however, meet with the unanimous approval of the Justices. The rival claims of Lancaster were strenuously upheld. In spite of a general understanding to regard the Preston meeting as the principal one, the Justices who met at Lancaster took it upon themselves, in 1795, summarily to dismiss so important an officer as the County Treasurer, and to appoint a successor without communicating with the Justices for the other Divisions of the county—an act which the Preston Quarter Sessions promptly declared to be "highly improper, and its legality also questionable."[3] For a couple of years the Lancashire Justices continued to quarrel furiously over the point. Those who belonged to the Hundred of Lonsdale stood out in flat rebellion against all the rest of the county. They refused to meet anywhere but Lancaster. They would have nothing to do with the "innovation upon the ancient usages of the county" proposed by the others. Backed up by the local municipal corporation, they denied the validity of any General Sessions of the Peace summoned in any other town than Lancaster.[4] Finally, the rest of the

---

[1] See the interesting statement in MS. Minutes, Quarter Sessions, Lancashire, 18th May 1795. No minutes or other records of this Sheriff's Board can be found. It is mentioned in 1784, when it seems to have consisted of three Justices from each Hundred, nominated by their colleagues at a preceding Quarter Sessions (*ibid.* 26th and 29th April 1784).

[2] *Ibid.* 8th February 1787.

[3] *Ibid.* 18th May 1795. The Lancaster Justices formally repeated their resolution of dismissal and appointment (*ibid.* 14th April 1796).

[4] *Ibid.* 30th January 1796 ; 30th March 1796.

county found itself driven to apply to Parliament for a Local Act establishing an Annual General Sessions at Preston, at which alone certain county business could be transacted. The Justices of the Lonsdale Hundred, stubborn to the last, opposed this bill in Parliament, and put the county to an expense of £2124, before it could be carried into law.[1] In all three Ridings of Yorkshire the same result was partially achieved in a cheaper way by getting a clause inserted in the public Act of 1803, relating to county bridges, by which, in each Riding, all orders and proceedings relating to the bridges chargeable to the Riding as a whole were to be dealt with only at the Easter Sessions.[2]

(b) *The Chairman of the Court*

Apart from mere ceremonial, the first business of the Justices in Quarter Sessions was to choose a Chairman for the Sessions, who gave the charge to the Juries, kept order during the proceedings, ascertained the decision of the Bench and pronounced the sentence or order of the Court. In the absence of the Custos Rotulorum no provision existed as to a Chairman to preside over the Court, and during the seventeenth century, as for some time after 1700, it seems frequently to have been the custom to have no Chairman at all. Even so important a county as the West Riding of Yorkshire had no president of the Court until 1709. In that year " it is ordered that, to prevent the disorder that is made in Court by persons applying themselves to several Justices of the Peace at one and the same time, that for the future . . . the Court shall proceed to elect a Chairman, and

---

[1] MS. Minutes, Quarter Sessions, Lancashire, 1792-1798. A detailed account of the legal effect of this Act (38 George III. c. 58), which has remained unique, will be found in the Minutes of the Annual General Sessions, Lancashire, 30th June 1881.

[2] 43 George III. c. 59. The West Riding tried to arrange that all appointments of officers should also be made at this Annual Sessions at Pontefract (MS. Minutes, Quarter Sessions, West Riding, 3rd April 1815). In some other counties all the business became eventually concentrated in one town. Thus in Dorsetshire, where Quarter Sessions had been habitually held in different quarters at Dorchester, Blandford, Sherborne, Shaston (Shaftesbury), and Bridport, it was decided in 1825 to hold them, unless by special adjournment, only at Dorchester (MS. Minutes, Quarter Sessions, Dorsetshire, 11th January 1825).

that all applications be made to the Chair."[1] In Shropshire, too, we are told that, between 1709 and 1726, "there is no indication of any Chairman having been elected, even *pro hac vice.*"[2]

The first innovation was for the Justices present at each Quarter Sessions to elect one of their number to preside for that Sessions only. So extensive and so experienced a body as the Middlesex Quarter Sessions was capable, in 1723, of deliberately resolving that no magistrate should be Chairman for more than one year.[3] As late as 1776 we find the Hampshire Justices taking steps to prevent even a customary chairmanship growing up. It is by them formally " ordered that the Clerk of the Peace do immediately before the opening of the Court put a question to every Justice present with regard to the choice of a Chairman; and that no one do presume to take the chair till the choice is determined in his favour by a majority of votes."[4] In less well organised counties this haphazard choice of a Chairman at each Quarter Sessions remained the practice right into the nineteenth century. As late as 1830, in the large and important county of Devon, where the finances had fallen into inextricable confusion, one of the leading reformers was aiming merely at regularising the periodical election.[5] Sometimes the convenience of placing

---

[1] MS. Minutes, Quarter Sessions, West Riding, 3rd May 1709 ; order to elect chairman repeated 19th April 1726.

[2] *Shropshire County Records*, part ii. edited by Sir Offley Wakeman, p. iii. In Dorsetshire no Justice is found designated as Chairman until about 1773 (MS. Minutes, Quarter Sessions, Dorsetshire, 5th October 1773). In Breconshire, though one Justice had apparently habitually presided for many years previously, we do not find the word Chairman mentioned in the minutes, nor any such appointment formally recorded until 1820 (MS. Minutes, Quarter Sessions, Breconshire, 11th July 1820).

[3] MS. Minutes, Quarter Sessions, Middlesex, 27th February 1723.

[4] MS. Minutes, Quarter Sessions, Hants, 8th October 1776. Except for the period 1773-1779, the Shropshire Quarter Sessions seems to have had no standing Chairman until 1785, when it was resolved that "many advantages and conveniences would accrue if such a Chairman were appointed " (*Shropshire County Records*, edited by Sir Offley Wakeman, part vii. p. 4, part ix. pp. 10, 11). The Chairman's casting vote does not appear in Quarter Sessions until the nineteenth century. In 1801, it was specifically allowed in Lancashire (MS. Minutes, Annual General Sessions, Lancashire, 19th November 1801). There was, it is said, no casting vote in Oxfordshire (*Oxfordshire Annals*, by J. M. Davenport, 1869, p. 105).

[5] At the July Quarter Sessions 1830, Captain Buller proposed a change in the mode of electing Chairmen. He was, he said, " convinced that no mode was less likely to give the county the Chairman it desired than that hitherto in use ;

upon some designated magistrate the responsibility for preparing the customary " charge," and of ensuring his attendance, led, as in Middlesex and Devonshire, in the middle of the eighteenth century, to the selection of a Chairman in advance at the next preceding Sessions.[1] We see another form in Norfolk in 1801, when four different Chairmen were chosen in a batch, each to preside in future over one of the four Quarter Sessions held at Norwich.[2] Gradually, however, the importance of maintaining some continuity of procedure and the convenience of utilising the expertness given by constant practice induced the Justices, in one county after another, to drift silently into standing chairmanships. In Oxfordshire, for instance, where the early records from 1689 to 1771 show constant changes of chairmanship, the post was from 1771 held for long terms of years by particular Justices, there being only seven successive Chairmen during the next century.[3] The county of Gloucester, distinguished from the end of the eighteenth century for its efficient administration, slipped silently about that time into the practice of permanent chairmanship; usually casting the office, be it noted, upon a Clerical Justice. In the important county of Middlesex, where the business of Sessions was heavy and difficult, we find the order of 1723 against a standing chairmanship quickly rescinded,[4] and the chairmanship gradually continuing into the same hands. Thus Sir John Hawkins was Chairman from 1765 [5] to 1780, and William Mainwaring, M.P., from

in fact, so far from securing in all instances the most efficient person, it was almost in the power of any gentleman so placed as to first catch the eye of the magistrate presiding at the time of appointment to elect himself into the chair. His sole object was to add to the dignity of the county." He proposed and carried a resolution providing that in future every magistrate in attendance at the Michaelmas Sessions should give the Clerk of the Peace a card bearing the names of the six whom he thought best qualified. The Clerk of the Peace would then place in order the six who had received most votes, "and then, dismissing all others, deliver a list of these six into Court " (*Western Flying Post*, 19th July 1830).

[1] MS. Minutes, Quarter Sessions, Devonshire, Easter 1762 and following quarters.

[2] "That in future James Mingay, Esq., shall preside as Chairman of the Court at Michaelmas Session ; Henry Jodrell, Esq., at the Christmas Session ; Thomas Blofield, Esq., at the Easter Session, and Charles Harvey, Esq., at the Midsummer Session of the Peace to be held at the Castle of Norwich " (MS. Minutes, Quarter Sessions, Norfolk, 16th July 1801).

[3] *Oxfordshire Annals*, by J. M. Davenport, 1869, pp. 105-107.

[4] MS. Minutes, Quarter Sessions, Middlesex, 25th February 1725.

[5] *Ibid*. 19th September 1765.

1781[1] to 1816. In Surrey from the latter end of the eighteenth century, whilst it continued the practice to have different Chairmen for the Sessions held at the different quarters or at the different towns, it became the custom for each such Sessions to retain its own Chairman for many years. Thus Lord Grantley was, down to 1808, eleven years Chairman of the Sessions regularly held by adjournment at Southwark ; and in 1825 Lord Midleton was eloquently thanked on retiring from his twenty-eight years' chairmanship of the Midsummer Sessions at Guildford.[2] A further specialisation was effected in Surrey, where certain Sessions, regularly held by adjournment for criminal business only, had their own Chairman "for the trial of prisoners"—a post for which Serjeant Onslow, a leading practising barrister, was chosen.[3] In Lancashire the criminal business at the Salford Sessions, which dealt with Manchester and the neighbouring manufacturing centres, became, towards the close of the eighteenth century, so onerous and of such gravity that it was recognised that a specially skilled Chairman was required, to act virtually as judge of this important criminal court. The county was fortunate enough to find, first in T. B. Bayley and then in the Rev. W. R. Hay, both of whom we have already described, unpaid amateur Justices who had acquired a legal training and great familiarity with the business. For more than thirty years these two gentlemen successively discharged the irksome and difficult duties of this office. Meanwhile, power had been obtained by Act of Parliament to appoint and pay a stipendiary Chairman—an expense which the devotion and public spirit of Mr. Hay rendered for twenty years unnecessary. On his resignation in 1823, however, a stipendiary Chairman of the Salford Quarter Sessions was

---

[1] MS. Minutes, Quarter Sessions, Middlesex, 22nd February 1781 and 30th May 1816. Mainwaring, as we shall subsequently describe, received a secret payment from the Treasury (chapter vi., *The Reaction against the Rulers of the County*).

[2] MS. Minutes, Quarter Sessions, Surrey, Epiphany 1808, and 12th July 1825.

[3] *Ibid.* 14th January 1806. Two years later Serjeant Onslow succeeded Lord Grantley (who retired with this object) as Chairman of the whole Southwark Sessions. In 1821 we note that Mr. Trotter resigned his chairmanship of "the adjourned Sessions at Newington for the trial of felonies, etc." (*Ibid.* 1st May 1821).

appointed, and from that date the office has been continuously
filled by barristers of experience.[1]

(c) *The Procedure of the Court*

At the close of the seventeenth century we do not find
that the half a dozen Justices who usually formed the Bench
at Quarter Sessions drew any precise distinction between their
criminal and administrative work. Administrative orders and
penal sentences, decisions on appeals and bills to be paid,
often appear higgledy-piggledy in the "Minute Books" or
"Order Books" in which the Deputy Clerk of the Peace
recorded the proceedings of the Sessions. Gradually, however,
a rough distinction is drawn between the business that needed
the presence of a Jury, or hearing the parties, or listening to
counsel, on the one hand, which commonly took place in
public, and that which the Justices could settle among themselves exclusively in comfortable privacy. Much of what
would now be considered mere administration, such as the
repairing of prisons, bridges, and roads, continued, as we shall
presently describe, to be embodied in judicial forms, and to
require the co-operation of Juries, if not also the hearing of
counsel, in the presence, nominally, of the county at large.
Appeals from the orders or sentences of the "Justices out of
Sessions"—whether from a "Single Justice" or a "Double

---

[1] 45 George III. c. 59, 1805 ; *An Account of the Expenditure of the
County Palatine of Lancaster*, by Robert Hindle, 1843, p. 197 ; *Abstract of the
Accounts of the County Treasurer . . . of Lancaster*, by James Rushton,
1885. The Salford paid Chairman remained—apart from the secret case
of Middlesex—unique for many years. When, in 1805, it was proposed to
take steps to appoint a paid Chairman of the Surrey Quarter Sessions at
£400 a year to deal with the heavy criminal business of the Metropolis South
of the Thames, the majority of the magistrates strongly objected, and
swarmed to the next Sessions to vote down the proposal (MS. Minutes,
Quarter Sessions, Surrey, 8th October 1805, and 8th January 1806). In
1832, however, when the criminal business had become enormous, a resolution
in favour of a salaried Chairman was carried. He was to preside over the
judicial business only, the Justices choosing another Chairman for "the County
Day." A proposal to place the appointment in the hands of the Lord Chief
Justice of the King's Bench was rejected (*Ibid.* 3rd January, 3rd April, 3rd
July 1832, and 1st January 1833). The necessary Act of Parliament was,
however, never obtained, partly because the Home Secretary refused to support
the proposal (Home Office Domestic Entry Book, 20th January 1833, vol. lxix.,
in Public Record Office). The Grand Jury of Devonshire petitioned in 1833
for a "travelling paid Chairman" of Divisional Sessions to cope with the
increase of crime and vagrancy (First Report of Poor Law Inquiry Commission,
1834, Appendix A, Chapman's Report, p. 457).

Justice," Petty Sessions or Special Sessions, though settled by
the Bench itself without a Jury—were frequently argued by
counsel for the respective parties, and therefore were heard in
open Court. The usual habit of Quarter Sessions during the
early part of the eighteenth century was, we believe, to deal
with all this business, together with the ordinary criminal
cases, in public, at the " Castle," or the " Shire Hall " ; [1] at a
room at the County Gaol or House of Correction; at the
private office of the Clerk of the Peace, or even in the largest
parlour of the principal inn. But as soon as the business
which involved the presence of outsiders was concluded, or at
any rate was ended for the day, the Justices would formally
adjourn to a private apartment in the most comfortable
ale-house of the town, where, over a convivial meal,[2] or
immediately after it, they would order payment of the

---

[1] At Gloucester it was called the " Booth Hall "; at Leeds the " Moot Hall."

[2] The dinner (which at the Assizes was usually paid for by the High Sheriff
or by the Under Sheriff) was an important event. At Quarter Sessions, when it
usually took place on the first day, it was evidently sometimes paid for out of
the county funds. Thus in Essex, in 1702, " it is ordered by this Court that
the Treasurer of the East Division do pay to Mr. John Clements, of Chelmsford,
inn-holder, the sum of £2 : 5 : 6 for Justices' dinner at the adjournment of the
Quarter Sessions " (MS. Minutes, Quarter Sessions, Essex, 14th April 1702).
In 1735 we find the Suffolk Quarter Sessions ordering the County Treasurer " to
pay to Philip Winterflood or order forty shillings for the Justices' dinners at the
present adjournment " (MS. Minutes, Quarter Sessions, Suffolk, 21st April
1735). The Suffolk Justices, by the way, dismissed their " chaplain " in 1705
for " neglecting to attend the Justices as usual at dinner" (*Ibid.* 20th April
1705). In other counties it seems to have been paid out of " the Justices' wages "
that we have described ; this course being followed in Shropshire (see order 4th
October 1788, in *Shropshire County Records*, part ix. p. 31) ; and certainly
in Middlesex in 1729, when the Sheriff had failed to provide a dinner as
had previously been done (MS. Minutes, Quarter Sessions, Middlesex, 14th
April 1729). The Middlesex Justices had, however, at their disposal " another
revenue called Colt Money, which belongs not to the County but to the Justices,
being collected from themselves " (*Ibid.* October 1723), probably from each
newly appointed acting magistrate on his first appearance ; and from this fund
(also called Honour Money or Socket Money) payments would occasionally be
made towards the Justices' dinners (*Ibid.* 6th December 1722, 14th April
1729). We find a Wiltshire Justice in 1743 paying half a guinea as " my
Colt Ale for my first acting " (MS. Diary of William Hunt, 1743 - 44, in
library of Wiltshire Archæological Society at Devizes). The Middlesex Justices
used habitually to summon " to dine with Mr. Chairman and the rest of His
Majesty's Justices " anyone of their number against whom a complaint had been
made ; and if he failed to attend " to answer such complaint," proceeded to pass
whatever resolution of disapproval the case required (Minutes, 6th December
1759). The Grand Jury also had a dinner, apparently separate from that of the
Justices. In Lancashire in 1752 the Court objects to the Grand Jury going far
away, as " this Court frequently meets with very great inconveniences by reason
of the Grand Juries . . . dining at too great a distance from the two public-

accounts due, fill any vacancies in the salaried offices of the county, and give such orders to the Clerk of the Peace, the Bridgemasters, or the Keepers of the Houses of Correction as were within their own competence. These primitive habits lasted, in some of the most remote and sparsely inhabited counties, down to the very end of the period that we are considering. Thus, of the Cumberland Quarter Sessions we are told, between 1820 and 1830, that "it was the custom of the magistrates, after the prisoners had been tried and parish appeals settled, to adjourn as a Court to an hotel—'The Bush' at Carlisle, 'The Globe' at Cockermouth—where, over their walnuts and wine, or, more generally, brandy punch, the said Court passed the 'quarterly accounts'—in other words, did the county business." In this instance, and we imagine also in others, the laxity of the procedure led to grave financial scandals. The Cumberland Justices, we learn, down to 1828, seemed "inert, supine, or asleep, as if caring little for balance sheets and the responsible and graver duties attached to their administrative faculty. . . . A pleasant settlement of the quarterly accounts at the borough hostelry was sufficient for the day, without giving a moment's thought for the morrow of the ratepayers. Everything requiring investigation was hurried through the Court by those whose policy it was to postpone the consideration of money disbursements to the last minutes of the sitting. There seems to have been no regular audit of bills and vouchers; the general debit was named under a few heads, and possibly glanced at by one or two of the less timid members of the Court. The Chairman, being assured by the Clerk that all was right, affixed his signature for 'pay, pay,' and so thousands of pounds were disposed of." [1] Towards the end of the eighteenth century, or at the beginning of the nineteenth, we note, in most counties, the coming in of more seemly arrangements. Thus, at the Devonshire Quarter Sessions in 1806, we find the Justices casting about for some

---

houses which His Majesty's Justices . . . frequently dine at," and it is formally ordered that for the future the Grand Jury is to dine at the public-house used by the Justices, taking each of the two in turn (MS. Minutes, Quarter Sessions, Lancashire, 7th April 1752).

[1] *The Worthies of Cumberland*, by Henry Lonsdale, 1868, vol. ii. pp. 75, 84. There seems to have been the same laxity in Norfolk, as we hear incidentally of a Justice objecting to "voting money in gross sums," and asking that the different items should be specified (*Norwich Mercury*, 1829).

better opportunity of " auditing the public accounts and for transacting the other general business of the county, which used formerly to be settled after dinner the first day of the Sessions." [1] One frequent expedient, which we find adopted in Norfolk, Hampshire, Somerset, and several other counties in the last quarter of the eighteenth century, was for the Justices to be summoned to a meeting in the " Grand Jury Chamber," either before the Grand Jury was sworn or after it concluded its business.[2] The Essex Quarter Sessions found another expedient, which was destined to become a common practice. As the criminal business involved an interval of several hours between the charging of the Grand Jury (who then retired to consider their " bills ") and the actual trial of the offenders against whom true bills were found, it became convenient to take the administrative or specifically " County Business " during this interval.[3] A further stage in Quarter Sessions procedure was reached in the exceptional county of Middlesex as early as the beginning of the eighteenth century. In this county the magnitude of the criminal business necessitated various special arrangements. Among these we find, from 1716 onwards, the keeping of a special set of books for recording all " general orders " of the Justices ; that is to say, all their decisions other than criminal convictions and appeals, and—certainly before 1723 [4]—the setting aside, at each Sessions, of a whole day during which nothing but the specific-

---

[1] MS. Minutes, Quarter Sessions, Devonshire, Midsummer 1806.

[2] See MS. Minutes, Quarter Sessions, Norfolk, 9th October 1799 ; ditto Hampshire, 5th October 1799 (see also advertisement in *Reading Mercury*, 22nd September 1788) ; ditto, Somerset, Midsummer 1811.

[3] This arrangement was adopted by Surrey in 1802 (MS. Minutes, Quarter Sessions, Surrey, 16th February 1802).

[4] See reference to "the County Day" in the Report of the Committee on the Accounts of the Treasurer, in MS. Minutes, Quarter Sessions, Middlesex, October 1723. It was on this day that the Chairman for the following Sessions was elected or re-elected. It was perhaps with the same object that the Surrey Quarter Sessions ordered, in 1788, "that the public day for doing the business of the county shall in future be on the second day of every General Quarter Sessions, and that the day on which the Sessions is opened shall be considered the first day, though the magistrates meet only to adjourn" (MS. Minutes, Quarter Sessions, Surrey, 23rd July 1788). See, for instance, *Leeds Intelligencer*, 9th April 1792. The same sort of arrangement was made by Essex in 1801. "It appearing to this Court that from the multiplicity of business of the present and several late Quarter Sessions it is highly expedient that an arrangement and provision be made so that the business of the next and every future Sessions may be gone through with as much despatch and regularity as possible," it is ordered that an advertisement be inserted in the local newspapers that the

ally "county business" was taken. The Quarter Sessions of the West Riding of Yorkshire distinguished itself in the latter part of the eighteenth century, not only by elaborately settling its order of business, but also by advertising it in the newspapers for the convenience of the public. "Notice is hereby given," runs the ordinary advertisement inserted by the Clerk of the Peace, "that the General Quarter Sessions of the Peace for the West Riding of the County of York will be opened at Pontefract on Monday . . . that the officers and Grand Jury will then be called over, the Chairman chosen and the vagrants passed. . . . On Tuesday morning . . . appeals will be heard. On Wednesday the Narrow Cloth Searchers will be sworn, and appeals to traverses tried. On Thursday morning the state of the bridges will be considered, the reports of the surveyors concerning them, and other reports relating to public works or business will be received, contracts for conveying vagrants treated upon, the Treasurer's, Clerk of the Peace's, and other accounts will be audited, and a Treasurer for the year ensuing elected. In the afternoon orders relating to the tolls of Castleford and Ferrybridge, to York Castle, the House of Correction, carriers' rates, wages of servants, artificers, and labourers will be settled. On Friday morning the felons will be tried; at noon the Grand Jury discharged and all recognisances called. In the afternoon highways and persons indicted will be called over and process awarded against them. All the remaining business will be dispatched and the Sessions closed that night if possible." Much the same procedure was publicly adopted by the well-organised county of Gloucestershire, where the Justices, in 1815, formally decided on the

criminal business would be taken first ; "after which (and the proclamation and Acts of Parliament being read, and the charge given to the Grand Jury) the Court will be immediately adjourned to the room upstairs . . . for the special purpose of doing all the business commonly known by the distinction of the County Business (except the inspecting and examining the Treasurer's Accounts and bills on the county, which will be done in the usual place and at the usual time on the Wednesday morning) ; and with a view that time may be given to the Grand Jury, whilst such County Business is going on, to proceed with their bills, and also to the counsel and attornies to be prepared in the appeals and other business of the Sessions. The Court will afterwards be adjourned to the Crown Court in the Shire House at the hour of five in the afternoon . . . or as early an hour after as the County Business will permit, when the general business of the Sessions will be resumed and proceeded upon . . . Persons attending to take the oaths may attend at the first opening of the Court" (MS. Minutes, Quarter Sessions, Essex, 14th April 1801.

following arrangements for their future Sessions. At ten
o'clock on the opening day of the Sessions, the magistrates,
having assembled at the " King's Head Inn," are to proceed to
the " Booth Hall," where the Court is to be opened by the
usual proclamation, and a Chairman elected. The magistrates
then adjourn to a private room at the " King's Head," " and
being attended by the Clerk of the Peace, do then and there
proceed to consider, discuss, and make orders concerning all
matters relating to the general police of the county ; to audit,
settle, and order payment of the bills and charges of the
Keepers of the Gaol, Penitentiary House, and Houses of
Correction, as well on account of their respective salaries as
for the maintaining, clothing, and employing prisoners ; to
examine the bills of Coroners and County Surveyors, and
order payment of the same ; and further to satisfy and discharge all other legal demands on the County Rate." The Court
adjourns at six o'clock (or earlier if the business is finished)
until eight the next morning, " for the purpose of discussing
and settling any general business that may have remained
unfinished at the close of the preceding evening." At ten,
the Court adjourns to the Booth Hall, and deals as a public
court of justice with indictments, traverses, and appeals, and
" delivers " the Gaol and Houses of Correction.[1]

Beyond this general allocation of the different kinds of
regular business to the different days, no provision was made
for notifying to the Justices the details of the cases or the
business proposals to be brought before them. The absence
of any efficient secretarial staff prevented the Justices from
developing that which is almost a necessity for good administration in a representative body, namely the prior circulation
of a detailed agenda. In no county do we find that a statement of the business to be done at any particular meeting was
sent round to the Justices before the meeting, or was even
prepared for their use at the meeting itself. Nothing more
than a bare notice of the day, hour, and place at which the
sessions was to be held was communicated to the acting

---

[1] MS. Minutes, Quarter Sessions, Gloucestershire, 11th July 1815. Another
elaborate order of proceedings will be found in MS. Minutes, Quarter Sessions,
Surrey, 4th April 1826. A brief account of the necessary formal and routine
business at this date will be found in *A Practical Guide to the Quarter Sessions*,
by W. D. Rastall, afterwards Dickinson, 1829, p. 90.

Justices before each Quarter or Special Sessions. The most that was done by way of notice was, on special occasions, to intimate that a particular office would be filled up at the coming meeting, and even this required an express order of the previous Sessions. In Hampshire, in 1775, it is, for instance, " Ordered that whenever any vacancy shall happen for the future in any office or offices belonging to or at the disposal of the County, a fortnight's notice shall be given by the Clerk of the Peace in the public papers previous to the day of election." [1] In Buckinghamshire, a generation later, the Court even goes so far as to order the Clerk of the Peace to " write to all the acting magistrates of the County, with notice that the appointment of a Treasurer of this County Stock will take place at the adjourned Sessions." [2] Occasionally, too, the consideration of business involving large expenditure would be expressly adjourned for a larger attendance of Justices. Thus the Suffolk Quarter Sessions in 1783 adjourns certain extensive repairs required by two of the Houses of Correction, and orders " the Clerk of the Peace to give notice thereof three weeks in the Ipswich paper, in order that a large attendance of Justices may be then had." [3] Nor was any attempt made to circulate among the Justices any information in the way of reports of committees or details of expenditure. Not until the close of the eighteenth century does any county appear to have printed a statement of accounts, even for the information of the Justices themselves.[4]

---

[1] MS. Minutes, Quarter Sessions, Hants, 11th July 1775. In Norfolk in 1795 they decided to defer the filling of vacancies in the chairmanship until the next subsequent meeting : " That in case of a vacancy in the office of Chairman such vacancies be declared at the next General Quarter Sessions of the Peace after such vacancy shall happen, and that the election of a new Chairman be made at the next General Quarter Sessions of the Peace after such vacancy be declared " (MS. Minutes, Quarter Sessions, Norfolk, 7th October 1795). As late as 1815, so important an authority as the West Riding orders that all appointments shall be made either at the Annual Sessions at Pontefract, or at a specially convened meeting for the purpose (MS. Minutes, Quarter Sessions, West Riding, 3rd April 1815).

[2] MS. Minutes, Quarter Sessions, Buckinghamshire, Easter 1814. So in Wiltshire in 1815 : "That previous to the next Sessions a circular letter be addressed to the several acting Justices of the County, requesting their personal attendance on the first day of the next Sessions at Devizes, and stating therein the several matters which will be then taken into consideration " (MS. Minutes, Quarter Sessions, Wiltshire, Michaelmas 1815).

[3] MS. Minutes, Quarter Sessions, Suffolk, 28th May 1783.

[4] The Derbyshire Justices printed such statements from 1783 onward

As a Court of Justice, Quarter Sessions was (unlike the subordinate tribunals of the Justices out of Sessions) always open to the public, and therefore to the press, as soon as any newspapers deigned to report its proceedings. "At Quarter Sessions," says a Devonshire reformer of 1834, "the magistrates occupy the bench and the counsel's table below. . . . All the rest of the Court is open . . . always attended by reporters. The Grand Jury frequently stay to hear the discussions."[1] Hence, so long as the local administration was judicial in character, or even cloaked in judicial forms, the county had at least the safeguard of publicity. But this safeguard vanished with the supersession, as we shall see in another chapter, of judicial processes and the judicial attitude towards county services, by a county executive, giving discretional orders to a staff of county officers. When the Justices adjourned from their Court of Justice to do whatever they came to consider as "County Business," their proceedings were, during the whole of the eighteenth century, shrouded in secrecy. No one who was not a magistrate (or a county officer in actual attendance upon them) was allowed to follow them to the "Grand Jury Room," or other private scene of their deliberations and convivialities.[2] Not until 1825, when the public agitation against the Rulers of the County

[1] (Three Centuries of Derbyshire Annals, by J. C. Cox, 1890, vol. i. p. 121). The County Treasurer of Lancashire was ordered to publish an annual statement in 1800 (MS. Minutes, Annual General Sessions, Lancashire, 26th June 1800). In Middlesex in 1723 a committee of the Justices recommended that a separate book of accounts should be kept, and after examination by a committee, "laid on the table after dinner on the County Days by the Clerk of the Peace för the perusal of the Justices" (MS. Minutes, Quarterly Sessions, October 1723). The Justices seem to have been extraordinarily loth to employ the printing press, even for their own convenience. Middlesex occasionally printed special reports of committees in the early part of the nineteenth century ; and Surrey, in 1835, ordered that any such committee might get its report printed (MS. Minutes, Quarter Sessions, Surrey, 30th June 1835). In 1818 the Somerset Quarter Sessions appointed a Committee which had printed an elaborate report of the county expenditure from 1759 to 1818 (preserved in Home Office Domestic State Papers, No. 332, in Public Record Office). The Lancashire Annual Sessions printed much of its agenda from 1821 onwards. The whole of its minutes for the 1829 meeting were printed, and from 1832 onward this was done as a matter of course. Most other counties did not print either minutes or detailed agenda right down to 1888.

[1] Report of House of Commons Committee on County Rates, 1834.

[2] At the Norfolk Quarter Sessions in 1824 we find the Court expressly ordering the Chairman to exclude all persons who were not magistrates both from the bench and "from the Grand Jury Room" (MS. Minutes, Quarter Sessions, Norfolk, 14th January 1824).

which we shall presently describe, had reached considerable
dimensions, was this secrecy broken into, and then not in all
counties. In 1825 Sir Peter Laurie induced the Middlesex
Justices to admit the public. In January 1828, the editor of
the *Carlisle Journal* applied formally for permission to report
the proceedings of the Cumberland Quarter Sessions. "After
some discussion the editor's request was complied with; so
that the financial affairs of the county became public." [1] In
the same year the Norfolk Justices resolved on a similar
concession to public opinion. [2] Most other counties did not
admit reporters until long after 1832. [3]

(d) *Administration by Judicial Process*

In the foregoing account of the general procedure of the
Court of Quarter Sessions we have followed the Justices out

---

[1] *The Worthies of Cumberland*, by H. Lonsdale, 1868, vol. ii. p. 78.

[2] MS. Minutes, Quarter Sessions, Norfolk, Michaelmas 1828 ; *Norfolk
Chronicle*, 31st January 1829. We should cite, by way of exception, the
action of the Berkshire Justices forty years previously in ordering an abstract
of the receipts and expenditure for the County Gaol during the past three years
to be printed and freely distributed by the Clerk of the Peace (MS. Minutes,
Quarter Sessions, Berkshire, 15th January 1788). We believe this to have
been very unusual, if not unique, at so early a date. The Dorsetshire Justices
in 1827 agreed to have an annual report of receipts and expenditure prepared
for publication (MS. Minutes, Quarter Sessions, Dorsetshire, 24th April 1827).

[3] In Devonshire, Latimer, the editor of the *Western Times*, forced his way
in some time in 1832 (White's *History of Torquay*, p. 178). Cheshire, in the
same year, was still obdurate, notwithstanding the fact that the Justices were
undertaking new and onerous burdens, in the shape of a salaried constabulary, to
which public objection was taken. Their extravagance, said one magistrate,
"was mainly owing to that inveterate practice of adjourning the public business
to a private room, where the public knew nothing of what was going on, and
were only permitted the privilege of paying the money " (*Chester Courant*, 24th
April 1832). So, too, was Dorsetshire in 1833, when a motion in favour of
publicity by the Hon. E. B. Portman, M.P., was rejected, and all strangers
were ejected (MS. Minutes, Quarter Sessions, Dorsetshire, 31st December 1833).
At the Derbyshire Quarter Sessions in 1833, Lord Vernon, the Chairman, said
that "with regard to the usual business of the county, which had hitherto been
transacted on the previous day in private, the magistrates had determined in
future to give publicity to it by making the Court an open one, and therefore
the public generally would be eligible to witness their proceedings should they
be so disposed" (*Morning Advertiser*, 12th July 1833). In 1834, at the
Somerset Epiphany Sessions, upon the question of adjournment to the Grand
Jury Room, Sir T. B. Lethbridge rose, not to object to the proposal, but merely
to have it clearly understood that the public had a right to be present upstairs
as well as in that Court. The right being fully recognised by the Chairman
and magistrates present, the Court adjourned to the Grand Jury Room, a large
number of persons following, and the doors remained open during the rest of
the day " (*Bristol Journal*, 4th January 1834).

of the open Court into the private meetings where they deliberated on what was coming to be called "County Business," now beginning to be separated from the criminal cases. We must, however, again remind the reader that, according to the legal constitution, all the authority of the Justices was in its nature judicial—that is to say, concerned with the enforcement of the obligations of the individual under the law of the land—and that even when they were discussing over wine and walnuts in the private parlour of a tavern their payments for bridges and prisons, they still, in theory, constituted the Court of Quarter Sessions, with all the prerogatives of a Court of Record.[1] We shall describe in the following chapter how the abandonment of the forms and procedure of a Court of Justice led to the development of an extra-legal constitution, under which more and more of the local government of the county came to be administered. But in 1689, and for many years afterwards, most of the county administration was transacted by judicial process, in open Court, with all the paraphernalia of a Court of Justice. To this part we for the moment restrict ourselves. This division of the subject enables us to bring into prominence the large part played in county government at the end of the seventeenth century by the Grand Inquest and the Hundred Juries, and the continuance, right down to 1835, of the device of presentment and trial, as a method of securing in each district the fulfilment of local obligations, the provision of local requirements, and the performance of local services.

(e) *The Grand Jury*

We do not nowadays associate Juries with local government. But, in 1689, and for many years afterwards, the Juries which formed an integral part of the Court of Quarter Sessions, as also of the six-monthly Assizes, had important functions in the civil as well as in the criminal business of

---

[1] So far did this assumption go that we find even the formal registration of dissenting chapels under 1 William and Mary, c. 18, sec. 19, taking the form of a judicial process. "The house of E. R. is at this Court presented to be a place intended by Protestant Dissenters to exercise their religion in" (MS. Minutes, Quarter Sessions, Breconshire, 15th January 1717; another case, 11th January 1704).

the county. The "Gentlemen of the Grand Jury," in
particular—the "Grand Inquest" of the County—were, it
was quaintly said in 1725, "the great or grand spring, or
Primum Mobile of the Court, that gives motion to all the
other wheels, their presentments being the key that opens and
shuts the proceedings of the Court." [1] Dissenters as well as
Churchmen, merchants and professional men, large farmers
and capitalist manufacturers, as well as landed proprietors—
"gentlemen of the best quality, estate, and understanding in
the county" [2]—would be summoned by the High Sheriff or
his deputy, to spend one or two days, entirely without
remuneration, at the time at which the Quarter Sessions or
Assizes were held; and neglect to obey this summons would
be followed by the infliction of a heavy fine. At the Assizes
the Grand Jury would frequently consist wholly or mainly of
Justices of the Peace. At Quarter Sessions these, of course,
were on the bench, and the Grand Jury had to be made up of
those who were not in the Commission. In the anomalous
County of Middlesex the Grand Jury, like the magistracy
itself, had its inferior elements; and we hear in 1723-25 of
the Sheriff's officers "contemptuously and for the sake of
corrupt lucre, wilfully neglecting to summon a great many
able, sufficient, and substantial men, and, in their room and
place," introducing others, "of mean capacity and in low
circumstances," [3] who, on one occasion, had "demeaned themselves with the greatest indecency in shouting and clamour-
ing" in the Grand Jury Room. [4] But in the ordinary county
the members of "the Grand Inquest" were, we believe, drawn
from among the substantial citizens of the county at large;
even if they did not "usually consist," as Blackstone declares,
"of gentlemen of the first figure in the county." "It is a
common order with us," says Lambard in 1581, "to have

---

[1] *A General Charge to all Grand Juries*, by Sir James Astry, 1725, p. 6.
[2] *The Second Charge of Whitelocke Bulstrode, Esq., to the Grand Jury of
Middlesex*, October 1718, p. 2.
[3] MS. Minutes, Quarter Sessions, Middlesex, 13th May 1725.
[4] *Ibid.* 10th January 1723. In the neighbouring county of Surrey we find
the Grand Jury, doubtless from neglect to attend it, partly made up of the
High Constables who were necessarily at Quarter Sessions. This led to complaints by the Justices, and an order specifically declaring the High Constables
to be unfit members of the "Grand Inquest for the body of the county" (MS.
Minutes, Quarter Sessions, Surrey, 12th July and 4th October 1743).

them of an odd number, as 17, 19, or 21, to the end (as it seemed) that if they should dissent in opinion somewhat equally yet there should be always one to weigh down the side and cast the balance. But if twelve of them do agree, the gainsaying of the residue cannot hinder the presentment."[1] With the business of the Grand Jury in considering the criminal "bills of indictment," hearing sufficient of the evidence for the prosecution to satisfy themselves that a *prima facie* case had been made out, and either returning them as "true bills" for trial, or "throwing them out," that is, "ignoring" them, by endorsing them "ignoramus"—we are here not concerned. Nor need we trouble the student with the, often, "too long and tedious charges," with which, we are told, learned Judges and eloquent Chairmen of Quarter Sessions wearied the Grand Jurymen, "at the General Assizes or Quarterly Sessions of the Peace."[2] More significant to the student of local government is the ancient habit of this "Grand Inquest" of acting as a sort of "third estate" of the shire, or county "House of Commons," giving the opinion of the county on matters of public concern, and even, in many cases, exercising a sort of right, if not to vote supplies, at any rate to sanction in advance the county expenditure.

The financial part of the ancient function of the Grand Inquest may, we think, be of some constitutional significance,

---

[1] *Eirenarcha*, by W. Lambard, 1581, p. 308.

[2] *A General Charge to all Grand Juries*, by Sir James Astry, 1725, p. 1. An excellent specimen of a charge, delivered by William Hay to the Grand Jury of Sussex in 1733, will be found in his *Works*, 1794, appendix. A more banal "model charge" was often printed in Justices' handbooks ; see, for instance, *The Complete Justice*, by R. Chamberlain, 1681, pp. 470-485. Others that were printed were *Three Charges delivered at the General Quarter Sessions for . . . Suffolk*, by Edmond Bohun, 1693 ; *Sir Richard Cocks his Charge to the Grand Jury of the County of Gloucester*, 1717 ; *Three Charges to Grand and other Juries*, by Whitelocke Bulstrode, 1718 and 1722 ; *Five Charges to several Grand Juries*, by Sir John Gonson, 1729 ; *Charge delivered to the Grand Jury of the Sessions . . . for Westminster*, by Henry Fielding, 1749 ; *Charge to the Grand Jury at Hick's Hall*, by Sir John Hawkins, 1770 ; *Charge to the Grand Jury of the County of Middlesex*, by the same, 1780 ; *A Charge to the Grand Jury for the County of Middlesex*, by Sir H. Ashurst, 1792 ; *A Charge . . . at the General Quarter Sessions . . . of Somerset*, by J. B. Burland, 1793 ; *Charge to Grand Jury at the Quarter Sessions for Norfolk*, by Henry Jodrell, 1793 ; *Charges delivered to the Grand Jury . . . for the County of Gloucester*, by Rev. John Foley, 1804 ; *Seven Charges . . . by Rev. Samuel Partridge, Chairman . . . Sessions for the Hundreds of Kirton and Skirbeck, Lincolnshire*, 1809 ; *Charges delivered . . . at the General Sessions of the Peace for Middlesex*, by W. Watson, 1816.

and it deserves further investigation. But by 1689 it was already far advanced in the course of decay which has since reduced the Grand Jury itself almost to insignificance. Yet, even in 1689, it was still taken for granted that, when the County Gaol or the County Hall was out of repair, or the county bridges needed amendment, it was for the Grand Jury to initiate the proceedings by a formal presentment, before any action was taken by the Justices. In the case of bridges, this presentment of the Grand Jury had been recognised as a necessary preliminary by the statute, 22 Henry VIII. c. 5 (1531). In the case of expenditure for other county purposes the legal position was not so clear; but there seemed much to be said for the view taken by some authorities that such a presentment by the Grand Jury was, strictly speaking, required, before the Justices could charge any payment (other than those expressly required by statute) on the county as a whole, or order each parish to contribute its quota of the amount.[1] In some counties there are signs that the Grand Jury acted, at any rate as regards the county buildings, as an independent Finance Committee. Thus, in Derbyshire in 1698, "when the roof of the County Hall required repair, it was no committee of the Justices that invited estimates or controlled the work, but ' We, the Grand Jury do suppose that for taking up the leads of the County Hall, and what lead may be wanting to make up the old which will not serve again, may amount to the sum of £40. And we, the Grand Jury, do desire that [three names] shall see the laying out of the said money to the best advantage, and shall employ such workmen as they think convenient, and give an account to the Grand Jury how they disburse the said money.' "[2] In 1762, when a bill for brick and stone work done to the

---

[1] Mr. Cox goes so far as to say confidently that "no payment was valid unless formally presented by the Grand Inquest of the freeholders, a remarkable survival of the old popular control of finance to which we are but now reverting under the County Councils" (*Three Centuries of Derbyshire Annals*, by J. C. Cox, 1890, vol. i. p. 117). We should be inclined to ask at what date is this popular control supposed to have existed?

In Ireland, it may be noted, the Grand Jury did become a financial and administrative authority, voting the "Grand Jury Cess" and (by statute of 5 George III. c. 14 of 1765) directing all road maintenance. See the reports of the various House of Commons Committees on the subject in 1815, 1816, 1822, 1827, 1842, and 1867-68.

[2] *Three Centuries of Derbyshire Annals*, by J. C. Cox, 1890, vol. i. p. 117.

County Gaol has to be paid, it is endorsed " We, the Jurors of
our Lord the King now assembled do hereby present the above
bill," and it is authorised by the signatures of the nineteen
members of the Grand Jury.[1]   In 1748, indeed, an expenditure of over £150, incurred pursuant to orders of Quarter
Sessions in 1744-47 for the purchase and adaptation of a new
House of Correction at Tideswell, was formally objected to as
illegal, because it had been incurred without express presentment
by the Grand Jury.   The Grand Jury had, in 1741, merely
directed the old building to be repaired, and had never
sanctioned a new building.   Quarter Sessions, in spite of its
own express orders, upheld the objection and ordered the
money to be refunded by the two Justices who had spent it,
though this drastic penalty was eventually not enforced.[2]   In
other counties the Grand Jury contented itself with formally
presenting the buildings needing repair, leaving both the work
to be done and the payment to be made to the Justices'
discretion.[3]   In 1739 Parliament so far endorsed this custom
as specially to enact that no money should be spent from
county funds on bridges, gaols, or houses of correction, except
after presentment by the Grand Jury;[4] and this enactment
was, in 1768, extended to shire halls.[5]

We accordingly find the Grand Juries, both at Quarter
Sessions and Assizes, making more or less formal presentments
that this or that county structure is out of repair.   This
definite ascertainment and legal record of a fact is, we are
inclined to think, in spite of the Derbyshire precedents, all
that the Jury was charged with.   It is the Justices themselves,
at the same or a subsequent Quarter Sessions, that we find
deciding what action should be taken, giving orders for the
work, arranging for its inspection, and passing the accounts
for payment.   Presently it was found inconvenient to wait for

[1] *Three Centuries of Derbyshire Annals*, by J. C. Cox, 1890, vol. i. p. 117.
[2] *Ibid.* vol. i. p. 117 ; vol. ii. pp. 35-36.
[3] We may, however, note that in Hampshire as late as 1788 we find the
Grand Jury at the Assizes formally resolving, in view of the fact that "some
difficulties have arisen respecting the salary to be allowed to the keeper of the
Felons' Prison," that he should be allowed £200 a year, without any fees ; and
that not more than £60 should be allowed for assistants. The Justices in
Quarter Sessions adopted the first proposal, but raised the latter sum to £75
(MS. Minutes, Quarter Sessions, Hampshire, 1st April 1788).
[4] 12 George II. c. 29, 1739.
[5] 9 George III. c. 20, 1768.

the Grand Jury's presentment. "That clause in the statute of
12 George II. c. 29," says Dr. Burn in 1764, "which enacts
that no money shall be applied to the repair of county bridges
till presentment be made by the Grand Jury at the Assizes or
Sessions, of the insufficiency of or want of reparation, carries
the matter evidently too far; for though it may be reasonable
that the High Constable, or other surveyors of bridges, and also
the Justices, should be restrained from bringing a charge upon
the county in such matters at their will and pleasure, and perhaps only for the private convenience of individuals; yet in
cases of emergency, and of small expense, as, for instance, under
the charge of 40s., it might be reasonable that the surveyors
had power to contract; lest before the Assizes or Sessions
the breach be made worse, or the bridge be broken down.
And in this last case, the Justices should have power immediately to meet and order the rebuilding with all convenient
speed." [1] For half a century the only relaxation allowed
was that, by Act of 1768, sudden repairs, up to £30 value,
could be ordered on an emergency by any two Justices. In
1812 ordinary repairs up to £20 were allowed to be executed
without a presentment.[2] Presently we have the Grand Jury
used as a consultative committee to suggest to the Justices
what works should be undertaken, and being expressly empowered to employ professional assistance. Thus in Northumberland in 1820, it is " Ordered that at each subsequent
Sessions the Clerk of the Peace do state to the respective
Grand Juries that the Justices request that whenever any of the
county bridges shall be reported to be in want of any extensive
repairs, that they shall take into their consideration the
propriety of taking the opinion of an experienced civil
engineer upon the proposed mode of repair, and the expense
thereof, for the guidance of the Bench." In this county,
indeed, the bridges had already been placed under the care of
two salaried Bridge Surveyors, one for the north and the
other for the south of the county, whose " Report Books "
furnished the information necessary for the formal indictments
or presentments, and who were each paid regularly sums " for
the repair of bridges as per his Report Book " . . . they being

---

[1] *The History of the Poor Laws*, by Rev. R. Burn, 1764, p. 246.
[2] 52 George III. c. 110, 1812.

under presentment for want of repairs."[1] In the case of a
bridge not plainly chargeable to public funds, county after
county strove to make the cumbrous machinery something
more than a formality. "No money," we read of Somerset in
1815, "can by law be granted for the repair of any bridge
until such bridge is presented or indicted for insufficiency,
inconveniency, or want of reparation."[2] "No allowance from
the Riding," declare the Justices of the East Riding, in 1824,
"towards building or repairing any bridge (which the East
Riding is not liable to support) shall be granted until the
person or township who ought to repair the same hath been
indicted and submitted to such indictment."[3] Right down to
the reign of Victoria the form of presentment was gone
through, but it evidently became, so far as the county buildings
were concerned, a mere formality, arranged beforehand by the
Justices, and drawn up in advance by the Clerk of the Peace.[4]

The presentments of Grand Juries for the first three
quarters of the eighteenth century extended to other matters
than bridges, gaols, and similar county structures. In the
sessions rolls of many counties[5] we discover Grand Jury

[1] MS. Minutes, Quarter Sessions, Northumberland, 13th January 1820 ;
18th July 1799. The Grand Jury of Hampshire in 1777, when the County
had been indicted at the Assizes for the non-repair of a bridge, express their
doubts whether this is a county bridge, and suggest that the Justices should
have a list of county bridges compiled (MS. Minutes, Quarter Sessions, Hampshire, 15th July 1777).

[2] *A Guide to the Practice of the Court of Quarter Sessions for the County of
Somerset*, by John Jesse, Junior, 1815, p. 43.

[3] *The Names of the Acting Magistrates and Public Officers of the East Riding
of the County of York, with several matters relating to the Practice and Proceedings of the Court of Quarter Sessions*, 1824.

[4] Already in 1776 we find it ordered by the Cambridgeshire Quarter Sessions
"that a Clerk of the Peace prepare or cause a proper presentment to be prepared,
to be made by the Grand Jury at the next Assizes, relative to the inconvenient
state and situation of the present Shire Hall for this county, that the Justices
may give directions to have the same altered at the next sessions" (MS.
Minutes, Cambridgeshire, 19th July 1776).

[5] It adds a difficulty to the student of local government that these presentments are seldom entered in the MS. Minute Books or Order Books of Quarter
Sessions. If preserved at all, they are usually to be found as separate documents,
rolled up year by year, in the "bundles," "sessions papers," "session rolls,"
or "miscellaneous documents," among the county archives. One of the best
collections is that of Gloucestershire ; see, for instance, the bundles for 1733-
1739. For Hertfordshire, the County Council has printed an elaborate
Calendar of the contents of many of the bundles from 1625 to 1859 ; but the
utility of the volume is diminished by an unfortunate omission to state whether
the presentments are by the Grand Jury, the Hundred Juries, High Constables,
Petty Constables, or individual Justices. We have already referred to the

presentments of particular highways, left "founderous" by parish or landlord under obligation to repair; side ditches unscoured by owners or occupiers; dung-heaps shot down by careless farmers on the highway itself, together with cases of the neglect of Parish Constables and Surveyors to fulfil their duties. In 1697 we find the Essex Grand Jury courageously presenting one of the County Coroners for "vexing the Jury . . . by reason they would not comply with his humour in finding a particular verdict"; and even making a formal presentment, which we have already quoted, of seven Justices of the Peace—three of them clergymen—for demanding excessive fees for issuing warrants, signing apprentices' indentures, and confirming the Poor Rate.[1] More usually the Grand Juries would present their complaints in general terms, leaving to High and Petty Constables the presentment of particular delinquents. Thus, when in 1678, "the Grand Inquest" of Gloucestershire presented to Quarter Sessions "the daily concourse and great increase of rogues and sturdy beggars," which had become "a great grievance and annoyance to the inhabitants of this county," it was to "the negligence or ignorance of those officers who have been entrusted in this concern" that they attributed the evil of the beggars having "now grown so insolent and presumptuous that they have oft by threats and menaces extorted money and victuals from those who live in houses far remote from neighbours." And the remedy which was suggested to and adopted by Quarter Sessions was the issue of an order to "all Chief Constables, Petty Constables, Headboroughs, Tithingmen, and all other officers herein concerned," to "forthwith cause all the laws and statutes . . . against . . . wandering and idle persons to be put in execution."[2] Such a quickening of the county executive we see, for instance, in the action of the Grand Jury of Essex, which in 1700 presented in a batch "all inn-keepers, victuallers, and ale-house keepers within the said county" as

publication of the records of the North and West Ridings, Worcestershire, Middlesex, and Shropshire. Some presentments are given in *Three Centuries of Derbyshire Annals*, by J. C. Cox, 1890.

[1] Presentment by Grand Jury at Chelmsford, 11th January 1697; in Sessions Bundle, No. 8, Essex Quarter Sessions Archives; given in full in Chapter III. County Administration by Justices out of Sessions, p. 416.

[2] Order of Quarter Sessions, 1678, in *Dursley and its Neighbourhood*, by J. H. Blunt, 1877, p. 45.

guilty, one and all, of " selling and uttering drink in measures not sealed according to the standard of the King's Exchequer"; a sweeping accusation which led to indictments being preferred by order of Quarter Sessions against many of the offenders.[1] In 1710, when royal proclamations had vainly endeavoured to keep down " the excessive price of corn," by fulminating against forestalling and regrating, the Essex Grand Jury drew attention to " the very great neglect of several Constables in this county," and incidentally to the remissness of the Justices themselves in not making arrangements to insist on the licensing, according to law, of " badgers, jobbers, and drovers." This led Quarter Sessions to sit by adjournment, in all the Divisions of the county, so that the persons concerned might the more conveniently take out licences, which required the entering into recognisances " in open court "; and that every Petty Constable in each Division might be notified to see that the law was obeyed.[2] In Merionethshire in 1654 the Grand Jury presented the township of Dolgelly for not having a pinfold.[3] In Devonshire, in 1713, the " Grand Inquest " presented that the statute of 1698 requiring the erection of sign-posts at cross roads " was of great use and benefit to Her Majesty's subjects . . . but the execution thereof hath in many places of this county been neglected, and wholly omitted, to the great inconvenience and damage of Her Majesty's liege people." On this the Court ordered the Justices in their several Divisions to order the Act to be put in execution.[4] The Grand Jury of Northumberland in 1744, " finding by experience that the good and salutary law to restrain and prevent the excessive increase of horse races " had not been put in operation, and that the frequent race meetings that being advertised, " together with the practice of cock-fighting (now so much in use) tend greatly to the encourage-ment of idleness . . . of the meaner sort of people," presented, in one swoop " all and every the contrivers and promoters of such illegal practices and diversions "; and peremptorily ordered the Clerk of the Peace to prosecute them at the

---

[1] MS. Minutes, Quarter Sessions, Essex, 8th October 1701.
[2] *Ibid.* 8th April 1710.
[3] MS. Sessions Rolls, Merionethshire, Midsummer 1754.
[4] MS. Minutes, Quarter Sessions, Devonshire, Michaelmas 1713.

expense of the county.[1] Throughout the whole century, indeed, the Grand Jury continues occasionally—but with ever-decreasing authority—to criticise the county administration, and to make specific suggestions for its improvement.[2] Finally, we have the Middlesex Justices, annoyed at the action of the Grand Jury in making what were declared to be inaccurate presentments about the state of the House of Correction, depriving succeeding Grand Juries of any official opportunity of visiting it. The members of this Grand Jury conceived that they had a right to make an independent inspection of the various county prisons, in order to see that the Justices were properly administering them. The Justices denied the existence of any such right; and, we are told, in 1827, "in order not to bring the matter to issue, have always discharged the Grand Jury as soon as they had concluded their inquiries into the bills laid before them, and before they had an opportunity to exercise their right." The Justices did not refuse admission to the prisons to the individual jurymen, and caused them to be "informed that an order for their admission had been sent to the gate of the prisons for 'the gentlemen of the late Grand Jury,'" who by this ingenious device found themselves unable to "embody their opinions in the form of a presentment to the Court, as they had been already discharged," and were relegated to the chilling pages of "the visitors' book."[3]

Another function of the Grand Jury was to formulate the opinion of the county on matters of common concern. In the seventeenth century we find "the Grand Inquest" still considered by Parliament, by the National Government, and by the Justices themselves, as the official exponent of the county. Hence in loyal addresses to the Crown, as in petitions to either House of Parliament, the "Gentlemen of the Grand Jury" usually figured first in the document, whilst in their frequent presentments at the Assizes and Quarter Sessions

[1] *Gentleman's Magazine*, August 1744, vol. xiv. p. 442.

[2] In Essex, we may note that the annual fixing of the rates of wages was not done by Quarter Sessions without the consent of the Grand Jury. "We consent that the Statute Wages may continue, and that they may be printed and sent to the Constables of every Hundred, and so to be sent to every parish" (Presentment of Grand Jury, Essex, 18th April 1594 ; in MS. Sessions Bundle No. 8).

[3] *Times*, 3rd November 1827. Complaint by the Grand Jury to the Home Secretary brought no redress (Home Office Domestic Entry Book, 29th May 1833, vol. lxix. in Public Record Office).

they were perpetually drawing attention to grievances. As might have been expected, it was the Grand Juries of the City of London and Middlesex who were the most forward with their views, and the most inclined to reliance on Parliamentary help. Their grievances varied from decade to decade. From the Restoration to the accession of the Hanoverian dynasty we find them mostly presenting Nonconformist fanatics and Papist recusants, unlawful assemblies and seditious publications. From the alarm set up in 1720 by the approach of the plague, these Grand Juries are concerned about the disorder and filth of the streets. They complain of the growing obstruction of traffic, the swarms of beggars, the increase of vagrancy, the disorderly shoe-blacks and other hooligans of the time, and the increase of robberies and assaults. Nor were their presentments always in vain. It was the eloquent denunciation of the ruin wrought by free gin, in the presentments of the Grand Juries of Middlesex, Westminster, the Tower Hamlets, and the City of London in 1733, that led to the Gin Act of 1736, suppressing the traffic in spirituous liquors. It was the presentment of the Middlesex Grand Jury in 1749 that caused the reform of the Middlesex County Court by the statute of 1750 (23 George II. c. 33). Such presentments continued right through the eighteenth century, though with diminishing frequency and a gradual loss of reality. By the end of the century they had come to be little more than sonorous generalities, loyal addresses, and declarations on national politics, usually " high Tory " in character.[1]

(f) *The Hundred Jury*

Besides the Grand Jury, on the one hand, and the lengthy panel of petty jurymen for the " Traverse " or " Felons' Juries " on the other—both summoned by the High Sheriff from " the

---

[1] The question of whether the Grand Jury has now any utility at all, even in criminal procedure, has often been discussed. Various bills for its complete abolition have been introduced but none passed. See the article (by Lord Denman) in *Edinburgh Review*, 1828 ; the Eighth Report of the Royal Commission on the State of the Criminal Law, 1845 ; the abortive bills of 1849 and 1852 ; and *Observations on the Inutility of Grand Juries and Suggestions for their Abolition*, by W. C. Humphreys, 1st edition 1842, 2nd edition 1857.

body of the county"—there were in attendance at the Quarter Sessions of the end of the seventeenth century other sets of jurymen summoned from the several Hundreds, Liberties, or Boroughs of the County, whose existence and duties have now been almost forgotten. These were the Hundred Juries or Petty Juries of Inquiry or Presentment, whose business it was " to inquire of such things as shall be given them in charge," [1] to present to the Court the delinquencies and derelictions of duty of their particular Hundreds or equivalent divisions, in the same way that the Grand Jury did for the county as a whole. These Hundred Juries, composed, like the Grand Jury, normally of between twelve and twenty-four men each, resembled the Grand Jury, and were distinguished from the other Petty Juries or "Felons' Juries," in that they did not require for the validity of their presentments or verdicts either any definite number, or even unanimity, so long as twelve jurymen agreed.[2] In the sixteenth and seventeenth centuries they seem to have been regularly summoned by the High Sheriff, acting through the High Bailiffs of the several Baili-wicks, Hundreds, Wapentakes, or Liberties, and the Mayors of Boroughs; and to have made regular presentments of nuisances and derelictions of duty.[3] Thus, at the Dorset Quarter Sessions, about the year 1630, "the Jury of the Hundred of Pimperne" presented that the blacksmith of that place persisted in making a fire "in the smith's forge there . . . not only for the use of his trade but also for the dressing his necessaries for his family, and for washing and other businesses, whereby the inhabitants . . . have been often endangered to have their houses set on fire"; whereupon Quarter Sessions orders, under penalty of commitment to the county gaol, that he shall "not use any fire in the time to come in the said forge, save only with sea coal, and that for the necessary use of his trade only."[4] So about the same

---

[1] MS. Minutes, Quarter Sessions, Essex, 6th October 1719.

[2] "If twelve of them agree, the dissent of the residue cannot hinder the presentment" (*The Office of the Clerk of the Peace*, etc., 1682, p. 103).

[3] Mr. Cox gives a translation of the Clerk of the Peace's precept to the Sheriff of Derbyshire in 1560 requiring him to summon these Hundred Juries, as well as the Grand Jury (*Three Centuries of Derbyshire Annals*, by J. C. Cox, 1890, vol. i. p. 114).

[4] Extract from Minutes of Dorsetshire Quarter Sessions, about 1630, in *Dorset County Chronicle*, 23rd May 1844.

time we have "the Jury and Constables of the Borough of
Shaston," in the same county, presenting that the said Borough
has no waste land on which to re-erect the archery butts,
whereupon the Court, at the instance of the Mayor, sanctions
the re-erection of the butts on a part of the churchyard not
used for burials.[1]

We infer that after the Restoration, in the general relaxation of manners and morals, and revulsion against the old
inquisitorial government, the presentments of these Hundred
Juries were very largely disused, and that the Juries themselves began to fall into abeyance, or, like so many other parts
of the judicial procedure of the Court of Quarter Sessions in
regard to civil affairs, to degenerate into mere formalities.[2]
At the close of the seventeenth century the Sheriffs were
still issuing their warrants every quarter to "the several
Bailiffs of Liberties and Bailiffs of Hundreds," requiring them
to return persons to serve on "the particular Juries of Inquiry
for Hundreds and Liberties" as well as "upon the Petty
Jury for the trial of prisoners"; but the Sheriffs were no
longer troubling themselves to select the names, and were
leaving it perfunctorily "to the discretion of Bailiffs to put in
and out whom they chose in that service."[3] The result was

---

[1] Extract from Minutes of Dorsetshire Quarter Sessions, about 1630, in
Dorset County Chronicle, 18th April 1844. For interesting examples from the
fourteenth to seventeenth century of elaborate presentments of public nuisances
connected with rivers, bridges, and roads, by the Juries of Hundreds and
Wapentakes to the Assize Judges and the "Justices of Sewers,"—it is not
clear whether any of the cases quoted came before Quarter Sessions,—and the
subsequent trials of the defendants by separate "Traverse Juries," see *The
History of Imbanking and Draining*, by Sir William Dugdale, 1662, pp. 41,
212-216, 277 of edition of 1772.

[2] In 1688-1700, at any rate, the Hundred Juries were still active in
Dorsetshire, where we have "the Constables and Jurors of the Hundred of
Sturminster, Newton Castle, presenting bridges" (MS. Minutes, Quarter Sessions,
Dorset, 10th and 11th July 1688); and in Surrey, for we find "the Jury for
the Hundred of Wallingford" presenting one Christopher Smith of Carshalton,
victualler, as "a person very much disaffected to their Majesty's Government";
whereupon he is bound over to appear at next Quarter Sessions to answer this
accusation (MS. Minutes, Quarter Sessions, Surrey, 5th April 1693). And in
1709 we are expressly told that the Borough of Blandford sent up to the
Epiphany Sessions to be sworn, besides its Bailiff, Sergeant at Mace, and two
Constables, six "jurors of the Grand Inquest," "five jurors to try cases,"
"and seventeen" sworn "jurors," who were evidently the Hundred Jury (MS.
Sessions Rolls, Quarter Sessions, Dorsetshire, January 1710).

[3] *The Office of the Clerk of Assize . . . together with the Office of the Clerk of
the Peace*, etc., 1682, p. 99.

that in county after county the High Bailiffs—or the underlings employed by them—made the summons to these Hundred
Juries an instrument of petty extortion, and an opportunity
for bribery to escape service. We hear, for instance, in
Devonshire in 1689 that " a great number of freeholders and
other owners of estates within this county have for several
years last past, been much burdened and oppressed, and annual
contributions have been exacted from them by subtle and
unjust practices of the Bailiffs of the Hundreds and Liberties
upon pretence of exempting them from serving in Juries at
the General Sessions and elsewhere." Owing to the failure of
the Sheriff himself to select names his High Bailiffs " have
often taken occasion . . . to warn a far greater number than
those whose names they certify to have been warned . . .
and upon pretence of favour have had or taken several sums
of money so that a great number of freeholders and many
others . . . have been and still are under constant composi-
tions and contributions towards such Bailiffs." [1]   Word for
word the same complaint is made in Essex thirty years later
" of the great abuse of the several Bailiffs of this county (to
whom the Sheriff left the return of the said Juries for the
several Hundreds) by pretending to have orders to return
much larger numbers than the said precept directed, and their
exacting money from many persons to excuse them from
such their service, and returning only those as would not
comply with such their exactions." [2]   It was apparently chiefly
in order to prevent this abuse that the Justices, by a sort of
tacit assent, let the Hundred Juries go entirely into disuse.
The Essex Quarter Sessions even went so far, some years
before 1719—we imagine, quite extra-legally—as to direct
the omission, from the precept to the Sheriff, of any order to
return these Juries.[3]   Elsewhere the ordinary citizen ceased
to attend for what had become a mere formality ; and, as we
learn already in 1682, when the number was insufficient, the
Under-Sheriff simply impanelled some of the Parish Con-

---

[1] MS. Minutes, Quarter Sessions, Devonshire, Michaelmas 1689.   The
actual insertion of the jurors' names by the Under Sheriff, before he delivers
the warrants to the High Bailiffs, was also ordered, in 1708, by the Breconshire
Quarter Sessions ; see MS. Minutes, 7th October 1708.

[2] MS. Minutes, Quarter Sessions, Essex, 6th October 1719.

[3] *Ibid.*

stables present in Court to "serve upon the particular Juries for Hundreds and Liberties,"[1] in order to keep the ceremonial of the Court complete. This became so much a matter of course that the Parish Constables were expressly summoned by the Sheriff to attend the Sessions in order to serve on these Hundred Juries, as well as in order to make their own presentments. This we find from a complaint of the Parish of Tring to the Hertfordshire Quarter Sessions in 1703, that the Sheriff insisted on summoning for this double purpose all the Constables of that large parish, whereas, it was urged, one "will serve the Queen and country as well as if they did all attend."[2]

Before, however, the Hundred Jury was quite forgotten, the Justices of one county made a gallant attempt to put new life into that ancient institution. In 1719 the Essex Quarter Sessions seems to have realised that the county administration was falling into decay. It was nobody's business to make the presentments from the several districts on which the Court had formerly depended. 'Many and great inconveniences," declared these magistrates, in their spirit of energy in 1719, " and many public nuisances and offences that have gone unpunished, have ensued by want of such Juries and their due inquiry and presentments, and particularly the said juries were enjoined to inquire into, and did from time to time present, the defects and decays of all bridges, causeways, highways, and common passages out of repair that were to be repaired by any private person or parish, and who to repair them . . . for want whereof many private bridges and cause-

---

[1] *The Office of the Clerk of Assize . . . together with the Office of the Clerk of the Peace*, 1682, p. 102.

[2] There was, as we have mentioned, even a tendency to utilise the Constables as members of the Grand Jury—a practice which led the Surrey Justices in 1743 to resolve " that the Constables . . . for the several Hundreds in this county, summoned to attend the Quarter Sessions for the special purpose of doing what appertains to their respective offices, are not proper to serve as the Grand Inquest for the body of this county " (MS. Minutes, Quarter Sessions, Surrey, 12th July 1743). Nevertheless the practice continued ; and we even find, in 1758 and 1768-69, Quarter Sessions itself ordering " that the Constables of the Borough of Southwark . . . do attend this Court . . . as a Grand Jury, to do and perform what shall be then and there enjoined them " (*Ibid.* 10th January 1758 and 12th January 1768, 10th January 1769). This led to protests by W. M. Godschall, an energetic reforming Justice, which resulted in the High Sheriff being directed in future to return only two Juries, "one to be Grand Jury, the other Traverse Jury " (*Ibid.* 11th July 1769).

ways have come upon the county to be repaired, and many
others are out of repair, and some altogether down and
demolished, the reparation of which in time may become a
charge to this county unless such defects are frequently
presented by such Juries of the neighbourhood as may well
know the same, and inquire and present what person or
parish are or ought to repair the same." The panacea of the
Essex Justices was the reconstitution of the old Hundred Juries.
A precept was ordered to be "sent to the Sheriff . . . for
returning the twelve men out of every Hundred . . . to serve
on such Petty Juries or Juries of Inquiry as has been time
out of mind used, and that the Sheriff do himself return the
said Juries and enjoin the Bailiffs to summon such only as by
him shall be returned, and that he likewise send notice to the
several Bailiffs that if they presume to summon or warn any
other persons on the said Jury than such as shall be by him
returned, or to take or demand any sum or sums of money to
excuse any person or persons from serving on the said Jury
that they will be presented according to law and incur the
highest displeasure of this Court." And as the very duties
of these Hundred Juries had been largely forgotten, the
Justices caused to be drawn up elaborate instructions for them,
which, as they give us not only the functions of this ancient
institution, but also some conception of the spirit of the county
government of the time, we venture to print in full.

"The Essex Justices' Charge to the Hundred Juries, 1719

"Imprimis, that you make due inquiry into the state, defects,
and condition of the several bridges or wharves (?) for either horse,
cart, or footman that lie in any highway, common passage, or footpath within your several Hundreds, together with the causeways to
them appertaining.

"2. That you particularly inquire what persons' lands', tenements', manors', places', or parishes' names are to repair them, or
any of them, together with the tenants', landlords', or persons' names
who ought to repair the same.

"3. That you make due inquiry into the state and condition
of the highways, causeways, and common passages within your
several Hundreds, with the defects and common nuisances therein,
and encroachments made upon them, and by whom.

"4. That you inquire into the abuses of ale-house keepers in entertaining people at unseasonable hours, or permitting people to tipple in their houses on the Lord's Day, in keeping of nine-pins, bowling-allies, shuffle-boards, or any other unlawful games, or in procuring any unlawful assemblies to meet at their houses on any pretence whatsoever.

" 5. That you inquire into such persons as kill and destroy the game, or keep guns, nets, or any other engines for the destruction thereof, not being qualified, and all other disorderly persons whatsoever.

" 6. And that you be ready to present such other offences as shall be given you in charge at the next General Quarter Sessions of the Peace to be holden for this County." [1]

Whether any transient or partial success rewarded this spirited attempt of the Essex Justices to revive the Hundred Jury, we have not been able to discover.

Of any activity of these local Juries of Presentment, whether in Essex or elsewhere, we hear no more. But in some counties, at any rate, they continued to be formally summoned by the Sheriff. In Surrey, for instance, we hear in 1751 of the Jury for the Liberty of the Archbishop of Canterbury in " the town of Lambeth, Vauxhall, and Walworth," which consisted continually " of poor, illiterate men, and not capable of making proper presentments to the Quarter Sessions . . . which defect has been and is still likely to be very prejudicial to His Majesty's liege subjects, inhabiting near the said Liberty." The summoning of this Jury, the Justices decided, should not be undertaken by the High Sheriff, but by an officer to be appointed by the Archbishop.[2] Nevertheless the Surrey Justices had no desire to dispense with these Hundred Juries, for as late as 1766 they are found ordering the High Sheriff that he " do for the future, at every Sessions, return the panels of the several Petty Juries, to be summoned to make presentments . . . for the different Hundreds in the County according to the precept sent to him, out of the free-holders' book returned to him after every Michaelmas Sessions." [3]

---

[1] MS. Minutes, Quarter Sessions, Essex, 1719.

[2] MS. Minutes, Quarter Sessions, Surrey, 16th April 1751.

[3] *Ibid.* 8th April 1766. We notice presentments by the jurors of various small Hundreds in Dorsetshire in 1752, etc. (MS. Sessions Rolls, Quarter Sessions, Dorsetshire, 3rd October 1752).

(g) *Presentments by Constables*

The Court of Quarter Sessions was provided with an instrument for the discovery of delinquencies less cumbrous than the Grand and Hundred Juries. The High Constables of the Hundreds and the Petty Constables of the townships and parishes were under legal obligation to bring to justice all those within their respective jurisdictions who offended against the law. More especially were they assumed to report to the Court, by way of "presentment," offences not usually prosecuted by private individuals. Murder and highway robbery, assault and larceny, might be left to the suit of the aggrieved parties or of those who for the sake of the reward payable upon conviction had actually arrested the criminals. But no private individual was likely to be at the trouble and expense of prosecuting all that large class of misdemeanours included under the head of public nuisance. When in a later volume we describe such services as the maintenance of roads, the paving and lighting of streets, and general sanitation, we shall find that this head of public nuisance comprised an extensive field—in fact, nearly the whole of the local government services of the time. If no man did anything that tended to the annoyance of the King's subjects, and if every man fulfilled his legal obligations [1]—that is, committed no nuisance, active or passive—there would, it was assumed, be no need for any collective action. To this wide range of public nuisances, we may add, as coming under the cognisance of the peace officers of the seventeenth and eighteenth centuries, the offences of the nature of national nuisances, such as sedition, recusancy, disaffection to the dynasty, blasphemy, disorderly drunkenness, and public gambling. Hence, in the charges by Chairmen of Quarter Sessions, and in the innumerable handbooks reciting the duties of parish officers, we see a constant emphasis laid on the obligation of Constables to make presentment to

---

[1] In a subsequent volume on municipal functions between 1689 and 1835 we shall describe how the various public services of maintaining, paving, cleansing, lighting, and watching the public ways all had their origin in, and were gradually evolved from, the immemorial obligation cast by custom or law upon every inhabitant to provide his quota of personal service. Failure to fulfil this obligation could be prosecuted as a public nuisance.

Quarter Sessions, as well as to the Assizes,[1] of all such delinquencies.

It may be that in this duty of the Tithingmen, Headboroughs, and Constables of every parish and township to attend Quarter Sessions and make their presentments, we have the explanation of "the Constable Jury," or the "Jury of Constables," of which we have some slight mention, but which does not seem to be known to the law. In various contemporary publications relating to the Middlesex and Westminster Quarter Sessions of the early part of the eighteenth century we find these Juries mentioned as distinct from the Grand and Petty Juries. They seem to have been honoured with separate charges by the Chairmen of Quarter Sessions.[2] We have found in Middlesex or Westminster no record of their proceedings ; nor, unless it was to hand in their individual presentments, can we imagine what their legal function was. With one remarkable exception, to be presently described, the only other specific reference to them that we have come across is that in an order of Quarter Sessions of Holland (Lincolnshire) in 1640, where the Constables of every township are directed with reference to certain elaborate instructions as to parochial assessments, "to certify under their hands to the Foreman of the Constable Jury upon Whitsun evening at Boston . . . to the end he may certify the same to His Majesty's Justices," the opinion of the parishes upon them.[3] But in the well-kept archives of the City and County of Coventry, where

---

[1] The Judges were equally insistent on their making their presentments to the Assizes. In 1656, for instance, the Judges animadverted on the neglect of the Constables and Tithingmen of Wiltshire in this respect, and ordered them to make their presentments in writing a fortnight before each Assizes, swear to them before a Justice of the Peace, and deliver them to the Constable of the Hundred, to be by him laid before the Court (MS. Order Book, Western Circuit, 21st July 1656).

[2] In the reports of "charges" about this time, we find the Chairman of Quarter Sessions addressing separately the Grand Jury, and "the other Juries" ; we come across formal prefaces and requests to print from " We, the Jury of Constables" ; these orations are occasionally "printed at the desire of the Justices and the Jury of High Constables and Constables" (*The Charge of Sir Daniel Dolins, Knight, Chairman of the Court of Quarter Sessions for Middlesex, 1725 ; The Second Charge* (of the same), *1726*). So, in 1728, we have a charge addressed to "the Grand Jury and Jury of Constables" ; another, at a different Quarter Sessions, to the Grand Jury "and to the High and Petty Constables" (*Five Charges to several Grand Juries*, by Sir John Gonson, 4th edition, 1742).

[3] *History and Antiquities of Boston*, by P. Thompson, 1856, p. 759.

the Court of Quarter Sessions was an active authority, we find
a unique collection of the presentments of what is specifically
called the Jury of Constables.[1] We see this anomalous body
forming evidently an integral part of the machinery of the
Court, and for more than a century actively presenting individual offenders. At the "General Quarter Sessions hólden
before the Mayor and Justices," between 1629 and 1742, a
whole series of presentments were regularly made by the Jury
of Constables, "being sworn to inquire for our Sovereign Lord the
King and the body of the City and County of Coventry." These
presentments included, apart from felonies and misdemeanours
affecting individuals, almost every conceivable offence against
the community—it might be " not coming to church," for which
eighteen persons were prosecuted in 1683, it might be "not
hanging out a lantern with light," or "not sending his team
to the highways"; it might be "not paying to the watch,"
or "selling ale without licence "; it might be "broken pavement," or "the nuisance of muck," for which in 1718 fifty-four
persons were prosecuted at a single meeting; it might be
" making a dunghill" or "keeping pigs "; it might be for
keeping "inmates" or having a "dangerous and offensive "
chimney; it might be "following a trade and not coming
into the company"; it might even be "cutting turf off the
commons," or "carrying several loads of gravel away," or
"destroying part of the common through digging." The Jury
of Constables would even present "the Mayor, Bailiffs, and
Commonality of the City " "for not mending the wall," or
"not mending the bridge." We have, in short, in this unique
collection a vivid picture of the Jury of Constables, formally
sworn as a Jury, serving practically as a Court Leet Jury of
Presentment, whose presentments, however, resembled those of
the Grand Jury in that they were nominally made to a Court
of Quarter Sessions.[2]

[1] See the scrapbook entitled "Constables' Presentments," in which these
presentments from 1629 to 1742 are attached with great care.

[2] The Court of Quarter Sessions of the City and County of Coventry met,
however, by the device of adjournment, practically weekly throughout each
quarter, and acted, in fact, much like a Petty Sessional Court. We infer that
the presentments of the Jury of Constables were treated, unlike the presentments of the Grand Jury of an ordinary Quarter Sessions, not as indictments to
be traversed and tried before a Petty or Traverse Jury, but as if they were what
we should now regard as police summonses to be summarily disposed of by the

Whether or not the Constables' presentments were made or delivered to the Court of Quarter Sessions by a formally sworn Jury, the fact that these presentments constituted a very real part of the local government for at least half a century after the Revolution is proved by the voluminous Sessions Rolls and bundles of documents in the county archives. At every Quarter Sessions there would be handed several dozens at least —sometimes a hundred or more—of separate pieces of paper, of all shapes and sizes, on which the High or Petty Constables had written a more or less literate account of the state of their districts. This bundle of papers was handed, with the ordinary criminal bills of indictment, to the Grand Jury. "Gentlemen," said the Chairman of the Gloucester Quarter Sessions in 1748, "peruse these returns, and write 'A True Presentment' on the back of those you find to be true, and 'Not a True Presentment' on the back of those you find not to be true."[1] The Constable's presentment, if endorsed by the Grand Jury, might then become the basis of an indictment which any person who chose to pay the necessary fees could prefer. In those cases in which the Justices so ordered, the Clerk of the Peace would prefer the indictment at the expense of the county.[2]

In this work of presentment the special duty of the High Constables was to stimulate the activity of the parishes and their officers within their respective Hundreds; to supervise the parochial presentments; and, if the Petty Constables did not themselves attend Quarter Sessions, to hand in the presentments on their behalf. For any default of duty the parish officers could be themselves presented. Thus, among the Derbyshire archives we find a presentment by the High Constable of the High Peak division in the following terms : " I present S. N., Constable of Youlgreave, for not putting in a presentment at this Sessions. I do also present the said S. N. for not paying in £2 for his part of the warrant of last

Bench without a Jury. We must be cautious in assuming that the Jury of Constables in Middlesex or at Boston occupied exactly the same position as that at Coventry.

[1] These words, evidently written out for the Chairman's use, are recorded on one of the Constable's presentments, dated 12th July 1748, among the Gloucestershire archives.

[2] "Ordered that the presentment of Rhyddllan Bridge . . . be turned into an indictment, and that the parishioners of the said parish be at liberty to traverse the same at the next Quarter Sessions" (MS. Minutes, Quarter Sessions, Cardiganshire, 4th October 1748).

Sessions for bridges. I do present the inhabitants of the township of Youlgreave for not having a Constable serve the office for three months last past." [1] In the Sessions Rolls of Berkshire, Buckinghamshire, Derbyshire, Essex, and Gloucestershire—to take only the five that we have most carefully explored—we find for seventy or eighty years after 1689 High Constables frequently presenting their Petty Constables for not returning " bills of presentment "; for not " bringing in lists of freeholders " for the Juries; for failing to pay in " quarterage " or " quarter-pay," " bridge money," or " sessions money," meaning always the County Rate; for refusing to give assistance in arrests; and for not accepting parish office. [2] In Surrey, as late as 1823, we see the High Constable of the Hundred of Kingston formally presenting the Headboroughs of the town of Kingston for neglect of duty. [3] But the High Constable had also his own presentments to make as to the state of his Hundred. In the early years of the eighteenth century these concerned Popish recusants, the harbouring of vagrants, and the keeping of disorderly houses or unlicensed ale-houses. We even see " the Chief Constable of the Hundred of Wangford " in 1760 formally presenting to the Suffolk Quarter Sessions certain inhabitants of Beccles " for a nuisance in suffering swine to go about the streets in Beccles," whereupon the offenders were at once fined. [4] More generally we find the independent power of presentment exercised with regard to parish highways or county bridges. [5] The various High Constables of Gloucestershire,

---

[1] MS. papers, Quarter Sessions, Derbyshire, 3rd October 1693 (Box iv. No. 8) ; printed in *Three Centuries of Derbyshire Annals*, by J. C. Cox, 1890, vol. i. p. 98).

[2] MS. Sessions Rolls and Miscellaneous Documents of Berkshire, Buckinghamshire, Derbyshire, Essex, and Gloucestershire, 1700-50.

[3] MS. Minutes, Quarter Sessions, Surrey, 3rd March 1823.

[4] MS. Minutes, Quarter Sessions, Suffolk, 6th October 1760.

[5] We give in full one such presentment from the Essex Quarter Sessions Archives, 1695 (Sessions Bundle 8). "The presentment of the Chief Constables of the Hundred of Winstree. At our Petty Sessions held at Colchester . . . we had no presentments come to our hands from our Petty Constables, therefore we have nothing to present as to their part ; but as to our part we present the parish of East Donyland for a piece of road called by the name of Roomand Hill . . . being unpassable for carts, and some of the horse-road very bad likewise. So we have nothing more to present but our service to the Honourable Jury.   JOHN TYE,   } Constables.
                                          RICHARD STONE, }

15th January 1694."

between 1733 and 1771, were perpetually drawing the attention of Quarter Sessions to the founderous state of particular roads, and the insecurity of certain bridges. Right down to the first quarter of the nineteenth century the High Constables of the various Hundreds of Somerset were frequently presenting parishes for non-repair of highways; and on these presentments the parishes were tried at the Sessions, found guilty, and fined.[1] Between 1806 and 1827 the Surrey Quarter Sessions successfully insisted that the High Constables of the Hundreds and Liberties of the County should regularly make presentments of bridges, roads, streets, and footpaths out of repair or dangerous to the public, and any such officer failing to present was peremptorily fined.[2] In 1825 a Committee of Quarter Sessions even framed elaborate instructions to High Constables as to the exact form and contents of these presentments, which evidently became a systematic means of effecting road repairs. Examination of the Session Rolls and miscellaneous documents of other counties would, we believe, yield innumerable examples of these presentments of highways, and especially of bridges, by High Constables. For " the High Constable," sums up a committee of the Middlesex Justices in 1826, " is, by virtue of his office, Inspector of Bridges, and . . . he is every term specially directed by a precept from the Grand Inquest . . .

---

[1] MS. Minutes, Quarter Sessions, Somerset, Epiphany 1812. In 1780 the High Constable of Scarsdale presents the House of Correction at Chesterfield as "very ruinous and in bad repair" (MS. Archives, Derbyshire, Box 4, bundle 8).

[2] See MS. Minutes, Quarter Sessions, Surrey, 1806, 1811, and almost every one of the next twenty years. In 1814 and 1816 the High Constables' presentments were rejected by the Court as incomplete, and the High Constables in question were summoned to attend an adjourned Sessions to explain their omissions. These presentments were, it appears, referred to the local Divisional Sessions for consideration, and, if approved there, were made the subject of a confirmatory presentment by the local Justices in Petty Sessions assembled, or any two of them, upon which indictments followed, at the county expense (MS. Minutes, Quarter Sessions, Surrey, 19th October 1824, and 12th April 1825). We infer, however, that the presentment of the High Constable was usually sufficient to set in motion the Surveyors of Highways in the parishes concerned, so that repairs of some sort were executed without waiting for an indictment (*Ibid.* 12th April 1825). In 1813 the High Constable of the Hundred of Woking presented a certain well at Merrow—not as insanitary or polluted—but as dangerous to passengers on the highway. Proceedings were suspended to allow the "nuisance" to be abated (MS. Minutes, Quarter Sessions, Surrey, 21st April 1813). In other cases (as in that of a dangerously steep footpath in Stamford Street, Blackfriars, in 1816) Quarter Sessions ordered the Surveyor of Highways to amend the defect (*Ibid.* 16th July 1816).

to make presentments of all defaults in not repairing bridges.'
Hence it appears that all informations and applications for the
repair of bridges ought properly to originate with the High
Constable, and might through that channel be brought to the
notice of the Committee." [1]

The innumerable tattered, dirty, and half-illegible scraps
of paper—a mere remnant surviving out of the mass of presentments by Petty Constables—yield in their picturesque
diversity, a graphic portrait of the village life of the beginning
of the eighteenth century. Inhabitants absent from church
for four successive Sundays,[2] or suspected of "recusancy,"
craftsmen exercising trades without having served a legal
apprenticeship, persons "keeping greyhounds," or "setting dogs,
nets, or guns without being qualified according to law," traders
engrossing provisions or forestalling the market, labourers
erecting cottages on the waste without licence from Quarter
Sessions, inhabitants refusing to keep nightly watch when
ordered by the Constable, or to labour on the roads when commanded by the Surveyor, householders "harbouring vagrants"
or "idle persons," "vile persons" abusing or beating the
Constable himself,[3] "using slanderous and baleful words" to
his wife,[4] or simply not "obeying our charge"—all appear
indiscriminately in the long procession of presentments made,
at every Quarter Sessions throughout the land, by the Constables of the ten thousand townships and parishes. After the

---

[1] *Report of Committee of the Magistrates of Middlesex on County Bridges,*
1826, p. 47. In Breconshire formal presentments of bridges by the High
Constables seem to begin in 1795 (MS. Minutes, Quarter Sessions, Breconshire,
14th April 1795).

[2] These, as we have elsewhere noted, greatly diminished after the Toleration
Act of 1689, though this in no way relieved the person who stayed away from
church because of a preference for the company of the ale-house or for an enjoyment of the open air. Renewed orders were, in fact, made in 1715 by Quarter
Sessions, in Middlesex, Shropshire, and doubtless other counties, for the enforcement of the laws against absence from religious worship (*Shropshire County
Records,* part ii. edited by Sir Offley Wakeman, p. 22). We find very few
convictions after 1715, but we note presentments by the Gloucestershire
Constables for this offence down to about 1740.

[3] "The Return of the Tithingman of Stoke Bishop, 13th January 1736.
That all things are peaceable and quiet to the best of my knowledge, except
Walter Huntley for keeping a disorderly house and for aiding and assisting some
vile persons harbouring in his house to beat and abuse me in the execution of
my office. James Church, Tithingman" (MS. Archives, Gloucestershire,
bundle No. 1).

[4] *Ibid.* 1748, bundle No. 3.

accession of the House of Hanover, recusancy and absence from church quickly disappear, in most counties, from the list of offences.   There is less notice taken of individual bad manners and ill-living.   Offences against the order and convenience of each little community as a whole begin to come to the front. Between 1730 and 1750 the favourite subjects for presentment are the unlicensed sellers of ale, the keepers of disorderly houses, the inn-holders who allow gambling or have skittle-alleys in their gardens, causing "much blaspheming and quarrelling," the householders entertaining "inmates"—that is, taking in lodgers—"against the consent of the whole parish," and the growing host of mere nuisance-mongers— persons "making dung heaps," "shooting stones on the road," "making stone-pits in the King's Highway," erecting posts in the village street, leaving ditches unscoured, digging up land-marks, diverting the village water or enclosing the village waste.   But by this time the presentments show signs of becoming perfunctory in character.   Already, in 1711, the Middlesex Court of Quarter Sessions upbraids the Parish Constables for "contemptuously withdrawing themselves" when charged by the Court to present public nuisances, "some of them making no returns at all, others often by writing or procuring to be wrote for them a pass in which is contained *omnia bene*, though many things are presentable, and deliver-ing the same to the High Constable or Beadle." [1]   In the course of the next generation we find in common use a printed form specifying under twelve heads the various defects and offences which ought to be presented, leaving spaces for the Constable's statements under each head.   The presentments of the Constable of Little Gransden, Cambridgeshire, in 1750 happen, by accident, to have been preserved and published. That happy parish was then described as follows :—

> *Imprimis.* We have no Popish recusants ; no common
>   drunkards.
> 2. Our Hue and Cries have been pursued ; watch and ward
>   kept.
> 3. We have not been remiss in apprehending vagrants.

---

[1] MS. Minutes, Quarter Sessions, Middlesex, 1711, and again in January 1714.

4. We have no unlicensed ale-houses or inns.

5. We have no unlawful weights and measures.

6. We have no new erected cottages or inmates.

7. We have no young persons idle out of service.

8. We have no ingrossers of corn, no fore-stallers of markets.

9. Our highways are in sufficient repair.

10. Our town stock is employed for the relief of the poor.

11. We have no profane swearers or cursers.

12. We have no riots, routs, or unlawful assemblies.

THOMAS DALE, Constable.[1]

The growing tendency of both High and Petty Constables to take lightly their duty of presentment met with criticism from Grand Juries who relied on these quarterly reports to save themselves the trouble of initiating presentments of their own. In 1744 the Middlesex Grand Jury makes a vehement complaint of the habit of the Constables " returning their several districts and divisions to be quiet and in good order, or to that effect; whereas the contrary does most manifestly appear." [2] " The Constables when they make their returns," protest the Hampshire Grand Jury in 1773, " are in general entirely ignorant of the contents, and deliver them in a printed form filled up without considering the substance of them, or being able to make the proper answers when required on the subject of them." The Grand Jury thereupon themselves order an advertisement to be inserted in the local newspapers, warning such Constables " that the strictest inquiry will be made into their returns, and if the Constables do not deliver in true and genuine returns, and such as they shall be able to give the strictest and fullest answers to every article, they will be prosecuted by indictment at the public expense." [3] In some counties the High Constables even began to neglect attending

---

[1] This presentment is specially printed in the *Northampton Mercury*, 3rd March 1787 ; we may thus infer that, only a generation after its date, such a document had become unusual. Here is a Berkshire presentment of 1736 : "The Return of the Tithingman of the parish of Markham in the County of Berks . . . 1736. The poor are provided for, the stocks and whipping-post in good repair, hues and cries duly pursued, highways and bridges in repair, warrants executed, watch and ward duly kept, and all things belonging to my office are in good order to the best of knowledge " (MS. Sessions Rolls, Berkshire, Michaelmas 1736).

[2] *Gentleman's Magazine*, May 1744, p. 278.

[3] MS. Minutes, Quarter Sessions, Hampshire, 5th October 1773.

the Quarter Sessions at all—a neglect which called for the
protest of Quarter Sessions in Lincolnshire in 1790, and Wiltshire in 1808.[1] The presentments went on, as mere formalities
for several more generations, growing, we believe, ever more
formal and empty. Occasionally the magistrates would try
to revive the old custom. In Surrey, in 1806, the High Constables are threatened with a fine of £5 if they neglect to
present any "decayed road, bridge, or other nuisance."[2] In
Buckinghamshire, in 1824, Quarter Sessions resolved to
appoint, at every Quarter Sessions, a committee of Justices "to
take into consideration the presentments made by the several
Petty Constables of this county, and to report thereon to the
Court."[3] But the end was now near at hand. In 1825, the
Norfolk Justices, moved by the difficulty of finding suitable
persons to serve as High Constables, appointed a committee to
see whether their work could not be reduced. It is significant
of the change in opinion that, to the members of this committee, the presentments of the Parish Constables, which in
this county had become merely "general printed negations" of
having anything to present on each subject-matter, seemed a
useless formality. Only a few years previously these Constables had, in this very county, been threatened with dire

---

[1] The Justices for "the Parts of Kesteven in the County of Lincoln," in
advertising the next ensuing Quarter Sessions, take occasion to warn "the Chief
Constables and Under-Constables of and for the several Wapentakes . . . that
unless they respectively attend such Sessions or show unto the Court reasonable
cause of absence, they will be fined for not attending" (*Lincoln, Rutland, and
Stamford Mercury*, 1st January 1790). The Wiltshire Quarter Sessions, on
codifying its "Rules and Orders" in 1808, peremptorily required "every
Constable or Bailiff of any Hundred" to be in attendance "with proper wands,"
during the whole time of the Sessions, not only to make their presentments and
returns "of all mandates and processes," but also "to assist in keeping peace
and good order" (MS. Minutes, Quarter Sessions, Wiltshire, Hilary, 1808). In
Middlesex, as we learn in 1817, the Cryer of the Court levied a fee of fourpence
on each Constable, for administering the oath by which his presentments were
authenticated (*Second Report on the State of the Police in the Metropolis*, 1817,
p. 398).

[2] MS. Minutes, Quarter Sessions, Surrey, 7th October 1806. On the neglect
of one of them in 1811 "to make a due presentment" he is peremptorily ordered
to do it within twenty-eight days (*Ibid.* 15th January 1811).

[3] MS. Minutes, Quarter Sessions, Buckinghamshire, Epiphany 1824. This
committee met at once, and examined thirty-one presentments, mostly about
bridges and footpaths, but also about stocks, pounds, etc. It suggested that it
would be well for each Petty or Special Sessions to inquire into the cases within
its division, as many of the Constables' presentments were "confused, irregular,
and sometimes unintelligible."

penalties if they neglected to attend on the first day of every Sessions and put in presentments of whatever was amiss in their parishes. Now the committee consulted the Home Office on the subject, and were officially informed in reply that the Secretary of State saw no imperative necessity for any such presentments. On this being reported to Quarter Sessions, it was resolved " that this Court was of opinion that the presentments which it has been customary for the Petty Constables of the several parishes to make, and the Chief Constables to deliver, at the Quarter Sessions and Assizes are altogether unnecessary, which is sanctioned by that of His Majesty's Secretary of State for the Home Department." [1] Within a couple of years the whole system of Constables' presentments was swept away. At one fell swoop, and with characteristic disregard for history, custom, and tradition, an Act of 1827 abolished all obligation of High or Petty Constables to make presentments of " popish recusants," persons not attending church, rogues and vagabonds, forestallers and regrators, profane swearers, servants out of place, false weights and measures, highways and bridges out of repair, riots and unlawful assemblies, and " whether the poor are well provided for and the Constables legally chosen " ; [2] or, as was customary in Middlesex, " of nuisances in the streets, and returns of the number of soldiers billeted at each public-house, and whether the public-houses have conducted themselves in an orderly manner ; " [3] without, it must be added, the provision of any substitute for the ancient supervision of the county organisation thus at one time exercised.

[1] MS. Minutes, Quarter Sessions, Norfolk, Michaelmas 1825 ; Home Office Domestic Entry Book, 15th April 1825 and 15th June 1826, vols. lix. and lx. in Public Record Office.

[2] 7 and 8 Geo. IV. c. 38 (1827) ; see House of Commons Return, No. 398, of 1827 as to the duties then performed, and *The Substance of the Charge . . . at the Quarter Sessions . . .* 1827 . . . *Wilts*, by T. G. B. Estcourt, 1827, p. 8. The Surrey Justices, who, as we have described, had latterly converted the High Constables' presentments into an organised system for securing road maintenance, thereupon formally "ordered that the High Constables attend the Courts of Quarter Sessions as heretofore, notwithstanding the Act of Parliament lately passed discontinuing certain presentments by them heretofore made" (MS. Minutes, Quarter Sessions, Surrey, 10th July 1827). The Cheshire Justices immediately asked that the Act should be repealed, so far as concerned the High Constables (Home Office Domestic Entry Book, 12th November 1827, vol. lxi. in Public Record Office).

[3] Second Report on the State of the Police of the Metropolis, 1817, p. 395.

(h) *Presentments by Justices*

There was one type of presentment—one form of administration by judicial process—which continued in vigour right down to 1835. The presentment by one of the Justices of the Peace, "upon his own view," constitutes an interesting transition from judicial to executive action. For bridges and highways at any rate, such a presentment by one Justice had been declared to be the equivalent of that of the twelve sworn men of the "Grand Inquest" of the county.[1] Hence we find coming to the Court of Quarter Sessions, from 1689 right down to 1835, no inconsiderable number of reports by particular magistrates of various public nuisances. To give one instance out of the many that the county archives afford, in Devonshire in 1714, "Bampfield Rodd, Esq., one of Her Majesty's Justices of the Peace for this county, upon his proper view doth present Thomas Bussell, Supervisor of the Highways in the Parish of Huxham, for not repairing the highway leading from Tiverton to Topsham; . . . and the inhabitants of the Parish of Poltimore for not repairing the highway in that parish leading from Topsham aforesaid to Tiverton, and other ways in the said parish, and for not cutting their hedges. And also the inhabitants of Silferton for not repairing the highway at the end of that town leading to the City of Exeter. And also William Warren of Rewe . . . for laying and making soil in the highway in that parish leading from Silferton aforesaid to the City of Exeter.[2]

---

[1] 13 Geo. III. c. 78, 1773.

[2] MS. Minutes, Quarter Sessions, Devonshire, Midsummer 1714. We give another case in which the formal procedure is more clearly set forth. "The King against the inhabitants of Chippenham. This day Gilbert Affleck, Esq., one of His Majesty's Justices of the Peace for this County, brought and delivered into Court a certain presentment under his hand and seal against the inhabitants of the parish of Chippenham in the said County for a nuisance in neglecting to repair and amend certain parts of the King's common highway lying and being within the said parish ; which presentment is ordered by the Court to be filed amongst the proceedings of the day. And it is also ordered that the Clerk of the Peace do issue out the process of this Court returnable at the next General Quarter Sessions of the Peace to be held for this County, directed to the Sheriff of the County aforesaid, commanding him to cause the inhabitants of the said parish of Chippenham to appear at the said next Sessions to answer the charge contained in the said presentment." At the next Sessions the parish appears (by counsel) and pleads guilty ; judgment is respited on condition that a

We trace, during the eighteenth century, a steady increase in the use of this device of presentment by the individual Justice as a means of improving the roads. Such presentments had the advantage over those by High or Petty Constables, and even over the Justice's own orders to a Surveyor of Highways, that they were not limited by the boundaries of any area less than that of the whole county. Thus, in every part of England in one decade or another, there emerges a squire or a clergyman who busies himself, for a year or two, in presenting all the ways of his neighbourhood as " founderous," and " in decay for want of preparation . . . to the common nuisance of all His Majesty's lieges " travelling along those roads. " Whereas," runs an order of the Essex Quarter Sessions, in 1721, " John Chewby, Esquire, has presented to this Court that great part of the highways within the Half Hundreds of Waltham and Harlow, and the Hundred of Ongar, are very much out of repair, and that the Surveyors of the Highways have been very negligent in performing their duty, . . . this Court doth recommend to His Majesty's Justices . . . of that Division . . . to cause the several Surveyors . . . to make due returns of the state and condition of their highways and of all such persons as shall make default of doing their work on the said highways." [1] At a Dorsetshire Quarter Sessions in 1752 one Justice presented eight parishes in a batch.[2] Sometimes this activity would be sufficiently extended and notorious to be mentioned in the local newspapers. Thus we hear of one Cumberland magistrate in 1829, " a gentleman of considerable experience in road-making," making a systematic tour of the county, giving peremptory orders to the Surveyors, and intimating his intention " to follow up his injunctions . . . by a personal survey or inspection of the lines of road in question previously to the commencement of the ensuing Sessions to enable him to present such parts of it at Sessions as he may find out of repair or slightly or insufficiently repaired." [3] The growing popularity of this device

recognisance is entered into, with one substantial surety for £40, binding the parish to appear at the next ensuing Sessions, and produce a formal certificate by a Justice that the necessary repairs have been executed (MS. Minutes, Quarter Sessions, Cambridgeshire, 15th January and 16th April 1779).

[1] MS. Minutes, Quarter Sessions, Essex, 18th April 1721.
[2] MS. Minutes, Quarter Sessions, Dorsetshire, 1752.
[3] *Cumberland Pacquet*, 15th December 1829.

of presentment did not escape criticism. " I have often been surprised," writes a correspondent to the *Gentleman's Magazine* in 1794, "at observing Justices presenting roads lying in their own districts. What could be their motive? Have they not all the power necessary for doing everything that can be done by a presentment? Some, I have heard, say they do it because they do not like to impose fines on their neighbours, and to be teased with applications for remitting them; others, that they get rid of the trouble of making orders and attending to their execution." [1] This way of repairing roads, explains T. B. Bayley, the Chairman of the Lancashire Quarter Sessions, is "very tedious and expensive," much of the money raised by the fine being lost in law charges, court fees, and other expenses. Moreover, as he points out, there was no certainty that the presentment would always be followed by the necessary indictment, unless the reforming Justice was prepared to advance the lawyer's charges and the court fees, at the risk of never being repaid. [2]

The Justices' presentments related to other "nuisances" besides those connected with highways. Bridges, as we have seen, were under the special cognisance of the Grand Jury and the High Constables, but we find them sometimes presented also by individual Justices. We give an example from the Gloucestershire Quarter Sessions as late as 1821. "The Court taking into consideration the presentment made and filed at this Sessions by the Rev. Wm. Hicks, one of the Justices of the Peace for this county, against the inhabitants of the county, for not repairing a certain common public stone bridge situate over the River Colne in the several parishes of . . .; and having received a report from Mr. Collingwood, the County Surveyor, that the probable expense of rebuilding and repairing the said bridge will not exceed

---

[1] *Gentleman's Magazine*, July 1794, p. 622. A presentment by a Justice of an individual farmer for dumping manure on the road, and thereby obstructing it, will be found in MS. Minutes, Quarter Sessions, Lancashire, 14th January 1752; and one against a landowner for not keeping open a watercourse (*Ibid.* 6th October 1772).

[2] *Observations on the General Highway and Turnpike Acts*, by T. B. Bayley, 1773, p. 25. In 1827 we see the Surrey Justices ordering that various presentments by individual magistrates of highways out of repair should be prosecuted at the county expense (MS. Minutes, Quarter Sessions, Surrey, 9th January 1827).

the sum of £30—ordered that the said work be executed immediately at the said expense."[1] It is uncommon to find a magistrate complaining of his neighbours, and there must, we think, have been something seriously wrong to have induced, in 1715, " William Ilbert, Esq., one of the Justices of the Peace" for the County of Devon, "upon his own knowledge and view," to "present that Richard Hawkings of Churchstow in this county is a very troublesome person amongst his neighbours and a common disturber of the peace."[2] Towards the end of the eighteenth century, when various Poor Law statutes had emphasised the responsibility of the Justices for the conduct of the parish officers, we find individual Justices using this device of presentment to compel some abatement of the scandals of contemporary workhouses. In the county of Kent, in 1795, we read that, "whereas James Roper Head, Esquire, one of His Majesty's Justices of the Peace for this county, hath certified to this Court . . . that the house kept and provided in the parish of Higham . . . for the maintenance of the poor of the said parish is not only inadequate in point of size, but is in a very dangerous, ruined, and decayed state, and that for several months preceding the date of the said certification, as well as at the present time, there had been and still continue in one room of thirteen feet by fourteen, two women and three children, and in another room of fifteen feet by thirteen a man, woman, and five children (one of which now lies ill of a fever), and in the next room, of only twelve by fourteen, a man and a woman, now ill, and five children. That the annual amount of the Poor Rate of the said parish amounts to nearly £200, scarce a shilling of which is now appropriated to the enlargement or repair of the said workhouse or poorhouse, which is not incorporated or regulated by any special Act or Acts of Parliament. Now this Court, after hearing the said James Roper Head in support of the said complaint, and John Prettle, Overseer of the Poor of the said parish of Higham, in answer thereto, doth order that a rate, not exceeding 6d. in the £ be immediately made on the occupiers of lands, tenements, and hereditaments in the said parish of Higham, and

---

[1] MS. Minutes, Quarter Sessions, Gloucestershire, 16th October 1821.

[2] MS. Minutes, Quarter Sessions, Devonshire, Easter 1715.

that the same be collected by the Overseers of the Poor of the said Parish, and laid out in making the said poorhouse more commodious, under the direction and superintendence of the said James Roper Head and John Longley, Esquires, two of H.M. Justices of the Peace for this county, acting as and for the North Division of Aylesford, wherein the said parish of Higham is situated."[1] So, in 1817, a Somerset Justice "duly presented to . . . Quarter Sessions that the poorhouse in the parish of Widmore was in a wretched state of decay and dilapidation, so as to prevent every useful purpose for which it was designed. . . . The Court . . . made an order for the poorhouse to be put in perfect repair."[2]

Perhaps the most interesting feature to the constitutional student, and one which no doubt endeared the device to the Justices themselves, was the manner in which these judicial presentments transformed themselves in the course of the proceedings into acts of direct administration. When a parish had been convicted of the misdemeanour of neglecting to repair a highway, or the county of failing to maintain a bridge, the sentence of the Court was a substantial fine. The fine was, however, not payable to the Sheriff on behalf of the King, but was, by special order, ordered to be spent on remedying the particular default. The usual custom was to require the amount of the fine to be levied by the Parish Surveyor of Highways or High Constable on the district convicted of default; and the amount to be spent either by or under the superintendence of the presenting Justice himself. Thus it was " ordered " by the Devonshire Quarter Sessions in one such case, "that the sum of £50 be levied forthwith on the parish of Drewsteignton, on the presentment of the Rev. Peter Davey Foulkes for not repairing a certain road lying in the said parish; and that

---

[1] MS. Minutes, Quarter Sessions, Kent, 7th October 1795.

[2] *Morning Advertiser*, 16th November 1818. The parish Vestry thereupon ordered the Overseers to have the poorhouse pulled down and rebuilt on the same site. The Overseers obeyed the first part of the instruction but utterly neglected to rebuild. They were indicted for disobedience to the order of Quarter Sessions, but got off on a technical flaw in the indictment. But Quarter Sessions did not let them escape. They had incurred expenses in defending themselves to the extent of £123, which sum they charged in their accounts. This being objected to by a ratepayer, was made the subject of appeal to Quarter Sessions, when the item was disallowed.

the same sum when levied be paid into the hands of the said Mr. Foulkes to be by him laid out towards the repair of the road so indicted, in such manner as he shall order and direct."[1] Similarly, in Wiltshire, in 1809, it is ordered " that the County Bridge at Compton Chamberlain, called Horse Shoe Bridge, presented by J. H. Penruddocke, Esq., as being out of repair, be forthwith repaired under the direction and superintendence of the said J. H. Penruddocke, Esq., and such surveyor as he shall think fit to employ; and that the expenses of such repairs be defrayed out of the county stock."[2] From the evidence before us we are inclined to suspect that, by the beginning of the nineteenth century, this attribute of the process of presentment—the direct expenditure of public money under the direction of the Justice himself—had become the substance of the device— the Clerk of the Peace, whenever a bridge needed repair, making out a presentment in the name of some complacent magistrate[3]—sometimes one who habitually attended to this branch of the county business—who was then deputed to superintend the work.

---

[1] MS. Minutes, Quarter Sessions, Devonshire, Easter 1792.

[2] MS. Minutes, Quarter Sessions, Wiltshire, 12th April 1809.

[3] " The most usual presentment at the present time," we read in 1829, " is that made by a Justice of the Peace himself under the statute " (*A Practical Guide to the Quarter Sessions*, by W. D. Rastall, afterwards Dickinson, 1829, p. 119). We find the Dorsetshire Quarter Sessions expressly ordering, in 1827, " that it be understood in future that any magistrate who takes upon himself to present or indict any county bridge without previous communication with the Court of Quarter Sessions, and receiving its instructions, be liable to every expense attending such proceeding " (MS. Minutes, Quarter Sessions, Dorsetshire, 16th October 1827).

CHAPTER V

THE DEVELOPMENT OF AN EXTRA-LEGAL CONSTITUTION

WE have seen in the preceding chapter that in the latter part of the seventeenth century it might have been taken for granted that the bulk of the local government entrusted to the Rulers of the County would be transacted by judicial process, in Open Court, according to the verdicts of Juries, the presentments of Constables and the findings, " on their own view," of particular Justices of the Peace. By 1835 the merest fragment of county business was done in Open Court, and that only as a matter of form; the Grand Jury had almost entirely ceased to concern itself about local government; the Hundred Jury and the enigmatical Jury of Constables had disappeared, whilst the High and Petty Constables were no longer semi-independent officers of judicial position, and had become merely the nominees, if not the hirelings, of the Justices of the Peace. The question inevitably arises, what kind of procedure had taken the place of administration by judicial process: what other structure had grown up to fulfil the functions of the organs which had decayed? For it was exactly in the period between the Revolution and the Municipal Corporations Act that the work of County Government was most largely augmented, and that the duties cast upon the Justices of the Peace, both collectively and as individuals, underwent the greatest development in extent, variety, and importance.

This increase in the work of the Rulers of the County occurred on all sides of their jurisdiction. The mere growth in number of the criminal cases, arising from the increase of population and the development of urban industry, necessarily

led to a more definite segregation of these cases from the
" County Business,"—sometimes even to the division of the
Court into separately sitting criminal tribunals in order to
cope with their number—and the elaboration of distinct
procedures.[1] Along with this criminal business there came
to Quarter Sessions, in bewildering variety, the ever-growing
mass of appeals, in which the Court, without a Jury, had to
revise the contested decisions of individual Justices or Petty
Sessions in the whole range of their work—misdemeanours
and nuisances, assessment and rating, bastardy and apprenticeship, and the enormous litigation connected with the settlement and removal of the constantly multiplying army of
paupers. Most important in its effects upon the actual
constitution and procedure of the Court was, however, the
continuous increase in the county services for which the
Justices were or became directly responsible. The maintenance and repair of the county bridges—in 1689 infinitesimal
in cost and extent—became, as the century wore on, a
business of considerable magnitude, involving, as we shall
describe, a specialised technique and large expenditure. The
problem of vagrancy, starting from mere suppression, led
Quarter Sessions into an elaborate organisation for conveying
a never-lessening horde of tramps from place to place. The
mere administration of the county gaol—once exclusively
the appanage of the High Sheriff—and of the county Houses
of Correction—originally simply " farmed " to their " Masters "
or " Keepers "—came, as we shall relate, to involve the
expenditure of no little time, money, and thought by the
Justices themselves. To this there began to be added, in
the first thirty years of the nineteenth century, yet another
expensive administrative service in the provision of county
lunatic asylums. To sum up, we may safely estimate that
Quarter Sessions, as the county administrative authority,
sprang, between 1689 and 1835, from a total expenditure
throughout England and Wales of less than a hundred
thousand pounds a year to one of more than a million ; whilst

---

[1] An Act of 1819 (59 Geo. III. c. 28) permitted the Justices, when the
business before the Court of Quarter Sessions was likely to occupy more than
three days, to divide themselves into two Courts. This course was presently
frequently adopted, but only for the trial of criminal cases (for instance, MS.
Minutes, Quarter Sessions, Dorsetshire, 15th January 1822).

the parish expenditure on highways and poor relief, for the superintendence of which the Justices of the Peace were responsible, increased from something like half a million sterling annually to seven or eight millions. How did the Rulers of the County cope with so vast a growth of their work?

The records of the various counties, explained and illustrated by the references in contemporary literature, enable us, in the following pages, to give the answer to this question. Coincidentally with the decay of Juries, and with the disappearance of the old type of semi-independent judicial officers, and with the consequent abandonment of administration by judicial process, there was taking place a gradual and unnoticed enlargement and differentiation of the constitutional structure of County Government. The changes do not begin at any one date, and they occur at different times and in different degrees in different counties. They are most apparent in the history of populous counties like Middlesex and Lancashire, or highly organised and progressive counties like the Gloucestershire of a century ago; they are least to be noticed in Wales, and in such stationary and remote counties as Westmorland and Somerset. But wherever changes occur the new developments are always in the same direction. From out of the Court of Justice there emerge two other organs of government, a County Executive, itself administering public services, and an Inchoate County Legislature, formulating new policies in respect to the prevention of crime, the treatment of criminals, the licensing of ale-houses, the relief of destitution, the maintenance of roads and bridges, the assessment of local taxation, and even the permissible habits of life of whole sections of the community. These developments were extra-legal in character; they were neither initiated by Parliament nor sanctioned by it. This enlargement and differentiation of what may be termed the central government of the county was accompanied by a considerable development of subordinate local authorities, in the Special Sessions and Petty Sessions of the Justices in the various Hundreds or Wapentakes. Moreover, both these separate developments happened to be coincident with subtle but substantial changes in the method of appointment and social status of the Rulers of the County themselves. Taken together, all these innovations resulted, as we shall show in the concluding pages of this chapter, in the evolution of an extra-legal constitution of an oligarchical type. Of all these new developments, the most important, the most complex, and, as it happened, the most durable, was the formation of a County Executive.

I. THE COUNTY EXECUTIVE

The county, like the parish, had, time out of mind, possessed certain executive officers, distinct from and independent of the Justices of the Peace, each charged by the law of the land with certain administrative functions. There was, as we have mentioned, the Custos Rotulorum and Lord-Lieutenant, who existed above and beyond the Justices and their Sessions. There was the High Sheriff, taking orders from the Judges of Assize and responsible to the King's Exchequer. There was the Clerk of Peace, appointed by the Custos Rotulorum, serving for life, selecting his own deputy and legally responsible for recording and reporting to superior authorities the proceedings of the Court of Quarter Sessions. There were the High Bailiffs of Hundreds, independently appointed by the High Sheriffs, to whom, with their hosts of subordinate bailiffs, was committed the execution of the summonses and writs upon which the very existence of the Court depended. Lastly, there were the High Constables of the Hundreds or Liberties, and the Petty Constables of the townships and parishes; all legally, and some actually, the nominees of the Leets of the Lords; and all directly responsible at law for the proper execution of the ancient duties of their offices. The congeries of separate and independent functionaries, each with his own distinct sphere of action, bound together by no tie, and owning allegiance to no other common authority than the King and the law, did not, in 1689, constitute anything like a County Executive. It is between the Revolution and the Municipal Corporations Act that we see this loose structure gradually transformed—not without analogy to the corresponding evolution of a parochial executive under an organised Vestry—either by alteration or super-session of particular parts, into an effective executive department carrying out the orders of the Court of Quarter Sessions. To trace this transformation in detail involves a long and, as we cannot but feel, tedious account of the several officers of the county, the gradual supersession of some of them, the institution of others unknown to the law, the relation of these officers to each other and to the Justices of the Peace, and finally the inauguration of the system of administrative committees of and under the Court of Quarter Sessions. The elaborate detail into which this description will lead us has the drawback of seeming to give disproportionate value to the County Executive in comparison with other organs of English Local Government. But it will have the incidental advantage of discovering to the student no small part of the actual working of county administration between 1689 and 1835.

(a) *The High Sheriff and his Bailiffs*

The main part of the duties of the High Sheriff were, in 1689, as before, primarily connected with the national organisation of government, rather than with that of the county. Though the High Sheriff was a local gentleman, unpaid, serving by compulsion, and in office only for a single year, it was on him that the King and his Ministers depended for the local work of national administration. Throughout the whole period he continued, as he does down to the present day, not only to be formally appointed by the Crown, but also to be actually selected for appointment by the King's Assize Judges.[1] It was the High Sheriff who was nominally

---

[1] Not finding in any of the constitutional text-books any explanation of the manner in which the three names are actually selected, which the Chancellor of the Exchequer, the Lord Chief Justice, and other high dignitaries annually present to the King, for him to "prick" one as the High Sheriff, we have ascertained that the process at the present day is as follows :—On "the morrow of St. Martin," all the Judges meet at the Courts of Justice, when the King's Remembrancer reads out, county by county (excluding the counties of Lancaster, Cornwall, and the "counties corporate") the one or two names remaining on the list. Each Judge has then to supply the names of eligible persons in the counties within his circuit, so as to make each list up to three names. The Judges are each supposed to decide on their Summer Assizes whom they will thus nominate. The responsibility is in all cases with them, and they have been known to reject names locally proposed to them. But the usual practice is for them to accept the suggestions made to them in accordance with the custom of each particular county. An attempt to "lobby" the Judge to get a favourable Sheriff nominated is mentioned in 1699 (*Calendar of Correspondence*

in charge of the King's defensive forces in the county. It was the High Sheriff who had to receive and entertain the King's Judges of Assize when they visited the county on their circuits, and to provide them with the paraphernalia of a Court of Justice. It was the High Sheriff who was responsible to the King's Courts for the safe custody of all debtors committed to prison. He had the keeping of the King's gaol in the county, and the custody of all felons. Above all, he was still the King's financial officer in the county, charged to collect all fines and forfeitures, and obliged to account for them to the King's Exchequer. But besides serving as the agent of the national government, he was responsible not merely for the constitution of the Court of Quarter Sessions, but also for the issuing of all its summonses and the execution of its judicial decisions. And as it was the county that had to maintain the King's gaol, he was, as its keeper, necessarily brought into close relationship with the Justices of the Peace. It is in the narrow range of Quarter Sessions procedure and prison administration that we see the High Sheriff and his underlings gradually superseded, in substance if not always in form, by officers appointed and controlled by the Justices of the Peace.

The country gentlemen, who took it in turns to act as High Sheriff, did not, it must be admitted, down to the advent of John Howard in 1773, seem at all aware of their personal responsibility for the state of the gaols and the

. . . *relating to the Family of Oliver Le Neve, 1675-1743*, edited by Walter Rye, 1895, p. 60). Generally the High Sheriff for the year suggests the necessary name or names. In some counties a list of five is kept running, in others of four, and in others, perhaps the majority, the list is of three. In Somersetshire the practice is for the Grand Jury at the Summer Assizes to make up the list, the part of the High Sheriff being merely ministerial. In some other counties, the magistrates are informally consulted by the High Sheriff for the time being. Similar local customs prevailed, we believe, in the eighteenth century. In 1828 Brougham refers to the fact "that with respect to the Sheriffs the Judges' opinion was taken," though he was apparently unaware exactly how it was done (Hansard, 1828, vol. xviii. N.S. p. 892). It would, however, be too much to assume that, during that period the Crown never exercised any influence in the choice of persons to serve. We have an instance of special ministerial selection of a High Sheriff in 1737, when "the appointment of Sir John Robinson for our High Sheriff" for Northamptonshire, in order to protect the Nonconformists from High Church mobs, is described by Doddridge as "a favour obtained by the condescension of the Duke of Montagu and Sir R. Walpole, with particular regard to the case" (*Diary and Correspondence of Philip Doddridge*, 1829-1831, vol. iii. p. 230).

treatment of prisoners. From one end of England to the other it was the invariable custom for the gaols to be " farmed " to the gaolers, who held them for life, and made their incomes out of fees and exactions from the prisoners. We shall tell elsewhere the hideous tale of this particular manifestation of the *régime* of the contractor, and discuss the extent to which it practically put it out of the power of the ordinary High Sheriff to effect any improvement. It was perhaps on account of the notorious supineness of the High Sheriffs that Parliament, in its spasmodic and feeble efforts, between 1689 and 1773, to stem the iniquitous traffic of the gaolers, was always trying to bring to bear the influence of the County Justices. Hence it was that Quarter Sessions found itself entrusted, under particular statutes, and in derogation of the authority of the High Sheriff, successively with the power to rebuild a prison after presentment by the Grand Jury ; to make tables of the maximum fees to be taken from prisoners, and even to draw up rules " for the better government " of the gaol.[1] Though John Howard was himself a High Sheriff and not a Justice of the Peace, he proposed to give the entire administration of the prisons to the Justices in Quarter Sessions, who were to employ the gaoler and his warders as their salaried servants. In the course of the half a century of prison reform that ensued, the High Sheriff accordingly found himself gradually ousted from all real power, and relieved (except nominally) of all personal responsibility in the administration of the county gaol. The staff of prison officers, which gradually grew up—the gaolers, warders, surgeons, and chaplains—became the salaried servants, not of the High Sheriff, but of Quarter Sessions. If the High Sheriff nominally retained the formal appointment of Keeper of the County Gaol, he could exercise it only in accordance with the decision of the Justices, who now provided the only emoluments of the office that were permitted by law.[2] Thus the connection of the High Sheriff with the County Gaol became, by 1835, purely honorary. At most,

---

[1] 11 and 12 Will. III. c. 19 (1699) ; 10 Anne, c. 14 (1711) ; 32 Geo. II. c. 28 (1759).

[2] Already in 1786 the High Sheriff of Berkshire removes from office "the Gaoler of this County," and appoints a successor, at the request of Quarter Sessions (MS. Minutes, Quarter Sessions, Berkshire, 3rd October 1786).

he found himself an *ex officio* member of a visiting committee of Justices, reporting to, and receiving instructions from, Quarter Sessions.[1]

The supersession of the High Sheriff and his particular subordinates, by officers responsible to Quarter Sessions, can also be seen in minor departments of the county service. In the records of many counties at the close of the seventeenth century the student becomes aware of an undercurrent of feeling, on the part of the Justices of the Peace, that they were unable to exercise any real control over the High Sheriff and his Bailiffs, even in matters concerning themselves and the efficiency of their administration. " Ordered," runs in deprecatory terms the resolution of the Devonshire Quarter Sessions in 1695, "that for the future, *as far as this Court can order,* the Sheriff of this county or his under-sheriff or other deputy do duly attend this Court for the future, and receive the fines and forfeitures to be imposed to His Majesty's use, and to pay the wages to the Justices of the Peace." [2] Loud and frequent are the complaints of the neglect of the High Sheriff to supervise the regular summoning of jurymen. The underlings of the High Sheriff—in this respect both the High Bailiffs of Hundreds and Liberties and the subordinate " foot " or " bound " bailiffs—seem sometimes to have defied the Justices and to have continued to use their power as a means of extorting money from those who preferred to avoid service. Hence we find Quarter Sessions striving to use the High and Petty Constables in the compilation of the jury lists. A similar tendency is to be noted with regard to the High Sheriff's duty of keeping order in the Court. "Whereas," declare the Surrey Justices in 1750, "the Sheriff's officers are not sufficient to keep the peace in this Court by reason of the great multitude of spectators and others whose business it is to attend this Court, it is therefore

---

[1] For instance, it was ordered in Surrey, as early as 1798, "that the High Sheriff for the time being," and eight named magistrates, "be . . . visitors of the County Gaol . . . to carry into execution certain rules and orders now established . . . pursuant to Act 31 George III." (MS. Minutes, Quarter Sessions, Surrey, 10th July 1798). A conflict of authority did occasionally occur, to be settled by mutual concessions (see, for instance, Home Office Domestic Entry Book in Public Record Office, for Home Office letters of 22nd November 1823 and 20th October 1828).

[2] MS. Minutes, Quarter Sessions, Devonshire, Michaelmas 1695.

ordered that the Constables of the Parish of Newington do attend with their long staves . . . at the Town Hall at St. Margaret's Hill [Southwark] in order to keep the peace."[1] Even more marked is the tendency to supersede the High Sheriff and his officers in the execution of the orders of the Court. The grave complaints of the negligence of Sheriffs and their Bailiffs in executing the processes of Quarter Sessions, "whereby many are allowed to stand in contempt of the Court," induced the Devonshire Justices to issue direct orders to the Constables forthwith to execute all warrants for arrest.[2] After the early part of the eighteenth century, the High Sheriff and his officers cease, in most counties, to be even nominally charged with the execution of the Justices' orders in the abatement of nuisances, the levy of fines for the repair of highways or bridges, sometimes even in the preparation of the lists of freeholders liable to serve on Juries,[3] and other matters of civil administration.[4]

---

[1] MS. Minutes, Quarter Sessions, Surrey, 9th January 1750. The management of the Court at this particular place offered special difficulties, partly, we imagine, because of the conflict of authority with the City of London, which claimed jurisdiction over Southwark, and which—to say the least—did not encourage the officers whom it appointed for Southwark to assist the Surrey Justices. From 1785 onward it became the practice of the Surrey Quarter Sessions to summon the "Constables and Headboroughs" of St. Saviour, Newington, Rotherhithe, Bermondsey, and the smaller Southwark parishes in rotation, to attend the Southwark Sessions, bringing "their long staves . . . to prevent all noise and disturbances" (MS. Minutes, Quarter Sessions, Surrey, 11th January 1785, 10th January 1786, 27th February 1787, etc.).

[2] MS. Minutes, Quarter Sessions, Devonshire, 8th April 1689.

[3] In Middlesex it was the High Constables who were ordered by Quarter Sessions to issue precepts to the Petty Constables to return lists of persons qualified to serve on Juries (MS. Minutes, Quarter Sessions, Middlesex, 11th July 1715).

[4] The High Sheriff equally ceased, during the eighteenth century to be called upon in practice to maintain the peace of the county. In Suffolk in 1695, when riotous mobs had destroyed corn waggons and stolen the corn, Quarter Sessions directs any Justice, in case of a repetition of such tumults, to "issue out his precept to the Sheriff of the County . . . requiring him forthwith to raise and bring the Posse Comitatus" (MS. Minutes, Quarter Sessions, Suffolk, 14th October 1695). We have come across no such order or precept to the High Sheriff in subsequent years : the Justices act through the High and Petty Constables, or, in later times, rely on "the invalids" (army pensioners) or the regular forces. But the Posse Comitatus was supposed to be a real force in 1798, when the Dorsetshire Justices allowed the Under-Sheriff and other officers two guineas a day each "for attending the several meetings of the High Sheriff, Lord-Lieutenant, Magistrates, and Deputy Lieutenants, in taking the necessary steps for the preparation and the arrangement of the Posse Comitatus in case of necessity against invasion, insurrection, or civil commotion" (MS. Minutes, Quarter Sessions, Dorsetshire, 15th December 1798). It is even said

(b) *The High Constable*

For the bulk of the ever-growing work involved in the actual administration of the county, Quarter Sessions had to rely on the Head, Chief, or High Constables of the several Hundreds or Liberties. By 1689, at any rate, these officers had, with the disuse of the Hundred Courts, come to be appointed, in the great majority of cases, by the Justices in Quarter Sessions.[1] It was invariably assumed that the High Constable should be a resident in the Hundred for which he was appointed;[2] and we gather that the appointment had originally been for a single year. But it seems to have been usual for the holder to continue in office, in some counties

that as late as 1830 the Sheriff of Oxfordshire nominally called out the Posse Comitatus of the county, summoning every male resident between 15 and 70 to attend, in order to put down the riots arising out of the enclosure of Otmoor (*Brief Annals of Bicester Poor Law Union*, etc., 1877, pp. 42-46). The Law Officers of the Crown advised in 1810 that the Sheriff had no right to interfere in the disposition of troops, or to control the magistrates, in suppressing civil tumult (Home Office Domestic State Papers, No. 216 of 1810). From 1812, many references will be found in the Home Office Records in Public Record Office under "Disturbances."

[1] The High Steward and Court of Burgesses of the City of Westminster continued to appoint a High Constable for Westminster under the Local Acts, 29 George II. c. 25 (1756) and 31 George II. c. 17 (1758) down to the middle of the nineteenth century, when the office fell into abeyance. It was not legally abolished until 1901 (Annual Report of the Westminster City Council, 1902-1903, pp. 30, 32). And there continued not a few such exceptional franchises. The Court Leet of Farnham, under the Bishop of Winchester, was appointing the High Constable for the Hundred of Farnham in 1805. The Surrey Justices considered the appointment of "a gentleman who was in the Commission of the Peace . . . as highly improper," and requested the Steward of the Court "to be more circumspect in his appointments in future" (MS. Minutes, Quarter Sessions, Surrey, 15th January 1805). In Berkshire the officers of the Hundreds, appointed at the Courts Leet of the Hundreds by the Lords thereof, were, in 1800, called Bailiffs, though they seem to have corresponded with those elsewhere called High Constables, and to have had no special relation to the High Sheriff. On their petitioning Quarter Sessions for further remuneration, the Justices referred them to their respective Lords, from whom it appeared they received £2 to £8 a year, though payment often remained in arrear (MS. Minutes, Quarter Sessions, Berkshire, 15th July 1800). One alone received payment from Quarter Sessions, and this was then discontinued (*Ibid.* 14th January 1823).

[2] In 1828, when the old traditions of the office were passing away, the Derbyshire Quarter Sessions appointed a "stranger to the county" as High Constable of Scarsdale, an appointment which evoked a storm of protest from the inhabitants, whose petitions declared that they viewed this innovation with "deep concern and regret" (MS. Papers, Quarter Sessions, Derbyshire, 1828 Box 5).

we find a practice of three years' service;[1] in others, the High Constables seem to have continued until they chose to resign; whilst in nearly half the counties the appointment eventually became one for life.[2] In some counties it was the habit to make the retiring High Constable "present the names of three fit persons residing in the said Hundred to succeed him in that office, to the end [that] the Justices of the Peace" acting for the Hundred in question might recommend to Quarter Sessions "which of the said three persons to make choice of to take the oath of the said office."[3] In one county, at least, this office was filled by lot.[4] As we have already

[1] Thus in Essex we read: "Upon application made this day to this Court by Mr. J. S., one of the Chief Constables of the Hundred of Dengie in this county, showing that he hath executed the said office for three years last past, and now praying to be discharged, this Court doth nominate and appoint Mr. M. H—— to succeed the said Mr. J. S. in the office of High Constable" (MS. Minutes, Quarter Sessions, Essex, 9th July 1711; for similar cases, see 14th January 1718). In other cases "the usual time" is referred to. The Middlesex Justices ordered, in 1719, that no High Constable should serve for more than three years (MS. Minutes, Quarter Sessions, Middlesex, 15th January 1722; 22nd February 1725). On the other hand, at the West Riding Quarter Sessions in 1721 it is "ordered that every Chief Constable within this Riding shall for the future petition for their discharge at every Christmas Sessions, and at the same Sessions return the names of persons to succeed him, that they may appear at Pontefract Sessions to be sworn" (MS. Minutes, Quarter Sessions, West Riding, 18th April 1721).

[2] "One of the Chief Constables for the Hundred of Cosford" in Suffolk, after twenty years' service, is discharged at his own request, and a successor appointed (MS. Minutes, Quarter Sessions, Suffolk, 14th October 1695). Ninety years later a Middlesex High Constable is similarly discharged, after more than sixteen years' service (MS. Minutes, Quarter Sessions, Middlesex, 7th April 1785). Apparently Quarter Sessions could dismiss a High Constable at any time for misconduct. A "High Constable of the Hundred of Woking" was summarily "removed from his said office" by the Surrey Justices, for "gross misconduct" (MS. Minutes, Quarter Sessions, Surrey, 27th February 1798). A Parliamentary Return of 1854-1855, No. 534, gives the names of 181 High Constables in sixteen counties then holding office for life.

[3] MS. Minutes, Quarter Sessions, Derbyshire, Midsummer 1700. We see the same nomination of three persons by the retiring officer in Middlesex (MS. Minutes, Quarter Sessions, Middlesex, 22nd February 1725). In Breconshire it was ordered in 1821 that "no High Constable shall go out of office until he shall have served the space of one year, and that he then deliver into Court a list of proper persons not less than three in number. . . . No High Constable to be discharged without producing such list (MS. Minutes, Quarter Sessions, Breconshire, 9th January 1821).

[4] In Breconshire in 1752 it was "ordered that a box be forthwith provided . . . for . . . keeping therein the several lists which the Chief Constables . . . shall from time to time return . . . of the names of proper persons to succeed them . . . and that the appointment of the new Chief Constables shall be made from such lists, to be divided into lots to be drawn out of the said box, by way of balloting, under the direction of the Court (MS. Minutes, Quarter Sessions, Breconshire, 7th April 1752). It will be remembered that

mentioned, service was compulsory, and there was no legal provision for any remuneration. In some counties at any rate, the office entailed not merely loss of time, but substantial expenses which were not reimbursed. " I have made inquiries," writes a Cheshire farmer in 1831, and I find . . . that a man cannot serve the office of High Constable without incurring an expense of not much less than £30 per annum ; and when a farmer is at a rack rent, this is no trifling addition to his difficulties." [1] The persons who served the office during the eighteenth century belonged, we gather, usually to the middle class ; in the rural districts they were the humbler gentry, the small freeholders or yeoman, or the more substantial tenant farmers,[2] whilst in the provincial towns they were the maltsters, millers, master manufacturers, and perhaps even the wealthier shop-keepers.[3]

The duties and functions of the High Constable were, like his social position, intermediate between those of the Justice of the Peace and the Constable of the parish. Between 1689 and 1835 they underwent a considerable change, the work constantly increasing in volume, whilst losing in dignity and independence. At the close of the seventeenth century, the office, though no longer carrying in practice any magisterial authority, was yet one of considerable position and autonomy. The High Constables seem to have held Sessions of their own in their Divisions, at which the parish and manorial Constables were summoned to attend.[4] At these Hundred

---

appointments to office were often made by lot in the archaic Swiss Cantons down to the beginning of the nineteenth century (*Les Alpes Suisses*, by E. Rambert, 1889).

[1] *Chester Advertiser*, 14th January 1831.

[2] In 1831 we have a Cheshire farmer saying, "from what class are the High Constables generally appointed ? Certainly from the most respectable farmers and yeomen of the Hundred " (*Chester Advertiser*, 14th January 1831).

[3] The Middlesex Justices in 1734 directed that no " dealer " in wine, by " wholesale or retail," should henceforth be nominated for High Constable (MS. Minutes, Quarter Sessions, Middlesex, 29th August 1734).

[4] Thus the North Riding Quarter Sessions in 1681 ordered the Constables in Richmondshire and Allertonshire to issue out their warrants to the Petty Constables to make returns of all servants that remain at home and are able to work, that such course may be taken by the Justices as the law directs ; and the C.C. [Capital, Chief, or High Constables] to hold their Petty Sessions and certify such returns and what other presentments they shall have before them at the next Sessions (*North Riding Quarter Sessions Records*, vol. vii. p. 47, 18th January 1681). In 1605 there are cases of Petty Constables being presented by the Grand Jury " for non-appearance at the Sessions held by the High

Sessions they made known the date and place of the next Assizes and Quarter Sessions of the Peace, and other proclamations of the Sheriff; they consulted with the Petty Constables with regard to the presentments of the latter, which they were supposed to overlook and to present to the Judges of Assize and Justices in Quarter Sessions; whilst at one such Sessions annually, coinciding with what became known as the Statute or Hiring Fair, they evidently supervised the annual hiring of servants in husbandry in accordance with the Statute of Labourers.[1] These High Constables' Sessions—the original "Petty Sessions"—lasted perhaps longer for the hiring of servants than for any other purpose. We find the Chief Constables of three of the Yorkshire Wapentakes in 1731 exhibiting lists of places where "meetings on the statute for hiring servants" were held; and Quarter Sessions thereupon deciding "that such meetings have been too many or too frequent, to the damage of masters and servants"; and ordering that such meetings be held in future only at two places, and only once a year.[2] In Suffolk, at any rate, the High Constable's Hiring Sessions appear to have continued to be held, in conjunction with the "Mop" or "Statute" fairs, down to the latter part of the eighteenth century.[3] But our impression is that, in most counties the

Constable of the Wapentake" (*Ibid.* vol. i. p. 1, etc.). On the other hand, in 1629 we find the Judges of the Western Circuit definitely ordering the Constables of Hundreds in Dorsetshire (where it must be remembered the Hundreds were exceptionally small) to attend and make their presentments at the Assizes only, not at the Quarter Sessions (Order Books of Western Circuit, 3rd August 1629).

[1] 5 Eliz. c. 4 (1562) ; see the suggestions for the more effective registration by the High Constable of such hiring agreements in *A Method Proposed for the Hiring and Recording of Servants*, by Sir Thomas Parkyns, Bart. (about 1720). These Hundred Sessions, held by the High Constables, need further study.

[2] MS. Minutes, Quarter Sessions, West Riding, 13th October 1731. In 1736 it is "ordered that for the future the Chief Constable of the division of Agbrigg shall hold his meetings at Wakefield and Huddersfield, with the Petty Constables of the said division, for all public business"—those living nearer one place than the other to attend such nearer place (*Ibid.* 15th January 1736).

[3] In 1765 we find the Suffolk Justices ordering that "Whereas many inconveniences have arisen from the Chief Constables of this Division holding sometimes two, sometimes three, Petty Sessions yearly within their respective Hundreds for the purpose of hiring and retaining servants, this Court doth order . . . the said Chief Constables for the future to hold only one Petty Sessions yearly in each Hundred for the purpose aforesaid, and that the same be holden in that place only where immemorially it hath been accustomed." (MS. Minutes, Quarter Sessions, Suffolk, 22nd July 1765). In Derbyshire we

High Constables' Sessions were, early in the eighteenth century, silently superseded by the gradual establishment of those Divisional Sessions of the Justices themselves which became known as Petty and Special Sessions. Thus, in the West Riding of Yorkshire in 1700, when Quarter Sessions wanted to make effective its wage assessment of that year, we may almost see taking place the transition from a Sessions held by the High Constable to a Sessions held by one or two Justices, with the High Constable in attendance. Quarter Sessions expressly urges "that one, two, or more of the next Justices of the Peace be present at the Statute or Petty Sessions, and that the Bailiff of every Hundred and their deputies, together with the Chief Constables and all the Petty Constables be summoned to give their attendance at the said Petty Sessions, and that the said Sessions be kept only in the month of October next upon such days as the Justices of Peace shall appoint." [1]

Whilst the High Constable was gradually losing his independent status, Quarter Sessions was devolving upon him a steadily increasing amount of laborious administrative work. He was, as we have described, charged with the duty of presenting founderous roads and decayed bridges, as well as of collecting and handing in the more multifarious presentments of the Petty Constables. Before this obligation to initiate judicial proceedings in county administration fell into disuse, the High Constable found himself required to carry out the executive decisions of Quarter Sessions. It was, in fact, on the High Constables that the Quarter Sessions of 1689 relied for the execution of nearly all their administrative orders. For the first generation after the Revolution we even find the High Constables occasionally charged with the duty, not merely of presenting faulty bridges, but also that of regularly inspecting all bridges whatsoever, and even of actually repairing them at the cost of the county. Thus the North Riding Quarter Sessions formally ordered the High Constables "to

hear, in 1714, of "the monthly meeting," at which a list of "drovers and badgers and swallers," within the Hundred of Peak Forest are given into the High Constable, though it is not clear whether this was his own Sessions or that of the Justices (MS. Papers, Quarter Sessions, Derbyshire, 1714, Box 4). See also for Norfolk in 1758, *Norfolk and Norwich Notes and Queries*, 1899, p. 433.

[1] MS. Minutes, Quarter Sessions, West Riding, 9th April 1700.

represent to this Court a state of all the county bridges within their Wapentakes at every Sessions; and the said Constables to be allowed twenty shillings per Wapentake for their trouble herein yearly." [1] In Suffolk, in 1695, it was often upon the High Constable that was imposed the execution of the works ordered by the Justices.[2] It is, however, in the whole range of " police," in the wide eighteenth-century meaning of that word, that the administrative work of the High Constable received the greatest enlargement. It was through him that Quarter Sessions gave orders to the Petty Constables, and it was to him that the Justices looked for their supervision and control. When Parliament, at the very beginning of the century, made the expenses of repressing vagrancy a charge on the county funds, it was the High Constable who was responsible for paying the Petty Constables, and consequently for their observance of the law and the orders of Quarter Sessions. In a subsequent volume on " English Local Government in relation to Poverty and Crime," we shall describe the gross ineptitude of these Vagrancy Laws, and the manifold frauds and collusions to which they gave rise. In county after county we see the Justices vainly striving, by innumerable orders and regulations, to compel the High Constables to check the peculations of the Petty Constables; to insist on their adhering strictly to the rules and rates of charges; and to stop, as far as possible, the indiscriminate relief of all " poor travellers." [3] When in 1714 " several persons" were reported " to ride armed in the night time within the Hundred of Munslow with an intent, as it is sup-

---

[1] *North Riding Quarter Sessions Records*, by J. C. Atkinson, 8th October 1728, vol. viii. p. 182. The unfortunate High Constables insisted, however, on being reimbursed their expenses for travelling over so extensive an area periodically to inspect the numerous stone bridges; and the economical Justices grudged even this expense, and were always casting about for some device that " would save the riding money" (*Ibid.* 14th July 1743, vol. viii. p. 244). " The business of surveying the bridges," writes Burn in 1758, " is usually annexed by the Justices to the office of the High Constables " (*Justice of the Peace*, vol. i. p. 158 of 1756 edition).

[2] See for " Blythborough Bridge and Causey," MS. Minutes, Quarter Sessions, Suffolk, 15th July 1695.

[3] See, for instance, the order made in Dorset in 1697 (MS. Minutes, Quarter Sessions, Dorset, 12th January 1697); the rules transmitted by the Essex Quarter Sessions, to the High Constables (MS. Minutes, Quarter Sessions, Essex, 11th July 1710); and the instructive report by a committee to the same Quarter Sessions in 1788 (*Ibid.* 15th July 1788); also *Shropshire County Records*, part ii., edited by Sir Offley Wakeman.

posed, to commit burglaries and robberies," it was the High
Constables of the Hundred whom the Shropshire Quarter
Sessions ordered to arrange for "watch and ward to be kept."[1]
Breconshire, in 1742, orders its High Constables to inform all
concerned that they must not act as drovers or cattle-dealers
without being licensed.[2]   It was through the High Constables
that Quarter Sessions spasmodically strove to put down the
disorders of the streets, and especially of every contemporary
assembly of the common people.   Thus, when in 1724 the
Middlesex Justices decided to regulate the disorderly fair at
Tottenham, it was to the High Constables of the Holborn
Division that they gave the orders; and that High Constable
thereupon assembled the Petty Constables of his division to
apprehend all persons keeping gaming booths at such fair.[3]
A similar order is repeated twenty years later, when Quarter
Sessions also recommends the Divisional Sessions for Finsbury
to give like instructions as to "the Welch Fair."[4]   In
Devonshire, in 1770, we find Quarter Sessions sending a
special order to the High Constables of the Hundred of
Roborough, in which Stoke Damerel, or Plymouth Dock, was
situated, to see that the Petty Constables of that parish "do
cause watch to be kept by night and ward by day, with able
men," for the next five months, in order to apprehend
vagrants.[5]   In the same year the Northumberland Quarter
Sessions sends a general order to all the High Constables, to
be by them transmitted to all the Petty Constables, commanding a "general search" throughout the county, for the
apprehension of all the "loose, idle, and disorderly persons
. . . now wandering about."[6]   It was on the High Constables that the North Riding Quarter Sessions relied in
1749-50 to put down the cattle plague then raging among
the herds; they were peremptorily ordered to attend every
fair and market within their respective Wapentakes to

---

[1] *Shropshire County Records*, part ii., edited by Sir Offley Wakeman, p. 17.

[2] MS. Minutes, Quarter Sessions, Breconshire, 5th October 1742.

[3] MS. Minutes, Quarter Sessions, Middlesex, 11th and 13th August 1724.

[4] *Gentleman's Magazine*, May 1744, p. 278.

[5] MS. Minutes, Quarter Sessions, Devonshire, 19th December 1770.   See a
similar order in 1793 in *Shropshire County Records*, part ix., edited by Sir Offley
Wakeman, p. 61.

[6] MS. Minutes, Quarter Sessions, Northumberland, October 1770 ; see also
Newcastle Chronicle, 20th October 1770.

prevent sales of cattle in contravention of the Act of 1749 ; and only where their personal attendance was impossible were they to arrange for some Petty Constable to be present in their stead. And when, six months later, the drastic step was taken of suppressing all fairs for three months, it was the High Constables who had to enforce this decree.[1] When, in 1787, the Justices throughout the whole of England and Wales were so stirred by Royal and episcopal pressure as genuinely to endeavour to act upon the Royal Proclamation against Vice and Immorality, it was mainly to the High Constables that they looked for a quickening of activities by the Petty Constables, and for the supervision of the latter.[2] It was the High Constables who were charged to make known and enforce all the complicated regulations of the successive new statutes that the Parliament of the eighteenth century was enacting.[3] The execution of the various statutes about weights and measures fell to their charge. Thus we see, in 1788, the Hampshire Quarter Sessions ordering "a set of wine measures from a quart to a gill" to be supplied for the use of each Chief Constable.[4] On the passing of the Act of 1795, many Quarter Sessions—like that of Berkshire for instance [5]—formally appointed the High Constables for the time being *ex officio* Inspectors of Weights and Measures.

[1] *North Riding Quarter Sessions Records*, by Rev. J. W. Atkinson, 1884-1892, vol. ix. pp. 2, 3, 24th April and 8th October 1750.

[2] See the order of the Essex Justices that the High Constables should be specially written to, 27th July 1787, in *Chelmsford Chronicle* of that date ; also that of the Shropshire Quarter Sessions, July 1787 (*Shropshire County Records*, part ix., edited by Sir Offley Wakeman, p. 23). Occasionally the High Constable's intervention seems to have been successful. "In the town of Stroud," we read in 1788, a "great diminution of irregularity and misbehaviour has of late been observed, to the comfort and satisfaction of the inhabitants. Such a change shows what may be effected in time by the uniform but gentle perseverénce of a worthy minister when supported by a few active and exemplary characters. The present High Constable has proved that our laws give full power for the suppression of every enormity, when the execution of them is consigned to men of spirit and integrity ; men who place not their happiness in indolence and ease, but in every exertion which can promote the welfare of the community" (*Bristol Gazette*, 10th April 1788).

[3] Thus, in Essex in 1759, the Justices direct "that the several Chief Constables of this County do order the printed clauses of the Acts relating to the drivers of carts, etc., be fixed up in every market town or some principal parish within their respective Divisions " (MS. Minutes, Quarter Sessions, Essex, 9th January 1759).

[4] MS. Minutes, Quarter Sessions, Hampshire, 1st April 1788.

[5] MS. Minutes, Quarter Sessions, Berkshire, 4th October 1796.

And when, in 1827, the Cheshire Quarter Sessions resolved to put in force the Weights and Measures Acts of 1822 and 1825, it was "to the High Constables of each Hundred within the County" that they delivered the new Imperial Standards, and issued instructions " to proceed to an examination of the Weights and Measures in their respective districts."[1] The Hampshire Justices not only peremptorily instructed the High Constables to execute all the work of the Weights and Measures Acts, but even minutely presented how they were to carry the standards. "You are expected," ran the order, " upon all occasions to carry them in a bag provided for that purpose, and in no other manner whatever "; bringing them in every Easter to the Quarter Sessions at Winchester, when " the County Brazier " would compare and rectify them.[2] The execution of the stringent policy of the regulation and suppression of public-houses, adopted by nearly all the Courts of Quarter Sessions of the English counties between 1787 and 1800, fell principally to the High Constables. By 1815, indeed, these officers were used by the Surrey Quarter Sessions as regular inspectors of public-houses ; they had to visit each ale-house once a week, they had to enforce closing at eleven o'clock at night, and they had to present, to the justices in their " Brewster Sessions," a detailed report upon the conduct of every publican in the Division throughout the whole year.[3]

But manifold as became the duties here and there placed upon the High Constables, the most important piece of administrative work that they all of them actually performed was the levy and collection of the County Rate. During the seventeenth century the county expenses were but small ; the prisons, as we shall subsequently describe, were self-supporting, and the judicial business paid for itself by fees and fines. There was, in fact, often no regular, periodical levy for county purposes. Expenses had occasionally to be incurred for repairs to the very few county bridges ; the " Treasurer of the funds for maimed soldiers " had to be reimbursed the small pensions that he had paid ; and every now and again the

---

[1] *Chester Courant*, 25th December 1827.

[2] MS. Minutes, Quarter Sessions, Hampshire, 22nd August 1812.

[3] Report of Committee appointed to frame an instruction to Constables as to their duty in connection with public-houses, MS. Minutes, Quarter Sessions, Surrey, 11th July 1815.

county had to meet a demand for its statutory contribution towards the maintenance of poor prisoners in the London prisons of the Marshalsea and the King's Bench. When the cash in hand was exhausted, Quarter Sessions, at irregular intervals, would order lump sums to be raised, to place these accounts in funds. These lump sums were apportioned among all the parishes of the county according to immemorial usage, each having to contribute its accustomed quota. It was the business of the High Constable to make known the demand to each parish, and to collect the amount, usually from the Petty Constable, but sometimes, by local custom, from the Churchwardens and Overseers. In default of payment, the High Constable could, it was assumed, levy the whole sum by distress on any inhabitant of the parish, leaving him to recover from his fellow-parishioners. In practice the Petty Constable was made to pay, as he could more easily levy from each occupier the sum actually due from him according to the parish assessment.[1] The High Constable who did not manage to collect in due time the quotas from his parishes would be peremptorily summoned to an adjourned Sessions "to show cause why he should not be committed for non-payment thereof."[2] And if nothing worse happened to him, he had at any rate to pay out of his pocket the fee for serving the summons.[3] If he did not find the money, he would, as in Breconshire in 1744, be actually "attached" for contempt;[4] and even taken in custody until it was paid.[5] This business of apportioning the County Rate, and its collection from the parish officers, became every decade more onerous, until, at the opening of the nineteenth century, the officers in such counties

---

[1] In 1705 the Hampshire Quarter Sessions made an order expressly empowering the High Constables to order the Petty Constables, Headboroughs, and Tithingmen of parishes and townships to levy by distress the arrears due (MS. Minutes, Quarter Sessions, Hampshire, 9th January 1705).

[2] MS. Minutes, Quarter Sessions, Hampshire, 7th October 1777.

[3] No less than £4 : 11 : 6 is charged for bailiffs for serving summonses on "Constables who have not paid in their quotas of County Rate, at one sitting of this same Quarter Sessions" (*ibid.* 24th April 1759). Warrants of commitment to the common gaol were actually made out by the Surrey Justices against three High Constables who had not paid in their quotas of the County Rate, but were suspended until the next adjournment of the Sessions (MS. Minutes, Quarter Sessions, Surrey, 6th October 1812).

[4] MS. Minutes, Quarter Sessions, Breconshire, 4th October 1744.

[5] MS. Minutes, Quarter Sessions, Cardiganshire, 10th May 1751.

as Middlesex, Lancashire, and the West Riding of Yorkshire found themselves charged with financial responsibility running into thousands of pounds.

The gradual change in the office of High Constable, and especially the steady increase in the routine administrative work devolving upon him, naturally led to a demand for some remuneration. " Why," asks an indignant Cheshire farmer, " are the High Constables to be burdened with the whole expense of performing the duties attached to that office without one farthing of remuneration ? Among the ' honours ' of the office may be enumerated the following : to attend four Quarter Sessions, two at Knutsford and two at Chester ; to attend two Assizes, and each month's meeting, without any allowance whatever ; to pay out of his own pocket the expense of printing all precepts to Petty Constables for each meeting, as also for each quarterly pay ; to pay out of the same fund the fees of swearing in at the month's meeting, as also to pay the Clerk of the Peace for administering the oaths at the first Quarter Sessions. . . . A ballot will shortly take place for the militia, an immense number of precepts and schedules will have to be delivered by the High Constables, which will increase the expenses very materially, and I may add that it has grown a custom for the High Constables to provide refreshments for the different Overseers, upon their bringing the quarterly pay." [1] For the greater part of the eighteenth century the High Constables were, in the absence of any provision for their remuneration or even for reimbursement of their actual expenses, left to pay themselves. That they did so pay themselves, by various illicit practices, some of which seem to have become customary, there is considerable evidence. In Suffolk, for instance, Quarter Sessions discovers in 1763 " that several of the Chief Constables . . . do demand and take of the Petty Constables the sum of one shilling for receiving the said Petty Constables' presentments and carrying them to the General Quarter Sessions and Assizes, and also the sum of sixpence for taking the lists of persons qualified to serve on Juries, which several sums of money this Court doth apprehend are illegally demanded and received by the said Chief Constables," whose exactions are for the future forbidden

---

[1] *Chester Advertiser*, 14th January 1831.

by public advertisement.[1]   To check the habit of the High Constables of Essex, of levying on "the Petty Constables of the several parishes within their divisions towards the Quarter-age and Bridge-money greater sums than ought to have been charged," Quarter Sessions in 1731 orders that they "do make out a fair list of the several parishes within their respective divisions, with an account of what sum or sums of money is charged upon every respective parish," as the quota towards a given County Rate, in order that the levy may be made known.[2]   The Suffolk Justices had long been equally suspicious of the High Constables, and already in 1695 had ordered them to produce to some of the Justices of each Hundred an exact account of all their levies on the parishes "for Bridge-money, and also to the Treasurers of the Mariners and Maimed Soldiers and King's Bench and Marshalsea."[3]   The Middlesex Justices were repeatedly considering some "method for obliging High Constables the better to account for moneys received."[4] Whatever may have been the result of these endeavours on the part of the Justices to keep the High Constables in the paths of honesty, it is clear that the office had, by the end of the eighteenth century, become in some counties an object of desire to its holders.   In Middlesex, for instance, already by 1774, the High Constableship was in some way sufficiently tempting to make it a favour to be allowed to continue in office ; otherwise we should not find the Justices for the Tower Division recommending Quarter Sessions to continue a certain gentleman as High Constable for that Division, notwithstanding that he had already served three years, "as well on account of his good behaviour in his office as his knowledge of the duties thereof."[5]

---

[1] MS. Minutes, Quarter Sessions, Suffolk, 10th October 1763.

[2] MS. Minutes, Quarter Sessions, Essex, 17th July 1731.

[3] MS. Minutes, Quarter Sessions, Suffolk, 22nd July 1695.

[4] MS. Minutes, Quarter Sessions, Middlesex, 26th February 1736.   We shall recur to the spread of corruption in this county in Chapter VI., The Reaction against the Rulers of the County.   As late as 1816, we have a case of obvious fraud elsewhere.   It is ordered in Gloucestershire, "That the Clerk of the Peace be directed to prosecute R. K., High Constable of the Hundred of Pucklechurch, charged with having demanded and received from several parishes in the said Hundred a sum and sums of money more than he was empowered to collect by the County Rate" (MS. Minutes, Quarter Sessions, Gloucestershire, 16th July 1816).

[5] MS. Minutes, Quarter Sessions, Middlesex, 1774.

In counties other than Middlesex the office of High Constable did not fall so low, partly, perhaps, because the duties were less onerous and some legitimate remuneration for the work done came to be provided. In county after county certain charges and expenses of the High Constables had, by the end of the eighteenth century, become customary, and were—often, we think, without legal authority—allowed as a matter of course. We find, for instance, the North Riding of Yorkshire allowing its High Constables a small but regular sum for inspecting the county bridges. To put down the cattle plague of 1749-50 the North Riding, and we imagine other counties, paid the High Constables a small sum for each day's attendance at the markets or fairs. In Norfolk it was ordered by Quarter Sessions, though not till 1825, that, in lieu of other customary but illegal fees, the Chief Constable should receive twenty shillings a year from each parish in his Hundred, payable as an addition to the County Rate.[1] In Derbyshire "a table of fees, consisting of thirteen items, to be taken by them was allowed at the Quarter Sessions in 1829," entirely, as was afterwards proved, without legal authority.[2] Many counties allowed the High Constables without question to deduct "poundage" on the amount of County Rate collected by them. For services in connection with statistical returns called for by Parliament—whether in connection with poor relief, vagrancy, or the census—the High Constables would often receive special fees. Towards the end of the eighteenth century allowances of this sort to the High Constables—together with the advantages to be derived from holding for longer or shorter periods the not inconsiderable sums of money passing through their hands—had transformed the office, even without unlawful exactions, into one of emolument. In one county, at least, it was eventually made—as we imagine, "extra legally"—into a definitely salaried appointment. In the West Riding of Yorkshire, where the work of the seventeen High Constables had become only less onerous than in Middlesex, we find them, by 1831, paid regular salaries from the Riding funds, averaging sixty guineas per

---

[1] MS. Minutes, Quarter Sessions, Norfolk, 1825.

[2] These fees were disallowed by the Auditors under the Poor Law Commissioners about 1838-1840 ; see *Three Centuries of Derbyshire Annals*, by J. C. Cox. 1890, vol. i. p. 104.

annum, and in one case reaching a hundred guineas; whilst so far were they from being at any charge that all their expenses (averaging £29 per annum) were reimbursed to them on a liberal scale.[1] The necessity for the payment of a salary to the High Constable became still more evident when it was realised that he was to be relied on for the organisation of the salaried professional police of the county. It was the county of Cheshire, as we shall hereafter describe, that in 1828 led the way in the establishment of a new police force on this model, and it was, from the outset, made part of the plan that each Hundred should have an officer, to be called Deputy High Constable, who should perform the more onerous of the duties of the High Constable, and receive a salary of £80 to £100 a year from the County Rate. " For it is in vain," said the local newspaper, " to expect that High Constables of Hundreds . . . will exert themselves to the extent that is in many cases rendered absolutely indispensable to the preservation of life and property." [2]

(c) *The Clerk of the Peace*

The High Constables of the Hundreds or Liberties and the Petty Constables of the townships and parishes provided the county with a numerous but rough-and-ready staff of outdoor officers, who found themselves between 1689 and 1835 gradually brought under the effective control of Quarter Sessions. But the orders of the Justices could not be executed until they had been drafted; nor, in most cases, until they had been transmitted to Constables living at a distance. For the clerical labour and administrative organisation that this involved the only officer of the Court of Quarter Sessions in 1689 was the Clerk of the Peace. Over this ancient officer the Justices had, at that date, but scant control. As we have seen in our chapter on the Legal Constitution of the County,

---

[1] Report of House of Commons Committee on County Rates, 1834 (Broadrick's evidence).

[2] *Chester Courant*, 15th January 1828. In this Cheshire experiment of 1828, slight and imperfect as it was, we have the form which the ancient office of High Constable was destined in a few years to take. By the statutes of 1839 and 1840 the High Constable was superseded as regards all police functions by the newly established "Chief Constable," a purely police officer; and by the Act of 1869 (32 Vic. c. 47), with certain formal savings, the five-centuries-old office was finally abolished.

they neither appointed him nor paid him a salary. The fourteenth-century statute which allowed the Justices four shillings a day provided also two shillings a day for the Clerk of the Peace,[1] which the Exchequer presumably continued to credit to the High Sheriff in his annual "bill of cravings." But the county owed him nothing. "For the whole of the duties appertaining to his office," says a report of the Committee of Accounts of the Middlesex Quarter Sessions, "the Clerk of the Peace was originally remunerated solely by customary fees received from individuals; and in no case was he paid for any official act as Clerk of the Peace by the Justices on the part of the county."[2] These fees in themselves made the office a valuable one, besides its indirect advantages and throughout the whole period that we are considering— indeed down to 1888—the Custos Rotulorum clung to his power of filling any vacancy in this life office; and the Clerk of the Peace for the time being tenaciously adhered to his right to exact the customary fees for all the operations that he performed. In practice, however, as the office became a lucrative one, it was usually filled by some friend or dependant of the Custos Rotulorum and Lord-Lieutenant, who seldom deigned personally to discharge the duties. Sometimes he would not even provide an office in the county town, letting his deputy get the work of the Court done as best he could at the actual time and place of its meeting.[3] What usually happened was that the titular Clerk of the Peace appointed as his deputy — as was specially authorised by statute[4]—subject to the approval of the Custos and the Justices, one of the leading solicitors in the county town, who under-

---

[1] 12 Richard II. c. 10.

[2] MS. Minutes, Quarter Sessions, Middlesex, 10th December 1829.

[3] In 1760 the Hampshire Quarter Sessions is driven to resolve "that it is the opinion of this Court that the Clerk of the Peace do either by himself or sufficient deputy (to be approved of by this Court) keep a public office at Winchester, where it has been kept time out of mind, complaints having been made to this Court for want thereof" (MS. Minutes, Quarter Sessions, Hampshire, 15th January 1760).

[4] 37 Henry VIII. c. 1, sec. 3 ; 1 William and Mary, c. 21, sec. 4. The office was almost openly bought and sold. When in 1754 the Clerk of the Peace for Surrey appointed a new Deputy Clerk, the Justices in Quarter Sessions refused to receive him or approve his appointment. The Clerk had become heavily involved in debt, and had practically sold his office for the sum of £1600. Failing to instal his new Deputy, he resigned and fled from the country to avoid arrest. The Custos (Lord Onslow) thereupon complacently appointed

took the whole of the work, and who dealt with Quarter Sessions as with any other important client, regarding it as no part of his duty to do more than see that the various statutory obligations of the Court were fulfilled and all the legal formalities complied with. We find in practice the post of Deputy Clerk of the Peace held, almost as a hereditary possession, by the principal firm of solicitors in the county town, one of the partners in which personally attended the Justices' meetings, drafted their formal resolutions, and advised them in matters of law, but left all the other work to his clerks. Under these circumstances it was with the utmost difficulty that he, or his clerks could be got to perform any official duty out of which they could extract no fee from some person or another. Everything beyond the criminal business of Quarter Sessions, the orders desired by private suitors, and those absolutely required by law tended to be neglected. The minutes of proceedings of the various counties during the eighteenth century, though differing greatly among themselves, all reveal the natural tendency of a solicitor's office to regard all administration as merely a matter of executing legal documents. Anything beyond the actual words of resolutions of the Justices is usually very imperfectly recorded. In Leicestershire no minutes or other books of record seem to have been kept.[1] In the important county of Middlesex, where the expenditure then already exceeded £35,000 a year, it was found, in 1824, that certain important books and documents, required to investigate grave charges, could not be found, having, as the Committee of Inquiry hinted, been purposely

as his successor the son of the man to whom the office had been sold, who promised to continue the same Deputy Clerk. Quarter Sessions greatly objected to the new appointment, and "doth not think fit to admit" the new Clerk, but had to succumb (MS. Minutes, Quarter Sessions, Surrey, 15th January, 20th February, 5th March 1754).

In Somerset, about 1830-1835, the same local attorney seems to have been Clerk of the Peace and Under Sheriff (letter of 29th August 1835 in Home Office Magistrates' Book in Public Record Office).

[1] Possibly the "Visiting Justices" of the gaols and lunatic asylum, as soon as any were appointed, kept their own minutes. But we are informed that no record of the resolutions of the Leicestershire Quarter Sessions on "County Business" during the eighteenth century can be found. Speaking generally, however, the actual minutes of Quarter Sessions have been well preserved (though those of Merionethshire seem to be missing, and those of Somersetshire to have been badly recorded). The bundles of Sessions papers, too, have been often saved from destruction by being forgotten—in many cases having apparently never been untied since they were put away.

made away with. The whole of the records were "in the utmost disorder." The Committee reports "that for a considerable time past great inconvenience has been felt for want of due attention in certain departments of the office of the Clerk of the Peace. Public business is often impeded and the time of the magistrates unnecessarily consumed by the irregular attendance of the proper officer and by the delays occasioned in searching for books and papers which, if found at all, are with much difficulty procured." In addition, either from negligence, or haste, or want of method, the orders of the Court and the proceedings of committees were often imperfectly "recorded, and sometimes wholly omitted. In short, the whole system is at present highly discreditable to the Clerk of the Peace, and to the county, and requires to be thoroughly reformed and properly organised." [1]

The Deputy Clerk of the Peace soon learnt to charge fees to the county, just as he charged them to individuals. It became customary for him to claim a payment, like a solicitor, for every letter that he wrote, every order that he transmitted, and every bill that the Justices passed for payment. Such charges were, in county after county, either passed by the Justices for payment without being noticed, or else tacitly admitted; and with the increase in the county business they swelled into large sums. [2] It was in order to check the growth of these items that the Clerk of the Peace for Shropshire was directed, in 1762, "to make out a bill of the business done by him yearly which ought to be put to the county charge, that the same may be examined and allowed by the Court." [3] The

---

[1] Report of Committee on the Records, MS. Minutes, Quarter Sessions, Middlesex, 9th December 1824.

[2] In Essex the demand of the Clerk of the Peace that he should be paid £6 : 13 : 4 "every time he sends out orders to all the High Constables, . . . and 3s. 6d. for every order he shall make out . . . upon the public account," was specifically agreed to in 1719 (MS. Minutes, Quarter Sessions, Essex, 4th July 1719). In the West Riding the Justices recorded in 1727 the fees to be taken by the Clerk of the Peace (*ibid.* West Riding, 11th April 1727). One early method of remuneration was to pay him £20 a year "for the carriage of the records and statutes" from one Sessions town to another (MS. Minutes, Quarter Sessions, Cardiganshire, 11th January 1774) ; or ten guineas a year, in addition to the usual fees, for conducting all prosecutions on behalf of the county (*ibid.* 12th July 1774).

[3] *Shropshire County Records*, Part V., edited by R. G. Venables, p. 185. In Shropshire, on the appointment of a new Clerk of the Peace in 1718, Quarter Sessions ordered a fee of one shilling to be paid to him on each ale-

Legislature, too, came to assume that the Clerk of the Peace should be paid from public funds rather than entirely by fees from individuals. "By certain late Acts of Parliament," reports the Committee of Accounts of the Middlesex Justices, "certain fees theretofore chargeable upon various classes of persons were no longer to be taken from them, but were directed in future to be paid out of the County Rate. . . . In some recent statutes wherein the Clerk of the Peace has been required to make official returns to the Government officers, it is directed that he should be paid for the same without saying from what quarter."[1] The fees exacted by the Clerk of the Peace were, in fact, regulated by local custom, and it was long uncertain to what extent they could be regulated by the Justices.[2] Throughout the century these fees and other payments became the subject of constant bickering between the Clerk of the Peace and Quarter Sessions, with the result that the former was often anything but a willing servant of the county.[3] The Middlesex Sessions, for instance, made a determined stand in 1829 against the growth of the Clerk's fees, and declared that " in no case can they admit that he is to be paid by the county for any services performed in his capacity

house licence by the Clerks to the Justices who granted it (*Shropshire County Records*, Part II., edited by Sir Offley Wakeman, pp. vi. 33, 34, 36). The income from fees amounted in Middlesex in 1829 to no less than £2088, of which the sinecurist Clerk of the Peace gave £855 to the working Deputy Clerk to cover all expenses (MS. Minutes, Quarter Sessions, Middlesex, 10th December 1829). In Lancashire the annual emoluments of the Clerk of the Peace were said to be at least £3000 a year in 1834 (Report of House of Commons Committee on the County Rate, 1834, Col. Williams's evidence).

[1] MS. Minutes, Quarter Sessions, Middlesex, 10th December 1829.

[2] Not until 1817 was there any express enactment on the subject. In that year power was given to Quarter Sessions by 57 George III. c. 91 to settle a table of fees, subject to confirmation by the Assize Judges. Even then the vested life interests of the existing Clerks of the Peace obstructed reform.

[3] The list of fees to be taken by the Clerk of the Peace for Berkshire was referred in 1727 to a committee "to adjust" (MS. Minutes, Quarter Sessions, Berkshire, Epiphany 1727). A new "Table of Fees to be taken by the Clerk of the Peace" was settled by the Hampshire Quarter Sessions in 1730 (MS. Minutes, Quarter Sessions, Hampshire, 6th October 1730). Thirty years later we find it "ordered," by the same authority, "that the Clerk of the Peace shall not for the future be allowed anything out of the County Rate for the making of Sessions Orders for the payment of salaries or bills" (*ibid.* 15th January 1760). As the work grew, the amount of the Clerk's "quarterly bills" led to attempts to commute his emoluments for a fixed salary. The Buckinghamshire Justices recommended this, and appointed a committee to settle the salary (MS. Minutes, Quarter Sessions, Buckinghamshire, Michaelmas 1832 and Epiphany 1833) ; but apparently failed to carry it out.

of Clerk of the Peace unless such payment is so directed by Act of Parliament." [1] In Cumberland, in 1828, Sir James Graham, then newly elected to Parliament for Carlisle, and alarmed at the rapid rise of the County Rate, began to over-haul the accounts. He objected to the bills presented by the Clerk of the Peace, who ran up his fees, and was in the habit of charging seven or ten pounds for attendance at each meeting. He insisted on scrutinising all the accounts and knocking off the illegal charges, much to the disgust of the Clerk of the Peace. He, for the first time, introduced a regular checking of the "quarterly bills" by one or two Justices before they were presented to the whole Sessions to be passed—a practice which, as we have seen, had already been adopted in other counties. [2] It was not from such an officer as the Clerk of the Peace, standing in such a relationship to the Justices, that Quarter Sessions could receive any assistance in the formulation of policy, or even in the construction of an efficient adminis-trative machine. [3]

(d) *The County Treasurer*

The first county officer to be added to the Clerk of the Peace was in most counties a Treasurer, to receive the contri-butions to the "County Stock," to make such payments out of it as he was directed, and (though this was hardly ever so

---

[1] MS. Minutes, Quarter Sessions, Middlesex, 10th December 1829.

[2] See *Life and Times of Sir James Graham*, by T. M'Cullagh Torrens, 1863, vol. i. p. 160-161. It is worth recording, as indicating both the laxness that had prevailed and the temper of the official, that the Clerk of the Peace demurred to the examination of his account by the Justices, observing, "It is a very unpleasant thing to have one's bill handed round for every one's inspec-tion" (Lonsdale's *Worthies of Cumberland*, 1868, vol. ii. p. 81).

[3] For many years after 1835 the Clerk of the Peace continued, in most counties, to hold practically the same anomalous position. An early attempt of the West Riding Justices in 1819 to give their Clerk of the Peace a salary of £400 in lieu of fees was revoked in 1828 (MS. Minutes, Quarter Sessions, West Riding, 14th April 1828). The House of Commons Committee on County Rates in 1834 recommended reforms in vain. After 1835 payment by salary was gradually substituted for the system of fees. By 1861 four-fifths of the Clerks of the Peace received fixed salaries of between £80 and £1600, though Middlesex, Surrey, Lancashire, Durham, and others continued the old system. It survived in Surrey until the death of Sir Richard Wyatt in 1904. Under the Local Government Act of 1888, a vacancy in the office is now filled by the County Council ; and as the survivors of the old system die out, they are replaced by working administrative secretaries having legal attainments.

much as mentioned) to keep all the accounts that were deemed necessary. It is characteristic of the slow development of the county administration down to the Revolution that, prior to that date, we seldom find any separate Treasurer or other financial or accounting officer whatsoever. In the West Riding of Yorkshire, at the close of the eighteenth century, one of the leading Justices would occasionally do duty for a few years.[1] In that county, as well as in Derbyshire and Hertfordshire, as late as 1700, we see the Clerk of the Peace himself discharging the simple duties of Treasurer.[2] From the beginning of the eighteenth century, however, most counties had a Treasurer under some title or another—not, it is true, a professional official, but usually a substantial person with some financial business interests in the county, which fitted him to act not only as bookkeeper and accountant, but also as a primitive banker to the county. He frequently was in a position to give security for a large sum, but he was during the eighteenth century not usually a magistrate, nor of the class from which magistrates were then drawn. Thus in Derbyshire, where the first definite appointment of a separate Treasurer dates only from 1708, the first four holders of the office, down to 1786, were never in the Commission of the Peace.[3] In Hertfordshire, in 1740, a draper of Hertford is chosen. In Hampshire, in 1780, it is a wine merchant of Winchester on whom the choice of Quarter Sessions falls. Dorset, in the first quarter of the nineteenth century, has as its two Treasurers the two partners of a firm of solicitors.[4] At the outset we often find, as in separate Treasurers for different county funds, such as " Bridge money," " maimed soldiers," " charitable use money," " Marshalsea money," " Gaol and House of Correction money," and " Turnpikes "; or, as in Essex,

---

[1] See MS. Minutes, Quarter Sessions, West Riding, 30th May 1698, 29th April 1701.

[2] *Three Centuries of Derbyshire Annals*, by J. C. Cox, 1890, vol. i. p. 119 ; MS. Minutes, Quarter Sessions, Hertfordshire, 8th April 1700-1703 ; *ibid.* West Riding, 14th April 1702. The Shropshire Justices merely chose two of their number annually to act as Treasurers down to 1739, when they appointed a permanent County Treasurer with a salary of £20 (*Shropshire County Records*, Part III., edited by Sir Offley Wakeman, pp. iii. 99).

[3] *Three Centuries of Derbyshire Annals*, by J. C. Cox, 1890, vol. i. p. 121/1.

[4] MS. Minutes, Quarter Sessions, Hertfordshire, 21st July 1740 ; *ibid.* Hampshire, 3rd October 1780 ; *ibid.* Dorsetshire, 1809-1819.

Berkshire, Devonshire, and many other counties, separate
Treasurers for different parts or divisions of the county.
Gradually we see these everywhere merged in a single office.[1]
The Treasurer confined himself for the most part to the
business of banker and bookkeeper, but during the earlier
part of the eighteenth century we not infrequently see Quarter
Sessions, in the absence of other administrative officers, putting
other duties upon him. Thus the Essex Justices in 1700
urged their several Treasurers to "use their endeavour" that
the "several High Constables" should pay over their collections as promptly as possible.[2] In 1724 the Hampshire
Justices entrust to their Treasurer the remodelling of the
primitive sanitary conveniences at the County Gaol.[3] Here
and there indeed we find him made use of as a general administrative officer. Thus we find the Berkshire Justices directing
"the Treasurer of the Hill Division," "to apprentice J. J. to
any person or trade that he shall think proper, and that he do
give with him . . . any sum not exceeding £10." The same
officer is directed to clothe a girl going out to service, and, as
she did not find a place, compulsorily to apprentice her.[4] It
is even ordered "that for the future no work or repairs be
done, or money laid out, on any account whatsoever," on the
County Gaol "but what shall be first view and ordered to be
done by the Treasurers of this County, or one of them."[5]
Occasionally, too, as in Essex between 1712 and 1719, we
find the office held by an active man of administrative ability,
who persuades Quarter Sessions to allow him to systematise
the accounts, check the bills of master-workmen and Petty
Constables, make a new assessment or apportionment on the
parishes, and introduce a regular poundage rate.[6] As a general

---

[1] Essex, starting with several Treasurers, merged them all in one salaried
office as early as 1712, with an efficient holder of it ; but reverted in 1719 to
two quasi-honorary Joint-Treasurers, whose accounts were quickly found unsatisfactory, and then to three separate Treasurers for different parts of the work
(MS. Minutes, Quarter Sessions, Essex, 9th April 1712, 14th April 1713, 7th
April 1719, 4th October 1720, 18th April and 11th July 1721). Dorset had
two Treasurers, but in 1815 decided to merge the offices into one as soon as a
vacancy occurred (MS. Minutes, Quarter Sessions, Dorsetshire, 17th October 1815).

[2] MS. Minutes, Quarter Sessions, Essex, 8th October 1700.

[3] MS. Minutes, Quarter Sessions, Hampshire, July 1724.

[4] MS. Minutes, Quarter Sessions, Berkshire, 15th July and 17th October
1735.

[5] *Ibid.* 4th and 5th May 1736.

[6] MS. Minutes, Quarter Sessions, Essex, 14th April 1713 and 6th April 1714.

rule, however, the Treasurer confined himself to "receiving and paying the moneys" of the county, and keeping its rudimentary accounts. How primitive was the conception of the office that the Justices entertained may be judged from the following order of the Essex Quarter Sessions in a year in which Pitt was building up a great colonial empire and London was already becoming the world's greatest banking centre: "It is ordered by this Court that the moneys which from time to time shall be received by the Treasurers of this County shall be locked up and kept in an iron chest provided for that purpose from the receipt thereof until the same shall be paid out again." [1]

It was of a piece with this conception of the County Treasurer's duties that during the whole of the eighteenth century he received either no specific remuneration beyond the honour and profit of holding the county balances—not as, we may believe, usually locked up in an iron chest—or else only an occasional gratuity or trifling annual stipend. In 1705, for instance, the Devonshire Quarter Sessions "doth think fit to allow Mr. Charles Inglett [the County Treasurer] the sum of £5 for writing 66 long warrants, and dispersing the same, and for several days' labours and attendance in settling the whole method of proceeding on the late Act of Parliament for repairing of bridges and other matters, and postage relating thereunto, his account being examined and allowed of by this Court." [2] In 1741 Hampshire pays its Treasurer a special gratuity of fifty guineas "for his extraordinary care and trouble for the several years past." [3] In 1759 the more economical Cambridgeshire awards its Treasurer a gratuity of six guineas for his "diligent and faithful services." [4] Breconshire in 1736 formally votes its Treasurer five shillings every quarter "for his trouble," but gave him a special gratuity of £10 in 1769.[5] Derbyshire paid its Treasurer £10 a year in 1708, and £20 in 1783.[6] Under these circumstances it is

---

[1] MS. Minutes, Quarter Sessions, Essex, 15th January 1760.

[2] MS. Minutes, Quarter Sessions, Devonshire, Midsummer 1705.

[3] MS. Minutes, Quarter Sessions, Hampshire, 6th October 1741.

[4] MS. Minutes, Quarter Sessions, Cambridgeshire, 12th January 1759.

[5] MS. Minutes, Quarter Sessions, Breconshire, 13th July 1736 and 10th June 1769.

[6] *Three Centuries of Derbyshire Annals*, by J. C. Cox, 1890, vol. i. p. 120. The "Treasurer of the County Bridges" for one of the Divisions of Devonshire

perhaps not surprising that county after county had trouble with its finances. The Treasurer was, to say the least of it, not prompt with his payment or quick in the settlement of his accounts. In Devonshire in 1690 Quarter Sessions is driven by the constant rise in the levy for " Bridge money " to inquire why " several sums of money still remain in the hands of the Treasurers for such bridges " for the preceding ten years.[1] In Hampshire in 1721 the Quarter Sessions has to dismiss the County Treasurer of the Gaol and House of Correction Money, " well satisfied that there hath been yearly and every year," during his term of office, " more money paid by the respective parishes . . . than hath been by him disbursed " ; and it is ordered that unless he produces a considerable balance he is to be prosecuted.[2] But whether or not the plan of entrusting the " County Stock " and the county bookkeeping to a local tradesman or one of the minor gentry resulted in financial security, it plainly did not afford the Justices much help in dealing with their problems of county administration.

With the great and sudden rise in the magnitude of the administrative and financial work of Quarter Sessions, which marked the close of the eighteenth century, the mere money-

got his salary raised in 1721 from £6 to £10 a year (MS. Minutes, Devonshire, Michaelmas 1721). Three years later we find "Treasurer and Supervisor of all the County Bridges" in another Division paid £14 a year (*ibid.* Easter 1724). But next year the Justices attempt to cut it down again (*ibid.* Midsummer 1725). In 1741 the "Treasurer of the County Rates" of Devonshire is paid £20 a year (*ibid.* Easter 1741). Essex paid its exceptionally active Treasurer between 1712 and 1719 as much as £100, and then £150 a year ; but reverted in 1719 to the quasi-honorary office (MS. Minutes, Quarter Sessions, Essex, 1712, 1719).

[1] MS. Minutes, Quarter Sessions, Devonshire, Michaelmas 1690. It was, we think, not on the advice of the County Treasurer, Giles Inglett, Esquire, that the Devonshire Quarter Sessions in 1719 ordered £680 of the county funds to be "put . . . into the South Sea Stock for the use of this county." At Easter 1720 the Treasurer reports having bought £500 South Sea Stock with the above sum, and that is "now worth £1500 and upwards to be sold." Prudently, it was resolved to sell and invest the proceeds in the East India Company's bonds. The sale was duly made for £1535, and the money received by the London Agent of the County Treasurer—one "Isaac Weare, of Lyon's Inn"—a name and address destined, by a coincidence, to have a tragic significance two centuries later. Alas, it has to be reported in 1726 that "the whole of, or the greatest part, hath been lost or embezzled." The County Treasurer, being legally responsible, gives his own bond for the amount, and we may hope that the county eventually got the money (MS. Minutes, Quarter Sessions, Devonshire, Easter 1719, Easter 1720, and Easter 1726).

[2] MS. Minutes, Quarter Sessions, Hampshire, 3rd October 1721.

handling and account-keeping work of the County Treasurer became exceedingly onerous, and though the balances doubtless increased accordingly, the counties had everywhere to pay increased salaries to their sole financial officers.[1] These salaries, it must be remembered, covered the whole cost of the necessary book-keeping, accounting, and cashier staff of the county administration, for which the Treasurer was at that time solely responsible. In view of this fact it is amazing to see how cheaply—if the mere salaries may be taken as the whole cost—even the largest counties got the work done. Northumberland in 1799 was only paying its Treasurer £40 a year, which was raised in 1823 to £120.[2] In 1822 the Quarter Sessions of Berkshire, which had before made cheaper arrangements, screwed up sufficient resolution to appoint a Treasurer at £150 a year, he giving security for £2000.[3] The Gloucestershire Quarter Sessions paid its Treasurer £120 a year in 1824.[4] In Lancashire the Justices seem to have drifted into an arrangement under which one person acted as Treasurer "without," as was complained in 1798, "the general concurrence of the Justices of the Peace." He had only £20 a year salary, but his current balance reached nearly £4000. He was then formally appointed as Treasurer at £200 a year, giving security for £10,000. In 1803 his salary was raised to £300, and in 1818 to £600 a year.[5] Even as late as 1834 the extensive and financially important West Riding of Yorkshire was allowing for all the expenses and remuneration of its Treasurer only £600 a year.[6]

(e) *The County Surveyor*

In no department of the county business does the Justices'

---

[1] In Buckinghamshire, on the other hand, as late as 1814, the Justices appointed the Clerk of the Peace to be himself "Treasurer of this County's Stock," saving a salary, but thereby removing all check on the payments, except their own amateur and perfunctory examination of the state of the county balances (MS. Minutes, Quarter Sessions, Buckinghamshire, Easter 1814). A separate Treasurer was not appointed until 1833, and then without salary.

[2] MS. Minutes, Quarter Sessions, Northumberland, 18th July 1799, 16th October 1823.

[3] MS. Minutes, Quarter Sessions, Berkshire, 16th April 1822.

[4] MS. Minutes, Quarter Sessions, Gloucestershire, 19th October 1824.

[5] MS. Minutes, Quarter Sessions, Lancashire, 1798-1803 ; 2nd August 1818.

[6] Report of House of Commons Committee on County Rates, 1834 (Broadrick's evidence).

rooted objection to the appointment of salaried officers stand out so conspicuously as in that of the execution of structural works and repairs. As we shall subsequently explain when we describe the maintenance of roads and bridges, every county was legally responsible for keeping up the larger bridges of wood or stone by which its rivers were crossed; every county had, too, its gaol and its Houses of Correction, usually also its Shire Hall, to keep constantly in repair at the expense of county funds. Nowadays it would be taken for granted that the constant supervision of these structures, and the execution of the repairs that they were perpetually requiring —to say nothing of the occasional need for new and additional buildings of one sort or another—rendered indispensable the appointment of a skilled professional architect, engineer, or surveyor, on whose expert inspection and advice, duly considered and endorsed by a standing committee of the Justices themselves, the necessary expenditure would be incurred. Nothing could have been further from the minds of the Justices of 1689, or indeed throughout the eighteenth century, than any such organisation. One favourite expedient in the early decades of the eighteenth century—just when "farming the poor" for a lump sum and "farming the workhouse" was being introduced by the Poor Law Act of 1723—was to "farm" the repairs to a local bricklayer, carpenter, or stonemason, who undertook, for a small lump sum annually, to keep a particular bridge,[1] or even all the bridges in a district, in proper repair, a neighbouring Justice certifying to Quarter Sessions that he had fulfilled his contract before his "salary" or "rent" was paid.[2] For the first three-quarters of the

[1] Such contracts abound, for instance, in the Merionethshire Sessions Rolls, 1747-1760.

[2] In 1712 the West Riding Justices, having spent over £538 a year during the past fourteen years in their casual bridge repairs, contracted, after tenders had been "heard in open court," with four men for keeping in repair all the Riding bridges for eleven years for £350 a year. Twenty years later they contract with another person for a ten years' term at £300 a year (MS. Minutes, Quarter Sessions, West Riding, 13th July 1712, 18th April 1732). So in Devonshire, in 1727, the Justices of "the East Grand Division" advertised for tenders from persons "to undertake the repair of the bridges in the East Division at a yearly salary for the space of seven, ten, fourteen, or twenty-one years" (MS. Minutes, Quarter Sessions, Michaelmas 1727). Two years later we find the Berkshire Justices ordering that the High Constables of the Hundred shall "yearly at Michaelmas pay to J. C. and W. R., bricklayers, . . . thirty shillings a year for their keeping in repair that part of the bridge"

eighteenth century we find the Lancashire and West Riding Quarter Sessions habitually putting out to contract the repair of all the bridges of a division, or of the county, for a fixed term of years, for an annual lump sum paid to the contractor, sometimes under the name of "salary."[1] There came, however, to be an impression in some counties that Quarter Sessions had no legal authority to enter into contracts for keeping bridges in repair,—owing, we assume, to the absence of Grand Jury presentments to support the expenditure,—and we find the Devonshire Justices accordingly petitioning Parliament to give them power to farm out "all the county bridges for such a term of years as they shall think proper."[2] In other counties individual Justices or groups of Justices undertook to superintend the work, a supervision which, as we have related, was elsewhere performed by the High Constables. Under such superintendence, we may well believe, with a Grand Jury of the West Riding in 1705 ("being freeholders of Staincliffe and Ewcross"), that "the county is put to . . . great and expensive charges," owing to "the abuses the workmen commit in the repairing of bridges."

over the Blackwater that belonged to the county (*ibid.* Berkshire, Easter, 1729). These little contractors urge that "there is £3 for two years' rent" due to them. The use of the word "rent," or in other cases "salary," may make it ambiguous to those unaccustomed to eighteenth-century terminology, whether or not the sum paid included (as we think is plain from the context of many such entries) the cost of labour and materials. Thus in Devonshire in 1725 we have in full the "memo. of contract made with R. S., bricklayer, for all repairs (except plumber's, smith's, and glazier's work) to all buildings, including the castle, the county workhouse, for a period of fourteen years," except the castle walls, and excepting damage from fire. For all this he is to have a yearly "salary" of £25, and be free to terminate the contract at the end of seven years (MS. Minutes, Quarter Sessions, Devonshire, Midsummer 1725).

[1] The Shropshire Grand Jury made a presentment in 1742 in favour of contracts being entered into for rebuilding certain bridges, and for keeping them in repair for a term of years (*Shropshire County Records*, Part IV., edited by R. G. Venables, p. 108). In the MS. Minutes of the Lancashire Quarter Sessions between 1750 (the date of the first existing Minute-book) and 1756 there are constantly recurring entries of fixed sums to be paid to the "undertakers of the common or public bridges" of the several Hundreds "pursuant to articles by them respectively executed" (see, for instance, MS. Minutes, Lancaster, 16th July 1751, January 1753). In 1756 the Justices begin to employ a "Supervisor" in some portions of the county employing workmen under the direction of local Justices, but they continue to "let" by open competition the repair of other bridges of this Hundred after 1768 (*ibid.* 22nd January 1756, 12th April 1768).

[2] MS. Minutes, Quarter Sessions, Devonshire, Michaelmas 1757.

They accordingly request that " a fit person may be appointed
. . . to take care of all the public bridges . . . and order the
repair of the same." Quarter Sessions accedes to the request
of this particular district, allowing the local Justices to select
such a person at £20 a year.[1] In other counties having
numerous county bridges to keep in order it seems to have
been usual, by 1689, for Quarter Sessions to appoint at a
small annual stipend a " Supervisor," " Surveyor," or " Bridgemaster," either for each Division, or for the county as a whole.
In Devonshire, in 1689, we find each of the three " Grand
Divisions " of the county (East, North, and South) having its
own Treasurer of the Bridge Money and its own Supervisor of
Bridges—minor landowners and substantial farmers, who were
periodically appointed by Quarter Sessions and paid salaries of
£8 a year to inspect all the bridges within their Divisions,
execute such urgent repairs as are necessary and approved by
two or four local magistrates, make presentments of other
works required for the decision of Quarter Sessions itself, and
raise the necessary funds, after special vote of Quarter Sessions,
by precept upon the parishes in the particular " Grand Division." [2] These arrangements were always being broken into
by the desire of the Justices to save the county the small
amount of the Surveyors' salaries. Thus the Devonshire
Justices, as we have seen, adopted in 1727 the device of
" farming " out the bridges to contractors, though in the next
decade we find them reverting to the old policy of salaried
Bridge Surveyors. In 1728 the Justices of the North Riding
of Yorkshire appointed, as an experiment, two Surveyors, each
taking six Wapentakes, for a salary of £15 a year; but they
quickly repented of it, and abolished the appointments within
the year.[3] Hampshire in 1777 was paying a " Surveyor to
the County " fees of a few guineas at a time for whatever work
he did, but dismissed him in 1784, " this Court having

---

[1] MS. Minutes, Quarter Sessions, West Riding, 10th July 1705.

[2] MS. Minutes, Quarter Sessions, Devonshire, 16th July 1689, March 1690,
March 1726, Midsummer 1727, Midsummer 1736, Easter 1745, Midsummer
1760, Easter 1787. At these dates salaries were from £25 to £30.

[3] *North Riding Quarter Sessions Records*, by J. C. Atkinson, 9th January
and 8th October 1728, vol. viii. pp. 179, 182. In this Riding they even
proposed to appoint a " General Surveyor of County Bridges " as early as 1743,
but the recommendation was not acted upon (*ibid.* vol. viii. p. 244).

adjudged such office to be unnecessary."[1]   Buckinghamshire
had a salaried "Surveyor of Bridges" from 1804 until 1822,
but then discontinued the office, and did not appoint another
paid officer until 1838.[2]   Breconshire first appointed one in
1810 at £20 a year.[3]   With the extraordinarily low salaries
which even the wealthiest counties consented to pay their
Surveyors or Bridgemasters we cannot wonder at the frequency
of the dismissals.   In Berkshire, as late as 1814, the officer
who was grandiloquently called Surveyor of Bridges was only
paid five guineas a year.[4]   In Lancashire, when the Justices
gave up letting the repairs of the bridges by contract, they
appointed five "Bridgemasters"—in one case a schoolmaster,
but usually small landowners or substantial farmers, who got
only a trifling annual salary for looking after all the bridges
in the Hundred.[5]   As late as 1825 this important county was
only aspiring to get a practical artisan as its only salaried
officer for all the engineering work in each of its Hundreds.[6]
The two "Bridge Surveyors," who had long been entrusted with
the care of the many stone bridges of the important county of
Northumberland, one taking the northern and the other the
southern half of the county, were, as late as 1825, only paid
fifteen shillings a week each, and were apparently only working
stonemasons.[7]   Sometimes the Justices had a "County Mason"
—that is, they appointed a master workman to whom they
gave all the small building jobs that occurred in the year—
and to this little contractor was entrusted the execution of the
bridge repairs.   Thus in Derbyshire in 1682 Quarter Sessions
made a lengthy order reciting that, it having previously been
reported, "upon the information of divers inhabitants residing

---

[1] MS. Minutes, Quarter Sessions, Hampshire, 15th July 1777, 20th April
1784.

[2] See MS. volume of "Minutes relating to Bridges," 1801-1814, Quarter
Sessions, Buckinghamshire.

[3] MS. Minutes, Quarter Sessions, Breconshire, 1st May 1810.

[4] MS. Minutes, Quarter Sessions, Berkshire, 11th January 1814.

[5] MS. Minutes, Quarter Sessions, Lancashire, 22nd January 1756, and
following years.

[6] Quarter Sessions declared its opinion "that the Bridgemaster for the
South Side of the Sands of the Hundred of Lonsdale should be a good practical
Stonemason," and resolved that the magistrates of the Hundred should elect
such a person at the next Quarter Sessions, the Deputy Clerk of the Peace to
give notice to magistrates of the Hundred accordingly (*ibid.* 12th January
1825).

[7] MS. Minutes, Quarter Sessions, Northumberland, 13th January 1825.

near several county bridges, . . . that the same were out of
repair, it was then referred to Simon Holt, the County Mason,
together with some of the respective inhabitants living near,
. . . to view the same and report their judgments to this
Court what repairs are necessary . . . and what such . . .
will cost." These reports show, the order continues, that ten
several bridges require to have spent on them the sum of
£306, which the "Head Constables" are directed to raise by
rate, and to pay in specified sums for each bridge to one or
two named persons, evidently local residents, who are to be
"overseers of the work done at the bridges. . . . And Simon
Holt, the County Mason," it is ordered, shall "be employed to
do the said work at the said several bridges, provided he undertake to do it as well and at as cheap rate as other masons." [1]
It is easy now to imagine how unskilful were the plans, how
lax the supervision, and how excessive were the charges under
such a system ; yet only slowly and reluctantly could Quarter
Sessions be induced to incur the expense of a salaried officer,
either to design and supervise the work, or even to check the
bills. The first device that occurred to the Derbyshire
Justices seems to have been to appoint, as "Surveyor of the
Bridges," at a fee of half a crown a day, the very Simon
Holt who, as "County Mason," carried out the work which he
reported to be required. What generally happened we may
infer from the exceptional case of Renishaw Bridge, in which
one of the Justices was specially interested, and which in
1699 he obtained leave to get repaired under his own supervision. His detailed account of the expenditure includes
an item of £2 : 3s. paid "to Simon Holt for his pains and
charges coming to view the decays of the said Bridge and
Causey by order of sessions, *and to keep him from coming to do
his work by reason we could do it much cheaper than he would
have taken it.*" [2] Yet the Derbyshire Justices continued the
same system for another twenty years at least. In 1713
Isaac Kirk, a mason, was appointed "Surveyor of the Bridges,"
or "Bridgemaster," at a salary of £10 a year; and at the
same time was employed to execute, without any agreement as

[1] Quarter Sessions, Derbyshire, January 1682 ; *Three Centuries of Derbyshire Annals*, by J. C. Cox, 1890, vol. ii. pp. 218-219.
[2] *Ibid.* p. 221.

to price, the various works that he recommended, under no more competent supervision than that of one of the Justices or other local residents named for each job.[1] The Essex Justices seem, early in the eighteenth century, to have brought themselves to face the expense of retaining the services of a Surveyor, at £40 a year; then they dismissed him as involving a needless burden on the rates; then, in 1711, "taking notice of many large extravagant bills and charges for workmen in repairing bridges and other public works and buildings for the service of this county," came deliberately to the conclusion that a " Surveyor is absolutely necessary to take care thereof and prevent their exorbitant demands. And therefore in full court *nemine contradicente* doth think fit to restore Mr. R. P. into that place again, and doth appoint him the same salary he formerly had of £40 . . . for his extraordinary pains and good service in saving the county from excessive unreasonable bills charged by workmen upon the public account."[2] Yet only four years later we read in the same volume of minutes that " it is ordered by this Court that the office of Surveyor of Bridges in this county be no longer continued."[3] But, before very long the Essex Justices again change their minds. In 1718 it appears to them " by long experience . . . that the county hath been notoriously abused and put upon by the workmen of several trades employed in the repairs of the public bridges belonging to this county, and in other public works and repairs done at the charge of this county for want of a proper officer to take care therein," whereupon they appoint one, Edward Turner, to be " the Public Surveyor of the bridges and other the public works and repairs to be done at the charge of this county, at a salary of £60 a year."[4]

The payment of a fixed salary to the County Surveyor or Bridgemaster remained, however, right down to the end of the eighteenth century, unusual. What seems to have been a more common practice was that adopted in Suffolk, where the Justices, in 1785, had a permanent County Surveyor, paid by a fee or a percentage for each job of bridge repair or other county work, who sometimes bought materials and hired labour

---

[1] *Three Centuries of Derbyshire Annals*, by J. C. Cox, 1890, vol. ii. pp. 215, 216, 222. [2] MS. Minutes, Quarter Sessions, Essex, 10th April 1711. [3] *Ibid.* 4th October 1715. [4] *Ibid.* 22nd April 1718.

at the expense of the county, at other times entered on behalf
of the county into contracts with master-workmen; and at
yet other times himself contracted with the county to do the
work for a fixed price at his own risk.[1] It was in vain that
Parliament, in 1737, sought to suggest to Quarter Sessions a
more carefully safeguarded financial procedure for executing
their bridge repairs.[2] Not until the latter part of the
eighteenth century, and then only in the more advanced
counties, do we find a complete separation of the functions of
the County Surveyor and the contractor; the execution of
formal plans and specifications; the submission of the work to
tender; and the conclusion of a contract with the lowest
suitable tenderer.[3] Gradually other counties reform their
procedure on the same lines. In 1809, by the West Riding
Justices it is wisely and prudently "ordered that during the
time Mr. Hartley is employed as Surveyor to the Riding and
receives the salary thereof, neither he nor any of his sons shall
be employed directly or indirectly in the execution of any
works carried on by the Riding.[4] Not until well into the
nineteenth century did it become established as a practice that,

[1] See, for instance, MS. Minutes, Quarter Sessions, Suffolk, 18th July and
6th August 1785, 28th April and 15th May 1786.

[2] By the 12 Geo. II. c. 29, sec. 14 (1739), it was enacted that "when any
public bridges, ramparts, banks or copes are to be repaired at the expense of
the county, the Justices at their General or Quarter Sessions, after presentment
made by the Grand Jury of their want of reparation, may contract with any
person for rebuilding, repairing, and amending the same, for any term not
exceeding seven years, at a fixed annual sum ; in order to which they shall give
public notice of their intention of contracting . . . and such contracts shall be
made at the most reasonable price which shall be proposed by the contractors,
who shall give sufficient security for the due performance thereof to the Clerk
of the Peace. And all contracts when agreed to, and all orders relating
thereto, shall be entered in a book to be kept by the Clerk of the Peace for that
purpose, who shall keep the same among the records of the county, to be
inspected by any of the Justices at all reasonable times, and by any person
employed by any parish or place contributing to the same, without fee."

[3] See the order for building a bridge in MS. Minutes, Quarter Sessions,
Middlesex, 23rd June 1796.

[4] MS. Minutes, Quarter Sessions, West Riding of Yorkshire, 10th April
1809. Presently we get even the Norfolk Justices formally resolving "that
the building and repairing of all county bridges, and the execution of all public
works to be done at the expense of this county, be offered by advertisements in
the Norwich and Norfolk newspapers, to be performed by contract of persons
desirous of executing the same ; such contracts to be delivered to the County
Surveyor, and having been submitted by him to the consideration of, and
approved by, five of the magistrates acting in and for this county ; and such
works to be done and executed under the direction and superintendence of the
County Surveyor " (MS. Minutes, Quarter Sessions, Norfolk, 15th July 1815).

before "the gentlemen of the Grand Jury" set formally in motion the proceedings for the repair or reconstruction of a bridge, they should have before them an expert professional report by a competent civil engineer as to the works that were required.[1]

It was thus rare, right down to the end of the eighteenth century, for the county to employ for its works and bridges any salaried professional engineer or surveyor, in the modern meaning of those terms. In 1787, however, we find the Devonshire Justices going to the hitherto unheard-of expense of getting a special survey of all the county bridges by a couple of surveyors, at a cost of fifty-five guineas.[2] Not until 1808, when there were in Devonshire no fewer than 250 county bridges to be looked after—one of which had lately gone to pieces owing to inefficient repairing—did the Justices of that great county make up their minds to appoint " a civil engineer of approved talent and ability," at a salary of £300 a year, " for the future direction and superintendence " of these 250 bridges, in place of the incompetent "surveyors."[3] It was thus almost unprecedented for the West Riding of Yorkshire, to employ, in the early years of the nineteenth century, the whole time of a professional "Surveyor of Riding Bridges," whose salary was raised in 1811 from £400 to £600 a year.[4] Moreover the Justices found it almost as difficult to place any confidence in their professional surveyor as to pay him. The old practice of entrusting the control of each work to a neighbouring magistrate long continued. Thus, in Gloucester-

---

[1] Thus, in Northumberland in 1820 it is "ordered that at each subsequent sessions the Clerk of the Peace do state to the respective Grand Juries that the Justices request that whenever any of the county bridges shall be reported to be in want of any extensive and substantial repairs, that they shall take into their consideration the propriety of taking the opinion of an experienced civil engineer upon the proposed mode of repair, and the expense thereof, for the guidance of the Bench" (MS. Minutes, Quarter Sessions, Northumberland, 13th January 1820).

[2] MS. Minutes, Quarter Sessions, Devonshire, Epiphany and Easter 1787. The only change made in immediate consequence of this report was the appointment of five new "Surveyors of Bridges" at salaries of £25 and £30 a year each, in supersession of the three former Supervisors.

[3] *Ibid.* Epiphany 1808. In the following year, at the instance of W. Morton Pitt, M.P., Dorset took a similar course, appointing an "Engineer" of the county bridges at £500 a year (MS. Minutes, Quarter Sessions, Dorsetshire, 24th June and 11th July 1809).

[4] MS. Minutes, Quarter Sessions, West Riding, Easter 1811.

shire, as late as 1825, " Mr. Collingwood, the County Surveyor, having made a report that it was absolutely necessary a new bridge should be erected at Preston-upon-Stour, and that the work was begun: Ordered that the building of the said bridge be placed under the direction and superintendence of the Rev. Charles Jefferson, whose orders the County Surveyor shall obey." [1] So in Norfolk the County Surveyor would be authorised to expend sums of £10 to £50 on particular bridges and causeways that he reported as needing repair under the personal direction of specified local Justices.[2] In one case, however, the country gentlemen were fortunate enough to put the county works into the hands of a practical genius. The greatest of these early professional advisers on the county gaols and bridges was, as we need hardly remind the reader, the promoted stonemason and self-taught architect and civil engineer, Thomas Telford, whom the Shropshire Justices had the wisdom, at the suggestion of Mr. Pulteney, M.P., to engage as " Surveyor of Public Works for the County of Salop," about 1787. On what terms Telford was employed, and exactly what work he executed, we have been unable to ascertain. His primary duty seems to have been the building of no fewer than forty-two new bridges, five of iron and thirty-seven of stone, over the innumerable streams of the county. But we find him also building and repairing the county prisons, and apparently contracting to employ the prisoners, whilst he also mends roads and rebuilds churches for particular parishes and undertakes the construction of the great Ellesmere Canal for its proprietors.[3]

(f) *Executive Makeshifts*

The inadequacy of the executive staff at the disposal of Quarter Sessions, and the scantiness of the control to be exercised over unsalaried officers, led to various makeshifts by which to supply the deficiency. Thus, the Court of Quarter Sessions necessarily had a Cryer, or officer to make the formal

---

[1] MS. Minutes, Quarter Sessions, Gloucestershire, Trinity Sessions, 1826.
[2] MS. Minutes, Quarter Sessions, Norfolk, 18th April 1792.
[3] See the interesting account of Telford in *Lives of the Engineers*, by Samuel Smiles, vol. ii. 1862 ; and the *Life of Thomas Telford* (edited by John Rickman, 1838) ; and *Shropshire County Records*, part viii. pp. iii.-v.

announcements, call out the names and demand silence.[1] This humble officer was used—in Middlesex, in 1718, for instance —to go on errands of inquiry for the Justices, or even to undertake special investigations.[2] The office, like so many others of the period, was, however, often "farmed," or at any rate performed by deputy, so that it did not easily lend itself to an extension of functions. In 1722 the Middlesex Justices found themselves compelled to appoint a committee to consider the quarrels between the owners and the lessees of the office of "Housekeeper and Cryer" at Hicks' Hall, the Middlesex Sessions House—the committee solemnly recommending to the Justices "that it is necessary for your service that the office of Housekeeper and Cryer should either not be rented at all by any tenant or servant, or if it be rented that it should be on more moderate and easy terms." Quarter Sessions thereupon determines that the business of "Housekeeper of Hicks' Hall and Cryer of the General and Quarter Sessions be not in future farmed or rented for any consideration whatsoever." [3]

Another expedient was found by the Dorset and Devonshire Justices. As the Judges of Assize had their Marshals, so could the Court of Quarter Sessions, and such officers could be used as special police agents for the county, or, as we read in 1689, "for the apprehending of all rogues and vagabonds begging and wandering"; and could be specially authorised "forthwith to carry them before some Justice of the Peace." [4] It was for such work that the Dorset Justices in 1631 voted

---

[1] A Cryer of the Court was appointed by Kent in 1694, to be paid by a fee of fourpence for every witness called (MS. Minutes, Quarter Sessions, Kent, 2nd October 1694). In the West Riding the Clerk of the Peace was directed to appoint "a Cryer to attend the several General Quarter Sessions of this Riding" (MS. Minutes, Quarter Sessions, West Riding, 29th April 1701). In Dorset, the Cryer had eight guineas a year, and was charged with making the payments to prosecutors and witnesses. In 1829, however, the newly appointed Finance Committee objected to such a salary as illegal (MS. Minutes, Quarter Sessions, Dorsetshire, 12th January 1796 ; *ibid.* 1829).

[2] We read "that the Constables, Headboroughs, and Beadles within this Liberty, refuse to go along with the Cryer of this Court who is ordered to make diligent inquiry after" certain persons who had been complained of as keeping unlicensed ale-houses ; whereupon the Court peremptorily orders all such officers, "as often as Lawrence Rendall, our Cryer, shall think fit and requisite, to go along with him to the houses . . . and assist him in taking a true and exact account in writing" of the names and addresses of the delinquents (MS. Minutes, Quarter Sessions, Middlesex, 5th March 1718).

[3] MS. Minutes, Quarter Sessions, Middlesex, 12th January and 2nd March 1722.

[4] MS. Minutes, Quarter Sessions, Devonshire, Michaelmas, 1689.

their Marshal forty shillings, "for the great pains and care" he had given "in the searching out and apprehending rogues and vagrants at fairs and other great places of meeting within this county."[1] In 1725 it was ordered in Devonshire "that for the future there shall be but four County Marshals who shall have each the yearly salary of four pounds and no more."[2] The office was, however, evidently found unsatisfactory, for, in 1742, "all the Marshals of the County" were summarily discharged, and the Clerk of the Peace was ordered to provide "two able men" to attend Quarter Sessions in their stead, at the old wage of a pound a quarter.[3] We infer from the lack of other mention of Marshals for purposes of local government that the seventeenth-century practice of Dorset and Devon was gradually abandoned, and did not generally prevail.

In one county at any rate, the decay and disuse into which the manorial courts fell, led to the appointment of entirely new officers by the county. Thus we learn in 1719 that "it appears by the records" of the Essex Quarter Sessions "that the Court has for many years appointed two officers by the name of Common Informers to inquire and present such offences as were public grievances and public nuisances to the county," and anything else that might be commanded by the Court. In 1719 the office is still in existence, "but the said officers have lately presented only the defects of weights and measures, and neglected to take any notice of any other" nuisance. Quarter Sessions accordingly enjoins them henceforth to include all the offences and public nuisances specified in a lengthy charge given to them, including various forms of poaching and illicit game destruction, all the common offences of ale-house keepers, the defects of bridges and highways, breaches of the Assize of Bread and the use of short weights or measures—in short, the whole range of offences cognisable by the Court Leet, the High Constable, the Hundred Jury and the Grand Inquest of the County.[4] How long these two

---

[1] Order of Quarter Sessions, Dorsetshire, Michaelmas 1631 ; in *Dorset County Chronicle*, 2nd May 1844.

[2] MS. Minutes, Quarter Sessions, Devonshire, Midsummer 1725. The salary was raised in 1789 to £4 : 10s. a year (*ibid.* Michaelmas 1739).

[3] *Ibid.* Michaelmas 1742.

[4] See the remarkable order in MS. Minutes, Quarter Sessions, Essex, 6th October 1719.

Common Informers continued to figure on the Essex County staff we have not ascertained. In 1739, however, we find a specialisation of the office, in that two persons are appointed "Surveyors and Searchers of Weights and Measures for the Eastern and Western Divisions of the county respectively, with orders so to "survey in the several towns, parishes, and places within their respective divisions, that the whole of the county may be surveyed once in every year, and that they do make a plain and distinct return on oath at every General Quarter Sessions . . . so that it may appear how far and in what manner they shall from time to time have respectively executed this order."[1] These officers were paid, from the outset, by fixed salary, at first £15, then £20, and eventually £25 a year. Thus, for a couple of generations prior to the Weights and Measures Act of 1795, we periodically hear in this county of these "Public Weighers, whose business it is to go to the several parts of the county and examine the weights of all millers and shopkeepers, and make returns of those in whose possession any light weight is found . . . and whenever complaint of this sort is made the suspected dealer is summoned to appear at the following sessions, where . . . he is sure to be exposed and otherwise punished, in proportion to his demerits."[2] Other inspectors appear from time to time, such as those who, in 1727, were appointed to ensure compliance with the Act of 12 Geo. I. regulating the making of bricks,[3] and those who in 1749-1750 vainly sought to ward off "the infection now raging among the horned cattle."[4] From 1771 onwards most counties appointed special persons in the several market towns to report the average prices of the corn sold, a service for which these "Corn Inspectors" regularly drew modest fees from the county funds. On their reports the Grand Jury would occasionally make the "average market price of the several sorts of middling English corn" the subject of a formal presentment on oath.[5]

---

[1] MS. Minutes, Quarter Sessions, Essex, 1st May 1739 ; 11th January 1763 ; 6th October 1778.

[2] *General View of the Agriculture of Essex*, by Messrs. Griggs, 1794, p. 26.

[3] MS. Minutes, Quarter Sessions, Essex, 10th January 1727.

[4] *Ibid.* 18th November 1749.

[5] See for instance such a presentment (Wheat 43s. per quarter) in MS. Minutes, Quarter Sessions, Essex, 5th January 1771.

It was, however, not by the makeshift use of subordinate officers or the sporadic appointment of an inspector or two, at the miserable stipends of the period, that the Justices could cope with the steadily growing mass of work thrust upon the county. Their main reliance for the fulfilment of these duties was in the characteristic device of eighteenth-century administration, the employment of a contractor. Up and down the country, in every conceivable service, the easiest way of getting the work done seemed to be to "farm" it, or put it out to contract to the man who offered the most advantageous terms.[1] It is the almost universal prevalence of this contract system in the eighteenth century that explains the exiguity of the executive staff. The prisons, like the workhouses, were "farmed" to the gaolers, keepers, governors, or masters; their wretched inmates, if fed and clothed at all, were fed and clothed by contract, and even physicked by contract; the bridges and roads, as we have seen, were often kept by contract, in what they were pleased to call repair; the vagrants were conveyed by contract, fed by contract, and even whipped by contract; and when the felons were sent beyond seas, they were habitually transported by contract and sold by auction on arrival to those who contracted at the highest rate to employ them. This contract system had naturally different results in different services, and we have therefore necessarily to defer examination of it until the subsequent volumes, in which we shall trace the evolution of such local government services as the Suppression of Vagrancy, the Prevention of Crime, the Administration of Prisons, the Relief of Destitution, and the Maintenance of Roads and Bridges.

---

[1] The interesting feature of the eighteenth-century contract for "farming" particular services was that, unlike the modern agreement with a contractor, they were usually, not for a specific amount of work, but to hold the local authority harmless, in the whole range of the department referred to, whilst leaving with local authority all the control. For a definite sum, the farmer undertook indefinite liabilities. Thus the vagrant contractor would undertake, for a lump sum, to convey all the vagrants who might be handed over to him; the bridge contractor would agree, for a definite payment, to maintain all the county bridges in repair; the contractor for the poor would promise, in return for a stipulated sum, to provide for all the poor who might become entitled to relief—even to comply with all the orders of the Justices for outdoor relief—whilst the Gaoler or the Keeper of the House of Correction would pay a fixed rent for his position, however few or many the prisoners for whom he had to provide.

(g) *Committees of Justices*

Concurrently with the slow accretion of a staff of paid officers, such as the County Treasurer, the County Surveyor, and the salaried High Constables, we may trace a distinct development of administrative structure among the Justices themselves. Their first idea seems always to have been to cope with the work by increased exertion in their individual capacities. When a magistrate, in riding about his neighbourhood, saw a bridge out of repair, he would mention the neglect at the next Justices' meeting—perhaps get it enforced by a formal presentment—and then be deputed to put the bridge in repair, himself engaging the master-workman, ordering the work, and reporting the cost to Quarter Sessions. When in the West Riding of Yorkshire, at the close of the seventeenth century, any sum of money " was estreated upon the said Riding " by Quarter Sessions, for the repair of a county bridge, it was invariably ordered to be paid to a particular Justice of the Peace, to be by him laid out for the necessary work.[1] Even if he had not superintended the work, it might be referred to him—as frequently in the West Riding between 1689 and 1700—to order what sum should be paid to particular workmen for the repairs they had executed.[2] He might even be asked to keep a particular bridge constantly in repair. The Derbyshire Quarter Sessions in 1713 directed " That John Harding, Esq., one of Her Majesty's Justices of the Peace . . . be desired to accept the trouble of Overseer of Swerkeston Bridge, and that he be Overseer accordingly, and from time to time as occasion shall require order such repairs and amendments thereof as he shall adjudge proper." [3] More usually Quarter Sessions preferred to trust the work jointly to two or three specified Justices. On " information being given to the Court of Quarter Sessions for Berkshire, that Blackwater Bridge within this County is very much out of repair, it is ordered by the Court

---

[1] MS. Minutes, Quarter Sessions, West Riding, 25th April 1693, and many other cases.

[2] *Ibid.* 1689-1700 *passim.*

[3] Quarter Sessions, Derbyshire, Midsummer 1713 ; *Three Centuries of Derbyshire Annals*, by J. C. Cox, 1890, vol. ii. p. 215.

that the same be viewed by [five named Justices] or any two or more of them, to order such repairs as they shall think fit, and to direct the Treasurer of the Hill Division of this County to pay such money as shall be necessary to defray the charges thereof." [1] No more elaborate was the procedure when the County Gaol needed repair. At the Hertfordshire Quarter Sessions we read, in 1715, "upon information given unto this Court by . . . the keeper of His Majesty's Gaol at Hertford . . . that the said Gaol is so ruinous . . . that the criminal offenders . . . sent thither cannot with safety be . . . kept therein," seven of the Justices are "desired to meet together with some able workman to view and examine into the condition . . . of the said gaol." Six months later, on their report, two Justices, with "a carpenter," are directed to execute the necessary repairs at a cost estimated at £73.[2] When the Wiltshire Justices in 1809 wanted to rebuild a county bridge at Melksham, the whole responsibility was thrown upon a committee of five local Justices, who consulted a surveyor chosen by themselves, presented his plan and estimate to Quarter Sessions, and were authorised to carry out the work.[3] Similarly, in other matters besides the execution of works, the Court of Quarter Sessions would get through its business by referring the points at issue to one or two Justices, who would be directed, for instance, "to determine the difference between the inhabitants" of two complaining parishes "touching their assessments,"[4] or to decide the appeal of certain absentee landowners who found the Overseer taking advantage of their non-resistance to "make very large assessments on the petitioners' lands and ease their own lands thereby."[5] And to prevent Quarter Sessions being again troubled, it would be ordained that "what order they shall make touching the same shall be conclusive to all parties concerned."[6] Even formal appeals would be similarly dealt with. When the Breconshire Quarter Sessions had an appeal against the action

[1] MS. Minutes, Quarter Sessions, Berkshire, March 1705.

[2] MS. Minutes, Quarter Sessions, Hertfordshire, October 1715 and April 1716.

[3] MS. Minutes, Quarter Sessions, Wiltshire, 11th July 1809.

[4] MS. Minutes, Quarter Sessions, West Riding, 17th January 1695.

[5] *Ibid.* 16th January 1695.   [6] *Ibid.* 17th January 1695.

of parish officers, it would refer it to the Justices "of the limits of the said parish," any order that any two of them made to stand ratified and confirmed by this Court.[1] In other cases, Quarter Sessions would make use of the Divisional Sessions. Thus, the West Riding Quarter Sessions frequently referred cases of settlement or bastardy to the Justices "at the next Private Sessions," or "at the next Special Sessions," held at a particular town.[2] The Essex Quarter Sessions in 1708, having received numerous complaints as to the inequality of assessment of parishes to the "quarterage" (or County Rate), refers them to the Justices of the respective Divisions to consider and report on in writing at the next ensuing Quarter Sessions.[3] Ten years later the Justices of the Division are to report what repairs are needed for one of the Houses of Correction; and three of them are then deputed to get the repairs done, at a cost not exceeding £30.[4] In 1739 Parliament authorised the consolidation of the Justices' levies into a single County Rate, and we see the Hampshire Quarter Sessions desiring "the Justices residing in and near Winchester to meet together before the next Sessions to consider of a method to make a regular general rate upon the county pursuant to the statute lately made . . . and to . . . report at next Sessions."[5] Fifty years later, when the Hampshire Quarter Sessions found itself responsible for the County Gaol, we find the Winchester Justices used as a committee of management.[6] When the Middlesex Quarter Sessions came to the conclusion in 1716 that the "Rag Fair" in Rosemary Lane was "a common nuisance to His Majesty's liege subjects," it directed the Petty Sessions for the Tower Hamlets Division "to give speedy orders to the High Constables and Petty Constables" to

---

[1] MS. Minutes, Quarter Sessions, Breconshire, 6th October 1719.

[2] MS. Minutes, Quarter Sessions, West Riding, 13th January 1691; 2nd April 1695.

[3] MS. Minutes, Quarter Sessions, Essex, 13th April 1708.

[4] *Ibid.* 22nd April and 15th July 1718.

[5] MS. Minutes, Quarter Sessions, Hampshire, 7th October 1739. The committee so appointed failed to solve the problem, and another was appointed the following quarter (*ibid.* 15th January 1740).

[6] "Ordered that the magistrates acting at the Petty Sessions in or near Winchester shall be authorised . . . to order such cloth and other necessaries to be furnished or sent to the Gaol and Bridewell as shall at any time appear to them to be immediately wanted" (*ibid.* 3rd October 1796).

suppress the so-called fair.[1] In Westminster, in particular, the reference to the various parochial Petty Sessions of all matters relating to Poor Relief and other parish business, otherwise than by way of appeal, quickly became habitual. We see the Petty Sessions for St. Margaret's, Westminster, in 1713, expressly ordering "that the clerk attending this Board do at the close of every Quarter Sessions apply to the Clerk of the Peace of this City and Liberty for all references made by order of the Justices of the Peace relating to the poor, to the end the Board make a quick despatch in the same."[2] It would be easy to multiply instances of this delegation from the very beginning of the eighteenth century. With the growing regularity and efficiency of these Divisional Sessions, so characteristic of the latter part of the eighteenth and the opening of the nineteenth century, the Justices in Quarter Sessions show an increasing tendency to make use of these monthly, fortnightly, or weekly meetings of magistrates as subordinate local committees, to report facts and execute orders appertaining to their respective localities.[3]

For all the affairs of the county as a whole the Court of Quarter Sessions gradually developed a system of administration by central committees. These committees were, for the first three-quarters of the eighteenth century, and in backward counties right down to the reign of Victoria, appointed only to deal with particular emergencies at particular times.[4] Like most of the contemporary committees of the House of Commons, these Justices' committees, though a nucleus was named, were open to any magistrate who chose to attend—in House of Commons phrase, "all who come to have voices." The first recognised need was for some committee to

---

[1] MS. Minutes, Quarter Sessions, Middlesex, 11th October 1716.

[2] MS. Minutes, Petty Sessions, St. Margaret's, Westminster 1713.

[3] In 1783 the Lancashire Quarter Sessions even deputed the walling in and arranging of the site for the new Salford prison to the "Justices assembled at the Royal Oak at next Special Sessions" (MS. Minutes, Quarter Sessions, Lancashire, 24th July 1783).

[4] The West Riding of Yorkshire seems to have been exceptionally backward in this development of committees—perhaps using instead its frequent adjournments of Quarter Sessions to particular towns (MS. Minutes, Quarter Sessions, West Riding, 1689-1750). The Welsh counties were even more backward. We did not notice in the MS. Minutes of Quarter Sessions, Breconshire, that the word "committee" was ever used until 1814.

examine the bills presented for payment out of county funds. We have seen that the financial arrangements of the Justices were, at the close of the seventeenth century, rudimentary in the extreme. There was no paid accountant or financial clerk. The various county officers—the Deputy Clerk of the Peace, the Gaoler, the Keepers of the House of Correction, the Coroners, the High Constables, and the various contractors—presented their " quarterly bills " at each Sessions, and these were habitually " ordered for payment " without discussion. Now and again, the magnitude of some charge, or some suspicion as to defalcation, would lead to the appointment of one or two Justices to look into the matter.[1] Other committees appear on particular emergencies. Thus the Surrey Quarter Sessions in 1705 appointed a number of specified justices " and such others as care to attend," to inquire into the manner of levying various County Rates.[2] In the following year the Justices " that shall be present at the Town Hall in the Borough of Southwark," at the adjourned Sessions, were made a committee to inquire what was owing by the County for the repair of " Foxhall Bridge," to let " Hangman's Acre," to consider how Wood Bridge in the parish of Stoke should be repaired, to discuss the best means of recovering arrears of County Rates and the propriety of erecting a new gaol, and to investigate the pensions payable by the county.[3] In Essex, in 1712, we find a committee of four Justices to choose a new Surveyor, at a salary of £40.[4] In 1714 the Shropshire Justices appointed a committee to visit the House of Correction, and see whether there were not " a convenient place for the running and dressing of hemp."[5] In 1721 the Court of Quarter Sessions of the County of Middlesex refer to a committee the burning question " of the most proper and effectual methods . . . of preventing and removing all public nuisances within the weekly Bills of Mortality." Six months later this committee favours the Court with a remarkable

---

[1] For instance see MS. Minutes, Quarter Sessions, Essex, April 1702, where a High Constable is suspected of keeping back part of his collections for " quarterage " (or County Rate).

[2] MS. Minutes, Quarter Sessions, Surrey, 2nd October 1705.

[3] *Ibid.* 8th October 1706.

[4] MS. Minutes, Quarter Sessions, Essex, 9th April 1712.

[5] *Shropshire County Records*, part ii., edited by Sir Offley Wakeman, p. 18.

survey of the condition of the London streets, enumerating
and describing, in vivid phrase, an amazing medley of
nuisances—broken pavements, maimed beggars, blood-reeking
slaughter-houses, illicit dram-shops, straying hogs, heaps of
manure, bawdy-houses, the practice of harbouring persons
likely to become chargeable to the rates, the neglect of
parish offices, the crowds of starving vagabonds, swaying signs
darkening the streets, the fever-spreading Debtors' Gaol of
Whitechapel, and all the other horrors of the Metropolis.[1]
From the middle of the eighteenth century to its close we find
county after county appointing special committees to report
upon the daily increasing burden arising from the "passing"
of vagrants; and the detailed and sometimes graphic reports
of these committees, describing the facts and suggesting
remedies are often the most interesting entries in the massive
MS. "Order Books" of Quarter Sessions of the period.[2] It is,
however, remarkable how slowly and hesitatingly Quarter
Sessions came to the customary modern device of appointing
definite standing committees to take charge of particular
branches of its business. We find such committees beginning
to be appointed in Middlesex in the third decade of the
eighteenth century. A special committee on the Treasurer's
Accounts in 1723 recommended (in a lengthy document)
that the county accounts should be annually "examined,
and a state thereof drawn up by a committee to be appointed
and approved of by the Sessions, which committee may be
also directed to report the arrears uncollected on all the rates
of the year preceding . . . and that these books of account
may be laid on the table after dinner every Sessions on the
"County Day by the Clerk of the Peace for the perusal of the
"Justices."[3] A further step was to provide in advance for
the regular reappointment of certain committees for particular

[1] For the Report see MS. Minutes, Middlesex Quarter Sessions, 12th October
1721.
[2] Three interesting series of such reports are to be found in the MS. Minutes,
Quarter Sessions, Surrey, 24th April and 2nd October 1759 ; Quarter Sessions,
Essex, 5th October 1784, 11th January, 22nd July and 4th October 1785, and
10th January and 25th April 1786, 10th July 1787, 15th July 1788, 5th
October 1791, and Quarter Sessions, Herts, 20th January 1786.
[3] MS. Minutes, Quarter Sessions, Middlesex, October 1723. The practice
was apparently adopted of the accounts being audited by such Justices as had
served the office of Treasurer.

administrative purposes. Thus, in 1752, it is "ordered that a committee be appointed on the County Day of every Sessions week, to see what prisoners in New Prison and in the House of Correction are not able to pay fees."[1] By 1759 we have similar provision for the annual appointment of what may be considered an incipient "General Purposes Committee." It is ordered that a committee be summoned on the Wednesday before the Quarter Sessions opens, and another on some day between Sessions, composed of such Justices "as shall be pleased to be present," to deal with "particular affairs concerning the public business of this county"— affairs including in practice all the various branches of county administration from vagrancy to bridge repair.[2] Not until the very last quarter of the eighteenth century, however, do we find Quarter Sessions habitually devolving any branch of its administration upon a standing administrative committee, and then only that of prisons. From about 1790 onward the periodical reports of the committees appointed by Quarter Sessions to manage the gaols—usually consisting of the "Visiting Justices," appointed under the Act of 1782—are a characteristic feature of the records of such highly organised counties as Gloucestershire and Middlesex, to be followed, in the nineteenth century, by Lancashire and the West Riding. By 1835 it is, in fact, rare to find a county without a standing "Prisons Committee." In the admirably organised County of Gloucester the system of committees, standing and special, was extended to all the county services—a General Audit Committee, a Vagrant Committee, various Bridge Committees, as well as special committees on the prison dietary, on the county archives, and on the actuarial basis of friendly societies,[3] are all to be found in these most in-

---

[1] MS. Minutes, Quarter Sessions, Middlesex, 20th February 1752.

[2] *Ibid.* 31st May 1759 ; see for instance the report of this committee on 17th January 1760. In the important Salford Hundred, Quarter Sessions in 1775 ordered that all matters relating to bridges should be dealt with before each Sessions by two Justices to be appointed for the purpose, who should report to the Court (MS. Minutes, Quarter Sessions, Lancashire, 4th May 1775).

[3] This committee, probably under the chairmanship of David Ricardo, consulted two great actuaries and drew up actuarial tables for the guidance of Friendly Societies desiring to be registered at Quarter Sessions, which such societies were required to adopt. See MS. Minutes, Quarter Sessions, Gloucestershire, 20th April 1819 ; *A Guide to the Practice of the Courts of Quarter Sessions of the Peace*, by Samuel Rogers, 1821, p. 54.

teresting minute books instructing and guiding the Court of
Quarter Sessions in its administrative work. In 1834 it is
even ordered that no account be submitted to Quarter
Sessions for payment unless it has "first submitted to" a
standing Committee of Accounts.[1] In other counties the
committee organisation was more slowly extended. The
county bridges were gradually placed under standing committees. By 1835 several counties—notably Lancashire, the
West Riding, and Northumberland—had reached, with
regard to this department of the county work, what may be
considered the most modern form—standing "Bridges Committees" of a small number of selected Justices, for each of
the Divisions of the county, appointed annually by Quarter
Sessions, to which they reported all important proposals for
approval, but each definitely charged with the care of all the
bridges within its area; carrying out their task by means of
salaried Bridgemasters or Surveyors, and executing the
necessary works partly by contract and partly by direct
employment.[2] It was, in fact, these standing committees,
with their permanent salaried officers, that were, by 1835,
rapidly taking the place both of the Grand Juries and of
what we have termed administration by judicial process.

II. An Inchoate Provincial Legislature [3]

We pass now to the most remarkable constitutional
development of county government between 1689 and 1835

---

[1] MS. Minutes, Quarter Sessions, Gloucestershire, 1st January 1834.

[2] See, for instance, MS. Minutes, Quarter Sessions, Lancashire, 2nd April
1833.

[3] We do not, under this designation of an Inchoate Provincial Legislature,
refer to the "county meetings," of which we hear so much in the political annals
of the latter part of the eighteenth century. It became part of the machinery
of politics for the "freeholders" of each county to be summoned to "county
meetings," presided over by the High Sheriff, for the purpose of passing
resolutions on public policy, or petitioning the Crown. Such meetings, it was
assumed, were part of the ancient constitutional machinery of the land—
presumably as the Shire Moot or County Court—not to be suppressed or
prohibited by the Crown. Whatever influence or importance these gatherings
may have had in national politics, they formed, as distinguished from the
gatherings of Justices, no part of what we understand by Local Government,
though we imagine that Quarter Sessions usually authorised the County
Treasurer to pay the cost of advertising them (see MS. Minutes, Quarter
Sessions, Dorsetshire, 12th July 1790); and they did not even discuss issues of

—the gradual and, we may add, usually unself - conscious development of a legislative assembly for the county, prescribing new rules of conduct for individual citizens and new policies for subordinate local authorities. In exercising what we cannot but classify as legislative functions, the Justices were not always proceeding illegally, or even extra-legally. Tudor and Stuart statutes empowered them, and sometimes directed them, in many departments of human conduct, to lay down the principles upon which the individual should proceed. In other cases their general discretionary powers under the Commission of the Peace were so wide and indefinite that it would be difficult to say whether, in making any given " General Order," they were or were not exceeding their legal powers. In many instances, however, no such authority can be discovered, and we think that even the eighteenth-century law courts must have held their orders, if they had been challenged, to have been either extra-legal—that is, not legally enforceable on any one who chose to disobey them—or else positively illegal—that is, in direct contravention of existing statutes. We have not the requisite legal knowledge to determine under which of these heads the various legislative orders of Quarter Sessions could be classed in particular counties at particular dates. To the modern constitutional student what is interesting is the extent, variety, and general acceptance of the legislative authority which Quarter Sessions assumed, in contrast with the narrow range and strict limitation of the by-law-making powers of modern local governing bodies.

For our present purpose we need not dwell upon the discretionary powers exercised by the Court of Quarter Sessions between 1689 and 1835 within the latitude expressly accorded to them by particular statutes ; in such matters, for instance, as the fixing of wages and rates of land carriage, or the selecting, by means of licences, of the persons to pursue certain occupations and of the premises on which they should be

Local Government policy. (For these county meetings, see *The Platform : its Rise and Progress*, by Henry Jephson, 1892. There is a vivid description of a great meeting at York in *Life of William Wilberforce*, by R. I. and S. Wilberforce, 1838.) Their place was to some extent taken in the nineteenth century by the political resolutions often passed by the Justices, or by the Justices and the Grand Jury, when they met at Quarter Sessions or the Assizes.

carried on. The importance of the Justices' discretion in these matters, and the extent to which they exercised it, will be dealt with in our subsequent volumes on the different local government services. Regarded from the standpoint of constitutional development they have practically no significance, as they in no way affected the constitutional position of the Court. Though the particular matters regulated varied from time to time, the total amount of this business did not, from 1689 to 1835, so appreciably change as to introduce any change in structure. From first to last we have the same, usually perfunctory, drawing up of a formal order by the Clerk of the Peace, the same formal reading of it in " Open Court," the same occasional discussion among the Justices about particular items, and the same spasmodic bursts of zeal in the promulgation and enforcement of the regulations so prepared. As compared with analogous discretional regulations by the local authorities of to-day we notice two important constitutional differences. The Justices between the Revolution and the Municipal Corporations Act enjoyed, in all these regulations, a complete and unshackled autonomy. Unlike a modern County Council making by-laws, Quarter Sessions was under no obligation to submit its orders for confirmation to the Home Secretary, or to any other authority. Moreover, the Justices were not only the law-makers, but, either collectively or individually, themselves also the tribunal to adjudicate on any breaches of the regulations. Thus when, in 1700, the West Riding Justices formulated their elaborate order fixing the rates of wages to be paid to all the artificers and labourers within the Riding, not only did they feel themselves free to exercise their discretion without the control of any central department or other superior authority, but they were also in a position to require every Petty Constable to report " what number of men and women servants each inhabitant within his constabulary hath, and what quality and what wages every master gives to every particular servant "; they could themselves individually be present at the " statute " or " Petty Sessions " of the High Constables at which the hirings took place; they could, in Quarter Sessions, order indictments to be preferred, at the county expense, against any person disobeying their orders; and finally, they were themselves, individually or collectively, the judges of such offenders against the regulations as were brought to trial before them.[1]

A wider field of legislative activity was open to the county Justices under their general instructions " to keep, and cause to be kept," the King's peace within their respective counties, and their general undefined powers of supervision of parish officers. Here, in particular, as Ritson complained in 1791, they considered " themselves a sort of legislative body." [2] Thus several counties objected, at different dates, to itinerant traders, who no doubt frequently committed offences, and certainly competed with the local tradesmen. It is, however, difficult for the modern student to understand how such objections could have warranted the Kent Quarter Sessions in 1785 in ordering " that no hawker, peddlar, petty chapman, or other trading person or persons going from town to town, or to other men's houses, . . . shall have liberty to vend his or their goods and wares within the . . . county, under pain of forfeiting for every such offence the sum of ten pounds." [3] In the early years of the eighteenth century we find county after county issuing " General Orders " against the holding of fairs, or indulgence in " revels and wakes," or the practice of some exciting sport or game by the wage-earning classes. Thus the Gloucestershire Justices in January 1710 resolve to put down " an unlawful revel or wake usually kept at Coaley in this county upon Sunday next after St. Bartholomew's " and three other days, and they direct the local Justices summarily to bind over to the next Quarter Sessions " to answer their contempt," any persons who " shall presume to assemble together on any such pretence." [4] At Easter in the same year they are moved, on the representations " of the ministers and principal inhabitants of . . . Coaley, Frocester, and Nymphsfield," that, " in those parishes, as well as in other places in this county, unlawful wakes and revels and other disorderly meetings " were held annually, at which much misconduct took place, peremptorily to prohibit all such "unlawful wakes and revels." [5]

---

[1] MS. Minutes, Quarter Sessions, West Riding, 9th April 1700 (see *History of Agriculture and Prices*, by J. E. Thorold Rogers, vol. vii. p. 610).
[2] *The Office of Constable*, by J. Ritson, 1791, p. xxviii.
[3] MS. Minutes, Quarter Sessions, Kent, 4th October 1785.
[4] MS. Minutes, Quarter Sessions, Gloucestershire, Epiphany 1710.
[5] *Ibid.* Easter 1710.

In 1718 we see these Justices still struggling against popular amusements, issuing a long order, not only against fairs, wakes, and revels, but also against meetings for wrestling and cudgel playing, under cover of which, they alleged, though we may nowadays doubt it, gatherings of persons disaffected to the Government were held.[1] We may cite, in conclusion, the peremptory printed orders which the same Court issued in 1731, "that no such wakes, revels, or other meetings for wrestling or cudgel playing for hats or other prizes be for the future held in any part of the county."[2] In the same way we see the Middlesex Quarter Sessions in the first half of the eighteenth century constantly enjoining the Justices in their Divisional Sessions to suppress the fairs held in the different suburbs of the Metropolis.[3] The Surrey Justices adopted the same policy in the second half of the century, repeatedly forbidding one suburban fair after another, and used all their efforts to prevent any such gathering from taking place. In this policy, however, they came sharply into conflict with the legal rights of the Lords of the Manors, to whom the fairs were sources of emolument. Thus in 1806 the Surrey Quarter Sessions issued a peremptory order suppressing Camberwell Fair, and declaring the Justices' intention to " employ the civil power to prevent the erection of any booths or stalls." But the Lord of the Manor stood on his legal rights, made known his intention of holding the fair as usual, and the Justices thought it more discreet not to seek to enforce the legislative power which they had assumed. Notwithstanding all their prohibitions "the fair was proclaimed, and commenced in the usual manner," and the magistrates prudently " resolved to confine their efforts . . . to the prevention of such abuses as the law enabled them to suppress."[4]

[1] MS. Minutes, Quarter Sessions, Gloucestershire, Epiphany 1718.

[2] *Ibid.* Easter 1731.

[3] See, for instance, the Order of Quarter Sessions, 1744, in *Gentleman's Magazine*, May 1744, p. 278.

[4] See for this, *Morning Advertiser*, 7th, 11th, 14th, 15th, 19th, 20th and 23rd August 1806; *Ye Parish of Camerwell*, by W. H. Blanch, 1875, p. 312. The Essex Quarter Sessions saved themselves the humiliation suffered by the Surrey magistrates by ordering the Clerk of the Peace to ascertain "who claims the right to hold" fairs, before putting in force their order for their general suppression throughout the county (MS. Minutes, Quarter Sessions, Essex, 1789). At Hampstead, the Lord of the Manor co-operated with the Middlesex Justices in 1819 in suppressing "West End Fair" (Home Office Domestic State Papers, No. 262 in Public Record Office).

A more ingenious way of legislating was for the Justices in Quarter Sessions to declare this or that act a common or public nuisance. We need not remind the student that, according to our present ideas, such a declaration in no way changed the character of the act in question; it did not make anything a nuisance or otherwise unlawful that was not so before the declaration. But as the Justices were themselves the tribunal that would deal with offenders, a public announcement by Quarter Sessions that any conduct of which the Justices chose to disapprove would be treated by them as a punishable offence amounted in effect—to all but the few who could pay for an appeal to a higher tribunal—to a legislative prohibition of such conduct. Thus, when the Kent Justices declared that Sydenham Fair, with its "great encouragement of drunkenness, gaming, and other vice, debauchery and immorality, . . . to the ruin of many apprentices and other young persons," had "become a public nuisance," their order to the Constables to arrest and bring before them all persons attempting to hold the fair, was an edict not lightly to be disregarded.[1] And many other things besides fairs could be thus prohibited. We see the Middlesex Justices, in 1710 and at other dates, issuing lengthy orders declaring to be public nuisances many of the common practices of the street life of an unpoliced Metropolis—for instance, merely "the going with, driving, and using of . . . wheelbarrows" in the hawking of "oysters, oranges, decayed cheese, apples, nuts, gingerbread, and other wares to sell," on the ground that such hawkers had frequently false weights and measures, and even used dice "to encourage unwary passengers and children to play" for their wares.[2] For the next forty or fifty years the Middlesex Quarter Sessions are constantly issuing "general orders" prohibiting one objectionable practice after another until Parliament relieved them from their thankless task by embodying their general orders in the clauses of innumerable Local Acts, giving to the Select Vestries, or to the Paving and Lighting Commissioners of the London parishes, statutory power to suppress all such specified offences against public convenience or health.[3]

[1] MS. Minutes, Quarter Sessions, Kent, 8th April 1766.

[2] MS. Minutes, Quarter Sessions, Middlesex, January 1710; repeated December 1710.

[3] In the nineteenth century we find the Justices taking similar action

The same power of themselves deciding the cases, coupled with the power to give commands to all officers of townships or parishes, enabled the Justices, in practically any detail of local administration, to convert their own opinions into mandatory enactments. They could, for instance, go far to create new disqualifications for particular offices, thereby increasing the burden of service on the rest of the inhabitants. Thus in 1712 we have the Middlesex Justices taking notice that several Constables and Headboroughs "keep public ale-houses, victualling houses, and sell brandy or other spirituous liquors by retail," order the Stewards of the respective Courts Leet "to appoint persons . . . who do not keep a public-house." [1] After half a century of controversy, the disqualification of publicans becomes a local rule, and we have Quarter Sessions directing that none be sworn in as Constables.[2] Similarly, in 1718 we see the same Quarter Sessions deciding that no Court Leet could appoint as Headborough any person "who hath had the honour of being one of His Majesty's Commission of the Peace," even if that person be no longer an acting Justice and was desirous of accepting the minor appointment.[3] Another form of legislative enactment was the direction that Quarter Sessions frequently gave to individual magistrates, limiting or regulating the powers which they were entitled, individually or in pairs, to exercise, either under the Commission of the Peace or even under express statutes. We have, for instance, already described the manner in which Quarter Sessions in Middlesex and in Gloucestershire cut down the jurisdiction of the individual Justices, by restricting them, in spite of the express words of the Commission, to, matters arising in the parishes or Divisions in which they resided. So, in 1701, we see the Kent Quarter Sessions peremptorily ordering that "all warrants and order made by Justices in any part of the county as to settlements shall be null and void, and so taken and deemed and construed, unless made after all parties concerned be legally summoned to be

against prize-fighting. "The magistrates of the County of Cambridge very laudably passed certain resolutions at the last Christmas Quarter Sessions to prevent the disgraceful practice of prize-fighting" (*Cambridge Chronicle*, 19th March 1808 ; in *Concise View of the Constitution of England*, by George Custance, 1808, p. 358).

[1] MS. Minutes, Quarter Sessions, Middlesex, April 1712.
[2] *Ibid.* 25th February 1785.   [3] *Ibid.* 7th July 1718.

heard." [1] In the West Riding of Yorkshire Quarter Sessions actually anticipated by a whole generation the action of Parliament in creating, by its own fiat in 1692, what afterwards became known as " Brewster Sessions." In that year it was "ordered that no year there shall be more than one Special Sessions for the licensing of ale-houses held in any division of this Riding, and that no ale-houses shall be licensed betwixt one Special Sessions and another, except it be done at some General Quarter Sessions of the Peace." [2] A century later the Surrey Quarter Sessions ordains " that licences refused at any or either of these meetings shall not be granted at any other time or place without the consent of the majority of the Justices present at the time of such refusal." [3] Even more remarkable, because permanently affecting the pecuniary obligations of individuals, seems the authority that the Justices assumed to themselves of altering local government areas and dictating the basis of the assessment to the local rates. In Northumberland, in 1711, Quarter Sessions decides that each of the six " Grieveships " into which the great parish of Allendale had always been divided, should thenceforth have its own Poor Rate. [4] In a settlement case arising out of a small hamlet in 1723, the West Riding Quarter Sessions takes it upon itself—seeing " that there is only eight acres of land within the said township of Foldby " and the Court thinks " that the said township is not of itself able to maintain its own poor "—to merge it in the adjoining parish, and order thenceforth only one Overseer to be appointed and one rate made for the newly created unit of area. [5] And up and down the country at the close of the seventeenth and beginning of the eighteenth century, in the important matter of the basis of assessment to local rates, we find Quarter Sessions not confining itself to its legal power of deciding individual appeals, but formally ordering one method of assessment rather than another—by annual rental value instead of by acreage—to be adopted for the

---

[1] MS. Minutes, Quarter Sessions, Kent, 29th April 1701.
[2] MS. Minutes, Quarter Sessions, West Riding, 5th April 1692.
[3] Surrey Quarter Sessions (see *Public Advertiser*, 17th August 1787).
[4] *Northumberland County History*, by A. B. Hinds, vol. iii. 1896, p. 11 ; vol. iv. 1897, p. 77.
[5] MS. Minutes, Quarter Sessions, West Riding, 16th October 1723.

future. Thus the Kent Quarter Sessions, "upon the complaint of the inhabitants of the parish of Erith in this county, considering the taxing of all the lands within the said parish to the Church and poor there, viz. whether such lands should be taxed by the acre or by a pound rate; and upon hearing of counsel in the said cause . . . ordered . . . that the taxation of the said lands within the said parish for the future shall not be by the acre but be made by a pound rate, that way of taxing by a pound rate appearing to this Court, upon proof and debate, to be the most equal for the said parishioners." [1]

The whole sphere of licensing afforded a wide opportunity for virtual legislation. We have sufficiently described elsewhere [2] the extent to which the Justices, at first in pairs and afterwards in Brewster Sessions, exercised their plain legal right to impose conditions on ale-house keepers seeking licences, and to bind them over, by "articles" attached to the statutory recognisances, to close at certain hours or on certain days, to follow this or that line of conduct, and to abstain from particular lawful acts of which these particular Justices chose to disapprove. Quarter Sessions, moreover, would send word to the Justices of a Division that they were expressly desired not to grant any licence at all to a particular person whom Quarter Sessions thought fit to exclude from the trade.[3] What is even more interesting is to see the Quarter Sessions of the county, which did not itself grant licences, coming to decisions, and sometimes laying down general regulations on the subject in its character of a provincial legislative authority. Thus in 1706 we find the Gloucestershire Quarter Sessions "recommending" to the Justices of the Berkeley Division "to license no more ale-houses in the parish of Winterborne than are absolutely necessary for that place, and that the rest of the ale-houses in that place be suppressed." [4] So, in 1713, we find this same Quarter Sessions recommending to the magis-

---

[1] MS. Minutes, Quarter Sessions, Kent, 5th April 1692. A similar order was made as to the parish of Yalden, *ibid.* 4th October 1692.

[2] *The History of Liquor Licensing in England, principally from 1700 to 1830* (1903).

[3] See, for instance, the formal letter to such effect that the Dorset Clerk of the Peace was ordered to write (MS. Minutes, Quarter Sessions, Dorsetshire, 16th April 1751).

[4] MS. Minutes, Quarter Sessions, Gloucestershire, Easter 1706.

trates of the Stroud Division " to be cautious what ale-houses they license there for the next year, and not to license any of the twenty-four persons complained of by the minister and parishioners there as supernumerary." [1] In Middlesex, in 1729, Quarter Sessions recommends the Justices in their several divisions " to consider and agree what number of persons are proper to be licensed in each parish . . . to sell brandy or strong waters by retail," and to report their conclusions to the next Quarter Sessions. When these are received, Quarter Sessions peremptorily orders the Justices not to grant any licences for selling brandy, etc., to persons keeping chandlers' shops. [2] In Dorsetshire, in 1752, we have Quarter Sessions expressly recommending that Brewster Sessions shall not license any ale-houses unless definitely recommended by the Incumbent, the parish officers, and the landowners of the village. [3] But the greatest outburst of this quasi-legislative activity on the part of Quarter Sessions was the result of the movement for the Reformation of Manners of the lower orders, engineered by Wilberforce in 1787. In county after county we find Quarter Sessions laying down general rules for the conduct of Brewster Sessions. In many counties Quarter Sessions adopted a formal resolution that no " new licence would be granted to any public-house but where the convenience of the public absolutely required it " ; [4] or "excepting the case where some other house in the same parish or place shall have been suppressed within the preceding twelve months " ; [5] or " until the present number shall have been considerably reduced " ; [6] or for any house situate upon the skirts or outparts of any village ; [7] or to any person intending to set up a dram-shop ; [8] and in any case to insist

---

[1] MS. Minutes, Quarter Sessions, Gloucestershire, Epiphany 1713.

[2] MS. Minutes, Quarter Sessions, Middlesex, 28th August and 16th October 1729.

[3] MS. Minutes, Quarter Sessions, Dorsetshire, 14th July 1752.

[4] For instance, Oxfordshire Quarter Sessions, 10th July 1787 (see *Bristol Journal*, 15th September 1787).

[5] Suffolk Quarter Sessions (see *Ipswich Journal*, 1st September 1787) ; Essex Quarter Sessions, 23rd July 1787 (see *Chelmsford Chronicle*, 27th July 1787).

[6] West Riding Quarter Sessions, 16th April 1787 (see *Leeds Intelligencer*, 1st May 1787).

[7] Nottingham Quarter Sessions (see *Nottingham Journal*, 21st July 1787).

[8] West Riding Quarter Sessions (see *Leeds Intelligencer*, 16th May 1786) ; Surrey Quarter Sessions (see *Public Advertiser*, 17th August 1787).

on four weeks' notice prior to the Brewster Sessions, in order to enable inquiries to be made.[1] The Nottinghamshire Justices in Quarter Sessions declared their intention of refusing, when they sat in Brewster Sessions, to grant a spirit licence to any person who did " not sell any wine, chocolate, coffee, tea, ale, beer, or other liquors."[2] But Quarter Sessions did more than decide on what lines new licences would be granted; we find them enacting new conditions under which the trade should be carried on by the existing publicans. In Gloucestershire, as in many other counties, Quarter Sessions decided on more or less Sunday closing; directing the publicans, for instance, not to serve on Sundays any one but travellers " until after the evening service," and then only up to eight o'clock.[3] In other counties all houses of public entertainment were to cease selling drink during the hours of divine service, during which time no one was to be received or remain in such houses.[4] The Berkshire Justices went further, and enforced complete Sunday closing, except for the " bona-fide traveller," making it a condition of all their licences " that on the Lord's Day they do not receive, or suffer to remain, any persons as guests to tipple, eat, or drink, other than travellers, or such as come upon necessary business."[5] The Shropshire Justices, " taking into their serious consideration the mischiefs arising from the practice of paying labourers and artificers their weekly wages at a public-house, and willing to exert their utmost power to suppress so pernicious a custom," practically anticipated Parliamentary prohibition of this practice by 93 years by the device of intimating, at the Quarter Sessions of April 1789, that they would regard such

---

[1] West Riding Quarter Sessions (see *Leeds Intelligencer*, 16th May 1786).

[2] Order of Nottinghamshire Quarter Sessions, Midsummer 1787 (see *Nottingham Journal*, 21st July 1787).

[3] Gloucestershire Quarter Sessions (see *Bristol Journal*, 24th January 1788).

[4] Essex Quarter Sessions, 11th July 1786 (see *Chelmsford Chronicle*, 28th July 1786); Oxfordshire Quarter Sessions, 10th July 1787 (see *Bristol Journal*, 15th September 1787); Nottinghamshire Quarter Sessions (see *Nottingham Journal*, 21st July 1787). It was the same desire for Sunday closing that led to the direction that no stage-waggon or cart was to be received at any time on Sunday, and the publican was required, at his peril, promptly to inform against the owners of public vehicles so breaking the Sabbath, so that they could be prosecuted (Oxfordshire Quarter Sessions, 10th July 1787; see *Bristol Journal*, 15th September 1787).

[5] Berkshire Quarter Sessions (see *Northampton Mercury*, 8th September, and *Leeds Intelligencer*, 18th September 1787).

gatherings in public-houses as breaches of the statutes against
tippling, involving non-renewal of licence.[1] The Gloucestershire Quarter Sessions, like some others, even adopted the
principle of Local Option, expressly requiring on every application for a licence that the statutory certificate of character be
in all cases signed by the clergyman and principal inhabitants
of the parish, and directing that it was to be signed "at a
Vestry to be called for that purpose with proper notice."[2]
The North Riding Quarter Sessions laconically requested the
ministers of all the parishes in the Riding "to state how
many ale-houses they think necessary in their respective
parishes."[3] More specific was the West Riding Quarter
Sessions, which decided, at Michaelmas 1787, that the
Justices should hold annually at Easter in each division an
adjourned Brewster Sessions, for the special purpose of inquiring into "the state and situation" of all the licensed houses,
prior to which "the Minister and Churchwardens of every
Township" were "to call a meeting of the Overseers of the
Poor, Constables, and all the principal inhabitants of their
Townships for the express purpose of making a return to the
Justices of such public-houses as they, or a majority of them,
shall think useful and necessary, and also of such others as are
either improperly situated, or on account of the past irregular
and disorderly conduct of the occupiers they would wish to
have suppressed in future."[4]

But the most remarkable of all these manifestations of
legislative activity on the part of the Justices in Quarter
Sessions were their well-known enactments as to poor relief.
We shall describe in a subsequent volume the development of
the Poor Law and the grave economic and social crisis of
1795, which compelled the Justices themselves to grapple
with the problem. Here it is sufficient to say that in the
famine years of 1794-1796 and 1799-1801 the magistrates
in all the agricultural districts found themselves individually
called upon to arbitrate between starving labourers and

[1] *Shropshire County Records*, part ix., edited by Sir Offley Wakeman, p. 33.
[2] Gloucestershire Quarter Sessions, Epiphany 1788 (see *Bristol Gazette*, 24th January 1788).
[3] North Riding Quarter Sessions, 10th July 1787 (see *Leeds Intelligencer*, 7th August 1787).
[4] West Riding Quarter Sessions (see *Leeds Intelligencer*, 9th October 1787).

penurious Overseers. The Justices turned for guidance to
Quarter Sessions, and the Leaders of the County did not fail
to respond. The procedure followed by the various Quarter
Sessions is interesting from its variety and informality. In
Buckinghamshire the Court of Quarter Sessions, taking into
" consideration the situation of the poor industrious labourers
and their families," determines on the abandonment of the
" roundsman " system, and straightaway orders the income of
each family to be made up from the Poor Rates to a minimum
of six shillings a week for a married couple, with additions for
children.[1] The Berkshire Court of Quarter Sessions decided
to summon to its assistance more than the little clique of
Justices who usually attended its meetings. It ordered a
" general meeting," to be called by public advertisement, " of
the Justices of this county, together with several discreet
persons, . . . for the purpose of rating husbandry wages."
At this meeting, held " at the Pelican Inn, Speenhamland," in
May 1795, when seven clergymen and thirteen squires were
present, a long series of resolutions, evidently prepared
beforehand, were unanimously adopted. These resolutions,
destined to become famous, declared that, whilst " the present
state of the poor " did require the Justices' intervention, it
was " inexpedient for the magistrates to grant that assistance
by regulating the wages of day labourers according to the
statutes." The Justices present announced that they would
" in their several Divisions make the following calculations
and allowances for the relief of all poor and industrious men
and their families," namely, " when the gallon loaf of seconds
flour weighing 8 lb. 11 oz. shall cost one shilling, then every
poor and industrious man shall have for his own support three
shillings weekly, either produced by his own and his family's
labour, or an allowance from the Poor Rates, and for the
support of his wife and every other of his family one and
sixpence," with corresponding variations according to the
price of the gallon loaf for the time being. It is specially
significant to us that this momentous declaration was, on the

---

[1] MS. Minutes, Quarter Sessions, Buckinghamshire, January 1795. The
"roundsman" was the pauper labourer who was offered to the various farmers
in turn at whatever wages they chose to pay—a Poor Law device that we shall
examine in our subsequent volume on *English Local Government in relation to
Poverty and Crime.*

same day, entered by the Deputy Clerk of the Peace in the
minute-books of the Berkshire Quarter Sessions as an order
of the Court. In the neighbouring county of Hampshire no
mention of the subject appears in the official records of Quarter
Sessions, but we learn otherwise that the Court, at the same
date, referred the state of the poor to a committee of Justices,
with directions to report to the ensuing Sessions. The report
so produced, adopted by the Court on the 14th of July 1795
(though again not recorded in the minute books), is perhaps
the most remarkable of the economic documents of the
eighteenth century. It was, we learn, drawn up by the Rev.
Edmund Poulter, a Prebendary of Winchester and Justice of
the Peace, and contains, besides a singularly interesting review
of the economic position of the labourer, an able argument in
favour of a physiological and non-competitive standard of
wages. It advocates, as a general principle to be followed by
masters in fixing wages, by Overseers in granting assistance,
and by magistrates in ordering relief, the determination of
" what is the proper subsistence, what its local amount, that
the several parts of the family do or may earn." But the
committee hesitate to recommend, at that moment, the
enforcement of a legal minimum wage. " We wish," they
say, " to be saved the necessity of interfering now, even to
regulate wages." They accordingly urge masters voluntarily
to give the physiologically sufficient wage, demonstrating with
genuine eloquence that such a course would really pay them
in the long-run. Where masters will not pay such wages,
the magistrate should " order in relief whatever may be the
deficiency, of the greatest income, under the best employment,
from the least outgoing, under the best management." In
this way the committee hope " to preclude the necessity which
may otherwise compel the Bench to have recourse to such
compulsory regulation of wages." [1]

---

[1] *Gentleman's Magazine*, December 1795, p. 1019 ; *An Inquiry into the
State of the Poor*, by Rev. Edmund Poulter, 1795.   In the following year
Arthur Young thought the report of sufficient importance to reprint it verbatim
in the *Annals of Agriculture*, vol. xxv. pp. 349-398, where it fills fifty pages.
The policy of the Allowance System, or " Rate in Aid of Wages," had been
publicly adopted in all its crudity three years before by the Dorsetshire Justices,
apparently on the occasion of some local insurrection, actual or apprehended.
At the Dorset Quarter Sessions in October 1792 " the Clerk of the Peace
reported that in consequence of a letter from . . . the Clerk to the Justices for

The decisions of the Courts of Quarter Sessions of Buckinghamshire, Berkshire, and Hampshire, followed as they were by most of the other counties south of the line from the Severn to the Wash, took the shape of printed tables, showing the weekly income to be ensured to each family, classified under eight or ten heads as to size, and varying according to more than a dozen expected prices of wheat. This complicated tabular statement was printed by Quarter Sessions, and issued by the Clerk of the Peace to every acting magistrate and to the Churchwardens and Overseers of every parish, to " be pasted in the books of the Overseers . . . in order to their regulating their allowance of relief to poor families accordingly." [1] The " Justices' Scale " thus became, in every county, the authoritative standard for poor relief. When any Overseer demurred to making up a labourer's earnings to the amount to which he was under the scale "entitled," both parties knew that an appeal to the nearest magistrate would lead to an instant order that such a sum should be paid. In this way the " Berkshire Bread Act, or Speenhamland Act of Parliament," as it was variously called, acquired, in county after county, all the force of law. In Norfolk we hear of the " Law of the Hundred of Freebridge Lynn." [2] The printed tables of scales were, from 1795 to

---

the Division of Dorchester, written by their direction, he had used the utmost despatch in summoning a General Meeting of the acting magistrates of the said county." At the next subsequent Sessions the Clerk reported that he had attended the meeting, and the resolution there carried was inserted in the Quarter Sessions Minutes as follows : " That having taken into consideration the difficulties the poor labour under from the present high price of corn and other necessaries, the Justices within their respective Divisions will make an order on the parish officers, on the complaint of any industrious and peaceable poor person, which shall appear to be well founded, to relieve him or her with such sum *as shall make up, together with the weekly earnings of him, her, and their family, a comfortable support for them* ; and that the Justices, having thus provided for the necessary subsistence of the industrious and peaceable poor, declare their determination to enforce the laws against such as shall meet together for any unlawful purpose " ; the resolution to be sent to every acting magistrate who was not present, and to be published in the local newspapers. Quarter Sessions thereupon itself orders copies of the resolution to be sent to every parish within the county (MS. Minutes, Quarter Sessions. Dorsetshire, 27th October and 1st December 1792).

[1] MS. Minutes, Quarter Sessions, Buckinghamshire, January 1795.

[2] *Observations on the Administration of the Poor Laws in Agricultural Districts*, by Rev. C. D. Brereton, 1824, p. 23. It is interesting to find that such scales were sometimes officially reported to the Government, which did not interfere. The printed circular of the Justices of the Hundred of Gallow,

1834, to be seen, framed and glazed, hanging up in conspicuous positions in the meeting - places of Vestries and
Incorporated Guardians, and occasionally in the "Justice
rooms" of the magistrates themselves. The sum fixed by the
scale became known as "the Government Allowance," and
even "the Act of Parliament Allowance." And when, in 1833,
the Assistant Commissioner inquiring into the Poor Law
entered the office of the Overseer at Bocking, in Essex, he
found himself confronted with a printed copy of the scale there
in force, bearing the magic heading "According to Act of
Parliament."[1]

We need not inquire whether the "Speenhamland Act of
Parliament," as a legislative enactment by the Court of
Quarter Sessions, was legal, extra-legal, or illegal. A generation later, when the tide of opinion had turned, we find the
same Courts of Quarter Sessions formulating no less explicit
enactments in a directly contrary sense. A whole generation
of argument had convinced many of the County Benches that

Norfolk, directing the Overseers to make certain allowances, is enshrined in the
Home Office archives (Home Office Domestic State Papers in Public Record
Office, No. 149 of 1799).

[1] First Report of Poor Law Inquiry Commissioners, 1834, Appendix A
(Majendie's Report), p. 229. We have given the "Speenhamland Act of
Parliament" as the most remarkable instance of quasi-legislation by Courts of
Quarter Sessions in the department of the relief of destitution. Many other
enactments of legislative character might be cited. Thus the Quarter Sessions
of Buckinghamshire in 1795 virtually prohibited the keeping of dogs by the
rural labourers, directing "that the magistrates of this county do, when application is made to them for relief of poor families, make particular inquiries whether
there is kept in such family any dog or dogs that may appear to such magistrates
to be unnecessary for such persons to keep, and if they find there is any such
dog or dogs kept, then that they forthwith see that such unnecessary dog or
dogs shall be destroyed, . . . and that the Clerk of the Peace do communicate
this Order to the Magistrates of the County" (MS. Minutes, Quarter Sessions,
Buckinghamshire, Easter 1795). In 1821 the Justices of the Hundred of West
Goscote in Leicestershire direct that no poor relief is to be granted to any
framework-knitter who does not give information as to who is guilty of certain
recent acts of destruction of machinery (Home Office Domestic State Papers,
No. 16, 1821, in Public Record Office). By contrast we may quote the order
of the Gloucestershire Quarter Sessions in 1816, when, "looking to the probable
scarcity of labour [*i.e.* employment] during the ensuing winter," the Court
decided to arrange for employment to be found for as many labourers as possible
by "recommending" the divisional magistrates, not only to enforce the Highway
Laws, but also "to suggest . . . various improvements . . . lowering hills and
widening roads," and to employ the destitute labourers who would be on the
hands of the Overseers "in this or any other work of public utility which local
or temporary circumstances may render expedient" (MS. Minutes, Quarter
Sessions, Gloucestershire, 15th October 1816).

the policy of "rate in aid of wages" was socially disastrous; and here and there a specially public-spirited and pertinacious landowner had successfully appealed to Quarter Sessions against the allowance of the Overseer's accounts, on the ground that such payments to labourers at work were illegal. The next step was for Quarter Sessions, by order, generally to forbid them. This we see done in 1830 in Buckinghamshire, the very county in which, thirty-five years before, the Overseers had first been officially instructed and commanded to make the labourers' incomes up to a fixed scale. At the Epiphany Sessions, 1830, the Clerk of the Peace laid before the Court a long letter from the Duke of Buckingham, as Lord-Lieutenant, drawing attention to the evil effects of this Poor Law policy. That letter was circulated "amongst the Justices in the several Petty Sessions in order that at a special adjournment of this present Sessions . . . some general resolutions may be proposed." At the adjourned Sessions, some weeks later, the Court resolves (without mentioning its own enactment of 1795) that the plan of giving relief to labourers in employment is pernicious and illegal; it pledges the Justices individually "to resist by all lawful means the continuance of that practice"; and it urges on the parishes as an alternative the provision in workhouses of suitable employment for the poor unable to maintain themselves. A printed circular to this effect was thereupon sent, by order of the Court, to the Churchwardens and Overseers of every parish in the county.[1] Other counties followed suit, not always so dramatic as the Buckinghamshire Quarter Sessions in the reversal of their own peremptory enactments of a generation before, but quite as effectively conveying to paupers and Overseers alike the new policy decided on by the Rulers of the County.[2] Thus—quite apart from the question whether the Court of Quarter Sessions had any legal authority at all to interfere with the discretion of the Overseers in the

---

[1] MS. Minutes, Quarter Sessions, Buckinghamshire, January and February 1830.

[2] Thus the Quarter Sessions of Surrey in 1832 emphatically denounced the "illegal practice . . . of paying labourers out of the Poor Rate," enjoining the magistrates in Petty Sessions "to exercise the greatest vigilance over the accounts of Overseers, and not to pass any in which such illegal proceedings are detected" (MS. Minutes, Quarter Sessions, Surrey, 3rd January 1832).

grant of poor relief—one or other of the contradictory enactments of the Buckinghamshire Quarter Justices, 1795 and 1830, must have represented a supersession of the Poor Law as laid down by Parliament itself.

III. An Extra-Legal County Oligarchy

The assumption by the Court of Quarter Sessions of quasi-legislative functions, combined with the organisation of a county executive, had an unforeseen, far-reaching effect upon the real constitution of county government. At the end of the seventeenth century the county was, as we have described, still administered by a quarterly Court of Justice, summoned by the High Sheriff at stated times and stated places; attended by separately appointed and gratuitously serving officers of the county and the parish; dependent on the co-operation of popular Juries from the various Hundreds and from the body of the county; considering only such issues as were by judicial process brought up for trial; and having its orders recorded by the independent Clerk of the Peace, and reviewable by the superior courts. We have now seen how, in the course of little more than a century, this judicial tribunal was, as regards the civil administration of the county, silently and almost imperceptibly replaced in every county by an organised local legislature and executive, composed exclusively of magistrates and such persons as they chose to consult; meeting privately at any dates and in any places; convened by chairmen, served by salaried officials, and advised by committees, all unknown to the legal constitution; deliberating on any matters without formality or notice; recording or not recording their " orders " as they chose; amending them, varying them, or rescinding them as the haphazard majority of the moment thought fit; and issuing them, with undisputed authority, as friendly " recommendations " to all the Justices of the county, as " requests " to local committees of Justices meeting in Special and Petty Sessions, or as private " instructions " to their salaried executive staff,—even publicly advertising them to the ordinary citizen as the principles according to which future judicial decisions would be given. And this silently evolved, entirely novel organisation of county government was as indefinite as it was extra-legal. As Cobbett indignantly pointed out in 1822, enactments vitally affecting the right of the destitute person to Poor Law relief were issued in the name of the Hampshire Court of Quarter Sessions by "two squires" and "five parsons" from behind the closed doors of the "Grand Jury Room."[1] Even the Justices themselves would occasionally complain of the informality and legislative assumptions of their so-called "deliberative assemblies." "I observed a paragraph and advertisement," deprecatingly writes an eminent Suffolk magistrate in 1795, who objected to the device of a formulated non-competitive wage, "in your paper of yesterday, reporting a resolution passed at the Quarter Sessions held at Bury. I assuredly did not concur in it; but as far as I understood it to be before the company as a matter of conversation (for I did not contemplate it as a question before the Sessions) I opposed it, and the resolve must have passed in my absence." "I opposed it," he subsequently adds, "as not advisable to be brought forward at that time, nor at any time without notice."[2]

These developments from the Court of Quarter Sessions were not the only changes that were being wrought in the working constitution of the county. There went on concurrently, as we have already indicated, a continuous transfer to Petty and Special Sessions of various classes of work which had formerly devolved upon the General Sessions of the Peace. At the close of the seventeenth century we find much of the time of Quarter Sessions taken up with petitions from distressed persons, and deciding what relief should be given to them by particular Overseers;[3] with discussing the state of particular

[1] Cobbett's *Political Register*, 21st September 1822.

[2] Capel Lofft to the Editor of the *Bury Post*, 15th October 1795; the same to Arthur Young, 21st October 1795; both in *Annals of Agriculture*, vol. xxv. pp. 317, 319. The "resolve" of Quarter Sessions, to which Capel Lofft objected, is in MS. Minutes, Quarter Sessions, Suffolk, 12th October 1795; and is reprinted, with all formality, as an order of the Court, in *Annals of Agriculture*, vol. xxv. p. 316. Eight clergymen and five squires were present.

[3] The following Order, taken from the MS. Minutes of Devon Quarter Sessions, is a typical specimen, found in the Orders of all the counties we have examined down to 1720, and occasionally as late as 1750. "Church-wardens and Overseers of Pilton ordered to relieve and provide for suich and such aged and infirm persons" (17th January 1689). More elaborate Orders are such as the following, also from the Devon Quarter Sessions MS. Order Book (Easter 1690):—"Upon the humble peticon of Edward Lethbridge himself and family and very poor persons and that they were last legally settled in the parish

highways, and the steps which the several parishes ought to take for their repair ; and with considering the conduct of particular ale-house keepers, and whether their ale-houses should continue to be licensed.[1] All this business was, as we have seen, gradually transferred to Divisional Sessions, either Petty or Special, Highway or Licensing. Similarly the extensive work connected with Poor Law apprenticeship and orders in bastardy was gradually left to Petty Sessions. It came, indeed, to be a rule of practice that wherever Quarter Sessions might have to act as a tribunal of appeal, it should decline to entertain the business as a court of first instance. What we have here to note is that all this shifting of work from Quarter Sessions to Petty or Special Sessions co-operated in the revolution that was silently taking place in the real constitution of county government. When at the end of the seventeenth century a distressed citizen or aggrieved ale-house keeper, a pauper apprentice, or a parish officer brought his grievance before Quarter Sessions—when a sixpenny rate was imposed on a parish to mend its highways, or when its public-houses were suppressed or multiplied—when the county bridges were repaired or County Rates levied, the business was dealt with " in open court," before the body of the " county," amid judicial surroundings, often at the instance or with the concurrence of a popular Jury, professedly as a matter of legal obligation.[2]

of Cheriton Bye in the County, and that the officers and p'ishioners of that p'ish are well satisfied that they are their p'ishioners and very poor and yet that the said officers and p'ishioners do confederate together not to afford him any habitation in that p'ish, by means whereof and of such confederacy the said Edward Lethbridge and his family are like to perish for want. This Court does desire any two or more of the Justices of the Peace of that Division, Quorum unus, to inquire into and examine the said practice and the necessity of the said poor p'sons and to make such order for the relief of the poor p'sons and for punishing the officers so confederating as the law directs."

[1] Orders suppressing licences abound. "It appearing to this Court upon oath that H. P. of B—— hath for some time past and still doth keep a very notorious and ill-governed and disorderly ale-house . . . said house . . . do stand absolutely suppressed" (MS. Minutes, Essex Quarter Sessions, 5th April 1720). The student of the printed records of Middlesex will find many such entries down to 1729, the date of establishment of Brewster Sessions.

[2] The student of the Minutes of Quarter Sessions from 1689 to 1730 will recognise the constant emphasis laid on administrative orders being given *after discussion in open Court*, or *after hearing Council on both sides*. To give a sample :—At the West Riding Quarter Sessions in 1712, when an important contract for maintaining all the county bridges for eleven years was under consideration, it is expressly noted in the minutes that the tenders were "heard in open Court" (MS. Minutes, Quarter Sessions, West Riding, 13th July 1712).

When, on the other hand, the "County Business" was differentiated from the rest of the Justices' work—still more when it was done in Petty or Special Sessions, instead of at "the General Sessions of the Peace for the County"—it was, as we have seen, dealt with in private, without the intervention of a Jury or other popular element, exclusively by the magistrates. Thus, alike in the differentiation of the business of Quarter Sessions itself, and in the transfer of so much of its work to Divisional Sessions, the result was that what had formerly been done "in open court," as a judicial proceeding, assumed to be in execution of the law of the land, came to be decided in private meetings, at the discretion of little knots of squires and parsons, acting upon their own views of social expediency.

It was perhaps an aggravation of this evolution that the Commission of the Peace had itself, as we have seen, become socially and politically more exclusive. With the cessation of courtly manipulation, and the slowly rising standard of manners and morals, the "Justice of Mean Degree" had, by the opening of the nineteenth century, been gradually eliminated. Meanwhile the tacit adoption by the Lords-Lieutenant of the principle of co-option, coupled with the real social apprehension and fierce political cleavages that marked the era of the French Revolution, had caused the Rulers of the County to be chosen, more than ever, exclusively from the members of one political party, one religious denomination, and one social class.

This gradual and unrecognised change in the working constitution of the county was accepted without disapproval by the public opinion of the whole governing class. "The system of magistracy," said Whitbread, the Whig leader in 1807, on proposing to add to its powers and duties, "had defects, but in what other country was there a body so excellent?"[1] The philanthropists, lawyers, and statesmen who busied themselves in the course of the eighteenth century with such matters as prisons and pauperism, highways and bridges, all alike proposed, in their various schemes of reform, to extend the powers of the County Justices, either as direct administrators of their own institutions and services, or as local

[1] Hansard, 13th July 1807, vol. ix. p. 803.

legislators dictating a policy to subordinate authorities.[1] And this attitude of complacent trust in the Rulers of the County was reflected in the Legislature of the time. Whenever the House of Commons, between 1740 and 1810, could bring itself to pass any general statute affecting a local government service, it was always the Justices who gained in power at the expense of the High Sheriff, the Grand Jury, the Surveyor of Highways, the Overseers of the Poor, or any other officer or authority. Even the new statutory bodies, created under Local Acts to perform the new services required by the new urban populations, found themselves compelled to submit either their constitution or their procedure, their by-laws or their expenditure, to the "confirmation" of the Court of Quarter Sessions. Parliament, in fact, throughout this period seemed to imply, alike in the occasional general statutes and the multitudinous Local Acts, that it assumed the Court of Quarter Sessions to stand, towards the other local authorities of the county, in much the same position as is to-day occupied by the Home Office, the Board of Education, and the Local Government Board. This unhesitating acceptance of the Justices as an autonomous county oligarchy is to be seen reflected in parliamentary procedure as well as in legislation. So far as the internal local administration of the rural districts was concerned the House of Commons felt itself to be but the legislative "clearing-house" of the several Courts of Quarter Sessions. The Knights of the Shire who sat at Westminster habitually regarded themselves as the spokesmen of these Courts, from which they received instructions as to bills to be promoted, supported, amended, or opposed. Such Parliamentary reformers of local government as Thomas Gilbert

---

[1] Thus, in highway maintenance, the repeatedly advocated panacea was the appointment of a county road officer, to act under the Justices' orders (see, for instance, *Proposals at Large for the Easy and Effectual Amendment of the Roads, etc.*, by a Gentleman, 1753, p. 23 ; *A Treatise upon Wheel Carriages*, by Daniel Bourn, 1763, p. 36 ; *Observations on the General Highway and Turnpike Acts*, by T. B. Bayley, 1773 ; Second Report from House of Commons Committee on the Highways of the Kingdom, 1808 ; and, as late as 1825, in the able anonymous pamphlet *Highways Improved*, 1825). So in Poor Law, the whole tendency of the proposals of William Hay, John Scott, Gilbert, Arthur Young, Wilberforce, and Whitbread, as well as the legislation of 1782-1810, was in the same direction. It was to the Justices, it will be remembered, that Whitbread in 1807 proposed to entrust the management of his system of parochial schools

were perpetually circulating their draft measures to the acting
Justices for their criticism. On one occasion at least, where
the magistrates were greatly concerned about prison administration and vagrancy, the Courts of Quarter Sessions even held
a convention of their own in London, attended by two Justices
from each county—a convention which formulated a common
policy, drafted a new vagrancy bill, and saw the measure safely
passed into law.[1] When a member of Parliament introduced
a bill relating to vagrancy or poor relief, prisons or roads, it
was usual throughout the second half of the eighteenth century
for it to be circulated to all the Courts of Quarter Sessions, or
even to every acting magistrate, before the House of Commons
was asked to vote the second reading. This practice continued
into the nineteenth century. When Whitbread brought in
his comprehensive Poor Law Bill in 1807 it was taken for
granted that it would be circulated to the Justices. Rose,
latterly Pitt's ablest subordinate, thought that " it might go
to Quarter Sessions in its present shape." Another Tory
member objected that " the opinion of the Justices could not
be collected at the next Quarter Sessions " on so extensive a
bill, and urged that it should " be divided into parts for their
consideration," a course which Whitbread thought it prudent
to adopt. Finally, Sturges Bourne, destined himself to be a
Poor Law reformer, suggested that Whitbread should take
care that the bill should be in the hands of the country
gentlemen at the Assizes as well as at Quarter Sessions, as it
would then meet with superior consideration.[2] When, a few
months later, Whitbread brought forward one of the parts, the
celebrated Parochial Schools Bill, he was commended " for his

---

[1] For particulars of this remarkable convention, see *Resolutions of the
Magistrates deputed from the several Counties in England and Wales assembled
at the St. Alban's Tavern, by desire of the Society for Giving effect to His
Majesty's Proclamation against Vice and Immorality* (1790).   Thirty - two
counties sent delegates, and among the Justices present were Sir G. O. Paul,
Bart. (Gloucestershire), T. B. Bayley (Lancashire), Rev. Henry Zouch (West
Riding), Rev. Dr. Glasse (Middlesex), and W. Morton Pitt (Dorsetshire),
and many of the Legislature.   "I was retained to attend them," relates
Christian, afterwards Chief Justice of the Isle of Ely, "as a legal assistant.
After many discussions and various resolutions, I was directed by them to
prepare a bill to be laid before Parliament to prevent a great abuse of the laws
respecting vagrants" (*Charges delivered to Grand Juries in the Isle of Ely*, by
Edward Christian, 1819, pp. 12, 144, etc.).   This bill became law in 1792
(32 George III. c. 45).

[2] Hansard, 19th February 1807 (vol. viii. pp. 919-920).

care in circulating it for the consideration of the magistrates throughout the country." "It had," said a Tory member, "been fully considered, but every magistrate with whom he had conversed was decidedly averse to it, and instructed their representatives to oppose it." Nor was this attitude confined to one party. Lord Henry Petty, one of the Whig leaders, gave as sufficient reason for opposition "that he understood that the magistrates in the North objected to the measure . . . as they already possessed within themselves sufficient means of education for the children of the poor in that part of the country." Needless to say, in face of this opposition the bill had eventually to be abandoned. When it came on in July the few county members who were still in attendance objected to its even being discussed " in the absence of the magistrates and country gentlemen, who were the persons competent to throw the most light on the subject." [1] This last objection was, in fact, often made in the unreformed House of Commons to any attempt to discuss local government questions whenever the Knights of the Shire were not in full force at Westminster, the plea being that " so many of the members were engaged at the several Sessions." The student will now realise what we meant by the assertion that, in spite of the apparently centralised legal constitution of English Local Government, and of the complete dependence in law of the Commission of the Peace on the will of the monarch and his ministers, at no period did the Rulers of the County enjoy so large a measure of local autonomy and irresponsible power as between the accession of the House of Hanover and the close of the Napoleonic wars.

[1] Hansard, 13th July 1807 (vol. ix. pp. 426, 492, 538, 739, 801, 804, 1049, 1054). When Henry Fielding, a Stipendiary Magistrate in the Metropolis, suggested to the Home Secretary in 1811 the "annual appointment of a committee of police in the House of Commons," he took it for granted that it would be composed of "all the county magistrates in the House" (Home Office Domestic State Papers in Public Record Office, No. 226, 1811).

CHAPTER VI

THE REACTION AGAINST THE RULERS OF THE COUNTY

THE reaction against the extra-legal autocratic oligarchy which had been established in county government was dramatic in its suddenness. The uncontrolled power of the Rulers of the County stood, in 1815, unchallenged either by Parliament or by public opinion. By 1835 the Justices had forfeited a great part of their administrative functions. The supervision of the Poor Law, the control of the ale-houses, the direction of highway repair, had passed out of their hands. In the administration of prisons and lunatic asylums, and even to some extent in the management of police, they had lost their autonomy, and had become subject to the supervision of the central government. They found themselves, individually and collectively, denounced on every platform and criticised in every newspaper. By one powerful party they were threatened with annihilation. Yet closer inspection shows that the County Justices survived these decades of iconoclastic fervour with less actual change than the other local governing authorities of the time. The immemorial parish, as we have seen, in spite of its evolution, between 1689 and 1815, into an extra-legal democracy, was effectually strangled by the legislation of 1818-34. The decadent municipal corporations were completely revolutionised by that of 1835. The statutory authorities for special purposes were, some of them, merged, others completely transformed, and all alike undermined by the establishment of the new Poor Law Unions, Highway Boards, and Town Councils. But the Commission of the Peace, as we described it in 1689, maintained, in 1835, its legal constitution intact, its ancient ceremonial procedure unaltered, and its membership increased, indeed, but virtually unchanged in character. It was destined even to withstand the subsequent assaults of Whigs and Radicals, and to continue for another half century as the sole county authority. And when, in 1888, county government was at last reorganised on a representative basis, it was only the administration of civil business that passed to the new County Councils; the Court of Quarter Sessions was continued in all its dignity, and the Justices retained at any rate all their judicial functions. We shall conclude our description of the county by tracing the causes of the reaction against its rulers, and by explaining why this reaction stopped short of a radical reconstitution of county government.

(a) *The Breakdown of the Middlesex Bench*

One insidious cause of the reaction against the Rulers of the County was the breakdown in efficiency and purity of administration of the Middlesex, and, in a lesser degree, of the Surrey magistracies. We have already described the notorious " Trading Justices " of Middlesex, and the infamous system of blackmail and oppression that they carried on in the Metropolitan parishes. Down to 1781, however, the Middlesex Court of Quarter Sessions—that is to say, the dozen or two of Justices who habitually attended at Hick's Hall [1]—seems to have been an honourable body, which had organised the county business on an economical and relatively efficient basis. It had even striven, though with scant success, to introduce some kind of decency and regularity into the individual jurisdiction of the crowd of " Justices of Mean Degree," who made up the bulk of the commission. It had, as we have seen, anticipated both the Parliamentary establishment of annual Licensing Sessions and the later practice of regular Petty Sessions.[2] It had made orders, which, we think, were beyond its legal competence, intended to obviate the overlapping jurisdictions of individual Justices eager for increase of business;[3] it had peremptorily forbidden them to act out of their own parishes

---

[1] The quorum for county business was reduced from twenty to fifteen in 1734, owing to the inconvenience caused by failure to get as many as twenty together (MS. Minutes, Quarter Sessions, Middlesex, 25th April 1734).

[2] *Ibid.* 25th February 1716.

[3] *Ibid.* 6th December 1716, 29th June 1738.

or Divisions, to grant licences to persons who had been refused at the annual Sessions, or to discharge from prison persons committed by other Justices. Moreover, the Court of Quarter Sessions had, through the charges of its Chairmen and the presentments of its Grand Juries, done its best to check the peculations and oppressions of the servants of the Justices—inquiring into the "indirect practices" of the Undersheriff [1]—denouncing and prosecuting corrupt Constables and Beadles,[2] limiting the fees of the Keepers of the Houses of Correction,[3] and also those of the Justices' Clerks,[4] preventing the latter from acting as attorneys in cases before Quarter Sessions,[5] and insisting that the Courts Leet and Divisional Sessions should not appoint or recommend ale-house keepers, spirit dealers, or wine merchants as High or Petty Constables. But the Court of Quarter Sessions had, between 1715 and 1781, done more than this. It had effectually stopped all allowances for refreshments to committees of Justices auditing accounts or viewing bridges.[6] When evidence was forthcoming of the iniquities of any particular Trading Justice, the Court, far from screening him, was quick to seize the opportunity formally to represent his misdoings in a detailed indictment to the Lord Chancellor, with a view to the removal of the culprit. Between 1720 and 1780 at least a dozen such corrupt Justices were thus removed from the Commission, whilst others were severely reprimanded by the Court.[7] And when, in 1774, one

---

[1] MS. Minutes, Quarter Sessions, Middlesex, 26th April 1723.

[2] *Ibid.* 2nd December 1717.   [3] *Ibid.* July 1720.

[4] *Ibid.* 2nd December 1715, 19th July 1753.

[5] *Ibid.* 21st May 1724.

[6] "For the future no allowance shall be made to any Justice of the Peace of this county" (*ibid.* 16th January 1719).

[7] We have noted the following "remonstrances" with peccant Justices, or representations to the Lord Chancellor of their misconduct, in the Middlesex Quarter Sessions Minutes :—

1720. Representation to Lord Chancellor as to Sir W. Moore's repeated acts of extortion and oppression (MS. Minutes, Quarter Sessions, Middlesex, 27th February 1720).

1720. Three Justices are similarly represented for corruption (*ibid.* 6th and 9th September 1720).

1724-1725. Samuel Newton, Sir Harry Dutton, and Charles Whingate are similarly represented (*ibid.* 3rd December 1724, 13th January and 23rd February 1725).

1727. Remonstrance with Simon Mitchell for improper bailing (*ibid.* 24th and 25th February 1727).

1728. Remonstrance with John Troughton for the same (*ibid.* 17th October 1728).

of the Justices, a certain Boulton Mainwaring, apparently a professional architect, claimed payment from the Court for the services he had during over ten years rendered in superintending the alterations of the new House of Correction,[1] and the repairing of Hick's Hall, such a claim was indignantly rejected, on the ground that he had not been employed by the County " in the capacity of a surveyor, but on the contrary," that the duties were entrusted to him, as the Court informed him, " conceiving that the services you have done the county were voluntary, and, in every sense of the word, disinterested."[2] There is, however, even more conclusive evidence of the purity of the administration of the Middlesex Court of Quarter Sessions in 1738. Having very creditably resisted the attempt of one of its own members, who had obtained a patent as " Clerk of the Market," to exact fees from all persons using weights and measures, the Court found itself subjected to a series of malicious attacks, culminating in a committee of inquiry appointed by the House of Commons. This committee investigated fully the whole of the financial arrangements of the Court, taking evidence from parish officers, High Constables, discontented Justices, and the discomfited " Clerk of the Market" himself. In the result we see all the loose allegations of misapplication and embezzlement fall to the ground : no accusation of corruption of any kind is sustained ; and the impression that remains is one of frugal and entirely honest administration.[3] We attribute this purity of adminis-

1738. Thomas Cotton represented for corruption (MS. Minutes, Quarter Sessions, Middlesex, 13th April 1738).

1751. Sir Samuel Gower represented for scandalous corruption and extortion (*ibid.* 28th February 1751).

1759. Palmer remonstrated with for improper pamphlet (*ibid.* 12th July 1759).

1769. John Sharratt represented for gross misconduct and unfitness (*ibid.* May 1769).

1777-1778. Committee to inquire into conduct of various Justices, report them guilty ; on representation to Lord Chancellor, John Gretton is removed (*ibid.* December 1777 and 30th April 1778).

1780. James Fielding and Wm. Hyde represented for corruption in connection with vagrancy (*ibid.* 13th January 1780).

[1] *Ibid.* 26th February 1761.

[2] *Ibid.* February and April 1774. He had formerly held the salaried post of Surveyor to the Tower Hamlets Court of Sewers, which he resigned in 1768 (MS. Minutes, Commissioners of Sewers, Tower Hamlets, 5th May 1768).

[3] For all this, see Report of House of Commons Committee upon the Taxes and Assessments raised in the County of Middlesex, 1739, extending over sixty pages of involved statement and counter-statement ; MS. Minutes, Quarter

tration of the Middlesex Court of Quarter Sessions down to
1781, partly to the non-attendance of the crowd of " Trading
Justices," whose gains still lay in the duties of the Single and
Double Justice, and who found no inducement to perform the
onerous work at Hicks' Hall; and partly to the fortunate
accident which gave the Court a succession of good and
honest chairmen in Whitelocke Bulstrode, Sir Thomas Abney,
Sir Daniel Dolins, John Milner, John Lane, and above all, the
sixteen years' service of Samuel Johnson's friend and biographer,
Sir John Hawkins, to whom we have already referred.[1]

Sessions, Middlesex, 24th February 1726, 24th February 1727, 5th December
1728, 29th April 1731, 23rd May, 18th October, and 11th December 1735,
7th July 1737 ; *The History of the Office of Clerk of the Market of the King's
Household*, by Thomas Robe, 1737 ; and *A Collection of all the Depositions and
Advertisements relating to the Charge brought against Mr. Robe of Clerkenwell*,
1737 ; *Our Weights and Measures*, by H. J. Chaney, 1897, p. 53. The
Justices contended that the King's Patent to Robe, the Clerk of the Market,
conveyed authority within " the Little Verge " of the Palace, whereas Robe
attempted to levy fees for examining weights and measures all over the county.
The Court of King's Bench in 1731 decided that the jurisdiction extended to
a twelve miles' radius of the Palace, but only when the King was in residence ;
and that he was not entitled to any fee for inspecting or reviewing weights and
measures, but only for sealing or marking them in the first instance, which
no one was obliged to have done. In revenge for the drastic reduction of his
profits thus caused, Robe carried on seven years' warfare against the Middlesex
Court of Quarter Sessions, harassing the Justices by every means in his power.
The only result was the Act of 1739, simplifying the levy of the County Rate.

[1] The Clerk of the Peace reported the election to the Home Secretary
(Magistrates Book in Home Office Archives in Public Record Office, 17th March
1781). As to Sir John Hawkins (1719-1789), see *Dictionary of National
Biography* and the sources there cited, especially *Memoirs of Lætitia Matilda
Hawkins*, his daughter, and *Calendar of Home Office Papers, 1770-2* (1881),
pp. 560-563. He was the son of a London carpenter ; became an attorney ;
wrote for the *Gentleman's Magazine*, and at the age of forty retired on a fortune
then inherited by his wife. He became a magistrate in 1761 and Chairman of
Quarter Sessions in 1765, continuing in that office until 1781. Already, as an
attorney, Hawkins had been an intimate associate of Dr. Johnson ; he was an
original member of the celebrated "club"; and on Johnson's death he became
his first biographer. He also wrote a voluminous *History of Music* and (of
more interest to the student of Local Government) a useful pamphlet on
Highway Administration, which may have led to the consolidating Acts of
1766 to 1773. Horace Walpole frequently mentions him as a "very worthy"
friend, grave and religious, and much addicted to angling. We retain (from
the MS. Minutes of the Middlesex Quarter Sessions, contemporary references
and other sources) an impression that Hawkins was an honest and public-
spirited magistrate, zealous in his duties, somewhat too obsequious to the great,
but a competent and devoted chairman of fair administrative ability. He, like
all others concerned, failed to cope with the emergency of the Lord George
Gordon riots in 1780, and this may have been partly the cause of his rejection
for the chairmanship in 1781. It is to be counted as his great merit that
during his sixteen years' chairmanship he kept the Middlesex Quarter Sessions
honest, and persistently strove to purify the Commission.

In 1781 the note changes. At the Spring Sessions of that year, Sir John Hawkins, notwithstanding his long and honoured service, was rejected for Chairman, by twenty-eight votes to twenty-three.[1] Whether this sudden fall from power was due to his unceasing vigilance of the morals of his fellow-Justices, or whether it was merely a reflection of the Government displeasure at the failure of the leaders of the Middlesex and Westminster magistrates to quell the Gordon riots, we have been unable to ascertain. The choice of the Justices fell on William Mainwaring, a banker of reputed piety, from 1785 member of Parliament for Middlesex. About this time—perhaps on the occasion of Mainwaring's election—we find recorded in the secret archives of the Treasury, as we shall presently mention, the payment of an annual salary to the Chairman of the Middlesex and Westminster Quarter Sessions, which never became known even to the other Justices. For the next forty years the Mainwaring family—one of whom we have already mentioned in an equivocal position—dominated the Middlesex Court of Quarter Sessions. Under their rule there was gradually introduced an extensive system of corruption. We note at once a complete cessation of all representations to the Lord Chancellor in favour of the removal of erring Justices. It was not that the need had ceased. When, in 1787, Quarter Sessions, acting on a vigorous presentment by the Grand Jury, urges all parish authorities to put an end to the growing disorder and licentiousness of the streets, the officers and inhabitants of Mile End Old Town have a sharp retort. " When we see," they reply, " individual Justices prostituting the dignity of their station to procure themselves a livelihood, opening offices in different parts of the town for the purpose of administering justice in the way of trade, and striving and contending against each other for business, with all the eagerness and jealousies attendant upon jarring interests, we cannot but draw the conclusion that to magistrates of such a description depravity and dissipation is as essentially necessary for the advancement of their interests as is a flow of business to that of traders of any other class." [2] Three years later we find a committee of Quarter Sessions itself reporting

---

[1] MS. Minutes, Quarter Sessions, Middlesex, 22nd February 1781.
[2] *Ibid.* 13th September 1787.

to the Court that one of the Justices, named Blackborough, besides other offences, " had threatened the Constables that if they took up thieves or prostitutes who live in Mr. Blackborough's tenements, he will protect his tenants, and, if they interrupt them, they will be punished." It was, moreover, proved that the same Justice had accepted money from publicans in return for licences.[1] The only action taken on this damaging report was to pass a resolution censuring Mr. Blackborough's conduct. After this date, even inquiries cease, and reprimands no longer appear in the records. Meanwhile, Mainwaring, the Chairman, outwardly fills his part with admirable propriety. He was in 1787 one of the founders of the " Proclamation Society " for enforcing the King's Proclamation against immorality and vice; and in 1794 we find him bringing in a bill for " promoting the stricter observance of the Lord's Day." [2] His annual charges to the Grand Jury as to the delinquencies of the parish authorities in permitting the disorders of the streets are so eloquent as to be reported in provincial newspapers, and even to obtain insertion in the *Gentleman's Magazine*.[3] But from the first years of his chairmanship certain ugly features appear in the administration of County Business. In 1784 the lucrative appointment of architect for the new House of Correction is conferred on a leading member of the Court.[4] Soon afterwards it appears that the new surveyor appointed by the Court under the Metropolitan Building Act is a brother of another leading member.[5] In 1793 Joseph Merceron, whose Napoleonic career as " Boss " of the parish of Bethnal Green we have already recounted,[6] becomes a Middlesex magistrate, and at once joins the governing clique, to be found, during the next twenty years, on every committee for auditing accounts and letting contracts. Sir Daniel Williams, his ally, if not his partner in corruption, first obtained a salaried appointment

[1] MS. Minutes, Quarter Sessions, Middlesex, 16th September 1790.
[2] *Life of William Wilberforce*, by R. I. and S. Wilberforce, 1839, vol. i. p. 394 ; vol. ii. p. 48.
[3] See, for instance, *Chelmsford Chronicle*, 21st April 1786, and *Gentleman's Magazine*, January 1812, vol. lxxxii. p. 85.
[4] MS. Minutes, Quarter Sessions, Middlesex, 21st May and 6th December 1784, 17th July 1786.
[5] *Ibid.* 10th January 1788.
[6] See "The Rule of the Boss " in Book I. Ch. II.

from the Government, and then was made, by Mainwaring's influence, Deputy Chairman of Quarter Sessions. It is evident that the little clique of magistrates who now ran the county put their relations and dependants into all sorts of minor offices and profitable businesses. Between them they built up, as was afterwards said, "a complex machine which . . . for some years . . . wielded, unseen, unnoticed, unopposed, the whole patronage of the county magistracy," the force directing "the secret springs which have given motion to the magisterial wheels" remaining unknown to "the body of independent men included in the Commission."[1] Meanwhile the successive Ministries cannot be absolved from a grave responsibility for this discreditable state of things. For at least thirty years, from 1782 to 1812, for which we have been able to explore the accounts of the "money issued for Special Service or Royal Bounty,"[2] the Treasury made a secret payment to Mainwaring for his services in keeping Middlesex quiet; at first of £350, and after 1799, of £750 a year. This payment was unrevealed to Parliament, and was evidently quite unknown either to Mainwaring's colleagues or to the many critics of his administration. Gradually, however, this salary failed to content the unscrupulous Chairman of the Middlesex Bench. The most important office of profit of the county, that of Treasurer, was conferred on G. B. Mainwaring, his son and partner, whose firm thus enjoyed the custody of the constantly large balances. But not satisfied with this, William Mainwaring used his position as a Commissioner of Sewers to get

---

[1] *An Address to the Magistracy of the County of Middlesex . . . on the motives that should influence their votes in the election of a Chairman of Quarter Sessions*, etc., 1815, p. 3.

[2] Among the Treasury archives in the Public Record Office are three "Special Service Books," Nos. 1, 2, and 3, extending from 1782 to 1821, and entitled "An Account of Money issued for Special Service or Royal Bounty, kept for that purpose in the Treasury in order to be produced to either House of Parliament if required, pursuant to . . . [22 George III.]." The payments to William Mainwaring occur from 1783 to 1812. He is generally described as "Chairman of the Sessions for the County of Middlesex and Chairman of the Sessions for the City and Liberty of Westminster." In all the contemporary criticism and discussion of the Middlesex Bench and Mainwaring's conduct, we have come across no mention of this salary. The failure of his bank is reported in *Times*, 21st November and 5th December 1814. The salary was continued to his successors down to 1833, when the Treasury stopped it (Home Office Domestic Entry Book, 13th March 1833, vol. lxix. in Public Record Office).

the current accounts of the Commissioners for Westminster, Holborn and Finsbury, and the Tower Hamlets transferred from other banks to his own, which was already on the brink of collapse. In 1814 the crash came. Mainwaring's bank failed, and the large public balances in his hands were lost. In an eloquent protest, one virtuous magistrate denounces him to his colleagues as a hypocrite and a defaulter. "As Chairman of the County," causticly observes this pamphleteer, " he expounds the law, expatiates on justice and virtue, and pronounces judgment ; as its public receiver or banker he forgets his precepts, neglecting to make good his payments to that county which raised him to his consequence." [1] Even then the Mainwaring family maintains its hold on the Court. No revelation is made that it had been for a whole generation secretly in the pay of the Treasury. Dominated by Sir Daniel Williams and Joseph Merceron, the Justices re-elect the father as Chairman and the son as Treasurer, this time actually awarding the latter a salary of £500 a year (" in addition to £250 a year which he had previously received for the management of the tontine "); and yet taking no steps " to reduce the balance in his hands." [2] In 1816 the elder Mainwaring, now an old man, broken in health, at last lays down his chairmanship, after a tenure of nearly thirty-six years ; and so far are the Justices from reprobating his conduct, that the Court officially memoralises the Government to grant him a pension from public funds. For six more years G. B. Mainwaring remains Treasurer. At last the scandal becomes too great ; various irregularities in the collection of the County Rates and in the accounting for balances come to light ; public meetings of parish officers and indignant ratepayers demand investigation of his accounts and inspection of his securities ; [3] and, finally, his fellow-Justices themselves compel him to resign. As he attempted to retain the account books in his possession, the Court of Quarter Sessions was driven to make a peremptory demand for their delivery, and only under threat of a

---

[1] *An Address to the Magistracy of the County of Middlesex . . . on the motives that should influence their votes on the election of a Chairman of Quarter Sessions*, etc., 1815, p. 15.

[2] *Ibid.* ; see also the article on "the Middlesex County Rates " in *Justice of the Peace*, 11th March 1837.

[3] See, for instance, the report in *Morning Chronicle*, 22nd April 1822.

mandamus from the Court of King's Bench were they handed over.[1] This virtual dismissal of the Treasurer in 1822, "under circumstances which created a considerable public sensation,"[2] was followed by a prolonged inquiry into the county administration of the past twenty years, in the course of which it was discovered that all the public records for certain crucial years had been suppressed, "for the purpose," as the Committee suggest, "of preventing the discovery of some irregular transactions," and of covering up the general increases in fees, salaries, and payments to contractors under the audits conducted by Merceron and his allies.[3] It was thought necessary for Parliament to pass a special statute "for the express regulation of the Treasurer of the County of Middlesex."[4]

It will be noticed that the corruption of the Middlesex Bench now dealt in larger figures, and was altogether more decorous, than the iniquities of the Trading Justices. One source of illicit gain had in fact been stopped and others opened. By an Act of 1792 the power of the Middlesex Justices to charge fees for judicial business was taken away from all but half a dozen definitely appointed stipendiary magistrates, sitting at the new public "police offices." Contemporaneously with this suppression of the profits of the Trading Justices, there came, however, a new source of corruption, offering opportunities of illicit gain to a larger circle of Justices than could participate in the perquisites attaching to the transaction of the "county business" at Hicks' Hall. Towards the latter part of the eighteenth century it was the Brewster Sessions, held in each Petty Sessional Division of the county—in Westminster apparently in each parish—that afforded most scope to unscrupulous magistrates. The rapid growth of population in the Metropolis, the rise of wealthy firms of brewers and distillers on a large scale, and the concentration of all the liquor traffic in the licensed houses, had made these licences of great and steadily growing pecuniary value. Brewers and distillers, publicans

---

[1] MS. Minutes, Quarter Sessions, Middlesex, February 1822.

[2] *Justice of the Peace*, 11th March 1837.

[3] MS. Minutes, Quarter Sessions, Middlesex, 9th December 1824, 9th June 1825.

[4] 3 George IV. c. cvii. 1822 ; see *Justice of the Peace*, 11th March 1837.

and owners of public-house property became ready to buy them for considerable sums. Many Justices did not hesitate, in the "hole and corner" Brewster Sessions held in the various parishes and Divisions,[1] to conduct a shameless traffic in public-house licences, which excited the animadversion of those of severer virtue. "Who, then, is there," wrote a magistrate in 1815, "but must have boiled with indignation when condemned to hear read a recent correspondence submitted to the magistrates at a late meeting, wherein individuals are openly charged with conniving, or something very like it, at a trafficking in public-house licences?"[2] Other magistrates did not perhaps sell licences, but we find them "placing their nearest and dearest relatives in warehouses for the sale of spirituous liquors and porter."[3] We have already described how, in the Brewster Sessions for the Tower Hamlets Division, Joseph Merceron consolidated his power over the parish of Bethnal Green, by corruptly licensing the numerous beershops in the occupation of his tenants and dependants. Nor did Merceron stand alone. In a confidential report to the Home Secretary, in 1787, we are told that "Turnmill Street [Clerkenwell] contains somewhat more than eighty houses, sixteen of which are licensed; most of them double the size of the unlicensed; every day, and I believe night too, open for the reception of the most abandoned of all descriptions. The Justice in that district owns a great proportion of the street, and in [to] his office almost all matters of complaint are referred."[4] So shameless a perversion of the Justice's licensing authority could not, of course, continue without the connivance of the other magistrates, including, we fear it must be said, Sir Daniel Williams, a Stipendiary Magistrate, a warm supporter of the Mainwaring interest in the Court of Quarter Sessions and Chairman of the Brewster Sessions for the Tower Hamlets Division. Williams, there is reason to suppose, had his own

[1] "In the various parishes in Westminster the public-houses" were in 1816 "licensed by the parochial magistrates in each parish" (Report of House of Commons Committee on the State of the Police in the Metropolis, 1816, p. 77).
[2] *An Address to the Magistracy of the County of Middlesex . . . on the motives that should influence their votes in the election of a Chairman of Quarter Sessions*, 1815, p. 6.   [3] *Ibid.* p. 7.
[4] Home Office Domestic State Papers in Public Record Office, No. 108, 13th August 1787.

equivocal transactions in public-houses, and his own jobbery of offices, contracts, and licences,[1] though his subsequent career as Chairman both of the Holborn and Finsbury Court of Sewers and of the Tower Hamlets Court of Sewers—both of which he dominated until his death—shows him to have been, not only an able administrator, but (at anyrate after his early struggles were over) apparently a man of upright conduct. So important a power was worth capturing, and captured it was. In contrast with the character even of the Middlesex Quarter Sessions during the third quarter of the eighteenth century, it could without contradiction be said fifty years later that " a considerable proportion of the magisterial interest is absorbed by rectifiers and dealers in spirits, and by the compounders of strong beer, not only in their own persons, but likewise through the less prominent and less ostensible medium of their friends and dependants." [2]

A similar morass of corruption is found in the Licensing Sessions of the rapidly growing Division of the County of Surrey which lay along the south bank of the Thames. From 1814 onwards we notice in the minutes a constant struggle between the noblemen, clergymen, and county squires who formed the Court of Quarter Sessions when it met at Reigate, Kingston, or Guildford; and the heterogeneous crowd of adventurers who dominated the Court at Newington, and practically filled the Brewster Sessions for "the Borough of Southwark and the East Half Hundred of Brixton." In 1816 this Division secured from Quarter Sessions the privilege of making its own separate rules for licensing,[3] and evidently

---

[1] See the particulars scattered over the various Reports of the House of Commons Committee on the State of the Police of the Metropolis, 1816-1817. His conduct was specifically brought before the Lord Chancellor by the Home Secretary himself (Home Office Domestic Entry Book, 21st October and 7th November 1816, vol. li. in Public Record Office).

[2] *An Address to the Magistracy of the County of Middlesex*, 1815, p. 5. Much information as to the lax practices of the Metropolitan Justices with regard to licensing will be found in the various Reports of the House of Commons Committee on the State of the Police of the Metropolis, 1816-1817. See also *A Letter to the Lord-Lieutenant of the County of Surrey on the Misconduct of Licensing Magistrates, and the consequent degradation of the Magistracy*, by Thomas Edwards, LL.D., J.P., 1825 ; the review of this able pamphlet by Sydney Smith in *Edinburgh Review*, September 1826 ; and the petition of Dr. Edwards, presented by Joseph Hume to the House of Commons in 1826 (Hansard, 13th April 1826).

[3] MS. Minutes, Quarter Sessions, Surrey, Easter, 16th July 1816.

made more rigid than ever the custom of excluding all Justices not belonging to the Division, which we also trace as existing in Middlesex.[1]   In Surrey, we are told, it came to be "deemed the very height of indecorum to disturb licensers in the management of their respective localities. . . . A magistrate sitting in a Division in which he does not dwell is called a foreigner, is frowned at, and perhaps personally insulted."[2] The result was, in this one Division—a district then made up largely of open commons and green meadows, only beginning to be covered with straggling colonies of mean streets, there soon came to be no fewer than 830 licensed houses, as compared with a total of only 503 for all the rest of the County. In spite of this fact, twenty-five new and additional licences were granted by this Brewster Sessions in the three years 1820-1823.[3]   The magistrates who attended this Sessions were almost entirely either brewers, or "brewers' backmakers," or tradesmen employed by the brewers, whilst the clerk, a practising solicitor, had most of the publicans as his clients. At every Brewster Sessions the Justices dined together, the custom being for the principal viands of the feast to be sent in by the brewers and tradesmen interested in the local public-houses.[4]   By 1824 the extraordinary multiplication of drink-shops in the riverside parts of Lambeth and Southwark, and their combination with disorderly houses of the worst kind, had become so scandalous, that Drummond of Albury, a leading Evangelical landowner, at last called attention at the Kingston Quarter Sessions to the conduct of the Brewster Sessions, declaring that the licences had "become so numerous that no respectable man would become a tenant of one of them"; he "could only hope to obtain a livelihood by giving gin gratuitously to prostitutes." The case which Drummond specifically brought before the Quarter Sessions as a sample of the Justices' proceedings was as follows: In 1824 the house of one Barton, a publican, was so notorious a brothel that even this prejudiced tribunal refused him a renewal of his licence, though only by

---

[1] It was an invariable rule with the licensing Justices not to interfere with each other's districts, as it is termed (Confidential Report to Home Secretary, in Home Office Domestic State Papers in Public Record Office, No. 108, 13th August 1787).

[2] *A Letter to the Lord-Lieutenant of the County of Surrey on the Misconduct of Licensing Magistrates*, by Thomas Edwards, 1825, p. 78.

[3] *Ibid.* p. 10.   [4] *Ibid.* p. 19.

a majority of one vote. " Several of the magistrates," continues a contemporary report, " not having a taste for the turtle which had been sent by a brewer for their dinner, went home, when, to their utter astonishment, they received a notice signed from the clerk, by which it appeared that in their absence upstairs in the dining-room (he, the same brewer, and also the High Sheriff of the County, who is a brewer's backmaker, and whose son was till lately a partner in the same brewery, being present), it was resolved to hold an extraordinary meeting to reconsider Barton's case. It appears that another brewer has a mortgage on Barton's house for £1400, that a considerable number of the publicans are clients of the magistrates' clerk, and that one day of the meeting a haunch of venison was sent for the magistrates' dinner by a distiller and on another day by a builder." [1] The country gentlemen of Guildford, shocked at this recital, passed a resolution expressly authorising every Justice of the county to attend any licensing Sessions, and peremptorily requiring the Clerk of the Peace to give notice of such Sessions to every acting magistrate of the county.[2]

The corruption that prevailed among the Justices of the Metropolitan Divisional Sessions naturally spread to their staffs. It was, for instance, in the Metropolitan area that the office of High Constable became most completely transformed, and finally reached its lowest degradation. The vast amount of business, and the odiousness of the work in the densely crowded Divisions of Middlesex, led to the office being avoided by every respectable citizen, and sought after only by those who would make a profit out of it. After the retirement of Sir John Hawkins, the Middlesex magistrates seem to have made no attempt to maintain the status and dignity of the office. They found it competed for admittedly for the sake of its illegitimate gains ; and they came, in the latter part of the century, habitually to treat it as an office of profit, making the appointment virtually one for life. The place was given to local tradesmen—grocers, coal merchants, second-hand clothes dealers, or shoemakers—who frankly looked to be remunerated

---

[1] *Morning Chronicle*, 20th October 1824 ; in confirmation, see MS. Minutes, Quarter Sessions, Surrey, 19th October 1824 ; and *A Letter to the Lord-Lieutenant of the County of Surrey on the Misconduct of Licensing Magistrates*, by Thomas Edwards, 1825.

[2] MS. Minutes, Quarter Sessions, Surrey, 19th October 1824.

for their work and reimbursed their expenses, partly by the extension of their trade among the publicans on whom they had to report, and partly by the bribes and perquisites obtained from them. For in the Metropolitan parishes of Middlesex the principal function of the High Constable (along with the levy of the County Rate) had come to be the supervision of the public-houses. "It is his duty," it was stated in 1816, " to see that the publicans do their duty upon the quartering of soldiers."[1] What was more important was that it was the High Constable who had to attend the Licensing Sessions of the Justices, and to report on the conduct of the publicans within his Division before their licences were renewed. "We consider," said a magistrate of 1816, "that a business peculiarly under the High Constable of the Division; it is his business to visit all the public-houses and to be acquainted with the conduct in them, and to report what is amiss."[2] It is an instance of the extraordinary ineptitude of the administration of the time that this responsible duty—practically the only supervision to which the licensed houses were subjected —should have been entrusted (as the same magistrate explains) to an officer who "has no pay, and the only way he can remunerate himself is by obtaining the custom of the publicans in the articles in which he deals." It is therefore not surprising to find that the High Constables were habitually in the pay of the publicans, and that the worst malpractices prevailed. If the publican kept on good terms with the High Constable, there was no excess that might not be committed with impunity. In return for their forbearance, the High Constables could exercise no little influence. In 1794 we hear that "circular letters have been sent to the different publicans in Westminster, signed Robert Jones, High Constable of Westminster, directing each to throw out the newspaper which he now uses, and take a particular morning paper, as he, Jones, has an interest in its welfare, and if they do, he promises to return the compliment by every means in his power."[3]

---

[1] Report of House of Commons Committee on the State of the Police of the Metropolis, 1816, p. 104. [2] *Ibid.* p. 78.

[3] *Times*, 11th January 1794. A circular asking for the publicans' custom for a High Constable who makes boots and sells coals, is reprinted in Report of House of Commons Committee on the State of the Police of the Metropolis, 1817, p. 256.

The cause of the breakdown of the Middlesex bench was plain even to contemporary observers. "The great and principal defects complained of in the magistracy of Westminster," says an able critic of 1784, "will be found to proceed from the absurdity of applying the same form of government to two very different subjects—to the various and intricate affairs of a city, as well as to the simple and unembarrassed regulation of a county."[1] Even assuming, as does this critic, that unpaid and amateur Justices were "fully sufficient for a wide district, thinly scattered with inhabitants, and removed from most of the temptations to disorder," it was obvious that this "loose and unsettled magistracy" could not be expected to cope with the perpetual corruption of three quarters of a million people, densely crowded into a Metropolitan City. In such a place where "the duties of this intricate and laborious, but constitutionally unrewarded office are of enormous weight, and require an exact and unremitting attention, gentlemen of knowledge and character are seldom induced to undergo the burden of them. Nor can it reasonably be expected," adds this typical eighteenth-century philosopher, "that persons of any description should forego their own private concerns, and without the smallest hope of a return, sacrifice their whole lives to the service of an interested public." In the Metropolis, unlike a rural county, there was no special class of landowners resident on their properties, whose rents, sporting amenities, comfort, and popularity were instantly and plainly injured by maladministration of local affairs. The duties of a Justice in the Metropolis being not only onerous, but also specially disagreeable in their character, and unrewarded by public esteem, it was almost inevitable that the Commission of the Peace should be, as we have seen, overrun with persons who made a profit out of it. As the character of the putrefaction changed, there was a corresponding change in the particular kind of parasite engendered. For a century after 1689 the most obvious and readiest source of profit lay in the fees to be

---

[1] *Observations on the Police or Civil Government of Westminster, with a Proposal for Reform*, by Edward Sayer, 1784, p. 17. It does not appear to have been publicly known that the Chairman of the Middlesex and Westminster Sessions received £750 a year from the Treasury in the secret manner that we have already described.

exacted for the judicial business transacted by the individual
magistrate. This produced the Trading Justice. After 1792,
when these fees were suppressed, contemporaneously with a
great increase in the expenditure on county services and a
rapid expansion of the licensing business, we have the development, instead of the ignoble petty extortions of the Trading
Justice, of a larger, costlier, and more insiduous type of
corruption, in the manipulation by the Mainwarings of the
county funds, in the dishonest jobbery of offices and contracts
by the little gang who ran the "county machine," and in the
lucrative trafficking in public-house licences by the Mercerons
who filled the benches at Brewster Sessions. The extra-legal
developments of county government fostered the spread of
corruption. The virtual adoption of the principle of co-
option led, as we have pointed out in the analogous case of the
Close Vestries, to an ever-growing homogeneity among the
magistracy.[1] Those Justices who were offended at the malpractices of their colleagues ceased to attend the Sessions,
whilst those who found their profit in them were perpetually
recommending new accomplices and dependants for appointment to the Commission. The same influences spread down-
wards throughout the staff. It is needless to point out how
the gradual transference of county business from the "Open
Court," with the co-operation of the Juries, to the secret
deliberations of the committee room at Hicks' Hall or the
tavern banquets of Brewster Sessions, facilitated every mal-
practice. Finally, we may observe that every increase in the
legislative or regulative authority of the Justices, under such
system and in such hands, merely gave new opportunities for
the sale of exceptions or immunities.

So complete and persistent a breakdown of the Commission
of the Peace, in so important an area as the Metropolis, had,
already in the middle of the eighteenth century, produced a
reaction in the mind of the Government. We need not repeat
our description of the gradual evolution of the "Court Justice"
into a secretly salaried official magistrate, sitting at the public
office at Bow Street, and taking his orders from the Secretary

---

[1] In Middlesex, in 1811, it was definitely said that "no person could be
appointed unless he was recommended by the other magistrates" (Report of
House of Commons Committee on the State of the Police of the Metropolis,
1816, p. 151).

of State.[1]   Under the able administration of Sir John Fielding, the "Bow Street Office," unknown to the constitution, gradually developed into a central bureau of information as to crime and criminals all over the country, publishing an early form of police gazette.[2]   In vain did Fielding, from 1768 onwards, urge the establishment of similar "public offices" in other parts of the Metropolis, served by salaried magistrates.[3] At last the calamitous Lord George Gordon riots of 1780 completed the demonstration—to use the words of Lord Shelburne—that "the police of Westminster was an imperfect, inadequate, and wretched system . . . a fit object of reformation. . . . It ought to be entirely remodelled, and that immediately."[4]   Such a loose crowd of jarring and contending individuals, as the Middlesex Justices had by this time become, were, it was felt, "the most unfit persons to look [to] for reform and steadiness in matters of police."[5]   It was plainly necessary "that some new authority should be devised to combine, direct, and control" the forces upon which the security of life and property depended.   The urgency of this need put out of sight for a time the need for reform of the arrangements for licensing public-houses and administering county business. At first the Government merely issued "Special Service money"—paying, as we have seen, a secret salary to the Chairman of the Middlesex Bench; and we may add dispensing large sums through the senior magistrate at Bow Street, Sampson, afterwards Sir Sampson, Wright, "to defray the expenses of a plan for preventing robberies, detecting offenders, and preserving peace and good order in the Metropolis."[6]   There was, indeed,

---

[1] See Chapter II. "The Rulers of the County."

[2] *The London Packet and Hue and Cry*, issued three times a week, and distributed to Mayors of Corporations and many acting Justices.

[3] *Extracts from Such of the Penal Laws*, etc., by Sir John Fielding, 1768, p. 5. Grenville, like all the other Prime Ministers of the time, "grudged spending money on the police of London" (*Political History of England*, by Rev. W. Hunt, 1905, p. 54).

[4] Lord Shelburne (afterwards Marquis of Lansdowne) in House of Lords, see *Morning Chronicle*, 5th June 1780.

[5] *Defence of the Police Bill*, by an Inhabitant of Westminster, 1786, p. 13. Lists among the Home Office papers in the Public Record Office show there to have been in 1783 about 900 persons in the Commission of the Peace for Middlesex, of whom, however, only 170 had qualified (Domestic State Papers).

[6] MS. Special Service Book, No. 1, among the Treasury archives in the Public Record Office.   Other special payments were occasionally made to Justices for exceptional work, as, for instance, in 1758, to three Middlesex magistrates

no sort of agreement as to the direction that the police reform should take. The Government were "told by one that the Justices can do all that is necessary to be done; by another, that the Vagrant Act is perfectly sufficient; by another, that caution in licensing ale-houses is all that is wanted; by another, take away the fees of Justices. One, exclaiming against pardons, advises to hang all thieves; another to hang all the Trading Justices; one to leave all justice business to gentlemen of independent fortunes; another, to professional persons who should have liberal salaries. No, says another, they are hirelings and cannot serve so well as those who act without salaries."[1] The Government first added thirty-five bankers and other wealthy citizens to the Commission. These are said to have done practically no duty.[2] The Treasury also secretly paid for "the hiring and employing a number of armed men to patrol the several roads leading into the centre of London and Westminster."[3] In 1785 a bill was introduced into Parliament by the Solicitor-General for the establishment of a Board of Police Commissioners for the Metropolis, to be paid substantial salaries, appointed by and responsible to the National Government, charged only with the executive or police work of the Justices, and controlling a Metropolitan paid police force; together with the provision of nine public offices, at each of which salaried Justices were to be constantly in attendance, for the judicial business of examining, committing or discharging defendants, and at which alone the charging of fees was to be permitted. The Justices within the Metropolitan area were, in fact, to be "restrained from acting

who had been exceptionally active in suppressing cattle plague (MS. Acts of Privy Council, 20th April 1758); and £700 to Rev. J. Becher of Southwell, Nottinghamshire, for his exertions in suppressing machine breaking (Home Office Domestic Entry Book, 11th June 1814, vol. xlix. in Public Record Office).

[1] Was this last objection urged by Jeremy Bentham? He was then an acting Justice for Middlesex, and he did subsequently express, not only an objection to stipendiary magistrates, but also a universal preference for unpaid public service, where it could be got, over paid service. "Never will I cease to remember that all pay given to him who would serve equally well without pay is given in waste." His naïve, not to say simple, argument was that the best guarantee of efficiency was desire to do the work, and that to give office to the person who would do it for the least remuneration (or even pay most to have it) would be to secure that it would be held by him who "desired" it most.

[2] See Home Office Domestic State Papers in Public Record Office, 1783; *Considerations on the Authority of the Magistrate commonly called the Police*, by Joseph Cawthorne, 1785, p. 21.

[3] MS. Special Service Book, No. 1, 1782, in Public Record Office.

anywhere but at a public office," and at the public office the salaried Justice "was to account to the Commissioners for all fees."[1] This proposal met with vehement opposition from the Middlesex and Surrey Courts of Quarter Sessions, as well as from the authorities of the City of London. The Lord Mayor and Aldermen protested loudly against the unconstitutional character of the change proposed. The Surrey Justices boldly resolved " that the present laws are sufficient for all the purposes of protection and security to the public." The Middlesex Justices were even more concerned. Defective as was their authority, independent men in the Commission besought the Government to consider before they passed a bill which, it was urged, would " annihilate it altogether." It was said that if the Government made stipendiary Justices as the bill proposes, the few remaining " respectable Justices who continue to act properly will immediately withdraw themselves from an office which they think cannot be executed with effect by hirelings."[2] When the bill was brought before Quarter Sessions at Hicks' Hall, " every one," we are told, " viewed it with an eye as much to his present situation as to his future prospects."[3] The Court eventually combined in a protest that any such Commission as the Government proposed, " invested with powers and authorities heretofore unknown in this country, is inexpedient and totally unnecessary ; that the creating a jurisdiction with the powers thereby given will be a dangerous innovation and encroachments on the rights and security of the people; and will annihilate the ancient and constitutional office of a Justice of the Peace within the intended district of the Metropolis."[4] The Middlesex Justices, under the politic guidance of Mainwaring, who had, as we now know, his own reasons for finding some way of serving the Government, did not stop at mere protest, but also put forward an alternative plan of reform. They suggested that the suppression of the business of the Trading Justices might be accomplished simply by

---

[1] *Defence of the Police Bill*, 1786, p. 15 ; *Morning Chronicle*, 24th June 1785 ; *London Chronicle*, 30th June 1785. The Bill—a remarkable measure, in many ways anticipating the reforms of a whole century—will be found in the British Museum, 816, l. 5 (43).

[2] Thomas Bishop, of Hayes, Middlesex, to Home Secretary, 4th April 1785 (Home Office Domestic State Papers in Public Record Office).

[3] *Defence of the Police Bill*, 1786, p. 17.

[4] MS. Minutes, Quarter Sessions, Middlesex, 6th July, 1785.

the institution of public police offices in the different districts of the Metropolis, as the Government proposed; the appointment to each office of a certain number of the existing Justices to act in rotation; the payment to such selected magistrates of definite salaries; and, instead of restraining the other Justices from acting elsewhere than at the public offices, the mere prohibition of the taking of fees within the Metropolitan area elsewhere than at those offices.[1] The Government plan of 1785 was meanwhile eagerly adopted for Dublin by the Irish Parliament in April 1786 — paid Police Commissioners, united constabulary force, public offices and all. But, as regards London, the Middlesex and Surrey Justices, together with the Court of Aldermen of the City of London, persisted in their opposition, and all reform had for the time to be laid aside. Seven years later, when Mainwaring was in Parliament as member for Middlesex, the emasculated plan to which he had got the Middlesex Justices to consent, was at last adopted. Nothing was done in the way of establishing a united force of metropolitan police under separate Police Commissioners. But by the Act of 1792—which was passed in the teeth of strenuous opposition of the Justices [2]—the Government was authorised to establish seven public offices, in addition to that existing at Bow Street, at which alone fees could be taken, each having attached to it three salaried Justices, who were to act in conjunction with such other Justices of the county as chose to attend. Salaries of £400 a year each were to be paid by the Government to the Justices who were required to be in attendance, the fees collected at their public offices being handed over to a new Government officer, the Receiver of Police. Instead of a Metropolitan Police Force under a

---

[1] This emasculated plan did not pass without objection. "I beg, Sir," wrote one critic to Mainwaring, "to ask you whether, after the experiment of the last three months [since Mainwaring proposed this plan in an address], you think the present set of Justices are to be left to themselves any longer, much less to be gratified with the accommodation of a new establishment, suited to their own ideas? I mean a number of offices, one in each Division, acting wholly independent of each other. . . . I would ask whether such an establishment would not confirm all the evils of the present lax and unconnected magistracy, whose jealousies, envies, and bickerings about the partial views of their respective offices are already a great cause that the small efforts they do make can never produce much benefit to the public" (*Defence of the Police Bill*, 1786, p. 21).

[2] MS. Home Office Domestic State Papers in Public Record Office, No. 122 of 1791.

central body of Commissioners, the stipendiary magistrates at
each office were to have the magnificent array of six "fit and
able men" at twelve shillings a week, to serve as Constables
under their respective orders.[1]

The twenty-four Justices to whom salaries were thus
paid were intended to devote themselves specially to the
detection and punishment of criminal offences, and their
appointment had therefore not necessarily any effect on
the organisation of the County Business. The suppression
of the business of the Trading Justices had, however, as we
have seen, a subtle result in deflecting the characteristic
corruption of the rank and file of the Middlesex magistracy
into other directions. As the salaried magistrates had the
same powers as the other Justices, and could give their whole
time, it might have been supposed that the bulk of the work
of civil administration would have passed into their hands.
This was not the case. We gather that the Government
added to the Commission a few competent men, drawn, not
from the bar, but from business. For the most part, however, the new appointments were apparently made the subject
of the usual contemporary jobbery, many of them falling to
the most pushing and self-seeking of the existing Justices.[2]
The best of them, notably Patrick Colquhoun, an ex-merchant
of Glasgow, the able and public-spirited author of the famous

---

[1] 32 George III. c. 53, continuing in force only for three years. It was
continued for another five years (36 George III. c. 75); re-enacted in 1802 by
42 George III. c. 76; and again in 1807 and 1812.

For many years some of the magistrates were allowed to keep the fees in
addition to their salaries, and it was not until well into the nineteenth century
that they were all credited to the revenue (see, for instance, Home Office State
Papers, Domestic, No. 156, 1801).

[2] Many petitions and requests for appointment exist in the Home Office
Domestic State Papers in Public Record Office. Many of the Justices chosen
were not the best even of their class. Nicholas Bond, for instance, appointed
to the Bow Street office in 1785, "had been a journeyman carpenter, and was
an illiterate, ignorant man." Sir Richard Birnie, an "unscrupulous and
dissolute" Scotchman, "was a journeyman and afterwards a master saddler"
(Place MSS. in Add. MSS. 27,827, p. 167; also "B." in *Times*, 10th January
1828). "Kinnaird, I remember, kept a little chemist's shop in Holborn. Sir
Daniel Williams was something of the sort" ("B." in *Times*, 10th January 1828).
Peel, in 1825, said that among the first batch were three clergymen, one major,
two starch dealers, one Glasgow trader (Colquhoun), and three barristers
(*Observations on Mr. Secretary Peel's House of Commons Speech . . . introducing
his Police Magistrate's Salary-Raising Bill, etc.*, by Jeremy Bentham, 1825,
p. 21).

Treatise on the Police of the Metropolis, and Henry Fielding, the nephew of the great novelist, finding unpleasant the moral atmosphere of Brewster Sessions, restricted themselves to police court work.[1] Others, however, like Sir Daniel Williams and Sir Richard Birnie, continued in close alliance with the Mainwaring and Merceron clique, taking leading parts in the Divisional and Quarter Sessions, and even in the Petty Sessions held at the offices of the Westminster Close Vestries for the transaction of the parish business about Overseers, assessments, and rates,[2] participating, we fear, in all the profits, jobs, and patronage that were to be had. Thus, it can scarcely be said that the transformation of twenty-four of the Justices of Middlesex and Surrey into salaried police magistrates effected much improvement in the reputation of the Metropolitan Benches, or in the honesty and efficiency of county government. Gradually, however, in the course of the next thirty years, successive Secretaries of State raised the status of the office by increasing the salary to £800 a year, and filling vacancies by the selection of barristers wholly un-connected with the unpaid magistracy. This new type of "blameless barrister" excited the dislike of the unpaid Justices. It is interesting to find the younger Mainwaring in 1821, a few months before his discreditable career was brought to an end, unctuously expounding the superiority of the "Great Unpaid"; "a national, independent, gratuitous magistracy, giving their time, their learning, and their efforts to the preservation of the peace and good order of society, and the due administration of the laws throughout the country, reconciles all even to their severest exercise, inasmuch as it proves that general good, and no sinister motive or interest, can actuate those who so engage in the public service. . . . Can such a feeling prevail with respect to a stipendiary body? . . . Will not the feeling be . . . that the members of such a body are the servants of the Government, instead of the independent guardians of the public interest?" For these

---

[1] This retiring tendency was strengthened by the fact that the other Justices resented the participation of the salaried magistrates in the "County Business"; see the protest of thirty-three Surrey Justices in Home Office State Papers, Domestic, No. 232, 11th January 1812.

[2] See *Times*, 27th March 1828, for the conduct of Sir Richard Birnie, at St. Paul, Covent Garden; and *ibid.* 18th February, in connection with St. Martin's.

reasons, this bankrupt peculator supplicates, from the King, "the gracious boon of an independent magistracy for the Metropolis."[1] But public opinion, and Robert Peel as Home Secretary, had had enough of the amateur Justices for Middlesex police business. The policy of raising the status and increasing the independence of the stipendiaries was continued, whilst the parochial constabulary, which had hitherto remained under the direction of the unpaid Justices, was presently superseded by Peel's new police, governed by separate Commissioners, directly under the Home Secretary. We accordingly leave the stipendiaries in 1835, now grown to thirty, all barristers, as "a set of quiet, gentlemanlike persons,"[2] perhaps the "failures" of their profession; concentrating their attention on trying the ordinary cases of a London police court; entirely divorced from County Business, and letting slip even their magisterial control of the Poor Law, for which they had neither desire nor aptitude.[3]

(b) *The Lack of Justices*

We have found among the County Justices, outside Middlesex and the Metropolitan divisions of Surrey, no trace

---

[1] *Observations on the Police of the Metropolis*, by G. B. Mainwaring, 1821, pp. 128, 129, 133.

[2] Letter from "B." in the *Times*, 10th January 1828.

[3] The stipendiary magistrates at the public office at Worship Street, Finsbury, are described, in 1833, as utterly unable to cope with the crowd of complaining paupers (First Report of Poor Law Inquiry Commissioners, 1834, Appendix A, Chadwick's Report, pp. 96, 136, etc.). For the institution and working of the public police offices and stipendiary magistrates in the Metropolis, see the Home Office Domestic State Papers in the Public Record Office, especially 1780-1812, the MS. Privy Council Register for their appointments and salaries, the Police Bill of 1785, the Dublin Police Act of 1786, and the Public Offices Act of 1792; *Considerations on the Authority of the Magistrate commonly called the Police*, by Joseph Cawthorne, 1785; *Defence of the Police Bill*, by an Inhabitant of Westminster, 1786; *Modern London*, 1804, ch. iii. p. 149; Reports of House of Commons Committees on the State of the Police of the Metropolis, 1816-1817; and on Mendicity, 1815; *Observations on the Vagrant Act*, etc., by John Adolphus, 1824, pp. 73-78; *Observations on Mr. Secretary Peel's House of Commons Speech . . . introducing his Police Magistrate's Salary-Raising Bill*, etc., by Jeremy Bentham, 1825; *Chronicles of Bow Street Police Office*, by P. Fitzgerald, 1888; *Police*, by C. T. Clarkson and J. H. Richardson, 1889; *History of Police*, by Captain Melville Lee, 1902. A stipendiary magistrate for Manchester was established by 53 George III. c. 72 (1813); see House of Commons Journals, April to June 1813, vol. lxviii.; Home Office Domestic State Papers, No. 247, 1813. The Home Secretary refused to support Brighton in a similar proposal (Home Office Domestic Entry Book, 15th December 1814, vol. xlix. in Public Record Office); and no more were created.

of anything even approaching the corruption and disorganisation that prevailed in the Metropolitan area. The faults of which the Justices throughout the rest of England and Wales were, between 1815 and 1835, freely accused, are, as we shall presently see, in themselves testimony to the freedom of the Rulers of the County from personal corruption, and evidence of a quite remarkable disregard among them of their direct pecuniary advantage. In another way, however, the breakdown of the magisterial system was, in many parts of the country, as patent as in Middlesex. Putting on one side for the moment the sharp differences of opinion that arose as to the policy of the Justices in such matters as the licensing of ale-houses, the relief of the poor, and the administration of the prisons and county expenditure, there were whole districts in which the grievance most severely felt was the scarcity of magistrates. Already in the middle of the eighteenth century Smollett depicts for us in *Roderick Random* the inconvenience of having to go miles to find a Justice of the Peace. We read in his lively pages of the capture of a highwayman by two servants; their "carrying him in triumph, amidst the acclamations of the country people, to a Justice of the Peace in a neighbouring village"; and their stopping at an inn to drink whilst their prisoner is placed "within a circle of peasants armed with pitchforks." When they arrived at the Justice's house, they found him away on a visit, with the result that the highwayman naturally escaped during the night.[1]

In many parts of the new England of mining and manufacturing industries which had grown up between 1760 and 1815, it became often impossible to find resident gentlemen who were legally and socially qualified to fill the office of a Justice of the Peace.[2] The Lord-Lieutenants of other

---

[1] *Roderick Random*, by T. Smollett, 1750, p. 57.

[2] By 1832 the number of county magistrates who had taken out their "Dedimus potestatem" had risen to 5131, of whom about a fourth were clergymen. But the bulk of the work was done by those who attended with any regularity the Divisional Sessions in the 550 districts—estimated by Rickman at an average of four each, or no more than 2200 in all (*Administration of the Poor Laws*, 1832; an anonymous and privately printed pamphlet by John Rickman). "A List of all His Majesty's Justices of the Peace . . . who appear to have taken out their Dedimus," dated 1819, gives about 2500 names (Home Office Magistrates' Book in Public Record Office), but this seems to omit some counties.

counties had steadfastly refused to follow the example of those responsible for filling the Commissions for Middlesex and Surrey with men whose circumstances laid them open to small pecuniary corruption. Nor would the public opinion of the County Benches permit the appointment, even if the Lord-Lieutenants had been willing, of the newly enriched manufacturers and traders of the neighbourhood.[1] The Rulers of the County preferred to leave districts of several hundred square miles without a single resident magistrate, and dependent, not only for judicial but also for administrative orders, on magistrates residing twenty miles away. The result was often an intolerable tax on such clergymen or country gentlemen as had to discharge the duties for half a county.[2] Such a state of things became increasingly serious as the once desolate regions were filled up by turbulent populations of potters, nailers, colliers, stockingers, weavers, or puddlers. In some such districts, notably in several of the unincorporated towns or suburbs, there developed, as we have described, an extra-legal Parish Democracy, dependent for its orderly administration on the ability and devotion of a few public-spirited citizens. In other cases, the local affairs were sometimes utterly neglected, sometimes abandoned to the uncontrolled discretion of the unpaid parish officers for the time being, under which—as at Manchester between 1790 and 1805—a system of wholesale peculation and squalid corruption might grow up.[3] When one of the frequent out-

---

[1] In spite of a great lack of magistrates in the mining districts of Monmouthshire, in 1827, the Lord-Lieutenant refused to recommend for the Commission of the Peace the younger son of an ironmaster, who had become a landed proprietor. He would have been willing to recommend the heir apparent, but not a younger son (Duke of Beaufort to the Lord Chancellor, 16th November 1827 ; in MS. Home Office archives in Public Record Office).

[2] The scarcity of Justices was specially felt in Wales. "Machynlleth," says the *Gentleman's Magazine* for September 1799, p. 756, "is a decent town . . . the want of a Justice is rather lamented." A Justice for the County of Anglesey complains in feeling terms to the Home Secretary in 1825 that, being the nearest magistrate, though eight miles from Holyhead, his house was daily besieged by applicants for vagrant passes, whom he dared not dismiss without food, on their sixteen miles' unnecessary walk. "No country gentleman or clergyman," he wrote, "can be expected to submit to the incessant calls upon his time and his feelings which was occasioned by the hordes of wretched objects who daily assailed my house during the last winter" (Home Office Magistrates' Book, and Domestic Entry Book, vol. lix. in Public Record Office).

[3] Such corruption might, of course, find its opportunities not only in the parish business, but also in that for which the Justices were themselves directly responsible. Thus, at Birmingham in 1818 it was complained that the Chief

breaks of riot or disorder occurred, there was no authority at hand to quell it at an early stage. At Birmingham, for instance, a serious tumult occurred in 1792, arising from an insignificant beginning, entirely owing to the absence of any Justice. "The situation of the inhabitants," we are told, "is really alarming . . . for although the two [neighbouring county] magistrates are always willing to afford the town every assistance in their power, yet they both reside some miles from Birmingham, and therefore could not appear at the head of the military before it would be too late." In the riots that had just taken place, when one house was, after a day's disorder, completely gutted, all that the Constables could do was to take "a post-chaise to fetch the magistrates to town. About seven in the evening the magistrates arrived. . . . At nine at night" they at last summoned up courage to deal with the mob, "read the Riot Act, persuaded them to disperse, and then returned to the hotel." [1]   What made the situation the more serious was that the absence of resident gentry tended to occur exactly in those places most prone to social disorder—in the growing villages of the Midlands, already beginning to be crowded with a turbulent population of coal-miners or potters, stockingers or weavers, and in the miles of unregulated hovels and mean streets rising up beyond the magistracies of the chartered municipalities.[2]   It was, as we have seen in our

Constable, who had to supervise and report on the publicans, and who directed the distribution among them of soldiers to be billeted, had set up in business as a maltster and hop-merchant. "The publicans at Birmingham are their own brewers . . . and purchase their malt and hops . . . The Patronage of the ale-house licences gives" the Chief Constable "the entire control of the publicans, amounting to upwards of 500, and a business which was open to all tradesmen is now confined to the monopoly of a public officer of the town. The evil tendency of such a system has been severely felt, and a memorial presented to the magistrates, without any desired effect. It is impossible for a maltster or hop-merchant to obtain orders from the publicans unless this influence is abolished" (*Birmingham Argus*, 31st October 1818).

[1] *Public Advertiser*, 23rd and 25th May 1792.

[2] A gentleman of Halifax (Yorkshire) writes to the Home Office in 1795 to point out that in all that great parish, as extensive in area as the whole county of Rutland, and containing 70,000 inhabitants, there was absolutely no resident acting magistrate. There were six residents in the Commission, including the writer, but none of them had taken out their Dedimus, nor would do so, for fear of being overwhelmed with business (Home Office Domestic State Papers in Public Record Office, No. 133A of 1795). Of Brighton in 1811, already a fashionable watering-place, we learn that "the nearest Justice of the Peace lives at Lewes, nine miles off" (*Letters to "Ivy," from the first Earl of Dudley*, by S. H. Romilly, 1905, p. 147, December 1811). This was still the case in 1814 (Home Office Domestic Entry Book, 10th May 1814, vol. xlix.).

chapters on Parish Government, the absence of any resident Justices in such parishes as these that led to the tyranny of the uncontrolled parish officers on the one hand, and, under favourable circumstances, to the development of an extra-legal constitution of parish autonomy on the other.

Under these circumstances the demand of such honest men as concerned themselves with local affairs was for Stipendiary Magistrates to fill the gap left by the practical breakdown of the system which had failed to supply their neighbourhood with the authority necessary alike for local government and for the administration of justice. In the rapidly-growing coal and iron district of Merthyr Tydvil in Glamorganshire, for instance, there were, in 1827, over 30,000 people dependent for justice either on the proprietor of the largest ironworks, who was frequently ill, and whose decisions, in what were largely his own concerns, were felt to be invidious, or else on a country gentleman six miles away, who was often absent, and who had so much magisterial business thrust upon him that he threatened to leave the county. The Incumbent, Churchwardens, Overseers, and Chief Constable inform Lord Melbourne that the parish business is "totally neglected," and that "a resident stipendiary magistrate" is "absolutely necessary."[1] At Sheerness in 1807, pervaded by sailors and crowded with sailors' alehouses, there was no magistrate within reach.[2] In Northumberland, the Grand Jury was driven formally to request the appointment of a resident stipendiary magistrate for the East Division of the Castle Ward, in which there were "twenty-two townships, containing a population of 40,000 souls . . . without the advantage of a single resident magistrate within reasonable distance."[3] At Chipping Sodbury, in Gloucestershire, a town of 1300 inhabitants, there was, in 1833, no magistrate within six miles. At Altringham, in Cheshire, in a neighbourhood where turbulent and disorderly canal-boatmen, miners, and factory operatives were to be found, the

---

[1] Joint letter to Lord Melbourne, 1827 ; in Home Office Magistrates' Book in Public Record Office.

[2] Home Office Domestic State Papers in Public Record Office, No. 201, 1807 ; ditto, Domestic Entry Book, 31st December 1811, vol. xliv.

[3] Duke of Northumberland to Lord Melbourne, 14th August 1833, in MS. Home Office Papers in Public Record Office.

nearest magistrate lived six miles away.[1] Similar petitions
poured in upon the Home Secretary from many of the
industrial districts. The upgrowth of a mining or manufacturing population round great industrial works was, in fact,
as Peel himself declared in 1828, " not only the means of
increasing crime, but also of diminishing the number of
magistrates, as such works . . . contributed to drive away
the country gentlemen." [2]

(c) *The Restriction of Public-Houses*

The breakdown of the Metropolitan Benches in integrity,
and the frequent absence, in mining or manufacturing districts, of any Bench whatever, were, between 1815 and
1835, fundamental and apparently permanent defects in the
organisation of county government. Both facts pointed to
the same conclusion. When either the work to be done was
onerous and disagreeable, or the place in which it had to be
done was lacking in amenity, it was impossible to rely on
obtaining a sufficient number of residents of leisure, competence, and public spirit to render so large an amount of
unpaid service to the county as had become necessary. But
in the popular clamour against county government that raged
between 1815 and 1835, this real and permanent defect in
the system was largely overlooked. What was fastened on by
all sorts of reformers, as the characteristic result of the rule of
the Justice of the Peace, was not the local breakdown of the
system, grave as were its consequences, but the particular social
policy pursued by the Justices in licensing, poor relief, prison
administration, and county expenditure, and enforced in certain
departments of their judicial work.

Perhaps the largest place is filled among the Radical

[1] First Report of Municipal Corporation Commissioners, 1835, Appendix,
vol. i. p. 37 ; vol. iv. p. 2576. Even in such a county as Kent, the dearth of
magistrates was felt. "In the whole Union" [Penshurst, Kent], writes an
assistant Poor Law Commissioner in 1835, "there is only one magistrate, and
as he is also the—and I may say the only—squire he is worshipped like a god,
except that the labouring classes have got into the habit of making him bend
the knee, instead of doing so themselves. He is a great, big, gentlemanly man,
but a being so irresolute I never met with ; and, look which way he will, he
sees nothing but what he calls difficulties " (17th June 1835, a letter from Sir
Francis Head to the Poor Law Commissioners ; unpublished).

[2] Hansard, 1828, vol. xviii. pp. 893-894.

criticisms of the unpaid magistracy between 1815 and 1835, by the denunciation of their licensing policy.[1] The modern student finds it difficult to understand the furious resentment that this policy excited. The legislation of 250 years had placed upon the Justices the responsibility for determining the number of persons to be licensed for the sale of intoxicating liquors, and the conditions under which the sale should be allowed. Down to 1787, as we gather, no uniform or consistent policy had been adhered to, each little knot of local magistrates taking its own line, usually that of granting licences freely to all applicants, and abandoning any effective control over the conditions of supply. The result was an enormous multiplication of ale-houses and dram-shops, often of the worst character. In 1787, as we have described, at the instigation of a Royal Proclamation which had been obtained by Wilberforce, the Courts of Quarter Sessions all over the country sought, in their character of provincial Parliaments, to discover some remedy for the drunkenness and disorder that were rampant. We find these county legislatures, with remarkable unanimity, everywhere adopting a definite and comprehensive licensing policy. The number of public-houses was to be strictly limited to the actual needs of each district. The local authorities (such as the Vestry, the Incumbent, and the parish officers) were to advise as to these needs. The public-houses thereupon licensed were to be regulated by a series of rules as to hours of closing, games, etc., and the holders of the licences were to be themselves held responsible for permitting drunkenness or disorderly behaviour among their customers. Unnecessary public-houses were to be peremptorily suppressed, whilst publicans who failed to observe the conditions imposed upon them were to have their licences transferred to other holders.[2] Up and down England —outside the Metropolis—these lines of policy appear to

---

[1] We shall deal more fully with this subject in our chapter on the Regulation of the Supply of Intoxicating Drinks, as one of the functions of Local Government. In the meantime, see our *History of Liquor Licensing in England*, 1903.

[2] This licensing policy was, it must be said, only part of the general endeavour to put down drunkenness, debauchery, and idleness among the lower orders, by the suppression of their coarse and disorderly amusements. The widespread suppression of pleasure fairs (at which, it must be owned, every kind of abomination took place) was another example of the Justices' vicarious Puritanism, calculated to arouse great popular discontent.

have been adhered to by the Justices between 1787 and 1815 with remarkable consistency, with results on the conduct and character of the people which, as we think, every student of the period would nowadays declare to be almost wholly good. There were, however, certain economic incidents for which the Justices were not responsible. The law did not permit them to make a charge for the licences; and there was, of course, even if this had been thought of, no public authority with power to undertake the sale of alcoholic drinks as a public service. It was therefore inevitable that any limitation of the number of public-houses to the proved needs of the locality should, with a traffic so peculiarly profitable, create, for those who were privileged to engage in it, a great monopoly value. No less inevitable was it that, with the rapid development of the industries of brewing and distilling, these great capitalist enterprises should obtain control over the publicans and their premises, and establish what is known as the " tied-house system."

It was these economic manifestations, together with the outcry of publicans deprived of their licences for some breach of the Justices' regulations, or merely as being unnecessary, that aroused the greatest outcry against the Justices. To the Whigs, and still more to the rising school of Philosophic Radicals, any interference with the freedom of the individual to invest his capital or to employ his leisure in any way that he thought fit was an offence in itself. They vehemently resented the fact that the working-man might be deprived of access to beer, the honest publican of his means of livelihood,[1] and the enterprising brewer of his property, by the fiat of a bench of squires and parsons acting on the recommendation of little parish oligarchies. Even where licences were not entirely refused, the restrictive policy of the Justices, by the mere fact that it led to great monopoly values, seemed inevitably to make the consumer pay " an extravagant price " for his beer.[2] Nor were the Tory politicians themselves at all

---

[1] Thus in 1828 Brougham brought specially before the House of Commons the hard case of a publican at Halifax, whom five Justices had deprived of his licence, without assigning any cause. The petition was ordered to lie on the table (Hansard, 7th March 1828, N.S. vol. xviii. p. 1059).

[2] See the whole statement of C. Barclay, before the House of Commons Committee on the Sale of Beer, 1830. Such a monopoly value " of course . . .

enamoured of the new-found Puritanism of the Rulers of the
County. If the lower orders, argued Windham, were restricted
in their pleasures, they would be all the more apt to be
seditious. It was, moreover, plain that any real restriction
of the consumption of beer would injuriously affect, not only
the revenue of the Government, but also the demand for
barley and hops, upon which the rents of so many landowners
depended. Thus, up and down the country, as well as in the
House of Commons itself, there gradually arose, in the decades
that followed the peace of 1815, an overwhelming reaction
against the licensing policy pursued by the Justices. It was
argued that "when the legislature empowered magistrates to
license publicans they could not intend that squires or rectors
or aldermen should enrich some men and ruin others, by controlling and curtailing the supplies and enjoyments of the
people. Yet magistrates have exercised this power during
the last fifty or sixty years with such rigorous industry as
to lessen the number of public-houses in many places, notwithstanding the great increase of population."[1] It was widely
resented that "what the poor shall drink—how they shall
drink it—in pint cups or quart mugs—hot or cold—in the
morning or in the evening; whether the 'Three Pidgeons'
shall be shut up and the 'Shoulder of Mutton' be opened;
whether the 'Black Horse' shall continue to swing in the air,
or the 'White Horse' with animated crest and tail no longer
portend spirits within," should "depend upon little clumps of
squires and parsons gathered together" at the September
Brewster Sessions.[2] The dominant idea became, to use Sydney
Smith's phrase of 1826, that of "Free Trade in ale and ale-
houses."[3] If every citizen were permitted to sell beer as
freely as groceries, in any place, at any hour, under any
conditions, the result, it was supposed, would be a harmonious

raised the price of everything that was sold" (Report of House of Commons
Committee on the Sale of Beer, 1833, p. 22); it must "create a necessity of
selling at such a price as may secure a trade interest on money so advanced"
by the purchaser of a public-house (Report of House of Commons Committee on
Public Breweries, 1818).

[1] *Hints on Licensing Publicans*, 1830, p. 11.
[2] *Edinburgh Review*, September 1826.
[3] Sydney Smith to Edward Davenport, 26th December 1826 (*Memoir of
Sydney Smith*, by Lady Holland, vol. ii. p. 271); see also the astonishing
article (by him; *ibid.* p. 266) in *Edinburgh Review*, September 1826, demanding complete freedom of the liquor traffic.

adjustment of supply and demand, fulfilling all requirements and satisfying all needs.[1]

(d) *The Justices' Poor Law*

From the standpoint of modern statesmanship the feeling that the Rulers of the County were blameworthy for their perpetual interference in the administration of the Poor Law is more comprehensible than the agitation against their licensing work. We have already described the power which any Justice of the Peace possessed, of ordering the Overseer to give to any pauper whatever relief the magistrate might think reasonable. With the ordinary kind-hearted country gentleman, such a power of overruling the decision of the Overseer could not fail to be subversive of discipline and order. Whenever the Overseer refused to give the customary dole, or gave less than the applicant considered his due, his decision was at the mercy of any neighbouring magistrate. " If," said an able observer in 1762, " the pauper is a meek and modest person, this is submitted to, and accepted, for such trouble not the magistrates, whereas at the same time a bold and noisy man who can get the ear of a Justice of the Peace, though he may not want help so much as the other, shall obtain more." [2] With the Acts of 1782 and 1795-1796,[3] enlarging the powers of Justices to order outdoor relief, their well-intentioned interference exercised, in many parts of the country, a paralysing influence on any attempt to improve the Poor Law administration. " The authority exercised by magistrates in ordering relief to the poor," reported a zealous clergyman in 1825, " has had effects upon the whole system

---

[1] "The trade in beer should be as open as the trades of the butchers and bakers," said one witness in 1833 (Report of House of Commons Committee on the Sale of Beer, 1833, pp. 57-58). This was, in fact, the current solution of the Whigs and Radicals. "Does anything pass at such licensing meetings but the eternally repeated phrase that public-houses must not be increased ? . . . There is a great deal of nonsense . . . about the supply of public-houses exceeding the demand. That it should do so for any length of time is absolutely impossible. . . . If the trade in public-houses were free, there would be precisely the number wanted, for no man would sell liquor to his ruin. . . . There is no end to this mischievous meddling with the natural arrangements of society " (Article by Sydney Smith in *Edinburgh Review*, September 1826).

[2] *The Christian's Magazine*, 1763, p. 26 (letter from Rev. Richard Canning of Ipswich).

[3] 22 George III. c. 33 (Gilbert's Act, 1782) ; 35 George III. c. 101 (1795); 36 George III. c. 23 (1796).

which were never intended, and could not have been contemplated . . . their jurisdiction originally extended only to
the prevention of abuses on the part of parish officers, but it
has subsequently been extended to the right of interfering
with every pauper's pension. . . . Magistrates when applied
to by a pauper for an increased allowance, whether at their own
homes, by which their domestic comforts or private affairs may
be disagreeably interrupted, or at the Bench, where they are
hurried by a multiplicity of business, are too apt to recommend
a compliance or a compromise with the applicants' wishes." [1]
It was to this incessant interference by the Justices that
the reformers attributed most of the maladministration. " A
poor man," wrote Sydney Smith, " now comes to a magistrate
any day in the week, and any hour in any day, to complain
of the Overseers." [2] When, after 1819, a Select Vestry had
been elected under Sturges Bourne's Act, the interference of
the Justices was still more resented, as an encroachment on
the authority of the popularly elected body. It was made a
special subject of complaint in a Durham parish that " the
magistrates still arrogate to themselves . . . the power of
ordering what relief they choose to paupers, and quite against
the opinion and decision of the Select Vestry." [3]

---

[1] *A Letter to the Rt. Hon. George Canning on the Principles and the Administration of the English Poor Law*, by a Select Vestryman of the Parish of
Putney [Rev. W. Carmalt], 1825, p. 63. The Justices interfered much less
where any body of "Guardians" or "Directors of the Poor" had been incorporated under Local Act ; and this was used as an argument in 1825 against a
reversion to relief by the Overseers. In an "incorporated parish," it was said,
"the pauper makes his complaint to the Overseer, and the Overseer takes it to
the Committee. If the complaint is unreasonable or experimental . : . the
Committee refuses relief, and there is an end of the business. The pauper
grumbles perhaps, but submits, because he knows there is no remedy. Not so
in an unincorporated parish ! The pauper who is refused relief to-day, comes
again to-morrow, frequently with abusive language, not infrequently with threats;
however often repulsed he returns again to the charge, drags the Overseer to half
the Justices in the county ; and at last by importunity and worrying obtains
an allowance that he ill deserves, and which is given rather to purchase quiet
and forbearance than because it is wanted. Whilst you are incorporated the
Directors and Guardians are judges of the measure of relief ; when you are
disincorporated it will be fixed by the Justices. And do you really believe that
these gentlemen are better judges of the real wants of the poor than a committee
of the House, composed of a mixture of gentlemen and men of business ; or do
you suppose that smaller allowances will be made at the Sessions Hall at
Woodbridge than in the committee-room of the House of Industry" (from an
able letter in the *Ipswich Journal*, 22nd January 1825).

[2] Article on the Poor Laws, in *Edinburgh Review*, 1820.

[3] Report of House of Commons Committee on Poor Rate Returns, 1823.

It is difficult for the modern student to share the indignation of the reformers of 1820-1830 at the "arrogation" by the Justices of the Peace of the power complained of. The Elizabethan legislation had expressly laid upon them the obligation of arbitrating between the destitute person requiring relief and parish officers refusing it. The intervention of the individual Justice had been expressly endorsed by the Parliaments of 1691 and 1723.[1] For three-quarters of a century after the latter date this intervention continued to be welcomed and encouraged by nearly every writer on the subject. Right down to the end of the eighteenth century it was relied on as a necessary protection of the poor; and the absence of a resident magistrate was felt not only as a personal loss to them, but also as a calamity to the parish as a whole. "Where the residence of a Justice is at the distance of six or seven miles from the existing grievance," says a correspondent of Arthur Young, "there is but little chance of its being removed; ignorance and want of leisure in the small occupier and pauper, secure the Overseer from any interruption in his peculations, or perversions of those laws which were enacted for the benefit of society, but which, I am confident, without the intervention of the magistrate, become . . . as oppressive as any . . . enacted by . . . despotism."[2] The reader who recalls our description of the oppressions, frauds, and administrative ineptitudes of the uncontrolled parish officers will readily appreciate this view of the Justices' intervention. It may well be that their intervention, though kindly intended, was not always well judged. Even in this respect, however, their conduct seems not to have merited the

---

[1] 3 William and Mary c. 11 (1691); 9 George I. c. 7 (1723).

[2] Rev. W. Butts of Suffolk, in *Annals of Agriculture*, vol. xxii. p. 49, 1794. The poetical exponent of the magistrate's duties put this intervention as a principal part of them.

> But chief thy notice shall one monster claim,
> A monster furnished with a human frame,
> The Parish Officer . . .
> . . . The sly, pilfering, cruel Overseer,
> The shuffling farmer, faithful to no trust,
> Ruthless as rocks, insatiate as the dust.

(*The County Justice*, by John Langhorne, 1774-1777, part ii., a poem written at the suggestion, and with the corrections of Dr. Richard Burn himself; see the life of Langhorne in *Worthies of Westmorland*, by G. Atkinson, 1849, vol. i. pp. 85-118.)

storm of denunciation to which they were subjected. When the Whig Cabinet of 1834 were considering how the Poor Law could be reformed, the exaggerations of the attack on the Justices called forth a protest from Nassau Senior himself. "Was not all the mischief," he was asked, "done by the magistrates acting as a court of appeal?" Mr. Senior replied that this was not so. The evidence against the magistrates could not be accepted. The mischief as a rule came from the Vestry. It was true that, forty years ago, the magistrates had contributed their share to the present evils, but now the magistrates had realised the nature of the crisis and were, with few exceptions, in favour of reform."[1]

But it was not only in their executive capacity that the Justices had incurred the blame of those who realised the evils of the Old Poor Law. In the emergency presented by the famine prices of 1795, the Rulers of the County had, as we have described, made a new departure in procedure, formulating, for the guidance of Overseers, definite scales of income to which the labourers' wages were to be made up out of the Poor Rate. This Allowance System had such calamitous results that it is not easy to be fair to its inventors. The Justices found themselves individually appealed to on all sides by labourers obviously unable to live on their wages. Matters looked so desperate that it became plainly desirable that the magistrates of each county, responsible alike for Poor Law administration and for the preservation of the peace, should deliberate on so grave a social crisis. Instead of deciding each case in a haphazard way, they everywhere consulted among themselves and dealt with the problem in their character as members of what we have termed the Inchoate Provincial Legislatures of the time. The alternative policies open for adoption by these deliberative assemblies were strictly limited by the state of the law and the circumstances of the moment. The Justices might conceivably have decided, at whatever risk of riot or arson, to leave the starving labourers to the mercy of the Overseers and the smaller ratepayers, without giving either counsel or direction. This would, however, only have postponed the difficulty, at the

---

[1] Nassau Senior's MS. Diary ; see *History of the English Poor Law* (vol. iii. of Sir George Nicholl's *History*), by Thomas Mackay, 1899, p. 121.

cost of untold suffering to the poor, and the trouble of
innumerable appeals. It is, we think, to the credit of the
Rulers of the County that the easy-going squires and benevolent clergymen who filled the rural Benches—quickened, it
may be, by the apprehension of such a revolutionary outbreak
as they had lately seen in France—put on one side this
policy of inaction as an impossible abnegation of their duty.
They might conceivably have anticipated the policy of the
New Poor Law of 1834, and advised the Overseers to refuse
all outdoor relief, offering "the House" to all applicants as
a test of destitution, and (as it must be added) providing
accommodation for the large numbers whose inability to
maintain their families was only too apparent. To any
student who has investigated the state of the workhouses of
the period—their incredible foulness and promiscuity, their
insanitation and utter inadequacy of accommodation, and the
demoralising cruelties and tyrannies of the contractors to
whom they were habitually "farmed"—the sudden enforcement of such a policy in the emergency of 1795 will appear
little short of criminal. It does not seem to have occurred,
even as a possibility, to any contemporary. Some Courts of
Quarter Sessions regarded as the proper solution of the
difficulty the compelling of the farmers to pay wages adequate
for the subsistence of such labourers as they chose to employ,
roughly in proportion to the price of the staple food; whilst
arranging that the Overseers should maintain completely from
the Poor Rate, either by finding work or by providing
adequate outdoor relief, such families as the farmers would
not engage on these terms. But the legal power of the
Justices to compel the farmers to pay such a rate of wages
was obscure and doubtful; the influence of Adam Smith
against any new interference with the conditions of employment was powerful; and the general faith of the governing
class in favour of the employers' freedom had become too
strong to admit of any public adoption of the policy of a
Legal Minimum Wage. The action of the Justices in this
direction went therefore no further than "earnestly recommending" the farmers to raise wages; and when this failed,
a policy had still to be found. There seemed to remain only
the obvious expedient of "standardising" the poor relief, by

recognising some minimum standard of subsistence, to which the Overseers should be directed to make up the income of such labourers as fell below it.   This policy, it is only fair to say, commended itself as the only possible one, not only to bucolic squires and humanitarian parsons, but also to the enlightened public opinion of the time—even to such disciples of Adam Smith as William Pitt, Arthur Young, and Malthus himself, who much preferred the Allowance System, with all the drawbacks that they foresaw, to any such authoritative interference with the conditions of employment as would have secured to the labourer the socially expedient Standard of Life.[1] The Justices can hardly be condemned for being no wiser than the most enlightened theorists and administrators of their age.   Where they were, we think, open to criticism, was in continuing the Allowance System after the crisis had passed.   But once " the Scale " had been adopted, there was set up, as we can now see, an automatic pressure against any rise in wages that would have been adequate to the continued high prices of the Napoleonic war-time.   It is only fair to remark that when, after 1815, convinced by observation of the disastrous results of their former policy, one county Bench after another turned against it, and strove to persuade individual Justices and parish officers to give up altogether the calamitous " rate in aid of wages," their new intervention was as much resented and reprobated by the fervent Democrats of the period, as the Allowance System was by the Philosophic Radicals.   Whether the Justices interfered with the parish

---

[1] Even Edwin Chadwick, in 1833, strongly prejudiced against the county magistracy, is brought to the conclusion that, " on a review of the circumstances of the introduction of the Allowance System by the Justices of the preceding generation . . . all that can be fairly alleged against them is that they were not before their age. . . . When reference is made to the speeches of the most distinguished and popular members of the legislature at that period . . . it cannot . . . be justly said that the magistrates were behind their age " (First Report of the Poor Law Inquiry Commission, 1833, Appendix A, Chadwick's Report, p. 168).   The account given by Malthus in 1800 is as follows : " The poor complained to the Justices that their wages would not enable them to supply their families in the single article of bread.   The Justices, very humanely, and I am far from saying improperly, listened to their complaints, inquired what was the smallest sum on which they could support their families at the then price of wheat, and gave an order of relief on the parish accordingly. . . . To say the truth, I hardly see what else could have been done " (*An Investigation into the Cause of the Present High Price of Provisions*, by the Author of the Essay on the Principles of Population, 1800, pp. 9, 11).

officers or let them alone, whether they adopted the newest economic philosophy or acted on the humanitarian principles in which they had been educated, it was, in 1828-1835, equally imputed to them as a crime.

(e) *The Growth of County Expenditure*

Meanwhile the Rulers of the County were giving more substantial grounds for unpopularity than any divergence of opinion about the policy for ale-houses or paupers adopted in their deliberative assemblies. Between 1774 and 1815 the different County Executives had been slowly but continuously building or rebuilding the gaols and Houses of Correction ; during the same half-century they had been steadily increasing the county expenditure on bridges ; and, in the early part of the nineteenth century, some Courts of Quarter Sessions even began to erect costly lunatic asylums. The cost of all these services had to be levied on the ratepayers. Parishes accustomed to pay out to the High Constable a few shillings now and again, for some occasional and scarcely heeded county levy, now found themselves compelled regularly to contribute each quarter an ever-rising County Rate of almost as many pounds as they had once paid shillings—even when they were not, in addition, asked for lump sums to defray capital expenditure.[1] Already, at the beginning of the nineteenth century, we become aware in the records of some of the parish Vestries of the first grumblings of discontent at this novel taxation. By 1830 these grumblings had swollen into a roar of complaint, and the extravagance of the county Justices had become part of the stock-in-trade of the Radical politicians. It was in vain that it was explained that both Parliament and public opinion insisted on reforming the insecure and insanitary county prisons, with their crowded yards and narrow dungeons, promiscuously packed with men, women, and children, the

---

[1] In 1830, at a county meeting in Cumberland, Blamire pointed out that, whereas in 1792 the county expenditure had been only £1600, it was then £13,000 per annum (*Cumberland Pacquet*, 8th February 1830). The expenditure of the West Riding Justices rose from £7279 in 1786 to £47,787 in 1826, of which about one-sixth was for prisons, one-sixth for the lunatic asylum, and one-sixth for bridges (Report of Special Committee on County Expenditure in MS. Minutes, Quarter Sessions, West Riding, 1832).

innocent with the guilty, in one putrefying mass of corruption and disease. It was useless to argue that the law itself threw upon the county the cost of repairing and providing the bridges necessary for the enormously increasing traffic; or that Parliament had enjoined the provision of county asylums to free the parish poorhouses from the disgrace and danger of the chained lunatic. The little ratepayer refused to consider either the causes or the results of the County Rate. What he felt as a grievance was the rise of a new impost, to which he had been, in the past, practically unaccustomed. Moreover, influenced by the "Administrative Nihilism" then current, even lawyers who were acquainted with the obligations of the county, and reformers who knew the needs, alike blamed the Justices for erecting such large buildings, paying so many officers, and spending so much money. Sydney Smith sneered at the "prison-fancying Justice," and the author of the most systematic work of criticism of the unpaid magistracy rated them soundly for indulging in such costly fads as the separation of male prisoners from female, of adults from children, and of the convicted from the unconvicted, whilst altogether disapproving of the extravagant cubic space required either for the cellular confinement or for the useful employment of any prisoners.[1] All this criticism of the public expenditure of the Rulers of the County reads, in the twentieth century, so strangely crude and unmerited that it is not worth our discussing it in detail. In the matter of prisons and lunatic asylums, at any rate, the most economical modern student blames neither the magnitude nor the celerity of the expenditure of the Justices, and criticises only the apathy, the procrastination, and the parsimony which, in all but a few of the most progressive districts, prevented the County Executives from adopting the reforms advocated by Howard—a dilatory policy all the more open to censure in that its adoption spared the pockets of those on whom lay the duty of improvement.[2]

---

[1] See *A Treatise on the Magistracy of England*, by Edward Mullins, 1836. The following is (p. 75) quoted with approval: "Your Justice must have a nice classification of criminals; the young must be separated from the old, the male from the female, the hardened offender from the fresh criminal . . . He must have tread-mills, too, and rigid inspection, which imply larger premises and more accommodation" (*Brighton Guardian*).

[2] Between 1828 and 1834 every Court of Quarter Sessions was assailed by petitions from parish Vestries and borough corporations, protesting against the

(f) *The Severity of the Game Laws*

In their administrative policy, as we have seen, the complaint against the Rulers of the County was not that they were influenced by their own self-interest. They did not use their opportunities of multiplying valuable liquor licences, to be given to their dependants or favourites ; they were only too lavish to the paupers, ultimately at the expense, as they must have known, of their own rents; and if they were extravagant in widening the county bridges, making the prisons sanitary or providing asylums for the village lunatics, it was on themselves and their fellow - landlords that fell the principal burden of the County Rate. Yet no small part of the reaction against the Rulers of the County was caused by a popular conviction that they had shown themselves grossly partial, selfishly biassed, and swayed by considerations of their own class interest, even to the verge of corruption. This accusation concerned, not their action as administrators of the County Business, but their behaviour on the judicial Bench ; and as regards two great classes of cases, it was, we think, frequently borne out by the facts. It is characteristic of the English country gentlemen that it was not to the love of money that their judicial impartiality and intellectual integrity succumbed, but to their overmastering desire to maintain their field sports and protect the amenity of their country seats. It forms no part of the plan of this work to explore the history of the Game Laws, or to examine the justification for the popular belief that the pursuit of wild animals is one of the inherent natural rights of every citizen. The law of England confined the privilege of killing game to the relatively small class of owners of freehold estates worth at least a hundred pounds a year, and protected this privilege

rise in the County Rate. In most counties the Justices, who were themselves alarmed at the burdens to which they were committing themselves, appointed committees to inquire into the county expenditure, and often effected some reduction in the total expenditure and many financial reforms. See, for instance, the proceedings and reports of such committees in the MS. Minutes of the Quarter Sessions of Devonshire, Michaelmas 1829 ; Buckinghamshire, Michaelmas 1832 ; Gloucestershire, Michaelmas, 1833 ; *Sherborne, Dorchester, and Taunton Journal*, 29th October 1829 ; *Manchester Times*, 28th April 1831 ; and the separate pamphlet entitled *Report of a Committee appointed at the Midsummer Sessions to inquire into the County Expenditure* [of Durham], 1833.

by elaborate outworks of penal prohibitions of trespassing in pursuit of game, and poaching of every kind, buying or selling game, taking or destroying the eggs of game birds, taking game out of season, and even killing a hare on one's own freehold land, if this land was insufficient in value to confer the treasured "qualification."[1] In order to facilitate the execution of these severe criminal statutes, offences against them could, as a rule, be tried summarily by any two Justices —sometimes even by one Justice—who had, moreover, large powers of arbitrarily confiscating or destroying instruments used for the taking of game. In the hands of the country gentlemen of the eighteenth century, and, still more, of the beginning of the nineteenth century, the Game Laws became, it is clear, an instrument of terrible severity, leading, not infrequently, to cruel oppression of individuals of the "lower orders" suspected of poaching. The same suspicion lent an additional vindictiveness to the zeal with which most Justices used their wide powers under the Vagrant Acts to "put away" from their villages any whom they considered "good-for-nothing" fellows.[2] In their ardour to protect their own

---

[1] As to the Game Laws, see *A Treatise on the Game Laws*, by Chitty, 1826 ; *A Treatise on the Game Laws*, by Pemberton Leigh, 1838 ; *Self-Government*, etc., by R. v. Gneist, 3rd edition, 1871, pp. 303-304 ; the House of Commons Returns, No. 504 of 1816, 260 of 1823, 235 of 1828, and 463 of 1846. Gneist points out with his usual acumen that, although the English Game Laws made the pursuit of game a class privilege, the class was nominally open to every rich man ; it was not, as in France and Germany, the privilege of a closed order of nobility ; nor did it confer the right to hunt on the peasants' land. The last observation is not strictly accurate. The Lord of the Manor had the right of killing game over the wastes of the manor ; by ancient reservation he might have similar rights over copyholds or even over the whole manor ; and similar rights were often given in Inclosure Acts (*The Law of Copyholds*, by C. I. Elton, p. 239 of edition of 1893).

[2] A clerical Justice of Bedfordshire took the trouble in 1827 to write to Peel, as Home Secretary, to inform him that the returns as to the number of convictions under the Game Laws, which Parliament had called for, were entirely untrustworthy. They did not, he alleged, show "the enormous increase of offences of that nature, it being the practice of magistrates out of sessions, or at Petty Sessions, to omit returning such convictions so generally that . . . not a tenth part, perhaps not a twentieth part of the actual number of convictions which lead to imprisonment and its pernicious consequences have been sent to the Clerk of the Peace." He urges that a return should be obtained from the keepers of prisons, showing how many have been committed after trial, and how many on summary conviction, whether as rogues and vagabonds, or under the Game Laws. "The demoralising effect which such proceedings have produced upon the peasantry is most deplorable " (Letter of 15th February 1827, in Home Office Magistrates' Book in Public Record Office).

monopoly of this particular form of sport, the Rulers of the County sometimes lost sight of every consideration of personal delicacy and natural justice. "There is not," said Brougham in 1828, "a worse constituted tribunal on the face of the earth . . . than that at which summary convictions on the Game Laws take place . . . I mean . . . a brace of sporting magistrates. I am far from saying that . . . they are actuated by corrupt motives, but they are undoubtedly instigated by their abhorrence of that *caput lupinum,* that *hostis humani generis* . . . that *fera naturæ*—a poacher!"[1] But it was not merely to the common poacher that they were unfair. "In 1822, a farmer coursing hares on his own land, with the permission of his own landlord, was summoned by the keeper of the adjoining landowner for doing so. The adjoining landowner in this particular instance was the Duke of Buckingham, and the farmer was literally convicted by the Duke himself, in the Duke's private house, at the instance of one of the Duke's keepers, and on the evidence of another of his keepers." The Duke refused to permit the defendant to bring in an attorney to help in the defence, and would not even allow a friend to take notes. The latter was told "that if he uttered one impertinent word there was a Constable in the room to take him to gaol or to the stocks."[2]

(g) *The Stopping up of Footpaths*

The other department of their judicial work in which the Rules of the County departed, we think, alike from impartiality and from personal integrity, was in stopping up public foot-paths. Unlike the grievances that arose under the Game Laws, those relating to footpaths occurred chiefly in the neighbourhood of the urban centres, and are not heard of during the eighteenth century. Until 1815 there was, indeed, no other legal machinery for stopping a footpath than that relating to the closing or diverting of a high road. On application at Westminster, the Lord Chancellor would issue

[1] Brougham's Speech in House of Commons, 7th February 1828, Hansard, N.S. vol. xviii. p. 166.
[2] *History of England,* by Sir Spencer Walpole, vol. i. p. 159 ; Hansard, N.S. vol. viii. p. 1292.

the writ known as *Ad Quod Damnum*, directing the Sheriff of
the county to summon a Jury, who were to inquire whether
the proposed closing or diversion would cause injury to the
public. On such a Jury returning a favourable verdict, the
Court of Quarter Sessions could make the necessary order.
Such a procedure made it difficult and costly—often practically
impossible—for the landowners legally to stop up the public
rights-of-way that traversed their fields. Nor do we find
them desiring to do so. The ancient footpaths by which
practically every landed estate was crossed were, we believe,
seldom resented or attacked by the landowners of the eighteenth
century. As, however, the urban population increased,
spreading out into the neighbouring country, we can easily
imagine that many of these footpaths, formerly unobjection-
able, but now incessantly frequented by townsfolk, became
serious drawbacks to the amenity of the country mansions.
From the very beginning of the nineteenth century we find
complaints of the footpaths being stopped up. "At present,"
writes a correspondent of the Board of Agriculture in 1809,
"any person who may possess only a few acres of land, and
finds that the footpath in his neighbourhood either spoils the
appearance of his grounds, or deprives them of that privacy
he wishes, immediately proceeds barricading the said footpath;
puts up a board 'No Thoroughfare,' 'Shut up by Order of the
Justices,' 'Shut up by Order of the Commissioners for Enclosing Waste Lands,' threatening prosecution for trespass 'as
the law directs,' and such-like intimidations to the labouring
peasant or artificer, who by such artifices are forced out of
their road."[1] Presently we see the country gentlemen in
Parliament giving themselves the power to do legally what
they had begun to do without the sanction of the law. An
Act of 1815[2] empowered any two Justices summarily to close
any footpath which they deemed unnecessary, subject only to
an instant appeal to the very next meeting of Quarter Sessions.
Unfortunately, as there is reason to believe, individual
magistrates up and down the country did not scruple to use
this power to their own personal advantage, whenever they

[1] H. Clifford to Sir H. Sinclair, 21st March 1809, in Report of House of
Commons Committee on Broad Wheels and Turnpike Roads, 1809.
[2] 55 George III. c. 68, sec. 2 (1815).

felt inclined to exclude the public from crossing their lands.
They seem to have ignored the fact that, as is expressly stated
by a grave legal commentator, " the closing of a public way
for the benefit of the proprietor is, in almost every instance,
. . . an absolute gift, without consideration, to an individual,
out of the possessions of the public." [1] They even assumed,
as the same authority declares, " that the powers for this
purpose which are given to Justices of the Peace are so given
to be exercised for the benefit of the proprietor . . . This
proposition has, in an especial degree, been reduced to practice
in the instance of footpaths." [2] The Justices, in fact, did not
scruple to give away the public rights-of-way at the request
of their neighbours ; they would even go so far as to make
such orders in the case of footpaths across their own estates.
It became common—so it was gravely asserted in the House
of Commons—for one magistrate to say to another, " Come
and dine with me : I shall expect you an hour earlier as I
want to stop up a footpath." [3] Yet the whole " supposition "
of the Justices, that the intention of the law was that they
should benefit one another, at the public expense—if such a
naïve supposition can ever have been entertained—was, as
our legal authority goes on to declare, " utterly untenable . . .
Justices . . . ought never to grant their assistance as a
matter of favour. The Act expressly declares that the alteration thereby authorised is to be made only when the change
will be more beneficial to the public : those who know how its
provisions have been carried into execution can best tell the
use which the magistracy have made of it." [4] It is therefore
not surprising to find, especially in the North of England, a
loud outcry against the grossly partial action of the Justices
in this branch of their work, and to see the Radical members
in the House of Commons protesting against so shameless a
robbery of the public. [5] Even so typical a representative of
the landowning class as the son of Lord Portman had to
deplore the " facility with which public and most useful

---

[1] *A Treatise on the Law of Highways*, by Robert Wellbeloved, 1829,
pp. viii. ix.   [2] *Ibid.* p. vii.
[3] Hansard, 3rd August 1831, p. 651.
[4] *A Treatise on the Law of Highways*, by Robert Wellbeloved, 1829,
pp. vii. ix.
[5] See, for instance, Hansard, 3rd August 1831, p. 651.

highways might be stopped up by the order of two magistrates, and the great difficulty of getting such orders quashed by appeal to the Quarter Sessions." [1]

(h) *The Stripping of the Oligarchy*

All these separate grievances against the Rulers of the County, some unsubstantial and others real, were merged and combined in a rapidly - growing discontent with county government as a whole, which manifested itself after the Peace of 1815, and reached a climax in 1830-1835.[2] The doctrinaire Radicals who blamed the Justices' restrictive policy in licensing ale-houses, the new economists who saw ruin in the Allowance System, the ratepayer to whom new prisons and lunatic asylums seemed wanton waste of public money, the sporting collier or puddler who found himself summarily imprisoned on suspicion of poaching, the ordinary citizen of Manchester or Leeds to whom access to the fields was closed by an arbitrary stopping up of immemorial footpaths—all alike attributed their grievances to the unrepresentative character, irresponsible authority, and secret procedure of the county magistrates in or out of Sessions. And the slow and almost imperceptible changes which, as we now see, had taken place in the actual county government between 1689 and 1815, went far to justify the half-conscious feeling that what was complained of was not so much an old abuse as a new usurpation. If the reformers of 1815-1835 had possessed more knowledge of the immediate past, they could have pointed out that the Justices of the Peace, in gradually discarding for civil government the whole machinery of a Court of Justice, in abandoning the use of the Jury, in ceasing to formulate their decisions "in Open Court," in slipping away from any control by the Privy Council or the Judges of Assize, in passing from a mere interpretation of the law and the enforcement of old obligations, to the creation of new services at the expense of the rates—in short, in developing out of the old Court of Quarter Sessions both a County Executive

[1] Hansard, 9th August 1831, p. 1035.

[2] See, for instance, the series of articles against the unpaid magistracy written by Albany de Fonblanque for the *Morning Chronicle*, 1821-1824 (*Life and Labours of Albany de Fonblanque*, by E. B. de Fonblanque, 1874, p. 63).

and an Inchoate Provincial Legislature, served by a salaried administrative staff—had, in the course of a century and a half, whilst retaining most of the form, vitally changed the substance of English Local Government. This fact, however, was as much unknown to the hostile critics of the county administration of 1815-1835 as it was to the Rulers of the County themselves. It is, perhaps, for this reason that the agitation for reform was less effective against the constitution of county government than against the extent of the Justices' powers. During the eight iconoclastic years, 1828-1835— for the loss of credit of the county magistracy preceded the accession to office of the Whig Ministry—we see all the efforts of the reformers concentrated, not on reorganising the local government of the rural districts, but on stripping the Rulers of the County of their powers; and either throwing away the control and supervision which these powers afforded, or else intrusting them to a department of the central government. The first to go was the Justices' authority over public-houses. By the Licensing Act of 1828, " Brewster Sessions " lost its power of requiring the applicant for a new licence to produce certificates of good character, and could not even refuse to renew a licence without having to justify its action against an appeal to Quarter Sessions. The Justices' powers of supervision were greatly weakened, and the right, which they had possessed since 1495, summarily to suppress an erring ale-house, was taken from them. More-over, the sale of beer for consumption off the premises was made free without licence.[1] In 1830, the still more hostile action was taken of depriving the Justices of the last remnant of control over the ale-houses, by permitting any ratepayer to open his house as a beer-shop, without any licence from the magistrates, merely on payment of two guineas to the local office of excise.[2] Within six months, 25,000 new beer-shops were opened, and rural villages which had formerly found custom only for a single inn, now rejoiced in half a dozen drinking-dens, free from any sort of restriction. No less a blow to the Justices' authority in the village was the New

---

[1] 9 George IV. c. 61 (1828); see our *History of Liquor Licensing in England*, 1904, p. 113.
[2] 11 George IV. and 1 William IV. c. 64 (1830).

Poor Law of 1834, which deprived them of all powers of supervision or control over what was then the largest branch of parish expenditure, entirely suppressed their own function in the management of vagrants, established new local authorities on an elective basis in which the magistrates had little more than an honorary position, and transferred the supreme control to the central Poor Law Commissioners.[1] Meanwhile, in the re-organisation of Metropolitan and other populous parishes under Hobhouse's Act of 1831,[2] and even in the establishment of a system of street lighting under the Lighting and Watching Act of 1833,[3] the Justices were practically ignored. The new Factory Act of 1833 [4] took from them the power which they had exercised since 1802 of inspecting cotton factories, and transferred the function to the Home Office. When reform of the highway administration was proposed in 1831 and 1833 and carried in 1835,[5] the Justices in Special Sessions lost the appointment of the Surveyor, and with it all authority over highway administration; the individual Justice found himself stripped of his century-old right of " presenting " any founderous road; whilst the power to stop up footpaths was peremptorily taken away from Petty Sessions, and practically from the Justices altogether, by being made dependent on the verdict of a Jury, in the open Court of Quarter Sessions.[6] Even the

---

[1] 4 & 5 William IV. c. 76 (1834). " The Poor Law Amendment Act," says Nassau Senior, " was a heavier blow to the aristocracy than the Reform Act . . . It . . . dethroned the country gentlemen. It found the country Justices each in his own circle the master of the property of the ratepayers and of the incomes of the labourers. It left them either excluded from influence in the management of their own parishes, or forced to accept a seat in the Board of Guardians and to debate and vote among shopkeepers and farmers " (Nassau Senior, 4th February 1851; in *Correspondence and Conversations of Alexis de Tocqueville with Nassau William Senior from 1834 to 1859*, edited by M. C. M. Simpson, 1872, vol. i. pp. 203-204).

[2] 1 & 2 William IV. c. 60 (1831).

[3] 3 & 4 William IV. c. 90 (1833); *The Law relating to Watching and Lighting Parishes*, by J. Tidd Pratt, 1834.

[4] 3 & 4 William IV. c. 103 (1833).

[5] It is characteristic of the time that this measure was framed by so mild a Whig as the Hon. E. B. Portman; see Hansard, 9th August 1831 and 1833, vol. v. p. 1035; and *The General Highway Acts*, by Leonard Shelford, 1835.

[6] 5 & 6 William IV. c. 50 (1835). The clause was not in the Bill as introduced in 1831, but was inserted in response to pressure from the members for Lancashire and Yorkshire. We learn, for instance, that in 1832 a petition was lying for signature at the warehouse of the Brothers Potter, Manchester, in favour of this clause (*Manchester Times*, 16th June 1832).

control of the county prisons began to pass out of their hands. By the Prisons Act of 1835,[1] their administration was made subject to rules framed by the Home Secretary, to which they were compelled to yield obedience, at the bidding of Government Inspectors. From 1828 to 1835 there was, in fact, hardly an alteration of the law touching any branch of local government which did not include some diminution of the authority of the county magistracy. Yet against the institution of the unpaid Justice of the Peace, the method of his appointment, or the comprehensive powers recited in the ancient Commission of the Peace, no adverse action was taken, even under the Reform Ministry.[2] Except for an abortive bill by Joseph Hume in 1835—and even this did not contemplate the abolition of the unpaid Justice of the Peace, appointed by Commission from the Crown—no attempt was made to give to county government any such organic reconstruction as was applied to the municipal corporations and the administration of the Poor Law.

(1) *Why the Justices survived*

It is difficult at first sight to understand why the reformers of 1832, supported by an apparently universal outcry against the Justices of the Peace, should, contented with a mere paring of their jurisdiction, have left them still the Rulers of the County, unchanged in their unrepresentative character, unchecked in their irresponsibility, unfettered in their powers

---

[1] 5 & 6 William IV. c. 38 (1835). By this Act, writes a contemporary, "Inspectors of Prisons were appointed and the management of every gaol in Great Britain vested in them virtually, though ostensibly in the Secretary of State for the Home Department, who is empowered to order the payment of any alterations he may consider it expedient to be effected on the recommendation of these inspectors" (*Prison Discipline and Secondary Punishments*, by P. Laurie, jun., 1837, p. 3).

[2] Even cases under the Game Laws continued to be dealt with by the country gentlemen Justices, though the position was greatly mitigated by the Game Act of 1831 (1 & 2 William IV. c. 32), which made many of the offences triable only by a Jury at Quarter Sessions or the Assizes (*Practical Treatise on the Game Laws as amended by the New Act*, by E. E. Deacon, 1831). By abolishing the qualification for taking game, throwing it open to any one who paid for a game licence, and legalising, under restrictions, the sale of game, this Act removed practically all the real objections felt to the Game Laws by the middle class. There was accordingly no subsequent reform of importance until the Ground Game Act of 1880 (43 & 44 Vic. c. 47).

of expenditure, and unreformed either in the method of their
appointment or in the secrecy of their procedure.[1] But the
way of the Radical reformer in county affairs was, in 1832,
peculiarly hard. By their history and by their name, no less
than by the most obtrusive side of their work, the Justices of
the Peace seemed still, in the main, to be judicial authorities.
For the appointment of judges by the direct election of those
whose delinquencies they were to try, not even the Radicals
were prepared. The obvious alternative to the unpaid
country gentlemen on the Petty Sessional Bench was the
Stipendiary Magistrate. But the Whigs and Radicals of
1832 hated, scarcely less than the Tories, the very idea of
Stipendiary Magistrates. To dislike of any increase of public
expenditure, there was added the jealousy of the growth of a
professional staff, and a rooted distrust of the central government, to which few were prepared to confide the making of so
many paid appointments. "What in truth," said Sydney
Smith, "could we substitute for the unpaid magistracy? We
have no doubt but that a set of rural judges, in the pay of
government, would very soon become corrupt jobbers and odious
tyrants, as they often are on the Continent. But the
magistrates, as they now exist, really constitute a bulwark of
some value against the supreme power of the State. They
would not submit to be employed for base and criminal purposes. They are tools, perhaps, in some cases, but still tools
that must be respected."[2] Those were days in which, in fact,
the influential Whigs and Radicals feared, even more than they
feared the prejudiced and class bias of the country gentleman,
what a writer in the *Morning Chronicle* called "the constant,

---

[1] "The Reform Bill," said one furious opponent of the Justices, "would be
a dead letter—a struggle without a triumph—if we are to be lorded over with
magisterial power and priestly pride after as before the reformation" (*A Letter to
the Rt. Hon. Lord Brougham and Vaux on the Magistracy of England*, 1832,
p. 24).

[2] Article on the Licensing of Ale-houses, in *Edinburgh Review*, September
1826, p. 441. The establishment of five hundred or a thousand Stipendiary
Magistrates at £500 a year seemed equally to the *Quarterly Review* an appalling
prospect. "Without consequence as lawyers, of no rank in their learned
profession, without the influence of property or birth, with no station in the
county or neighbourhood where they administer justice . . . surrounded by
powerful landowners possessing all these ties and all these qualifications . . . is
it likely that they would be above the influence of peers and landholders . . .
that they would be proof against the temptations to which indigent authority
surrounded by wealth is exposed?" (*Quarterly Review*, 1828, p. 268).

artful, yet specious operations of a pensioned servant of the Government, well skilled in the subtleties of the law." [1] Hence the dispensation of petty justice in the rural districts remained still in the hands of unpaid amateurs, " appointed by irresponsible advisers " to an office from which they were in practice " irremovable without a conviction for some tangible offence." [2] It was to Whigs and Radicals an anomaly that such unrepresentative persons should collectively have the power of spending the County Rate. But an elaborate Parliamentary inquiry of 1834 [3] had revealed no financial corruption; the expense and difficulty of travelling, and the exceptional degradation into which the rural labourer had sunk, put out of the question any county board elected like the new Town Councils; and no alternative administrative body for the rural county could then be invented. Yet the survival of the Justices of the Peace, unchanged in constitution and with only a partial curtailment in their powers — whilst the Parish Vestry was strangled and the Municipal Corporation was revolutionised— is due, we think, in the main, to the fact, that in spite of all the extra-legal developments that we have described, both Quarter Sessions and Petty Sessions still seemed to the public, not county administrative authorities, but essentially Courts of Justice.

[1] *Morning Chronicle*, 14th October 1825.

[2] *A Letter to the Right Hon. Lord Brougham and Vaux on the Magistracy of England*, 1832, p. 8.

[3] Report of the Select Committee appointed to inquire into the County Rates and Highway Rates in England and Wales, and to report whether and what regulations may be adopted to diminish their pressure upon the owners and occupiers of land, 1834. This committee did not recommend any change in the constitution of county government, but advocated contributions from the national exchequer and the reforms of highway administration which were embodied in the Act of 1835.

INDEX OF SUBJECTS

Bastardy, 46, 55 ; cases, revenue from, 75 ; dealt with by salaried overseers, 137 ; referred to Divisional Sessions, 528 ; orders, making of, by Justices, 299 *n.* ; at Petty Sessions, 552; appeals against, 420, 481

Beadle, 35, 470 ; as Overseer, 59, 127 ; corruption of, 69, 254 *n.* ; control of, 102 *n.*, 236 ; appointment or election of, 106, 109, 126-128, 205, 207, 225, 254, 272 ; duties of, 126-127 ; salary of, 127-128, 207 ; number of, in London, 127 *n.* ; of Liberties, 522 *n.* ; inquiry into unlicensed ale-houses by, 522 *n.* ; prosecution of, in Middlesex, 559 —— assistant, 129 *n.*

Beadman. See *Beadle*

Bearbaiting, 357

Beer, supervision of Justices over price and quality of, 400 ; free trade in, 588, 589 *n.* ; restriction of consumption of, 588

Beershops, in Bethnal Green, 82, 567 ; absence of control of Justices, 603. See also *Ale-houses, Licences, Licensing*

Beggars, employment of, 338

Bellman, 34, 127 *n.*, 225

Bell-ringer, 33, 404

Bishop, responsibility of Churchwardens, 10, 20 ; as judex ordinarius, 190 *n.* ; appeals to, for establishment of Select Vestry, 193 ; appointment of commissioners for church building by ; jurisdiction of, over counties palatine, 313, 316-317

Bishop's faculty. See *Faculty*

Blasphemy, 463

Boonmasters, 29

Booth Hall, at Gloucester, 438, 442

Boroughhead, 27 *n.*

Boroughreeve, 71, 107, 167 *n.*, 169

Boroughs, municipal, relation of, to parishes, 12 ; oligarchical structure of, 176 ; "rotten," 268 ; metropolitan, 276 ; exemption of, from County jurisdiction, 280, 284 ; as subdivisions for County purposes, 285 ; juries of, 457. See also *Manorial boroughs*

Borsholder, 27 *n.*

Boss, the rule of the, 79-90

Bound Bailiffs. See *Bailiffs, bound*

Boundaries of parish, 5, 9, 10, 12 ; of various local government areas, not coincident and uncertain, 11-12 ; perambulations of, 10, 12 ; alteration of, by Vestry, 53 ; intersection of, with County, 283-284 ; beating of, 10, 12, 53, 404 ; of County, 283-284

Bounds, beating of. See *Boundaries*

Bow Street, 339 ; police office in, 341, 342

Brazier, County, 497

"Bread Act," "Berkshire." See *Speenhamland Act*

Brewers, Justices as, 569

Bricks, Inspectors of, 524

Bridewell, committal of criminals to, 352. See also *House of Correction*

Bridge master, 439, 515, 516. See also *Surveyor of bridges*

Bridge money, payment of, 388, 526 ; collection of, 466-467, 500, 517 ; raising of, 497 ; accounts of, 500 ; Treasurer of, 508, 510-511 *n.*, 515

Bridgereeve, 34

Bridges, repairs of, 296, 307, 308, 353, 415 *n.*, 418, 427, 451-452, 479, 481, 488, 497, 512, 513-514, 515-520, 525, 525 *n.*, 526, 530, 532, 533 ; maintenance of, 282, 307, 429 *n.*, 446, 481, 513, 525 ; presentments of, 308, 449, 451-452, 458 *n.*, 460-461, 465, 467-469, 471, 472, 473, 474, 476, 478-479, 493, 514, 515, 523, 526 ; laws relating to, 368, 510 ; supervision of, by Justices, 392 ; business relating to, only done at Easter Sessions, in Yorkshire, 433 ; reports of surveyors concerning, 441 ; expenditure on, 450, 595, 596, 597 ; inspector of, 468 ; inspection of, 559 ; by High Constables, 493-494, 494· *n.*, 501 ; survey of, in Devonshire, 520 ; surveyor of, see *Surveyors of bridges*

Building Act, Metropolitan, 563

Bull-baiting, 48-49 *n.*, 357

Bullock hunting, 83, 85, 87

Burgesses, Court of. See *Court of Burgesses*

Burglars, payments for apprehension of, 115 *n.*

By-laws, power of Vestry to make, 39 ; for suppression of nuisances, 57 ; of County Council, 535

Canal, construction of, 521

Canons, ecclesiastical, 22, 23 ; chapter of, of Southwell, 317 *n.*

Cantrev, 284 *n.*

Capitation Act, 416 *n.*

Carnival, 34. See also *Flesh-taster*

Carriage, land, regulation of rates of, 297, 441, 534-535

Castle, Court of Quarter Sessions held at, 438

"Catchland," 10

Cattle, distempered, inspectors of, 524

Cattle plague, suppression of, 495-496, 574-575 *n.*

Cemetery, purchase of ground for, at Liverpool, 140

Certiorari, writ of, 336, 390 *n.*, 419 ; definition of, 419-420 *n.*

cal resolutions passed at, 534 *n.*;
autonomy of, 535 ; alteration of areas
by, 540 ; policy of, as to rate in aid
of wages, 545 - 550 ; abolition of
roundsman system by, in Bucks, 545 ;
transfer of business from, 552, 553,
573 ; promotion of Bills in Parliament
by, 554-555 ; submission of Bills in
Parliament to, 555-556 ; Vagrancy
Bill, drafted at Convention of, 555 ;
purity of administration of, 560 ;
Opposition of, to Police Bill in
Middlesex and Surrey, 576-577 ;
directions of, to individual Justices,
594 ; alleged extravagance of, 595,
596, 597 ; irresponsible authority at,
602, 604-605 ; powers of, to close footpaths, 604 ; trial of offences against
Game Laws at, 605 *n.* ; survival of, as
a Court of Justice, 607
Sessions, Quarter, Assessment of Wages
by. See *Wages*
—— Quarter, Chairman of. See *Chairman*
—— Quarter, Committees of. See *Committees*
—— Quarter, Presentments to. See
Presentments
Sessions, Special, 396-400, 401, 405 *n.*,
408, 550 ; origin of, 297, 396 *n.*, 493 ;
judicial definition of, 396 *n.* ; in West
Riding, 406-407, 413 *n.* ; for appointing parish officers, 408 ; dinners at,
paid for out of fees, 409 *n.* ; business
at, 412 ; functions of, 418 ; frequency
of, 415 ; Clerk to, 417, 418 *n.* ;
appeals from orders of, 438 ; notices
of, 442, 443 ; investigation of Constable's presentments by, 472 *n.* ;
development of, 482 ; delegation of
powers of Quarter Sessions to, 528,
529 *n.* ; transfer of powers of Quarter
Sessions to, 551, 552 ; privacy of, 553 ;
powers of, in Highway administration,
604. See also *Sessions, Highway.*
See also *Sessions, Licensing*
—— Statute, 493 ; of High Constables,
535
"Sessions' money," 467
Settlement, law of, 4, 14, 15, 16 *n.*,
53 *n.* ; disputes about, 65 ; orders for
removal to place to, 299, 309, 539-
540 ; appeals against, 420, 481 ;
cases of, referred to Divisional Sessions, 528
Sewers, construction of, by Vestry at
Tooting, 58
—— Commissioners of. See *Commissioners, Court of.* See *Court*
—— Jury of. See *Juries.*
Sexton, 33, 34 *n.*, 47 ; right of women
to vote at election of, 15 ; polls for

election of, 109, 169 *n.* ; salary of,
140
Sheriff, Deputy, 447, 487
—— High, 30, 280, 287-291, 319, 365,
373 ; of Bedfordshire, 365 ; of Berkshire, 288 *n.*, 486 *n.* ; of Cambridgeshire, 288 *n.*, 317 ; of Cornwall, 289 *n.*;
of Devonshire, 487 ; of Gloucestershire, 368 ; of Huntingdonshire, 288 *n.*,
317 ; of Kent, 428 *n.* ; of Lancashire,
366 ; of Middlesex and the City of
London, 288 *n.*, 310, 312 ; of Surrey,
427, 570 ; of the City of Oxford, 311 ;
of Suffolk, 427 ; of Westmoreland,
288 *n.* ; office of, held by same person
for two counties, 288 *n.* ; Report of
Committee of House of Lords and
House of Commons on, 288 *n.* ; woman
as, 288 *n.* ; characteristics of, as
representative of the Crown, 288 *n.*,
306 ; as Conservator of the Peace ;
generally, 375-377 ; powers, duties,
and functions of, 289, 295, 305, 484-
485 ; to proclaim new Acts, 291 *n.* ;
to summon juries, 296, 387, 428 *n.*,
447, 456-462, 600 ; to attend Quarter
Sessions, 296, 422, 425 ; to attend
Assizes, 306 ; to levy fines, 308 ; to
issue summons for Quarter Sessions,
421, 550 ; to present lists of Hundred
and parish officers to Quarter Sessions,
421 ; to supervise gaol, 481, 485-487;
to appoint High Bailiffs of Hundreds,
483 ; fees of, 304, 316 *n.* ; profits of
office of, 305-306 *n.* ; of counties
corporate, 310 ; places exempt from
jurisdiction of, 310-311, 312 ; one,
for three parts of Lincolnshire, 311 ;
oath of, 316 *n.* ; accounts of, 316 *n.* ;
social position of, 375-377 ; responsibilities of, 376 ; allowance from
Exchequer to, 423 *n.* ; precept to, for
summoning Quarter Sessions, 426 ; to
keep order in Court of Quarter Sessions,
487 ; military duties of, 488-489 *n.* ;
to raise Posse Comitatus, 488 *n.* ; to
preside over County meetings, 533 *n.* ;
appointment of, 287, 304, 484-485 *n.* ;
in Lancashire, 289 *n.*, 317 ; in
Counties Palatine, 289 *n.* ; by lord
palatine, 314 ; by the Crown, 484 ;
influence of Judge of Assize in, 380 ;
of Crown in, 485 ; qualification of,
302, 304 ; office of, compulsory, 304 ;
dinners at Assizes paid for by, 438 *n.* ;
process directed to, 474 *n.* ; payment
of fines to, 478 ; nomination of, by
Judges of Assize, 484 ; of successor
by, 485 *n.* ; authority of Judge of
Assize over, 483 ; officers of, 485, 487 ;
suppression of, by paid officers, 485,
486, 488, 554 ; relation of, to Justices,

levying of fines by, 478 ; decrease in powers of, 554

Surveyor of Highways, Assistant, 129 *n.* ; collection of rates by, 136

—— under Metropolitan Building Act, 563

—— to Tower Hamlets Court of Sewers, 560

Surveys, 12

Swearing, punishment of, 372 *n.*

Synods, 25 *n.*

Synodsmen, 25 *n.*

Tax, Income, resolution against, 107

—— Land, as basis for rates, 178 ; collection of, 307

—— Property, 360 *n.*

Taxation, parochial, 4

Taxes, assessed, collection of, 148

Collectors of. See *Collectors*

Tests, religious, for parish officers, 19 ; for members of Close Vestries in Metropolis, 39 *n.*, 242 ; for Justices, 303

Thirdborough, 27 *n.*

Tied-house system, establishment of, 587

Tithes Bill, 24

Tithingmen, nomination of, 27 *n.* ; appointment of, 38 *n.* ; presentments by, 422, 464, 469 *n.*, 471 *n.* ; enforcement of Vagrancy Acts by, 453

Tithings as units of administration, 10, 27 *n.*

—— Constable of. See *Constables*

Toleration Act, 64, 469 *n.*

Tolls, bridge, settlement of, by Quarter Sessions, 441

Tories, control of Court Leet by, in Manchester, 71 ; demands for poll by, 168, 169 ; support of, by Metropolitan Close Vestries, 252, 253 ; attitude of, towards Hobhouse's Bill, 272 ; influence of, in appointment of Lords-Lieutenant, 374-375 *n.* ; objections of, to Stipendiary Magistrates, 606

Toryism, High Church, participation of Close Vestries in wave of, 242

Town Councils, establishment of, 557, 607

—— Hall, Vestry meetings adjourned to, in Manchester, 101

"Town-meeting," 39 *n.*

Towns, separate Commissions of the Peace for, 320

"Town's Husband," 34

Townships, as units of administration, 10 ; number of, 13 ; separate Churchwardens for, 22, 72; separate Overseers for, 31, 71, 72 ; separate Surveyors for, 71 ; of the parish of Manchester, 70 ; division of parishes into, 156 ; separate Vestry meetings for, 157, 159 ; rating of, 72, 181 *n.*, 292 ;

autonomy of, 280 ; presentments of, 452, 454 ; officers of, 539 ; maintenance of poor by, 540 ; union of, with adjoining parish, 540 ; meetings of inhabitants of, 544

"Townsmen" of Braintree, 221

Trade, exclusive right to. See *Freemen*

Traders, itinerant, suppression of, by Quarter Sessions of Kent, 536 ; of Middlesex, 538

Trading Justices. See *Justices, Trading*

Transportation, 299, 353, 367, 525

Traverse Jury. See *Juries, Petty*

Traverses, trial of, at Quarter Sessions, 442

Tread-mills, 596 *n.* ; use of, for untried prisoners, 371

Treasurer, County, 507-512 ; appointment of, 432, 441, 443, 508, 512, 526 ; payments to, by High Constable, 292, 497 ; inspection of Sheriff's accounts by, 423 *n.* ; dismissal of, in Lancashire, 432 ; in Hampshire, 511 ; payment of Justices' dinners, etc., in Suffolk, 438 *n.* ; accounts of, 441, 510, 512 *n.*, 531, 566 ; functions of, 507-508, 509, 510, 512 ; duties of, performed by Clerk of the Peace, 508, 512 *n.* ; late development of office of, 508 ; separate, for different County funds, 508-511 ; for different divisions, 509 ; social status of, 508, 511 ; salary of, 508 *n.*, 510, 510-511 *n.*, 512 ; security given by, 508, 512 ; default of, in Devonshire, 511 ; in Hampshire, *ib.* ; payments by, 527, 533 *n.* ; of Middlesex Quarter Sessions, election of G. B. Mainwaring as, 564-565 ; resignation of, 565-566 ; Act of Parliament for regulation of, 566

—— parish, in Bethnal Green, 81, 84, 86, 87 ; salaried, appointment of, in Liverpool, 136 ; proposed election of, by Vestry Committees, under Hobhouse's Bill, 272

Treasury, grants to Court Justice from, 339, 340 *n.* ; payment of Justices' wages by, 424 *n.* ; secret payments from, to Chairman of Middlesex Quarter Sessions, 436 *n.*, 564, 565, 572 ; payments from, to Justices, for special services, 574-575 *n* ; secret payments from, for patrol, 575

Trev, 284 *n.*

"True Bills," 440, 448

Trustees, of Church lands, in St. Pancras, 208

—— estate, 228

—— for municipal administration at Richmond, 221

—— for the parish, Churchwardens as, 24

INDEX OF AUTHORS AND OTHER PERSONS

647

INDEX OF PLACES

END OF VOL. I